Radically Speaking

Radically Speaking

Feminism Reclaimed

edited by

Diane Bell and Renate Klein

SPINIFEX

Spinifex Press Pty Ltd
504 Queensberry Street
North Melbourne, Vic. 3051
Australia
spinifex@publishaust.net.au

Published by Spinifex Press, 1996

Edited by Jo Turner
Indexed by Patricia Holt
Cover design by Liz Nicholson, Design Bite
Typeset by Claire Warren
Page set up SPG
Made and printed in Australia by Australian Print Group

National Library of Australia
Cataloguing-in-Publication entry:

Radically speaking: feminism reclaimed.

  Bibliography.
  Includes index.
  ISBN 1 875559 38 8.

  1. Feminism. I. Bell, Diane, 1943– . II. Klein, Renate, 1945– .

305.4201

Acknowledgements

"Truth Versus Loyalty: Speaking out on genital mutilation." © 1996 Evelyne Accad. "Towards Global Feminism: A Muslim perspective" © 1994 Mahnaz Afkhami, originally published as "Women in Post-Revolutionary Iran" in *In the Eye of the Storm* published by I. B. Tauris & Co. Ltd. "Amidst the Smoke We Remember: Mothers of the Plaza de Mayo" © 1989 Marjorie Agosin, originally published in *Women of Smoke: Latin American Women in Literature and Life* published by Williams Wallace, Canada. Photograph from *Circles of Madness*, © 1992 Alicia D'Amico and Alicia Sanguinetti published by White Pine Press. "The Great Incest Hijack" originally published as "Incest: A Journey to Hullabulloo", Reprinted with permission, work originally appeared in *Women and Therapy*, 17 (1/2), © 1995 Haworth Press Inc. Binghampton. NY, USA. "A Feminist University: The thrill and challenges, conflicts and rewards of trying to establish an alternative education" © 1996 Berit Ås. "Deconstructing Deconstructionism (or whatever happened to feminist studies?)" © 1991 Kathleen Barry, reprinted by permission of *Ms. Magazine*. "The banned professor, how radical feminism saved me from men trapped in men's bodies and female impersonators, with a little help from my friends" © 1996 Pauline Bart. "Speaking of things that shouldn't be written: Cross cultural excursions into the land of misrepresentations" © 1996 Diane Bell. "Beware: Radical feminists speak, read, write, organise, enjoy life, and never forget" © 1996, Diane Bell & Renate Klein. "The narrow bridge of art and politics" © 1996 Suzanne Bellamy. "Take Your Pageant and Shove It" © 1983 Angela Bowen originally published in *Village Voice*, November 8, 1983. Enabling a Visible Black Lesbian Presence in Academia: A Radically Reasonable Request" © 1996 Angela Bowen. "Nothing mat(t)ers" © 1992 Somer Brodribb, originally published in *Nothing Mat(t)ers: A feminist critique of postmodernism*, Spinifex Press. "Withdrawing Her Energy" © 1996 Somer Brodribb. "'Generation X', the 'Third Wave' or just plain radical: Reviewing the reviewers of Catharine MacKinnon's *Only Words*." © 1996 Deirdre Carraher, Sharon M. Cox, Elizabeth Daake, Michele Gagne, Patricia Good, Jessie McManmon & Marjorie O'Connor. "The Race for Theory" © 1987 Barbara Christian, by permission of Oxford University Press. "The Last Post for Feminism" from *Out of the Frying Pan: Inflammatory Writing 1972–89* © 1990 Sandra Coney, published by Penguin Books New Zealand. "The Witches Return" © 1992 Mary Daly from *Outercourse: The Witches Return* reprinted by permission from HarperCollins Publishers Inc. and from Spinifex Press. "'French Feminism': An imperialist invention" © 1996, Christine Delphy. "I'll take the low road: A look at contemporary feminist theory." © 1996, Carol Anne Douglas. "Surfing the edge of the alphabet" © 1996 Beryl Fletcher, Susan Sayer & Cathie Dunsford. "Dworkin on Dworkin" © 1990, Andrea Dworkin reprinted from *Trouble and Strife, 19* Summer, 1990. "Feminist Education Research De-Radicalized: A Warning From Germany" © 1996 Uta Enders-Dragässer & Brigitte Sellach. "The Posse Rides Again"

Action" © 1990 Robyn Rowland and Renate Klein, originally published as "Radical Feminism: Critique and Construct" in *Feminist Knowledge: Critique and Construct* with permission from Routledge London. "US pornography invades South Africa" from *Women and the Law* © 1994 Diana E. H Russell reprinted with permission of the Human Sciences Research Council, Pretoria, South Africa. "Declaración de Propósito/Mission Statement" © 1994 Santa Barbara Rape Crisis Center, reprinted with permission of the Santa Barbara Rape Crisis Center/El Centro Contra la Violación Sexual, from *Outcry*, Mayo/May 1994, 1, 6. "The Personal is Political" © 1994 Jocelynne A. Scutt originally published in *The Sexual Gerrymander*, Spinifex Press. "A (Political) Postcard from a Peripheral Pre-post-modern State (of mind) or How Alliteration and Parentheses can knock you down dead in Women's Studies" from *Women's Studies International Forum*, 15 331–37 © 1992 Ailbhe Smyth reprinted by permission of Elsevier Science Ltd, Pergamon Imprint, The Boulevard, Langford Lane, Kidlington OX5 1GB UK. "The Disembodied Worldview of Deconstructive Post-modernism", excerpt from "Epilogue" from *States of Grace* © 1991 Charlene Spretnak reprinted with permission from HarperCollins Publishers, Inc. "Lest We Forget" words and music by © Judy Small 1981 and 1983 Crafty Maid Music. "Maori–Lesbian–Feminist Radical" © 1996 Ngahuia Te Awekotuku and from *Women Who Do and Women Who Don't Join the Women's Movement*, 1984, Routledge, UK and *Mana Wahine Maori: Selected Writings on Maori Women's Art, Culture and Politics*, 1991, New Women's Press, Auckland, pp. 17–21. "The self-contradiction of 'post-modernist' feminism" © 1996 Denise Thompson. "The Backlash on Campus: Chilly Climate Report Opens Floodgates" from *Herizons*, 8 (3), 28-9 & 46-7 © 1994 Ellen Travis, reprinted as "Stranger than Fiction: The Backlash on Campus at the University of Victoria" with permission from *Herizons* Magazine, PO Box 128, Station Main, Winnipeg, Manitoba, R3C 2GI. "Chilly Climate Committee" photograph © 1994 Allan Edgar reprinted with permission. "People's Perspectives on 'Population' Symposium" © 1993 UBINIG. "(Re)turning to the Modern: Radical Feminism and the Post-Modern Turn" © 1996 Kristin Waters. "The Queer Backlash" © 1996 Sue Wilkinson & Celia Kitzinger.

Every effort has been made to trace copyright-holders but in a few cases this has proved impossible. The publisher would be interested to hear from copyright holders not acknowledged here or acknowledged incorrectly.

Contents

Section 1: Speaking Radically

Section Two: Radical Feminists Under Attack

Section Three: Radical Feminists "Interrogate" Post-modernism

Section Four: Refusing to be Silenced

Section Five: Feminism Reclaimed

Robin Morgan

Monster*

May my hives bloom bravely until my flesh is aflame
and burns through the cobwebs.
May we go mad together, my sisters.
May our labor agony in bringing forth this revolution
be the death of all pain.

May we comprehend that we cannot be stopped.

May I learn how to survive until my part is finished.
May I realize that I
                  am a
                  monster. I am
        a
            monster.
I am a monster.

And I am proud.

* Extract from Robyn Morgan (1972) *Monster*.

Diane Bell and Renate Klein

Foreword — Beware: Radical Feminists Speak, Read, Write, Organise, Enjoy Life, and Never Forget

> *If it does not track bloody footprints across your desk, it is probably not about women. Feminism, the discipline of this reality, refuses to abstract itself in order to be recognized as being real (that is, axiomatic) theory. In terms of existing theory, the distinctive intellectual challenge of feminism is to retain its specificity without being confined to the parochial; its distinctive practical challenge is to stay concrete without being crushed. In feminist terms, it is difficult to be narrow if you are truly talking about the situation of 53% of the population, but it is almost impossible to survive if you do – which makes these one and the same challenge.*
>
> Catharine MacKinnon,
> *Feminism Unmodified* (1987, p. 9)

An Introduction in Five Acts with Two Speaking Parts and an Ever-increasing Cast of Characters Who Eventually Get Organised into Thematic Groups and Begin to Speak in Prose

Act One: Where radical feminists rant and rave about being attacked all the time by all manners of persons

Chorus: We need a book.

Renate: I'm sick and tired of radical feminist bashing. It seems we have become the target of post-modernists, the right, the media, and . . .

Diane: . . . and the "faux feminists" who churn out one book after the other saying that radical feminism is the problem and that things aren't really that bad for women.

Renate: And this preference for calling everything "gender" – "gender feminists", "gender studies" – anything to avoid putting men on the spot. And look at the media attention they get when they say radical feminists are "male bashers".

Diane: To me that's a real misuse of language. Women get assaulted, raped and murdered and when we speak out, we're called "male bashers".

Renate: Yeah, and they also call us "victim feminists". Strange, isn't it? We speak out against male aggression. We demand safe spaces for women. We work for social change. We insist on women's health centres, Women's Studies, shelters – you name it – and we're called "passive victims".

Diane: And what about being called essentialist? That's a favourite put-down. What does "essentialist" mean? Didn't we talk about social constructs since the 70s?

Renate: Ahistorical! Universalising! Who is it that remembers? Who is it that makes global connections? I guess that is dangerous and needs to be put down too.

Diane: Post-modernism! If I hear one more person expound on her multiple subject positions . . . Radical feminists have always understood that race, class, sexuality, age are intertwined, but they hold fast to the identity of woman.

Renate: That's crucial. It's the basis of political action. How can we speak if we are fragmented into so many partial and shifting identities? How can we engage in joint actions, if we are merely "thinking fragments?"

Diane: Isn't it interesting that just as "woman" began to speak, in her own voice, of her own realities, she was told that was naive: there was no unitary self.

Act Two: Where radical feminists get to speak for themselves and a book is conceived

Renate: Yes, we do need a book.

Diane: One that celebrates what women have achieved and has confidence that there is a feminist future.

Renate: I want a book about why post-modernism is bad for your health, about why radical feminists are such a threat.

Diane: OK, but let's be clear about what a healthy woman is.

Renate: She is physically safe, economically secure, and is able to enjoy her human rights to the full.

Diane: She might live in Bangladesh, in South Africa, Russia, the Lebanon, Chile, Taiwan, the USA, Canada, Europe, the UK, Australia or New Zealand/Aotearoa. She could live in the cities or the bush and don't assume she speaks English.

[*Conversation dissolves . . .*] We agree she works, plays, studies, raises children, lives alone, in families, with other women, makes art, talks back, takes action. She is discriminated against, harassed, raped, the object of pornography; she bears the burden of caring for, and feeding, her loved ones, but is paid less than her male counterpart, if she is paid at all. This woman finds strength with other women. They are her best friends, her support. She knows that despite the differences in personal background, geography, class, history, and culture, she is vulnerable because she is a woman. Stubbornly, defiantly, we hold on to that truth. There is such a thing as woman.

Remember Robin Morgan's 1972 collection of poems, *Monster* and her "I want a Women's Movement like a lover?" We still need that capacity to unite the emotional and political, as Suzanne Bellamy does in her art. We need to listen to many women: working-class women, lesbian women, Indigenous women, Black women, women who took on the hard issues and have stayed with them. The brave, prophetic voices of the late 60s and early 70s are still speaking. We need to hear them, more than ever joined by new ones. Do you see the violence against women getting any less?

We need to make it plain that radical feminism is global and that it is and always has been driven by issues; that the theory arises from the practice; and that it is women of all classes, creeds, colours and dispositions that are the basis of the movement. The "Black Women in the Academy: Defending our Name" conference in Boston in January 1994 was a stunning statement about the involvement of women of colour in the Women's Movement, and the Sixth International Feminist Book Fair in Melbourne in July 1994 celebrated "Indigenous, Asian and Pacific Women's Writing". It brought women together from around the world. As far as possible, the book should be international, inclusive, and grounded in the actual experiences of real live women. It will tell a story.

We'll also have to "interrogate" post-modernism. Of course, Barbara Christian's "The race for theory" is a fabulous starting point, Somer Brodribb's *Nothing Mat(t)ters* is already a classic, and there are so many dedicated radical feminists who, albeit trained in different disciplines, are saying the same thing. The post-modern turn is apolitical, ahistorical, irresponsible, and self-contradictory; it takes the "heat off patriarchy"; just look at what is happening in some Women's Studies programmes and in academic publishing. Ailbhe Smyth's wonderfully irreverent postcard from Ireland and Diane Richardson and Victoria Robinson's revealing account of the gender politics of publishing show how feminists are being marginalised.

It has all happened before, as Marcia Ann Gillespie points out: women have been set against other women and the focus of serious research has drifted back to a male standpoint. Who is the focus of Gender Studies, or lesbianandgay theory? Ask Sheila Jeffreys that one. Or queer theory? Sue Wilkinson and Celia Kitzinger call it a backlash. Post-modernism has created a climate in which the rationalist project is being abandoned. Just as women were poised to become part of the world of reason, we have been thrown back on to the troubled terrain of desire. Post-modernism dislocates and fragments while claiming to create discursive spaces for a multitude of voices. But, they are so elitist and obscure in their language and this reliance on "French feminism" is spurious. Christine Delphy is strong on that move and Carol Anne Douglas puts it bluntly, "I'll take the low road . . . and I'll be in Scotland, Peoria, Bangladesh, or any other actual place before you." It's not that radical feminists are "theory shy", it's just that we know a theory that is good in theory but doesn't work in practice is not much of a theory worth knowing. This book will be about crossing boundaries, about women taking control of their lives, refusing to buy the cheap, tawdry, and sentimental depictions of their place in society. It will have humour, compassion, dedication, hard work, and dangerous work. It will engage all generations. Here goes the proposal.

RADICALLY SPEAKING is a collection of radical feminist voices distinguished by their continuity through time, global reach, politics of engagement and passionate determination to create a better world for women. In bringing these voices together, we seek to tell a story of a particular past, present and hopes for the future: one that concerns justice, dignity and above all safety from all forms of violence. We see this as an urgent undertaking. Radical feminists' knowledge of the past has been misrepresented, fragmented, and indeed abused in the retelling by others, such as liberal and Marxist feminists, post-modernists, the right and the media. Furthermore, our ability to act in the present is being severely curtailed by the post-modern insistence that there are no subjects, with the consequence that woman has been virtually erased as the author of her own life. Women, reduced to an assemblage of texts and multiplicities of identities, no longer exist as a sociological category. From this perspective, women's on-going multifaceted oppressions by men as a social class are deemed at best irrelevant, at worst non-existent. Thus, envisaging a feminist future is rendered impossible: woman disappears.

Act Three: Where during an extended pregnancy, the manuscript grows larger and larger

In June 1992 we composed a letter which spelt out what we wanted to accomplish in putting together our collection of radical voices. We sent that initial letter and the proposal to twenty-eight colleagues, all women who had been involved in radical feminist campaigns over the years. Of this first group, some twenty stayed with us and appear in the present volume. We asked for suggestions of others we might involve in the project and the list grew. As the word spread that we were putting together a book on radical feminism and were serious about critiquing post-modernism, feminists came to us with papers that might be appropriate. We made lists of the themes we wanted to address and sought out authors. The book grew. Our publisher shuddered. By now it was obvious the book had a life of its own. This was no single-issue, monolithic work; it was as diverse as radical feminism. It refused to be constrained and it had an underlying coherence: all our contributors were committed to working for social change.

As we read and talked, patterns emerged from the manuscript and we realised that this was what we wanted: to tease out themes that would be reflections on the feminism we'd set out to document. Short, snappy, previously published pieces, which we called "Memorable Media Moments", such as Sandra Coney's "The Last Post for Feminism", and Kathleen Barry's "Deconstructing Deconstruction" would frame the sections. While there are many expressions of radical feminism, at core is agreement that under patriarchy women can not be fully self-determining human beings and a commitment to transforming society so that women may enjoy their full personhood. Patriarchy assumes different forms under different conditions: it may be classism, sexism, racism, homophobia and ageism – and it is their multiple intersections that we need to understand. Hence radical feminist strategies have included law reform, speak-outs, sit-ins and marches; the establishment of various centres for women. Radical analyses have focused on the violence against women in its many forms, from rape and pornography, through sexual harassment to reproductive technologies. These we understand as manifestations of the oppression of women. But radical writings have also celebrated the power of resistance and passion when women are each other's best friends.

At first glance, the politics of the 90s appears to be fertile ground for an inclusive, interdisciplinary, problem-based approach. Likewise, global communi-cation networks seem to facilitate inclusive, rather than piecemeal approaches. However, tracing interconnections and drawing macro-maps are no longer fashion-able activities for sophisticates. Rather, the fracturing of nation states, shrinking of budgets, growing specialisations and sub-fields, have spurred a return to the safe harbours of individual disciplines, where one may plumb the depths of a sub-discipline. To attempt to be a Renaissance woman in the late 90s is quite a task: little wonder radical feminists who still try to keep in touch with the many fields with which they need to be conversant are called dinosaurs. However, in our view, a radical feminist analysis is more pertinent than ever; maybe that is why we are so feared.

When our students set out to do independent research, it reflects their lives. One focuses on sexual harassment, and she has already learnt that the law alone will not protect her; another explores violence against women tennis stars, she is herself a fine athlete; several examine women's health issues, and find their female kin have stories yet to be told. Population control and genetic engineering are as eagerly researched as are the daily realities of female friendship and similarities between the "second" and the "third" wave of the Women's Movement. These young women are involved in women's organisations that are working for change. Through vigils, condom distributions on Valentine's Day (on a Catholic campus!), fundraising for lesbian centres, speak-outs, marches, and demonstrations, they continually emphasise the relationship between practice and theory.

Mid-1995, we printed out the table of contents and found that we had 66 articles, and 68 contributors. Anyone who thought that radical feminism was dead should think again. These were brave, witty, incisive, inclusive voices that spoke out of practice. They exude a gritty determination which refuses to be cowed, an irreverence for boundaries (disciplinary or canonical), a willingness to tackle issues as they arise and to address them in all their specificity and messiness. The scholarship is rigorous, and unrelenting in the recounting and accounting. For those who are more comfortable with representations than real lives, such voices are shocking. Still there is a playfulness with language, a well-honed sense of humour – as the Po-mo Quiz demonstrates – and experimentation with style, poetry, fiction, photographs, metaphors.

As the manuscript came into being, we wondered if there were any glaring omissions. We knew we were going on to produce a companion volume, *Essential Readings: A Source Book* (forthcoming) which would contain many of the classic writings of radical feminists, so we would be able to republish pieces by authors already in *Radically Speaking*. Often we felt that one piece hadn't done justice to the range of a particular contributor's work and by now the publisher was in a dead faint. Basically, given the constraints of time, space and other peoples' workloads, we were happy with the range of issues covered. More on work and health would have been welcome. On sexuality, we would have liked to add to the critiques with something positive, as Susan Hawthorne evokes in her wild politics and Robyn Rowland addresses in her piece on radical feminist heterosexuality.

Act Four: Where the hard part, giving birth, demonstrates that labouring internationally is worthwhile

Scene One: Speaking Radically

March 1995 was our first opportunity to behold the entire (well almost) manuscript and the book was already a monster (in the nicest possible Robin Morgan sense). Diane had flown in from the USA, where an ice storm had ground most transport to a halt. Renate had rescheduled her teaching for the week. Our only plan was to celebrate International Women's Day on 8 March by attending the launch of Zelda D'Aprano's book in the afternoon and POW (Performing Older Women's Circus made up of women who ranged in age from 40 to 64) in the evening. The Melbourne weather was balmy; we went into retreat, and began to work our way through the manuscript. The book had almost organised itself into sections. It was as if our contributors were engaged in a lively set of conversations. On the basis of the number of shared texts, we decided that a consolidated bibliography was in order.

We did, however, decide to honour/honor and emphasise/emphasize the specificity of language by retaining the regional renditions of English spellings.

For us, a striking feature of the radical voices in this collection is the diversity of their standpoints. From Angela Bowen, Ngahuia Te Awekotuku, and Joy James comes an insistence that we not sever our experience from our analysis; that we do more than pay lip service to the sex/race/class mantra; that we ground our theorising in the lives of women from different communities. Joy James is blunt: "Without a history, philosophy is not indigenous to us as a people and "contemporary" theorizing becomes disconnected from its tradition." From Pat Mahoney and Christine Zmroczek comes a fierce reminder that working-class women have always been part of the Women's Movement and that many are radical feminists. Education *per se* has not cut them off from their roots: working-class values still resonate.

A corollary to the diversity of standpoints is that radical feminists are not single-issue feminists. It would simplify all our lives, not to mention our careers, if we were dealing in single issues, but we know from the nineteenth-century struggle for suffrage and the US women's struggle to pass the ERA in the 1970s and 80s of the dangers of having all one's eggs in one basket. Women's history, as Joan Hoff points out, is a critical component of developing a consciousness about the ways in which knowledge has been politicised and women written out of historical scripts. Our contributors are well aware of the need to keep many fires burning. In fact many could have written three or more pieces for us and still not exhausted their repertoire. Janice Raymond has written on women's friendships, reproductive technology, trafficking, the politics of lesbianism. Angela Bowen works on biography, dance and lesbian theory. Inés Talamantez' poem is an excerpt from a longer piece that commemorates the long walk from San Francisco to Washington DC which was undertaken to awaken the consciousness of US society to the struggles of Native Americans. A poet, journal editor, teacher of Chicano/a Studies and Native American Religions and an environmental activist, she protests injustice wherever it occurs. Noteworthy is that a sizeable proportion of our contributors are involved in establishing and running Women's Studies programs, as well as editing journals, newsletters, and book series.

Radical feminists, like radishes, go to the root. Thus, when Louise Armstrong takes on therapy she de-centres Freud; when Catharine MacKinnon and Andrea Dworkin speak of pornography as an infringement of women's civil rights, rather than an exercise of free speech, the male basis of the legal order is revealed; and when Morny Joy identifies the radical questions in religion, she demands an ethical accounting from the patriarchs. Radical challenges to these cornerstones of patriarchy, law, religion and medicine are rightly recognised as constituting a threat and not surprisingly there is a price to pay for naming the locus of oppression.

The "personal is the political", perhaps the best-known radical feminist slogan is, as Jocelynne Scutt illustrates, a powerful analytical tool; it is at once both simple and complex, but it means just what it says. When Robin Morgan's collected poems, *Monster*, appeared in 1972, she demanded that Ted Hughes be called to account regarding his relationship with Sylvia Plath. In explicit terms she told the story of the destruction of a talented woman by an overweening male ego. Random House, the USA publishers, felt her poem "Arraignment" was "unfair" and "libelous" and Robin Morgan was faced with the choice: rewrite or be silenced. Believing her collection constituted personal/political/aesthetic poems "to be used as real tools/ weapons in the hands and heart and minds of my sisters," she rewrote "Arraignment" in a hypothetical form. *Monster*, in the USA, included this version, but feminists in Australia, Canada, and Great Britain prepared pirate editions that included both versions (Morgan, n.d. p. iii). "How can I accuse Ted Hughes?" she asked . . .

> . . . myths of freedom are actually atrocities of co-optation or of out and out censorship . . . male bonding around power is all-pervasive; . . . those who keep silent about murder are indeed accomplices in the act . . . it is a wiser and more serious revolutionary feminist who communicates the above to her readers rather than misleading them about free speech fairy-tales.

Two decades later, in Yorkshire, as commemorated in Robyn Rowland's poem, five feminists, intent on remembering Plath, chiselled the name of Hughes from her gravestone.

Scene Two: Radical feminists under attack

With acts such as these, no wonder radical feminism is the feminism that everyone loves to hate. The attack on radical feminism as both a theory and a praxis has continued since the first Take Back the Night marches and collectives theorising from experience. It is evident in the present characterisation of radical feminism as essentialist and therefore perilously close to right-wing platforms; in the charge that radical feminism universalises and therefore masks differences amongst women; and in the assertion that radical feminism is ahistorical and therefore non-cognisant of the specificity of time and place. "Liberal feminism is the feminism that the media plays back to us," says Andrea Dworkin and Tania Lienert looks at the conflation of radical and cultural feminism. Similarly, Diane Richardson asks, whose interests are served by such labels as "essentialism", "moralistic", "monolithic", and "oversimplification"? Given that for us social change is the most important item on the political agenda, it is difficult to understand why we would hold on to a belief in essential, unchangeable selves as the basis of social order.

When radical feminists are attacked, the depths to which the attackers will sink know no bounds. When Carlin Romano begins a review of Catharine MacKinnon's *Only Words* with "Suppose I rape MacKinnon before I write this review . . .", we have to wonder what is going on. Seven young Women's Studies students have an answer. The attackers are not addressing the substantive issues raised by MacKinnon. We find over and over again that when radical feminists are attacked it is not through engagement with their analyses but through demonising the authors. Attacks come from persons with well-known and long-established hostilities to radical feminists and thus we spend valuable time just correcting and refuting, rather than being able to advance the debates and map strategies for social change. Rejecting any notion that they are separated from the issues by a generation, these seven young feminists claim the radical feminist agenda as their agenda. They know that violence against women has not abated. The personal is the political for them as much as it is for many older women.

Despite the attacks, radical feminists refuse to be silenced and, instead of being intimidated, explore the dimensions of the strategies of silencing. This may entail a task as pragmatic as the archiving of our history, as Jalna Hanmer recounts. Silencing may also be about threatening your job. Pauline Bart's defiant narrative about the University of Illinois and Ellen Travis discussing Somer Brodribb's bizarre saga illustrate this all too well. Or, as Uta Enders-Dragässer and Brigitte Sellach argue, when your research is dismissed as narrow-minded and unprofessional, as happened to German educationalists, feminists are also silenced. The insidiousness of such practices is that they are not about men versus women, but about the power of patriarchy to co-opt, silence and make complicit. The marvel is the wit and irony with which deep hurt and betrayals are confronted and recounted.

Isn't it strange how in attacks on radical feminists, the whistle-blowers become the troublemakers and are then identified as the problem? This is what happened to Diane Bell in writing about intra-racial rape when she was attacked by a unholy alliance of angry urban Aboriginal and white women who preferred to dissect the prose rather than confront the extent of the violence. Similarly, critics of reproductive technologies find that, instead of their critiques forming the basis for an informed discussion of the inhuman and dangerous nature of reproductive and genetic engineering, they are blamed for being cruel to infertile women. The first response is to shoot the messenger, and in so doing, to deflect attention away from the substantive issues. Unfortunately, this often sets women against women. "Faux-feminists", as Susan Faludi (1995, p. 30) calls Camille Paglia and her ilk, purport to present a "feminism" for our times. They denounce the second wave of feminists and their concern with violence against women, delight the media, pander to the right wing, and set young women against older women. In Australia in 1995 Helen Garner's *The First Stone* charmed misogynists across the land with its trivialising of two young women's use of sexual harassment laws. Bemoaning a feminism that had ". . . mutated into – these cold-faced, punitive girls" with "hard hearts" (p. 100), Garner depicted the third wave of feminism as fragile and mis-guided. The media celebrated the "wisdom" of her words and the Eros Foundation, a libertarian pro-pornography national lobby group fittingly awarded her their 1995 Book of the Year prize (as reported in *Australian*, 18 December 1995, p. 3).

In another of these about-face moves, older feminists, Sheila Jeffreys, Catharine MacKinnon and Andrea Dworkin have been labelled the "New Victorians": the anti-sex puritans of the pornographic wars. But, how many of the free speech proponents have actually read the texts or seen the images? Too often they pass judgement based on the descriptions of pornographic acts and sexual attacks on women that are illustrative case material in radical feminists' critiques. It facilitates quite remarkable misreadings of attempts to reform the law, such as the Butler

Diane Bell and Renate Klein

decision in Canada which takes an equality approach to pornography's harm to women. Taking a stand means making judgements that one can act on. Sexual and reproductive liberals are more comfortable talking about "choice" and how radical feminists make women into victims, than spelling out an explicit agenda of human rights for women. Janice Raymond has the political courage to ask the hard questions about victimhood, coercion and complicity in a way that offers a framing for a nuanced understanding of radical feminist strategies in a post-modern climate.

Scene Three: Radical feminists "interrogate" post-modernism

The critiques of post-modernism are consistent. Whereas post-modernists occupy the borderlands looking out over the wastelands created by their deconstructive brilliance, radical feminists have been busy crossing boundaries in order to integrate modes of understanding. The common ground thus generated constitutes what Mary Daly has mapped as a kind of "collective feminist memory" which makes action on many and diverse projects possible. While we can understand the attraction of retreating into disciplines where there is some limit on what one is asked to do, the possibility of addressing actual issues as they arise in the lives of particular women is curtailed.

So what do our contributors have to say about post-modernism? Post-modernism is self-contradictory as Kristin Waters and Denise Thompson demonstrate: by declaring the end of all truth, it makes a truth claim! Post-modernism is politically irresponsible as Katja Mikhailovich shows with reference to violence against women. Post-modernism has (dead) bodies floating in cyberspace, writes Renate Klein. Sheila Jeffreys argues that post-modernism disappears women with reference to lesbianandgay theory and, in the queer theory turn, lesbians are disappeared. Post-modernism relies on a most partial, ahistorical and decontextualised reading of high theory (mainly French) as Christine Delphy explains. Post-structuralism is a "friend of Phallic Drift," writes Joan Hoff. "Like the tendency of a compass to drift north no matter how you turn the instrument, Phallic Drift is the powerful tendency . . . to drift inexorably to the male point of view."

Post-modernism is not about change, it is about wallowing in dystopias and doing it with glee. Post-modernism represents women by differences, not similarities, and the power of the representer is masked. Because it declines to identify domination in general and male domination in particular, post-modernism cannot contest the relations of power. The post-modern turn has depoliticised feminist theory. Post-modernism prioritises pleasure over political analysis, as Sue Wilkinson and Celia Kitzinger explain. The move from reason to desire, the emphasis on style rather than content, take feminism away from its roots in politics. Post-modernism may make feminism safer for the academy, but not safer for women, Kristin Waters concludes. On the surface, post-modernism is about making a discursive space available to the "other". In fact, it is elitist, as Barbara Christian and Joy James demonstrate.

Feminist theory, Kristin Waters argues, can interactively illuminate analyses made from standpoints of race, class and culture. In fact, feminism has already traversed much of the terrain currently claimed as newly articulated by the post-modernists. "So, genealogically," Kristin Waters writes, "feminist theory in the US largely precedes and informs post-modernism, not the reverse." It is feminist theory which, from the beginning, has provided self-conscious critiques of modern theories from the Enlightenment to the present. Post-modernism, on the other hand, with its move to "destabilize the subject," is a reiteration of the modern argument against abstract ideas.

Scene Four: Refusing to be silenced

Words may fly in the academy, but radical feminists refuse to be silenced. There is too much important work to be done. Take violence against women. Radical feminists have been talking about the various ways in which women are silenced, abused, coerced, exploited, and trafficked. They have documented these forms of violence from the local level to the international, but they haven't stopped there. Some, like Yenlin Ku in Taiwan, have worked through grassroots organisations, the legislature, and feminist publishing to create a safer world for women. Some, like Tatyana Mamonova in the Commonwealth of Independent States, who has spent decades publicising the plight of Russian women, now find that changes in the geopolitical structures have facilitated an intensification of pornographic markets and prostitution. Teboho Maitse, from South Africa, turns her attention to the nationalism of the new South Africa, and finds that women are poorly served. In her view, it offers women no protection from male violence. "Instead rape, battering, harassment, molestation and sexist jokes continue under the umbrella of nationalism and serve to keep women in their place." Diana Russell began by addressing issues of rape, pornography, femicide and sado-masochism when she was a tenured professor at Mills College, California. Frustrated by the restraints of the academy, she took her activism to the streets on a full-time basis, was arrested, but continued. More recently she has returned to her native South Africa, and there kept working for women, only to learn that US pornography has found a profitable market in this newly liberated country. As with Tatyana Mamonova's experience in Russia, freedom and democracy do not necessarily mean a better world for women.

Telling a woman's story can be a revolutionary act: but, under certain circumstances, so can silence. When Evelyne Accad speaks out about genital mutilation, she raises the most difficult of questions regarding sensitivity to others: how to speak? Like other feminists caught in this cross-cultural dilemma, Evelyne Accad chooses to name this form of violence against women. Like Marjorie Agosin she is prepared to experiment with style. Through poetry and fiction, these women take us into their worlds. Agosin takes us into the Plaza de Mayo, where the mothers of the disappeared stand mute. In the accompanying photograph by Alicia D'Amico and Alicia Sanguinetti, we witness the importance of silence as a female strategy of protest. Finding a way of framing stories of horror, such as those coming out of Croatia, Bosnia-Hercegovina, is another example of feminist balancing "tradition" against human rights. Making the argument that rape in war is a human rights crime and that what has happened in this region of Europe is genocidal femicide has required enormous courage, but silence in this instance would be complicity. Silence kills. But how to speak and in what voice? WHISPER, when it stands for Women Hurt in Systems of Prostitution Engaged in Revolt, makes anything but a small noise. Rather, Eveline Giobbe's organisation supports women quitting prostitution.

Scene Five: Feminism reclaimed

From the very beginning of the second wave of the Women's Liberation Movement, radical feminists have lobbied for, established and maintained women's health centres, rape crisis centres, refuges, and a range of other collectives for women in the field of the arts, science, law and medicine. Radical feminists understand the need for safe places. Berit As struggled to establish a feminist university in Norway, and in Santa Barbara, California, a rape crisis centre is explicit about its feminist politics and its cross-cultural mission. Likewise, the Pitjantjatjara Women's Council has developed a health service that is finely tuned to the needs of Aboriginal women in desert Australia. Little by way of tribute attaches to those who work in woman-focused organisations, as we have seen in the USA with the murder of employees of Planned Parenthood. Making women's spaces and women's rights visible is a direct threat to patriarchal structures and is punished accordingly by those whose sense of entitlement is infringed upon.

Although involved in the immediacy of a particular struggle, be it the daily demands of working in a rape crisis or a women's health centre, and scarcely able to draw breath, we write. Despite putting in the long grinding years of strategising, fundraising, networking, and petitioning that it takes to pull together an international Coalition Against Trafficking in Women, the International Feminist Book Fair, the Sisterhood is Global Institute, or the Feminist International Network of Resistance to Reproductive and Genetic Engineering (FINRRAGE), we write. Sometimes our writing issues in a declaration like that at Comilla in Bangladesh where sixty-one women from twent-three countries opposed population control. When radical feminists write they are theorising from practice.

How do we speak across difference? One thing is sure, radical feminists have refused to give in to despair. Mahnaz Afkhami, speaking from a Muslim perspective, holds out the hope that Third World feminists can develop a sense of empathy with their western sisters in other parts of the globe. Despite the difficulties, women have persevered with collaborative structures, collective action and cross-cultural communication, and have experimented in their writing, organising and businesses. Powhiri Rika-Hike and Sigrid Markmann write from within their cultures, but do so in a common language. They have found ways to build coalitions despite the dilemmas of speaking as Maori, lesbian and German. These complex undertakings demand finding ways of overcoming the strictures of the dominant culture while remaining faithful to one's own experience. Collaborative work requires dedication, but it can also be exciting as Cathie Dunsford, Beryl Fletcher and Susan Sayer demonstrate through their exchange about writing, editing, and publishing. The work of such women offers glimpses of the quality of knowledge that might be generated through co-operation rather than conflict. This is a radical thought.

So where do we go from here? Susan Hawthorne's "Wild Politics" are inspirational. "Let us not eradicate all meaning from the world," she writes:

> Wild politics is feminist and in keeping with the resistance of Indigenous peoples, the poor and the marginalised. It resists Coca Cola colonisation and accumulation, over-consumption, fundamentalist and repressive ideologies, mass communications, the military and interference by international scientific, monetary and cultural elites. Wild politics is a politics of joy.

[Scene as for Act 4, Scene 1]

It was a wonderful International Women's Day. Zelda D'Aprano held us spellbound. "We need feminism with a heart," said this activist of three decades. The republication of her autobiography *Zelda* brought together feminists across the generations. Radical women celebrated radical women.

Act Five: Where our production schedule threatens to overwhelm us, but with the help of many, *Radically Speaking: Feminism Reclaimed* launches forth

Somewhere in a course on publishing, that neither of us has taken, it is probably explained that to bring an edited collection from idea to reality requires that we not exceed a certain number of contributors. It may also be explained that you need access to faxes, frequent flyer-miles and photocopiers. A big fat grant would help too, as would a sabbatical. *Radically Speaking* certainly pushed the limits of our resources and time, and we could never have made it without the help of many, many good women and several key institutions. We had no grant, but we did grab every possible opportunity to create working spaces for our book. Renate thanks Deakin University for Outside Study Program Support, 1994, during which time she was able to work with Diane in the USA. Diane thanks the College of the Holy Cross for support on her sabbatical 1993–4 and the generous funding of her position by the Henry Luce Foundation. We both thank our respective institutions for their facilitation of international communications.

We thank each and every one of our 68 contributors, who have filled in countless forms, have been patient and were forthcoming with ideas and contacts. Above all, they have sustained us with their unwavering enthusiasm and insistence that this critically important book had to be published. Our publisher, Spinifex Press, has been all that a feminist press can be and although Susan Hawthorne declared that never again would she publish a book with fifty-plus contributors, she did. We thank her for her humour, skill, and commitment to *Radically Speaking*. Likewise, Louise Murray's enthusiasm at Zed Press, London, was heartening. Michelle Proctor and Jo Turner bore the brunt of administration, entering data and keeping those files ordered. Jo, in particular, did an extraordinary amount of work in the last phase of this (gigantic) project and we really appreciate her going the extra mile. Sarn Potter did the page design and Claire Warren, typesetter extraordinaire, one more time outdid herself and despite the pressure remained her usual cheerful self. And we thank Liz Nicholson for making waves with the elegant cover.

Diane: I thank my daughter Genevieve for listening and offering helpful suggestions as over and over I enumerated the merits of this book and declared it done. I also thank my students for their wonderful examples of what young feminists can be. Working on *Radically Speaking* has consumed much of my time over the last three years and the best part of this has been being able to spend time with Renate, sometimes in the USA, sometimes in Australia, but always in moving forward with a project we both passionately believe in. Renate's capacity to work intensely on three projects at the same time is one I envy. I have enjoyed her sharp wit, marvelled at her global knowledge, and looked forward to golden moments in her gardens.

Renate: I thank students and staff in Women's Studies at Deakin University where radical feminism is proudly taught. In particular I thank Alison Brookes, Tania Lienert, Kathy Munro and Laurel Guymer for their support and Robyn Rowland for being an unwavering radical feminist colleague and friend. From afar, I thank Janice Raymond and Christine Zmroczek for always being there. Kelly McElroy and Jane Rocca deserve a medal for keeping the paperwork at bay and doing bibliographic tasks. Debra Voogt and Dorthe Rusz scanned pages, typed articles and addresses, and generally provided secretarial assistance without ever losing their cool. The best thing about editing *Radically Speaking* was the opportunity to work with Diane, whose generosity of spirit, awesome intellect, and great sense of humour made hard work pleasurable. I learned, however, that she too has a weakness – don't disturb her files – but even when I did, she still cooked fabulous meals.

Our collaboration has been a joy. Especially pleasant has been discovering how easily we can write together and *Radically Speaking* is not our last word on the subject of radical feminism. *Essential Readings: A Source Book*, now in preparation, is a collection of classic texts that feminists need. Radical feminism has a past, a present and a future.

Diane Bell and Renate Klein,
1995, Leicester and Melbourne

I

SPEAKING RADICALLY

Inés Maria Talamantez

Woman of all Nations

Deep within
I am wild in my sorrow
I am a woman

       a working woman
       a good Apache woman
       a gathering woman
       a Red World woman
       a brown Chicana woman
       a mother woman
       a loving woman
       a blue woman
       a eucalyptus woman
       a soft woman
       a loud woman
       a resisting woman
       a trouble making woman
       a hunting woman
       a moving woman
       a quiet woman
       a dancing woman
       a singing woman
       a pollen woman
       a spirit woman
       a desert woman
       a mountain woman
       an ocean woman
       a White World woman

a trail making woman
a changing woman

Look around you
Look around you

What do you see
What do you see

What will you do
What will you do

When will we walk together
When will we walk together

Robin Morgan

Light Bulbs, Radishes, and the Politics of the 21st Century

Radical feminism – that wilfully misunderstood, frequently maligned state of political being, consciousness, and action that reputedly makes journalists snarl, funders wince, "post-modern" academics tremble, and strong men go catatonic — well, you ask, what is it *really?*

I could reply with one of the notorious feminist light bulb jokes: Q – How many radical feminists does it take to change a light bulb? A – Thirteen. One to change the bulb and twelve to argue over the definition of "radical feminist".

Or I could point out that etymology is usually revealing: the word "radical", for example, refers to "going to the root" (as in radish) of an issue or subject. (That is to say, why waste time on political superficialities when you can wrestle with the most primary, basic oppression of all?)

Or I might suggest that we use deduction as a method of defining. For example, radical feminism is not:

* socialist (or Marxist) feminism. This is because radical feminists reject a politics positing: (a) that sexism is merely a by-product of capitalism, (b) that patriarchy, like the state, will wither away under communism, (c) that women automatically become free and equal snap! in socialist or communist societies, (d) that boring words ending in "–tion" and "–ism", written by white, heterosexual, middle-class, nineteenth-century European Jewish men (however bright or bearded), could actually constitute feminist theory, or (e) that imitating leftist men could possibly be good for women.
* liberal (or reformist) feminism. This is because radical feminists refuse to settle: (a) for the individual solution – otherwise known as a piece of the pie as currently and poisonously baked, (b) for pornography and prostitution as faux sexual liberation, (c) for "wonderfully supportive" male lovers or spouses who "permit" a woman to be a feminist, (d) for a politics that refers to "women's issues" (as if all issues weren't women's issues), thus ignoring the organic connections

between sexism, racism, class and homophobic and ethnocentric bigotries, environmental degradation, and, well, everything else, or (e) for playing by the boys' rules, e.g. thinking that imitating establishment men could possibly be good for women.

- cultural feminism. This is because radical feminists – while affirming the existence of an emerging global cross-cultural "women's culture" – nevertheless do not believe that profound societal change can be brought about solely: (a) by women dancing shirtless in a circle under the full moon, (b) by shaking tambourines and singing lesbian love songs to women-only audiences, (c) by praising the Goddess without also passing the petition, (d) by putting the making of political mischief second to the making of pottery, teas, tie-dyed garments, hand-dipped candles, tofu casseroles, or a stunning sister, or (e) by believing that imitating pseudo-counter-culture men – to get stoned, laid, or away from it all – could possibly be good for women.

Well, that's a start toward definition (and whoever said radical feminists had no sense of humor, had no sense). But seriously, folks. Although the list isn't high in number (but it is in quality), there are anthologies of/on radical feminism that are sister to the one you hold in your hands. Among them: *Radical Feminism* (Koedt *et al.*: 1973), forty-five articles ranging from the personal to the theoretical, although all US voices; *Take Back the Night: Women on Pornography* (Lederer: 1980), indispensable for an overview of the radical feminist position against pornography; *Against Sadomasochism: A Radical Feminist Analysis* (Linden *et al.*: 1982), twenty-six writers able to tell the difference between libertarianism and freedom; *For the Record: The Making and Meaning of Feminist Knowledge*, a collection short in pages but long on strength (Spender: 1985); *Femicide: The Politics of Woman Killing* (Radford and Russell: 1992), an international collection of powerful politics and impassioned words; *Making Violence Sexy: Feminist Views on Pornography*, a furthering of the Lederer cited above, both scholarly and radical (Russell: 1993); and of course *Sisterhood Is Powerful* (Morgan: 1970), the first anthology of the contemporary feminist wave, containing voices of primarily, although not exclusively, US women; and *Sisterhood Is Global: The International Women's Movement Anthology* (Morgan: 1984), presenting radical feminist contributors – plus encyclopedic statistics, "herstory", analysis, and bibliography – from more than eighty countries.

Well, when you've fortified your spirit and stiffened your spine with some of the above work on radical feminism, dear reader, you will, as they say, "recognize it when you see it".

The strength of this politics lies, in fact, in its dynamism, in the fluid energy that links unapologetic intellect with unashamed passion; it is a means, not an end; a process, not a dogma. Consequently, what a radical feminist in Brazil (the nation's debt, for example) might consider her cutting-edge issue, need not be the same as that considered a priority by a radical feminist in Thailand (combating sex tourism) or in Kuwait (winning women's suffrage) or in Sudan (ending the practice of female genital mutilation) or Nepal (gaining inheritance rights) or the Pacific Island nations (halting French nuclear testing, the fallout of which creates "jellyfish babies" – children born with no spines), and so on – and so on, and on.

What radical feminists have in common, though, includes a stubborn commitment to the people of women, the courage to dare question anything and dare redefine everything, a dedication to making the connections between issues, a sobering comprehension of the enormity of this task – freeing more than half of humanity and, by so doing, saving the other half – and perhaps most importantly of all, *radical feminists share an audacious understanding of this politics' centrality to the continuation of sentient life itself on this planet.*

This is no hyperbole. Women constitute the majority of the human species, so the female condition is hardly a marginal or minority issue. Furthermore, all the ills that afflict humankind – from pollution to war to poverty – impact first and worst on women, who are also the last to be consulted about solutions to such problems.

Two-thirds of all illiterates are women. Women and children comprise ninety per cent of all refugee populations (whether fleeing war or environmental disaster), and eighty per cent of all poverty populations. One-third of all families on earth are woman-headed. Less than one-third of all women have access to contraceptive information, and more than half have no trained help during pregnancy and childbirth. Complications from pregnancy, childbirth, and abortion – which kill more than half a million women per year – are the leading cause of death among all women of reproductive age. With non-pregnancy-related reproductive tract infections (RTIs) factored in, the death toll rises to more than a million, with another hundred million maimed every year. Toxic waste, pesticides, nuclear fallout, and other pollutions take their first toll as cancers of the female reproductive system, and in stillborn infants and birth deformities. The global pandemic of HIV/AIDS now affects more female human beings than males. Women are more than one-third of the world's formal labor force, but receive only one-tenth of world income and own less than one per cent of world property. Outside the formal labor force – whether as homemaker, nun, farmer, or domestic servant – women's work is regarded as unskilled, marginal, transient, or simply "natural", and is invisible in the Gross Domestic Product accounting of virtually all nations. Nowhere does the work of reproduction of the species count as "productive activity". The environment is a "woman's issue" because women are the fuel gatherers, water haulers, and fodder collectors of the world, as well as most of its farmers (eighty per cent of farmers on the African continent alone are women). Violence against women is global, cross cultural, and epidemic, in diverse forms not restricted to rape (including date/acquaintance rape and marital rape), battery, sexual molestation and abuse, and sexual harassment. It is evident in the practice of sati – the forced "suicide" of an otherwise property-inheriting widow on her husband's funeral pyre – still prevalent, though outlawed, on the subcontinent of India. It is conspicuous in female infanticide, still practiced, though illegal, in China.

It is apparent in the "traditions" of bride sale, child marriage, polygyny, dowry murders, and forced seclusion in purdah. It is blatant in the international traffick in sexual slavery of women and children. It is manifest in the denial of two basic human rights – reproductive freedom and freedom of sexual choice – by fundamentalists of all patriarchal religions.

Perhaps it becomes clear why all issues are feminist issues – and why bandaid reforms, or equality with men in a male-defined society, or "empowering" women to have "self-esteem" while leaving intact a status quo with a perforated ozone layer – all are pseudo-solutions that a radical feminist finds unacceptable; the beautifully irascible voices in this collection cannot be bought off so easily.

Of course, "feminism" itself – even without a qualifying prefix – can be the subject of debated definitions. At its most basic, it can mean simply the struggle for female freedom against a male supremacist society – certainly a vital, valid fight in itself. It also can be, in part, an ethics, an esthetics, even a metaphysics. For me, feminism (inherently and potentially so radical in itself as to make the prefix "radical" almost redundant) is also something more: it is the politics uniquely capable at this moment in history of, quite literally, saving the fragile blue and green biosphere named Earth.

Which is why I call feminism The Politics of the 21st Century.

To me, this is obvious, sensible, and reasonable.

To me, this isn't even radical.

Robyn Rowland and Renate Klein

Radical Feminism: History, Politics, Action*

Introduction

Because of its very nature, radical feminism has concentrated on creating its theory in the writing of women's lives and the political analysis of women's oppression. Little time has been devoted to defining and redefining our "theory" for theory's sake. Where socialist, liberal, and more recently post-modernist feminisms have convenient existing theoretical structures to manipulate and re-manipulate, stretching them like a skin across the drum of women's experiences, radical feminism creates an original political and social theory of women's oppression, and strategies for ending that oppression which come from women's lived experiences.

So Janice Raymond writes her theory of women's friendships, their passion and the obstacles involved in befriending women. In doing so she critiques hetero-reality: the value system of women as being "for" men, upon which patriarchy rests. Kathleen Barry, Catharine MacKinnon, Susan Griffin, and Andrea Dworkin document the international trafficking in women and children, pornography and rape, creating a power analysis of violence against women and the abuse of women's bodies as international currency. Radical feminists frequently combine creative writing and theory, such as in the poetry and prose of Adrienne Rich, Audre Lorde, Robin Morgan, Susan Griffin, and Judy Grahn. Here the passion of radical feminism can be fully expressed, because it is a theory of the emotional as well as the rational intellect.

Theory and practice are interdependently intertwined. Anne Koedt, Judith Levine, and Anita Rapone touched on this in their introduction to *Radical Feminism* in 1973 when they wrote: "... the purpose in selecting and organising this anthology was to present primary source material not so much *about* as *from* the Radical Feminist Movement" (our italics, p. viii). Radical means "pertaining to the root"; Radical Feminism looks at the roots of women's oppression. As Robin Morgan says:

---

* This is an expanded version of "Radical Feminism: Critique and Construct" (Gunew, Ed., 1990a).
We would like to acknowledge Christine Zmroczek's invaluable contribution in unearthing early radical feminist writings.

> I call myself a Radical Feminist, and that means specific things to me. The etymology of the word 'radical' refers to 'one who goes to the root'. I believe that sexism is the root oppression, the one which, until and unless we uproot it will continue to put forth the branches of racism, class hatred, ageism, competition, ecological disaster, and economic exploitation. This means, to me, that the so-called revolutions to date have been *coups-d'état* between men, in a halfhearted attempt to prune the branches but leave the root embedded for the sake of preserving their own male privileges (1978, p. 9).

Radical feminism's revolutionary intent is expressed first and foremost in its woman-centredness: women's experiences and interests are at the centre of our theory and practice. It is the only theory *by* and *for* women. Radical feminism names *all* women as part of an oppressed group, stressing that no woman can walk down the street or even live in her home safely without fear of violation by men. But French feminist Christine Delphy points out that like all oppressed people, many women do not like to accept that they are part of an oppressed group, misunderstanding a power analysis for "conspiracy theory" and mistakenly feeling a threat to their sense of agency.

Feminism itself has often marginalised radical feminism, moving into a comfortable and easy libertarianism, stressing individualism rather than collective responsibility; or into socialism with its ready made structures to attack, withdrawing the heat from the main actors of patriarchy: men themselves.

More than sixteen years after the publication of *Feminist Practice: Notes From the Tenth Year* (1979) – a self-published pamphlet by a group of English radical feminists – many of the comments about the place of radical feminism still ring true.

> We are all agreed that we would call ourselves Radical Feminists and that we want to do something about the fact that we feel our politics have been lost, have become invisible, in the present state of the WLM [Women's Liberation Movement]. We feel that this was partly Radical Feminism's own fault, for in England we have not written much for ourselves – concentrating on action – and so being defined (maligned?) by others by default.
>
> We feel that Radical Feminism has been a, if not *the*, major force in the WLM since the start, but as factions started to emerge it has rarely been women who called themselves radical feminists who have defined radical feminism. For a long time it was used as a term of abuse to corral those aspects of WL which frightened those concerned with male acceptability, those aspects which most threatened their image of respectability. Radical Feminists became a corporate object of derision which these women and men could then dissociate themselves from (p. 1).

Post sixties radical feminism also had its history in women's activism in the past. For example, Hedwig Dohm in Germany, Susan B. Anthony, Matilda Joslyn Gage, and Charlotte Perkins Gilman in the US, Christabel Pankhurst (before her socialism) and Virginia Woolf in England, and Vida Goldstein in Australia are but a few of our predecessors.[1] In November 1911, in England, a radical feminist review, *The Free Woman*, began publishing weekly as a forum for revolutionary ideas about women, marriage, politics, prostitution, sexual relations, and issues concerning women's oppression and strategies for ending it. It was banned by booksellers, and many suffragists objected to it because of its critical position on the fight for the vote as the single issue which would ensure women's equality. "Feminism is the whole issue, political enfranchisement a branch issue," they wrote (in Tuttle: 1986, p. 117).

Definitional Statements From Radical Feminism

As space is limited, we concentrate on the general principles shared by the various streams within radical feminism rather than on the differences between them. The first and fundamental theme is that women as a social group are oppressed by men as a social group and that this oppression is the *primary* oppression for women. Patriarchy is the oppressing *structure* of male domination. Radical feminism makes visible male control as it is exercised in every sphere of women's lives, both public and private. So reproduction, marriage, compulsory heterosexuality, and motherhood are primary sites of attack and envisaged positive change.

Robin Morgan catches the excitement of radical feminism in her definition in *Going Too Far*.

> ... it wasn't ... a wing or arm or toe of the Left – or Right – or any other male-defined, male-controlled group. It was something quite Else, something in itself, a whole new politics, an entirely different and astoundingly radical way of perceiving society, sentient matter, life itself, the universe. It was a philosophy. It was immense. It was also most decidedly a real, autonomous Movement, this feminism, with all the strengths that implied. And with all the evils too – the familiar internecine squabbles (1978, p. 13).

A second central element characteristic of radical feminism is that it is created by women for women. Christine Delphy points out that people from the Left for example, are fighting on behalf of someone else, but that

> ... the contradictions which result from this situation are foreign to feminism. We are not fighting for others, but for ourselves. We and no other people are the victims of the oppression which we denounce and fight against. And when we speak, it is not in the name or in the place of others, but in our own name and in our own place (1984, p. 146).

---

1. See Dale Spender (1983), for a collection of historical writings on feminist theorists.

Radical feminism stresses that "emancipation" or "equality" on male terms is not enough. A total revolution of the social structures and the elimination of the processes of patriarchy are essential. In her paper published originally in 1979 titled "I Call Myself a Radical Feminist" British writer Gail Chester outlined her position, clearly defining herself as "active in and believing in the need for, a strong, autonomous, revolutionary movement for the liberation of women" (p. 12). To her radical feminism is both socialist in its intent and revolutionary.

Mary Daly defines radical feminism in terms of the selfhood of women. Reclaiming and remaking language she exhorts women to take their true Selves back, and become self-acting, self-respecting. In *Gyn/Ecology* (1978), she calls radical feminism a "journey of women becoming" (p. 1). Mary Daly has a unique style in which she reworks language for radical feminist purposes. Her work is impassioned, poetic and deals with the spiritual dimension. She sees the radical feminist task as changing consciousness, rediscovering the past and creating the future through women's radical "otherness". In her own words (p. 39): "Radical Feminism is not reconciliation with the father. Rather it is affirming our original birth, our original source, movement, surge of living. This finding of our original integrity is remembering our Selves."

In the introduction to the first issue of the French feminist journal *Questions Feministes* (1977) – a journal of radical feminist theory – the editors identify their political perspective as radical feminist, recognising that the political struggle they are involved in is that against "the oppression of women by the patriarchal social system" (p. 5). They outline some of the underlying principles of radical feminism: the notion that the social existence of men and women was created rather than being part of their "nature"; the right of women not to be "different" but to be "autonomous"; and a materialist approach to analysing women's oppression based on a premise that women form a social class based in sex. As Kate Millett (1971) wrote: "sex is a status category with political implications."

That women form a group that can be likened to a social class is an inherent part of radical feminist theory. Ti-Grace Atkinson wrote in 1974 that "the analysis begins with the feminist *raison d'être* that women are a class, that this class is political in nature, and that this political class is oppressed. From this point on, radical feminism separates from traditional feminism" (p. 41). She saw the "male/female system" as "the first and most fundamental instance of human oppression", adding that "all other class systems are built on top of it". She writes:

> Women will not be free until all oppressed classes are free. I am not suggesting that women work to free other classes. However in the case of women oppressing other women, the exercise of class privilege by identification in effect locks the sex class into place. In identifying one's interests with those of any power class, one thereby maintains the position of that class. As long as any class system is left standing, it stands on the backs of women (1974, p. 73).

In the Introduction to *Feminist Practice: Notes from the Tenth Year* (1979), the principles of Women's Liberation were clearly delineated. From this manifesto we can pull together some common threads: radical feminism insists that women as a social class or a social group are oppressed by men as a social group as well as individually by men who continue to benefit from that oppression and do nothing to change it; the system through which men do this has been termed patriarchy; radical feminism is women-centred and stresses both the personal as political and the need for collective action and responsibility; it is "power" rather than "difference" which determines the relationship between women and men. And finally, that "whatever we do we mean to enjoy ourselves while we do it!"

Theory and Practice

Because the theory is based in the experience of women's lives, it is part of the value system of Radical Feminism that "the personal is political". In Gail Chester's words (1979, p. 13): "Radical Feminist theory is that theory follows from practice and is impossible to develop in the absence of practice, because our theory is that practice and our practice is our theory". Misunderstandings have occurred because critics claim that radical feminism has rejected theory. But it has always maintained that we *do* need theory for understanding women's experiences, for evaluating the causes of women's oppression, and for devising strategies for action. But we *have* rejected theory which is too esoteric, too divorced from the reality of women's experiences, too inaccessible to the majority of women whom feminism is supposed to serve: theory which we have elsewhere titled "disengagement theory".[2]

Chester argues that radical feminist theory has not been recognised as "a theory" because it hasn't always been written down (p. 14): "If your theory is embodied in your practice, then the way you act politically has as much right to be taken as a serious statement of your theoretical position as writing it down in a book which hardly anybody will read anyhow".

Charlotte Bunch has written that theory is not "simply intellectually interesting", but that it is "crucial to the survival of feminism". It is not an academic exercise but "a process based on understanding and advancing the activist movement" (1983, p. 248). To this end, radical feminist theory is not an objective exercise, disengaged from women themselves. A theory which begins with women, places women and women's experiences at the centre, and names the oppression of women, involves an holistic view of the world, an analysis which probes every facet of existence for women. It is not, as Bunch indicates, a "laundry list of 'women's issues'", but "provides a basis for understanding every area of our lives ... politically, culturally, economically, and spiritually" (1983, p. 250).

Bunch cautions radical feminists against becoming tired and feeling that feminist theory is too slow in bringing about change. At these times "feminists are

---

2. Renate Klein and Robyn Rowland, Feminist Theory into Action: The Politics of Engagement, Australian Women's Studies Association Annual Conference, University of Sydney, September, 1992 (unpublished).

tempted to submerge our insights into one of the century's two dominant progressive theories of reality and change: democratic liberalism or Marxist socialism" (p. 250). Bunch argues that while feminism can learn from both of these streams of theory, it must not become embedded within them or too tied to them because our view of the world is an alternative view which is autonomous and women-centred.

For her, theory "both grows out of and guides activism in a continuing, spiralling process" (p. 251). It can be divided into four interrelated parts: a description of what exists and the naming of reality; an analysis of why the reality exists and the origin of women's oppression; strategies on how to change that reality; and determining a vision for the future (pp. 251–53).

An example of the coalescence between theory and practice is the development of collective action. Through collective work radical feminists have attempted to eliminate the concept of hierarchy which places power in the hands of a few over the many. Working in a co-operative fashion towards a common goal gives value to each woman, allowing her a voice, yet making all members collectively responsible for action.

An example of the grounding of activism in theory emerges in the analysis of the painful and unsanitised issues centering in the many violences against women: battering, rape, incest, reproductive violence and femicide. Grassroots organising at the level of women's daily existence and survival, for example within the Rape Crisis Centre Movement and the Domestic Violence Movement, stresses the ongoing struggle against patriarchal abuse. It also stresses the belief that in every day of our lives women can contribute to the erosion of the negative self-image and sense of powerlessness which male-dominated society hands to us. So the revolution takes place every day, not in an imagined future. In Gail Chester's words:

> Because Radical Feminists do not recognise a split between our theory and practice, we are able to say that the revolution can begin now, by us taking positive actions to change our lives . . . it is a much more optimistic and humane vision of change than the male-defined notion of the building towards a revolution at some point in the distant future, once all the preparations have been made (1979, pp. 14–15).

Patriarchy

Radical feminists see patriarchy as a universal value system, though it exhibits itself in different forms culturally and historically.[3] Ruth Bleier defines it thus:

> By patriarchy I mean the historic system of male dominance, a system committed to the maintenance and reinforcement of male hegemony in all aspects of life – personal and private privilege and power as well as public privilege and power. Its

---

3. For examples of its universality see Morgan (1984) and Seager and Olson (1986).

institutions direct and protect the distribution of power and privilege to those who are male, apportioned, however, according to social and economic class and race. Patriarchy takes different forms and develops specific supporting institutions and ideologies during different historical periods and political economies (1984, p. 162).

Patriarchy is a system of structures and institutions created by men in order to sustain and recreate male power and female subordination. Such structures include: institutions such as the law, religion, and the family; ideologies which perpetuate the "naturally" inferior position of women; socialisation processes to ensure that women and men develop behaviour and belief systems appropriate to the powerful or less powerful group to which they belong.

The *structures* of patriarchy which have been established in order to maintain male power have been clearly analysed by radical feminists. *Economic* structures have been dealt with by, for example, Lisa Leghorn and Katherine Parker (1981); Marilyn Waring, (1988); Prue Hyman, (1994). Hilda Scott (1984) clearly demonstrates the increasing feminisation of poverty. *Political, legal,* and *religious* structures are dominated by men who ensure that they maintain those positions. Women's right to vote is only a recent event historically. Within the legal profession, few women sit on the higher benches in the court system. Within the private domain of *the family*, marriage, and reproduction, men have structured a system whereby woman's reproductive capacity leaves her vulnerable, domestically exploited, and often entrapped in economic dependence.

Patriarchal *ideology* maintains these structures. The family is maintained through the concept of romantic love between men and women, when in fact marriage contracts have traditionally had an economic base. Women's labour within the family, which has been unpaid and unacknowledged, and which includes the emotional servicing of members of the family as well as their physical servicing, continues to be defined as a "labour of love". Men have managed to create an ideology which defines men as the "natural" owners of intellect, rationality, and the power to rule. Women "by nature" are submissive, passive, and willing to be led. Processes such as the socialisation of children encourage this situation to continue. So, for example, in playground games, boys soon learn that they are to act and girls to create an "audience" for male performance.

The construction of the *family* and of the economic dependence of women on men also interrelates with the ideology of hetero-reality and the structures of heterosexuality. Adrienne Rich (1980) has analysed the compulsory nature of heterosexuality and its function as a political institution. She argues that men fear that women could be indifferent to them and that "men could be allowed emotional – therefore economic – access to women *only* on women's terms" (p. 643). The compulsory nature of heterosexuality defines men's access to women as natural and their right.

In a broader analysis Janice Raymond (1986) has created the term hetero-reality, that is the belief that in our world woman's purpose is to be "for men". Hetero-reality determines that the single woman is defined as "loose" in the promiscuous sense. So the state of being free and unattached with respect to men is translated into the negative state of being available to any man.

The patriarchal system is located within a language and knowledge system which constructs masculinity and femininity in support of the established power imbalance. Dale Spender has addressed these issues through her analysis of language, showing how men have constructed and controlled language in order to reinforce women's subordinate position (Spender: 1980). She also reclaims "women of ideas" historically and the knowledge that they have created. In *Women of Ideas and What Men Have Done to Them* she writes:

> I have come to accept that a patriarchal society depends in large measure on the experience and values of males being perceived as the *only* valid frame of reference for society, and that it is therefore in patriarchal interests to prevent women from sharing, establishing and asserting their equally real, valid and *different frame* of reference, which is the outcome of different experience (1982, p. 5).

Spender stresses that men have controlled knowledge and therefore made women invisible in the world of ideas. Structures within patriarchy are established in order to maintain the view that there is no problem with the fact that men are more powerful than women. As she says (1982, p. 7): "Patriarchy requires that any conceptualisation of the world in which men and their power are a central problem should become invisible and unreal. How could patriarchy afford to accept that men were a serious problem?"

Patriarchy also has a material base in two senses. First, the economic systems are structured so that women have difficulty getting paid labour in a society which values only paid labour and in which money is the currency of power. It is extremely difficult for women without economic independence to sustain themselves without a breadwinner. It is difficult to leave a brutal husband, to withdraw sexual, emotional, and physical servicing from men, to have an equal say in decisions affecting their own lives, such as where they might live. Radical feminism has therefore stressed the necessity for women to exercise economic power in their own right.

Women's unpaid domestic service in the home is primary in supporting the patriarchal system. Christine Delphy, whose Radical Feminism stems from a Marxist base, argues that "patriarchy is the system of subordination of women to men in contemporary industrial societies, that this system has an economic base, and that this base is the domestic mode of production" (1984, p. 18). It is also a mode of consumption and circulation of goods and differs from the capitalist mode of production because "those exploited by the domestic mode of production are not *paid* but rather *maintained*. In this mode, therefore, consumption is not separate from production, and the unequal sharing of goods is not mediated by money" (1984, p. 18). Delphy argues that the analysis of women's oppression using a traditional class analysis is not adequate because it cannot account for the particular exploitation of unwaged women. Men are the class which oppresses and exploits women and which benefits from their exploitation.

The second material base which radical feminism names as crucial to Women's Liberation is that of woman's body herself. Internationally, it is a woman's body which is the currency of patriarchy. Kathleen Barry has shown in *Female Sexual Slavery* (1979), and in *The Prostitution of Sexuality* (1995), that the international traffic in women operates extensively to socially control women. Women in marriage are seen to be "owned" by their husbands and cannot bring a civil case of rape in many countries. Women's bodies are used in advertising and pornography alike, objectified and defined as "other" and available for male use. As Delphy notes "feminism, by imprinting the word oppression on the domain of sexuality, has annexed it to materialism" (1984, p. 217). Men control the laws of reproduction, for example male-dominated parliaments and male-run pharmaceutical companies determine the forms of contraception available and the extent of their use.[4] Male-controlled government determines women's access to safe abortion. Law developed by men determines the civil power or powerlessness of women in bringing rape or incest charges against men.

Men as a group enjoy the privileges of power. It is in the best interest of men to maintain the existing patriarchal system, and the world has been structured in order to maintain this power imbalance, for example, in their structuring of pay inequality, and the sex-segregated work world. They need to maintain the unpaid labour of women; emotional and physical servicing by women; the sense of being in control which they feel individually and collectively. Men experience both a fear and an envy of women's reproductive power (O'Brien: 1981; Rowland: 1987b). It is an area of life which is owned by the less powerful group, women. In order to wrest control back, men develop laws regulating and controlling abortion and contraception. Historically they have fought midwives for control of birth and through the new reproductive technology developments, seek to control conception itself (Rowland: 1992/1993).

Male power is maintained and defined through a variety of methods: through institutions within society, through ideology, through coercion or force, through the control of resources and rewards, through the politics of intimacy, and through personal power. The simplistic labelling of an analysis of patriarchy as "conspiracy theory" conveniently allows critics of radical feminism to dismiss this analysis of women's oppression (see also Chesler: 1994 on patriarchy from an "expert witness" perspective).

---

4. Radical feminists also stress the importance of applying a woman-centred analysis to the various forms of population control as they oppress women in so-called Third World countries. See for example Vimal Balasubrahmanyan (1984) and Viola Roggenkamp (1984) on India, and Farida Akhter (1987, 1992) on Bangladesh and Betsy Hartmann (1995).

Universality: Class and Race Issues

Radical feminism has been accused of a "false universalism"; an unjustified assumption of female commonality (Eisenstein: 1984). Indeed, radical feminism does see the oppression of women as universal, crossing race and culture boundaries, as well as those of class and other delineating structures such as sexuality, age and physical ability. Radical feminists make no apologies for that. Sexual slavery within marriage was an accusation of Christabel Pankhurst's in the nineteenth century in Anglo-Saxon England, and sexual slavery as a trade has been documented and traced by Kathleen Barry (1979, 1995) in many countries in the twentieth century. We have been accused of ignoring difference – of being indifferent to difference. Yet radical feminism has always welcomed and *acknowledged* the diversity of women, while stressing our commonality.

The concept of sisterhood has been important within radical feminism, underlining a belief that to undermine male power women need to form a cohesive revolutionary group. Sisterhood is a moving and potentially radicalising concept of united women. Sonia Johnson ran an historical campaign for the US Presidency in 1984 on a radical feminist platform. She writes (1986, p. 14): "One of the basic tenets of radical feminism is that any woman in the world has more in common with any other woman regardless of class, race, age, ethnic group, nationality – than any woman has with any man."

In *Sisterhood is Global* (1984) Robin Morgan draws together contributions from feminists in seventy countries, the majority of which are Third World countries. She begins with a quote about the global position of women in the Report to the UN Commission on the Status of Women, which has improved little since it was written and is still often cited (p. 1): "While women represent half the global population and one-third of the labour force, they receive one-tenth of the world income and own less than one per cent of world property. They also are responsible for two thirds of all working hours." Morgan then proceeds to draw together the commonality of women through the various feminist representations in the book. These include, among many, the following aspects which we will briefly summarise.

Two out of three of the world's illiterates are women, and while the general literacy rate is increasing, female illiteracy is rising. Only a third of the world's women have access to contraceptive information or devices. In the developing world women are responsible for more than fifty per cent of all food production. In industrialised countries women still are paid only one-half to three-quarters of men's wages. Most of the world's starving are women and children. Twenty million people die annually of hunger-related causes and one billion endure chronic undernourishment and poverty. The majority of these are women and children. Women and children constitute more than ninety per cent of all refugee populations. Women in all countries bear the double burden of unpaid housework in association with any paid work they do.[5]

---

5. The Beijing Platform for Action which emerged from the United Nations Fourth World Conference on Women, reinforced this picture.

Many countries have stories of the invisibility of women's history. Organised patriarchal religion operates world-wide in order to maintain women in subservient positions. The right to safe abortion is under constant attack in most countries. Reproductive autonomy is still a theory rather than a practice in most countries. Laws concerning marriage continue to militate against women's independence and freedom. The basic right to divorce has still to be won in many countries. Trafficking in women and children is increasing and this is particularly true in Asia and the Pacific. Violence against women through rape, pornography, and battery is a continuing global issue.

And the connections continue. Robin Morgan comments that the contributions in *Sisterhood is Global* cross culture, age, occupation, race, sexual preference, and ideological barriers, and so does the Women's Liberation Movement itself. She speaks of the resistance shown in all countries to patriarchy, and the sense of solidarity and unity that the women express:

> Contributor after contributor in this book contests a class analysis as at best incomplete and at worst deliberately divisive of women. Article after article attempts valiantly not to minimise the differences but to identify the similarities between and among women ...
>
> Rape, after all, is an omnipresent terror to all women of any class, race, or caste. Battery is a nightmare of emotional and physical pain no matter who the victim. ... A human life in constraint – such suffering is not to be computed, judged or brought into shameful competition (1984, p. 19).

Radical feminism thus holds that women are oppressed primarily and in the first instance as *women*. But because of differences in our lives created by, for example culture and class, women experience that oppression differentially, and it expresses itself differentially. Radical feminism has from the beginning striven to deal with such differences. As Susan Griffin remembers:

> And of course, we carried the conflicts and differences of society into our world. Within us there were working-class women, middle-class women, white women, women of colour, Jewish women, Catholic women, heterosexual and lesbian women, women with and without children. We had to learn to speak among ourselves not only about our shared oppression but about the different conditions of our lives, and like any movement, we have at times faltered over these differences, and quarrelled over the definition of who we are (1982, p. 11).

As early as 1969 there was a "Congress to Unite Women" in which many of these issues were raised. In workshops women addressed the question "how women are divided: class, racial, sexual, and religious differences". Conclusions included the following:

> We will work with all women recognising that the uniqueness of our revolution transcends economic, racial, generational, and political differences, and that these differences must be transcended in action, in the common interest of our liberation, self-determination and development of our political movement.
>
> All women are oppressed as women and can unite on that basis; however, we acknowledge that there are differences among women, male-created – of economic and social privilege, race, education, etc. – and that these differences are real, not in our heads. Such divisions must be eliminated. They can only be eliminated by hard work and concrete action, not by rhetoric (Koedt *et al:* 1973, p. 309).

In the late spring of 1971 there was a radical feminist conference in Detroit, USA. The many issues discussed there are outlined by Robin Morgan (1978). Among them were the difficulties of relationships with men, the difficulties about decisions concerning children and lesbianism. "What about our ageism and older women? How can white feminists concretely support the growing feminism among minority women?" (p. 156).

In 1978, the problems of racial differences were discussed by Adrienne Rich in her prose piece "Disloyal to civilisation: feminism, racism, gynophobia" in which she writes about the separation of black and white women from each other and points out the difficulty and the pain and anger involved in these delineations. Rich acknowledges "the passive or active instrumentality of white women in the practice of inhumanity against black people" (1979a, p. 284). But she argues against what she calls the ludicrous and fruitless game of "hierarchies of oppression" including the liberal guilt reflex on the part of women whenever racism is mentioned. There is a danger, she argues, that guilt feelings provoked in white women can become a form of social control, paralysing rather than leading women to relate honestly to the nature of racism itself. She warns white women against the possibilities of colluding with white male power to the disadvantage of black women.

But as bell hooks (1984) points out, there are also cultural differences. She stresses the importance of learning cultural codes. She quotes an Asian American student of Japanese heritage who was reluctant to participate in feminist organisations because she felt feminists spoke rapidly without pause. She had been raised to pause and think before speaking and therefore felt inadequate in feminist groups.

This example raises the varieties of categorisation which delineate different groups of women. Robin Morgan (1984) points out in her global analysis of the Women's Liberation Movement the many forms of division that can operate, including clanism, tribalism, the caste system, religious bigotry, and rural versus urban living. Looking at the various possible categories reminds us that racism itself is an ideology. As Rosario Morales, of Puerto Rican background, comments:

> . . . everyone is capable of being racist whatever their colour and condition. Only some of us are liable to racist attack . . . guilt is a fact for us all, white and coloured:

and identification with the oppressor and oppressive ideology. Let us, instead, identify, understand, and feel with the oppressed as a way out of the morass of racism and guilt (1981, p. 91).

The criticism that radical feminism has not dealt with class is meant to imply that we do not consider economics to be of importance, and that we do not understand the battle against capitalism. This is patently not true in the work for example, of Lisa Leghorn and Katherine Parker, and of French theorist Christine Delphy. But, as Delphy comments:

> . . . but we materialist feminists, who affirm the existence of several – at least two – class systems, and hence the possibility of an individual having several class memberships (which can in addition be contradictory); we do think that male workers are not, as victims of capitalism, thereby absolved of the sin of being the beneficiaries of patriarchy (1984, p. 147).

The delineation of women as a class itself implies that men benefit in concrete and material ways from their oppression and exploitation of women. Whatever the political regime, it is women who do the unpaid domestic labour and men who gain from it. It is women who service sexually and emotionally.

Radical feminism acknowledges that women experience their oppression differentially depending upon class. In the early 1970s, two members of the US collective The Furies, published an anthology on *Class and Feminism* (Bunch and Myron: 1974) in which radical feminist authors grappled with the problems engendered by class differences among feminists. Consistently since that time Charlotte Bunch has stressed a class analysis within radical feminism. In her words:

> Women's oppression is rooted both in the structures of our society, which are patriarchal, and in the sons of patriarchy: capitalism and white supremacy. Patriarchy includes not only male rule but also heterosexual imperialism and sexism; patriarchy led to the development of white supremacy and capitalism. For me, the term patriarchy refers to all these forms of oppression and domination, all of which must be ended before all women will be free (1981a, p. 194).

In her discussion of sexuality she points out that there can be a breaking of class barriers among lesbians where "cross-class intimacy" occurs. This is particularly true for middle-class women because

> . . . lesbianism means discovering that we have to support ourselves for the rest of our lives, something that lower- and working-class women have always known. This discovery makes us begin to understand what lower- and working-class women have been trying to tell us all along: "what do you know about survival?" (1981a, p. 71).

Again, the personal is *political.* Radical feminists will not devote women's energy to the traditional socialist revolution, though we share some values in common, such as the oppressive nature of capitalism. We do not have faith that such man-made revolutions will ensure women's autonomy. Bonnie Mann analysed socialism in action in Nicaragua, pointing out the positive values inherent in the work of the Sandinista government, but noting also that there were no known lesbians in Nicaragua and no safe abortion. She writes:

> But there is a lesson here that history teaches her radical feminist students who have long since rejected the ideological reduction of patriarchy to capitalism by the left, for those of us who know a socialist or communist revolution is not the answer to the global slave-status of women. The lesson is this: anything that strikes a blow to such a large root of suffering, of evil in this world, sends reverberations through the very foundations of patriarchal power. And these reverberations ring with the possibility of radical, lasting change (1986, p. 54).

Women's Bodies

Radical feminism has stressed women's bodily integrity and autonomy as essential to liberation. The issue has been dealt with in three primary ways; through the Women's Health Movement; through an analysis of the body as a primary site of women's oppression; and through a discussion of sexuality.

The Women's Health Movement

As part of its analysis of the structures of patriarchy, radical feminism has argued that medicine is male-controlled, operating to control women socially to the detriment of our health. In the late 1960s the Women's Health Movement gathered momentum, developing since then in international scope with diverse approaches to women's health. It has revised the way women's health has been viewed, stressing self-help and prevention rather than a reliance on hi-tech, expensive, and dangerous technologies and drugs.

Radical feminists argued for safe and freely available abortion and contraception. "The right to choose", in the issue of abortion, was a slogan which encapsulated the right of a woman to decide whether or not she wished to maintain a pregnancy and rear a child. Women of colour made us aware of the limitations of the concept of choice within this slogan by stressing that while white women were being controlled by their lack of access to abortion, black women were being controlled by constant sterilisation without consent. The British anthology *No Turning Back* documents this.

> Obviously, the fact that the black women are sterilised against their will while white women are finding it harder and harder to get abortions, is related to the attempts to limit the black population on the one hand, and to force white women out of paid employment on the other. A campaign around "a woman's right to

choose" must relate to the different needs and demands of all women and in so doing recognise that the problems of black women do not mirror those of white women (Feminist Anthology Collective: 1982, p. 145).

The recognition that "choice" has to be redefined has also led to the analysis of the way women in the Third World have dangerous provider-controlled contraceptive drugs dumped upon them, such as the increasing use of Depo-Provera and Norplant, and the analysis of the way international aid is tied to such things as sterilisation programs for women (see Akhter: 1987, 1995).

One of the landmarks of the Women's Health Movement was the initial revolutionary action of self-help gynaecology. In April 1971 in Los Angeles, Carol Downer showed women for the first time how to use a speculum to examine their own vagina and cervix and the bodies of other women. These actions demystified women's bodies and made the gynaecological ritual more obvious in its humiliation of women. Ellen Frankfort remembers:

> I hate to use the word "revolutionary", but no other word seems accurate to describe the effects of the first part of the evening. It was a little like having a blind person see for the first time – for what woman is not blind to her own insides? The simplicity with which Carol examined herself brought forth in a flash the whole gynaecological ritual; the receptionist, the magazines, the waiting room, and then the examination itself – being told to undress, lying on your back with your feet in stirrups . . . no-one thinking that 'meeting' doctor for the first time in this position is slightly odd (1973, p. ix).

The development of women's health centres was an essential part of this form of activism. The intention was to develop alternative health measures for dealing with some of the most common ailments that women suffer from, such as candida and cystitis, with a focus on developing preventative procedures. And these were to be women-centred: services run *for* women, by women.

In 1969, when little information was available on women's health, the Boston Women's Health Collective put out the first edition of *Our Bodies, Ourselves* which became a basic reference text for women all over the world. Further editions have continued this tradition with an expanded view of women's health and the medical system which attempts to control it. Stressing preventative measures, and the need for women to understand how our bodies work, this book is an act of resistance against misogynist health care throughout the world.

Women's Bodies as a Primary Site of Women's Oppression

More than any other theory of women's oppression, radical feminism has been unafraid to look at the violence done to women by men. It has shown that this violence to women's bodies and women's selves has been so intrinsic to patriarchal culture as to appear "normal" and therefore justifiable. Many myths about its specificity developed as a control mechanism on women's behaviour. For example, rape, pornography, and sexual slavery supposedly affect one particular group of "bad" women (see Barry: 1979) and not other "good" women. The message is that if women "behave" they will be spared. This process ensures the intimidation of women in their daily behaviour, and splits women from each other, classifying one group of women as justifiably abused.

A large amount of empirical work has been done by radical feminists on violence against women, particularly sexual violence (Susanne Kappeler: 1995), documenting the evidence on rape (for example Susan Brownmiller: 1975; Bart and O'Brien: 1985); incest (for example Elizabeth Ward: 1984; Armstrong: 1994); pornography (for example Andrea Dworkin: 1981; Susan Griffin: 1981; Diana Russell: 1993); sexual slavery (Kathleen Barry: 1979/1995), and woman killing (Radford and Russell: 1992). There is no space here to deal with such an extensive body of work, but Kathleen Barry's work on female sexual slavery is an example of the development of Radical Feminist theory and practice.[6]

Barry has documented sexual slavery on an international level (1979). She begins by tracing the original work carried out by Josephine Butler in the first wave of women's protest against sexual slavery in the nineteenth century. She then goes on to detail current practices of sexual slavery. For example, since 1979, agencies promoting sex tourism and mail-order brides have been operating in the US and many European countries. This amounts to the buying of women from Latin America and Asian countries: ". . . this practice, built upon the most racist and misogynist stereotypes of Asian and Latin American women, is a growing part of the traffic in women which is a violation of the United Nations conventions and covenance" (p. xiii).

Female sexual slavery is used to refer to the international traffic in women and forced street prostitution, which, as Barry amply shows, is carried out with the same methods of sadism, torture, beating, and so on which are used to enslave women internationally into prostitution. She points out that although there is a white slave trade in eastern countries, there is an Asian slave trade in western societies.

Barry resists the argument that prostitution is purely an economic exploitation of women. When economic power becomes the cause of women's oppression "the sex dimensions of power usually remain unidentified and unchallenged" (p. 9). Touching again on the resistance even of feminists to deal with the sexual oppression of women in its raw form she writes:

> Feminist analysis of sexual power is often modified to make it fit into an economic analysis which defines economic exploitation as the primary instrument of female oppression. Under that system of thought, institutionalised sexual slavery, such as

---

6. See also *The Sexual Liberals and the Attack on Feminism* by Dorchen Leidholdt and Janice Raymond (1990).

is found in prostitution, is understood in terms of economic exploitation which results in the lack of economic opportunities for women, the result of an unjust economic order. Undoubtedly economic exploitation is an important factor in the oppression of women, but here we must be concerned with whether or not economic analysis reveals the more fundamental sexual domination of women (1979, p. 10).

She goes on to point out that people are justifiably horrified at the enslavement of children, but this has become separated from the enslavement of women. This process distorts the reality of the situation, implying that it is tolerable to enslave women but not tolerable to enslave children. She writes (p. 9): ". . . as I studied the attitudes that accept female enslavement, I realised that a powerful ideology stems from it and permeates the social order. I have named that ideology cultural sadism".

Barry explores the economic reasons for the cover-up of the international trade in women and the basis of male power which is involved in it. She instances, for example, the INTERPOL analysis of sexual slavery which is conveniently hidden from public scrutiny. INTERPOL has prepared comprehensive reports based on their own international surveys "which they have suppressed" (p. 58). In their 1974 report, contained in Barry's appendix, one of the conclusions is that "the disguised traffic in women still exists all over the world" (p. 296).

Initially Barry herself had flinched from the task of unveiling the traffic in women. She talks about the difficulties of coming face to face with this raw brutality towards women, which includes the seduction of women into slavery by promises of love and affection, or the brutal kidnapping and forcible entry of women into prostitution and sexual slavery. But much as radical feminism has dealt with the horror of pornography, rape, and incest, Barry believes that for women it is important to know the truth about the sexual violence against women. Women have been bullied into denying that it exists. We have been forced into colluding in the secrecy of sexual violence against women. We are unable to bear the feeling of vulnerability which that gives to all women:

> Hiding has helped keep female sexual slavery from being exposed. But worse than that, it has kept us from understanding the full extent of women's victimisation, thereby denying us the opportunity to find our way out of it through political confrontation as well as through vision and hope . . . knowing the worst frees us to hope and strive for the best (Barry: 1979, p. 13).

As theory and practice are intertwined in radical feminism, Barry has been involved since 1980 with the establishment of the International Feminist Network Against Female Sexual Slavery which launched its first meeting in Rotterdam in 1983. From twenty-four countries women came to expose the traffic in women, forced prostitution, sex tourism, military brothels, torture of female prisoners, and the sexual mutilation of women. In each country the network operates collectively to deal with their specific culturally based problem areas. For example, the most effective work against sex tourism and the mail-order bride industry (which operates quite effectively between Australia and Thailand among other countries) has been done by Asian feminists, particularly the Asian Women's Association in Japan and the Third World Movement Against the Exploitation of Women in The Philippines. Again, this demonstrates the global perspective of radical feminism. This Network has now become the Coalition Against Trafficking in Women (see Barry pp. 448–455 in this volume).

From the empirical work of women in the area of sexual violence has come the development of theories of what Barry calls "sexual terrorism". This terrorism she explains "is a way of life for women even if we are not its direct victims. It has resulted in many women living with it while trying not to see or acknowledge it. This denial of reality creates a form of hiding" (p. 12). Radical feminism will not collaborate in this blindness, but names and addresses the basic and primary violence done to women as a social group and to individual women at the level of their daily lives.[7]

Similar work is occurring within the area of the new reproductive technologies. Here, radical feminists are analysing the way patriarchal medicine is brutalising women's bodies in the name of "curing" infertility. No preventative measures are offered. Little attempt is made to understand the causes of infertility. No analysis takes place of the structures which create the desperate desire to have children.

Radical feminism names the alliance between commercial interests and reproductive technologists or "techno-patriarchs" within the structures which currently wrench power from women in the procreative area. We refuse the naive political analysis which posits that it is possible for women to gain some control over these technologies, and that then it will be acceptable to use them. Our analysis shows that the technology is not value-free but is part of a pattern of male-controlled birth, pregnancy, and now conception. (See for example Arditti *et al*: 1984; Corea: 1985; Corea *et al*: 1985; Spallone and Steinberg: 1987; Klein: 1989; Rowland: 1993; Raymond: 1994). Again, from this theoretical and empirical work has come the development of an international network, the Feminist International Network of Resistance to Reproductive and Genetic Engineering (FINRRAGE). Based on national regional groups working in a collective fashion, radical feminists are educating women at the grassroots level as well as working on political strategies in order to stop the control and abuse of women's bodies.

---

7. Pornography is another crucial site for radical feminist theory and practice. The work of Andrea Dworkin and Catharine MacKinnon would deserve a chapter of its own. Due to limitations of space, however, we have to refer the reader to the following references: Dworkin (1981); Griffin (1981); Lederer (1980); Linden *et al.* (1982); Marchiano (1980); Rhodes and McNeill (1985); MacKinnon (1993b).

Sexuality

Because of the radical feminist analysis of the oppression of women through male-defined sexuality and power, and because of the demand to take back our bodies, radical feminism has identified sexuality as political. The interrelationship between heterosexuality and power was named.

In 1982 Catharine MacKinnon argued that heterosexuality is the "primary social sphere of male power" (p. 529) and that this power is the basis of gender inequality. It is to feminism what work is to Marxism – "that which is most one's own yet most taken away" (p. 515). Heterosexuality as an institution is the structure which imposes this appropriation of woman's self, "gender and family its congealed forms, sex roles its qualities generalised to social persona, reproduction a consequence, and control its issue" (p. 516).

It was within radical feminism that lesbian women began to demand their right to choose a lesbian existence. In a summary article first published in the *Revolutionary and Radical Feminist Newsletter*, (1982), the London Lesbian Offensive Group expressed their anger at anti-lesbian attitudes within the movement and at heterosexual feminists because they:

> . . . do not take responsibility for being members of an oppressive power group, do not appear to recognise or challenge the privileges which go with that, nor do they bother to examine how all this undermines not only our lesbian politics, but our very existence (1984, p. 255).

When heterosexual feminists do not acknowledge their privileged position, lesbian women feel silenced and made invisible. The article outlines clearly the privileges which heterosexual feminists experience over lesbian feminists in spite of the real fact of the oppression of heterosexual women. For example, many have access to male money, they have the privilege of the assumptions of being considered "normal" instead of "deviant". In short, they have automatic benefits by virtue of the fact that they are either attached to a man or have a place within the heterosexual normative culture.

Lesbian feminists suffer under the law in a variety of ways. Often they are not free to claim their lesbian lifestyle for fear of retaliation in the workplace, in terms of housing rights, in terms of being ostracised. In issues over custody of children, the battles for lesbian women are bloodier and more likely to fail (see, for example, Chesler: 1986).

In retaliation for the oppression of lesbian women by hetero feminists, in 1979 the Leeds Revolutionary Feminist Group published a stinging attack. They accused women in heterosexual couples of supporting male supremacy (p. 65): "Men are the enemy. Heterosexual women are collaborators with the enemy . . . every woman who lives with or fucks a man helps to maintain the oppression of her sisters and hinders our struggle." Part of the basic argument against hetero feminism is the argument that heterosexual women service male power and privilege. By directing their energy towards a specific man within the social group men, women's energy is once more taken from women and given to men.

Although there are substantial difficulties and dangers in being lesbian in a heterosexual world, the pleasures of living a lesbian existence were also clearly outlined in the Leeds article:

> The pleasures of knowing that you are not directly servicing men, living without the strain of the glaring contradiction in your personal life, uniting the personal and the political, loving and putting your energies into those you are fighting alongside rather than those you are fighting against (1979, p. 66).

In an afterword which was added before republication in 1981, the Leeds group commented that this paper had been written for a workshop at a radical feminist conference in 1979. Some of their comments they later found to be offensive and inconsistent. For example, "we now think that 'collaborators' is the wrong word to describe women who sleep with men, since this implies a conscious act of betrayal" (p. 69).

For some women within the Women's Liberation Movement the issues of lesbianism and heterosexuality caused an irreparable split. For others, the debate increased their awareness, as did discussions around class and culture, about their own positions of privilege or oppression within the social group woman, and within feminism itself. Some lesbian feminists moved to develop an analysis of the position of lesbian feminism within the Women's Movement. More recently radical feminists have begun to theorise a radical feminist heterosexuality (for example, Rowland: 1993; Wilkinson and Kitzinger: 1993; Maynard and Purvis: 1995; see also Rowland, pp. 77–86 this volume).

Charlotte Bunch named lesbian feminism as the political perspective on "the ideological and institutional domination of heterosexuality" (1976, p. 553). As she put it, lesbian feminism means putting women first in an act of resistance in a world in which life is structured around the male. Discussing the first paper issued by radical lesbians, "The Woman-identified Woman", she takes up the expanded definition of lesbianism as the idea of woman-identification and a love for all women. Behind this is the belief in the development of self-respect and a self-identity in relation to women, rather than in relation to men.

In 1975 Bunch had already said that "heterosexuality means men first. That's what it's all about. It assumes that every woman is heterosexual; that every woman is identified by and is the property of men" (1981a, p. 69). Bunch thus stated what Adrienne Rich later theorised in her influential paper on compulsory heterosexuality (1980) and Janice Raymond developed in her work on female friendship (1986). Bunch argued that heterosexism supports male supremacy in the workplace and is supported through the oppressive structure of the nuclear family. It is being fed by the actual or more often supposed benefits to women who continue life within the accepted norm of heterosexuality: the privileges of legitimacy, economic security, social acceptance, legal and physical protection – most of which do not hold true anyway for the majority of women in heterosexual relationships.

Adrienne Rich (1980) analysed the way in which heterosexuality had been forced upon women as an *institution*, and the way women had been seduced into it (in the same way as she had previously analysed motherhood as an institution; see Rich: 1976 and Hawthorne 1976/1990). Lesbian existence represents a direct assault on the male's right of access to women.

Most importantly, though, was the term she coined: the "lesbian continuum". It was to have a major effect in reuniting lesbian and heterosexual feminists in their attempts to both validate the differences between their lives and strive towards developing a common political platform. Her lesbian continuum includes:

> . . . a range – through each woman's life and throughout history – of woman-identified experience; not simply the fact that a woman has had or consciously desired genital sexual experience with another woman. If we expand it to embrace many more forms of primary identity between and among women, including the sharing of a rich inner life, the bonding against male tyranny, the giving and receiving of practical and political support; . . . we begin to grasp bits of female history and psychology which have lain out of reach as a consequence of limited, mostly clinical, definitions of 'lesbianism' (1980, p. 649).

Extending this analysis of heterosexuality and the way it has controlled women's energy, women's sexuality and women's culture, Janice Raymond created the term "hetero-reality". She writes:

> While I agree that we are living in a heterosexist society, I think the wider problem is that we live in a hetero-relational society, where most of women's personal, social, political, professional, and economic relations are defined by the ideology that woman is for man (1986, p. 11).

Smashing the myth that women do not bond together and that heteroreality has always been the norm, Raymond traces the history of women's friendship, of women as friends, lovers, economic and emotional supporters, and of companions. She attacks the dismembering of female friendships arguing that this represents a "dismembering of the woman-identified Self" (p. 4). She emphasises the intimacy in women's relationships, stressing that passionate friendships need not be of a genital-sexual nature.

Raymond coins the term *Gyn/affection* in order to be inclusive of all women who put each other first, whether lesbian or not. At the basis of her discussions of sexuality is the radical feminist belief in the political necessity of woman-identified feminism. It means that a woman's *primary* relationships are with other women. It is to women that we give our economic, emotional, political, and social support. In the words of Rita Mae Brown:

> A woman-identified woman is one who defines herself in relationship to other women and most importantly as a self apart and distinct from other selves, not with function as the centre of self, but being . . . a woman can best find out who she is with other women, not with just one other woman but with other women, who are also struggling to free themselves from an alien and destructive culture. It is this new concept, that of woman-identified woman, that sounds the death knell for the male culture and calls for a new culture where cooperation, life and love are the guiding forces of organization rather than competition, power and bloodshed. This concept will change the way we live and who we live with (1975, p. 66).

Implicit in many of these statements is an assumption of separatism, which has been seen as a political strategy, a space in which to create women-identification and the regeneration of women's energy and women's Selves. Charlotte Bunch writes of her time living in a totally separatist community of women as one in which personal growth and political analysis could be more readily developed. Despite the fact that she ultimately rejected total separatism because of the isolation it involved, as a political strategy it still has its uses. In Bunch's words (1976b, p. 556): "Separatism is a dynamic strategy to be moved in and out of whenever a minority feels that its interests are being overlooked by the majority, or that its insights need more space to be developed."

In her paper "In Defence of Separatism" (1976/1990), Australian, Susan Hawthorne has outlined the degrees of separatism which operate within radical feminism. She points out that it is impossible to be a feminist and not believe in separatism in one of its degrees. She includes among acts of separatism: valuing dialogue with other women and engaging in women only groups; engaging in political and social action with other women; attending women-only events-including events where women can have a good time!; working in an environment which is run by and for women; giving emotional support to women; engaging in sexual relationships with women; participating in groups which are concerned with women's creativity and the creation of women's culture; living in an all-women environment without contact with men.

It is this last degree of separatism which is predominantly understood as its definition. This is perceived as the most threatening form of separatism because it suggests that women can successfully live in the world independent of men. Indeed, this conception of separatism within the radical feminist framework is an empowering one. As Marilyn Frye writes:

> When our feminist acts or practices have an aspect of separatism, we are assuming power by controlling access and simultaneously by undertaking definition. The slave who excludes the master from her hut thereby declares herself *not a slave*. And *definition* is another face of power (1983, p. 105).

Motherhood and the Family

The institution of the nuclear family is a primary institution of patriarchy. Chained to the theory and practice of hetero-reality and compulsory heterosexuality, the traditional father-dominated family, with its dependent motherhood for women, has enslaved women into sexual and emotional service. For many women this still includes unpaid domestic labour. In the bastion of the family, the private oppression of women is experienced on a daily level. It may be expressed through its physical manifestation in assault, its economic manifestation in male control of resources and decision-making, its ideological control through the socialisation of women and children, and/or its control of women's energy in emotional and physical servicing of men and children. In addition, as Andrea Dworkin says (1974, p. 190): "The nuclear family is the school of values in a sexist, sexually repressed society. One learns what one must know: the rules, rituals, and behaviours appropriate to male-female polarity and the internalised mechanisms of sexual oppression."

Marriage itself has been seen as prostitution, where a woman trades sexual servicing for shelter and food. Sex is compulsory in marriage for women, ensuring heterosexuality within the economic bargain. As Sheila Cronan wrote:

> It became increasingly clear to us that the institution of marriage "protects" women in the same way that the institution of slavery was said to "protect" blacks – that is, that the word "protection" in this case is simply a euphemism for oppression (Cronan: 1973, p. 214).

The patriarchal ideology of motherhood has also been scrutinised. During the sixties and seventies, many women rejected motherhood as an enslaving role within patriarchal culture. Since that time, feminists have tried to rewrite the definitions of motherhood, leading us to a more positive vision of what the experience might be like if women could determine the conditions (Rowland and Thomas: 1996). Adrienne Rich has written:

> This institution – which affects each woman's personal experience – is visible in the male dispensation of birth control and abortion; the guardianship of men over children in the courts and the educational system; the subservience, through most of history, of women and children to the patriarchal father; the economic dominance of the father over the family; the usurpation of the birth process by male medical establishments (1979b, p. 196).

Although motherhood is supposedly revered, its daily reality in patriarchy is tantamount to a degraded position. The pressure on women to undertake the mothering role is intense, yet it is only admirable when the mother is attached to a legal father.

In *Of Woman Born* (1976) Rich delineated two meanings of motherhood: the *potential* relationship of a woman to her powers of reproduction and to children, and the patriarchal *institution* of motherhood which is concerned with male control of women and children. One of the most bewildering contradictions in the institutionalisation of motherhood is that "it has alienated women from our bodies by incarcerating us in them" (p. 13).

Just as heterosexuality is compulsory, so too is motherhood. Women who choose not to mother are outside the "caring and rearing" bond and attract strong social disapproval. Women who are infertile, on the other hand, are subjects of pity and even derision. The institutionalisation of motherhood by patriarchy has ensured that women are divided into breeders and non-breeders. So motherhood is used to define woman and her usefulness.

Women's Culture

Emerging out of the concept of separatism as an empowering base and a belief in establishing and transmitting traditions, histories, and ideologies which are woman-centred, radical feminism strives to generate a women's culture through which women can artistically recreate both their selves and their way of being in the world outside of patriarchal definition. So, for example, Judy Chicago creates "The Dinner Party" with two hundred places set for women of history who have made important contributions to women's culture as well as society at large. So radical feminist artists, painters, and writers resist the male-stream definitions of art and culture, redefining both stylistically and in their content what culture and art are and might be for women. Many radical feminists are involved in writing (prose and poetry), film making, sculpture, theatre, dance, and so on in their daily practice of radical feminism. For radical feminist poets and novelists, language becomes an essential code in redefining and restructuring the world with women as its centre. As Bonnie Zimmerman put it "language is action" (1984, p. 672).

Within the creation of a woman's culture, the arts are not the sole areas of work. Feminist scientists for example are trying to generate visions of a new science and technology which would not be exploitative of people and the environment. Having critiqued masculine science, radical feminists are developing new ways of conceptualising science (Bleier: 1986; Rosser: 1990).

Mary Daly attempts to reconceptualise the world as it might look from a perspective in which women's different needs and interests form the core of cultural practices and their theoretical underpinnings (1978; 1984; 1993). In her unique analysis of the oppression of women, including her stress upon the daily physical and mental violence done to women, she recreates language, a sense of the spiritual, and a sense of physical being. She emphasises the importance of naming, in that to name is to create the world. She also stresses the need to recreate and refind our original Selves, before women were mutilated by patriarchy and subjugated to patriarchal definitions of the feminine self. She refuses to accept the woman-hatred within existing language, redefining for example "spinster" and "hag" in a positive way.

As radical feminism struggles to refind our cultural history and recreate culture around women, it is constantly misunderstood, labelled "cultural feminism", and defined as "non-political". This is a false representation as the redefining of culture is interrelated with the development of a liberating ideology in tune with the autonomous being of people. It attacks male control of the concept of culture and patriarchal use of culture for the purposes of indoctrination of both women and men into patriarchal ideology. It is essentially *political*.

Biological Essentialism

A frequent criticism of radical feminism is that it supports a biologically based "essential" division of the world into male and female. In particular this accusation is charged against radical feminists working in the area of violence against women who name men as a social group, as well as individual men where relevant, as oppressors of women.

The facts are that men brutally oppress women as radical feminists have empirically shown. But why do men do this? Can it be changed? Kathleen Barry has addressed these issues in her analysis of sexual slavery which we discussed earlier. She states that men do these things to women because "there is nothing to stop them" (1979, p. 254). Her analysis of the *values of patriarchy* and theories which supposedly account for male violence is too detailed to discuss here. The important point to stress is that radical feminism cannot be reduced to a simplistic biological determinist argument. That its critics often *do* thus reduce it is a political ploy which takes place in order to limit the effectiveness of its analysis. Women have good reasons for being frightened to name men as the enemy, particularly when they live in hetero-relationships: punishment is often meted out for exposing patriarchy and its mechanisms (see Cline and Spender: 1987).

Christine Delphy argues that the concept of gender – that is the respective social positions of women and men – is a construction of patriarchal ideology and that "sex has become a pertinent fact, hence a perceived category, because of the existence of gender" (1984, p. 144). Therefore, she argues, the oppression creates gender, and in the end, gender creates anatomical sex (p. 144), ". . . in a sense that the hierarchical division of humanity into two transforms an anatomical difference (which is in itself devoid of social implications) into a relevant distinction for social practice".

Radical Feminists are well aware of the dangers of basing analysis in biology. If men and women are represented as having "aggressive" and "nurturing" characteristics because of their biology, the situation will remain immutable and the continuation of male violence against women can be justified. But this is not to say that there are not differences between the sexes. This is patently so. These differences, however, do not need to be rooted in biology nor do they need to be equated with determinism. As the editors of *Questions Feministes* put it (1980, p. 14): ". . . we acknowledge a biological difference between men and women, but it does not in itself imply a relationship of oppression between the sexes. The struggle between the sexes is not the result of biology".

Men are the powerful group. But men need women, for sexual and emotional labour, for domestic labour, for admiration, for love, and for a justification of the existing power imbalance (see Cline and Spender: 1987). In order to maintain the more powerful position and so feed on their need of women without being consumed by it, men as a powerful group institutionalise their position of power. This involves the need to structure institutions to maintain that power, the development of an ideology to justify it, and the use of force and violence to impose it when resistance emerges (see also Rowland: 1988).

It is possible that differences between women and men arise out of a biological base but in a different way to that proposed by a reductivist determinism. The fact that women belong to the social group which has the capacity for procreation and mothering, and the fact that men belong to the social group which has the capacity to, and does carry out, acts of rape and violence against women, must intrude into the consciousness of being female and male. But this analysis allows for *change* in the sense that men themselves could change that consciousness and therefore their actions. It also allows women to recognise that we can and must develop our own theories and practices and need not accept male domination as unchangeable.

Existing differences between women and men may have been generated out of the different worlds we inhabit as social groups, including our experience of power and powerlessness. Again this is not to say that these differences are immutable. The history of women's resistance is evidence of resistance to deterministic thinking, as is the history of the betrayal of patriarchy by some men who support feminism.

Women's Resistance, Women's Power

In our relation to men as the more powerful group, women do have some crucial bargaining areas: withdrawing reproductive services, emotional and physical labour, domestic labour, sexual labour, and refusing consent to being defined as the powerless, thereby verifying man's right to power. The withdrawal of services from men is an act of resistance; in Dale Spender's words (1983, p. 373): ". . . making men feel good is *work*, which women are required to undertake in a patriarchal society; refusing to engage in such work is a form of resistance."

In *Powers of the Weak* (1980) Elizabeth Janeway lists the power of *disbelief* as a form of resistance. The powerful need those ruled to believe in them and believe in the justice of their position. But, as Janeway points out, if women refuse to endorse men's domination it signifies a lack of sanction of the authority of the ruler by the ruled, and destabilises their sense of security.

Importantly, women can also exercise the power of disbelief with respect to the self of woman as defined by man. Janeway explores it thus:

> Ordered use of the power to disbelieve, the first power of the weak, begins here, with the refusal to accept the definition of one's self that is put forward by the powerful. It is true that one may not have a coherent self-definition to set against

the status assigned by the established social mythology, but that is not necessary for dissent. By disbelieving, one would be led toward doubting prescribed codes of behaviour, and as one begins to act in ways that deviate from the norm in any degree, it becomes clear that in fact there is just not one way to handle or understand events (1980, p. 167).

A further "power of the weak" lies in the collective understanding of a shared situation. Through collective political action and through consciousness-raising techniques, women have developed a sense of female identity and solidarity. The collective action and networking of the Coalition Against Trafficking in Women, and the Feminist International Network of Resistance to Reproductive and Genetic Engineering are examples of women educating for activism against violence against women. Women's health centres and the development of refuges and rape crisis centres are other examples of collective actions of resistance.

Radical Feminists are also developing women–centred approaches to changing the law. Catharine MacKinnon and Andrea Dworkin attempted to introduce a law in the United States to ensure that the victims of pornography had a right to take civil action against their abusers (MacKinnon: 1987 and 1993b).

The creation of radical feminist knowledge itself, such as that contained within the works described above, represents an act of women's resistance. Radical feminism has often been described as a state of rage. People – men and women – who have comfortable, seemingly safe lives, fear that rage. It implicates them in the oppression of women, either as members of the oppressing group or of the oppressed group. Radical feminism reminds women of their own moments of exploitation or abuse, and these memories are not welcome. Such down-to-earth knowledge intimates the possibility of a lack of control. As Susan Griffin remembers:

> As I became more conscious of my oppression as a woman, I found myself entering a state of rage. Everywhere I turned I found more evidence of male domination, of a social hatred of, and derogation of women, of increasingly insufferable limitations imposed upon my life. Social blindness is lived out in each separate life. Like many women, I had been used to lying to myself. To tell myself that I wanted what I did not want, or felt what I did not feel, was a habit so deeply ingrained in me, I was never aware of having lied. I had shaped my life to fit the traditional idea of a woman, and thus, through countless decisions large and small, had sacrificed myself. Each sacrifice had made me angry. But I could not allow myself this anger. For my anger would have told me that I was lying. Now, when I ceased to lie, the anger I had accumulated for years was revealed to me (1982, pp. 6–7).

Radical feminists are angry because patriarchy oppresses women, but we are also filled with a sense of empowering well-being through bonding with other women and a joy in the liberation from accepting patriarchy and hetero-reality as immutable ingredients of human existence. Radical feminist writings are sometimes rejected because of their openly voiced anger and passionate call to end women's oppression.[8] But radical feminism *is* passionate. We are passionately committed to Women's Liberation and through our work we hope to impassion others. Nothing less will do if we are to develop theories and practices for a future in which women can live autonomous as well as socially responsible lives.

---

8. See Frye (1983), *A Note on Anger*, for an excellent discussion of the meaning of this anger.

Joy James

Experience, Reflection, Judgment and Action: Teaching Theory, Talking Community*

Contemporary African American theorists think within an African and community-centered tradition in which the creativity of a people in the race for theory sustains humanity. Barbara Christian writes that theory not rooted in practice is elitist (1987, p. 336). However, teaching theory as non-elitist, and intending the liberation and development of humanity, specifically African communities, contradicts much of academic theory[1] which is Eurocentric.

Making Our Presence Known

Before I can even teach theory, given its current social construction as biologically marked, I seem continuously challenged to "prove" that I am qualified. Comparing my work experiences with those of other African American women academics, I notice that despite our having been hired through a highly competitive process, we seem to be asked more routinely, almost reflexively, if we have PhDs. We could attribute this, and have, to our "diminutive" height, youngish appearance or casual attire. Yet I notice that White women about our height, unsuited, and under sixty, seem not to be interrogated as frequently about their qualifications. Continuously asked my "qualifications" as a "theorist" I cited to the inquisitive or inquisition: my *training* – a degree in political philosophy; my *research* – a dissertation on a European theorist; or my *employment* – teaching theory courses in academe. These

---

* Excerpt from Teaching Theory, Talking Community originally published in Joy James and Ruth Farmer (Eds.) (1993).

1. Native American writer Lee Maracle (1990, p. 3) notes the circular logic of academic theory: "Theory: If it can't be shown, it can't be understood. Theory is a proposition, proven by demonstrable argument. Argument: Evidence, proof. Evidence: demonstrable testimony, demonstration . . . Argument is defined as evidence; proof or evidence is defined by demonstration or proof; and theory is a proposition proven by demonstrable evidence. None of these words exist outside of their inter-connectedness. Each is defined by the other".

are prerequisites for institutional membership but not measurements of competency. I accept that nothing will qualify me to students and faculty who do not struggle with their racism, fear, and hostility towards Black/African people, philosophy, and theorizing centered on liberation. For me, teaching theory courses on the praxis of African American women permits me to claim that I think. Connecting my teaching to community organizing allows me to say I theorize. Service in African/Black liberation qualifies me.

These qualifications make me a suspicious character if not "unqualified" for academe. A hydra for teachers and students who do not set them, criteria established without our input appear like shrouds. The issue is not whether there should be academic standards and qualifications; there always are. The issue is who sets and will set them, and for whose benefit they function. The reward of transgressing conventional academic standards is re-establishing connections to some community wisdom and practice larger than academe. The spectre of failing to meet institutional standards and "qualifications" inhibits the search for new models of knowledge and teaching.

In teaching, I try to learn and share more about the history of social thought. Teaching about the origins of the "academy", "philosophy" and "theory" as predating the "Greek ancestors" of "Western civilization" broadens the scope of both the time and space in which theory takes place; it expands academia's concept of who theorizes. Changing the concept of time or the time-line changes the context for philosophy and theory.[2] Philosophy extends beyond the appearance of Europeans (and their designated ancestors) in history; so theory extends beyond the spaces they occupy or dominate. To restrict our discussions of the contributions of Black/African cosmology and philosophy to the "contemporary" period implies that we have no "ancient" or "modern" history in philosophizing. Any people of gender labelled as being without a history of philosophy is a people of gender for whom philosophy is not indigenous; often for the marginalized, "contemporary" theorizing becomes disconnected from culturally diverse traditions. That is why women and Blacks or other people of color must reinsert ourselves in time and history on the continuum, and confront academic disciplines attempting to erase us from that line. The ways in which I approach theory are changing.

---

2. Academia's presentation of time and consequently the history of thought promotes the delusion that philosophy (and civilization) began with "Greeks". The role and contributions of Black/African scholars who preceded and taught them and the African civilizations often erased before Athens are ignored. Voids in timelines manufacture artificial "origins" which, legitimizing European dominance elide African contributions in philosophy. "Ancient" becomes the "sui generis" thinking of "Europeanized" Greeks; "Medieval" the European Christian Church, with a de-Africanized Augustine; "Modern" European Enlightenment *philosophs;* and "Contemporary" European (American) writers and thinkers. "Ancient", "Medieval", "Modern", and "Contemporary" as categories for time also become categories of space and "race", denoting geography and ethnicity. Theorists assigned in each category are invariably "White" men in masculinist theory (where a few such as Hannah Arendt might qualify as the "exceptional" woman) and "White" women in feminist theory.

Extending time to find other origins of theory, I encounter more comprehensive spaces and thoughts. Hypatia, the (Egyptian) woman philosopher, sits with the "Ancient" philosophers of academic masculinist theory. The Kongo women kings theorize in a unique cosmology coexisting with the space occupied by Locke, and Rousseau and other *philosophs* of the European Enlightenment. Angela Davis and Black/African revolutionary theorizing coexist with the European (American) liberalism of Rawls, Arendt, and Bentham in contemporary political theory. In "essential feminist writings", Ida B. Wells is taught alongside Mary Wollstonecraft and Susan B. Anthony; Virginia Woolf and Mary Daly are placed beside Assata Shakur and Audre Lorde.

The ways in which I teach theory are changing. Cultivating respectfulness in myself and seeking it in my students, I ask my classes: "Who are you? Do you know your personal and political relationship to the knowledge studied?" I find that autobiographical theorizing discourages appropriation and objectification, while encouraging students to identify themselves as potential theorists and embark in self-reflections that include critiques of racist, classist and (hetero)sexist assumptions (a "backlash" usually follows any sustained critique of entrenched, dominant biases). I urge students to carefully consider the claim by revolutionary African American women who write that the roles of living thinkers are open to all and that they are not "exceptional" (those who participate in a legacy follow rather than deviate from the normative).

Students encounter the women's images and voices through video and audio tapes that supplement readings for discussions on women's contributions to and roles in liberation struggles. These images, along with exploring our relationships and responsibilities to writers, stories, and theories, pull us off the sidelines as "spectators" and consumers of Africana "performance" towards our own roles as actors. Contending with my own "consumerism", I find that progressive activists give me more than subject matter for courses; they also provide instruction in philosophy and democratic pedagogy. I am pushed most as a teacher-student when wrestling with the implications of philosophy and theorizing in the autobiographies of revolutionary African American women. More than any other type of writing, this form prods me to confront my personal and political responsibilities to ancestors, youth, and future generations. Attempting to share what I learn, the internal obstacles appear. They emerge out of my physical and sometimes intellectual alienation from work for community liberation and the philosophers and theorists of the community. They coexist with the ever present external obstacles of indifference and hostility towards Black liberation theorizing. Despite the internal and external obstacles, I begin to fear less being dismissively ignored by academics and fear more my own ignorance about and faltering ties to our ancestors' loving, radical traditions. Although it grates the academic norm, responsibility means that legitimacy and authority come from the humanity of my communities.[3] If respect

---

3. Bernice Johnson Reagon (1991) argues this about the work of Martin Luther King, Jr.

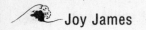

and recognition mean communicating our wisdom and humanity in struggle, regardless, then pedagogy will be the transport.

Talking Theory: Activism in Pedagogy

Pedagogy rooted in ethical concerns and an epistemology based on a four part process of experience, reflection, judgment, and action[4] organize my courses. Readings stimulate and challenge students to expand their experiential base. They then enter their reflections in journals, essay papers and compare their insights in small student work groups. Judging dominant norms, students design activities or projects to demystify and challenge economic and racial-sexual oppression, and evaluate their own ideologies. Through organizing, they obtain a greater experimental base to reflect on philosophy and theorizing, cosmologies, freedom and liberation struggles. The last step in this epistemological framework is action. Ethical action expands experiences, stimulates self-reflections, and judging. A pedagogy that denies the validity of personal experiences, that makes no space for self-reflection, that discourages judgment, and severs action from insight confuses fragmented thinking with knowledge. Guided by ethical concerns to think and organize to resist oppression, we walk closer to the place where humane political thinkers stand. There, hopefully with a less distant and more substantial awareness of their theorizing, we begin to comprehend and critique.

To respectfully teach about theorizing by African American women activists requires such a pedagogy based on ethics and active commitment to community liberation. So, I reject the concept of education as value-neutral and use "extracurricular" activities as a lab component (for instance, the hands-on experience of "applied" knowledge or "labs" to supplement "book" knowledge is indispensable in disciplines such as chemistry or architecture). These activities, encouraging students to take an active rather than passive role in their self-development, advance critical analyses of: child abuse; sexual violence; adultism; racism; (hetero)sexism; and classism.

For example, in my senior seminar on "Women and the State", students wrote papers and organized educational forums for the campus and local community on relevant topics. Their educationals in the campus center, held on Tuesday afternoons in March during Women's History Month, were: "Women and Militarization", "Women and Occupation", and "Women Political Prisoners". "Women and

---

4. Theologian Bernard Lonergan (1957) discusses an epistemology similar to the African (Afrocentric) ethical paradigm in which knowledge exists for the sake of communal good and individual human liberation (which are not presented as oppositional). Experience, reflection, judgment, and action are part of the process by which people (knowingly or unknowingly) learn. Action is indispensable to the learning process: you know how to ride a bicycle or drive a car not from merely reading books about bicycles or cars, but from riding or driving one as well (building furthers your knowledge). One knows how to live, learn and teach without patriarchal, White supremacist, or classist elitist assumptions by doing activities that confront and diminish racism, sexism, heterosexism, and classism.

Militarization" occurred around the time of the US bombing of Iraq. Over 100 people attended this educational, which students organized as a tribunal or mock trial in which African American, Caribbean and Native American and European American women activists and teachers testified on US crimes against humanity, specifically violence resulting from racism and sexism in US domestic and foreign policies. The students performed-educated as poets, defence and prosecution lawyers, judge, and witnesses. They staged guerilla theatre to disrupt their mock trial: dressed in mourning garb, the "ghosts" of several women murdered by their male companions in domestic violence interrupted the proceedings, bitterly denouncing the court for ignoring their desperate petitions, as living women, to stop their batterers.

Although the majority of students in the "Women and the State" seminar stated that they found organizing their forum and attending and critiquing the others as one of their most difficult and most rewarding educational experiences, interrelating doing and knowing for ethical–political action is not a popular practice in academe. White students have told me that they resent not the request to engage in activities outside the classroom (they do for other classes), but the request to act against racism, believing it unjust to require, as proper and necessary, that students (staff and faculty) confront adultism, classism, racism, and (hetero)sexism in their courses and themselves. (Other more liberal advocates of multiculturalism have argued that critiques of texts are the only responsible action in academic classes.)

I argue for activism as an indispensable component in learning. Action promotes consciousness of one's own political practice; such self-consciousness is a prerequisite to literacy. "Interest" in the lives of Black women and democratic struggles is superficial and the "knowledge" acquired specious if one remains illiterate in the language of community and commitment spoken by the women activists. Activism promotes literacy. It is usually the greatest and most difficult learning experience, particularly if it is connected to communities and issues broader than the parameters of academic life.

Theory and philosophy "born in struggle" carry extremely difficult lessons. Activism concretizing ethical ideals in action, allows us to better comprehend a form of thinking unfamiliar in abstract academic thought – theorizing under fire or under conditions of confrontation or repression. Thinking to stay alive and be free is the heart of liberation praxis. For half a millennium, Indigenous and African peoples in the Americas and Africa have theorized for their individual lives and the life of the community. Theorizing as a life and death endeavor rather than leisured, idle speculation, embodies revolutionary praxis. As faculty we may find ourselves in positions where living by our beliefs and theory carries the hazards of not receiving grants, promotion or tenure; students may lose scholarships and higher grades. We rarely though find ourselves in positions where living by our ideals carries the possibility that we may die for them. We generally never have to risk our lives to claim our ideals and freedom, as have radical thinkers

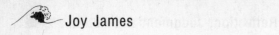

and activists such as: Harriet Tubman; Anne Moody; Assata Shakur; Martin Luther King, Jr.; Malcolm X; and Fred Hampton.[5]

Several years ago, while a visiting scholar at a mid-western university, I was able to learn more about how risk-taking and radical organizing test ideas, ideologies and commitments. During my semester tenure, the Ku Klux Klan based in its national headquarters in Indiana decided to march and stage a rally in the local campus town. The general response against the march and rally centered on individual comments of fear and anger. There was little collective, organized response until one night, as part of a women's film festival, a small number of students viewed William Greave's video, "A Passion for Justice" on the life of Ida B. Wells. An African American woman senior facilitated the discussion session that followed the video during which students shared how they were impressed by Ida B. Wells' courageous and influential activism, which began at such a young age, their age. They were silent when asked about the relationship between their feelings of inspiration for the story of Miss Wells' resistance and their feelings of anger and fear about the upcoming Klan march. Exploring these issues later that night in their dorm rooms, students began strategy sessions: they decided to allow their admiration for Miss Wells to lead them to organize a counter-educational critiquing racism, homophobia, sexism, and antisemitism in response to the impending KKK march.

African American women students led the organizing and formed a coalition with European Americans, European Jewish Americans and gay and lesbian activists. Some of these African American women students had experienced the most violent racial/sexual assaults on the campus. At an early organizing meeting, one African American senior spoke of being dragged off a catwalk into bushes as her White male assailant yelled "nigger bitch" while repeatedly punching her. As she struggled away she noticed White student spectators who made no effort to assist or intervene. The woman student stated that the university's investigation and handling of the attack were equally unresponsive.

Faculty criticisms and complaints about White dominated universities did not translate into support for the student initiated organizing. Most African American faculty and administrators, like their White counterparts, were reluctant to publicly support a student "speak-out" against racist, sexist, and homophobic violence critical of the university. University employees mirrored the divisions among African American students in which more cautious or conservative students dismissed student organizers as "radical" and ridiculed them for "over-reacting". Political differences among African American students, faculty and administration were exacerbated during the KKK organizing.

---

5. Prior to his assassination by the FBI and Chicago police in 1971, Fred Hampton prophesied: "I'm going to die for the people because I live for the people." Quoted in A Nation of Law? (1968–71), *Eyes on the Prize – Part II* which documents Hampton's political work for the African American community, the FBI's disruption of the Black liberation movement and its eventual assassination of Fred Hampton and Mark Clark.

Fear of criticizing the administration or faculty, along with homophobia, sexism and caste elitism allowed faculty and more conservative African American students to distance themselves from student activists. Yet students and youth face the greatest dangers from racial-sexual violence on campus and in society. Alongside community women and men, only two European American women and I as faculty actively organized with students educating against, in the wake of the Klan rally, increasing racist/antisemitic verbal abuse and physical violence on campus. The Klan rally highlighted faculty ambivalence and refusal to support student organizing and the university administration's unwillingness to publicly take an uncompromised stance against and responsible action for diminishing racist, antisemitic, homophobic, and sexual violence on campus.

It seemed that we faculty and administrators believed our class and caste status in academe granted us immunity from the violence assaulting many African American youth, women, and gay, lesbian and bisexual students. My own inabilities, with others, to always speak and talk to community in the midst of organizing conflicts, were compounded by my impatience and frustration with the political rhetoric and passivity of non activists. The confusion and strains impressed on me the precarious balance of teaching and talking for justice and my own uncertainty and anger, with others, about the terrain of struggle and community.

Community

Individual changes in classroom teaching to deconstruct racist–heterosexist curricula and build community are marginal if not supported by the department or program and other instructors. Often the struggles for more accuracy and accountability in education are labelled and depoliticized as personal (personnel) whims of faculty rather than responsible action. I have found that personalizing my confrontations with Eurocentric thinkers or academic careerists is a form of depoliticization that contributes to my own isolation and ineffectualness. Supporting progressive curricula and pedagogies demands political change. Yet, my experiences show that few are willing to engage in the type of activism and restructuring necessary to supplant tokenism.

I share Toni Morrison's observations in "Rootedness: The Ancestor As Foundation", applying her thoughts on writing to teaching, another art form:

> If anything I do in the way of writing ... isn't about the village or the community or about you, then it is not about anything. I am not interested in indulging myself in some private, closed exercise of my imagination that fulfils only the obligation of my personal dreams – which is to say, yes, the work must be political. It must have that as its thrust. That's a pejorative term in critical circles now: if a work of art has any political influence in it, somehow it's tainted. My feeling is just the opposite: if it has none, it is tainted (1984, pp. 344–45).

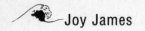

Academics and students, if not always content, seem comparatively "safe" from the political-economic conditions destroying African communities and villages. Educational status and economic "stability" grant us space to move about the world as if our survival were guaranteed, despite the increasing impoverishment and death of Africans worldwide.[6] Privilege may reduce our primary preoccupation in academia to struggles for accreditation and legitimacy from the intellectual representatives of the "new" old world order.

I am paid – and so I pay my bills and taxes to the military – by teaching "theory" in a White university's White Women's Studies program in a White suburb called "Amherst". On my better days, I think freely about a people loving and theorizing for liberation. I try to think in the traditions in which philosophy and theory are the tools of initiates and "slaves"[7] to the community, rather than the techniques of academic employees; this is problematic in places where people talk and write about life and death in and to abstraction. Although at times afraid to forget and to always remember my indebtedness to the militant Black praxis that forced open the doors of White academia, I am grateful to the call to be in a tradition of midwifery to philosophizing and theorizing, a tradition that intends community and respect for African ancestors, the living, and future born.

---

6. The US dominates international financial institutions such as the World Bank and International Monetary Fund (IMF). These institutions have underdeveloped Africa, Latin America and the Caribbean so that we as a people are poorer in the 1990s than we were in the 1960s. According to UNICEF's 1988 report, *State of the World's Children,* the "Third World" is in debt to the US and western European nations/financial institutions for over $1000 billion (US currency).

7. According to Bunseki Fukia, in Kongo philosophy the Nganga – the initiated elders and teachers – are "slaves" to the community (lecture, Caribbean Cultural Center, New York City, February 1991).

Catharine A. MacKinnon

From Practice to Theory, or
What is a White Woman Anyway?*

And ain't I a woman?

– Sojourner Truth[1]

Black feminists speak as women because we are women ...

– Audre Lorde[2]

It is common to say that something is good in theory but not in practice. I always want to say, then it is not such a good theory, is it? To be good in theory but not in practice posits a relation between theory and practice that places theory prior to practice, both methodologically and normatively, as if theory is a terrain unto itself. The conventional image of the relation between the two is first theory, then practice. You have an idea, then act on it. In legal academia you theorize, then try to get some practitioner to put it into practice. To be more exact, you read law, review articles, then write more law review articles. The closest most legal academics come to practice is teaching – their students, most of whom will practice, being regarded by many as an occupational hazard to their theorizing.

The postmodern version of the relation between theory and practice is discourse unto death. Theory begets no practice, only more text. It proceeds as if you can deconstruct power relations by shifting their markers around in your head. Like all formal idealism, this approach to theory tends unselfconsciously to reproduce existing relations of dominance, in part because it is an utterly removed

* Reprinted from *Yale Journal of Law and Feminism,* (1991b), 4 (13) pp. 13–22. This paper benefited from the comments of members of the Collective on Women of Color and the Law at Yale Law School.
1. Bert J. Loewenberg & Ruth Dugin (1976, p. 235).
2. Audre Lorde (1984, p.60). The whole quotation is "Black feminists speak as women because we are women and do not need others to speak for us."

elite activity. On this level, all theory is a form of practice, because it either subverts or shores up existing deployments of power, in their martial metaphor. As an approach to change, it is the same as the conventional approach to the theory/practice relation: head driven, not world driven. Social change is first thought about, then acted out. Books relate to books, heads talk to heads. Bodies do not crunch bodies or people move people. As theory, it is the de-realization of the world.

The movement for the liberation of women, including in law, moves the other way around. It is first practice, then theory. Actually, it moves this way in practice, not just in theory. Feminism was a practice long before it was a theory. On its real level, the Women's Movement – where women move against their determinants as women – remains more practice than theory. This distinguishes it from academic feminism. For women in the world, the gap between theory and practice is the gap between practice and theory. We know things with our lives, and live that knowledge, beyond anything any theory has yet theorized. Women's practice of confrontation with the realities of male dominance outruns any existing theory of the possibility of consciousness or resistance. To write the theory of this practice is not to work through logical puzzles or entertaining conundra, not to fantasize utopias, not to moralize or tell people what to do. It is not to exercise authority; it does not lead practice. Its task is to engage life through developing mechanisms that identify and criticize rather than reproduce social practices of subordination and to make tools of women's consciousness and resistance that further a practical struggle to end inequality. This kind of theory requires humility and it requires participation.

I am saying: we who work with law need to be about the business of articulating the theory of women's practice – women's resistance, visions, consciousness, injuries, notions of community, experience of inequality. By practical, I mean socially lived. As our theoretical question becomes "what is the theory of women's practice", our theory becomes a way of moving against and through the world, and methodology becomes technology.

Specifically – and such theory inhabits particularity – I want to take up the notion of experience "as a woman" and argue that it is the practice of which the concept of discrimination "based on sex" is the legal theory. That is, I want to investigate how the realities of women's experience of sex inequality in the world have shaped some contours of sex discrimination in the law.

Sex equality as a legal concept has not traditionally been theorized to encompass issues of sexual assault or reproduction because equality theory has been written out of men's practice, not women's. Men's experiences of group-based subordination have not centered on sexual and reproductive abuse, although they include instances of it. Some men have been hurt in these ways, but they are few and are not usually regarded as hurt because they are men, but in spite of it or in derogation of it. Few men are, sexually and reproductively speaking, "similarly situated" to women but treated better. So sexuality and reproduction are not regarded as equality issues in the traditional approach.[3] Two intrepid, indomitable women, women determined to write the practice of their lives onto the law, moved the theory of sex equality to include these issues.

In her case, *Meritor Savings Bank v. Vinson*,[4] Mechelle Vinson established that sexual harassment as a working environment is sex discrimination under civil rights law. Her resistance to her supervisor Sidney Taylor – specifically, her identification that his repeated rape, his standing over her in the bank vault waving his penis and laughing, were done to her because she was a woman – changed the theory of sex discrimination for all women. In her case, *California Federal Savings and Loan Association v. Guerra*,[5] Lillian Garland established that guaranteeing unpaid leaves for pregnant women by law is not discrimination on the basis of sex, but is a step in ending discrimination on the basis of sex. Her resistance to her employer, the California Federal Savings and Loan Association, in its refusal to reinstate her in her job after a pregnancy leave; her identification of that practice as illegal treatment of her because she was a woman, gave sex equality law a decisive spin in the direction of promoting equality, away from its prior status quo-mirroring regressive neutrality. The arguments that won these cases were based on the plaintiffs' lives as women, on insisting that actual social practices that subordinated them as women be theoretically recognized as impermissible sex-based discrimination under law. In the process, sexual assault and reproduction became sex equality issues, with implications for the laws of rape and abortion, among others.

So what is meant by treatment "as women" here? To speak of being treated "as a woman" is to make an empirical statement about reality, to describe the realities of women's situation. In the USA, with parallels in other cultures, women's situation combines unequal pay with allocation to disrespected work, sexual targeting for rape, domestic battering, sexual abuse as children, and systematic sexual harassment; depersonalization, demeaned physical characteristics, use in denigrating entertainment, deprivation of reproductive control, and forced prostitution. To see that these practices are done by men to women is to see these abuses as forming a system, a hierarchy of inequality. This situation has occurred in many places, in one form or another, for a very long time, often in a context characterized by disenfranchisement, preclusion from property ownership (women are more likely to be property than to own any), ownership and use as object, exclusion from public life, sex-based poverty, degraded sexuality, and a devaluation of women's human worth and contributions throughout society. This subordination of women to men is socially institutionalized, cumulatively and systematically shaping access to human dignity, respect, resources, physical security, credibility, membership in community, speech and power. Comprised of all

---

3. I detail this argument further in Reflections on Sex Equality Under Law (1991a, p. 100).

4. Meritor Savings Bank v. Vinson, 477 U.S. 57 (1986).

5. California Fed. Sav. & Loan Ass'n v. Guerra, 479 U.S. 272 (1987).

its variations, the group women can be seen to have a collective social history of disempowerment, exploitation and subordination extending to the present. To be treated "as a woman" in this sense is to be disadvantaged in these ways incident to being socially assigned to the female sex. To speak of social treatment "as a woman" is thus not to invoke any abstract essence or homogeneous generic or ideal type, not to posit anything, far less a universal anything, but to refer to this diverse and pervasive concrete material reality of social meanings and practices such that, in the words of Richard Rorty, "a woman is not yet the name of a way of being human . . ."[6]

Thus cohering the theory of "women" out of the practice of "women" produces the opposite of what Elizabeth Spelman has criticized as a reductive assumption of essential sameness of all women that she identifies in some feminist theory.[7] The task of theorizing women's practice produces a new kind of theory, a theory that is different from prior modes of theorizing in form, not just content. As Andrea Dworkin said quite a long time ago, women's situation requires new ways of thinking, not just thinking new things.[8] "Woman" as abstraction, distillation, common denominator, or idea is the old way of thinking, or at most a new thing to think, but it is not a new way of thinking. Nor is thinking "as" a woman, as one embodiment of a collective experience, the same as thinking "like" a woman, which is to reproduce one's determinants and think like a victim.

Some recent work, especially Elizabeth Spelman's, could be read to argue that there is no such thing as experience "as a woman" and women of color prove it.[9] This theory converges with the elevation of "differences" as a flag under which to develop diverse feminisms.[10] To do theory in its conventional abstract way, as many do, is to import the assumption that all women are the same or they are not women. What makes them women is their fit within the abstraction "woman" or their conformity to a fixed, posited female essence. The consequence is to reproduce

---

6. Richard Rorty (1991, pp. 231–34) states "MacKinnon's central point, as I read her, is that 'a woman' is not yet the name of a way of being human – not yet the name of a moral identity, but, at most, the name of a disability."

7. Elizabeth V. Spelman (1988, pp. 158–59).

8. "[O]ne can be excited about ideas without changing at all. [O]ne can think about ideas, talk about ideas, without changing at all. [P]eople are willing to think about many things. What people refuse to do, or are not permitted to do, or resist doing, is to change the way they think." Andrea Dworkin (1974, p. 202).

9. Spelman (1988, pp. 164–66, 174, 186) defines "essentialism" largely in terms of central tenets of radical feminism, without being clear whether the experience "as a woman" she identifies in radical feminism is a social or a biological construct. Having done this, it becomes easy to conclude that the "woman" of feminism is a distilled projection of the personal lives of a few comparatively powerful biological females, rather than a congealed synthesis of the lived social situation of women as a class, historically and worldwide.

10. Spelman implies that "differences" not be valorized or used as a theoretical construct (1988, p. 174) but others, building on her work and that of Carol Gilligan (1982), do.

dominance: While much work subjected to this criticism does not do this,[11] one can trace it, surprisingly, in the works of Simone de Beauvoir and Susan Brownmiller. De Beauvoir, explaining why women are second class citizens, says:

> Here we have the key to the whole mystery. On the biological level a species is maintained only by creating itself anew; but this creation results only in repeating the same Life in more individuals . . . Her [woman's] misfortune is to have been biologically destined for the repetition of Life, when even in her own view Life does not carry within itself its reasons for being, reasons that are more important than Life itself (de Beauvoir: 1971, p. 64).

Here women are defined in terms of biological reproductive capacity. It is unclear exactly how any social organization of equality could change such an existential fact, far less how to argue that a social policy that institutionalized it could be sex discriminatory.

Susan Brownmiller argues the centrality of rape in women's condition in the following terms:

> Man's structural capacity to rape and woman's corresponding structural vulnerability are as basic to the physiology of both our sexes as the primal act of sex itself. Had it not been for this accident of biology, an accommodation requiring the locking together of two separate parts, penis and vagina, there would be neither copulation nor rape as we know it . . . By anatomical fiat – the inescapable construction of their genital organs – the human male was a natural predator and the human female served as his natural prey (Brownmiller: 1976, pp. 4, 6).

Exactly how to oppose sexual assault from this vantage point is similarly unclear. Do we make a law against intercourse? Although both theorists have considerably more to offer on the question of what defines women's condition, what we have in these passages is simple biological determinism presented as a critical theory of social change.

The problem here, it seems to me, does not begin with a failure to take account of race or class, but with the failure to take account of gender. It is not only or most fundamentally an account of race or class dominance that is missing here, but an account of male dominance. There is nothing biologically necessary about rape, as Mechelle Vinson made abundantly clear when she sued for rape as unequal treatment on the basis of sex. And, as Lillian Garland saw, and made

---

11. The philosophical term "essentialism" is sometimes wrongly applied to socially based theories that observe and analyze empirical commonalities in women's condition. See for example, Angela P. Harris (1990). One can also take an essentialist approach to race or class. In other words, a theory does not become "essentialist" to the degree it discusses gender as such nor is it saved from "essentialism" to the degree it incorporates race or class.

everyone else see, it is the way society punishes women for reproduction that creates women's problems with reproduction, not reproduction itself. Both women are Black. This only supports my suspicion that if a theory is not true of, and does not work for, women of color, it is not really true of, and will not work for, any women, and that it is not really about gender at all. The theory of the practice of Mechelle Vinson and Lillian Garland, because it is about the experience of Black women, is what gender is about.

In recent critiques of feminist work for failing to take account of race or class,[12] it is worth noting that the fact that there is such a thing as race and class is assumed, although race and class are generally treated as abstractions to attack gender rather than as concrete realities, if indeed they are treated at all. Spelman, for example, discusses race but does virtually nothing with class.[13] In any event, race and class are regarded as unproblematically real and not in need of justification or theoretical construction. Only gender is not real and needs to be justified. Although many women have demanded that discussions of race or class take gender into account, typically these demands do not take the form that, outside explicit recognition of gender, race or class do not exist. That there is a diversity to the experience of men and women of color, and of working class women and men regardless of race, is not said to mean that race or class are not meaningful concepts. I have heard no one say that there can be no meaningful discussion of "people of color" without gender specificity. Thus the phrase "people of color and white women" has come to replace the previous "women and minorities", which women of color rightly perceived as not including them twice, and embodying a white standard for sex and a male standard for race. But I hear not talk of "all women and men of color", for instance. It is worth thinking about that when women of color refer to "people who look like me", it is understood that they mean people of color, not women, in spite of the fact that both race and sex are visual assignments, both possess clarity as well as ambiguity, and both are marks of oppression, hence community.

In this connection, it has recently come to my attention that the white woman is the issue here, so I decided I better find out what one is. This creature is not poor, not battered, not raped (not really), not molested as a child, not pregnant as a teenager, not prostituted, not coerced into pornography, not a welfare mother, and not economically exploited. She doesn't work. She is either the white man's image of her – effete, pampered, privileged, protected, flighty, and self-indulgent –

---

12. I am thinking in particular of Spelman (1988) and Marlee Kline (1989, p. 115), although this analysis also applies to others who have made the same argument, such as Harris (1990). Among its other problems, much of this work tends to make invisible the women of color who were and are instrumental in defining and creating feminism as a movement of women in the world, as well as a movement of mind.
13. This is by contrast with the massive feminist literature on the problem of class, which I discuss and summarize as a foundational problem for feminist theory in *Toward a Feminist Theory of the State* (1989a). Harris (1990), discusses race but does nothing with either class or sexual orientation except invoke them as clubs against others.

or the Black man's image of her – all that, plus the "pretty white girl" (meaning ugly as sin but regarded as the ultimate in beauty because she is white). She is Miss Anne of the kitchen, she puts Frederick Douglass to the lash, she cries rape when Emmett Till looks at her sideways, she manipulates white men's very real power with the lifting of her very well-manicured little finger. She makes an appearance in Baraka's "rape the white girl",[14] as Cleaver's real thing after target practice on Black women,[15] as Helmut Newton's glossy upscale hard-edged, distanced vamp (1976), and as the Central Park Jogger, the classy white madonna who got herself raped and beaten nearly to death. She flings her hair, feels beautiful all the time, complains about the colored help, tips badly, can't do anything, doesn't do anything, doesn't know anything, and alternates fantasizing about fucking Black men with accusing them of raping her. As Ntozake Shange points out, all Western civilization depends on her (1981, p. 48). On top of all of this, out of impudence, imitativeness, pique, and a simple lack of anything meaningful to do, she thinks she needs to be liberated. Her feminist incarnation is all of the above, and guilty about every single bit of it, having by dint of repetition refined saying "I'm sorry" to a high form of art. She can't even make up her own songs.

There is, of course, much to much of this, this "woman, modified", this woman discounted by white, meaning she would be oppressed but for her privilege. But this image seldom comes face to face with the rest of her reality: the fact that the majority of the poor are white women and their children (at least half of whom are female); that white women are systematically battered in their homes, murdered by intimates and serial killers alike, molested as children, actually raped (mostly by white men), and that even Black men, on average, make more than they do.[16] If one did not know this, one could be taken in by white men's image of white women: that the pedestal is real, rather than a cage in which to confine and trivialize them and segregate them from the rest of life, a vehicle for sexualized infantilization, a virginal set-up for rape by men who enjoy violating the pure, and a myth with which to try to control Black women. (See, if you would lie down and be quiet and not move, we would revere you, too.) One would think that the white men's myth that they protect white women was real, rather than a racist cover to guarantee their exclusive and unimpeded sexual access – meaning they can rape her at will, and do, a posture made good in the marital rape exclusion and the

---

14. Imamu Amiri Baraka is also known as LeRoi Jones (Baraka: 1964, pp. 61, 63).

15. "I became a rapist. To refine my technique and modus operandi, I started out by practicing on black girls in the ghetto . . . and when I considered myself smooth enough, I crossed the tracks and sought out white prey." "[R]aping the white girl" as an activity for Black men is described as one of "the funky facts of life." In a racist context in which the white girl's white girlness is sexualized – that is, made a site of lust, hatred and hostility – for the Black man through the history of lynching. Eldridge Cleaver (1968, pp.14–15).

16. In 1989, the median income of white women was approximately one-fourth less than that of Black men; in 1990 it was one-fifth less. U.S. Bureau of the Census, Current Population Report (1991, p. 60).

largely useless rape law generally. One would think that the only white women in brothels in the South during the Civil War were in *Gone With the Wind*.[17] This is not to say there is no such thing as skin privilege, but rather that it has never insulated white women from the brutality and misogyny of men, mostly but not exclusively white men, or from its effective legalization. In other words, the "white girls" of this theory miss quite a lot of the reality of white women in the practice of male supremacy.

Beneath the trivialization of the white woman's subordination implicit in the dismissive sneer "straight white economically privileged women" (a phrase which has become one word, the accuracy of some of its terms being rarely documented even in law journals) lies the notion that there is no such thing as the oppression of women as such. If white women's oppression is an illusion of privilege and a rip-off and reduction of the civil rights movement, we are being told that there is no such thing as a woman, that our practice produces no theory, and that there is no such thing as discrimination on the basis of sex. What I am saying is, to argue that oppression "as a woman" negates rather than encompasses recognition of the oppression of women on other bases, is to say that there is no such thing as the practice of sex inequality.

Let's take this the other way around. As I mentioned, both Mechelle Vinson and Lillian Garland are African-American women. Wasn't Mechelle Vinson sexually harassed as a woman? Wasn't Lillian Garland pregnant as a woman? They thought so. The whole point of their cases was to get their injuries understood as "based on sex", that is, because they are women. The perpetrators, and the policies under which they were disadvantaged, saw them as women. What is being a woman if it does not include being oppressed as one? When the Reconstruction Amendments "gave Blacks the vote", and Black women still could not vote, weren't they kept from voting "as women"? When African-American women are raped two times as often as white women, aren't they raped as women? That does not mean their race is irrelevant and it does not mean that their injuries can be understood outside a racial context. Rather, it means that "sex" is made up of the reality of the experiences of all women, including theirs. It is a composite unit rather than a divided unitary whole, such that each women, in her way, is all women. So, when white women are sexually harassed or lose their jobs because they are pregnant, aren't they women too?

The treatment of women in pornography shows this approach in graphic relief. One way or another, all women are in pornography. African-American women are featured in bondage, struggling, in cages, as animals, insatiable. As Andrea Dworkin has shown, the sexualized hostility directed against them makes their skin into a sex organ, focusing the aggression and contempt directed principally at other women's genitals (1981, pp. 215–16). Asian women are passive, inert, as if dead, tortured unspeakably. Latinas are hot mommas. Fill in the rest from every demeaning and hostile racial stereotype you know; it is sex here. This

---

17. This is an insight of Dorothy Teer.

is not done to men, not in heterosexual pornography. What is done to white women is a kind of floor; it is the best anyone is treated and it runs from *Playboy* through sadomasochism to snuff. What is done to white women can be done to any woman, and then some. This does not make white women the essence of womanhood. It is a reality to observe that this is what can be done and is done to the most privileged of women. This is what privilege as a woman gets you: most valued as dead meat.

I am saying, each woman is in pornography as the embodiment of her particularities. This is not in tension with being there "as a woman", *it is what being there as a woman means*. Her specificity makes up what gender is. White, for instance, is not a residual category. It is not a standard against which the rest are "different". There is no generic "woman" in pornography. White is not unmarked; it is a specific sexual taste. Being defined and used in this way defines what being a woman means in practice. Robin Morgan once said, "pornography is the theory, rape is the practice" (1978, p. 169). This is true, but Andrea Dworkin's revision is more true: "Pornography is the theory, pornography is the practice."[18] This approach to "what is a woman" is reminiscent of Sartre's answer to the question "what is a Jew?" Start with the anti-Semite.[19]

In my view, the subtext to the critique of oppression "as a woman", the critique that holds that there is no such thing, is dis-identification with women. One of its consequences is the destruction of the basis for a jurisprudence of sex equality. An argument advanced in many critiques by women of color has been that theories of women must include all women, and when they do, theory will change. On one level, this is necessarily true. On another, it ignores the formative contributions of women of color to feminist theory since its inception. I also sense, though, that many women, not only women of color and not only academics, do not want to be "just women", not only because something important is left out, but also because that means being in a category with "her", the useless white woman whose first reaction when the going gets rough is to cry. I sense here that people feel more dignity in being part of a group that includes men than in being part of a group that includes that ultimate reduction of the notion of oppression, that instigator of lynch mobs, that ludicrous whiner, that equality coat-tails rider, the white woman. It seems that if your oppression is also done to a man, you are more likely to be recognized as oppressed, as opposed to inferior. Once a group is seen as putatively human, a process helped by including men in it, an oppressed man falls from a human standard.[20] A woman is just a woman – the ontological victim – so not victimized at all.

---

18. Personal communication with Andrea Dworkin. *See also* Andrea Dworkin (1991, pp. 304–7).

19. "Thus, to know what the contemporary Jew is, we must ask the Christian conscience. And we must ask, not 'What is a Jew?' but *'What have you made of the Jews?'* The Jew is one whom other men consider a Jew: that is the simple truth from which we must start. In this sense . . . it is the anti-Semite who *makes* the Jew." Jean-Paul Sartre (1948).

20. I sense a similar dynamic at work in the attraction among some lesbians of identification with "gay rights" rather than "women's rights", with the result of obscuring the roots in male dominance of the oppression of both lesbians and gay men.

Unlike other women, the white woman who is not poor or working class or lesbian or Jewish or disabled or old or young *does not share her oppression with any man*. That does not make her condition any more definitive of the meaning of "women" than the condition of any other woman is. But trivializing her oppression, because it is not even potentially racist or class-biased or heterosexist or anti-Semitic, does define the meaning of being "anti-woman" with a special clarity. How the white woman is imagined and constructed and treated becomes a particularly sensitive indicator of the degree to which women, as such, are despised.

If we build a theory out of women's practice, comprised of the diversity of all women's experiences, we do not have the problem that some feminist theory has been rightly criticized for. When we have it is when we make theory out of abstractions and accept the images forced on us by male dominance. I said all that so I could say this: the assumption that all women are the same is part of the bedrock of sexism that the Women's Movement is predicated on challenging. That some academics find it difficult to theorize without reproducing it simply means that they continue to do to women what theory, predicated on the practice of male dominance, has always done to women. It is their notion of what theory is, and its relation to its world, that needs to change.

If our theory of what is "based on sex" makes gender out of actual social practices distinctively directed against women as women identify them, the problem that the critique of so-called "essentialism" exists to rectify ceases to exist. And this bridge, the one from practice to theory, is not built on anyone's back.

Ngahuia Te Awekotuku

Maori–Lesbian–Feminist Radical*

This article draws a pattern of autobiography, describing certain phases of my school life, and initial years in Auckland. Growing up in a village environment, coping with being outside the sexual "norm", discovering feminist and gay politics, and getting to know Auckland against high odds.

I came aboard this planet with Aries rising, a Taurus sun, and the moon in mercurial Gemini, thirty-three years ago. Raised in many different households, Maori fashion I enjoyed the featherdown soft cuddles of a doting, gentle Kuia (grandmother), graced by the warm safety of a tribal environment. I was fortunate in having a school teacher aunt, whose attentive ministrations and private needs had me reading at four years old: precocious and alien.

School. I loved it, particularly as I grew older, and the cosy security of early childhood years fell away to the temerity of death, illness, violence, and change. The classroom became my safe place, especially the convent of inter-mediate school. Wonderful, fierce, strong nuns politicised me radically, nourished me with stories of the IRA, the horrors of Auschwitz and the Klan, the heroism of Violette Szabo, female freedom-fighter. And my fearless, stroppy mother, at home. Then off I went to high school, to be expelled for insolence, perversion, and numerous escapades, at the end of my first year.

Delinquency soon bored me. All my wild mates got pregnant – god! Loathing that option, which the world was convinced was my fate, I settled down, started my retreat into study-books, writing, fantasy and politics. These have persisted, as I gathered degrees – a challenging, often sour harvest – along the way: BA and MA (Hons) in English Literature; a Doctorate in social sciences.

The Doctorate is important for my people: a study of the social and cultural impact of tourism on my tribal community. In many ways it is a gift to them, and to our descendants, for it records the stories, memoirs, anecdotes and

---

* Reprinted from *Women Who Do and Women Who Don't* (1984) and *Mana Wahine Maori* (1991).

reminiscences of many who have since gone on. And although I wrote the pieces in between, the story itself, the actual, substantive and substantial fabric was woven by the people, by Te Arawa, my principal tribe.

I have spent four years in the Hawaiian Islands, cherishing each balmy moment, and on the North American continent, aghast; then around the various states of the Pacific, wondering.

Briefly, some basic facts about myself that won't change. I love women, cats and ducks. Actually, I love animals. Make myself run a little, swim a lot. Have an insatiable appetite for fantasy science fiction, particularly feminist. Enjoy eating, and Mozart, Vivaldi and Grace Jones. Adore, need, cherish the ocean, Hine Moana, her savagery and calm, her enveloping, enlightening beauty. Her smell. And I dream crazy creative dreams.

> Whaia ki te iti kahurangi
> Me tuohu koe, he maunga teitei
> Seek after your innermost wishes
> And bend only to the highest mountain.

This is a proverb of my people, the Maori of Aotearoa: New Zealand, where the White Man came, imposing his God, wielding his technology, indulging his avarice and greed. Generations later, resilient and resourceful, we reconstruct and regenerate, drawing some knowledge from within ourselves, and celebrating our language once condemned. Land, culture, language – all threatened, now emerging with new meanings and form. Particularly for women, because as the refurbished tradition develops, a potent and ironic misogyny appears. Cluttered beneath the superficial structure of Maori-tanga – a generalized Maori-ness – are concepts, roles and notions that put woman down, reinterpret her story, and shove her into a latterday Judaeo-Christian line. Following what the missionaries taught – the debasement of women as unclean; the elevation of God the Father, God as Man.

And woman suffers, while the warrior snarls within her. I am one such woman.

Maori – lesbian – feminist. Born into a colonized tribal patriarchy in the thermal districts of Aotearoa, I discovered my lesbianism relatively early, although I certainly did not survive the stormy years of late adolescence a maiden intact. Years of study at university fashioned a cosmopolitan exterior, and the galloping madness of antipodean hippiedom and anti-war actions soon sharpened my political edge, making me aware and verbal in the white, middle-class world. Particularly on issues I felt affected me directly: class, and deeper still, colour. Despite a lightish skin – my people's delight – and an educated accent, I was still visibly, boldly, Maori. Nothing could ever change that – it was/is permanent, wonderful, and as inexorable as my femaleness.

Working with flatmates, other female members of our ghetto student activist community, I often considered how we were still chained to the stove or sink, still mute when the actions, excitement, indulgences of that late 1960s early 1970s world were decided. Any opinions offered by women were shrugged off, blown away as so much froth atop the ubiquitous beer mugs of the period. And as a lesbian – "like that" – I had even less validity. Apart from being Maori, good god! I wasn't even a *real* woman.

Our day did come, the first gentle ripples that precede a rising tide. *Notes from the Second Year* arrived at the local political bookshop. And never was a volume so cherished: articulating our grievances, exposing our pains, releasing us from our own doubt and self-denial. Suddenly, we women realized, like the valiant Viet Cong, like the Blacks, like the working class, we were an oppressed people, a voiceless, hushed, unseen majority – with the right to demand equality. Over the summer of 1971–72 it did the rounds of radical households. By March, Women's Liberation Groups were meeting in Auckland, including the readers of that book, and many other politically involved but exploited women. Most of us felt we'd had an utter gut full of the macho radical left or hippie "gentle" men. Ideologically, I felt I'd finally come home, despite being a Maori, despite being a dozen conflicting, different, contradictory selves.

Throughout my life, I have never doubted that women are stronger, braver and more resourceful – regardless of men's rules, men's games, and men's petty triumphs. My role models – of the fierce women fighters, shamans and poets of Maori legend and myth; of the resilient, courageous women of my own extended family – demonstrate this to me. For as much as colonial and contemporary ethnography and tribal record attempt to annihilate the relevance and radiance of their achievements, it is my responsibility to them, as their inheritor, to ensure their stories are not lost in a mawkishly romantic middle of male-translated history.

The movement in Aotearoa – the contemporary feminist wave of the last dozen years or so – had predictably bewildering beginnings. Issues were relatively tame; men were often active group members; we focussed on equal opportunity in education and employment, child-care, and the end of sex role stereotyping. We aimed for the end of oppression of *all* women, whatever their credo, perspective, or accountability. We had loads of fun in comic actions, commanded extraordinary media space, and indulged in shrilly competitive bickering while engulfed in massive ideological confusion. Other women noticed us, joined, argued, mobilized. They became aware, became involved, became excited by the reality of feminist revolution. And over the years, The Movement gathered momentum.

For me, feminism means working as much as one can to end the oppression of women, to break our dependence on men, and to subvert, challenge, and ultimately destroy those bastions of male power that enslave us. Strategy may vary. So may commitment. The feminism I ascribe for myself is in many ways markedly different from that of my friends. Yet our intention is basically the same. Being a woman-oriented woman whose lifestyle is as much as possible – socially, politically, sexually – focussed on women, I attempt to define a clear line for myself by as complete and uncompromised a commitment to women as I can possibly sustain.

Yet inevitably the line shifts, for being a Fourth World woman I must also function within the vividly determined tribal world of female and male, and function effectively. My ethnicity sharpens my focus brutally, essentially, because racism is an integral part of cross-cultural relationships in post-colonial Aotearoa. We strive to acknowledge and exterminate those attitudes through countless hours and days and weeks of gut-searing workshops, sobbing confrontations, and exorcising guilt. Yet so many pakeha, including feminists, remain safely locked into the inertia of not looking, not seeing, but still "wanting so much to help, to understand".

The disease must be dealt with, though I feel that racism is the responsibility of the racist – and they, not I should work it out. Nevertheless, I count women, initially, as my allies, because I believe sexism to be the primary offence against humanity, whatever terse prioritizing the other issues may engender. However, some thinkers may refute that any one issue or struggle is more loaded than another. Until women are free to choose, to chance, to challenge, to change, *no one* is truly free. And the planet is deprived of half its creative potential.

As a Maori lesbian, I am often compelled to consider the colliding urgencies of my life. I have risked the brand of "house nigger", for I will defend the middle-class white rape victim before the disadvantaged and deprived brown rapist – for his act violates *all* women, and welds the manacles of sexist oppression more fixedly than ever. I move within many worlds, yet share the confidence and security of my community of tribal women, and a branching global network of lesbian sisters.

With all of them, I experience highly textured, often tragic, visions of our future. Change is painfully slow; progress for us may take generations, as the waves of consciousness and direct confrontation rise, then recede. The small or substantial moves we make, jagged or gentle, subtle or violent, contribute to that process of growth, of revolution. And we are all part of it.

Frequently, the contradictions of my life are harrowing, but I refuse to reject any one facet of myself. I claim *all* my cultures, all my conflicts. They make me what I am; they will shape what I am becoming.

Postscript, 1995

Shrill, the birds still sing.

And I write here, twelve years later, responding to an invitation from this collection's editors.

To contribute a postscript.

The shaping, of course, continues:

I am still becoming and will do so until my final breath. As each year's complexity of events and adventures, disappointments and triumphs, painful or joyous lessons, form the spirals of my life. So much has happened.

So much more will, I am sure!

What astonishes me most of all is that I've hardly shifted from the position described above. On one level, I certainly don't swim as much and the running is less than a little, but the appetites remain; ditto the dreams. And I've discovered the slow, graceful, silent mystery of rivers. The newness of my doctorate has faded – though only three Maori women, tribally nurtured and identified, hold the academic degree as I write this, surely an indictment of the academy and its inadequacies, which each one of us three is trying to confront. But there are still only three, and that hurts. Eagerly, we pressure, encourage, heave, cajole, motivate, shove, mentor and await the others coming through. There is a healthy handful of Maori female doctoral aspirants – some of them are almost there – from a population of 404,000 people who claim Maori descent. Two-thirds of this number are tribally nurtured and identified; while the question persists, what is a Maori? Certainly, if it means being of part Maori descent, as in a great-great-great-grandmama being a Maori princess, then certainly, there are more than just three of us. It is the nurturing and identification, the commitment and self-knowledge that means Maori to me.

I now smile at my own phrase – "post-colonial Aotearoa" – for these miserable statistics indicate that the colonial process continues, that the Maori people are still oppressed. That land, culture, language issues engage us all in day-to-day confrontation and dilemma. Unlike those African, Pacific and Asian states whose political sovereignty has been realized and reasserted in the last two generations, Aotearoa is still fettered by a majority white population who dominate and control; who have an investment in the colonial ethic. They are threatened by Maori ideas of sovereignty and make pronouncements about this country's multi-cultural future on their own, mono-cultural, terms.

Dealing with the indigenous is a different dialogue indeed; because the boundaries, though possibly redefined by goodwill and contrition, nevertheless, remain. So my islands may never experience a post-colonial condition; demographic reality, as well as simple racism and the politics of ownership, will not allow it.

Maori women have developed many dynamic initiatives to counter this. The resistance and protest of the 1970s and early 1980s germinated the Kohanga Reo movement: unique Maori preschools that ensured the language's survival; various health outreach programmes, one notably on nicotine addition, based in both tribal and urban communities; and the development of a nationwide domestic violence intervention project. Tribal radio, legal services, expansive business ventures, have all engaged the energies of the Maori, and lesbian Maori women.

Despite this, in the last decade, the five private boarding institutions for Maori girls have been threatened with, or experienced, closure. Meanwhile, the boys' schools flourish, in a manic macho frenzy of reconstruction, computer purchasing and rugby.

Racism still flourishes in Aotearoa. And sexism, too.

The issues of role-modelling and radicalism continue to confound. So many have been seduced by high salaries, designer cars and clothes, and the fevered prestige of political influence and electoral gamesmanship. But a few of us haven't. The hardcore radicals. The boring 1970s left-overs. The dreary outdated dreamers.

Are we dreary and outdated? Are we boring? Are we radicals?

All of those and yes and no.

Do we look at the generation that followed us, and despair?

I confess. Sometimes, I do. Despair.

If radical lesbian means, to them, a lesbian-identified, female-born woman who does sex with a man, i.e. male-born man, then I do. Despair.

If radical lesbian sex, to be "really radical" to them, means a baldheaded butchette pumping a latex strap on dildo into the welcoming anus of a twittering fem trannie, then I do. Despair.

And I ask, what has become of our work? And our works?

So much has been swallowed by a miasma of fanciful semantics. So that we are left with what we have retreated into, within the boundaries we have drawn. For radicalism is about boundaries. Breaking them, and testing them. Pushing against them, and resetting them. Sealing them, and risking them. And smashing them down.

The last few years have also had me thinking about what it means, for me, to be a feminist. As I've watched the convulsively painful convolutions and birthing (in which I laboured myself, for a while) of Women's Studies at both Auckland and Waikato Universities, and as I've observed the diverse indulgences of white heterosexual careerists on the feminist platform, I've wondered, seriously, if that word still describes me.

Being Maori, being lesbian, I have no choice. Being feminist means *choosing*: do I want to share my spirit with a global "community" which doesn't really give a damn about the urgencies of incest, unemployment, disease, homelessness, suicide, escalating debt in my immediate, residential, environment? I doubt it. But if I am committed to working for, and with, women, what other word is there? None; so I take the word, and I make it fit me, I make it mine. My way.

Maori. Lesbian. Feminist. Radical.

The International Dyke March and Stonewall 94 in New York City; the 1.1 million lesbians/gays/queers/bi's and sexual renegades in Central Park during my three speaking minutes of heady soaring terror, revealed to me the global changes of a generation. They represented the outcome of radical action of years of hard work; large disappointments, small triumphs.

I am still conscious of what, and who, encircle me: my own community of women. Maori lesbians – tribals, urbans, moving as graciously as one can to an elderly women – crone – Kuia status. And we call ourselves Kuia 2000 – organized to share our knowledge, prepare for the ritualistic expectations of tribal ageing, take care of ourselves, our health, our finances, our burgeoning needs, this group, rough and very ready, always resilient, celebrates our survival. To our straight contemporaries, such action – so many ageing tribal women so visibly without men – is radical indeed.

So much has happened.

So much more will, I am sure.

And I look forward to it.

Oh yes. I do.

Angela Bowen

Enabling a Visible Black Lesbian Presence in Academia: A Radically Reasonable Request*

When I met with the admissions committee for graduate school, a woman on the committee who was about my age asked, "Why do you want to be entering graduate school now at this stage of your life? They're very ageist in the academy, you know." My mental response was, "Oh, really, and not racist, sexist and homophobic as well?" In spite of my reputation as a smart-mouth, I managed to deliver a more considered response and gain entry.

I do not see my age, or my color, or my sex as my biggest problems, but as a series of obstacles to step over in my determination to do this work. What do I see standing more firmly in my way? Not the difficulty of the academic work; not the patriarchal structure of the institutions; not the disdain, disregard and erasure of my Black, middle-aged, woman, lesbian, feminist, community-connected self by an omniscient, omnipotent eurocentric patriarchy (although I am familiar with all of the above). What I am more apprehensive about is the disdain, disregard and erasure of my lesbian self by my Black heterosexual sisters, from whom I would rather anticipate comfort, encouragement, a safe retreat. So I pose these questions: Will our Black heterosexual sisters enable Black lesbians to do our work? Will they be allies or obstacles? Will they enable us to survive? For if we are all to fulfill our mission — to water the thirsting spirits and intellects of our precious young Black women and men — we visible Black lesbians in the academy must not only survive, but thrive.

If we are not out there visibly as Black lesbians, our young Black college students will not be able to locate us. They need to be able to look us in the eye and have us honestly say who we are. People have all kinds of reasons for not being

---

* A different version of this article appears in Angela Bowen (1996).

able to do so, some valid ones, I'm sure. But I remember being at a university a couple of years ago co-facilitating a workshop about lesbian visibility within academe. There were about sixty women in the room, nearly all of them white, only a few of whom were out; and those few were generally teaching part-time or in community colleges. The reasons given for being closeted were those we are all familiar with: being out would retard careers; or make tenure difficult or impossible; or cause hostility; or keep the students from being able to relate to them. After about forty minutes of this, a woman named Vivien Ng spoke up. As I recall, she was the only woman of color in the room. She said that she went as an out lesbian to teach at the University of Oklahoma because the students were her priority, and she wanted to be visible as a lesbian for them. If she didn't rise in the academy, so what? She made enough to live on whether she ever got tenure or not, and that was the right decision for her regardless of the outcome. However, she had received tenure with no trouble and was very well liked and respected.

I read a similar story by Toni McNaron (1982) called "Out at the University: Myth and Reality". The myth was that if she came out "they" would attack her. The reality was that once she came out, she respected herself so much that she began liking herself and became freer, which made other people see and appreciate who she was. McNaron had received tenure at the University of Minnesota in record time, only three years, but stayed in the closet for nine more, suffering panic, overeating, being an alcholic, and suffering from a variety of other ills until she gained the courage to come out. After reaching bottom, she took a year's leave to decide whether she could ever work at a university as a lesbian, or even as a feminist, and was encouraged to stay by Florence Howe and by Adrienne Rich who, she says, gave her "an afternoon of her self and a small piece of raw amethyst (given Rich in turn by Audre Lorde), for clarity." She stayed, announced her identity to her chairman, and began doing the most powerful and creative work she'd ever done. Of course, McNaron didn't have the added oppression of being Black, or being Asian, as is Vivien Ng; nor do all stories of lesbian oppression end so happily — although mine does. Being out has been glorious for me.[1]

True, every Black lesbian cannot afford to come out within academia, for a variety of perfectly valid reasons. Still, closeted lesbians can help us to live visible lesbian lives by not fearing us, but nurturing us, not killing us with hostility, but encouraging us, not undercutting us, but helping to watch our backs by feeding us the information we need to avoid traps, enabling us to be as out as possible, for all of us. That sounds like a bargain to me. It's the kind of bargain that sociologist Aldon Morris refers to in *The Origins of the Civil Rights Movement* (1984), where he writes about the bus boycotts and lunch counter sit-ins in the south in the 50s. Black businessmen who had money and goods to offer but were vulnerable to white retaliation if they were open in their support, kept silent but contributed in the background, keeping the movement going while the churches served as movement

1. Thanks to Vivien Ng and Toni McNaron for permission to relate their stories.

centers. The ministers, who were not directly dependent on the white economy, could take the lead because they bore less risk. Is it too much for us to expect similar support from Black women in academe?

Building such networks of support would allow us to provide a visible presence to all our students, thus helping them understand that we are existing and flourishing everywhere, even on college campuses, as professors. Our visible, proud and matter of fact acceptance of ourselves would show them that all of our lives are valuable, precious and meaningful. Students would see that we command respect for who we are and what we know, just as all their professors do. This in turn would help foster respect in heterosexual students for their peers who are lesbian, gay or bisexual or may be struggling with sexual identity issues. And our visibility would allow them to carry positive images of Black lesbians into their lives beyond college. If we offered them this broader outlook, they, as well as we, would survive, thrive and contribute to the future of Africanas throughout the diaspora.

Nelson Mandela in a recent public statement embraced South African lesbians and gay men as part of the new South African liberation. By embracing them, Mandela honors their total humanity, for of course we are more than lesbians, just as we are more than Black, more than women, or mothers, or daughters, or teachers. The point is not that we want to make ourselves into one gigantic walking capital "L". No. We insist on claiming the lesbian identity because without it we are not whole; and without a sense of wholeness we lose our strength, our creativity, our sense of adventure, our vision.

If we accept W. E. B. Du Bois' concept of the "two-ness" of Black folks' vision, we must then accept that Black women bring a "three-ness" of vision to all societal relations. How, then, can Black women who accept this concept not acknowledge that Black lesbians carry a "four-ness" of vision that pushes scrutiny and clarification to yet another level? If we are truly seeking more analyses that will broaden our approaches to our feminist politics, scholarship, history, our very lives, then the vision of Black lesbian feminists is crucial.

Sometimes Black lesbians who are quite brave about being out in all other aspects of their lives are paralyzed with fear when it comes to being themselves within academia because the Black sisterhood makes it clear that it will not abide a lesbian who brings attention to her sexual identity on campus. It's alright to be one, just keep quiet about it. This silencing tactic is a reactionary holdover that refuses to recognize the radical oppositional stance of claiming lesbianism as a valid identity, not merely a "sexual preference", that old liberal canard which glosses over the political ramifications of choosing an out lesbian life. For some of us living as an open lesbian is not a choice but a necessity, although the difference between deciding and doing so are two vastly different realities. Still, as Audre Lorde said, difficult though it is to be out, living in the closet is even more difficult.

But should we Black lesbians expect support from Black women in the academy who are not out lesbians? I believe so. Because every Black woman in the academy, whether she is a heterosexual, a closeted lesbian, or somewhere on the continuum between (Rich: 1980), benefits from lesbian visibility. Our radical stance, the chances we take, the issues we choose to write and talk about, allow us to be seen as "bad girls", "fringe folks", the "nutcakes", if you will. As we keep pushing the envelope closer to the edge of the table, knowing that we must take the heat, can we expect support and succor, or condemnation and chastisement? Living as a lesbian is no game, says Adrienne Rich:

> For us, the process of naming and defining is not an intellectual game, but a grasping of our experience and a key to action. The word lesbian must be affirmed because to disregard it is to collaborate with silence and lying about our very existence; with the closet-game, the creation of the unspeakable (1979, p. 202).

Audre Lorde almost commands us to speak:

> What are the tyrannies you swallow day by day and attempt to make your own, until you will sicken and die of them, still in silence? Perhaps for some of you here today I am the face of one of your fears. Because I am woman, because I am black, because I am lesbian, because I am myself — a Black woman warrior poet doing my work — come to ask you, are you doing yours? (1984, pp. 41–2).

And Joy James and Ruth Farmer remind us of the compelling reasons that we Black women are in the academy:

> We have chosen academe because of our commitment to education, to serving ourselves and our communities. Yet often it appears that the only way to survive is through silence. Silence is the absence of our words and the presence of our complicity. If silent, we lose our ability to challenge (1993, p. 223).

Silences, gaps, erasures, lies. Who will rectify them if not out Black lesbians? Who has more of an investment in expunging the myths, distortions and stereotypes and exposing the reality of our lives than out Black lesbians? Who will fight harder against the exhortations which entice us to conform, to abandon our voices and our communities and stay within the walls, within the confines of language? Who has more need to resist the insidious pressures of cooptation, the rewards of security and comfort dangled before us, urging us not to say too much, do too much, identify with our communities too much?

Yet the Black lesbian's investment in withstanding the pressures, in struggling against cooptation, does not guarantee that we will be able to call up the strength to keep doing it over and over, coming out repeatedly, writing articles without knowing if they will be rejected — not because of the worth of the work, but because of their content. Having the investment and commitment does not mean you don't have to walk the line, knowing that your honesty and openness can lead people to attack you on every imaginable front because you insist on claiming all parts of yourself; that no matter how much you may talk or write about being a woman, being Black, a mother, a historian, a writer, or whatever else, as soon as you say you are a lesbian — and radical feminist — you are being "essentialist", "blatant", "political", "unprofessional", or in some other way unacceptable. Black women know the routine because we get the double dose of racism and sexism. Add homophobia to the mix (which, when it comes from Black women, raises the intensity exponentially) and you might just begin to fathom the level of pain.

The truth is that we're all in this together, and we need each other. So who among our Black heterosexual and hidden lesbian sisters will provide a safety zone when we stagger back from the front line of hostility, hatred, homophobia — the war zone? We need steady, unwavering support and encouragement. Our heterosexual sisters need the "fourth" dimension of our vision; and we all need each other's strength, courage and fortitude. Do we Black lesbians have allies? This is not an academic question, for we are all beneficiaries of our struggle and the war really is the same, said Sister Audre:

> We choose the earth
> and the edge of each others battles
> the war is the same
> if we lose
> someday women's blood will congeal
> upon a dead planet
> but if we win
> there's no telling
> we seek beyond history
> for a new and more possible meeting
> I look to meet you
> upon whatever barricade you erect or choose.
>
> (1984)

*Pat Mahony and Christine Zmroczek**

Working-Class Radical Feminism: Lives Beyond the Text

Radical feminism changed our lives! This is not a cliché, but a statement which captures our experiences and lived reality. Radical feminism provided us with understandings about our experiences of the ways patriarchy operates and, given that we have been involved in radical feminism for the last twenty years, we have also had the opportunity to contribute to those understandings. So far, radical feminism has been liberating, inspiring, exciting, thrilling and above all empowering, precisely because it tells us that every woman's experiences are to be taken seriously. This does not mean that what every woman says is a universal "truth", but nor is it "untrue". Radical feminism values women and women's experiences whilst recognising the partiality of each woman's experience and the specificities. It also allows for connections to be made between those experiences, so that we can see the systems and structures which operate in societies and cultures and so we can begin to decode and challenge them when they are harmful to women. In other words radical feminism gives us tools of analysis which enable us to begin from our own experiences and to go on to understand the social, cultural and political world beyond them.

Our account of radical feminism does not fit easily with the all too common criticisms of the Women's Movement as monolithic, middle class and heterosexual. Whilst we would agree that many of the agendas of radical feminism as with other feminisms, have been set by White middle-class women, working-class women have been involved. For example, we are just two of the working-class women who have been radical feminists for over twenty years.

We are both from working-class backgrounds and have benefited from a number of years in higher education. Between us we have several degrees and full time salaried positions in universities in London. We each have a car and a

---

* No order of seniority implied.

mortgage and many other of the accoutrements of a middle-class life style; so how can we say we are working class? It took us a number of years to find out.

We begin with a story of two conferences, where we each made a different choice about whether to attend a session "for working-class women". At an early Women's Studies conference, believing that by virtue of her education she no longer qualified, Chris stayed away but on hearing the report back later in the conference, she realised that the women who had taken part in the workshop had also been through higher education. She remained unsure about whether she could still call herself working class whilst also being very confused with any notion of herself as middle class. At another women's conference around the same time, Pat decided she would attend the session but once ensconced felt she had made a mistake. As one of the few women in the room who had gone on to higher education and with a relatively well paid job in a university she felt like an imposter and almost voyeuristic. The event evoked painful memories of the pride versus the treachery of passing the selection examination at eleven and going to the "snob" school and she concluded by the end of that conference that in class terms she did not belong anywhere. At that time neither of us thought to challenge the analyses of class which stratified us into invisibility. We did not then insist on our own definitions of class; that came some years later.

When hearing for at least the two hundredth time that radical feminism – in which by that time we had both been active for some fifteen years – "is middle class", we began to share our frustration and to ponder the effects of this criticism which in rendering us invisible, also stole our contributions. The more we talked, the more urgent it became to find out how to place ourselves as two White women distanced from our undoubtedly working-class backgrounds but certainly not always comfortable in and at times positively enraged by the oppressive behaviour of the largely middle-class world which we now inhabited. We knew two Black[1] women who were also concerned about these issues and the four of us formed a group. We intended to write a book which would contribute to challenging the expectations of, and attitudes and behaviour towards, working-class girls and women.

After two years of intense discussion the four of us had only just begun to scratch the surface of the ways in which the constant drip of negative and oppressive experience operates at a personal level to recreate gendered class and race divisions in England. We learned a great deal about our similarities and our differences, despite the very real differences for Black and White women living in a racist society. We were all excited by the unities which we as feminists found through sharing our experiences of class and what this enabled us to learn from each other. We shared our strategies for coping with and overcoming the obstacles which had faced us at school and in higher education, at home and in our workplaces. Another important theme of our meetings was the rediscovery and revaluing of

---

1. We use Black in this context as a shorthand for one woman of Scottish, African and Asian background and one of English Asian background.

some of the strengths which accrued to us by virtue of our working-class backgrounds and we will say more of this later. But we did not write the book before new jobs, moving house, increased pressure of work and various family crises fractured our meetings. There always seemed too much to talk to each other about to get down to writing.

Whilst meeting regularly the four of us came up with the formulation of a concept which although still partial spoke clearly to two of the aspects of ourselves which we were discussing. We decided that we would name ourselves "educated working-class women" thus refusing the stereotypes of working-class people as uneducated and "thick" – refusing the disqualification from our own class background and our new class positioning. We were delighted to find out much later that other working-class women were struggling with the same ideas and had also arrived at the very same concept or definition. Valerie Walkerdine's words sum up the feelings of our group well:

> I call myself an "educated working class woman" . . . it allows something to be spoken and some things to come together – educated, working class and woman – three terms which I thought were hopelessly fragmented. Terms which assert my education and my power with pride and claim back my education, not as alienation and a move to another class but as part of a narrative which allows me a place from which to struggle, a sense of belonging (1990, p. 158).

This is for us a strong confirmation of the radical feminist premise that whatever one woman is thinking, feeling or theorizing, there is almost certain to be others going through the same or similar struggle.

Four years have passed since the group stopped meeting, but the two of us, Pat and Chris, continued to discuss these issues with women friends, students, colleagues and each other. In addition to these conversations which are on-going, we have also organised conference workshops and discussion groups for working-class women in Women's Studies.

Before reporting on the content of some of these discussions, let us explore further what we mean by "educated working-class woman". We suggest that it means a woman from a working-class background who has taken part in higher education, or who is self educated, who is able (mostly) to live in several worlds and be more aware of the ignorant, romanticized and insulting nature of the attitudes towards working-class women. We are only just beginning to grasp those aspects of our experience, past and present, which shape how we negotiate life as educated working-class feminists, not only in the hostile world "outside" but also in the Women's Movement – the supposedly "inside" world of feminism where we have found that working-class women and some of the issues particularly relevant to us are also often excluded.

Some of the women with whom we have talked have reported that when they have tried to raise issues of social class in the classroom (including Women's

Studies) they have been rebuked for introducing "diversions". Radical feminism has always emphasised that women experience patriarchal oppression differently and that we are positioned differently in relation to a complex web of power relations. It has also emphasised that we share a world in which women and men, femininity and masculinity, are constructed in ways which privilege men at the expense of women. This does not mean that every man is more advantaged than any woman – that would clearly be absurd. Rather, radical feminism has argued that where women are awarded power, privilege or status, it is by virtue of some characteristic other than sex or gender (Mahony: 1992). For example, where a woman has privileged status in relation to a man, it will be because she is white and he Black, she is middle class, he working class, not because she is a woman. These beliefs would suggest that each woman can contribute but a partial perspective from her own position within the complicated network of power relations which at times render her disadvantaged and powerless and at others, relatively advantaged and powerful. We each need a voice to describe this complicated web of relations if we are to develop theories which enable us to understand the political significance of the particular and how to act upon it. In what sense then can working-class women's experience constitute a *diversion*, as reported above, within an arena which seeks to address *women?* It seems crucial to continue what other women have begun (Taking Liberties Collective: 1989; Steedman: 1986, 1984; Penelope: 1994; Tokarczyk and Fay: 1992) by documenting our experiences as working-class women.

It may of course come as a surprise that we claim that the literature on class is incomplete. There is after all a considerable body of work on the subject and there may be many, who feel that class has been "done" (to death). But while a great deal has been written about social class, particularly by Marxists, there is much less about women and social class and a significant lack of published material which actually deals with women's own experiences. Few feminist analyses of class have the power and resonance of feminist writings about the experiences of sexism. For example, the act of naming "the sexually appraising look" enabled us to move beyond our isolated feelings of discomfort and towards a political analysis. Having discussed this particular kind of sexually objectifying gaze and named it, we were able to identify when it happened again, to understand the way it operates to objectify us and how, in conjunction with many other mechanisms, it contributes to the positionings of women within society at large. There is little equivalent analysis of the ways in which working-class women experience the structuring of class relations. Perhaps there is an equivalent look – one which appraises the speaker with a working-class accent, as in some way a less valid speaker. When it is added to a sexually appraising look then a working-class woman attempting to speak out in the academy, for example, is in danger of being objectified – and ignored or belittled – twice over.

The absence, as yet, of thorough feminist analyses of class grounded in the experiences working-class women leaves us with a legacy which is unhelpful in our striving to become strong women in control of our own lives. To be precise, it leaves us in confusion and uncertainty about who we are and where we fit, if indeed we do fit at all. It leaves us with an inability to identify, name and locate the feelings of shame, humiliation, invisibility and under-confidence which are the felt effects of oppressive experiences described over and over again by women with whom we have spoken. While these experiences remain unnamed and unidentified, working-class women are powerless to challenge them in an articulate and effective way when they recur. It takes practice to recognise and to explain what is wrong and why. Finally our invisibility as working-class women in higher education leaves us dislocated from our pasts and makes it difficult to acknowledge the source of some of what we know, *precisely* because we are working class. It leaves us feeling bereft rather than enriched by knowing how to operate in the two different working-class and middle-class arenas. In our view, the advantages of this dual cultural knowledge are many and we will refer to them later. Predictably, however, our "difference" and "middle-class ways" are often highly visible within our working-class families, so that we often become "outsiders" here too.

How then shall we begin to explore the precise ways in which girls and women experience oppression through social class? In the following we discuss some of the themes and offer some examples of what we understood so far from our research with educated working-class women.

Material Resources

Poverty seems to be a common experience for many women we spoke with, at least in childhood. This is a significantly different experience from not having much money to spare. We have seen the struggles of our mothers to put food on the table let alone meet the demands of school:

> I was surprised the first time I went to a middle-class school friend's home for a meal to find that the food was in bowls on the table and you helped yourself. In our house the food was eked out and carefully arranged on each plate to make it seem as if there was enough to go round – there were no seconds, and it was no good asking for any. I think I helped myself to rather too much at that first meal at my friend's, I hadn't yet learned that there were rules to this game too.

Economic hardship often expressed itself in painful memories about clothes:

> I remember vividly the tears and worries about how to afford a school uniform for me when I passed the eleven plus exam, which completely overshadowed the congratulations. How could I be other than ambivalent about success now?

The lack of clothes also structured our social lives:

> It was often impossible to accept social invitations from school friends because I had nothing suitable to wear. In fact I had one set of clothes (which were hideous) other than my school uniform.

71

Others remember that lack of money for school equipment, sports gear, musical instruments and school trips led them to pretend not to be interested in school in an attempt to keep a sense of dignity. Our school reports portray us at times as "sullen", "diffident" and "unwilling to participate". Some of us took Saturday jobs which branded us as "not seriously academic" or to be more precise "common" – all the more so if these jobs were in Woolworths. All these experiences played a part in structuring our choice of jobs or career. Some of us left school as soon as we could either because we were so alienated by the whole experience, or because we knew it was not possible to stay on:

> I knew my parents couldn't afford another uniform for my sister who had just got a scholarship to the same school as me. So I left and got a job.

Others said that they chose to go to college near home so that they could avoid the financial pressures of a residential life as a student. All these experiences live on in the present. As one woman put it:

> My current economic privilege is as long or short as the job lasts. The terror of redundancy looms large when you've not been able to accumulate savings and material goods. I'm contributing to my parents' upkeep by paying their rent and unlike some of my friends I can't look forward to inheriting their property – its a council house.

The memory of the hardships experienced by our parents are hard to put aside. Several of us have confessed to each other that we find it difficult not to calculate the cost of a meal out with friends in terms of what our parents live on each week. It is true of course that not all working-class people are grindingly poor, some are quite comfortable, some are even quite rich. Lack of economic resources are not always or only what working-class women have to face.

Cultural Resources

The middle-class world is one with a particular culture and particular rules. Because it is taken for granted as the norm, the knowledge which is needed to negotiate it is rarely made explicit. Middle-class women usually do not realise what they know in this respect and because it is not explicit it is difficult for working-class women to learn (and learn it we must if we want to survive in middle-class occupations). We are not talking here about the useful connections which open doors to jobs and other opportunities, these have been documented within the literature on access to social institutions. What we are referring to is the "know how" which is needed to feel at home, to maximise opportunities for oneself and other women in higher education for example. The learning process for some of us has been perplexing.

When I first went to university I felt as though I was constantly trying to crack the codes. I used to watch to see how to eat things I'd never come across before. I remember being invited round to dinner and I turned up six hours early at one o'clock!

What to wear or dressing appropriately for the occasion has been a constant preoccupation and for some of us continues to be a source of disquiet, even when we have attained positions sufficiently high in the academic hierarchy to receive social invitations from the Vice Chancellor:

What do you wear to the Vice Chancellor's house when you've been invited to lunch and it's "Dress Informal"? Thank God I asked around and didn't wear my tracksuit!

Another woman remembers:

My painful memories of being laughed at and teased about what I was wearing as a child seem to have stuck with me so that I know that I'm overanxious about wearing the "right" things to the point where I'm practically obsessed with buying clothes in case I need them for any particular occasion.

In addition we know there is an enormous range of other "cultural" resources which have to be learned if working-class women are not to miss out. We are referring here to enjoyable experiences such as theatre, music, and art which have not necessarily been accessible through prior knowledge in our own homes. It also needs to be recognised that having high expectations – and knowing how to go about fulfilling them is another cultural resource from which working-class women often seem to be excluded. One woman described it as:

... like walking along a cliff path in a thick mist with no signposts. You are on your own, there is no one to ask directions from. You have only the vaguest idea of where you are going and you don't know how to get there and at any moment you might put a foot wrong and crash down the cliff face.

One of the intriguing things about having to learn another set of codes is that the workings of those codes are often clearer to an outsider. Almost as anthropologists, educated working-class women are in a position to accumulate knowledge about what goes on in middle-class cultures. This allows us to analyse what has previously been almost hidden from view – in the same ways as feminists have analyzed the previously invisible workings of patriarchy and male institutions in society.

An area in which radical feminist theories have been especially enlightening (Spender: 1980) and which has particular significance for educated working-class women is language.

Language

The issue of language figures largely in our experience as one of the major ways in which we were put down. Many middle-class people retain a hint of a regional accent and this can be quite acceptable and even fashionable in some circles. But the systematic attack on strong regional accents which instantly reveal a working-class background, left many of us unable or unwilling to speak in public. We were then caught in a vicious circle of lacking the confidence to explore our ideas and thus missing the opportunity to gain the practice we needed to become articulate. Women have their own particular versions of this all too familiar story:

> At my selective school not a year went by but my school report criticised me for not being able to express myself. No-one ever suggested how I might learn and it never occurred to me to challenge how this and the criticism that I was too talkative, could both be true.

Elocution lessons have particular painful memories for some of us:

> Double barrelled names, orfully nice accents and oodles of poise is what I remember of my first day of my Teacher Training course. I was glad I was a day student and could go home despite the long journey else I doubt I would have stayed. The staff too, were terribly jolly and I soon learned that I was at what had been, until my year, a fee paying college. There were about half a dozen of us who were very obviously not "of the class" and two of us whose accents placed us more with the kids we would teach than with our peers. We were sent to elocution lessons to learn not to flatten our vowels. While a Welsh or a Northern accent was tolerable, (though there weren't many of those either) a London accent was perceived as not speaking properly. And so we sat week after week with a tape recorder and mirror trying to change how we spoke. My aunt phoned one evening after one of these sessions. "Oh," she said. "Haven't we gone posh?" And I felt ashamed. The effect of all this trying to learn to "speak properly" was disastrous at college too. I became so self conscious that I was unable to speak at all in class and after a term the Principal told me I was an uncooperative student. It wasn't until years later that I learned that Received Pronunciation was invented by the boys' public schools to exclude "new money".

The seriousness of these accounts cannot be underestimated for we know that there is an intimate connection between language and thought, confidence and "ability". Learners simply do not flourish unless their ideas are treated seriously and we do not share our ideas or rehearse and practice them unless it is safe to do so. Written language has proved equally problematic for some women. The failure to distinguish between "proper" English and "Standard English" (which underpins many of the recent controversies in the school curriculum for England and Wales) caused many of us unnecessary difficulty. Not all of us were born into conditions where the evil of the split infinitive was at the forefront of our minds. We were not stupid in not knowing the rules of standard English and if it is important for us to learn the language of power (which we believe it is) then these rules need to be made explicit for what they are, that is, as part of what distinguishes the powerful from the powerless.

Many working-class women entering higher education will need continued support if they are to develop their writing skills in this language of power. The sensitivity with which this task is approached is crucial to their intellectual development.

As well as being a source of distress, a number of women have also cited higher education as the place where they finally learned how to learn.

> I never understood how the other girls knew what Shakespeare meant. How did they know who wrote this or that piece of music or where bits of the world were? We had no reference books at home and the idea of going to the library didn't occur to me. Anyway what would I have looked up? As far as I was concerned what you knew was what you'd learned in school and how anyone knew what we hadn't been taught could only be explained by invoking their cleverness. Not until I was twenty-three did anyone show me how to use a library and not until twenty years after that did I learn about Bourdieu's theory of 'cultural capital'.

Often one good teacher has transformed women's lives:

> Sometime during the first year we had a new lecturer. He had a reputation for being subversive. He encouraged the exploration of different accents and dialect forms and he validated them all. He railed against the use of unnecessarily mystifying language and debunked for us the myth that unintelligibility was a mark of a writer's brilliance. He taught me how to write essays using resources beyond my own head and lecture notes. It was breathtaking and I remember to this day what he said – "Do what everyone else does, including me. Go to the library, find a few books on the subject you're discussing, look up the index for the relevant bits, read those extracts and form your essay by discussing what you agree with and what not." It was a complete revelation. That five minutes transformed my life and I went on to get a 1st Class Honours Degree. More importantly I gained the confidence to be able to ask "What do you mean?" and "How do you do this?"

Other women have stories to tell about the confidence they gained from teachers who valued their potential and encouraged their self expression even if it was unorthodox:

> I will never forget the woman who taught my first ever feminist course. She gave me such a boost of confidence when she encouraged me to write a feminist analysis of menstruation, at that time a very under researched area. She actually thought

I could do it – I can still feel the thrill, the challenge and the power her confidence gave me. It has probably propelled me through the last twenty years of struggle as a working class radical feminist! I didn't realise that it was possible to write what I thought, that it was valid was a revelation, that it was necessary and part of the feminist struggle was a gift from my feminist tutor.

Confidence

The issue of confidence emerges consistently in what women have said. Many of the experiences outlined above have conspired to undermine us and have sometimes left us feeling stupid, socially inept and ignorant. It is also true that working-class women who have gone through higher education emerge if nothing else, more confident – perhaps also more angry. As we learned more about how to "play the game" we became more aware that there is a game being played: it is one of exclusion. However as we have already explained, educated working-class women inhabit a number of worlds and although this has its price, there are also tremendous advantages. We are familiar with the middle-class world from the perspective of the spectator as well as the participant. We suggest that this can enable us to not only identify but to expose what has hitherto been so intangible as to appear "natural". This is knowledge which can be developed in the same ways as feminists have developed understandings of the ways in which other forms of oppression operate; starting with our own experiences.

Future Directions

For the future we propose that working women and in particular working-class feminists within the academy insist upon developing our knowledge and making our contributions to the future of feminism; that we refuse to be silent, refuse to be invisible any longer. Our contributions to radical feminist thought, along with others, are essential.

In writing this piece our aim has been to begin a debate which our discussions with working-class women have led us to believe is important. In addition, the absence of analysis which we have identified in relation to working-class women, applies equally to middle- and upper-class women who also have inadequate knowledge about their collective experiences of social class. In good radical feminist tradition, we invite women of those classes to investigate the issues for themselves though we hope that our analyses and suggestions about the issues for working-class women will prove to be useful, enlightening, thought and theory provoking.

Robyn Rowland

Politics of Intimacy:
Heterosexuality, Love and Power

Perhaps the most powerful contribution lesbian radical feminist gave us during the 1970s and the 1980s has been the analysis of the institutions of motherhood and heterosexuality. These have been crucial to our understanding of the ways in which the power of men as a social group has been used to control women in both the public and private spheres. During this period, many feminists decided to remain child-free and/or to be lesbians. The socialisation into our feminist sub-culture encouraged it. These analyses were so powerful and so strong that some saw the entrapment of motherhood as irreversible; the heterosexual life as "colluding with the enemy" (see Rowland and Klein in this volume, pp. 9–36; Jackson: 1995; Thompson: 1993). Motherhood as an institution, was differentiated from motherhood as experience. Our analysis of heterosexuality likewise critiqued the institution and made visible the experience of heterosexuality in its most oppressive forms.

Institutionalised heterosexual violence against women operates across national boundaries on a global scale in the trafficking of women and the imposition of heterosexual prostitution and forced marriage. Genital mutilation, rape in war, sexual exploitation and prostitution, as well as the sex trade in women and girls, abuses women's human rights. Internationally, a woman's body forms a kind of currency in male-dominated societies. Kathleen Barry has shown in *Female Sexual Slavery* (1979) and in *The Prostitution of Sexuality* (1995), that the international traffic in women operates extensively to socially control women. The trafficking of women is particularly strong in the Asian region, fed by the sex industry that has been industrialised and incorporated into the economic infrastructure of many countries. Statistics in this area continue to horrify: Lawyers for Human Rights estimate that about 200,000 Bangladeshi are in slavery, bonded labour, marriage or prostitution in Pakistan. Around 200–400 young women and children are smuggled every month from Bangladesh to Pakistan and India. They are usually sold for US $1,000 to US $2,000 to brothels in Pakistan (Barry: 1995).

Human rights researchers working on the trafficking of Burmese women and girls into Thai brothels have reported anecdotes confirming the extent of sexual slavery:

> One young girl explained to us that she was told that as soon as she had served one thousand men she could go home. So she served one thousand men in three months. She was then told that she would have pay back for the clothing, food, medicine and anything else she had received in that time. When the brothel was raided two years later, she was still there.

Heterosexual violence is frequently used by states in controlling the population of women, particularly refugee women and girl children. A refugee woman fleeing Ethiopia describes her journey:

> We were four people: my two children, four and two years old, our guide and myself. I was five months pregnant. On our way we were stopped by two men who asked us where we were going. When we explained, one pulled me aside and said: "No safe passage before sex" . . . [He] forced me down, kicked me in the stomach and raped me in front of my children. He knew I was pregnant, but that made no difference to him (*Amnesty International:* 1995, p. 25).

To heterosexual feminists, the continuity of this horrific violence against women is particularly painful as it includes the weaponry of sex: men's bodies used as battering rams, men's hearts objectifying women, humiliating and violating women sexually.

Examples of rape and incest, of forced sex in marriage, serve to highlight the smudged line between normalcy and abuse, such that many theorists have argued that force is central to the definition of normal masculine sexuality. In Nicola Gavey's study (1993) women expressed their difficulty over defining coercive or unwanted sex *within* their close relationships. It would be a rare heterosexual woman who has not at some point experienced forced sex or sex engaged in to avoid coercion or out of politeness: what Gavey described as "for pragmatic reasons" (1993, p. 112).

Knowing all this, then, why do some feminists still decide to remain heterosexual. I say "decide" because I agree with Sheila Jeffreys that we can be wilful about our sexuality. I do not say we "choose" to be heterosexual, because I feel the concept of "choice" to be problematic within the context of patriarchal society (see Rowland: 1992/1993 and Raymond, this volume pp. 231–246). But women *do* exercise agency in general in constructing our lives, admittedly within many and varying constraints. Yet deciding on heterosexuality is seen by many lesbian feminists as merely falling in with the easy options; going with the flow. As Celia Kitzinger and Sue Wilkinson put it: "In sum, heterosexuality is not a *political* identity for heterosexual feminists in the way that lesbianism is a political identity for lesbian feminists. Several of the contributors [to this volume] recognised the apolitical nature of their heterosexualities" (their emphasis, 1993, p. 6). In patriarchal society, being lesbian entails definite risks (Rowland: 1990). Heterosexuality does not. But in the part of the Women's Movement that radical feminism occupies, being heterosexual definitely is not "going with the flow". It opens us to assumptions that we are in a "pre-lesbian" phase; it labels us as lacking the strength of our politics at a personal level and implies that at that personal level, no struggle or sites of contestation are part of our daily experience of intimacy.

It also encourages a binary view of sexuality. In the 70s, as feminists we really had to declare our sexual allegiances, and once declared we were expected to stick to those labels. Yet surely we can contest those labels without being apolitical or aligning ourselves with libertarians, just as we can contest that heterosexual experiences and relationships must always include intercourse. Shulamit Reinharz (1993) prefers a notion that we "move around, perhaps on a continuum, in different stages of our lives" and Mary Crawford points out that feminism has taught us "to question oppositional categories" and that the opposition of heterosexual and homosexual may obscure "the many dimensions along which an individual might choose to place herself as a sexual, sensual and social being" (1993, p. 43). Surely in a society centred on feminist values, breaking the categories of masculine male and feminine female would allow us to freely love the human qualities of a person we are attracted to, regardless of sex.

As Renate Klein and I point out in our chapter in this volume (pp. 9–36), the idea of a "lesbian continuum" was articulated by Adrienne Rich in her analysis of the institution of heterosexuality. Her analysis of sexuality as a continuum was extremely useful to many feminists when it was written, but it has since been criticised as letting heterosexual women off the hook. Janice Raymond's further exploration of hetero-reality, extended our understanding of the pervasive philosophy that women are "for men" which permeates all of our social relations. Again her work reinforced the concept of woman-loving and opened up a history of passionate friendships between women which were not necessarily genital or erotic. For many heterosexual feminists, Raymond's work reaffirmed the importance of women's friendships, the difference in these relationships from those between women and men, and the necessity of those relationships in our personal lives.

Because these analyses came from lesbian feminists, and because of the nature of their analysis, it is difficult even to think of feminist heterosexuality without comparing it to lesbian feminism. But lesbian feminism, once presented to us as the ideal of politically correct woman-loving, has itself changed since the 1970s. On the positive side, these changes have included the refinding of an entire culture of lesbian history which has reaffirmed lesbian identity. On the negative, there has evolved a conservative libertarianism (Raymond: 1989a) and indeed a mimicking of what Sheila Jeffreys calls sado-society (Jeffreys: 1993). As a heterosexual woman who survived domestic violence and rape within a "close and loving" relationship with a man, I have been appalled at the claims of normalcy for sadomasochism in lesbian sexuality by libertarians. Dominance and submission are conceptualisations which male-defined heterosexuality has deified. To replicate them within pur-portedly woman-loving relationships cannot hope to create a sexuality empowering women with dignity and autonomy.

Heterosexual feminists know well that sex as part of a relationship cannot be divorced from issues of domestic labour or economic power. The bedroom, the kitchen, the boardroom, the chambers of parliament – are spaces where power has traditionally been in the hands of men. But when feminist women fill these spaces, we hardly expect a replication of male oppression. The personal is still political and relationships based in hurt and/or pain cannot generate feminist visions of equality. Within them, a self has to be denied, submerged, lost. As Janice Raymond writes: "sex is a whole human life rooted in passion, in flesh. This whole human life is at stake always" (1989b, p. 156).

Kitzinger and Wilkinson (1993) claim that lesbian feminists have theorised lesbianism effectively and heterosexuals have failed to do the same with heterosexuality. Recently heterosexual feminists are tackling heterosexuality from within our own experience, theorising from the personal to the political *positively*. Collections by Wilkinson and Kitzinger (1993), and Maynard and Purvis (1995) explore these experiences. As Stevi Jackson has pointed out, this revolves around analysing our heterosexuality critically "without conflating heterosexuality as an institution with heterosexual practice, experience and identity" (1995, p. 11). Her analysis is based in materialist feminism as a form of radical feminism and draws particularly on the work of Christine Delphy. She argues that it is not the physical relating of male to female sexually which is problematic but "the social relations under which those bodies meet" (1995, p. 21). It is these social relationships which can be and are challenged. Questioning Jeffreys' (1990) argument that we need to "eroticize sameness and equality", Jackson questions whether sameness is *necessary* for equality. "From a materialist feminist perspective, it is not difference which produces hierarchy, but hierarchy which gives rise to socially significant differences" (p. 21). Reaffirming the idea that heterosexual feminists also struggle against male dominance in their lives, she explicates that struggle as one in which "we have asserted our right to define our own pleasure, questioned phallocentric models of sexuality, tried to deprioritise penetration or reconceptualise it in ways which did not position us as passive objects" (p. 21).

The collection by Wilkinson and Kitzinger (1993) which originally emerged from an issue of *Feminism and Psychology* is a unique and important contribution to discussions on heterosexuality in the 1990s. However, their intro-duction does a disservice to a considerable amount of work within the volume by heterosexual feminists. In the Introduction as lesbian feminists they find it an "irony that lesbians should be creating the space that heterosexual women have, apparently, been unable or unwilling to create for themselves" (1993, p. 3). They support Denise Thompson's argument that the lesbian/heterosexual split "is not so much a split between women of different sexual identities, but rather between those with differing political commitments" (1993, p. 11). They describe the material in the collection as "a long grey stream of heterosexual misery" which is, I think, a misrepresentation of the material in the volume. They are certainly content in their introduction to selectively use much of the negative or contradictory or difficult material on heterosexuality generously contributed by many of the authors as they struggle in public with the confusion and contradictions of feminist heterosexuality. The decision to be in heterosexual relationships is not acknowledged by the editors as forging any kind of challenge or resistance to male defined sexuality, but rather referred to as accepting the "eroticising of powerlessness" (1993, p. 17).

In contrast, the contributions cover a wide range of issues, including the conflicts and contradictions involved in living within heterosexuality and striving to redefine it within feminist politics. A number of women note the influence of having sons in bringing them face to face with the reality of the difficulties within patriarchal culture. These experiences are further reinforced by women writing about the specific challenges of a feminist mothering of sons in a special issue of *Feminism and Psychology* (Rowland and Thomas: 1996). Caroline Ramazanoglu points out that loving men brings masculinity up close; "close relations with men can bring home the damage that heterosexuality can do to males, and the many ways in which men can damage each other". Like relationships with sons, relationships with men mean that feminists cannot blame "men" for women's oppression without looking at the role of power and how it affects both men and women.

The pieces in the Kitzinger and Wilkinson collection stress the struggle that heterosexual feminists are involved in with respect to changing their own experiences of sexuality as well as focusing on the political impact of changing hetero-relations in general. In my piece in that collection, I wrote of both negative and positive experiences of heterosexuality. I want to try and expand that here to envision sites within heterosexuality where change is/might be occuring; where resistance to the old ways of being can and are happening; and to incorporate some strategies for living a radical feminist heterosexuality. Feminism is not just critique. We are also involved in "anticipatory vision" (Rowland: 1996); in constructing a new kind of society with feminist ethics and politics as its base. Part of that vision must include healthy loving relationships with men, or there is no point in being part of a social movement for change. Activism is about creating that change not just about understanding our current gender-relations.

Contextual reforms to what Janice Raymond called hetero-reality are crucial to any reconceptualisation of heterosexuality. Feminists working for social change also work for change at an individual level. Though patriarchal institutions and ideologies are implicit in our intimate relationships, at that level there is sometimes more room for negotiation. Sheila Jeffreys (1990), in her thorough dissection of male-defined heterosexual desire, has located it within marriage. But marriage too is changing. Just as feminist mothers are trying to redefine mothering sons, so women who are married are trying to redefine marriage. In her study of *Heterosexual Women Changing the Family: Refusing to be a "Wife"*, Jo VanEvery considered the ways in which women resist the traditional definitions of marriage and wife. She drew up some possible directions for a feminist politics in this area. Apart from changes in domestic and non-domestic work, and in the definitions of "husband" and "wife", she discusses what I think is a very important concept. Reinvigorating Marilyn Frye's delineation of "feminist separation" and reminding us of the differentiation Frye makes between separation and separatism, she names this as a crucial part of the rejection of the role/identity of "wife". Various kinds of separation are discussed but the important issue is the struggle to keep identity and life roles separate within heterosexual relationships. This role of separateness is echoed by writers in the Wilkinson and Kitzinger volume who maintain their separateness in terms of their identity in a variety of ways, including separate domestic arrangements. Conceptualising the self as single, but in partnership is one way of doing this.

A feminist heterosexual relationship would include an equitable power distribution in terms of economic independence, where the woman does not engage in domestic, sexual and emotional servicing; a relationship in which sex or intercourse is not the primary way of relating, but merely part of the relationship alongside other important dimensions, such as friendship and companionship. It would include a respect for the independence of the working lives of each partner; and it would include a recognition and respect for other networks of intimacy and closeness, particularly woman to woman relationships, which enable the woman to retain a sense of separateness, an intimacy companionably outside the heterosexual partnership. With these kinds of changes, there is more possibility of "eroticizing equality" (Jeffreys: 1990).

Love and sexuality are at the core of intimate relationships. Yet love has understandably been given a bad press by feminists (Carol Anne Douglas: 1990). Shulamith Firestone (1972) severely criticized love as being "the pivot of women's oppression today". She did not mean the open exchange of caring which love can be, but the patriarchal definition: a total of submerging and submission of a woman's self to the physical and emotional service of man. In love, women are expected to self-destruct or to de-self (Rowland: 1988). Love is supposed to be a merging, a loss of separateness, a giving up of individuality, instead of a strengthening of it. Our critiques of love are understandable when love has always been defined for women as this self-abnegation, self sacrificing or self disappearing act. "Romantic" love was used to convince women of the economic bargain of marriage. But these misuses do not mean that love cannot be created which involves equity, trust, reciprocity, knowing another and being known, a sustenance and vulnerability, a wisdom and friendship.

Within a close intimacy, there is also a need for separateness; a retaining of emotional space that allows for growth outside that particular relationship. Perhaps in some ways that space is more easily found within heterosexual relationships than within lesbian relationships. There, dissimilarity makes the way into separateness more open and available. Writing of intimacy and relationship,

Anne Morrow Lindbergh quoted the poet Rilke describing a "love that consists in this, that two solitudes protect and touch and greet each other" (1955/1992, p. 90). She advocates a self-sufficiency in both men and women; a greater wholeness, a greater separation. Again quoting Rilke (1955/1992, p. 94):

> ... once the realisation is accepted that, even between the closest human beings, infinite distances continue to exist, a wonderful living side by side can grow up, if they succeed in loving the distance between them which makes it possible for each to see the other whole and against a wide sky!

Morrow Lindbergh critiques the acceptance of the definitions of love which feed us a vision of relationship in which we are loved wholly and all the time from moment to moment. She writes:

> We have so little faith in the ebb and flow of life, of love, of relationships. We leap at the flow of the tide and resist in terror its ebb. We are afraid it will never return. We insist on permanency, on duration, on continuity; when the only continuity possible, in life as in love, is in growth, in fluidity – in freedom, in the sense that the dancers are free, barely touching as they pass, but partners in the same pattern. (pp. 105–106)

Intimacy is not often discussed by feminists; nor need; nor loneliness; nor sexual longing. The hard day-to-day issues of the woman alone – single or single mother – by choice or chance – are rarely open to the light. Discussions of recreational sex, intimacy without relationship, are not part of our theory while it revolves around assumptions of long term partnerships. So too the issue of monogamy is neglected – its positive aspects of commitment and security, its negative aspects of possessiveness and jealousy. And we have neglected to look at other variations on living heterosexually: the possibility of commitments to more than one intimate relationship concurrently – a kind of poly-fidelity.

And what about sexuality itself? One of the reasons heterosexual feminists have continuing relationships with men is that we like sex with a man. Heterosexual sexuality is not always intercourse. And intercourse does take place which is not degrading. Penetration is not always rape. Having experienced penetration which was, I know the enormous difference between the feeling of fear, anxiety and disembodiment which comes with forced sex, and the feeling of intimacy, oneness and sensuality which comes with intercourse which is not. With regard always to the meanings of words, I note with interest the varied meanings of "to penetrate" in my grandfather's old Webster dictionary which reflect in a way the range of experiences of heterosexuality feminists have delineated: to pierce, to enter into, to diffuse itself through, to affect profoundly, to move deeply, to understand.

Robyn Rowland

We should also be careful that in our own analysis of heterosexuality, we do not fixate sexuality on intercourse. Discussing new ways of being male, Allan Hunter points out that it should not be in mind as the "goal of erotic expression – or for that matter any goal other than intimacy and sharing and pleasure" (1993, p. 167). He reminds us that sex itself cannot be disconnected from the emotions: "sexual sensations have emotional content in and of themselves, and have a tendency to create or strengthen empathic connections and shared identity" (p. 161). In a new sequence of poems, I have tried to capture that fluidity:

Connection

Your kisses barely touch my flesh,
the long golden storm of your hair
thrown forward whispering
along the curve of my back.
You make love as a man should
opening, giving,
not vehement for closure.
Sex is not binding us
but the naked tenderness of holding.

No kiss is unsoft
lips honeyed from our exchange of secrets.
Your blue eyes are open as the summer sky
still shimmering with the quiet shock
of flourishing closeness.
the planes of your face change constantly
as the script of your thoughts range
intense to laughter.
You are lovely in every sense.

The seduction of talk has brought us here,
every coincidence propitious to intimacy,
the saffron swirl of our conversation
winding chrysalis-like about us,
through us, within.
Silk-skinned you glow sensuous amber
in the lamp light.
Touch is everywhere –
on the skin
in the mind
through the soul.
Not yet love,
this is a beginning.
The tawny fluid maleness of you
floods me still.

It is important in a sexual relationship that each partner feels integrity, self-respect and self-empowerment, and not at the cost of another. Perhaps the greatest test for a woman within a heterosexual relationship is her ability to say no and to have that respected particularly within an existing partnership. Issues of celibacy both within and outside relationships again are rarely canvassed in our discussions of sexuality. Yet celibacy can mark the centring of sexuality in a new and deep way. Within celibacy, sensuality is more heightened and identity more focused on the self and on relationships outside of the sexual.

The heterosexual relationship for a feminist can be a site of struggle and resistance. Andrea Dworkin encapsulates this struggling resistance well in her book on intercourse when she writes:

> Women have also wanted intercourse to work in this sense: women have wanted intercourse to be, for women, an experience of equality and passion, sensuality and intimacy. Women have a vision of love that includes men as human too: and women want the human in men including in the act of intercourse . . . these visions of a humane sensuality based in equality are in the aspirations of women . . . they are deep humane dreams that repudiate the rapist as the final arbiter of reality. They are an underground resistance to both inferiority and brutality, visions that sustain life and further endurance (1987, pp. 128–9).

But finally, no possibility of change can occur without men changing. And here I mean not just men as a social group – powerful and controlling (the institution of masculinity, if you like), but as individuals we know – flawed, difficult, but struggling to find a way of being male that has integrity within our feminist-influenced western society. And it is true: our politics have been working. Men do, and are, and have been changing. Some men. The heterosexuality expressed by many men now has changed considerably under the pressure of women's new sexual self-assertion and self-confidence; the understandings of feminism and its political theory; or even the understanding that men's own pleasure can be enhanced by mutually exploring with women new definitions of men and women's sexuality. But there are dangers here too: men can change their relationship to women's sexuality without a concurrent political commitment to equality with women in other spheres, without an acceptance of a changed politics and daily practice.

Under the influence of feminism and ignited by some of the men's movement literature, men are undergoing difficult changes. The nature of the men's movement itself is problematic, promising on the one hand a liberation of men in partnership with women with all the hope of understanding and growth, and on the other, a resurgence of androcentric justification for male separation and dominance. James McBride (1995) warns against a men's movement that reinvents the fear of the woman/mother, and he challenges the courage of men to seek liberated partnerships with women rather than a new version of phallocentric culture. Finding new definitions of being male within patriarchy without losing their passion, wildness and uniqueness is quite a challenge for men. Allan Hunter discusses the fear of "risking love with another free person"; the fear of vulnerability for men. The vulnerability and trust required on the part of men in heterosexual relationships with feminists is only now being tackled by men themselves.

Some of these issues are leading to new definitions of heterosexuality for women and for men. Heterosexual feminists are as committed to political change in our society as are lesbian feminists. Learning from the analysis of heterosexuality within feminism, heterosexual feminists are striving to develop a politics of intimacy that is self-respecting, self-enhancing and generates social change. The politics of intimacy for heterosexual radical feminists continues to be a site of resistance and change, enriching our understanding of the personal as political.

Louise Armstrong

The Great Incest Hijack

We have heard a lot, in recent years, about what incest causes (disorders like depression, drug-addiction, dissociation). I suppose you could say that, in me, it caused feminism.

That may be a shade facile, but still – you could not have found an *unlikelier* candidate to pin *radical feminist politico* on in all of early 1970s New York City. An advertising copywriter, no less, and *married,* and with twin sons. Sure, I was also publishing books, but they were humorous little things that explained a few puzzling phenomena – like Freud (Armstrong: 1963), economics, micro and macro (Armstrong: 1975 and 1978a), and international relations (Armstrong: 1979a).

Surely there was nothing *feminist* in trying to follow and explain the logic of common belief systems. Or was there?

Perhaps once you make the discovery of the power of junk system-language to construct a reality everybody *believes,* once you intuit that power systems run on group faith in them – you've taken a step toward intuiting the power of *naming.* And perhaps once you've begun to question thought systems that are taken for givens, once you've begun to analyze their relationship to your experience of reality – you can no longer draw the intellectual capital you need in the currency available at the Automated Belief Machines.

But if, in me, incest caused feminism, it did not do so in a vacuum.

In the 1970s, feminist literature boldly addressed the need for social change – as distinct from later emphasis on social and economic access. It was a vibrant force, both in the market and in the marketplace of ideas. Women were speaking out forcefully on rape as a male crime of violence against women. Wife-battering, too – now widely referred to as "spousal assault" – was analyzed as an issue of male prerogative, male right.

It was in this climate that I began thinking about what had happened to me – and wondering why no one was talking about that. (I did not know, then, that a few radical feminists like Florence Rush already had.) It was in this climate that

I absorbed the concept: the personal is political. The idea formed to offer a forum within which women would explore our common experience, and see what we could identify as the commonalities of our experience – that would help us identify what it was that had happened to us that had meaning beyond the individual.

I was certain there *were* other women out there. The publishers were less so. ("Incest is certainly a sensational subject, but since it's so rare, who would the readers be?") But I did get a book contract (Armstrong: 1978b). I advertised, mainly in the then-abundant feminist press. And letters poured in from women, and they phoned, and we met, and we talked, and we corresponded.

And what emerged was a sharing that was truly elegant: a collective journey of discovery.

And what we discovered was brilliantly simple, and utterly inescapable: different though our individual stories may have been, our fathers had all done this to us, not in spite of the fact that they knew it was wrong, but because they believed it was *their right*, or at least justifiable. What we discovered was that incest was among the forms of male violence against women and children long-permitted through history – sometimes tacitly, sometimes explicitly. And that abuse of the child was often intended as violence against the wife (our mothers) – that, in a crazy way, we'd been caught in the cradle of sexual politics.

To know this was to know that children's issues were inextricably linked to women's issues – that both belonged under the umbrella of feminism.

This was epiphany. This was the "click".

One thing more I learned: that because I was calling for social change, for social censure of male behaviours that had historically been routine and uncensored – I was not only a feminist. I was a radical feminist.

And what *was* the mainstream view of the widespread paternal rape of children (which it had taken feminists to expose)? It was perceived as a mental health problem. Virtually from the moment we spoke out, mental health professionals became society's appointed social sanitation engineers. It was to new-found "experts" among their ranks that the powers-that-be turned to defuse the "discovery" of the rampant patriarchal tyranny, the sexual slavery, that is incest.

They said it should be "de-criminalized." They said it was no more than a "symptom of family dysfunction". "Family dysfunction", it quickly turned out, was code. Code for: *She* made me do it, my wife. (This was change of a kind: it *had* been, *She* made me do it, my daughter.) And so they unveiled, for our oohing and ahing – the real culprit, the "incest *mother*". And I began speaking and writing about this turn of events, the medicalization of child-rape and of all crimes in the home.

And even as I wrote, paternal child rape was being tied into a noose with which to hang those the new experts identified as the real culprits: the mothers who "failed to protect". Those who "knew or *should have known*". And I watched as mental health ideology, mental health language coalesced into a great shield covering the entire issue, impermeable by reality. I watched as, in 1984, social work sentimentality promised salvation for Amelia in the ABC made-for-TV movie, "Something About Amelia" – and the actor-daddy said he was ashamed of himself, and the actress-mother looked as though, after a suitable period of *family* "treatment" (during which she acknowledged she had made him do it), she might welcome poor-ashamed-of-himself daddy back into the marital bed.

This occured even while (as I watched) more and more kids in real life were being yanked from mothers who not only did not know she'd made him do it, but didn't even know until just this minute he *was* doing it. Even while more and more mothers were being charged with "failure to protect".

Hot damn, I said then, What next? They'll arrest the women? Sure enough, next thing – they were arresting the mothers who, the minute they did find out, rose up and acted to protect the children; mothers who were having none of this "family treatment" – mothers who then, alas, discovered they were not now co-operating, not now fulfilling their role of "incest mother" as recently scripted. And so now – with psychiatrists and psychologists eager to certify these mothers as vindictive – the women were now "diagnosed" as hysterical, they were found to be *in contempt* for refusing to turn their child over to a rapist. And so I included this new assault by mental health medical personnel in what I wrote. (Armstrong: 1983).

Was I contributing to feminist mental health with this assault on the mental health scions? I thought so. (I think so still.) Because by now it was clear to me that what they sought was dominion over this now visibly sizeable and potentially profitable issue. And it seemed clear to those scions (as it was to me) that for mental health ideology to win, feminist analysis had to lose.

And so I spoke about this, wrote about this. And what is funny is – I still thought we could win. Even as I watched, the celebration of treatment was joined by the celebration of "prevention", and more experts arose selling programs to teach children about the sanctity of their "bathing-suit area" (as though little kids, thus armed, could stop daddies). Even then, I still thought we could make ourselves heard.

And even as I thought that, things got worse. Under glossy theories about children's "best interests" (being the right to a loving father), more and more kids were court-ordered to live with their rapists – removed from the mother who attempted rescue, though in the eyes of the experts she was attempting to impede the child's best interests.

More and more kids were, alternatively, subjected to "social rescue" – the opportunity to experience foster care. And here, too, the mental health professionals were busy. Their dire warnings about what incest *caused* placed more and more kids who spoke up under mental health surveillance, at risk of psychiatric institutionalization. And so I (what else?) spoke and wrote about this (Armstrong: 1979b and 1993).

But mental health ideology had already triumphed. And one sign of that triumph was that these issues – of what happened to child-victims of incest in this brave new world following feminists' breaking the silence – were not perceived as

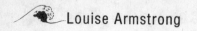

being feminist. By now the issue of "children-now" had been segregated from the issue of adult survivors, swallowed by child welfare experts, dominated by that set of mental health professionals specializing in "incested" children.

Because by now (I am speaking of the late 1980s, early 1990s here) all that was recognizably feminist had been obliterated from the entire issue of incest, as more and more adult survivors were swallowed into the great Recovery Movement Maw; as we were inundated with evangelical calls to Healing; as women were everywhere importuned to Gain Empowerment – by turning their power over to psychological experts. Instead of – as we had hoped – feminist analysis prevailing on the issue of incest, the recovery movement had hijacked the issue and silenced feminist analysis.

By now, incest had long since been declared "gender neutral". Victims were genderless; offenders were genderless. Indeed, they were almost spectral. Those few who were spotlighted had long since learned to recite the exculpatory mantra: not only had their wives made them do it, but their mothers had made them rapists by letting their fathers "do it" to them when they were children.

The entire focus was on what incest *caused* – all those disorders, all those diseases. No one, any longer, spoke of the societally, the historically, sanctioned right of males to sexually violate their children. No one spoke of the grotesque abuse of power, of the sense of male entitlement, that caused incest.

It is common, now, to speak of the *backlash* on the issue of incest. It is most often referred to in connection with the newest manufactured "syndrome", False Memory Syndrome. (The one that followed False Accusation Syndrome, and Parental Alienation Syndrome.) No one points out that the rise of the mental health ideology – beginning at the very moment when we first spoke out – was itself backlash.

"De-criminalization" was backlash. "Family dysfunction" was backlash. The "cycle of violence" is backlash: it feeds the idea that incest is a public health problem, not a problem of male predation. (Worse, it acts as a prediction of doom, telling "children-now" that it is their destiny to become that which they so fiercely hate in the now – molesters.) The recovery movement with its primary focus on incest as the victim's pathology is backlash: it individualizes – makes the problem medical; it infantilizes women, and makes of their suffering a medical curiosity. It sells community in frailty, not in feminism. The sequestering of the "children-now" issue, the issue of protective mothers, from the adult survivor issue is backlash: it fractures the picture, it is divisive. It leads to status quo, not social change.

And it is all cozily capitalism-compatible.

What is my major contribution to the field of feminist mental health? (Smile.) Simply to, one way and another, keep trying to remind women that the therapeutic *ideology* – which turns women into patients and inmates – has always been antithetical to feminism: that when this ideology wins, feminism loses. All of which I now, again, say.

The 1 September 1994 *Kirkus Review* says of my recent informal history of the issue of incest (Armstrong: 1994): "An important, incendiary, unapologetic history written in hopes of rekindling the possibility of radical change – nothing less than a redistribution of gender power".

Such language.

And in 1994, no less.

Shocking.

As for me. How did my life change personally? (Older and wiser, girls; older and wiser.) I've come a ways, certainly – from product campaigns to social change campaigns. (I'd certainly have made more money the old way.) On a more serious plane, the personal remains, for me, profoundly tied to the political.

Optimism is a struggle (far more than it once was). Pessimism is unbearable. To stand on neither side of an ever-tensing polarity is to feel excluded, to feel – well, yes: alone. The energy and passion that informed our early protests are now dismissed as unstylish. The clarity, the naming, is labeled simplistic. The humor that leavened the early stages of the journey is now taken for sacrilege.

Do I believe there will come a time soon when women will, on this issue, once again listen to their own voices, follow their own moral compass toward their own defined goals – independent of "experts"? I need to believe that if I continue to hope for change.

For all the talk of *listening to the children*, in a very important sense the children continue unheard. Their voices come to us through interpreters. Do I believe we will ever start really listening to the kids themselves? Again, I need to believe that if I continue to hope for change.

And of course I *do*, quite profoundly, hope for change.

I've been down all the fascinating highways and byways that radiate out from this issue so far.

It's been one hell of a trip.

For all the curlicues, filigree, and baroquery, however – and for all the syndromes, disorders, and experts – I remain as convinced as ever that we were not incorrect the first time out in identifying incest as the cradle of sexual politics.

We gave it a push.

The bough is still holding.

The cradle's still rocking.

And I'll be watching (and most likely writing and speaking about) whatever it is that happens next.

Celia Kitzinger

Therapy and How it Undermines the Practice of Radical Feminism*

One of the great insights of second wave feminisms was the recognition that "the personal is political" – a phrase first coined by Carol Hanisch in 1971. We meant by this that all our small, personal, day-to-day activities had political meaning, whether intended or not. Aspects of our lives that had previously been seen as purely "personal" – housework, sex, relationships with sons and fathers, mothers, sisters and lovers – were shaped by, and influential upon, their broader social context. "The slogan . . . meant, for example, that when a woman is forced to have sex with her husband it is a political act because it reflects the power dynamics in the relationship: wives are property to which husbands have full access" (Rowland: 1984, p. 5). A feminist understanding of "politics" meant challenging the male definition of the political as something external (to do with governments, laws, banner-waving, and protest marches) towards an understanding of politics as central to our very beings, affecting our thoughts, emotions, and the apparently trivial everyday choices we make about how we live. Feminism meant treating what had been perceived as merely "personal" issues as political concerns.

This article explores the way in which the slogan, "the personal is political", is used within feminist psychological writing, with particular reference to therapy. The growth in feminist therapies (including self-help books, co-counselling, twelve-step groups, and so on, as well as one-to-one therapy) has been rapid, and has attracted criticism from many feminists concerned about their political implications (Cardea: 1985; Hoagland: 1988; Tallen: 1990a and b; Perkins: 1991). However, many feminist psychologists (both researchers and practitioners) state explicitly their belief that "the personal is political".

According to some, this principle has "prevailed as a cornerstone of feminist therapy" (Gilbert: 1980), and qualitative methodologies have often been adopted by feminists precisely because they permit access to "personal" experience,

---

* Excerpt from Celia Kitzinger (1993). Depoliticising the Personal: A Feminist Slogan in Feminist Therapy.

the "political" implications of which can be drawn out through the research. It would be unusual to find a feminist psychologist who denied believing that "the personal is political," despite the existence of feminist critiques of some of its implications (its false universalising of women's experience, for example, see hooks: 1984, and the – ironic – tendency of some women to perceive the slogan's categories of "personal" and "political" as polarised and in competition, see David: 1992). However, widespread concurrence with this slogan amongst feminist psychologists conceals a variety of interpretations. This article illustrates four of those differing psychological interpretations of "the personal is political," and argues that far from politicising the personal, psychology personalises the political, focuses attention on "the revolution within," concentrates on "validating women's experience" at the expense of political analysis of that experience, and seeks to "empower" women, rather that accord real political power.

Two caveats before launching into my main argument.

First, this article does not claim to present a thorough overview of the whole of feminist psychology – a huge and growing area. Moreover, unlike other critiques (e.g. Jackson: 1983; Sternhall: 1992; Tallen: 1990a and b), this article is not an attack on any one particular brand of psychology, or a discussion from within the discipline (e.g. Burack: 1992). Rather, its aim is to stand outside the disciplinary framework of psychology and to draw attention to the political problems inherent in the very concept of "feminist psychology" *per se.*

Second "it doesn't seem fair", said one referee, "to scoff at institutions that help women live their lives in less pain." Many women have been helped by therapy. I have heard enough women say "it saved my life" to feel almost guilty about challenging psychology. Many women say that it was only with the help of therapy that they became able to leave an abusive relationship, to rid themselves of incapacitating fears and anxieties, or to stop drug abuse. Anything that saves women's lives, anything that makes women happier, must be feminist – mustn't it? Well, no. It's possible to patch women up and enable them to make changes in their lives without ever addressing the underlying political issues that cause these personal problems in the first place. "I used to bitch at my husband to do house-work and nothing happened", a women from Minnesota told Harrit Lerner (1990, p. 15); "now I'm in an intensive treatment program for codependency and I'm asserting myself very strongly. My husband is more helpful because he knows I'm co-dependant and he supports my recovery". For this woman, the psychological explanation ("I'm codependant and need to recover") was *more successful* than the feminist explanation (women's work as unpaid domestic labour for men, Mainardi: 1970) in creating change. With the idea of herself as sick, she was able to make him do housework. As Carol Tavris (1992) says, "women get much more sympathy and support when they define their problems in medical or psychological than in political terms." The codependency explanation masks what feminists see as the real cause of our problems – male supremacy. Instead we are told that the cause lies in our own "codependency". This is not feminism. Although it's clear that "many women have been helped by therapy", it is equally clear that many women have been helped, and feel better about themselves, as a result of (for example) dieting, buying new clothes, or joining a religious cult. Historically, as Bette Tallen (1990a, p. 390) points out, women have "sought refuge in such institutions as the Catholic church or the military. But does this mean that these are institutions that should be fully embraced by feminist?" The reasons behind the rush into psychology, and the benefits it offers (as well as the price it exacts) are discussed in more detail elsewhere (Kitzinger and Perkins: 1993). In this article, I focus more narrowly on psychological interpretations of "the personal is political", and the implications of these for feminism.

Personalising the Political

In this interpretation of "the personal is political", instead of politicising the "personal", the "political" is personalised. Political concerns, national and international politics, and major social, economic, and ecological disasters are reduced to personal, individual psychological matters.

This wholesale translation of the political into the personal is characteristic, not just of feminist psychology, but of psychology generally. In the USA a group of twenty-two professionals spent three years and $73,500 (£448,000) in coming to the conclusion that lack of self-esteem is the root cause of "many of the major social ills that plague us today" (The *Guardian*: April 13, 1990). Sexual violence against women is addressed by setting up social skills training and anger management sessions for rapists (now available in sixty jails in England and Wales, The *Guardian*: May 21, 1991), and racism becomes something to get off your chest in a counselling workshop (Green: 1987). Many people now think of major social and political issues in psychological terms.

In fact, the whole of life can be seen as one great psychological exercise. Back in 1977, Judi Chamberlin pointed out that mental hospitals tend to use the term "therapy" to describe absolutely everything that goes on inside them:

> ... making the beds and sweeping the floor can be called "industrial therapy", going to a dance or movie "recreational therapy", stupefying patients with drugs "chemotherapy", and so forth. Custodial mental hospitals, which offer very little treatment, frequently make reference to "milieu therapy", as if the very hospital air were somehow curative (1977, p. 131).

A decade or so later, with psychology's major clientele not in mental hospitals but in the community, everything in our lives is translated into "therapy". Reading books becomes "bibliotherapy"; writing (Wenz: 1988), journal keeping (Hagan: 1988), and art are all ascribed therapeutic functions. Even taking photographs is now a psychological technique: Feminist "phototherapist" Jo Spence drew on the psychoanalytic theories of Alice Miller (1987) and advocates healing (among other "wounds"), "the wound of class shame" through photography. And although reading, writing, and taking photographs are ordinary activities, in their therapeutic manifestation they require expert guidance: "I don't think people can do this with friends or by themselves . . . they'll never have the safety working alone that they'll get working with a therapist because they will encounter their own blockages and be unable to get past them" (Spence: 1990, p. 39). While not wishing to deny that reading, writing, art, photography, and so on might make some people feel better about themselves, it is disturbing to find such activities assessed in purely psychological terms. As feminists, we used to read in order to learn more about feminist history and culture; write and paint to communicate with others. These were *social* activities directed outwards; now they are treated as explorations of the self. The success of what we do is evaluated in terms of how it makes us feel. Social conditions are assessed in terms of how the inner life of individuals responds to them. Political and ethical commitments are judged by the degree to which they enhance or detract from our individual sense of well being.

Feminist therapists now "prescribe" political activities for their clients – not for their inherent political value, but as cure-alls. The "Guidelines for Feminist Therapy" offered by therapist Marylou Butler in the *Handbook of Feminist Therapy* (1985) includes the suggestion that feminist therapists should "make referrals to women's centres, CR groups, and feminist organisations, when that would be therapeutic for clients" (p. 37). Consciousness Raising – the practice of making the personal political – was never intended to be "therapy" (Sarachild: 1978). Women who participate in feminist activism with the goal of feeling better about themselves are likely to be disappointed. In sending women to feminist groups, the primary aims of which are activist rather than therapeutic, therapists are doing a disservice to both their clients and to feminism.

Our relationships, too, are considered not in terms of their political implications, but rather, in terms of their therapeutic functions. Therapy used to name what happened between a therapist and a client. Now, as Bonnie Mann points out, it accurately describes what happens between many women in daily interactions: "any activity organised by women is boxed into a therapeutic framework. Its value is determined on the basis of whether or not it is 'healing'":

> I have often seen an honest conversation turn into a therapeutic interaction before my eyes. For instance: I mention something that has bothered, hurt, or been difficult for me in some way. Something shifts. I see the woman I am with take on The Role of the Supportive Friend. It is as if a tape clicks into her brain, her voice changes, I can see her begin to see me differently, as a victim. She begins to recite the lines, "That must have been very difficult for you," or "That must have felt so invalidating" or "What do you think you need to feel better about that?" I know very well the corresponding tape that is supposed to click into my own brain: "I think I just needed to let you know what was going on for me," or "It helps to hear you say that, it feels very validating," or "I guess I just need to go off alone and nurture myself a little" (1987, p. 47).

Psychological ways of thinking have spilled out of the therapist's office, the AA groups, and self-help books, the experiential workshops and rebirthing sessions to invade all aspects of our lives. The political has been thoroughly personalised.

Revolution from Within

Another common feminist psychologising of "the personal is political" goes something like this:

> The supposedly "personal" activity of therapy is deeply political because learning to feel better about ourselves, raising our self-esteem, accepting our sexualities and coming to terms with who we really are – all these are political acts in a heteropatriarchal world. With woman-hating all around us, it is revolutionary to love ourselves, to heal the wounds of patriarchy, and to overcome self-oppression. If everyone loved and accepted themselves, so that women (and men) no longer projected on to each other their own repressed self-hatreds, we would have real social change.

This is a very common argument, most recently rehearsed in Gloria Steinem's *Revolution from Within*. As Carol Sternhall points out in a critical review, "The point of all this trendy, tied-dyed shrinkery isn't simply feeling better about yourself – or rather, it is, because feeling better about all our selves is now the key to worldwide revolution" (1992, p. 5).

In this model, the "self" is naturally good, but has to be uncovered from beneath the layers of internalised oppression and healed from the wounds inflicted on it by a heteropatriarchal society. Despite her manifest differences from Gloria Steinem in other areas, lesbian feminist therapist Laura Brown (1992) shares Steinem's notion of the "true self". She writes, for example, of a client's "struggle to recover her self from the snares of patriarchy" (pp. 241–42), by "peel(ing) away the layers of patriarchal training" (p. 242) and "heal(ing) the wounds of . . . childhood" (p. 245); in therapy with Laura Brown, a woman is helped to "know herself" (p. 246), to move beyond her "accommodated self" (p. 243) and discover her "true self" (p. 243) (or "shammed inner self" p. 245), and live "at harmony with herself" (p. 243). In most feminist psychology, this inner self is characterised as a beautiful, spontaneous little girl. Getting in touch with and nurturing her is a first step in creating social change: It is "revolution from within".

This set of ideas has its roots in the "growth movement" of the 1960s, which emphasised personal liberation and "human potential". Back then, the central image was of a vaguely defined "sick society".

> "The System" was poisoned by its materialism, consumerism and lack of concern for the individual. These things were internalised by people; but underneath the layers of "shit" in each person lay an essential "natural self" which could be reached

through various therapeutic techniques. What this suggests is that revolutionary change is not something that has to be built, created or invented with other people, but that it is somehow natural, dormant in each of us individually and only has to be released (Scott and Payne: 1984, p. 22).

The absurdity of taking this "revolution from within" argument to its logical conclusion is illustrated by one project, the offspring of a popular therapeutic program, which proposed to end starvation. Not, as might seem sensible, by organising soup kitchens, distributing food parcels to the hungry, campaigning for impoverished countries to be released from their national debts, or sponsoring farming cooperatives. Instead, it offers the simple expedient of getting individuals to sign cards saying that they are "willing to be responsible for making the end of starvation an idea whose time has come." When an undisclosed number of people have signed such cards, a "context" will have been created in which hunger will somehow end (cited in Zilbergeld: 1983, pp. 5–6). Of course, Laura Brown, along with many other feminist therapists, would probably also want to challenge the obscenity of this project. Yet the logic of her own arguments permits precisely this kind of interpretation.

Such approaches are a very long way from my own understanding of "the personal is political." I don't think social change happens from the inside out. I don't think people have inner children somewhere inside waiting to be nurtured, re-parented, and their natural goodness released into the world. On the contrary, as I have argued elsewhere (Kitzinger: 1987; Kitzinger and Perkins: 1993), our inner selves are constructed by the social and political contexts in which we live, and if we want to alter people's behaviour it is far more effective to change the environment that to psychologise individuals. Yet as Sarah Scott and Tracey Payne (1984, p. 24) point out, "when it comes to doing therapy it is essential to each and every technique that women see their 'real' selves and their 'social' selves as distinct." This means that the process of making ethical and political decisions about our lives is reduced to the supposed "discovery" of our true selves, the honouring of our "hearts desires". Political understandings of our thoughts and feelings is occluded, and our ethical choices are cast within a therapeutic rather than a political framework. A set of repressive social conditions has made life hard for women and lesbians. Yet the "revolution from within" solution is to improve the individuals, rather that change the conditions.

Psychology suggests that only after healing yourself can you begin to heal the world. I disagree. People do not have to be perfectly functioning, self-actualised human beings in order to create social change. Think of the feminists you know who have been influential in the world, and who have worked hard and effectively for social justice: Have they all loved and accepted themselves? The vast majority of those admired for their political work go on struggling for change not because they have achieved self-fulfilment (nor in order to attain it), but because of their ethical and political commitments, and often in spite of their own fears, self-doubts,

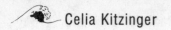

personal angst, and self-hatreds. Those who work for "revolution without" are often no more "in touch with their real selves" than those fixated on inner change: this observation should not be used (as it sometimes is) to discredit their activism, but rather to demonstrate that political action is an option for all of us, whatever our state of psychological well-being. Wait until your inner world is sorted out before shifting your attention to the outer, and you are, indeed "waiting for the revolution" (Brown: 1992).

Validating Women's Experience

A third psychological version of "the personal is political" as applied to therapy goes something like this:

> Politics develops out of personal experience. Feminism is derived from women's own life stories, and must reflect and validate those. Women's realities have always been ignored, denied or invalidated under heteropatriarchy; therapy serves to witness, affirm, and validate women's experience. As such, it makes the personal, political.

The politics of therapy, according to this approach, involves no more than "validating", "respecting", "honouring", "celebrating", "affirming", "attending to", or "witnessing" (these buzz words are generally used inter-changeably) another woman's "experience" or "reality".

This "validation" process is supposed to have enormous implications: "When we honour our clients, they transform themselves" (Hill: 1990, p. 56).

There is obviously a lot of sense in listening to each other and in being willing to understand the meaning of other women's experience. We used to do this in Consciousness Raising groups; now we do it in therapy. Because it has been transformed into a therapeutic activity, it now carries all the risks of abuse of power endemic to the therapeutic enterprise (Kitzinger and Perkins: 1993, chapter 3; Silveira: 1985). In particular, therapists are selective about which experiences they will or won't validate in therapy. Those of a client's feelings and beliefs which are most similar to those of the therapist are "validated"; the others are more or less subtly "invalidated".

Few feminist therapists, for example, will uncritically validate a survivor of child sexual abuse who talks of being to blame for her childhood rape because of her seductive behaviour; instead, she is likely to be offered an analysis of the way in which victim-blaming operates under heteropatriarchy. Similarly, few feminist therapists will validate the experience of a woman who says she is sick and perverted for being lesbian: instead, as Laura Brown (1992) herself argues, her "dysfunctional thoughts" (p. 243) will be challenged and therapy geared towards modifying them to the belief that "patriarchy teaches that lesbianism is evil as a means of socially controlling all women and reserving emotional resources for men and dominant institutions (an analysis that I have offered, in various forms, to women wondering out loud in my office about why they hate themselves so for being lesbian)" (Brown: 1992, p. 249). While claiming to "validate" all women's realities, in fact only a subset, consisting of those realities with which the therapist is in agreement, are accepted as "true" reflections of the way things are. The others are "invalidated", whether as "faulty cognitions" (Padesky: 1989) or as "patriarchal distortions" (Brown: 1992, p. 242). In other words, all this talk about "validating" and "honouring" clients' reality is thin disguise for the therapeutic shaping of women's experience in terms of the therapist's own theories.

In any case, "experience" is always perceived through a theoretical framework (implicit or explicit) within which it gains meaning. Feelings and emotions are not simply immediate, unsocialised, self-authenticating responses. They are socially constructed, and presuppose certain social norms. "Experience" is never "raw"; it is embedded in a social web of interpretation and reinterpretation. In encouraging and perpetuating the notion of pure, unsullied, presocialised "experience" and natural emotion welling up from inside, therapists have disguised or obscured the social roots of our "inner selves". Placing "experience" beyond debate in this way is deeply anti-feminist precisely because it denies the political sources of experience and renders them purely personal. When psychology simply "validates" particular emotions, it removes them from an ethical and political framework.

Empowerment

A fourth psychological interpretation of "the person is political" relies on the notion of "empowerment". It goes something like this:

> Therapy empowers us to act politically. Raising one's personal awareness through therapy enables individuals to release their psychic energies towards creative social change. Through therapy, lesbians can gain both the feminist consciousness and the self-confidence to engage in political action. Many radical feminist political activists are empowered to continue through their ongoing self-nurturing in therapy.

Those in therapy often use this justification: according to Angela Johnson (1992, p. 8), therapy (along with rock-climbing) "gives me the energy to continue my activism with renewed excitement." And therapists concur. According to clinical psychologist Jan Burns (1992, p. 230), writing on the psychology of lesbian health care, "it seems intuitively reasonable that an individual may prefer to engage in self-exploration prior to choosing to engage in more political action, and may in fact need to, before being able to take other action". Laura Brown (1992) says that many of her clients "have precious little to give to the larger struggle from which many are disengaged when I first see them" (p. 245). Her client, "Ruth", was helped to understand that "ultimate healing lies in her participation in cultural, not only personal change" (p. 246) and was shown by Laura Brown "how to move her healing process into a broader sphere" (p. 245). As a result of therapy, her "energies" were "freed" (p. 245) and she became a speaker, poet, and teacher about women and war, and engaged in public anti-war activism. Similarly, clinical psychologist Sue Holland (1991), in an article entitled "From private symptoms to public action," promotes a model of therapy in which the client moves from "passive, 'ill' patient/ victim" at the start of treatment to a "recognition of . . . oppression as located in the objective environment" which leads to a "collective desire for change" in which "psychic energies can . . . be addressed outward onto structural enemies" (p. 59).

According to this interpretation, the "personal" consists of "psychic energies" (never clearly defined) which operate according to a hydraulic model. There is a fixed amount of "energy" which can be blocked, freed, or redirected along other channels. The "political" is simply one of these "channels". Therapy can (and some would say *should)* direct feminist energy along "political" channels. Often, of course it does not, and women remain perpetually focussed within - a problem noted with regret by the more radical lesbian/feminist therapists. But *their* therapy (they say) does result in their clients' becoming politically active.

Far from embodying the notion of "the personal is political", these ideas rely on a radical *separation* of the two. The "person" business of doing therapy is distinguished from the "political" work of going on marches, and having severed the "personal" and "political" in this way, the two are then inspected for degree of correlation.

The "empowerment" argument totally ignores the politics of therapy itself. It is seen simply as a hobby (like rock climbing) or personal activity with no particular ethical or political implications in and of itself. Shorn of intrinsic political meaning, it is assessed only in terms of its presumed consequences for "politics" – defined in terms of the old male left banner-waving variety. If "the personal is political", the very *process of doing* therapy is political, and this process (not simply its alleged outcomes) must be critically evaluated in political terms.

In conclusion, and despite the frequency with which feminist therapists routinely state that "the personal is political", it seems utterly wrong to claim that this aim is a "cornerstone of feminist therapy" (Gilbert: 1980). Certainly the notions of "revolution from within", the importance of "validating" women's reality, and "empowering" women for political activism *are* central to the thinking of many feminist psychologists. These overlapping and interrelated ideas are braided throughout a great deal of lesbian/feminist psychological theory and practice. But such notions are a long way from the radical feminist insight that "the personal is political", and are often interpreted in direct contradiction to it. They often foster naive concepts of the mechanisms whereby social change is achieved; involve uncritical acceptance of "true feelings" and/or manipulative "reinterpretations" of women's lives in terms preferred by the psychologist; lead women to revert to "external" definitions of politics in contradistinction to the "personal" business of therapy; and leave us shorn of ethical and political language. Acknowledging that the personal really is political means rejecting psychology.

I recognise that some women whose politics I admire and respect have not rejected psychology: Many are "in therapy" or are providers of therapy. This observation is sometimes used to counter our arguments. After reading a chapter (Kitzinger and Perkins: 1993) which cites Nancy Johnson's class action suit against the US government for condemning the people of Utah to cancer (because of nuclear nesting), one reader commented that Nancy Johnson now works as a psychic healer in a manner which I was likely to find politically problematic. "I think the situation is more complicated than you've presented it: Feminism and psychology don't seem to be mutually exclusive", she said. Obviously, feminist activists are sometimes practitioners or consumers of psychology: many feminists clearly find it possible to include both in their lives. But then, health campaigners sometimes smoke cigarettes; ecologists sometimes drop litter; and pacifists sometimes slap their children. The observed coexistence of two views or behaviours in the same person does not render them logically ethically, or politically compatible.

Argument about the ethical and political compatibility of people's different ideas and behaviour is an important part of what feminist political discussion is all about. My argument is that feminism and psychology are not ethically or politically compatible. It's not, necessarily, that women involved in psychology are apolitical or anti-feminist. Many are serious about their feminism and deeply engaged in political activities. But in-so-far as they organise their lives with reference to psychological ideas, and in-so-far as they limit their thoughts and actions to what they learn from psychology, they are denying the fundamental feminist principle that "the personal is political".

Jocelynne A. Scutt

The Personal is Political

People see peace as a destination but it is not. It is a way of travelling
Stella Cornelius: 1986, p. 3.

When the Women's Liberation movement took as its slogan "the personal is political", it was saying in shorthand to the world at large that it is time to give up the fragmented view of reality which has persisted in accordance with dominant views. The women's liberation movement was putting down a statement of the need to cease viewing reality as a jigsaw where the pieces never fit. It demanded that reality be reintegrated; that the world view become one wherein individual lives are seen as part of a whole, instead of being isolated away from general events. It articulated a need to recognise that what happens to each one of us, in our private lives, directly affects and is affected by what happens to all of us in the public sphere. The need is to see that the private lives of citizens are a part of the public world, of the standards set in the public world, and the events occurring "out there".

"The personal is political" has a direct relevance to calls for peace and ecological compassion. Accepting or subscribing to standards of violence, exploitation and abuse in the private world makes a mockery of any calls for peace and environmental care in the public arena. In Australia, the calls for peace and an end to the pillaging of the earth are drowned out, in the ears of those who are open to them, by the cries of women and children who are beaten, abused and raped in their own homes. Demands for peace and environment are drowned in the debasement of everyone living in a world where class and race violence are everyday events.

The violence of war and ravaging of the earth are too often replicated in the personal lives of ordinary, everyday Australians – and those who would not describe themselves as "ordinary" but are, nonetheless, in their acceptance of home-based violence as the norm. And the violence against women and Black Australians,

* Excerpt from Jocelynne A. Scutt (1994). *The Sexual Gerrymander.*

class-based violence and ethnic-based violence experienced on a personal level by many in Australia is replicated on the world stage when international differences are fought out in the wartime arena. Calls for an end to war, to an end to exploitation of the earth, for peace, will always be uttered from hypocritical lips and therefore never result in fulfilment, for as long as violence on a personal level is not seen as closely aligned with, indeed inseparably a part of, the political violence of war and environmental degradation.

Violence Against Women

Indisputably the major violence taking place the world over is violence exercised against women and girls. This violence takes place on a global scale. Every country is involved. All of our countrymen are involved, so long as they condone that violence by letting it go on.

Since the first feminist refuges and rape crisis centres were set up in 1974 and 1975 in New South Wales and Western Australia, the women's shelter movement has burgeoned, so that around Australia today there are more than 300 women's refuges. But women and children are often turned away from these sanctuaries because the numbers are beyond the level with which the shelters can cope. Before that period, women's voices were lifted on behalf of women suffering from violence at home. Louise Lawson at the end of the last century published impassioned pleas against criminal assault at home, furious in her anger at the brutality to which women and children were subjected.[1] Her ire was matched by that of other women, and by the less passionate, but no less felt, calls for changes to divorce laws so that bashed, beaten and abused women could be freed from their brutal mates.

But the violence – and recognition of the violence – does not end there. Rape is common within the family, and more common where the aggressor knows his victim than where he does not. As a crime against daughters, and less often sons, rape and sexual exploitation at home is euphemistically called incest, which implies there are two consenting parties. More realistically, the Women's Movement labelled the event in accordance with the girls' (and boys') reality (Ward: 1984). By the mid-80s, Elizabeth Stanko (1985, p. 24) had spelt out the realities:

- between 90 and 97 per cent of offenders in all cases are male;
- in over 87 per cent of cases, the assaulted is female;
- sexual assault of children is coercive, and often but not always violent; coercion exists within the structural positions of the offender and the assaulted;
- the assaulted suffers emotional trauma; the longer the behaviour has been going on, the deeper the trauma is likely to be;
- incestuous assault, like other forms of violence against women, is steeped in myths about seductiveness, and consequently the blameworthiness, of the assaulted;
- the incidence is grossly underestimated.

---

1. Louisa Lawson spoke out in *The Dawn*, the feminist newspaper she established in the latter part of the nineteenth century and published from Sydney, Australia.

Arising out of the evidence, Strauss (1978) has said: "Although there may be exceptions, such as the police or the army in time of war . . . the family is the most violent institution, group, or setting that a typical citizen is likely to encounter".

Ironically, the truth is that the army in time of war lives out not a new form of violence, but the old violence learned on the home front.

In the 1970s small groups of women took to the streets to mourn for all women raped in all wars. They chose Anzac Day to do this, in defiance of the bellows of indignation from self-appointed spokesmen who claimed the day was reserved for returned servicepersons. The rape of women had nothing to do with war, they proclaimed. The women were not deterred. Each year, on April 25, women went back out to march. The numbers swelled. The opposition did not cease. Representatives of the Returned Servicepersons League (RSL) attested they were affronted for all service personnel. The notion that home-grown, Aussie soldiers might be implicated in rape of women, any women, was absurd, they claimed. It was a slur on every man who fought for his country. It was a slur on every man who died for his country. The women ought to be ashamed of themselves and their perfidy, it was said. They were an insult to Anzac Day and to Australia.

The women sought only to have the truth spoken. They wished only that their presence should be seen and their voices heard in mourning for women ignored in remembrances of the dead and injured: "There is no acknowledgment of them in casualty lists".[2] Now that (some) women raped in war are being remembered, and governments are purporting to take some responsibility for the rape, the grand euphemism "comfort women" has been invented. Whose "comfort" was in issue, when women were used and abused as objects to be raped and ravaged by soldiers in wartime, with the imprimatur of governments? Certainly not the comfort of the women, who should rightly be named survivors of rape, survivors of war, survivors of rape-in-war, (Daly and Jellie: 1993; Daly and Porter: 1993).

Women demanded a right to mourn their sisters who not only met death as war spoils, or lived on after rape, but were forgotten by the dominant culture at the same time. In the words of Judy Small's song, "Lest We Forget":

> Lest they forget the countless children
>   burned alive in napalm's fire
> Lest they forget the dead civilians lying
>   tangled in the wire
> And the faces of the women raped and
>   shattered to the core
> It's not only men in uniform who pay the
>   price of war.

---

2. Rayner Hoff, sculptor of three female figures supporting on their shoulders a corpse upon a shield, at the Hall of Memory in Sydney's War Memorial, Hyde Park, circa. 1934.

The violence of war and its depiction in the popular mind as extreme, extraordinary, the result of unusual circumstances shades the reality of violence in the domestic sphere – on the home ground and in the national arena. Violence against women covers the field: no woman is immune, whatever her race, her class or class origins, her ethnic background. But women and men suffer added burdens of violence and exploitation by reason of class or ethnic background, or race. In Australia, as elsewhere, the major group filling prisons is from the lower socio-economic strata. The violence of prison is simultaneously notorious and hidden. Nonetheless, stories surface with some frequency in Australian states of violence said to be meted out on persons in custody – most often Black Australians (Elliot Johnson: 1992). Women – particularly women working as prostitutes – are also at risk, and the violence comes not only from those in authority (Report: 1985). It comes from fellow inmates. In the United States, although the Constitution forbids "cruel and unusual punishment", it is reported that the overwhelming majority of judges, attorneys, police officers and gaolers "have long known about the vicious sexual assaults among male as well as female inmates of jails and prisons throughout the country". Writing in the journal *Victimology*, Tom Cahill points out that instead of trying to stop this brutality, "makers and enforcers of the law have consistently turned a deaf ear to inmate rape". Loretta Tofani of the *Washington Post*, who won the Pulitzer Prize in April 1983 for her series exposing rape and violence in the American prison system, reported one judge as saying "you shut your mind to it" (Cahill: 1984).

Sexual violence is not confined to United States prisons. In New South Wales in 1978 a series of vicious gang and individual rapes in New South Wales prisons gained the headlines for a short time. Over the years, stories continue to be related by those involved in prison activism, fighting for the rights of the imprisoned not to be raped by fellow inmates. In Victoria in mid-1986 similar tales reached the public through the news media. Dormitory living arrangements were scheduled to be replaced by individual accommodation as a result of this exposé (Victorian Attorney General: 1986).

Yet the irony for women (who may be raped or sexually harassed in prison also) is that women live in a world where rape and sexual harassment are everyday events. Women do not have to go to prison to be bashed, abused and sexually assaulted. For too many, this exploitation and brutalisation occurs too often in their own homes. In their own homes, there are "written and unwritten" rules; failure to conform with the rules results in violence inflicted upon them, not infrequently of the magnitude meted out on the men in Grafton prison and other gaols. Unwritten rules consist of "opening the cornflakes packet from the wrong end" (what is the "right" end?); "squeezing the toothpaste tube from the middle"; not cooking to the satisfaction of "the master of the house". "I felt like a slave in prison", wrote one woman of her thirteen years of intolerable violence, abuse and damaging psychological battering (Scutt: 1983).

The violence is not always overt. It takes more subtle or psychological forms, as described by Elizabeth Williams, Koori activist, who experienced the negative effects of racism in a New South Wales country town:

> In December 1981 I was appointed by the Minister for Health as director on the Queanbeyan Hospital Board. My experience in community work and being Aboriginal helped. The following year, in December, I was nominated as chairperson by two other women directors, and was elected by majority. I had no idea of the flak in store for me. My election upset a few people – some on the board. At that December meeting tension was high. I was stunned. This was the first time I had experienced such strong feelings against me ... People I thought would be happy with my new appointment now presented a complete turn about. Some showed outright rudeness, ignoring me. Some were disgusted I would even consider myself capable of performing the duties of chairperson. Others urged me to resign. To avoid further abuse I found myself walking the back streets and staying home. Just when I thought calm had arrived, I received a letter from my predecessor. My first reaction on reading it was shock. I read it many times before the words sank in. Before the letter arrived, I was under tremendous pressure to resign. Now I was angry. This man has such a nerve to send me what was an awful letter. Little did he realise his words would have the opposite effect of what he intended. I would now do the job and do it well, in fact better than any of my white male pre-decessors ... (1987, p. 70).

Violence of War

During wartime, race, sex and class violence are meted out on a grand scale, although that grand scale does not begin to match the violence meted out along sex, race and class lines the world over. During the war in Vietnam, women were raped and beaten and killed as "kikes" or "goons", words depicting them as less than human. Chris Domingo (1984, p. 11) writes:

> an ex-marine
> who had been to
> Vietnam
> raped me.
> He saw
> my small
> dark female body
> in the woods.
> He had learned to rape.
> He had learned to kill.
> He pointed his
> rifle
> at my head
> He had learned this

somewhere
maybe
on tv.

Maybe
over there
in a country
of small dark
people.
He had learned to rape.
He had learned to kill.

At a slide show
about violent pornography
i see the photographs
that some men use
to ejaculate by.
Among the slides
of nude wimmin
bound by ropes,
in a meat grinder,
misrepresented, degraded,
demeaned
in various ways
was an actual photo
from Vietnam
of a small dark
womin's
dead body
under a tree,
taken from a series
of such photos
in a popular porn magazine.
i affirmed aloud
THAT COULD
HAVE BEEN ME.

But where did he learn it? The violence of bashing, raping, killing; the violence against women, against those of another race, or another class: in Vietnam, at war; or at home – in so-called peace?

To be trained for war, men learn domination, control, and violence. Or they build on the learning that has already been done through socialisation in the broader world. To learn to kill, one must learn to despise the killed, to debase them as a group, to downgrade them from human beings to less than human. Violence is an issue for the military not only on the battle field, but in their own homes.

The Dominance of Silence

As long as those ruling the world continue to ignore the violence endemic in the everyday lives of the ruled, and as long as those in power see "peace" and environment as narrow political issues to be used for personal political gain, peace and a cared-for and caring environment will never be "at hand". Rather, the hypocrisy that currently goes for "peace" and ecological concern will continue. And in its continuing, women will continue to be raped, bashed and beaten by those whom they (thought they) loved and who (they thought) loved them. Those of minority racial and ethnic background will continue to be scorned, attacked, verbally demeaned by the bully boys. The state will continue to imprison, in intolerable conditions of violence and despair, women who defraud social security in order to feed themselves and their children, or who "go on the game" of prostitution for the same purpose. And men who grow up in a violent milieu, being taught to believe that their only design for living is a replication of the violence meted out against them by an unfriendly world, will continue to fill prisons and police lock-ups. For these men, their problem (in dominant-ethic terms) is that they are unable to exploit and abuse their physical strength or brains in "res-pectable" middle-class ways – such as engaging in extortionary activity on the stock exchange and the ultimately debilitating competition so often applauded in the financial pages of newspapers by pundits who should know better.

Where the violence of men's world has penetrated the world of women, women have been trained to be silent about it. And where women have been permitted to enter into the violent world of men, women have similarly been frightened into maintaining that same silence. Cynthia Enloe talks of the militari-sation of women's lives, noting that the armed forces "get nervous" when nurses start telling their stories of wartime, because "they reveal so much about the nature of the war itself". In *Does Khaki Become You?* Enloe points out that it is not only the military gender structure that is protected by the silence of military nurses, but "the basic legitimacy of the military as a pillar of civilised society is being protected ...". A nurse who talks of war as seen from a military hospital or a Mobile Army Surgical Hospital (MASH) unit is, writes Enloe, "a dangerous woman" (1983/ 1988, p. 113).

And where women are raped, children are sexually abused and exploited, they are ordered by their attackers to maintain silence. The fear of shame and humiliation, or guilt that they are "responsible" for the attack, "wanted" it, or "led him on", compounds this silencing. Where they do speak out, women's voices, women's truths, are barely listened to, or are dismissed as fiction, sham or bitter lies.

But men too maintain the silence. Writing in *The Sexuality of Men*, Tony Eardley recalls a discussion amongst a group of men who had begun to think about their need to reassess their dominant attitudes:

One of us distributed copies of an article from the American radical journal *Mother Jones*, which reported the story of the rape and mutilation of Mary Bell Jones, a teenage girl attacked while hitch-hiking in California. We didn't know how to begin talking about it and found ourselves avoiding each other's eyes. When our reactions came they varied from "I can't bear to read this", and "we cannot be expected to take responsibility for these atrocities simply because we are men", to "we have to accept that at the bottom this is what men are about". It soon became clear that any notion of responsibility was meaningless unless we started from our own violence and our experiences both as perpetrators and victims, as a way to some understanding of how men acquire such a capacity for brutality. We found it was essential to develop a political analysis which looked toward possibilities for change, and a concept of personal responsibility not based on guilt but on positive challenge to destructive aspects of masculinity (1985, p. 88).

One can start such a challenge, he writes, by asking what lies behind men's silence.

Men's violence has been meted out against women while a vast silence prevails. Where women have spoken out, our voices have often been swamped in that male silence. Men have been silent too about class and race violence, or speak out in numbers which falter against the silences of many.

Rightly it is said that it is doubtful whether the power to demand or force sexual services from women "has led to any widespread sexual satisfaction or happiness amongst men" (Eardley: 1985, p. 89). Similarly it is doubtful whether the power to demand or force services from black men or women, or others racially or ethnically in the minority, has led to any widespread satisfaction or happiness amongst those who perpetrate the oppression. Yet the silences about this violence remain. But within the peace movement, if the full force of the demand for peace is to be maintained and realised, it would be well for all within it to end the silences about this violence which is endemic in our society and which founds the very nature of war. That so called personal violence is inseparable from the violence of war. Without concern for the environment of the hearth, there can be no concern at all. Without peace on the home front, there can be no peace at all.

Power, Autonomy and Peace

There is another vision of the world, a vision that can be reached if the personal is recognised as political and the political in turn acknowledged as personal responsibility and trust. What is needed to make peace a reality, to put an end to the earth's ravishment, and end to all war, is a recognition of what goes on in our own lives as crucial to the question of what goes on in the world. Our lives are a part of the world. Women have recognised that truth, probably for millennia, sometimes in greater numbers, sometimes in less. Talking about women's position, in *The Powers of the Weak*, Elizabeth Janeway writes: "Distrust, the first power of the weak is already ours . . ." (1980, p. 318).

To talk about distrust, as if it is positive, is frightening at first. We have been taught that trust is one of the most important emotions we can express. And we are right, but the pity is we have been taught to trust those who have no right to our trust, those whom we should distrust. The potential for peace is subverted for as long as we trust those who are in positions of power, who abuse the power and move us so surely down the road to disaster, their "little" violences strewing the way. We must learn to think more clearly about the value of our emotions and refuse to debase them as we are expected to do. Thus will it become more easy for us to progress toward autonomy and peace. This takes courage:

> There is a kind of courage that's very familiar to the weak; endurance, patience, stamina, the ability to repeat everyday tasks every day, these are the forms of courage that have allowed generations of the governed to survive without losing ultimate hope. The knowledge of one's own vulnerability, the choice of restraint in the face of provocation, the ability to hear oneself described as unworthy without accepted the stigma as final – that takes courage of a high order. We do not want to lose it, for it's still a source of strength when the time comes to be patient no longer, when direct confrontation with the powerful for independent aims must be risked if not sought (Janeway: 1980, p. 292).

Many people may be driven to say: Why raise issues of violence on the home ground, when nuclear war and depletion of the ozone layer stare us in the face? In response I say, so long as violence in our everyday lives goes unchecked, unremarked, left alone or ignored, then repeating "peace" and environment as a litany will never prevent any expression of war, whether national or international, "contained" or of holocaust proportions. The status of women is crucial to the way what we say, and what we demand, is perceived. So long as women's claims are denied because we are women, our status as women is used against us. Our standing is valued less than the standing of men. Race, class and ethnic discrimination play an important role, too, in depriving many women of full status. Our determination to have women recognised as human is central to the claims we make for all women. Not being recognised as fully human means that those great male silences will never be penetrated. Women's power to refuse to accept a downgrading of our opinions, our rights, our demands, is the beginning of a fundamental change in the way we are seen and way the world operates. We need the courage to continue to speak out loudly again and again against violence and aggression in whatever form it takes. The importance of any peace and environmental movement is its recognition of the value of working for peace at various levels. It is also its recognition that isolating forms of violence is precisely what is needed to depoliticise and downgrade the origins of violence as a way of life. Peace too has its origins in a way of life:

Peace is not a destination. It's a way of travelling.

Morny Joy

Looking for God in All the Wrong Places: Feminists Seeking the Radical Questions in Religion

In the seventies, the terms "radical" and "revolutionary" in Religious Studies referred to writers such as Carol Christ (1979) and Naomi Goldenberg (1979) who advocated the abandonment of traditional religion as irredeemably patriarchal. In contrast, those who believed that religion, as a system of beliefs, behaviours and structures, could change to meet the demands of women, were named "reformers". Today, such a simplistic dichotomy has outlived its appropriateness, even in the opinion of those who first applied it (Plaskow and Christ: 1989, pp. 6–8). For what has become apparent is that many feminists in religion have been at the forefront in articulating radical agendas on issues such as sexuality, birth control and abortion, violence against women, pornography and racism.[1] These matters, they insist, are central to both the study and practice of religion if it is to honour its responsibility to fostering the well-being of all peoples without distinction.

On the other hand, there are many feminists who believe that no woman in her right mind would have anything to do with religion – of all institutions it is the most conservative, the most recalcitrant to change. Yet, as the resurgence of interest in the Goddess has illustrated, many women still have divine intimations, if not more ambitious aspirations (Eller: 1993). At the same time, there is a staggering revival of fundamentalism in this seemingly secular age (Boone: 1989; Hawley: 1994). How can one negotiate this minefield-like mixture of religious ideals and desperation that continues to attract the loyalties of the majority of

---

1. Unfortunately, this essay can but survey some of the main currents and thinkers involved – without expanding on the controversies. I will also confine my observations to the work of prominent Jewish and Christian feminist thinkers. This essay is part of a more comprehensive study of the topic that is forthcoming (see *Women's Studies International Forum*, 1996).

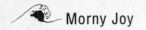

humankind?[2] The very fact of religion's pervasiveness and its continuing influence on virtually all contemporary social structures (whether intentional or not) is, I believe, sufficient reason for a concerned, if suspicious feminist analysis. And, as radical feminists have demonstrated, their questions constitute a fundamental and irreducible challenge to the basis of religion where, until recently, men alone have been the founders, recorders and policy-makers. Further, the vehemence of the responses to their proposals illustrates that these women's questions challenge deeply entrenched biases, that thwart the calls for transformation not just for religion, but for all who envision a just society wherein women, no less than men, may live, love, play, work, think, dream, desire and express their most deeply held commitments in safety, with security and dignity.

From my perspective, as a religiously unaffiliated person and an unrepentant feminist scholar in Religious Studies (Joy: 1989), I would nominate three topics that are crucial areas for religious reform. First, there is the institution itself and its accompanying paraphernalia of text and ritual;[3] second, the symbolic dimension, which concerns the various representations of God or the absolute;[4] and third, ethical issues.[5] Here, I will focus primarily on ethics. That some women have chosen to remain within the orbit of religious institutions and to attempt reform should not be taken as a measure of their docility and conformity – rather it bespeaks a certain indomitable courage in the face of overwhelming odds. Indeed, without the ground-breaking investigations, critiques and re-interpretations of Elisabeth Schüssler Fiorenza (1983), Rosemary Radford Ruether (1983) and Judith Plaskow (1990) – to name but a few of the trail-blazers who have questioned not only the blatant discriminatory practices, but also the textual omissions and distortions – other feminists who have proposed reconsideration and reformulation of ethical issues would be severely handicapped.

It is an extraordinarily difficult task to draw together the diverse interests and undertakings of the women in both Christianity and Judaism who seek to transform their traditions. But perhaps the core insight is that which can

---

2. An article in *Newsweek*, November 29, 1993, pp. 80–2, stated that approximately 70% of Americans were religiously committed in the following categories: strongly, 19%; moderately, 22%; nominally, 29%.
3. Here I refer to the books of sacred scripture and their interpretation and implementation. Until recently, education to be a qualified commentator on these texts in the public domain has been confined to male-only institutions. In most cases, the right to conduct public rituals or other sacred ceremonies was also conferred as a result of graduation from such exclusionary religious seminaries, divinity schools or yeshivas.
4. Official representations of the divine mirror the scriptural foundations, if not descriptions, though Christian theology has mostly been an intriguing exercise in trying to coordinate scriptural pronouncements with the formulas of the reigning philosophical school. In Judaism there has been the Talmudic commentary. Needless to say, the tone and attributions have been decidedly male in orientation.
5. Ethics is a broad term which has come to incorporate both accumulated tradition as well as those laws which are considered as mandatory obligations because they featured in the original religious revelation. Both aspects are under intense scrutiny by contemporary religious feminists.

be distilled from the changing conceptualizations of God. No longer is there a paternalistic father-figure proclaiming from on high his omniscient decrees. Instead, God is very much in and of the world. Whether, as in some forms of liberation Christianity, Christ becomes an insurgent figure, fighting inequitable appropriations of power, or whether, as in other forms of Christianity and Judaism, God is envisioned as an intrinsic element in the creative process, a watershed in theology has been reached. The consequences of this feminist theological inception cannot but decisively alter the complexion of religion as it has appeared until now. God will no longer reside in outmoded institutions, archaic laws, and indefensible desecrations of life. God becomes allied with what is deepest, strongest and most affirmative in a vital synergism of feminist forces that seeks not a kingdom in another world or time, but a space where women, and not just men, may flourish. Perhaps, as some feminists attest, this was the radical intention of religion in its initial impetus, but this was somehow displaced by an alleged alignment of the male hierarchy with heavenly potentialities and earthly powers. If this is the case, it is time to reclaim the original radical agenda, for too long it has rested in the hands of those who have failed to understand the innate fullness of life that is the birthright of all human beings.

Radical "Re-visionings"

Perhaps the most vibrant contemporary heretic (I use this term in a complimentary way) is Mary Daly (see Joy: 1994). Her trajectory from Catholicism to the further galactic reaches of post-Christian lusty life with its affirmative capacities has charted a course many women have followed with verve and delight. Daly (1993) is uncompromising in her rejection of exclusionary practices and formulations that she perceives as denying women their rightful place in the universe. Yet she has not abandoned her metaphysical impulses, affirming that today, as women come into their own, they provide the appropriate, if not definitive, revelation for our time.[6] Declaring that it is time to abandon that bad historical habit of anthropomorphism – that unfortunate propensity of conceiving God in our own image, replete with our own neurotic needs for protection and/or punishment, Daly's preference is for Meta-Being, as source of energy and creative dynamism. Despite its traditional metaphysical baggage, this conception of God as a verb rather than a noun appeals to many who wish to identify with cosmic processes as the locus of divine manifestation.

Another strong challenge to habitual God-talk is coming from African-

---

6. In *Pure Lust* (1984, pp. 26–30), Daly refines her notion of the classical metaphysical understanding of Being. Instead of regarding it as a static noun, Daly prefers to see it as a vibrant verb Be-ing. She then revolutionizes the stagnant transcendental categories by appealing to the spirited realms of Meta-Being which inspire the radical activities of women who refuse to be contained by traditional deformations. Metaphors, moving beyond literalisms, give access to these transformative powers of Meta-Being which draw their energy from Be-ing.

American or womanist theologians.[7] Dissatisfied with western metaphysical posturing, womanist thinkers such as Grant (1989) and Williams (1993) look to Jesus, rather than to an omnipotent and remote God, as their religious figurehead. The Jesus of their belief and practice, however, is not a meek and mild teacher but a revolutionary figure who came to bring justice to all. Particularly in the work of Dolores Williams, Jesus does not save by his death on the cross, nor is the resurrection viewed as a vindication. In fact, in Williams' reading, the powers of evil were victorious. As a result, the bleeding agony of the cross should never be promulgated as vicarious suffering that redeems human sinfulness and also compensates for all unjustified misery, whether inflicted or encountered. Such a God-figure simply endorses sado-masochistic abuses in the guise of education for subservience. For Williams, the call to be religious is to imitate Christ not in his suffering, but in his mission to bring freedom to all. Williams argues that this interpretation requires a commitment to change not just the patriarchally affiliated black churches, but all forms of social and political oppression that deny people their freedom.

A further challenge is that emerging from the liberatory theologies of *mujerista* (Tamez: 1989), Asian (Kwok Pui-Lan: 1992; Chung Hyun Kyung: 1990) and African (Fabella and Oduyoye: 1990) women. They are part of a multifaceted confrontation with traditional Christianity yet, in this struggle, they can also represent the specific needs, self-definition and agendas of their peoples. While religion is thus not exculpated from its legacy of colonial, magisterial exploitation, it can be critically employed as an agency for change.

One Jewish woman, Judith Plaskow (1990) and Plaskow and Christ: 1989, takes full advantage of the fact that Jewish feminists need not be restricted in their exploration of God-talk and imagery by the demand to satisfy established theological dogmas. This is because the Jewish tradition (unlike Christianity) did not become preoccupied with philosophical proofs of the existence of God. With reference to the foundational basis of her tradition, in the book *Standing Again at Sinai* (1990), Plaskow envisages the forms of renegotiation that are needed if the Covenant is to include women as full participants. Among her recommendations for reviewing the notion of God, Plaskow stresses two aspects in particular. One is that of conceiving of God as woman – either in the guise of mother or goddess. Plaskow (1990, p. 42) acknowledges the Bible as a source for even this seemingly heterodox practice: "Indeed, if one reads the prophetic accounts carefully, it seems clear that an indigenous polytheism flourished in Israel up until the exile".

The other mode Plaskow recommends investigating is a reinvestment/ revitalization of feminine modalities that have been associated with God – most specifically that of *Shekinah* – the biblical term used to refer to the spiritual

---

7. The term "womanist" is the name used by African-American women to distinguish themselves from the white middle-class perspective which has informed much of North American feminism. It was first used by Alice Walker in *The Color Purple*.

presence of God as it pervades creation. But, as Plaskow also qualifies this suggestion:

> The Shekinah is the subordinate bride and consort within God. Just as in the Bible, Israel is the bride of God, so the Shekinah is the subordinate bride and consort within God. It is the female as the male understands the secondary aspect within himself, not as experienced by women (1990, p. 169).

Such a reservation regarding reclamation of traditional imagery is crucial, not just with regard to Judaism, but to all male-centred traditions. How sacrosanct is a tradition where all authority has been vested in the male? How essential to its constitution is the male figurehead who presides? Is it the case, as secular feminists charge, that changes which incorporate women are just cosmetic, and thus do not disrupt the quintessentially masculine ambience that has permeated all western religious constructions? It seems to me that unless western religions are willing to challenge the major presupposition that sustains their core – that God is male – very little substantial progress can be made either in transforming the tradition or in ameliorating the condition of women.

Understandably, there are those feminists who would question these modifications in the conception of God as mere superficial dabbling. In response, however, one could indicate the outraged reaction to a ecumenic gathering of approximately two thousand women and men in November 1993 in Minneapolis. The aim of this consultation, which was entitled "Reimagining", included many already mentioned "heretics", such as Dolores Walker, Chung Hyun Kyung and Kwok Pui-Lan, was to investigate, among other topics, that of "Reimagining God". A short article in *Religious Studies News* (1994) by the American Academy of Religion Committee on the Status of Women, relates that as a result of partici- pating in this conference, one church official has lost her job, while other scholars have been harassed and their work taken out of context and misrepresented. What seemed to have especially exercised the offended traditionalists, both men and women, was the evocation of God as Sophia – a tradition that has an impeccable scriptural lineage.[8] Yet this celebration was referred to as a reversion, if not degeneration, to pagan beliefs with rituals honouring the goddess. The furore that resulted is evidence that an extremely sensitive nerve has been touched, and that such breaching of the boundaries is a needed corrective in a society that has invested all its symbolic structures (not just religious ones) with masculine privilege. I believe that the repercussions of such movements will not be limited to religious circles.

---

8. Appealing to such sources as *The Book of Wisdom and Sirach* from the Apocrypha, but also to the New Testament where Jesus is referred to as the Wisdom of God, Elizabeth Johnson, in her recent work *She Who Is* (1993), provides a ground-breaking theology where God is conceived according to the exemplar of wisdom, and Christ is understood as a unique manifestation of this wisdom.

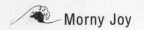

This is but one instance of a growing self-confidence of women in that most sensitive and contentious of religious spheres – the meaning of God. For it does seem imperative for women to be able to envisage themselves as a locus of power and self-affirmation in their efforts to confront in constructive ways outmoded forms that continue to circumscribe their self-determination and expression. Perhaps it is the French thinker Luce Irigaray, in her more recent work, particularly "Divine Women" (1993a) and *Je, tu, nous* (1993b), who can provide insight into the complex situation? In these works, Irigaray (who is not religious in any conventional sense) seems to be responding, whether consciously or not, to those who regarded her earlier work as essentialist and solipsistic. Irigaray appreciates that two mutually reinforcing efforts are necessary. One is the advocacy of an ethical system that protects women and honours her difference, specifically as it concerns her body and its sexual/reproductive integrity. But the other, more remarkable pronouncement is that women should be able to consider themselves divine. By this, Irigaray is not making a facile recommendation for the literal appropriation of divinity in a female manifestation. Instead, she is exhorting women to find the source of their power and ultimate allegiance within themselves, without resorting to any external agency of endorsement. This internalization of self-worth has long been denied women by both secular and religious authorities. The implication is that by so confirming her being, a woman finds the confidence to discredit those barriers, endemic to all patriarchal structures, that have denied her both psychological and social parity and worth. Ultimately, it would seem that unless religious institutions are willing to grant this autonomy to women, they will sustain those rearguard forces in society that wish to believe, as did Aristotle and Aquinas, that woman is both an aberration and a deficiency in creation (Børresen: 1981).

Sin and the Moral Incapacity of Women

One of the great anomalies that becomes apparent on reading the ideas of the Christian Church fathers on women is their various comical attempts to disparage women's sexuality at the same time as acknowledging her existence as part of the blessed pattern of creation. She is invariably described as the weaker vessel, hence more easily prey to temptation and deficient in moral capacity. At the same time, however, this inferior being can be the cause of the downfall of the stronger male. This is because her bodily charms and wiles are vehicles of sin and depravity for all those stalwart souls who wish to maintain their spiritual (and anti-corporeal) integrity. A woman's only exit from this impasse was to maintain the state of virginity, which thereby miraculously freed her from her carnal disadvantages, even conferring on her the honoured equivalency of male status (Ruether: 1974, p. 159). Such a dubious honour fails to impress contemporary religious feminists.

In this regard, one of the most striking developments in recent work by Christian women in religion is their repudiation of traditional notions of sin, based as they are on male defects of character, such as the proclivity to pride and domineering behaviour. These failings have not been the provenance of women who were educated for compliance with authority – be it religious or secular. As Anne Carr observes:

> Women's temptation or 'sin', conversely relates to a *lack* of self-assertion in relation to cultural and familial expectations, failure to assume responsibility and make choices for themselves, failure to discover their own personhood and uniqueness rather than finding their whole meaning in the too-easy sacrifice of self for others (1990, pp. 8-9).

Thus, as women reject these previously male-based conceptions of sin, they are also reclaiming both their bodily and moral integrity. This is occurring in many areas, but I would like to focus on three specific, though interrelated, instances. These are sexuality, abortion and violence against women.

Sexuality

Perhaps the initial hurdle in all of these endeavours is to establish a reinterpretation of Eve. As scapegoat figure, Eve has acquired the accumulated projections of male distrust of and aversion to women over the years. She bears the opprobrium of causing the fall of humanity from the plenitude of the Garden of Eden. Mythic as such a tale may be, it has been used as justification for all the suffering that has been inflicted on women, for she is regarded as needing male supervision and control as well as deserving the travail and suffering of childbirth. Literally interpreted, the female of the species becomes relegated to a mere breeding machine, whose reproductive activities must be carefully monitored. All behaviour that would question such a designation must be eliminated by appropriate punishment and re-education. (Margaret Atwood's *The Handmaid's Tale* is a chilling reminder of the ever-present threat of such a scenario).

How are women to combat such ingrained attitudes in ways that can challenge their pernicious influence as it lingers on in our laws and sexual mores? Judith Plaskow's lovely rejoinder, "The Coming of Lilith" (1992), is a retelling of the first of the two depictions of the creation of humanity in Genesis 1:27. This first woman, created in the image of God (who becomes Lilith in later Jewish lore) is a spirited creature, the equal of Adam.[9] Adam, however was not willing to live with such an indomitable partner and Lilith was replaced by the more deferential Eve, who appears in Genesis 2:21–24 as suitably subordinate and fashioned from Adam's rib. In Plaskow's version, Lilith awakens Eve to her condition and together they plot the possibilities of a changed order of reality. Other writers, such as Kim Chernin

---

9. Lilith is a mysterious figure that haunts Jewish scriptures and mysticism. She makes a relatively late appearance, however, as the first mention of Lilith in association with the notion of "a first Eve" is found in the book of pseudonymous *Alphabet of Ben Sirach* which is variously dated sometime between 600–1000 C.E. See Cantor (1983).

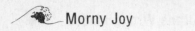

(1987), reinterpret Eve as the prototype of the woman who dares to disobey convention – who moves beyond the dilemma of obedience versus knowledge to break through to new vistas of self-awareness and authentic power. These revisions are of course troubling variants to those who wish to maintain the irrevocable and binding nature of the biblical mandate that proscribes women as inferior from the beginning.

What the reclamation of the figures of women in scripture brings to awareness is the fact that, at the time of the recording of scripture, women were considered to be the property of men. It is the attempt to vindicate women as independent ethical agents rather than objects of male legislation that marks the distinct changes in contemporary religious ethics. This is reflected in diverse ways in both Christianity and Judaism.

In Christianity, this is particularly noticeable in works that deal with sexuality. Christianity, or more particularly Catholicism, had been so preoccupied with procreation that it is only in this century that it was acknowledged that sexual relations could be an expression of mutual love and pleasure for two people who happened to be married. But perhaps the definitive parting of the ways occurred when in 1968, Pope Paul VI decided, contrary to the recommendation he had been offered by the lay advisers consulted, to forbid the use of the contraceptive pill. This was the beginning of a divide that saw many women take matters into their own hands. Since then the gap has widened on many other matters that deal with sexuality. In a recent work (1989), Anne E. Patrick, who has been the President of the Catholic Theological Society of America, examines the traditional notion of chastity with its in-built prejudice against women. In the contrasting egalitarian paradigm that she promotes, reason itself becomes appreciated as embodied – no longer the abstract instrument of a spiritually decapitated creature who strives to remain uncontaminated by corporeal connections. Within Patrick's exemplar of an equal and integrated creation, the concept of respect for all created reality is essential. This approach values a woman's body not simply as the bearer of life, but on its own grounds, where embodiment and all of its associated carnal qualities are now virtues rather than vices.

Lisa Sowle Cahill develops the communal implications of this model:

> In discussing the links between male and female embodiment and natural equality, feminist authors push the moral relevance of embodiment and its cultural shaping beyond reproductive roles. All human beings exist in spatial and material relationships which not only are constitutive of individual identity but are also the conditions of possibility of human communities and institutions (1990, p. 55).

Christine Gudorf's recent publication, *Body, Sex and Pleasure: Reconstructing Christian Sexual Ethics* (1994), develops the radical notion of respect for *bodyright* as a way of redressing the wrongs not just of religious ethics, but the treatment of human bodies in all areas of private and public life, including the military. She realizes that this will not be an easy task:

> Moving our culture toward a more complete respect for bodyright will require even more massive changes. A starting point would be for ordinary competent individuals to be understood to have complete control over their own bodies, and for such individuals to understand themselves as part of an integral human community and cosmic biosphere (1994, p. 201).

As yet, a detailed depiction and the ultimate philosophical/theological ramifications of this position are in the formative stages of articulation, but its evocations resonate with many women. For this affirmation of embodiment reflects the passion with which many women insist on not just their sexual inviolability, but also on its vital connectedness to the core of their being. Mary Daly describes this organic awareness as a biophilic energy or lust (1984), while Audre Lorde appreciates this dimension as erotic power, over and beyond simply sexual connotations:

> [Erotic power is] an assertion of the life force of woman; of that creative energy empowered, the knowledge of which we are now reclaiming in our language, our history, our dancing, our loving, our work, our lives (1984, p. 55).

Carter Heywood, a lesbian Episcopal minister, infuses this notion of erotic power with the presence of God that can be realized in loving partnerships:

> In the context of mutually empowering relationships, we come to realize that our shared experience of our power in mutual relation is sacred: that by which we are called for the more fully into becoming who we are – whole persons, whose integrity is formed in our connection with one another. And our shared power, this sacred resource of creation and liberation, is powerfully erotic (1991, p. 238).

Such modes of connection move beyond monolithic or hierarchical notions of power that are regarded as endemic to patriarchy, particularly as it has been practised in religious structures. Erotic power in its more integrated understanding of body/spirit also moves beyond the false binary system that has informed theology. In Rita Nakashima Brock's work *Journeys by Heart* (1988), the divine dimension of existence as participating in relationship is realized. As such, it is the precursor, if not the initiating impulse, of a new theology (or Christology), whereby Christ is now understood as intimately involved in the fullness of human life.

In contrast, the Jewish tradition ostensibly has not been burdened with a prejudicial bias against all things carnal. Indeed in its scriptural repertoire, the *Song of Songs*, is one of the most unabashed celebrations of sensual love ever written. But Judith Plaskow is not so sanguine in her estimation of Jewish attitudes

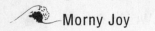

to sexuality as to infer that, as a result, women's bodies and persons have always been accorded the respect they deserve. She detects instead a profound ambivalence. This allows that, though sexuality is honoured as a gift of God, it needs to be guarded by specific restraints. These regulations strongly reinforce the suspicion that outside of marital relations, indiscriminate sexuality could lead to communal breakdown. This anxiety manifested itself particularly in the male need to harness female procreative activity to legitimate (i.e. patriarchally dictated) ends. Plaskow makes a telling comparison:

> Though Jewish attitudes toward sexuality are often contrasted favourably with Christian asceticism, one might argue that the energy the church fathers devoted to worrying about sexuality, the rabbis devoted to worrying about illicit sexuality – and with similar implications. While the desire to extirpate the sexual instinct is certainly not the same as the desire to channel and control it, both lead to a consuming focus on the difficulty of containing male sexuality, the lure of female sexuality, and strategies for circumventing sexuality's attraction and power (1990, p. 183).

In Plaskow's recommendations, she appeals to the work of Audre Lorde (1984) as well as the ethicist Beverly Wildung Harrison (1985) for a similar revaluation of sexuality that appreciates it as a dynamic element that informs all personal and communal interactions, not just genital expressions. Plaskow (1990, p. 209) also concedes that for many people today who profess themselves to be Jews, relationships are not strictly confined to those of a marital or heterosexual variety. These commitments obviously do not support the primary Jewish emphasis on progeny and, as in Christianity, acknowledgement of such sexual arrangements is controversial. In both religions, acceptance of a more inclusive appreciation of sexuality, as a dimension of connectedness to the world that embraces all types of encounters and is not restricted to propagation, needs urgently to be articulated. In their struggles to name and claim their embodied experiences, perhaps for the first time in history, women are inevitably eroding the masculinist monopoly that has previously dictated the requisite behaviour for the whole community.

And it is this area of formal legalistic training and implementation that is perhaps one of the most insurmountable barriers for women. Until very recently, women have been denied access to the training in both Christianity and Judaism (as canon lawyers and rabbis who rule on *halakhah*[10] respectively) that would qualify them as juridical experts and administrators (Adler: 1983; Biale: 1984). Small inroads have been made, but the fundamental question remains that is still a matter of great debate in both secular and religious arenas: is the law itself irretrievably hostile to women, or is it just that legal precedents and pronouncements reflect the cultural and historical condoning of the violation of women's

---

10. *Halakhah* can refer to the cumulative tradition of Jewish law, or a specific judgment on an issue.

integrity? The secular legal system itself is under intense scrutiny and review on these very issues. Until more women are in place of authority in legal procedures, whatever its provenance, the law will continue to operate to the disadvantage, if not desolation of women.

From the juridical perspective, the compensatory evocations of erotic pervasiveness may seem to some to be a rather flamboyant attempt to demonstrate women's dissatisfaction with men's single-minded and perfunctory injunctions. From another perspective, such erotic indulgences could be dismissed as simply narcissistic pretensions. What such experiential innovations represent, however, is a revolution in understanding the way that God is present in the world. In Christianity, the incarnation need no longer be reduced to arid and convoluted maxims; instead God becomes "enfleshed" in all human relationships, particularly those of an intimate nature. The poor old Church fathers are probably doing more than turning in their graves at what would appear, to their pathological distrust of the flesh, to be perversion, if not nymphomania (Ruether: 1974).

Abortion

It is against the framework of these same Church fathers that the Protestant ethicist, Beverly Wildung Harrison, introduces her discussion of abortion in the book *Our Right to Choose* (1983). Obviously the object of an incendiary reaction from conservatives, this book was written because, as Harrison remarks, so little of the heated debate surrounding abortion took into account the context of the life of the woman who was concerned with making the decision. Today's denunciations hardly differ in tone (or content for that matter) from the vituperative condemnations of the early Church.

> Nearly all extant early Christian objections to abortion, when any moral reasons were enunciated, either directly condemn wanton women (those who seek to avoid pregnancy) or denounce the triad of adulterous pleasure-oriented sex, contraception and abortion. These were undifferentiated elements in a disparaging attitude to non-procreative functional sexuality . . . grounded in what was, within Christianity, the antisensual spirituality of its most ascetic, frequently celibate theologians (1983, p. 130).

Though the higher moral ground has shifted somewhat today to incorporate an appeal to family values, Harrison is accurate when she locates the impetus for opposition to abortion in male supremacist tendencies that wish to control women's reproductive choices. In response to such unilateral posturing, Harrison does not wish to insist on individual rights on the part of women, but to emphasize their moral and creative power to inform a society's moral ethos. Harrison promotes "a consensus favouring the legal availability of safe surgical abortion", at the same time as she holds that "the act of abortion is sometimes, even frequently, a positive moral good for women" (p. 16), but she insists that a personal

decision needs to be undertaken so as to illuminate the question: "What practices and policies ought to characterize a genuinely moral or good society?" (p. 15) Harrison does not attempt to delineate specific policies, as she believes the diversity of women's situations will have their specific justifications. Her whole argument addresses the need for all women to be acknowledged in their full capacity as moral agents. This implies a thoroughgoing reformulation of cultural attitudes towards women, for Harrison contends that the tenor of so-called right-to-life policies is exacerbating the hostility toward women on which the reality of social violence against women feeds" (p. 248). Uncompromising in her indictment of not just abortion policy, but of the social and economic conditions that make abortion a necessary option for many poor women while allowing the rich the customary consolation of privilege, Harrison's work is a benchmark in contemporary Christian ethics, placing the question of abortion in the perspective of generalized societal discrimination and violence towards women.

Jewish women who reflect on the abortion issue (Greenberg: 1976; Biale: 1989; Davis: 1992), are aware that the Jewish position has not been as stringent in its opposition to abortion, particularly where the life of the mother is at stake, as in the traditional Christian view. Basically, however, the rabbinic judgments have dealt with the dangers of childbirth, not matters of contraception and pro-choice stands. In this territory the debate seems very similar to that in Christianity between liberals and conservatives, as to whether a woman has the right to determine to end a pregnancy. And here the halakhic tradition of law is of no help because the decision-making process has never included women. As Davis observes:

> If women's experiences of childbearing and childrearing were part of the halakhic data, taken on their own terms and not mediated through male sensibilities, then the results would be more credible to the women (and men) who are expected to live by them (1992, p. 322).

Such a drastic rethinking implies not just a review of the abortion issue alone, but of its location in the whole sad and sorry mess of male attitudes to female sexuality with all their accompanying expressions of violence, both social and physical in nature.

Violence Against Women

One only has to look at the issue of violence against women, where there is an inextricable mixing of religious and state interests, to realize the magnitude of the problem. Until very recently, the ubiquity of violence against women was not regarded as an issue of paramount importance. That men abused women was almost part of the natural scheme of things: clergymen sent battered wives back to violent households to perform their marital duty; incest and sexual interference with daughters or females in one's protection was condoned – in the sense that there was no appropriate and adequately sympathetic public or religious forum that could deal effectively with such situations (it was hushed up); women could be stalked and killed without protection from the law and without outcry from religious leaders; vicious pornography is tolerated. All too often legitimate complaints by women were met with malignant silence or an attitude that blamed the victim – "she must have been responsible for this".

This systemic distortion of the most pernicious type is only slowly coming to public consciousness because of the unrelenting efforts of outraged women in all areas. In a chapter entitled, "Marriages made in heaven? Battered Jewish Wives", Mimi Scarf challenges the sacrosanct image of Jewish family life that is part of a woman's upbringing. Scarf believes that this attitude instills guilt and shame so that:

> Their Jewish-family-centered socialization not only prevents such women from being prepared to defend themselves against their husbands and from believing it has happened, but makes them feel guilty and responsible for their husband's actions (1983, p. 60).

Scarf advocates recognition of this paragon of the Jewish family for what it is: "an idealized concept, a myth" (p. 63). Sophia Benjamin surveys her own experience of abuse and declares:

> Having survived a childhood in which I was powerless to defend myself or fight back against adult abuse, I see no reason to recast myself in the role of helpless child in a relationship to an omnipotent parent. The overwhelmingly images of God as a human male and especially as a father were and are completely untenable for me as a survivor of abandonment, sexual violence, and physical abuse by the father, grandfather, and stepfather present in my life (1992, p. 332).

With regard to Christianity, feminist activists (Fortune: 1983; Gudorf: 1992) have called attention to the confusion within religion (but also not absent in society at large) between sexual activity and sexual violence. This is because our sexual conditioning has reflected the prevailing view, since Biblical times, that the female is the property of the male, and that heterosexual relations have predominantly been regarded within a dominance/submission syndrome. As Karen Lebacqz stated in her presidential address to the Society for Christian Ethics:

> We are accustomed to male power because it surrounds us. However, the point of interest is not simply that men *have* power. Rather, the key factor is that male power has become *eroticized.* Men and women alike are socialized not only to think that being a man means being in control but also to find male domination sexually arousing. The overpowering of a woman is a paradigm for "normal" heterosexual relations, at least among young people and in segments of popular literature.

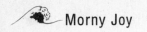

Studies of pornography demonstrate the eroticizing of domination in this culture (1990, p. 7).

Women who work in battered women's shelters often find this syndrome couched firmly in a framework of religious legitimation. Susan Brooks Thistlethwaite, a theologian and counsellor, describes her experience:

> Battered women frequently bring their religious beliefs to the process of working through a battering relationship. Phone calls to shelters often begin, "I'm a Bible-believing Christian, but . . ." We begin to develop a feminist interpretation because the Bible is part of the fabric of the oppression of battered women (1985, p. 97).

As she elaborates:

> Christian women are supposed to be meek, and claiming rights for oneself is committing the sin of pride. But as soon as battered women who hold rigidly traditional beliefs begin to develop an ideological suspicion that this violence against them is wrong, they react against it (1985, p. 99).

There are other religious feminists, however, who, while accepting the necessary strategic adoption of these procedures, do not feel they address the ultimate issue of systemic deformity that supports violence in the first place. What they advocate is major structural change – not just for the churches, but for society at large.

To achieve this, the whole tradition of a victorious Christ and the doctrine of atonement need to be jettisoned. Such a tradition has upheld a belief that suffering is redemptive and that even if one is not recompensed in this life, an eternal justification awaits in the next. In opposition to this interpretation, in their introduction to "Christianity, Patriarchy and Abuse," Joanne Carlson Brown and Carole R. Bohn state:

> We need not be saved by Jesus' death from original sin. We need to be liberated from the oppression[s] of racism, classism, and sexism, that is from patriarchy. If in that liberation process there is suffering it will be because people with power choose to use their power to resist and oppose the human claim to passionate and free life. Those who seek redemption must dare to live their lives with passion in intimate, immediate love relationships with each other, remembering times when we were not slaves (1989, p. 27).

In company with Dolores Williams (1993), the womanist theologian, Christ's death can no longer be viewed as a triumph; it is in fact a triumph of the forces of evil. Neither can the resurrection be viewed as a supernatural act of corroboration. Christ came to establish a world where justice was to prevail.

Ironically, not just the civil and religious authorities of his time conspired in its failure, but the ecclesiastical structures that have proliferated in the wake of the Jesus movement have exacerbated the problem. Whether the vision of those feminists who believe that to be a Christian today is to remain faithful to Jesus' teachings on radical justice can prevail is a moot point. What is decisive is that these women have become a conscience not just for the church itself, but for the violence that is an inevitable, and seemingly irrevocable consequence of a patriarchal hegemony.

Conclusion

Women in western societies who argue for a fundamental realignment of not just society's unjust structures, but of its ingrained habits and embedded prejudices against women, are labelled feminist and immediately consigned to the neurotic category characteristically employed to describe radicals. Pressures are brought to bear from many sectors, but most often the media, that depict these women as deviant. Yet it is interesting that, in many religions, these "deviants" are increasing in number as women realize the vehemency of the opposition to their full inclusion in mainstream religions. But these women, unlike their uneducated sisters of earlier centuries, know that men can no longer claim that they alone are made in God's image and thus have an innate prerogative to pontificate with divine impunity. And it is this move to dislodge the trappings of power that men have unjustly wielded in matters both sacred and profane, that is the common cause for all feminists, both religious and secular. The manoeuverings and defences against this sharing of resources – the derision, the offended righteousness and the blatant attempts at censure and discreditation – are tactics familiar to all feminists. But women are drawing strength from their shared agenda. This is a commitment that refuses to allow discrimination to continue and that encourages every woman to seek, affirm and share the source of her own power in egalitarian communities where no one can play God – no matter what his lineage or credentials.

Suzanne Bellamy

The Narrow Bridge of Art and Politics*

The political weaponry of linguistics has dominated the 20th century, and the naming battles of the 1990s for radical feminists are neither new nor shocking. We have swum in a sea of names, within the broad range of feminism, of Women's Liberation, of the whole phenomenon of the Women's Movement. This movement itself is only a piece of a whole, with a historic pedigree defying measurement, of voices, names, images, all equally problematic to language. Naming is part of the game. From whose tongue flows the sound, for what strategic purpose, in whose interests? If I can be named into being, can I be named out? I think not. The key is the agency of naming. Naming myself gives me extended being. Another person un-naming me just makes me mad.

I'm fussy about naming, about the relationships between dynamic changing forms and their labels. As an artist I work also in the world of the non-verbal. I know the limpness and inadequacy of descriptions by words of complex forms, thoughts and deeds in time, from sculptures to political movements to individuals. I'm fussy about my political and philosophical commitments too, re-negotiating my liberty within the whole as part of the deal. The whole process of re-negotiation is at the core of radical feminism itself, and is the principle reason why I have chosen to swim in that company for so long.

Twenty-five years is a short time to map a multi-faceted political philosophy, but a fair slice of my individual lifetime. How goes this partnership, and how would I tell its story from this place in this life? The young anarchistic artist/intellectual of twenty has become a mid-career professional artist/writer. In the myriad changes which made that happen, none feels bigger than the one I am feeling now.

There is a shift happening in the Women's Movement, a process of shedding, an emptying out and preparing new ground. I resist the premature urge

---

* Virginia Woolf. (1927/1958). "The Narrow Bridge of Art".

to label this which abounds in the reactionary critical theories of recent times. They seem to clutter the foreground noisily, with intellectually unsatisfying glibness and pompous judgement – a kind of boutique thinking, using fashion and cynicism and hands too clean for the battles of actual women.

All the philosophical systems of the planet are in a shake-down time, across all the interlocking systems of patriarchy. For a radical feminist, an archaeologist of patriarchal forms, this is a unique period of study. Fragmentation, resurgence, nostalgia, *fin de siecle* nihilism, recanting, rehashing, malaise, millenarianism, fundamentalism, various forms of cultural criticism mocking political radicalism, especially feminism – like 1930s aesthetes claiming all is narrative, nothing matters. Short memories and bad history abound in the competition to reorder the recent past, even in the Women's Movement. Turbulence of this nature touches all things, and can be creatively grasped. I choose this time to renegotiate, to find new clarity, and give full attention. What do I keep, what do I leave behind?

Women's Liberation burst into our lives, as the 60s ended, as if unique. But we quickly had to acknowledge its antecedents, to learn to recognise the core ingredients of a sporadic autonomous philosophical feminism as old as recorded history. There was rarely unity of goals, methods or language between the sectarian groups, but a great deal of invention in that fusion. Within a couple of years a coherent philosophical position emerged which sought no alliances with male ideologies or existing parties, no grafts with Marxism or socialism or liberalism, no goals of success within the dominant culture – an independent core philosophy giving primacy to women's experience, participation and visions. It was always a minority position, an irritant for many, a source point of great originality in ideas and methods. This movement came to be called *radical feminism,* and it became for me an expanding universe.

It is a truism in the Women's Movement that radical feminism has been "defined" mainly by its opponents, rarely by its adherents. From the outset the boundaries of this newly released energy defied pinning down. This is the principle reason why radical feminism attracted and nourished artists, creative writers and poets, radical philosophers, independent scholars. Unlike the dogmatic and doctrinaire belief systems and hierarchies of the old left, it seemed to embrace the eccentric, the experimental, anarchistic boundary breaking ideas and projects. And being much maligned and caricatured, it had few fellow travellers, which necessarily created great bonds of trust among us. To this movement I brought youth and optimism, hunger for a passionate struggle which demanded response from all of my senses and faculties. My baggage, even at twenty, was full of paradox: a working-class family and a middle-class education, zealous new left student politics, a fine classical education in revolutionary theory and practice, historical studies in co-operative anarchism, a distaste for socialist sectarianism and party discipline, an artist's wariness of ideologies and verbal dominance. I had an educated political desire for something new, and the youthful arrogance to find it.

I read Robin Morgan's collection of poems *Monster* (ND) in early 1973. It was electrifying. "I want a women's revolution like a lover" (p. 82). "May we comprehend that we cannot be stopped" (p. 86). "... We must all become guilty of attempted apocalypse" (p. 67).

Here was a language new yet utterly familiar, here was a poet/activist working on the boundary of art and politics. It transformed my life. Artists are traditionally an "endangered species" in political movements, and I have never forgotten this in all my years of activism. Revolutionary movements historically mistrust, misuse and often murder their artists – unable otherwise to control the creative spirit, valuing poor graphics more than new forms. And while the Women's Movement charted new territory, we were all carrying old ways. I was a passionate participant, a hard-working activist, but I was also my own authority, committed ultimately to my own spirits and demons, my own story. If there was no breathing space for that process, it did not work for me. This was the first meaning of the personal is political. For radical feminism, this is still the first principle. What do I keep, what do I leave behind?

On reflection, I see I have required a number of other core ethical principles for my participation. "Freedom from unreal loyalties", Virginia Woolf's theme in *Three Guineas* (1938/1966), helped to free me from excessive devotion to the work and ideas of others – to maintain some detachment – and alerted me to the subtle evils of zealotry and idolatry. We used heady language, words that could send you, dreams that could knock you off your feet, passions that could fling your brains up a tree, visceral dynamite. Idealism floated on lust, jealousy, rage. The lid had been taken off an imposed patriarchal rationalism, and the jewels tumbled from the chest. Again Virginia Woolf helped me. She described her madness as her brains exploding like fireworks. In the ashes were her core ideas. But first it was necessary to survive the explosion. Could this long repressed and controlled desire in women be let out without casualties? It seemed not. I learned a sense of balance through hard work and difficult experience, and managed to balance a great capacity for devotion with equal mistrust for elites, and an old old wariness of betrayal. An independent mind had to be worked for vigilantly, as much within radical feminism as anywhere. This I also keep.

An enduring principle flowing from this was the insistence that we are peers, equals. Diversity, freedom to experiment, life-affirming flexibility, self-mockery, heresy, humour. The genius of Mary Daly exemplifies this principle. I still remember the thrill of reading the last section of *Beyond God the Father* (1973), when it was published, my heart shifting. In all her works to date I know I am in the presence of someone so cerebrally original that I can only try to meet the work halfway – like coming to a great painting, and returning to see new depths. I would say that a lot of my art work has been deeply influenced by Mary Daly's works, but in inexplicable ways to me, as yet. I came to the work not from a Catholic background, nor even a philosophic background, and I came with self-confidence. While *Gyn/Ecology* (1978) was most widely read and fought about, it was her great work *Pure Lust* (1984) which astounded me. Here was creative and intellectual liberty on the most exotic journey. I could not conceive that there were women alive in the time of this kind of writing and thinking who did not read her. Her work heightened my sense of perfect timing, being in, of, and for my time.

There was a sense of abundance, of choice, of a kaleidoscope for the imagination, not locked away in some eccentric abbey of illumination, but side by side with our work on the ground – of economic struggle, birth control, sexual slavery, genetic manipulation, child abuse, refuges, rape, domestic violence, racism, genocidal rape, war. Real women, real lives, real struggles - radical feminists do not go off into an elusive theory and forget their activism, but balance action with the exploration of new ideas and forms wherever we are drawn. There were no limits to the new territories. And this was another core principle, being prepared to risk going to unlikely places to find what you needed to know, and making the process visible.

I came to realise this was very important, seeing the process, seeing the journey, keeping only the best – a creative shake-out. This emphasised again the theme of experiment, shedding, letting things go, inventing while going along, visible movement in thought. This is the key to lasting, to recreating the self. This may be my most precious tool, and I keep that too.

It was around the time of the end of the 70s when I settled more consciously on a personal way of being in the Women's Movement, which maximised my pleasure, my education and my room to move. It occurred to me that we were on an epic/comic journey not unlike *The Canterbury Tales* (1951), and that I was not only of the party but able to watch it, move about within it, and picture it in my work. Having had the great benefit of a classical historical education and a rich imagination, my brain effortlessly releases images of other times and places, real and ridiculous. It's like a tap. I began in earnest my enjoyable career watching my peers and associates, body language, posturings, idiosyncrasies, reading through lenses of other imagined periods, past and future. Some of this went into clay figures and salon studies, lots into my journals for future work.

I decided to explore the idea of a women's culture as an imaginative construct. Perhaps there had been one, perhaps not. That wasn't the point. A retrospective dream still has potency if it informs the actions of the present, and it was clear to me that this idea was welling up in women across cultures. I also knew the archaeological literature and the problematic reinterpretations which began to mesh with the dreams of a women's culture. In this imaginary culture I created for myself the imaginary role of an artist/scholar who could be witness, commentator, creator of dynamic artefacts and stories, and most importantly traveller on the trade routes which crisscrossed the geography of this rich hypothetical Reality. At this point I have devoted several years of my life to this creative experiment. It differs from a play/performance only in that there are no seats and tickets, no script, and it cannot be repeated, being pure improvisation.

The gatherings of the 1970s (marches, conferences, meetings) gave way to the more absorbing experiments of the 80s and 90s. Festivals, craftings, longmarches, peace camps, NGO forums, village setups where 24-hour-a-day living in groups allowed the new geography of women's culture to sprout and tantalise memory and imagination. I started making things for this culture (artefacts), and images of it (figures, journey sculptures, maps). Women appeared to adopt this work, feeling it authentically belonged in the wider world and had meaning for them. One thing led to another, one place led to another, oceans, deserts, cities, farms, other lands, other languages. Finally I worked for five years in a row as an artist at the Michigan Womyn's Music Festival as a long-crew worker. Eight hundred women work for five weeks preparing for the arrival of up to 10,000 women who come to the festival, the biggest village cultural gathering of mainly lesbians on the planet. My trade routes were expanding, my sails full.

It seemed to me that certain women on this planet were behaving in most remarkable ways, expressing in palpable forms the shapes and behaviour of independent women's culture, for short periods usually focussed on great projects or events. Not only great gatherings like Michigan, which has lasted twenty years, but smaller regional festivals and gatherings ring the planet, linking women in grids of common purpose, knowledge of which seems mysteriously not to bridge back to the world they leave and to which they return. I know there is a certain cynicism among some feminists that these events are goddess-cult-magic-lost-crazywomen backwaters, but this is a real misreading of the phenomenon, where diversity rules, and it is possible to explore and express a new potency. Not in themselves expressions of radical feminism *per se*, they nonetheless base themselves on the principle of women's space, creative invention of new ways, and pleasure in community. It was within these new spaces that I began to experiment further, running workshops to collect stories and images for my work.

My first observation about these gatherings of community was that they were transitory, that it seemed impossible to conceive of them going on without end, without a clear time-frame and focus. This was not "life" as it were, so much as an experimental space from which women returned to the battles, the issues, the campaigns. Nor were these experiments in culture to be read as utopian. All the dilemmas were visible, and in fact made more available for investigation. Those issues not so easily named in the 1970s and early 80s could no longer be hidden, including violence between women, the promotion of sado-masochism in the lesbian community, profitmaking businesses trading off the free labour and idealism of women, the influence of New Age slick commercialism, battery, sexual abuse, disease, drugs, showbiz hypocrisy, cultural appropriation, and a pervading racism and class elitism. I have sat in huge democratic community meetings of women in which all of the above were named in some form, as well as the problems of paper plates, sewage and plumbing. If nothing is resolved, also nothing is ultimately unnamed. Such is the many-headed figure of a wounded people.

Paradox abounds; idealism shadowed by greed, great creative image-making and debased symbols and fetishes. I invented the term "house matriarchal" (as in house wine or house music) to describe the creation of an embarrassing array of simplified borrowed and repeated images – ultimately often clichés from a splendid archaeological heritage. The research of Marija Gimbutas (1974 and 1989) and other archaeologists, since the Catal Hüyük discoveries of the 1960s, covering many ancient cultures, have not only inspired many artists, but sometimes fed a commercial fetish market which has thrived in the Women's Movement. The new hunger for non-verbal symbols and images grew faster than the ability of artists to respond with integrity and authenticity. Bad taste and cultural theft exist in the same spaces as thrilling new music, new images, new words.

What also flourished was a therapeutic profession and healing industry with the same extremes of creative original work and also ill-trained profiteering. Just like *The Canterbury Tales*, we have it all – and all of it needs to be seen with clarity, and with critical generosity. There is no future in despairing or railing against this mix. Take the long view, find a point of personal balance, and weigh in.

I invented a series of information gathering and sharing workshops, which were intended to posit certain core constructs of my imaginary geography. They were presented with a lot of humour, in the pinch-of-salt tradition. "Sustainable Lesbian Culture in the Twenty-First Century" worked off the ecology-based notion of diversity as strength, and the efficient use of physical and spiritual resources. It addressed the damaging wound carried by many lesbians that we have no "natural" place in the ecology of our planet. What is our work, how can we work in community, how can we address our own wounding and that of our planet, as lesbians? In an imaginary journey format, we visited the Council of Old Laughing Women. "What is my job?" each woman sought an answer, based on the conviction that each woman *has* cultural/political work which can only be done by her. Humour and a little healthy scepticism were crucial ingredients. In the spirit of Mary Leakey, I named our people Lesbia Sapiens Magnificata. The report-back storytelling after these journeys, in big circles, hundreds of women over time, was amazing to me, rich diverse knowledge and revelation, poignant and hilarious.

The "Lesbian Passion Play" workshop worked from the old medieval miracle and passion plays, asking the core question, "What is the Lesbian Life Cycle?" Traditional passion plays, which move in actual landscape, invoke agricultural cycles to embody the magical year and stages of life from birth to death, and are invariably heterosexual and patriarchal. Again I wanted to put the lesbian and the woman in the sacred landscape, belonging to the planet, enduring a life cycle of great turning points, passion, pain and transformation, as lesbians, in an ecologically ethical sustainable landscape. The wounded link between the spiritual and the erotic in women, planetary agency was again the focus.

I moved my own studio to an Australian rural landscape in 1983. When not moving about among women, I spent long periods alone in the bush, thinking about land, animals and water. Animal workshops which flowed out of this included the series on "Ants", which were very funny to do. I have been studying ants and their sculptural mounds, journeys and communities for a long time. Thinking about them raises lots of useful themes for women – about ordered community, collective work, repair, commitment to enormous journeys. It's amazing what grown women will do in the pursuit of knowledge and a good time. Ant sisterhood was born! Underlying all these experiments was my own deepest question, did we have memory of another way to live, another time frame? Was it possible to speak of neurological patterns of prior knowledge, could we imagine a transformation that our brains could make real?

It goes almost without saying that radical feminist experiments often require the risk of making a fool of yourself. In fact I have found the role of the Fool my mainstay in this work, and the political use of comic energy crucial to independent thinking. The path of the Fool can be perilous in a play without an audience. But by now I had crossed "the narrow bridge" of art and politics, myth and reality. I was in the imaginary culture as much as anyone, generating and generated by the released energy.

If radical feminism is a process of moving thought – not ideology, not fixed form, not static philosophy – was I in the flow? Could I claim that my sculptures and earth works, my workshops, stories, and observations were part of an emergent pattern of women's knowledge, or eccentric individual expressions? This unanswerable question brings me again to the initial attempt in radical feminism to fuse art and politics, thought and feeling, and to imagine the possibility of women grasping our life force in our own two hands. *Where Do Ideas Come From?* is the name of a recent sculpture I made of my own hands, old land forms with my lifelines at 45, the fingertips transforming into figures of women in rapt connection with each other. Like the many huge boatloads of women I have also made over the years, I see here the attempt to invoke the company of women, and yet know that it only works if each one is uniquely charged with difference. There's the risk and the reward on the road to Canterbury or anywhere else.

"Boat", Porcelain, 1991, 40cm x 25cm.
Photo: Suzanne Bellamy

Virginia Woolf, in "The Narrow Bridge of Art" (1927/1958) faces the difficulty for artists who, in trying to do their work, must invent a form which can hold all they have to pour out. "The mind is full of monstrous, hybrid, unmanageable emotions . . . It is in this atmosphere of doubt and conflict that writers have now to create." (p. 12)

She talks about "a vague mysterious thing called an attitude to life." Artists can "stand at an uncomfortable angle whence they see everything askew", or they can "use their faculties to the full upon things that are of importance . . ." Those who do, "seem alive all over . . . They grasp something hard; when they come into action they cut real ice." (p. 13)

Creative thought and ideas cut ice within radical feminism because the narrow bridge exists. I can do my work, we can do our work, alone, in studios, at desks, and there is still a fine thread of agreement, of peers and common purpose. The bridge has synaptic strength but, like individuals, needs constant renewal.

In 1991, I made a series of clay figures called *What Is This Thing We Keep Holding Up?*, women in the habit of bearing a great weight, shaped by their burdens, but on the edge of wondering why. It could be read as the layer upon layer of habit supporting the weight of patriarchy, but it actually came from my own questions about feminism itself. I had been moving among a generation of feminists who were expressing resentful tiredness, about keeping newsletters going, courses running, keeping journals appearing, keeping projects afloat, struggling with a malaise of energy and vision. Duty and responsibility drove out passion and renewal.

"I want a women's revolution like a lover" (Morgan: ND, p. 82), not a burned out affair. I started asking questions about this widespread feeling, and found common threads – a holding on to outmoded forms, structures, words and ideas, a fear that if projects were ended we would return to a bleak past of nothing for women – and in some women a sense of failure, a despair that some of the great experiments of the 70s and 80s had withered and died, failing to bridge to new generations of younger women. Like the baby and the bathwater, some parts of this mattered more than others. A generational shift can be fearful, and it is hard to cop some of the ageism, and intentionally wounding rhetoric of the wishful "post-feminism". But opposition is not new, and it is only internal dilemmas which create weakened will. I know from my own journeys that women in their late teens and early twenties care passionately for radical change. Among my work crew at Michigan, I was, at only forty-five, the oldest woman, which was an exhilarating experience for me who had always been younger than my peers in the 1970s. When I was twenty I was allowed a hearing – now I find I am equally thrilled by the explorations of young radical women. As Virginia Woolf said, it has something to do with "a vague mysterious thing called an attitude to life" (1927/1955, p. 12).

As an artist I had to learn a long time ago how to let go of what I made, to empty out the space so that the next thing could emerge. It's a horrible business but it's part of the deal. The dilemma of feminism historically is *itself* – forever being seemingly interrupted by cross-currents of hostile forces, just as we get started. It's the same in an individual life cycle. Never enough time.

There is however another point of view, in which we can read malaise as an unfamiliarity with the deeper processes of change, and of letting go. Here is an opportunity to learn to do this well. What do I keep, what do I leave behind?

At the Nairobi Women's Conference in 1985, I felt a sudden sense of insignificance as 25,000 women from mainly Third World countries took on the questions of food, water, hunger, genital mutilation, genocide, racial oppression, illiteracy, sexual slavery, global biocide. This crushed sense of self was a real educational corrective, which renewed my commitments and my energy. I had witnessed women sit down to the business of the planet, women's business. This business has not stopped, and I have my work within that, as we all do. It takes a great many ants a very long time to move a very large object even a very little way. There is no mileage in being daunted, in panic, or in cynicism and mockery.

There have always been organised forms of opposition to feminism and the political expressions of women. The current labelling frenzy within some parts of post-modernism carry on the tradition of straw figure mockery, the cult of youth, the posturing of an old aestheticism. In fact artists have much to be concerned about here, as did Virginia Woolf in the 1930s when she wrote *Three Guineas* in a similar time of backlash cloaked in critic-driven theory. Critic-driven culture is like fast-food, it fails to nourish the creative spirit. Artists have become again an endangered species in the domain of the post-modern.

We are living in a time of great shift, perilous and thrilling.

What do I keep, what do I leave behind?

I keep my tools, my stories, my memory, my clarity. I keep the lives of actual women in clear view. I keep my commitment to the idea of women's spaces, women's business. I exercise the muscles of my brain, I expand my neurological patterns, I follow the fault lines of change, I hold divinity in my own life, I continue to integrate wounded and fractured parts of myself. I respect our elders and our young, recognising threads in the differences.

I leave all the work, all the projects, all the little points of certainty. I will always wonder who we are, as a gender, as a species, as a planet, going where? And as for that women's revolution? She is not for keeping or for leaving, she is for loving, which is another matter altogether.

Angela Bowen

Take Your Pageant and Shove It

When I was growing up in the 40s in Roxbury – which was then in the middle of its transformation into the black ghetto that we know today – the whites who were left to exist side by side with us were only bitter that they had not yet managed to escape. The apartments were just this side of shabby, not quite respectable or desirable by their standards. For us, they were a cut above what many working-class blacks could afford or expect. So, when they ran, it made more room for us.

The recent crowning of the first black Miss America reminds me of that situation – when whites have had their fill of something, stuffed themselves with all the richest part of it and thrown the leavings to the poor blacks, who ought to be glad to get it, whatever shape it's in. Just as they throw us their left-over food, their worn-out clothing, their run-down neighborhoods where everything is left in disrepair in preparation for us, so they have handed over a beauty pageant that has seen far better days – thanks to those feminists who descended on Atlantic City back in 1968 to let the world know the shame of women on display.

So now that white America has ODed on beauty contests, any young black woman can dare to dream of walking that runway at Convention Hall before 25,000 people, crying tears of joy, as did Vanessa Williams, our first black Miss America on Saturday, September 17, 1983.

The tears that stream down a woman's face when she wins such a contest certainly belong there. But the tears from a black woman ought to make deep, deep tracks indeed. Oh, have we not been on that auction block for centuries already? We've had our bodies examined and exposed from every conceivable angle – legs, teeth, breasts, and buttocks. White American women came happily to the block in 1922, the year of the first Miss America pageant. Black women were onstage that year also – portraying slaves in a show included as entertainment in the pageant.

For three decades black women were officially excluded as participants until the ban was lifted in the late 50s. In 1970, Cheryl Brown of Iowa was the first

black to enter, followed by eleven others since then. This year, pageant officials set out to find an acceptable black, and discovered Vanessa Williams onstage in a production at Syracuse University, where she is a junior majoring in theater and planning to take on Broadway when she graduates. According to the *Los Angeles Times*, they urged her into the contest, whereupon she took the New York state prize, and sailed to victory in Atlantic City. For many beautiful and talented black women who have made a career of contests, but who couldn't get to first base even in their own state pageants, this must have been a bitter pill to swallow. But according to Vanessa, who says she had never even thought about entering a contest before, "I was chosen because I was qualified for the position. The fact that I was black was not a factor." Interestingly, the first runner-up, Suzette Charles of New Jersey was also black. There appears to be a clear mandate that this was to be the year of the black woman.

Although Vanessa at 20 can be forgiven her naivete, don't we have a right to expect more than the delight expressed by some of our leading black figures?

"It is good that another of America's *cultural institutions* [emphasis added] has ripped off the curtain that excluded American women who are young, gifted and black", said Joseph Lowry, of the Southern Christian Leadership Conference in the *Los Angeles Times*.

"I am delighted. It's exciting at a time when we do find separation of the races that her color was not a factor, and her talent won", said Charles Rangel, congressman from New York in the *Amsterdam News*.

Shirley Chisolm has known sexism at its greatest heights. Yet she, who couldn't convince her own black male colleagues to support her clearly symbolic bid for the presidency, said, "My first reaction is that the inherent racism in America must be diluting itself." She told another reporter: "Because it didn't put bread on the table, people might say, 'So what?' But the event was not trivial because it shows in a sense that the country, for whatever the motivation might be, seems to be trying desperately to move toward a more equalitarian set of circumstances."

Another woman who has long fought for black rights, Dorothy Height, president of the National Council of Negro Women, said: "I think it is a very proud moment to witness – to know they will be given equal opportunity, that has meaning to everyone." There was a more considered and restrained approach from Benjamin Hooks, executive director of the NAACP: "Miss Williams' selection will also wake up America to the tragedy of excluding blacks from the competitive arenas of life like law, medicine and physics."

But a vociferous attack came from the Congress of Racial Equality (CORE), whose spokesman, Roy Innis, called the selections a "bittersweet victory" and a "small step forward, a giant step backward". In his carefully worded statement, he made the case that Vanessa Williams is a light-skinned, green-eyed beauty, hardly your traditional black woman with kinky hair, thick lips, and a dark complexion. These "ironic selections", according to CORE, are supposed to bring long-term damaging effects to the self-image of "truly" black women. He went on to say, "In one broad, insidious and far from accidental blow, the Miss America pageant denigrated and attempted to cancel out much [sic] of the gains of the 1960s 'Black is Beautiful' movement."

Although Innis condemned the victory, he was particularly careful not to condemn the woman herself, stating that he spoke for the grassroots community and was issuing his statement "in the cause of true (honest) black unity." Score five points for Innis' understanding that the achievement was hollow indeed. But he seemed to be saying that if a "truly" black woman had won, all would be well. Leave aside his contention that only women of a certain type can be considered "truly" black. We understand his point, but let us refuse to squabble among ourselves over skin color, hair texture, or fineness of features; too many years and tears, and entirely too much of our energy has been wasted on that madness. The real tragedy is that Innis and all the rest still missed the essential point.

Such an issue, which cuts across the whole spectrum of black lives, gives black spokespersons a national forum to take a moral position and give black consciousness a new direction. It's disturbing that the leading black figures had a chance to speak out on a degrading practice and failed to do so. Shirley Chisolm is right; this is not a trivial issue. But the point is: WE SHOULD NOT BE PLAYING THIS GAME, PERIOD! When you join someone else's game, you play by their rules. White men don't see African-looking black women as beautiful. So what? Not only is it self-defeating to attempt to change their sense of beauty, but we should assure them that this is one bit of the leftover mess that we will not pick up.

As it begins to dawn on white males that those are their daughters and sisters they are putting up there on display, as it begins to sink in ever so slowly that it's not nice to display women like that, now it becomes our turn. When do we decide that they can't buy us like that any more? I'm glad that a *black* black woman didn't win. I'm glad that they don't consider us beautiful enough. If we get ourselves together, maybe by the time they get around to us, we'll have enough pride, as blacks and as women, to say, "Thanks, but no, thanks".

Black people living here must find ways to make it work for us. We need fun and games too. But allowing the white man to lead us willingly up the aisle to pick up that tacky, disheveled crown that white women of any thought, taste, or sensibility are beginning to discard, makes no sense at all. Let's leave it there. In fact, let's help white women stomp it into the ground.

Originally published in *Villlage Voice* (1983, November 8).

II

RADICAL FEMINISTS

UNDER ATTACK

Marcia Ann Gillespie

The Posse Rides Again

Maybe it was the weather in the USA this winter. Snowstorms practically every week in some places, an earthquake in Los Angeles. Maybe it started with the floods last summer, those forty days of rain, all that muck and ooze. Maybe there was a disharmonic convergence: Mars in blue flux, Jupiter in slide, Mercury in retro-retrograde. How else to explain not only that feminism had become a big topic of discussion by too many of the wrong people in all the usual places, but also that even some feminists were talkin' *weird*.

A few years ago the media and the "experts" proclaimed the post-feminist era, the implication being that women had moved beyond feminism and/or that here in the good ole USA, women were all doing peachy-keen. No sooner had Anita Hill burst that backlash bubble, than out came all that "radical feminist equals antifamily, anti-God-and-country" attack-yak again.

But then suddenly last spring, the "feminism is passé" posse moved into high gear. This time the tack was that the movement was nothing more than one big pity party, where we gathered to wallow in our victimization and trade tales of woe. They trucked out a twentysomething "Paglia-ette" who'd written a book that supposedly proved the point [Katie Roiphe]. Of course the "feminist friendly" media lapped up her assertion that date rape on college campuses is blown way out of proportion mainly because too many girls can't tell the difference between bad sex and rape, or worse, they make it all up to garner sympathy from Take Back the Night feminists.

Come autumn, we were being called victim feminists not only by our foes but also by some of our sisters. Next came odes on "why feminism has failed" because it's "too white, too dyke, too radical, too combative . . ." On the heels of that came a men's magazine's discovery of a "new" breed of feminists, who worship men and adore sex – or is it worship sex and adore men? Or is just do sex? Forget those "feminazis", make way for the "Do Me's" – in other words, Girls Who Gotta Have It.

By the time the earth quit quaking and the snow falling, there were so many different discussions going on that I began to lose track. Were we feminazi, man-hating, penis-cutting, pity-partying, hopelessly confused, victim-loving crybabies? Or were we male-adoring, sex-obsessed, muscle-flexing powerhouses? And then, lo and behold, the next thing I knew the hot question making the rounds was "Has the movement become too divisive?" Followed by "Why can't you all focus on a single issue? Why so many different agendas?" So the one-note sobsisters of the summer were by winter's end an orchestra playing different tunes out of synch.

Frankly, all this "attention" was beginning to work my last nerve.

And then with spring only a few days old, along came one of the newsmagazines with the cover story "The War Against Women" – about time, I would say. I expected that they would write about violence, poverty, and abuse as if they'd just discovered something none of us had heard of before. OK, fine, I say to myself, as long as the issues are being raised. But those smug hypocrites acted as if we were part of the problem. First they do the "Critics charge that mainstream feminism hasn't done enough for women in poverty", and then in their conclusion the writers declare, "Now that American feminists are looking beyond abortion, their priorities may be more relevant to the forgotten women at home and overseas."

So to add insult to injury, feminists haven't done enough about poverty and have ignored the "forgotten women". Twenty-some years of work to raise the issues of poverty and abuse and violence and battery and rape just don't count. I'll be damned. I guess we've just been sitting around contemplating our navels. Maybe Ronald Reagan and George Bush never happened.

Well, what's next? Perhaps a feminazi, do me, pity-partying, abortion-driven, forgetful-of-forgotten-women, divisive, one-dimensional, radical, mainstream, muscle-flexing, power-hungry, antifamily conspiracy to put all the men in the USA on Prozac? Or maybe we'll be told of the discovery of FFMS – the False Feminist Memory Syndrome – caused by "victim feminists" brainwashing women into believing that they've been cheated, mistreated, and abused, and that the FFMS Foundation has been launched to organize Give Up the Night marches.

Originally published as an Editorial in *Ms. Magazine* (1994, May–June).

Diane Richardson

"Misguided, Dangerous and Wrong"[1] on the Maligning of Radical Feminism

Despite its richness and diversity, radical feminist thought is frequently caricatured, criticised and marginalised. Its most vigorous critics include socialist feminists, sexual libertarians, former radical feminists and more recently both lesbians and gay men associated with queer and post-structuralist theory. What are their main criticisms?

Recognising Radical Feminism: Now You See It, Now You Don't

One of the most common misreadings of radical feminist thinking is that it is essentialist; that it locates the source of women's subordination in female biology and/or male biology. For example, although they state that not all radical feminists accept "biological theories", British sociologists Pamela Abbot and Claire Wallace nonetheless feed this caricature of radical feminism as biologically determinist when they claim in their introduction to feminist perspectives in sociology that:

> Women's oppression is seen as rooted in women's biological capacity for motherhood or in the innate, biologically determined aggression of the male, as manifested in rape (1990, p. 12).

The supposed essentialism of radical feminist perspectives can be seen, in part, as the outcome of a tendency, which in some cases would seem to be deliberate, to reduce the diverse strands of radical feminist thought to a relatively few sources. For instance, Shulamith Firestone's *The Dialectic of Sex*, first published in 1970, is still frequently cited twenty-five years later as if it were representative of what is termed the radical feminist "position". Although issues of sexuality and

---

1. The title is prompted by Gayle Rubin's piece, of the same name, in Gillian Rodgerson and Elizabeth Wilson (1991) *Pornography and Feminism: The Case Against Censorship.*

reproduction remain central to radical feminist theorising in the nineties, few radical feminists nowadays would agree with Firestone's view that gender divisions are the outcome of natural biological differences between the sexes.

Other works, frequently used to illustrate early radical feminism, include Kate Millett (1970), Mary Daly (1978), Susan Brownmiller (1975/1976), Christine Delphy (1984), Monique Wittig (1979, 1981) and Adrienne Rich (1977, 1980). While these are all important works, to cite them repeatedly becomes problematic, especially in the absence of little or no discussion of more recent radical feminist writing. Often one could be forgiven for thinking that, with a few exceptions, radical feminist writers are a thing of the past. I am not suggesting that feminist texts from the seventies and early eighties have no relevance for feminist theory and practice today, rather I am pointing out that one mechanism by which contemporary feminists can discredit and dismiss radical feminism is through claiming it is outdated and therefore old-fashioned. Also, in addition to potentially undermining the assumed relevance of radical feminism for contemporary debates and issues, this limited list suggests radical feminist views exist in a rather narrow range.

One important consequence of this tacit stereotyping of radical feminists is that it ignores important differences among writers. It is little wonder then that radical feminism gets caricatured as "monolithic"! In fact, there are many kinds of radical feminists and a wide variety of radical feminist theories. As Carol Anne Douglas remarks in the introduction to her review of radical and lesbian feminist theories:

> What is radical feminism? A whole book seems scarcely long enough to delimit radical feminism. It is hard to find one single definition that encompasses radical feminism, and lesbian feminism, which has stemmed from it (1990, p. 1).

Even whilst acknowledging the often monolithic and out-dated portrayal of radical feminism, I still have to say that the characterising of radical feminist analyses as "essentialist" has always struck me as very odd (not to mention irritating), especially in relation to sexuality. Although some feminists writers have alluded to an essential female/male nature, they are not typical of radical feminist theories. Those few among feminists (generally) who appear to be arguing for essential differences between the "sexes" include some American feminists, such as Carol Gilligan (1982),[2] who argues that women and men have different moral sensibilities; some eco-feminists and some following the work of French feminists such as Luce Irigaray (1985) who, whilst herself denying the charge of essentialism, has prompted investigation into the specificity of a feminine writing (l'écriture féminine), culture and sexuality. Within most radical feminist writing it is abundantly clear that sexuality and gender difference is understood to be socially

---

2. Gilligan has herself consistently denied the charge of essentialism, see, for example, the preface to the 1993 edition of *In a Different Voice*.

constructed, not biologically determined, and that, contrary to what many seem to want to believe, radical feminists have consistently challenged essentialist conceptions of sexuality and women (see, for example, Coveney *et al.*: 1984; Dworkin: 1987; Richardson: 1992).

Where the basis in social constructionism is recognised, radical feminists are sometimes accused of a different form of essentialism. In Ann Ferguson's view:

> Though these social constructionist theories may not technically be biologically essentialist, they are still a form of social essentialism: that is, they assume a social divide between male and female sexual natures which is unconvincingly universal, static and ahistorical (1989, p. 54).

Once again, and acknowledging the relativity of the terms constructionist/essentialist such criticisms are frankly misplaced.[3] Most radical feminist analyses recognise the social variability of sexuality in different social and historical contexts. They do not see female and male sexuality as pre-given and unchanging and, therefore, offering little hope for women's liberation. On the contrary, central to radical feminist perspectives is the belief that if sexuality is socially constructed, then it can be reconstructed in new and different ways; sexuality need not be coercive or oppressive, it can be challenged and changed.

The construction of radical feminism as essentialist is nothing new. However, in recent years the increasing influence of post-modernist ideas within feminism (and the media) has revitalised this perception of radical feminism as essentialist in its attempts to theorise women's oppression. Most feminist post-modernists, along with some Marxist and Black feminists, regard the use of the notion of "patriarchy" as problematically essentialist. Many post-modernists also label radical as well as other feminists as essentialist for their use of the categories "woman" and "man". Such critiques stem from emphasis within post-modernism on deconstructing these categories in order to demonstrate that they are "regulatory fictions" which have no fixed, consistent, unitary meaning, rather than natural categories. In this respect Stevi Jackson is right to ask, "So what's new?" Most radical feminists assume the category woman is socially constructed and recognise its diverse meanings, being "just as concerned as any post-modernist to challenge essentialist conceptions of women" (Jackson: 1992, p. 28).

Indeed, although it is rarely acknowledged, many of the ideas associated with post-modernism are products of radical feminist thinking: the idea of knowledge as contextual and situated; the recognition of the importance of

---

3. In her book *Essentially Speaking*, Diana Fuss (1990) makes the point that essentialism and social constructionism are not two distinct and opposing terms. These are relative terms (though I would suggest it may make more sense to talk of theories being more or less essentialist than more or less constructionist) and it may be more helpful to think of a social constructionist/essentialist continuum along which theorists may be placed.

language in constructing difference; the questioning of notions of "truth" and "the self" as unitary and consistent. The important difference, of course, is that within post-modernism women are in danger of being deconstructed out of existence. Instead of rejecting such categories, radical feminists continue to argue that, however diverse and varied our experiences may be, women exist as a political and as a socially constructed category whose lives are materially shaped by belonging to that category.

If some critics have misread radical feminism as essentially essentialist, conceptualising sexuality as universal and unchanging, others have accused radical feminism of over-emphasising the possibilities for change and the potential for transforming our sexual practices and ideas about sexuality. In this case the charge is one of voluntarism, that radical feminists have simply assumed that sexual practices and desires can be changed through our individual efforts, ignoring the social and economic constraints to "choice". Such criticisms seem particularly unfair when one considers the groundbreaking work of Adrienne Rich (1980) and other radical feminists since (see, for example, Jeffreys: 1990; Wilkinson and Kitzinger: 1993; Richardson: 1995) who have written about ways in which hetero-sexuality is socially instituted and maintained, creating the prescriptions and the conditions in which women experience sexual relations. Similarly, although lesbianism has been written about as a political choice, the possibility of women living independently of men is also acknowledged to be socially and economically determined (Jeffreys: 1990).

As well as being misrepresented, in particular as essentialist, moralistic, unconcerned with race and class issues, radical feminism is often ignored in published accounts of feminist theory and feminism's history. An example of the omission of radical feminist thinking in British feminist accounts is Terry Lovell's (1990) *British Feminist Thought* and Maggie Humm's *Feminism Reader* (1992). Alternatively, radical feminism may be portrayed as history, as a "spent force" in feminist politics.

An example of this form of erasure is Alice Echols' (1989) book *Daring To Be Bad: Radical Feminism in America* 1967–1975, in which it is suggested that radical feminism ceased to exist as a movement in the United States after the mid seventies, evolving into what Echol's labels "cultural feminism" (see Cameron: 1993) for a fuller discussion). Echols distinguishes the two in the following way:

> In the terminology of today, radical feminists were typically social constructionists who wanted to render gender irrelevant, while cultural feminists were generally essentialists who sought to celebrate femaleness ... whereas radical feminists were anti-capitalist – if often only implicitly – cultural feminists dismissed economic class struggle as "male" and, therefore, irrelevant to women (1989, pp. 6–7).

Echols acknowledges that others would use the term contemporary radical feminism rather than cultural feminism, and that those she labels as cultural feminists would most likely call themselves radical feminists. Thus we have radical feminism, post 1975, identified once again as essentialist and unconcerned with class issues.

A serious consequence of this kind of misrepresentation and over-simplification of radical feminist thinking is that radical feminists are dismissed as out-dated, misguided or, at best, theoretically naive and unsophisticated. Such stereotypic assumptions implicitly inform accounts which single out radical feminism for being too simplistic, especially in relationship to its "oversimplified conception of power and of gender . . ." (Hollway: 1993, p. 412). Thus, for example, in her review of *The Real Facts of Life* by Margaret Jackson (1994), Paula Bartley comments that, "To her credit, Jackson is too sophisticated a radical feminist to see women as a homogenous group" (1994, p. 28).

What this implies is that radical feminists are not usually sophisticated in their analysis, in particular of differences among women. It is ironic that one of the consequences of oversimplification and overgeneralization of radical feminism is the encouragement of a belief that radical feminism tends to ignore differences among women. In particular, that it is insensitive to race and class issues, as well as other forms of inequality. Writing on the radical feminist critique of new reproductive technologies, Elaine Denny comments that:

> The radical feminist tendency to treat women as a homogeneous group, universally oppressed and passive, and to treat all relationships with men as exploitative, leads to an oversimplification of the issues. One way this is manifested is in the widely held feminist assumption that the experience of women as an oppressed group has led to similarities in all women that outweigh differences of class, colour, ability, etc. (1994, p. 75).

I would not want to claim that radical feminism has, in the past, dealt adequately with class, ethnic variation and racism, because I do not believe it has. But then no other brand of feminism has either! Where I disagree is with the suggestion that radical feminism is inherently more likely than other forms of feminism to result in a denial of the different interests between, especially, Black and white women. For example, in a paper which raises critical questions about the racism embedded within contemporary feminist thought, Kum-Kum Bhavnani argues that

> . . . a position such as that which is the basis of all forms of radical feminism, and which urges all women to unite as "sisters" against the patriarchy, is the one that is the most likely to lead to a Denial of differing and contradictory interests between Black and white women (1993, p. 34).

The argument seems to be that in claiming women are universally oppressed through patriarchy, differences between women and the existence of other forms of oppression (and their interconnection with gender) are likely to be ignored or marginalised. However, the "universalism of women's oppression" and the theorisation of "difference between women" are two different issues. As Jackie Stacey points out:

> ... the two debates, that of universalism and that of differences between women, cannot simply be mapped on to each other: For example, plenty of feminist theory which is not claiming the universality of women's oppression can be challenged for its racist assumptions, and likewise generalised theories of oppression are by no means the prerogative of white feminists (1993, p. 63).

This is a very important point, as by confusing the two issues writers have been able to argue against radical feminism. To clarify the position: for radical feminists the concept of patriarchy is an important concept for theorising the common and specific oppression of women. However, most radical feminists also challenge the notion of some essential female nature and the use of the category "woman" as a unitary, absolutist category, which leads to the denial of difference. In offering accounts of women's subordination most radical feminists are keenly aware of the need to theorise how and why patriarchal structures affect women differently according to, for instance, class, race, ethnicity, and sexual identity.

To put it another way, it is important to distinguish between the production of radical feminist explanations of women's oppression in terms of patriarchy and the claim for the universal validity of theoretical models developed from an understanding of white, and here one could also add heterosexual and middle-class women. The question surely is whether sufficient attention is given within radical feminist writing to the relationship of patriarchy to class inequality and racism, and the particular ways in which ethnicity and gender relations interact historically. This is an important criticism and one which radical feminists continue to need to address in their work. However, such a criticism can be made of most (white) feminist accounts, including liberal and socialist writing; it is not specific to radical feminism.

Radical Feminism as a Form of Oppression

Another attempt to discredit radical feminism is to claim that far from aiding the liberation of women, it is dangerous and oppressive. This is commonly linked to the perception of radical feminism as narrow, moralistic, judgmental and reactionary – a social purity movement by any other name. For example, Margaret Hunt refers to revolutionary and radical feminists as "new purity feminists", claiming that:

> Most of us – some of us to our great personal distress – are familiar with the attempts revolutionary and radical feminists have made to purify sexual practices within the British and North American women's movements ... The resemblance to past social practice is, once more, striking (1990, p. 38).

In Britain such criticisms have been voiced in the main by Marxist feminists, sexual libertarians, and, more recently, by some advocates of queer and poststructuralist theory, with radical feminism often being described as "prescriptive feminism". In the United States, writers who formerly identified with radical feminism but who now reject its political agenda have also been prominent in the trashing of radical feminism as conservative and moralistic (see, for example, Echols: 1989).

This caricature of a "politically correct Stalinist feminism" has routinely been invoked to discredit radical feminist work, especially in relation to sexuality. In the current rush to celebrate sexual diversity and difference in all its many forms, there is a tendency to define those who question certain forms of sexual practice as seeking mandatory sexual homogeneity. David Evans (1993), following Gayle Rubin, identifies the perspective of radical feminism, which he falsely labels "cultural feminism", as that which "condemns almost all forms of sexual expression as anti-feminist" (Evans: 1993). Not only are radical feminists accused of being narrow, we are also accused of being "sex negative" or anti-sex, making women, in particular, feel guilty and ashamed of their sexual feelings. For example, in relation to theorising heterosexuality, a commonly expressed view is that heterosexual feminists have been silenced as a result of radical feminists making them feel guilty about their sexuality and, more especially, sexual pleasure. This is evident in the recent interest in theorising heterosexuality (see various voices in Wilkinson and Kitzinger: 1993) as well as in debates about heterosexual feminism and political lesbianism that occurred in the late 1970s (see for example, Onlywomen Press: 1981). In *Straight Sex*, for example, Lynne Segal claims that:

> Straight feminists may have succumbed, by and large, to the pressure to keep silent about their sexual pursuits and pleasures in the face of impassioned campaigns against men's sexual abuse of women, and the commodification of women's sexuality . . . (1994, p. xiii).

In a similar vein, Wendy Hollway writes:

> Of course heterosexual feminists have good reasons for dwelling on the contradictions [of heterosexuality], since they are trying to engage in intimate relationships based on mutuality and reciprocity in the wider context of women's subordination. Not to find any would smack of denial and defensiveness. But dwelling on the difficulties is also motivated by guilt; a guilt which reproduces and is reproduced by the dominant radical feminist discourse on heterosexuality (1993, p. 413).

Others, myself included, would argue that it will not do to continue to blame radical feminism for the reluctance on the part of heterosexual feminists to discuss their (satisfactions and pleasures in) sexual relationships with men (see

Rowland this volume, pp. 77–86). As Robinson (1993a) points out, this cannot "adequately explain the continued silence (mainly) from heterosexual women on their sexuality". The responsibility for this must lie primarily with heterosexual feminists and the "initial reactions to lesbian demands to be made visible within the movement" (Tsoulis: 1987). The history of anti-lesbianism within the feminist movement, especially in the early days of the women's liberation movement, resulted in pressures on lesbians to downplay their sexuality to avoid "giving feminism a bad name" or scaring off heterosexual women. In this historical context, feelings of defensiveness and guilt on the part of many heterosexual feminists can be understood as largely self-imposed.

Others such as Caroline Ramazanoglu have questioned whether, in any case, radical feminism has the power to constrain heterosexual women's voices in this way, suggesting instead that:

> ... if heterosexual women persistently report negative sexual experiences in their relationships with men, it seems more obvious to look at their relationships with men, than at the failures of feminism, in order to explain this (1993, p. 320).

It is true to say, of course, that radical feminists have problematized concepts of desire and pleasure, and have been critical of current constructions of sexuality. But to equate this with being anti-pleasure and anti-sex is fundamentally flawed. Being opposed to certain sexual practices such as, for instance, S/M does not in itself imply one is against either sexual diversity (or pleasure) in desires and practices, or engaging in "sex" itself. The distinction to be made is whether sexual diversity *per se* is valued, or sexual diversity based on practices that do not eroticize dominance and submission (see Jeffreys: 1990, 1994).

We are also told that within British feminism, radical feminism has achieved hegemonic control of sexuality, and with supposedly atrophying effect. Beatrix Campbell makes this point when she claims that a "feminist sexual politics was defeated indirectly by the hegemony of radical feminism." (Campbell: 1987). Her view is shared by other writers (see, for example, Segal: 1987; Evans: 1993). There are a number of very worrying aspects attached to this general assumption. First, we are informed that radical feminism has served to police sexual practice, both heterosexual, gay and lesbian, through the enforcement of hegemonic cultural norms which define what is "politically correct" and "politically incorrect" sex. Then, following on from this, it is suggested that the recent popularisation of certain forms of practice, such as butch/femme and lesbian S/M pornography, is the result of a desire to transgress radical feminist "norms" (Faderman: 1993). Here we have it: radical feminism identified with a political agenda that is seen as leading to the promotion of sexual transgression and sado-masochist sexual practices in particular. How queer!

This notion of radical feminists as the "thought police", making women feel guilty over expressing a sexuality that has previously been denied them, is one version of the radical feminism as the repressor/oppressor scenario. Radical feminists have certainly criticised certain forms of sexual practice and desire, but then so have other feminists and, for that matter, so have so called sex radicals and queers. Despite the appeals to pluralism, it would seem that the valorisation of sexual diversity clearly has its limits. It would seem that all things are not equal. For example, socialist feminist Sheila Rowbotham has this to say about what she terms "anti-porn feminism":

> Its challenge to male-defined sexual culture is in terms of a feminist convention of a woman-centred "good" sexuality, in which the tangled range of women's sexual desires are nicely sorted. Out goes a lot of scruffy unlabelled jumble and we are delivered a salutary, nurturing, non-violent, co-operative loving (1990, p. 256).

What some women wouldn't give! To want sex that is reciprocal, egalitarian, less goal-oriented is, it seems, somehow unacceptable. It is, Rowbotham implies, a turn off, unlikely to arouse either passion or desire.

Some writers (for example Nichols: 1987) use the term "politically correct sex"; an expression that is generally used negatively to imply a curtailment of sexual desires and practices and which provides a context for understanding critiques of "vanilla sex"[4] as dull and unexploratory. If you don't turn on to power and if you don't want to "fuck with gender" you run the risk of being seen as prudish, immature or boring (Richardson: 1992). For example, queer, Cherry Smyth claims lesbian feminism silenced "anything but 'right on' forms of sexual expression" and propagated the belief that "lust was a gentle wild orchid" (Smyth: 1992). For those who are unfamiliar with Georgia O'Keeffe's paintings, this is meant as a put down!

For women to feel they have to defend the right to have "vanilla sex" – Be Vanilla and Proud – could well be dubbed the consequence of "policing". Actually, this is a term I neither like nor, more to the point, think is very useful in theorising sexualities (not to mention crime). The point I am really making is why pick on radical feminists? Here, the issue seems to be the claim that radical feminist discourse has dominated sexual politics and has therefore had more disciplinary power to influence events than other perspectives. Radical feminists have certainly made a very important contribution to theoretical and political debates around sexuality; unfortunately, however, in many (feminist) texts radical feminist thinking on sexuality is either ignored or discredited.

The view of radical feminism as oppressive – hence "powerful" – is also related to the belief advocated by certain writers that the discourse of radical feminism constructs "woman" as passive victims without agency, with potentially

---

4. The term vanilla sex is ill-defined, most commonly it is used in an oppositional sense by writers affirming certain sexual desires and practices, most notably S/M.

negative and far reaching effects on women's attitudes and behaviour. (Again, this is influenced by the inaccurate portrayal of radical feminist theory as over-whelmingly essentialist and deterministic.) For example, Lynne Segal writing from a socialist feminist perspective, claims that:

> The identification of sexuality as "the primary social sphere of male power" was ... disastrous in my view, because it encouraged "all women" to identify them-selves as the victims of "all men" (1987, p. 70).

For a more recent and very graphic example of the view that radical feminism portrays woman as weak and helpless victims, and thereby encourages women to position themselves as vulnerable and at risk, one need look no further than the characterisation of Catharine MacKinnon's work in a recent interview in the British newspaper the *Guardian* which refers to her

> ... fatalistic depiction of women as so many little bunny rabbits hopping around in the middle of the road, waiting for the next juggernaut to come thundering round the corner (Bennett: 1994, p. 27).

At the same time that radical feminists are accused of making women feel powerless, they are also criticised for failing to acknowledge that women do not experience themselves as powerless. The charge here is that radical feminism misrepresents women. For instance, Elaine Denny states that "the experiences of individual women have been lacking from most radical feminist literature, women have been portrayed as powerless victims" (Denny: 1994).

Similarly Lynne Segal , speaking of the experiences of women in Britain in the 1980s, claims that there was

> ... a dramatic lack of fit between what one very visible group of feminists were saying about women's experience of sexual victimisation, and what the over-whelming majority of women were reporting as their experiences of sex, and its importance in their lives (1994, p. 67).

Radical feminism is thus construed as "theoretical and highly specu-lative", out of touch with what women's lives are really like and, by failing to legitimise women's experiences, oppressive. As with so many caricatures of radical feminism, this is (doubly) ironic. The stress on the importance of women's experience and the understanding that the personal is political, the significance of "consciousness-raising" as a political strategy, the insistence on the relationship between theory, activism and personal life, the importance placed on making radical feminist ideas more accessible and to de-mystify theory, are all fundamental aspects of radical feminist politics. Indeed, some writers regard radical feminism as being overly reliant on personal experience, a reliance which is criticised for being too atheoretical and/or "subjectivist" (Beechey: 1986).

Radical Feminist Strategies

Many of the critiques of radical feminism have focused on political strategy. Radical feminists have been accused of siding with the right wing and thus betraying feminist causes in the process (see, for example, Segal: 1994). Radical feminists have also been accused of attributing tremendous power to sexual activity as a political strategy and a means to social change (see, for example, Hunt: 1990). In fact, very few radical feminists focus on private sexual activity as a political strategy. The notion that we can change the world through what we do – or don't do – sexually is more often critiqued by radical feminists, as part of the discourse of sexual liberation. Having said this, it is important from a radical feminist perspective not to depoliticise private sexual interactions. Not only do these reflect wider social relations, but they can also shape social practices and meanings. Sexual practices within the home, for instance, "help shape the character and meaning of home-life" (Cooper: 1995). The important theoretical distinction to be made here is between a radical feminist approach to changing sexual practice and desire through cultural and social struggle, and the libertarian assumption that one can transform gender relations through (private) sexual practices and interactions.

Radical feminism encompasses a number of political strategies. However, it is separatism which has attracted particular critical attention both in the past and more recently. It seems nowadays as if it is simply assumed without question that separatism is beyond the pale, dangerous and wrong, to be resisted and challenged. Another critique of separatism is that it is self-indulgent, a "luxury" (Yuval-Davis: 1993).

Cherry Smyth, for instance, critiques the "gender-polarised feminism" of the 60s and 70s which she claims produced a "moralistic feminist separatism". She both desires and sees the possibility for new alliances across gender, as well as sexuality and race, through queer politics:

> ... one of the most vital, engaging aspects of queer politics for dykes: (was) working with gay men, gaining an understanding of and appropriating their sexual culture (1992, p. 42).

Queer theory and politics is often expressed in terms "explicitly opposional to feminism, especially radical feminism" (Kitzinger and Wilkinson: 1994, p. 457; see also this volume pp. 375–382), characterized as moralistic feminist separation. In this queer discourse we find that separatism and misogyny are often represented alongside each other as equally "oppressive", rendering the reasons why women come to feel separatism to be politically and personally necessary as equal in status to woman-hating by men. Here is another version of the separatist as "man-hating feminist" – and the equation of man-hating as equivalent in significance to woman-hating.

Queer is one of the ways of identifying with a mixed movement and challenging both separatism and misogyny at the same time (Boffin cited in Smyth:

1992, p. 21). And again from Cherry Smyth:

> The huge wave of energy unleashed by queer politics has enabled powerful alliances between lesbians and gay men, defying the separatism of the lesbian feminist movement and the misogyny of the gay male community (1992, p. 60).

Conclusion

I have attempted to highlight some of the main ways in which radical feminism is caricatured and criticised, the effect of which is to often discredit or even dismiss radical feminism as a strand of contemporary feminist thought. There are of course criticisms that we do need to take account of, serious gaps in our understanding, and areas that remain under-theorised within radical feminist accounts.[5] Yet in an important respect the (mis)representation of radical feminism works against this.

The danger is twofold. As I have indicated, radical feminists get criticised, defined and known largely for what they haven't said, whilst at the same time what they actually have said is very often ignored. As a result we often are faced with the task of having to correct misconceptions, at the risk of being labelled "defensive", rather than spending time articulating and developing radical feminist theory and practice. Now, for my next article . . .

---

5. For example, until recently relatively little attention has been given to theorising women who commit acts of violence in the public domain as distinct from the private sphere (Birch: 1993). Such work is all the more necessary in a context where evidence of women's violence towards others, but more especially sexual abuse by women, violence within lesbian relationships, the murder of men and children outside of the domestic sphere, is being used to discredit the validity of a gendered understanding of (sexual) violence and abuse.

Tania Lienert

On Who is Calling Radical Feminists "Cultural Feminists" and Other Historical Sleights of Hand*

> *... by the early 70s radical feminism began to flounder, and after 1975 it was eclipsed by cultural feminism – a tendency that grew out of radical feminism, but contravened much that was fundamental to it ... by 1975 radical feminism virtually ceased to exist as a movement. Once radical feminism was superseded by cultural feminism, activism became largely the province of liberal feminists.*
>
> Alice Echols (1989, pp. 4–5)

In 1989 Alice Echols published *Daring to be Bad: Radical Feminism in America 1967–75*, adapted from her dissertation in history which she had begun in 1983. Her thesis appears to herald the *demise* of radical feminism in the US in the mid-1970s and its *takeover* or replacement by cultural feminism. Throughout her discussion of the 1980s she calls radical feminists cultural feminists. Her idea of cultural feminism is not about the political role of culture, which many feminists have written about (e.g. Bunch: 1976b, p. 190; Rowland and Klein: 1990, p. 296; see also this volume pp. 32–33), but rather she argues that radical feminists are guilty of an apolitical retreat or escape into a feminine culture in which women are seen as superior beings to men. She equates this with biological determinism or essentialism and also with women being passive victims of men. As a consequence she dismisses radical feminist contributions. Echols' thesis, or the view that radical feminists are biologically determinist, appears to have found favour with numerous others in the

* I thank Renate Klein, Susan Hawthorne, Sheila Jeffreys, Marilyn Frye, Petra Bueskens and Suzanne Bellamy for their discussion on this topic; and the School of Social Inquiry publication support fund for assistance in the form of teaching release from Deakin University.

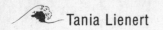

US, Britain and Australia (Alcoff: 1988; Tuttle: 1986/1987).

However, the radical feminists who are called cultural feminists do not claim this label for themselves and reject it outright. Most work from within a social constructionist framework, yet the misrepresentation continues, and has become the ruling orthodoxy in academic feminist theory. Why might this be so?

What follows is a documentation of some of the misrepresentations, and a brief discussion of why they might have come about. I will conclude that what Denise Thompson (1994) calls the denial of male domination in what are perceived as conservative times lies at the heart of the issue. Radical feminists who work against pornography and violence against women are not hesitant about naming men and male supremacy as a problem. However, many other feminists do not think it a good strategy to be so explicit – it might offend men and get them offside. So radical feminist theories are dismissed or trivialised as being biologically determinist – and hence not really feminist – and theories that are less threatening to the status quo are put forward in their place. These theories include socialist feminism, where capitalism is faulted rather than men themselves, sexual libertarianism where "anything goes" and post-modernism, where "woman" does not even exist.

It is also my perception that in this misrepresentation the terms "essentialism" and "biological determinism" have become confused, if not fused, and are used incorrectly. A mere acknowledgement that we all, male and female, have a sexed body in which we live before culture has any impact on it is called "essentialist". But analysis of this body may draw on what are often seen to be esoteric concepts such as the interconnectedness of all life – ideas which many ecofeminists have pursued further without being biologically determinist about it.

Biological determinism, moreover, is something very different from essentialism – it is about whether women's biology, our *capacity* to have children for example, becomes our *destiny* or our only role in life. Feminists, especially radical feminists, have explicitly renounced biological explanations for women's and men's roles, knowing that if it is accepted that men are naturally violent and women are naturally passive, then there is no point in working for change. Biological determinism would accept that women are victims and this cannot be changed so there would be no point to a feminist movement (Bleier: 1984; Rowland: 1988; Kaplan and Rogers: 1990; Star: 1990; Hubbard: 1990; Rowland and Klein: 1990, see also pp. 9–36 this volume; Hawthorne: 1976).[1] Again and again radical feminists have given evidence of women who have resisted deterministic classifications and demonstrated agency under oppression, and of men who work to betray patriarchy (Rowland and Klein: 1990, p. 298, see also this volume p. 34; Hoagland: 1988). For one set of feminists to then deride radical feminists for being biologically determinist is in effect to undermine them and destroy their credentials.

---

1. This view was also expressed in an interview I conducted with Susan Hawthorne in 1993.

So What Do the Critics of Radical Feminism Say?
Alice Echols points out the differences between the early radical feminists and the cultural feminists who took over the movement:

> Most fundamentally, radical feminism was a political movement dedicated to eliminating the sex-class system, whereas cultural feminism was a countercultural movement aimed at reversing the cultural valuation of the male and the devaluation of the female. In the terminology of today, *radical feminists were typically social constructionists who wanted to render gender irrelevant, while cultural feminists were generally essentialists who sought to celebrate femaleness* [emphasis added]. Thus, we find radical feminists mobilising women on the basis of their similarity to men and cultural feminists organising women around the principle of female difference (1989, pp. 6–7).

Echols argues that to add to the conceptual confusion, "cultural feminists almost always identified themselves as radical feminists and insisted that they were deepening rather than jettisoning radical feminism" (1989, p. 7). However she states that she has chosen to use the term cultural feminism to "underscore its disjuncture from radical feminism". Those she names cultural feminists include Robin Morgan, Kathleen Barry, Mary Daly, Susan Griffin, Adrienne Rich, Andrea Dworkin, Susan Brownmiller and Janice Raymond

In Robin Morgan's (1970) article "Goodbye to all that", Echols sees "foreshadowings of cultural feminism . . . And there was the essentialism – the claim that women were by nature ecologists . . . (1989, p. 252).

Echols is also critical of "The Fourth World Manifesto" drafted in 1971 by Barbara Burris and others and published in the edited collection *Radical Feminism* (1973). She argues that the manifesto was an embryonic but highly influential expression of cultural feminism, one that should be read as a transitional work as it straddled the line between radical and cultural feminism. As she puts it:

> Finally, the authors of the "Manifesto" contended that the goal of feminism should be the assertion "of the long suppressed and ridiculed female principle". They characterised female culture – which they attributed to women's colonisation, not to their biology – as one of "emotion, intuition, love, personal relationships, etc, as the most essential human characteristics" [sic] (1989, p. 247).

Echols argues that cultural feminists have demonstrated less interest in effecting structural change than in nurturing an alternative female consciousness, or what Mary Daly terms "the spring into free space" (1984, p. 53). She is strongly critical of Mary Daly, and indeed Daly is the most consistent target of those who call radical feminists cultural feminists, in particular for her writing in *Gyn/Ecology* (1979).

Alice Echols also speculates about Janice Raymond being essentialist in her 1979 book *The Transsexual Empire.*

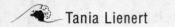

At best, there has been a curiously cavalier disregard for whether these differences are biological or cultural in origin. Thus Janice Raymond argues: "Yet there are differences, and some feminists have come to realize that those differences are important whether they spring from socialization, from biology, or from the total history of existing as a woman in a patriarchal society". For Raymond the source of these differences is irrelevant because as women "we know who we are" (1983, p. 35).

Linda Alcoff also calls radical feminists cultural feminists in her often-quoted article "Cultural feminism versus post-structuralism: The identity crisis in feminist theory" (1988). She compares cultural feminism with post-structuralist theory and is is highly critical of cultural feminists – she interprets Mary Daly and Adrienne Rich as such – for their essentialism:

> Cultural feminism is the ideology of a female nature or female essence reappropriated by feminists themselves in an effort to revalidate undervalued female attributes. For cultural feminists, the enemy of women is not merely a social system or economic institution or set of backward beliefs but masculinity itself and in some cases male biology. Cultural feminist politics revolve around creating and maintaining a healthy environment – free of masculinist values and all their offshoots such as pornography – for the female principle. Feminist theory, the explanation of sexism, and the justification of feminist demands can all be grounded securely and unambiguously on the concept of the essential female. Mary Daly and Adrienne Rich have been influential proponents of this position. Breaking from the trend toward androgyny and the minimizing of gender differences that was popular among feminists in the early seventies, both Daly and Rich argue for a returned focus on femaleness (1988, p. 408).

Alcoff speculates that Daly and Rich are essentialists even though she notes that neither espouse biological reductionism. She quotes from each and argues that:

> Certainly, it is difficult to render the views of Rich and Daly into a coherent whole without supplying a missing premise that there is an innate female essence (1988, p. 412).

She quotes Rich's definition of a "female consciousness" that has a great deal to do with the female body, and argues that Rich, like Daly

> . . . identifies a female essence, defines patriarchy as the subjugation and colonization of this essence out of male envy and need, and then promotes a solution that revolves around rediscovering our essence and bonding with other women (1988, p. 410).

In Alcoff's opinion,

> To the extent cultural feminism merely valorizes genuinely positive attributes developed under oppression, it cannot map our future long-range course. To the extent that it reinforces essentialist explanations of these attributes, it is in danger of solidifying an important bulwark for sexist oppression . . . (1988, p. 414).

Another author who is often quoted as an authoritative source on feminism is Lisa Tuttle in her encyclopaedia of feminism (1986/1987). In the entries on radical feminism, cultural feminism and the peace movement she calls radical feminists cultural feminists:

> Cultural feminism emphasizes the importance of a woman-identified life style and is usually unconcerned with mass reforms or public changes, preferring to concentrate on individual solutions and the creation of alternatives to the mainstream of society. Far from denying the importance of biological differences, or seeing in them the cause of women's oppression, cultural feminists tend to glorify the differences between the sexes, to imply that they are unchangeable, and to accept the idea that women are by nature less violent, more co-operative, more caring, etc. than men. The same idea also lies behind the women's peace movement. Some of the major theorists of cultural feminism are Mary Daly, Adrienne Rich and Susan Griffin (1987, p. 73).

Others who name radical feminists cultural feminists include Joan Cocks (1984), Juliette Zipper and Selma Sevenhuijsen (1987/1988, p. 125), Janet Sayers (1982, pp. 187–92), Lynne Segal (1987), Lynne Segal and Mary McIntosh (1992), Gayle Rubin (1992) and Jane Ussher (1991).

While not using the tag cultural feminist, others label radical feminists biological determinists. Hester Eisenstein is one. Her book *Contemporary Feminist Thought* (1984) is a key text on feminist theory. She argues (1984, pp. 111–12) that Mary Daly's *Gyn/Ecology* "identified women as wholly good, and men as wholly evil . . . women embodied the force of light and men the force of darkness".

Further, Eisenstein argues, Mary Daly:

> . . . portrayed women as fundamentally innocent, the powerless victims of male cruelty and violence throughout the long history of civilisation since the lost paradise of the Goddess (1984, p. 112).

Eisenstein also takes Susan Griffin to task for her book *Pornography and Silence* (1981). She maintains that:

> Griffin appeared to agree, at some level, that real women, or at least women in their role as nurturers, did embody feelings and eros, and did inhabit, therefore, a world located in some way outside of culture and language (1984, p. 120).

Tania Lienert

In a conference paper presented at Melbourne University, Barbara Creed called anti-pornography activist Andrea Dworkin essentialist. When I challenged her on this, stating that my research revealed her to be a thorough social constructionist, she rephrased her argument and said instead that Andrea Dworkin's position on pornography meant that she *fell into the trap* of essentialism (1993). Like other critics of radical feminism, Creed is *interpreting* Dworkin's work as essentialist rather than backing up her statement with evidence that Dworkin herself admits to essentialism.

Similarly, Judith Butler labels Dworkin's partner in much of her activism, Catharine MacKinnon, a biological determinist (1993a, pp. 238–39). And Elizabeth Grosz defuses Robyn Rowland's radical feminist critiques of reproductive technologies by placing her with Simone de Beauvoir and Shulamith Firestone in a new category called "negative egalitarians" who are also biologically determinist (1994, pp. 15–16), while claiming social constructionism for Marxist, psychoanalytic and post-modern feminists (pp. 16–19).

In other historical sleights of hand, Ann Snitow, Christine Stansell and Sharon Thompson connect cultural feminism and the anti-pornography movement:

> The anti-porn movement emerged in the late 70s as the most dramatic expression of cultural feminism . . . Like other cultural feminists, they often implied that these images of female vulnerability were fixed, universal, natural. The anti-pornography movement . . . based its tactics and its message on a dichotomous view of erotic nature – male sexuality as violent and lustful, female secuality as tender and gentle (1983, pp. 37–8).

Ann Snitow is even more explicit in a 1992 article about the anti-pornography movement. She is critical of the movement for seeing men as having an intrinsically violent sexual drive, which is different from a more consensual and loving female sexual nature.

Parallel to the renaming of radical feminists as cultural feminists appears to be the appropriation of the term "radical" by lesbians who promote and defend lesbian sadomasochism. They describe themselves as "sex radicals", for example Teresa de Lauretis draws divisions between "sex-radical or S/M lesbians" and "mainstream or cultural feminist lesbians" and refers to the essentialism debate (1991). Carole Vance discusses the dilemmas "sex radicals" had over what to name themselves. Were they pro-sex feminists? Were they anti-anti-pornography feminists? She concludes:

> Perhaps the term feminist sex radical does the least violence to their project, as long as radical is understood to mean "less a matter of what you do and more a matter of what you are willing to think, entertain and question"[2] (1992, p. xxiii).

---

2. Also Gayle Rubin (1984); Sue O'Sullivan (in Susan Ardill and Sue O'Sullivan: 1987, pp. 287–300); Lillian Faderman (1991); and Judith Butler (1990) discuss sex radicalism.

Today, the work of critics of radical feminism is predominantly cited without reference to the original radical feminists, for example Biddy Martin and Chandra Talpade Mohanty quote Carole Vance, Alice Echols and Gayle Rubin on the cultural feminism of Griffin, Rich and Daly (1986). I have also noticed this lack of reference to the original texts in student publications and at conferences, for example Sarah Lowe (1991) and students at the 1992 Network of Women Students of Australia (NOWSA) conference seemed to take it for granted that Mary Daly and other radical feminists are essentialist and that this is not the kind of feminism to support. In fact at the 1995 NOWSA conference students so thoroughly schooled in these ideas insisted that I was a biological determinist despite a paper on transsexualism I had delivered explicitly rejecting biological determinism.

What Do the Radical Feminists Themselves Say?

Having shown what the critics of radical feminist say, I will now look at the work of the radical feminists so misrepresented above to see if there is any justification for calling them biologically determinist.

Robin Morgan's "Goodbye to all that" is an angry denouncement of and farewell to sexist left men and the sexist male-designed left movement, which includes women as well as men. On ecology, she says:

> Goodbye to a beautiful new ecology movement that could fight to save us all if it would stop tripping off women as earthmother types or frontier chicks, if it would right now cede leadership to those who have not polluted the planet because that action implies power and women haven't had any power in about 5000 years, cede leadership to those whose brains are as tough and clear as any man's but whose bodies are also unavoidably aware of the locked-in relationship between humans and their biosphere – the earth, the tides, the atmosphere, the moon. Ecology is no big shtick if you're a woman – it's always been there (1970/1992, p. 63).

I interpret this as a *criticism* of the fact that women are lauded as earthmother types, rather than an embracing of it, as Echols argues. At the same time Morgan acknowledges women's connections with the cosmos, a connection that is an obvious biological fact. Nowhere in her writings does she say that men *do not have* this connection also, although obviously they would not experience it in the same way as women, and she has decided *not* to focus on men in her writing.

"The Fourth World Manifesto" by Barbara Burris and others is illustrative placed in its full context:

> We are proud of the female culture of emotion, intuition, love, personal relationships etc. as the most essential human characteristics. It is our male colonisers – it is the male culture – who have defined essential humanity out of their identity and who are "culturally deprived". We are also proud as females of our heritage of known and unknown resisters to male colonial domination and values (1973, p. 355).

This passage demonstrates clearly how the authors are aware of how men have "defined" women. It also refutes Alice Echols' claim that radical/cultural feminists portray women as passive victims. The manifesto does not evade the issue of male supremacy. It demonstrates how men, as part of their colonisation of women, have suppressed any female culture and put forward their own as universal. As Burris says:

> It is simply a truth that there is a split between the female and male and that the female half of life has been suppressed by the male half of life (1973, p. 355).

The manifesto is explicitly anti-biologically determinist. Although this was perhaps not so clear in earlier versions, in a postscript to the 1973 publication the manifesto warns of the dangers of glorifying the oppressed and of "a split between men and women being made into a new feminist orthodoxy":

> The female culture and the male culture are not natural; *they are artificial creations of a male-dominated world.* [emphasis added] The artificial split between what has been defined as female and what has been defined as male has nothing to do with the inherent nature or potential of females or males. The definitions . . . are social definitions only (1973, p. 357).

Alice Echols (1989, p. 247) contradicts herself twice about the cultural feminism of the manifesto in her own quoting of extracts from it. The first is with regard to the processes of colonisation, not biology, being the reason for the development of female culture. The second is where she quotes the manifesto as saying that aspects of female culture are human characteristics. Presumably her use of "*sic*" means that she thinks the authors should have said emotion, intuition and the like were essential female characteristics and their use of "human" was a mistake. But I read the manifesto as a long overdue call to value women's culture as human, rather than what has happened in the past, i.e. the valuing of male culture *only* as human.

In *Gyn/Ecology* Mary Daly (1979, p. 379) writes about role-defined masculinity; and how patriarchal socialisation has numbed women's brains and blocked our original Be-ing (pp. 21–2). Her "spring into free space" (p. 12) criticised by Echols is not about a retreat, but about the importance of women working together to uncover and rediscover our pre-patriarchal Be-ing, and to *create* a new world:

> Radical feminist consciousness spirals in all directions, dis-covering the past, creating/dis-closing the present/future. The radical be-ing of women is very much an Otherworld Journey. It is both discovery and creation of a world other than patriarchy. Patriarchy appears to be "everywhere". As a rule, even the more imaginative science-fiction writers (allegedly the most foretelling futurists) cannot/will not create a space and time in which women get far beyond the role of space stewardess (1978, p. 1).

> Moving into the Background/Centre is not navel-gazing. It is be-ing in the world
> . . . enabling the Self to act "outwardly" in the cosmos as she comes alive. This
> metapatriarchal movement is not Afterlife, but Living now, dis-covering Life (1987,
> p. 7).

Referring to Rachel Carson's *Silent Spring*, and women's role in the ecology movement, Daly argues:

> I am not suggesting that women have a "mission" to save the world from ecological
> disaster. I am certainly not calling for female self-sacrifice in the male-led cause of
> "ecology". I am affirming that those women who have the courage to break the
> silence within ourselves are finding/creating/spiraling a new Spring (1987, p. 21)

This is a follow-on from Daly's previous work in *Beyond God the Father* (1973, pp.
2, 23, 168–9) where she discusses in detail how women's potential is blocked and the
process by which women *become* what is expected of them. It follows that to achieve
revolution, women must *unbecome* what they have become. It is interesting that
it is *Gyn/Ecology* which is targeted by critics of radical feminism in this debate
rather than Daly's two earlier books. The *whole* of the *The Church and the Second
Sex* (1968/1975) is a refutation of biological determinism as used by the Christian
church to justify and legitimate the subordination of women. In *Beyond God the
Father* Daly (1973, pp. 49, 121) explicitly rejects biological determinism in favour of
sex-role socialisation.

Similarly, Janice Raymond's *one* speculation in *The Transsexual Empire*
about biological differences between men and women is seized upon and taken
right out of context by Echols (1983, p. 35). It is interesting to read the whole passage:

> Men, of course, have defined the supposed differences that have kept women out of
> (truck driving and engineering) jobs and professions, and feminists have spent
> much energy demonstrating how these differences, if indeed they do exist, are
> primarily the result of socialization. Yet there are differences, and some feminists
> have come to realize that those differences are important whether they spring
> from socialization, from biology, or from the total history of existing as a woman
> in a patriarchal society. The point is, however, that the origin of these differences
> is probably not the important question, and we shall perhaps never know the total
> answer to it. Yet we are forced back into trying to answer it again and again.
> (Raymond: 1979/1994a, pp. 113-14).

In a footnote to the above Raymond says a parallel is the abortion issue, where the
key question asked by men for centuries has been "when does life begin?" This
question, Raymond says, is posed in men's terms and on their turf, and is essentially
unanswerable: "Women torture themselves trying to answer it and thus do not
assert or even develop our own questions about abortion" (1979/1994a, p. 114).

Raymond argues that the question of who is a woman may well be a non-question, and that:

> ... the only answer that we can give to them is that we know who we are. We know that we are women born with female chromosomes and anatomy, and that whether or not we were socialized to be so-called normal women, patriarchy has treated and will treat us like women (1979/1994a, p. 114).

Biology is thus not irrelevant for Raymond as Echols claims, nor does she have a "curiously cavalier disregard" (Echols: 1983, p. 35) for where differences come from. To the contrary, in the bulk of her work Raymond consistently argues it is history and culture that make the differences, not biology. My own reading of *The Transsexual Empire* confirms this – it is thoroughly anti-biological determinist. Further, in her following book, *A Passion for Friends* (1986), she repeatedly emphasises she is not a biological determinist.

Adrienne Rich, too, rejects biological determinism. At the very beginning of *Of Woman Born*, she argues that women *learn* to nurture:

> Motherhood is earned, first through an intense physical and psychic rite of passage – pregnancy and childbirth – then through learning to nurture, which does not come by instinct (1976, p. 12).

She then distinguishes quite clearly between two meanings of motherhood:

> the *potential relationship* of any woman to her powers of reproduction and to children; and the *institution*, which aims at ensuring that the potential – and all women – shall remain under male control [her emphases] (1976, p. 13).

However she is nonetheless called essentialist! While Alcoff in her criticism of Rich understands the point of women valuing what has been devalued by men, she still insists on calling Rich's philosophy essentialist. Further, to say radical feminists "merely valorize" womanhood (Alcoff: 1988, p. 414) is a put down of all the other things that radical feminists have done. Like most feminists other than radical feminists, she does not consider the political strategy of bonding with other women to be as effective as working with men.

Susan Griffin is also quite clearly anti-biological determinism in her work. *Throughout Pornography and Silence* she argues that it is a myth and a delusion that men are inherently violent. She instead states quite clearly that male violence against women is as a result of powerful socialisation (1981, pp. 94–9). Like Daly, she remarks on the phenomenon of the self-fulfilling prophecy, or how we become what we are taught (pp. 108–9). For example:

> We see a film in which a woman is murdered. Or a series of women are murdered, or beaten, or raped. The next day, we read in the newspaper that a woman has been shot to death by a stranger. We hear that the man next door has several times

"broken down" and threatened the life of his wife, his son. An advertisement for a novel depicts a woman's throat cut open and bleeding. And in our minds all this is woven into a fabric which we imagine is inevitable. We begin to look on the violence of men toward women as a kind of natural phenomenon. And slowly, our own behaviour becomes a part of this delusion which we have called reality. If we are women, we grow up with a fear which we come to believe is as common as hunger, or thirst, or anger . . . If we are men, acts of violence toward women become part of a range of behaviour which we think of as human (1981, p. 157).

Robyn Rowland too is not a biological determinist as Elizabeth Grosz charges. In her introduction to her 1988 book, *Woman Herself*, Rowland states:

> I argue that men have created an identity for women, based in biology, which is intended to reinforce difference and to tie women to a "natural" position in such a way as to make woman the negative or "other". Through patriarchy men direct and try to impose this self on woman for the purposes of controlling her and maintaining woman as a servicing class for men. Part of the feminist struggle has been resistance to this imposition of negative selfhood and I will also consider examples of these acts of resistance (1988, p. 2).

Radical Feminist Responses

I think it is quite clear from the examples that none of the radical feminists so accused are biological determinists. Radical feminist responses to this charge have varied. Mary Daly, the most oft-misrepresented, has chosen not to respond.

Instead she continues working and developing her ideas. One gets the feeling from stories of other attacks during her career in her "New Intergalactic Introduction" to *Gyn/Ecology* in 1991 and from *Outercourse* in 1993 that she does not want to waste time on attacks but prefers people to read her work and make up their own minds. However others have defended her. Marilyn Frye,[3] for example, says Mary Daly's work in creating a new world is in fact practising social construction (1993).

In *Reading Between the Lines* (1991), Denise Thompson has a detailed explication of what she calls the libertarian construction of "the straw woman" of cultural feminism. As she puts it:

> . . . so-called "cultural" feminism is not an identifiable form of feminism in the sense that it is not chosen by the feminists who supposedly subscribe to it, but rather a label applied to writings of which the labeller disapproves. The socialist feminist/"cultural" feminist split is not a confrontation between two equally matched adversaries, but a demarcation dispute set up by some socialist and libertarian feminists to distinguish their own position from that of an opponent *who is not there*. [emphasis added] (1991, p. 8).

---

3. Personal correspondence with Marilyn Frye, 1993.

She documents misrepresentations and puts examples into their full contexts, much as I have done above. These include defending Susan Griffin's and Andrea Dworkin's use of myth and allegory – acknowledged powerful tools for social construction – in their factual writing. One defence is of a passage in Susan Griffin's *Woman and Nature*, which Thompson identifies not as a realist text but as an extended poem or song. Thomson argues that Lynne Segal in her critique of Griffin fails to see this due to her own literalist and empiricist bias (1991, pp. 108-9). Similarly, Thompson criticises Alice Echols for misperceiving the nature of Andrea Dworkin's argument against male sexuality being "the stuff of murder not love". This, Thompson argues, is taken out of context from her 1977 paper "Why so-called radical men need and love pornography". In the quote the argument is couched in allegorical terms and is about myth and meaning and the patriarchal articulation of power struggles between men, she says. Further:

> It is not possible to counter the force of myth by citing "facts" since myth is either impervious to "the facts" or has already constructed them to fit. Myth can only be challenged by exposing its grounding in the relations of power it serves to uphold. That is the task which Dworkin was engaged upon (1991, p. 173).

Andrea Dworkin herself rejects biological determinism:

> I am a Jew who has studied Nazi Germany, and I know that many Germans who followed Hitler also cared about being good, but found it easier to be good by biological definition than by act . . . I would not be associated with a movement that advocated the most pernicious ideology on the face of the earth. It was this very ideology of biological determinism that has licenced the slaughter and/or enslave-ment of virtually any group one could name, including women by men (cited in Carol Anne Douglas: 1990, p. 84).

Janice Raymond, herself misrepresented over her book, *The Transsexual Empire*, has taken the issue up repeatedly. In her introduction to the new edition of *The Transsexual Empire*, she expresses surprise at the criticism that she is essentialist, pointing out that a whole chapter of the book criticises the theories of biological essentialism that ground the etiology of transsexualism in biology, for example in prenatal hormonal or in genetic factors (1994a, p. xix).

Raymond is even more explicit in her 1989 article "At Issue: Reproductive technologies, radical feminism and socialist liberalism". Those who call radical feminists cultural feminists, she says,

> . . . quote selectively from radical feminist authors such as Andrea Dworkin, Kathleen Barry and others including myself who have specified at great length and in great detail our own critiques of biological determinism and female essentialism (1989, p. 135).

Raymond also addresses the issue in her latest book, *Women as Wombs* (1994b, pp. 90–2).

Other radical feminists have also written about the misrepresentation. Somer Brodribb argues that in the context of post-modernism and radical uncertainty whenever women speak about women's bodies they are labelled essentialist (1992, xviii). Marilyn Frye too observes that when women like Daly and Griffin try to give new meaning and value to the concept *woman,* they are read as being essentialist (1993). Robyn Rowland and Renate Klein argue that the reduction of radical feminism to biological determinism is "a political ploy which takes place in order to limit the effectiveness of its analysis (1990, p. 297; see also p. 33 this volume). And as Sheila Jeffreys points out, "a quite new meaning of the word essentialist has been invented so that it can be used against all those who maintain some belief in the possibility of social action to create social change" (1993, p. 83).

Why the Misrepresentation?[4]

As the above-mentioned radical feminists have observed, and from my own reading of the literature on both sides of the debate, it is clear that the underlying theoretical position of most of those engaged in misrepresenting radical feminism is a brand of socialist feminism that in the mid-1980s turned into an odd mixture of socialist feminism, post-modernism and sexual libertarianism. (In the 1990s, many of these critics of radical feminism have also embraced the new queer politics and theory of the lesbian and gay movement which includes a celebration of lesbian sadomasochism). The main reason for the misrepresentation can thus be seen to be a battle over which *strategies* are the best for social change, and obviously radical feminism, because it conflicts with the feminism of its critics, has to be argued against. As I said at the beginning of this discussion, I concur with Denise Thompson (1994) that the critics of radical feminism deny male domination

---

4. In questioning why this misrepresentation has occurred it must be noted that *some* radical feminists *did* stray into biological determinism. The women's spirituality, peace and ecology movements today contain women who do believe that women are naturally superior to men. (They also contain women who have radical social constructionist views). Susan Hawthorne remembers that in the 1970s a minority of lesbian separatists did retreat into these movements (Interview, 1993). Charlotte Bunch (1976a; 1976b), Janice Raymond (1986, p. 21) and Carol Anne Douglas (1990) have also discussed this. Further, Suzanne Bellamy (Interview, 1993) discusses how early second-wave feminists were *still uncovering* details about whether men and women were the way they were because of their innate natures or because of socialisation. There was "a passionate cauldron of ideas" about what women really were. "We were delving – there was never a peaceful moment", Bellamy (Interview, 1993) remembers. Certainly to this day the debate still rages.

So the misrepresentation can partially be seen to have roots in the *actual* desertion of the social constructionist framework by a *minority* of women. However as I have shown, those so named and discussed in this article, in particular Robin Morgan, Mary Daly, Susan Griffin, Adrienne Rich and Janice Raymond are not biological determinists.

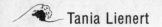

while radical feminists do not shy away from naming it. Many of them even celebrate dominance and submission in their celebrations of sadomasochism. In these post-modern times, it is inevitable that those who continue to name men as a problem will be labelled essentialist.

It is interesting that these battles occur mainly in academia: perhaps they reflect the required structure of work in universities where to prove your argument you have to consider and then disprove contesting theories. Denise Thompson says the battles in Marxism "have more often been fought in the groves of academe than on the barricades or the factory floor (1991, p. 90); perhaps the same can be said about feminist theory.

Firm in our conviction about the social causes of inequality, and our desire and belief in the possibilities of social change, radical feminists must continue our work. However, the criticisms mean that we must be vigilant and constantly explicit about social constructionism in everything we write. We need to be clear about the insidious post-modern imperative to say nothing, not even woman, exists, and stand up and say that yes, we do exist. We are real women, with bodies, minds and spirits, we do live in the world, and we do say no to the social construction of male domination and women's subordination.

Ailbhe Smyth

A (Political) Postcard from a Peripheral Pre-Postmodern State (of Mind) or How Alliteration and Parentheses can Knock you down Dead in Women's Studies*

NOTE
(Non-Explanatory Preface)

This **Note** is supposed to explain the peculiarities of the **Paper** that follows. Of course, if I could explain it succinctly, there would be no need for the paper. The **Abstract** which follows the **Note** was constructed, as is usual in these matters, some time before the **Paper** and (evidently) a long time before the **Note**. The **Postcard,** now placed last, was actually what I wrote first. All of which simply proves that nothing is ever as it first appears and that academic narratives are as subject to "modification" (falsification?) as any other kind. Like anything else, the truths of feminist academic life are fraught with paradox. The **Note,** which precedes your reading of the **Paper,** was itself generated by a (previous) reading (aloud), and is "strictly" peripheral to everything that follows. The **Paper,** a critique of (some) kinds of feminist theory-making, was (half-)written to be read aloud (with appropriate gestures, expression and inflections), in a working session at a Women's Studies conference ("Women in a Changing Europe", University of Aalborg, Denmark, August 18–22, 1991). The aim was to provoke, neither more nor less – debate, discussion, a response of some/any kind. But **The Paper,** in all its sacrosanct wholeness, consumed the allotted time and conversation happened later, unprescribed, fragmented, casual, laughing, pleasurable (for me). None of that is here. The best is always elsewhere, although remembered. "Here", then, are **The Abstract,**

---

* Originally published in *Women's Studies International Forum* (1992, May–June).

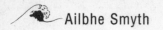

The Paper – the given order (more or less) of disciplined academic exercise. Ripe for interruption? I believe so – hence The **Postcard**. Act of faith and of necessity, not reason. As I hurtle ever more rapidly through middle age, pleasure becomes less and less resistible. And pleasure is, by definition (more parenthetical paradox), undisciplined. In a way, this has become a paper about writing a "feminist" paper (a meta-paper?) and, pleasure apart, I'm not at all sure it has any use or function.

Abstract

Not strictly a "paper" from the disciplined perspective of a "discipline", this is more a questioning conversation with myself (and others) about the relationship between the Women's Liberation Movement and Women's Studies in the 1990s. The conversation is located in Ireland, but Ireland itself is a post-colonial and deeply divided state located on the edge of one continent, directly confronting (or exposed to) another. The insecurities and vulnerabilities which flow from this location inevitably ground the questions raised. And especially questions about trends and directions within western feminist thought which appear to be exacerbating distinctions between activism and theory-making or, more concretely, increasing the distance between Women's Movement activists, feminist theorists – and women. Specifically, the conversation queries whether the attraction of (some) feminist theorists to post-modernism is enabling or disabling for Women's Liberation and processes of social, economic and political change – or whether it matters at all. The final question of the conversation concerns the "place" of Women's Studies (in particular places) and its relation to feminist practices and theories.

Paper

1. Apology (With Necessary Repetition)

This is definitely not a paper, "strictly" speaking, more the questions hovering just beneath the surface of my mind as I go about my very strictly disciplined Women's Studies business. These are the fears and anxieties which have become (for me) the rhythm of that business, disturbing surface rationality and the calm practice of my academic life. A disruptive conversation – interruption – impossible to smooth away, out of mind.

Actually, I don't usually go to conferences, far less write papers, with an up-front "I" and a disorderly list of truculently personal questions. Polemics, like doubts, should happen somewhere else, preferably peripheral, or so I have learned, at some cost. But it seems, at the least, more direct to put the questions rather than pretend to have answers which I don't possess. Although I do indeed have views, opinions, feelings, passions – not at all the stuff of papers.

The conventions of academic life, of conferences, of our "disciplines" require that we mask (even deny) uncertainty, confusion. Our job is to be clear, not to admit to not knowing. Women's Studies is not exempt from these conventions. It is caught up in them, which is no small part of the problem and the reason why this has to be a paper, not a conversation.

Why so defensive? Why all this preambular apologetics, this heavy Latin metal? Why should it feel so difficult to ask questions? Especially when they seem (to me) to be so urgent. My language, voice, everything, feels clumsy, naive.

Defence seems necessary for survival, even in Women's Studies. Increasingly so. Women's Studies was not always Feminist Studies, now confusingly is sometimes (often) Gender Studies. Where next? Multi-internationalised, with corporate take-overs, smart moves, career plans and all the rest of it? Which I hate.

I hate the hierarchies. Appropriative apex to self-defensive base. The big boys are everywhere still in place, rapidly growing big girls in tow (or are they, more properly, in thrall, these big girls?) Women's Studies (or whatever's flavour of the circuit) has its stars, its gurus, and its power-brokers. And you don't, generally speaking, find them on the edge of anything – geographical, cultural, social – they are the very centre. What is Women's Studies – and especially all our thinking and our theorising – doing to shift the place of the centre? What of all those zones, regions, states, states of mind where even whispers cost you dear? Where resources are few and power is not? Pyramids or peripheries – mixing metaphors doesn't matter: it's all much the same sort of power play.

I'm a local girl at heart, still full of the facts and fictions of my own place, whatever occupies my mind. Post-colonial habits of deference and subordination, a history of inferiorisation, these die hard. I have also to remember, to be sure, a history of resistance, revolution. (It's hard to resist the prevailing discourse when you're on the edge, hard to refuse assimilation, hard to recognise when it's already happened.) Coming from – and remaining within – a very small, not very rich, very conservative (President Robinson notwithstanding), very recent state physically on the edge of continental Europe and economically on the edge of just about everywhere in the "developed" (by whom? for whom?) world is not designed to give you a sense of your own power. The risk of self-centredness is not exactly major. Hence the irony, of course, of my up-front "I". There is a difficulty in standing your ground when you haven't much ground to speak of.

My interrupting voice insists that the issues and priorities of the Women's Movement in Ireland have, of course, their particularities, dismissed by (some) others as peculiar, in- or non-significant, worthy but boring. They've been there before, know all the answers, have rushed on somewhere else. But those issues are in our Women's Studies too. For a long time, we eclectically imported theory to deal with them and, for a while, the fit seemed smooth, felt good. Far less so now. Is that "us" or, may be, the theories? Are we more wary of appropriation? More aware that even stars have feet of clay, not always firmly rooted? Certainly, we are less trusting, less credulous, less willing to be taken for a ride.

The Women's Movement gave new and particular meaning to the global, not deleting the local, seeing both in relation, conversation. In the post-modern age (or

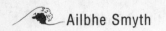

so the big boys say), the local is where it's at and meanings are (may be) all fictions. The problem is, big girls (perplexing sound-alikes) are trans-multinationals who speak from dislocated heights. No doubt they have a cooler view. But does this mean that local girls must maintain defensive deference?

2. Question

I think my question is not many but one, although two-sided, and the title, for all its trickery, does mean to put it plainly.

The question is: what is dying in Women's Studies – or killing it? I know this begs another question and appears absurd when Women's Studies is growing all the time, developing in universities, research institutions, even schools, publishing (of a certain type), beginning to get funding from "established" sources, credence, credibility. But if the profile has never been higher, what is that profile, who's constructing and projecting it and who's it aimed at? What is the price we pay for growth? It would be naive indeed to think there is no price. Can we pay it without selling out? Yes, I know that's an old question, we have "all" been there before. But since I haven't heard or seen the answer just recently, I'm going to keep on asking: What is the politics of Women's Studies? Why do I feel, experience, such disconnection between Women's Studies and political action? Is there a wilful disengagement from activism? What is the meaning of feminism (in all its global plurality) within Women's Studies? Or have one or both become so vast and distant that the very notion of meaning is meaningless?

There is, for me, a loss of politics in the Women's Studies I know – defeminism, in Kathleen Barry's phrase (Barry: 1991; see pp. 189–90 this volume). Is this a "personal problem" (my state of mind)? Generational, perhaps (the weary disillusionment of middle age)? Internal to Women's Studies (institutionalisation, "professionalisation", Americanisation)? Culturally and/or regionally specific (worse "here" rather than "there")? Is it an effect of shifts in the global economy and politics? How is it connected with the state(s) of the Women's Movement? It's all of these, I know, and more, which complicates the issue. But does that mean it's necessarily foolish to raise the question?

I do want to know what is de-radicalising Women's Studies. Why words (realities on their other side) like oppression, patriarchy, resistance, struggle, community, collective (action), liberation (and more) are so suspect. Why is it so un-cool to use them? Who has taken them away from us – and where have they put them? I want to know why Women's Studies feels so unpolitical – and who actually cares about that?

3. Opinion

The view is limited, of course, where I'm sitting, in some comfort, be it said, before my sturdy computer, with my white middle-class western European upbringing, my academic job with tenure till I'm sixty-five – generous compensations for "my" radical feminist politics, Irishness and other such discomforts. (More apologetics). I try to maintain objectivity and balance (why?), to bear in mind all the complex interactive reasons why it feels like this but it's no good. Anger gets the better or the worse of me: anger with a certain kind of feminist theory-making – academic, Anglophone, assured, plugged in to powerful resource points most of us have never even heard of. And apolitical, utterly abstracted from the "issues and priorities" of the Women's Movement anywhere.

I want to focus, with my limited view and for the moment, on the magnetic pull within feminist theory towards post-modernism (deconstructionism, if you will). Not because it's the only problem (it is not), nor the only kind of theory being made by feminists in Women's Studies (it is not), but because it is an increasingly sophisticated, articulate and prevalent strand which threatens to occupy (if it's not already there) and dominate hard-won space for women's thought and knowledge, paralysing action. The world is not, after all, reducible to a text, is not a matter of rhetoric.

You cannot expect feminist theorists and researchers to be activists. Oh no? I don't expect to construct my theories, write my paper, teach my class, sitting on a barricade. I do expect the issues and the theories, the causes and the courses, to be informed, illuminated, activated by one another as part of the same desire for transformation.

You're being paranoid, feminist theory hasn't really been appropriated, you've got it all out of perspective and proportion. Oh yes? When a collection of essays about literary theory, published by a prestigious Anglophone academic press, can be called *Feminism and Institutions*, I do get a mite worried (Kauffman: 1989). *Dialogues on Feminist Theory*, the discreet sub-title, does nothing at all to alleviate my anxiety. The provision of bending-over-backwards space for essays by men and a free and generous use of the word "gender" throughout (where "women" or "women and men" is what is meant) bewilders and disturbs me very much. Why bother fighting so hard for space if we're just going to hand it back again, neatly processed in the oppressors' language with a sweetly compliant smile? I think the joke's on us.

You can't seriously base a critique on one example. No, indeed. Mindful of correct academic procedure, let us quote chapter and verse, no fantasising:

> Postmodernism has become an unavoidable issue for feminists – activists and theorists alike. It calls into question and overturns the basic practices and concepts grounding feminism: from identity, difference and the category of woman/women to the very nature of politics and the "real" . . . (Ebert: 1991).

I quote from the opening paragraph of a review in a feminist journal of a collection of essays entitled *Feminism/Postmodernism* (Nicholson: 1990), which in fact includes (some) critiques of post-modernism. Nonetheless, the baldness of that opening phrase struck me with great force. I assumed at first it was ironic – a post-modern strategy *par excellence* – or at any rate provocative, but no, I found

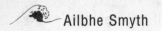

not a trace of irony subsequently, nor any conscious intention to provoke. Strangely, both "feminism" and "post-modernism" remain unquestioned terms. The review centralises a number of the questions nagging away in my mind:

- *Who has determined that post-modernism is an "unavoidable issue for feminists"?* It is still reasonably avoidable in the peripheral state I inhabit – except within some very ivory towers. Perhaps, of course, only "real" feminists don't avoid it.

- *For which feminists is it an issue?* Listening to women from other peripheries – racial, cultural, linguistic, geographical – it clearly is no such thing. "The local", of course, is the great stamping ground of post-modernism. The concept is deftly wielded by those who wage war on "totality", who also, not at all incidentally, "acknowledge" that feminism is a "totalising, hegemonic discourse". *At what point does acknowledgement become accusation become devastation?* The post-modern "local" bears no relation to localities, particular places, that I (you, we) actually inhabit. I have the greatest difficulty, in my mundanely literal way, in fitting disembodied "feminists" into a concept of the local.

- On what grounds can it be claimed that the "basic practices and concepts of feminism" have been overturned? Assuming that "we" know what they are, have all of "us" colluded in this extraordinary event? And why were (some of) "us" kept in the dark about all this overturning? It occurs to me again that if "we", i.e. feminists anywhere and everywhere, accept so readily that this is so, there is little need for those whom we used to call our oppressors to seek to control "us". We are doing it for ourselves. I know the "we" of sisterhood is problematic, but must "we" kill it stone dead?

- Is the theory/activism* split as watertight as the phrase suggests ("activists and theorists alike")? Does one not flow into the other, or has "doing feminist theory" become a substitute or compensation for political engagement? Has Women's Studies, for some, become a substitute for Women's Movement? But what are the origins of Women's Studies and why deny those roots? *A proper post-colonial, post-Catholic girl, I well know the smell of shame and how it leads you to deny your own place.* Why, even more bewilderingly, should we think so highly of academia that we would seek to suppress all knowledge of our origins?

---

* But theorists, I remember, are different from activists (and presumably everyone else). Has "difference" (now so different from diversity) become such an overriding element that in seeking to conceptualise it, we neglect the point/strategy of working with and around it/them? (Why singular "difference" anyway?). Recognition of differences is not new – at least not within radical feminism. The difficulty is not in locating the differences, but rather in remaining determined, despite our differences, to identify the common ground, the connections. Where once there was diversity within community, post-modernism has claimed to discover only a desert of difference. I categorically and passionately and politically and unacademically do not want an "inexhaustible heterogeneity" of "unassimilated otherness" (Young: 1990). I am appalled by the dismissal of community as an ideal. Are no ideals permitted? If that is so, there is no point at all in feminism which strives to give reality to the (an) ideal of liberation.

Barbara Christian, reflecting passionately (she does) on "the race for theory", explains its hegemony thus: "Theory has become a commodity because that helps determine whether we are hired or promoted in academic institutions – worse, whether we are heard at all" (1989, p. 225; [see p. 311 this volume]). In the race for jobs, sadly, feminist elbows perform the same function as any other kind. I still don't really understand why theory can't talk politics and why politics can't talk back to theory. Can feminism afford two languages? Why should we *need* two languages?

- Taking up Barbara Christian's point, what is professionalism doing to Women's Studies? Is professionalism (whatever it means) a symptom of severe theory-stress or its cause? Or both? Professionalism stultifies, keeps you on the straight and narrow, makes you fearful. Professionalism (never defined) keeps you in your place and, in the case of academia, hardens the divide between political and intellectual work. The abstract must not be polluted by contact with the concrete. Professionalism is about control. Like Patriarchy.

   To be sure, the problems faced by feminism and the Women's Movement socially, economically and politically (and on a global scale) make it difficult for women privileged to have jobs in academia or anywhere else to protest in our libraries and classrooms. But since we (and now I mean feminist academics) are so privileged and, relatively, safe, should we just sit there quietly, lost in abstractions? Need we accept so readily strategies that so blatantly dilute and disempower women's movements? Must we mimic those strategies in our theory? And should the concerns and fears of academic women (like me, indeed) become the overriding issues of feminism? How can we possibly know what these issues are if we stay securely perched on our career ladders? *Conflicts in Feminism* – yet another contemporary collection of essays on my bookshelves (Hirsch and Fox Keller: 1990). Stimulating essays – but the title is mesmerically, hegemonically arrogant. What feminism? Whose conflicts? Where?

- Are there hierarchical reverberations in all of this? Some do theory and those who do not do something more or less unmentionable. Of course, if speaking theory is the only way to be heard, questioning it is presumably a redundant exercise. In fact, I'm not questioning feminism's/feminists' need for theory: we must strive to comprehend the world and our experiences. The problem is that not all theoretical work is recognised or valued as such – hierarchies again. The fact, increasingly, is that some do *post-modern* theory (or versions thereof) and others do something less, not quite *comme il faut*. If you are not a philosopher or at least in cultural/textual studies – can you exist? That's the "real" question for "real" feminist theorists.

- How comprehensible are the results of all these strivings? The accusation of incomprehensibility is usually treated with contempt, as old hat, impossibly naive, absolutely from another level of being. But it ought not to be. If feminist theorists cannot or will not make ourselves understood to women who resist and revolt in other settings, what is the point of making theory? If it is

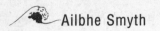

incommunicable, it is unusable, doomed to en-closure. We might as well be talking to ourselves – and I fear that is what we're doing, through our (old) hats.

- What does this mean for women? Are women realities, categories, neither or nothing at all? Isn't it an amazing coincidence all the same, how, as soon as women begin, diversely, to discover selfhood, to make our own self-definitions, to name our selves as subjects, "woman" becomes obsolete. A text-book example of the patriarchal process of control. How to name trouble out of existence. The proliferation of "gender" and "Gender Studies" is the ultimate denial of women, women's oppression and desire for liberation and the unequal power relations between women and men. *You see, "Gender" is not a loaded word, they told me patiently, in all seriousness.* Well, quite. My problem, precisely, with "Gender Studies" is that it carefully *unloads* women and women's multiple oppressions from the programme.

- If we do not exist (*it's absurd!*), how can we act to transform the world? Which is a stupid question: if we do not exist, we don't need to change anything at all. In whose interests is it that women should continue not to see ourselves as subjects, capable of agency? Such an old, old question. Post-modern decon-struction of the subject leads, logically and promptly, to nihilism, political paralysis, disempowerment – stylish, of course, but anomie nonetheless.

- The "real" is not a matter of style, is not a parenthesis, is not a fiction if you are living on or below the breadline. The real has a material base which cannot be conceptualised away. You know with absolute certainty (nothing relative) that survival is not guaranteed. You don't deny the real when you are in it – poverty, unemployment, racism, violence and abuse, physical, sexual and reproductive control, homophobia, censorship and represssion – you cannot afford to. You need tools which above all will enable you to change it. Reconceptualising power relations will not change their operation in the everyday unless that recon-ceptualisation is part of a politically engaged project. The dismantling of the notion of identity, the *eclatement*/explosion of power into atomistic relation-ships or the privileging of the concept of fragmentation as process are extraordinarily unhelpful in enabling women – or other groups – to develop collective practices. The concept of the local does indeed shift us away from generalising, universalising discourses, but can also be used as a cop-out to avoid thinking about the complicated global systems which affect how women live. Notions of multiplicity, openness, ambivalence, ambiguity and so on are rarely applied to the everyday (not at all a smart word). It must be said that the world economy is remarkably impervious to their cool charm.

4. Proposal

It's no good knocking something down if you have nothing to replace it with. Not necessarily something new – it may be that we do not always have to reinvent our strategies. Although that goes against the grain, for a condition of academic survival and "success" is the constant production of the new or, at least, the cunning recycling of the old so as to appear "new" and "original". I don't want to discard ideas or strategies which are still fresh and usable. I want, instead, to propose that we use Charlotte Bunch's *Reform Tool Kit* (1975b/1981b) to evaluate the theories we make. These are the criteria that she suggests we can apply to reforms of one kind and another. They work a treat with post-modern and deconstructionist theory – I really do recommend most warmly that you never be without it.

Charlotte Bunch's Reform Tool Kit

* *Does it materially improve the lives of women and if so, which women and how many?* And where? And how quickly? And can we understand it?
* *Does it build an individual woman's self-respect, strength and confidence?* What is the price we must pay to "master" it? How long does mastery take to achieve? Do we really want to be masters anyway?
* *Does working for it* (i.e. making that theory) *give women a sense of power, strength and imagination as a group and help build structures for further change?* Words alone do not change worlds. Sticks and stones . . .
* *Does the struggle to make it* (i.e. theory) *educate women politically, enhancing their ability to criticise and challenge the system in the future?*
* *Does it weaken patriarchal control of society's institutions and help women gain power over them?* And does it enable/encourage us to construct alternative institutions? Or does it replicate the big boys, originators of the Word?

Theory is not, or should not, be a way of making it to the top, a self-indulgent in-group activity. Feminist theory is, or should be, a tool for women's survival and growth. If we are making it, doing it, whatever – and calling ourselves feminist as we go – we need to be accountable above and before all to feminism and the project of Women's Liberation. And that means not giving a fig for the big boys (and even some of the big girls).

Postcard

But first there was, after all, a postcard.

Just now, as I sit down to write this paper, I hope (the fear I won't be able to do it this time is always there), I think a postcard is just about what I can manage (maybe more), and the style is right, so convenient: brief, elliptical, ambiguous, open-ended, faintly impersonal, anodyne, replica of millions of others.

> Not what I expected – crowded, confusing, exhausting – words fail me! Having a hard time trying to work out what's what, who's who but sticking with it. On the look-out for things to bring home – not sure about what I've found. Keep the faith and keep in touch – it's lonely sometimes on the edge.

> Love to all in sisterhood and solidarity.

> A. XXX

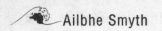

Postscript

From where? Postmark illegible. Women's Studies? Feminist Theory? Women's Studies Conferences? A State or state of mind?

To whom? "Unknown at this address." The Women's Movement? (where does it live now?). Women. (What is "women"?)

That won't do – is done already. And repetition is not allowed. Abstracts are well named: *Separated from matter, practice or particulars; ideal or abstruse (Oxford English Dictionary)*. But is separation from practice and particulars ideal? Could I not write a Concrete? Embodied in matter.

A postcard has, at least, "a picture on the reverse side" *(OED)*. Two sides, not one-dimensional – saying more than its mere words. A kind of dialogue – verse, reverse, converse. Possibilities of exchange. Not abstract and abstruse. No separation.

Abstracts and Ideals. What I think I have written (is that not repetition?) or – more honestly for most – what I think I would like to write, abstracted from the chaos of ideas half-formed, confusions, fears, feelings, the concrete always interfering (reverse – the other side).

A paper is expected – even in Women's Studies, no subversions, for all our fine talk and wild desire. Fully formed, clear, coherent, and entire. Substance, not style. Finished. Copies in advance, say what you are going to say, then say it. No deviations, no digressions, no tricks.

Yes, I think now, the title was a trick. I thought it clever at the time, the time of abstraction, separated from the practice. High-flown, smart, abstruse enough. But is the trick a trap? Marketing strategy? Alliteration sells, just at the moment, preferably in parentheses (abstruse alliterative abstractions/attractions, or any combination).

Parentheses (and postcards) can be seductive, hiding insecurities, leading astray, away from concrete, matter, practice and particulars. Particular politics and much else besides.

Victoria Robinson and Diane Richardson

Repackaging Women and Feminism: Taking the Heat Off Patriarchy*

> *Women's Studies exists in Britain, primarily because feminists have been sufficiently ingenious creating new alliances between the movement and the market; thus the publishing houses are among feminism's best allies* (Hilary Rose: 1993, p. 13)

Introduction

In recent years there has been a growth in the publishing of feminist texts by mainstream publishers, which has gradually expanded to include gender studies and masculinity. Through an examination of a selection of recent catalogues from major academic publishers we explore how these books are represented and sold, as well as the issues and themes that are prioritised. Given the high profile of feminist publishing in Britain and elsewhere marketing is influential in shaping both perceptions of research as well as debate within Women's Studies and the development of feminist theory. So is the optimism about the relationship between feminism and the publishing houses well-founded? What are the implications of recent trends for feminism and Women's Studies? How are we to understand the increasing attention given to gender studies, masculinity and men's studies?

Defining the Shift

> ... issues of gender and masculinity are now central to social theory and philosophy, while in the early eighties Marxism and feminism were (Victor Seidler: 1992).

Interestingly, Women's Studies, gender studies, men's studies, feminist studies, sexual politics, men and masculinity, used as organising categories within recent publishers'

---

* An earlier version of this article was published in *Journal of Gender Studies* (1994).

catalogues, do not always exhbit a linear progression from year to year. Different publishers may include the same book(s) under different headings, reflecting a degree of interchange between the categories used and the books being advertised. There are, however, certain recognisable trends. Since the late eighties gender studies and/or books on masculinity by men have gained prominence in terms of the headings used and space allocated.

For example, the HarperCollins 1991 "Culture, Media and Gender Studies" catalogue had two pages on Perspectives on Gender, including titles such as Patricia Hill Collin's *Black Feminist Thought* and other books with the word feminist highlighted in the title; two pages entitled "Feminist Theory"; four pages on "Gender, Culture and Society"; and three on "Men and Masculinities". Polity Press is another good example of recent trends. In 1991–92 they published a "Feminism and Women's Studies" catalogue, but by 1993 this ceased to exist was replaced by one entitled "Gender Studies". Similarly, in Macmillan's 1992–93 catalogue, incorporating the "Women in Society" list, only one of the books advertised uses the word gender in the title, while many include women and/or feminist. None specifically concern men and masculinity. Despite this, the catalogue is entitled "Gender Studies". In this instance, it could be argued that gender is being used as a marketing strategy. Our own edited volume, *Introducing Women's Studies: Feminist Theory and Practice* (Richardson and Robinson: 1993), an introductory text to various issues in Women's Studies including chapters that are overtly critical of gender studies and men's studies, is nonetheless placed under "Gender Studies".

The fact that gender is increasingly emphasised over "woman" and "feminism" as a distinct category is also reflected in the cover design. For example, Routledge's "Gender and Women's Studies" catalogues, depicted a woman and a man on the cover and unbelievably, for the 1993–94 catologue, two bronzed, muscular, naked men, one of whom is worshipping at the feet (and cod-piece) of the other who is standing on a pedestal! (see fig. 1). The 1995 cover is a photograph of a Black male bodybuilder in a bra. This contrasts starkly with previous advertising strategies that employed representations of women either symbolically or pictorially.

Publishing is big business and the relationship between writers, readers and publishers could in one sense be interpreted as the social relations between producers and consumers. Feminist publishing appears to make money. The emergence of new feminist presses such as Scarlet Press, in 1992, whose aim is to market feminist non-fiction, suggests that even in a recession feminism is a buoyant area. On the other hand it has been primarily mainstream publishers who have reaped the profits, often at the expense of specifically feminist publishing houses such as The Women's Press and Pandora.

Most major bookshops now have a Feminist/Women's or Gender Studies section. Clearly feminism, of a kind, sells which Susan Faludi's *Backlash* (1992) blockbuster, number one on the New York Times Bestseller list, and American media feminism represented by the likes of Naomi Wolf's *The Beauty Myth* (1990) and, more recently, *Fire with Fire* (1993) exemplify. Witness Andrew Neil, former

Figure 1

editor of the British newspaper *The Sunday Times*, who recently chaired Naomi Wolf, Katie Roiphe and Erica Jong in an all-American feminist debate. This "packaging" is the acceptable face of non-lesbian and/or non-radical feminism. Writers such as Camille Paglia (1992) and Katie Roiphe (1994) are classic examples of the media attention and willingness to publish writers who attack radical feminism and/or lesbian feminists. Success depends on playing the media game and distancing themselves from or attacking lesbian and/or radical feminists, who do not fit easily into a mainstream context. Feminist writers such as, for example, Andrea Dworkin (1991) with their radical and/or lesbian politics have difficulty getting into print. In addition, in Britain there are still relatively few Black women writers who are published in the Women's Studies field. Working-class women also often do not have access to resources, or contact with publishers.

Publishing books relating to masculinity and the "men's movement" is also a money maker. Robert Bly's best seller *Iron John* (1992), which focused on "male-healing", and Sam Keen's *Fire in the Belly: On Being a Man* (1992) are prime examples of this. In the United States their success has prompted a host of self-help manuals for men to understand themselves and their feelings, including titles like *The Grown-Up Man* and *Heroes Healing*. Men's rights groups in the United States have also declared February 7, International Men's Day. In Britain, the publication of books by anti-feminist male writers such as Neil Lyndon (1992) and David Thomas (1993), who claim that as a result of feminism men are now the disadvantaged sex, have also attracted media attention.

Routledge is a prominent mainstream publisher and leader in the field of publishing works on gender and men and masculinity. For this reason it is useful to examine, as a case-study, the process of categorisation and organisation of books within their catalogues in recent years. Routledge have two series on men and masculinity: "Male Orders" edited by Victor Seidler, which first appeared in 1991, and "Critical Studies on Men and Masculinity", edited by Jeff Hearn, originally launched in 1990. It is informative to examine the language used to publicise these series. In 1993 the "Critical Studies on Men and Masculinities" series describes its aims in the following terms:

> In recent years, and inspired particularly by important research in the field of women's studies, scholars have turned their attention to the study of men. [The series] . . . provides a publishing forum for some of the best work emerging in this new field.

Routledge acquired this series from HarperCollins, who inherited it from Unwin Hyman. It is interesting to compare the text used to launch the series, in 1990, with that in the Routledge catalogue. A number of deletions have been made which, it could be argued, deradicalises the series, from a feminist perspective. For example, in the first round of cuts the following was left out: "Overall, the attempt has been made to produce a series of studies of men and masculinities that are anti-

sexist and anti-patriarchal in orientation". The 1991–92 Routledge catalogue nevertheless continued to define the series as "pro-feminist", its task being "the critique
of men and masculinities" stating that "Each volume in the series approaches its
specific topic in the light of feminist theory and practice." By 1993, though the
series title remains the same, all reference to feminism has disappeared.

The description of the "Male Orders" series has also undergone a number
of changes. Whereas in the 1991 publisher's catalogue the series is "sympathetic to
feminism", in 1992–93 it merely acknowledges "the challenges of feminism . . .".
There is no attempt to explicitly identify it with the aims of feminism, as was
initially the case with the series edited by Hearn. Male Orders now ". . . attempts to
understand male forms of identity, practice and association in the modern world.
The series explores how dominant forms of masculinity have helped shape
prevailing forms of knowledge, culture and experience".

The themes and issues that are prioritised over others under the study
men and masculinity are primarily concerned with masculine subjectivity, in
particular father and son relationships, men's feelings about their own sexuality,
male bonding/friendships, men's response to feminism, and masculinity and the
media. Why not focus on research which would "contribute to our understanding
of how men gain, maintain, and use power to subordinate women?" (Hanmer: 1990,
p. 37).

An example of a publisher very specifically promoting books written by
men in the area of masculinity is Sage. Their 1990 brochure entitled "Women's
Studies" included Michael Kimmel's book *Changing Men: New Directions in
Research On Men and Masculinity* which in their view "contributes to the
demarcation of the new field of men's studies . . . and future directions for men's
studies". A later 1990–91 brochure entitled "Gender Studies and Sexual Politics"
contains a separate "Men's Studies" section, which includes Kimmel's book previously
defined as "Of Related Interest" to "Women's Studies". By 1992, men's studies has its
own separate catalogue with "An Impressive New Series", edited by Kimmel, on
"Research on Men and Masculinities". Since then Sage have continued to produce a
Men's Studies brochure.

One possible response to this is to assert that, until recently, all academic
study has been "men's studies", both because of the omission of women's experience
and in theorising the masculine as universal. Dale Spender and others drew
attention to this in *Men's Studies Modified: The Impact of Feminism on the
Academic Disciplines* (Spender: 1981).

More recently, Kimmel has asserted the need for "men's studies" as a
distinct subject area. He states that: "Men's studies doesn't seek to supplant women's
studies. It seeks to buttress, to augment women's studies, to complete the radically
redrawn portrait of gender that women's studies has begun" (Kimmel: 1988b, p. 20).
Others might argue that the very name men's studies is a threat to Women's
Studies, given that it assumes Women's Studies and men's studies are complementary. Another concern is that its development before the security of Women's

Studies is established will ironically put the focus back on men, with resources being diverted away from Women's Studies. Some male researchers though, such as Jeff Hearn referenced in David Morgan (1992), have recognised the politics involved around naming the study of men and masculinities and prefer "male dominance" studies and "the critical study of men" as an alternative title.

It could also be argued that the shift towards the use of the term gender in preference to "woman" poses a threat to feminism and Women's Studies (for a fuller discussion see Robinson: 1993b; Richardson and Robinson: 1994). For example, the backcover of Harry Brod's book *The Making of Masculinities: The New Men's Studies* (1987) states that:

> There has been a marked trend in feminist scholarship during the past few years away from a focus exclusively on women to a broader conception of gender. The study of men is a fundamental part of this trend.

Not all publisher's catalogues have reflected these trends. For example, The Open University Press list for 1994 is called "Women's Studies" although many of the books represented have the word gender in the title and male authors are included in the list. This highlights an interesting contradiction, where despite Women's Studies continuing to be used as the title, the use of the term gender appears more regularly. Similarly, even where publishers have continued to produce separate Feminist and/or Women's Studies catalogues most now include a Gender Studies section (see for example Harvester Wheatsheaf 1994 catalogue).

There are four main categorisations used by publishers in their catalogues a) Gender Studies, Women's Studies, Men and Masculinity, b) Gender Studies/Women's Studies, c) Gender Studies/Men's Studies, d) Gender and Women's Studies.

The term "Gender Studies" may be used as a catch all/superordinate category incorporating Women's Studies and, in some cases, men's studies and/or "men and masculinity" as in category (a). Books on sexuality, including women and sexuality, are also sometimes placed under the heading gender studies, as for example in the 1994 Harvester Wheatsheaf Women's Studies catalogue where Lesbian Studies appears under "Gender Studies". (Some publishers are now developing separate Gay and Lesbian Studies lists, for example Sage and Cassell.) Interestingly, where Women's Studies is submerged under Gender Studies, men's studies may still be distinguished, for example, Sage 1994 catalogue.

Gender Studies may be regarded as a distinct category of study from Women's Studies. For example, in the 1994 Harvester Wheatsheaf catalogue Gender Studies is distinct from Women's Studies/Feminist Theory as in category (b). In some cases, the terms Women's Studies and gender studies are used interchangeably, as if they are synonymous as in category (c). Finally, the two may be amalgamated into one category "Gender and Women's Studies" with no clear distinction between the two, for example in the case of the 1994 Routledge and

Macmillan catalogues, as in category (d). Women's Studies, and the feminist research and theory which informs it, is clearly under threat as a subject area in its own right, but most particularly in (a) and (c) where gender is seen as incorporating or representing women.

As we have already indicated, there has also been a move away from using feminist, as well as "woman", in preference to the term gender. During the 1980s a number of publishers ran feminist series, Hutchinson's "Explorations in Feminism" being one example. In the 90s, however, feminist seems to have given way to "woman" and latterly "woman" to gender; for example, Taylor and Francis' "Gender and Society" series; Sage's "Gender and Psychology", and Routledge's "Thinking Gender" series. As we have argued elsewhere, such shifts are not simply the result of redefining terminology in the light of theoretical developments, they signify "political processes at work and shifts in power relations". (Richardson and Robinson: 1994, p. 18). It is clear, for instance, that those book series which are defined primarily by their theoretical orientation, such as Routledge's "Thinking Gender" series, are heavily dominated by post-modernist positions and for the most part do not include radical feminist perspectives. By failing to encompass a full range of feminist perspectives in their catalogue series and lists publishers are thereby contributing to a form of censorship of radical feminism that, inevitably, will have a significant effect on the development of contemporary feminist theory and debates. It is partly for these reasons that we are highly critical of such developments because they may lead to a narrower political and theoretical agenda in terms of analyses of women's experience.

Related to this, we also need to consider how different feminist theoretical approaches may influence how gender studies is becoming defined as a subject area. To give an illustrative example, at a Women's Studies conference we attended recently one woman remarked, after giving a paper criticising radical feminism – rather poorly as it happened – "Don't worry I'm moving into gender studies!" What this anecdote highlights is the question of whether theoretical and conceptual developments in gender studies will reflect only certain strands of feminism, in particular those critical of radical feminist contributions? A question that becomes all the more significant in the context of the insitutional and cultural shifts towards gender studies that we have outlined.

Further Implications of these Shifts

Confusion over the use of the terms gender studies, feminism, Women's Studies and sexual politics by publishers partly reflects how they are sometimes used seemingly interchangeably in educational institutions for practical or strategic reasons. For example, sometimes the term "gender studies" is used even though the staff running courses would have preferred to use the term Women's Studies, because of concern over getting courses safely through the system, as gender is seen as less threatening than either women or feminist. Others may actively choose to use the title gender studies for intellectual reasons, because they believe that it represents both women and men equally and thus signifies a more democratic course.

The so called move of Women's Studies "out of the margins and into the centre" (Aaron and Walby: 1991) has meant that both female and male students may now take such courses as they would any other i.e. not necessarily for personal/political reasons. Therefore to call such courses gender studies is less likely to alienate those students who may have preconceived ideas about the "bias" of Feminist/Women's Studies[1] and hold the notion that Feminist/Women's Studies is of relevance for women only. Similarly, as more male tutors and students engage with/appropriate feminist theoretical issues, gender and men's studies are safer, less controversial places for them to do so in preference to an "alienating" or separatist Feminist/Women's Studies course.

A parallel can be drawn with gender studies. For instance, the first *Reader in Gender Studies* published in Britain (Polity Press: 1994) was the result of a "collaborative editorial enterprise"(!) Out of those involved, five were men and two were women. Nearly a quarter of the articles included were by men. This contrasts with recently published readers and collections in Women's Studies and feminism which do not include men as either editors or contributors (Humm: 1992; Evans: 1994).

With the move towards gender studies it can also seem that the reasons for not letting men teach in certain areas are not as justified. In the United States, for example, it would seem that the potential of a male take-over of Women's Studies is already becoming a reality. For example, the first chair in gender studies went to Harry Brod. There are also parallels here with current debates about the development of lesbian and gay studies, and the concern with the field's domination by gay men and, related to this, the question of whether it is preferable to establish lesbian studies and gay studies rather than lesbian and gay studies or queer theory/studies?

Such shifts in the institutions towards gender and men's studies parallels publishers' increasing use of the headings gender and men and masculinity, as they are perceived as being safer and more acceptable to a greater number of potential readers. Feminism and Women's Studies tends to be seen as a more specialist/ separatist market, and many publishers believe that to construct a readership based on gender means a wider audience and increased profits. The marketing strategy is that men, for instance, are more likely to buy books defined in terms of gender and masculinity rather than feminist or Women's Studies because, it is assumed, they feel they are being addressed specifically.

The proliferation of journals such as, for example, *Gender and Education, Gender and Society,* and *Gender and History,* as well as the growing tendency for bookshops to rename Women's Studies or feminist sections as Gender Studies, is also symptomatic of the marketing and packaging of feminism into a diluted and more

---

1. In using the category Feminist/Women's Studies we would want to acknowledge that there is debate over whether Women's Studies is necessarily feminist. Our own position is that this is a political necessity.

widely acceptable form. Moreover, some bookstores now have separate Men's Studies sections and a journal of Men's Studies has been established.

It could be argued that such shifts undermines Feminist/Women's Studies as a field of study before it is even "established". Feminist theory and Women's Studies has not yet fully or systematically taken on the diversity of the experiences of Black women, lesbians, older, working-class and disabled women. But is gender studies more likely to engage with the issues of, for example, racism and anti-lesbianism, if the use of the category gender rather than "woman" (even if the latter term is problematic) depoliticises the relations between the sexes? Will the new men's studies engage with these complexities any better? Canaan and Griffin (1990) argue:

> We still have a long way to go, and it has not been a smooth ride, but TNMS can draw us all back to a narrow political agenda. Radical analyses of "race", class, age, disability and sexuality can all be marginalised as just another set of "variables".

Conclusion

From an examination of recent academic publishing a number of trends can be identified. Firstly, there has been a shift in the amount of space given to Feminist/Women's Studies as a definite subject area, with increasing attention given to gender studies and men and masculinity. Also, men's studies has emerged as a distinct field. Secondly, Women's Studies and feminist theory is often subsumed under the organising principle of gender. Arguably, the terms of the feminist debate are being moved from discussing women's oppression in terms of the (problematic) category of "woman" to using gender as an interrogating and organising category, and by focussing on men and masculinity. Thirdly, words such as feminist, anti-sexist and patriarchy are being used by publishers less and less frequently. It can be argued that these shifts, the latter in particular, represent a re-packaging and a deradicalisation of Women's Studies.

These trends could be seen to support Seidler's suggestion that feminism has been superseded and "issues of gender and masculinity are now central to social theory and philosophy". The question for us as feminists is do we agree with Seidler's pronouncements and, if not, how do we subvert these shifts to maintain a feminist and woman-centred perspective in the 1990s?

Kathleen Barry

Deconstructing Deconstructionism (or, Whatever Happened to Feminist Studies?)

In the beginning there was sex. Sex as in male and female sexes, sex as in sex drives, and sex as in reproduction. Sex was biology as destiny. That was patriarchy's version.

Then along came feminists.

Feminists challenged patriarchal sex and showed that sex is not "natural" rather, sex (as in being able to reproduce) and sex (as in being sexual) are what they are *because* of how we regard and use them. Among all the ways sex could be perceived and used, sex is used to oppress; sex (as in male and female) is constructed into a male hierarchy of domination. Feminists redefined what patriarchy had called "sex" and termed it "gender."

If the patriarchal definition of "sex" was inherent, fixed, natural, and biologically determined, in the feminist concept of gender the whole gamut of sexual labels, attributions, behaviours, and acts are *socially shaped* by the meaning patriarchy gives them; socially shaped to form *sex classes* (that is, women are not just oppressed as a *sex class*).

Now, feminists did not make this up; we simply observed and became conscious of what patriarchy had done to sex. This sex-class analysis became the foundation of feminist theory: the social definition of sex was the *political* condition of women. What we meant by gender no longer tied woman's destiny to her "nature," or to any man's "drives." Gender meant the possibility of change, self-determination, even liberation.

No wonder patriarchy fought back.

The religious right was determined to reduce women to a "natural function" – baby making. The secular left campaigned relentlessly to reduce women to *their* definition of women's "natural function" – sexual availability (as in the sexual liberals' defence of pornography). The collusion of the left and right has been systematic. Unfortunately, the feminist response has been mixed. We

188

continue to organise and march to protect our reproductive rights. But feminists who fight against the reduction of women to pornographic functions are met with bitter hostility from women (within the movement) who defend sexual liberalism. Such debates have raged throughout the movement; academia has been no exception.

Feminism first moved into the university connected to feminist action on the streets: demonstrations, manifestos, sit-ins. In speak-outs, legislative hearings, and research, feminism focused on women's lives to connect theory to politics, research to action. We found common ground, discovered that gender was women's class condition, that sexism and racism were inextricable.

Revolutionary feminist knowledge was put in motion

Almost immediately, reaction set in: *feminist* studies started to become "Women's Studies". Many academics drifted away from political action as their research began to move away from a feminism rooted in women's real lives, and they no longer wanted to be called feminists because it might jeopardise their careers. Most Women's Studies research stopped using gender to mean how patriarchal power shapes sex and sex class. The word disappeared and gender no longer had anything to do with sexuality. "Sex drives" returned to biology as "women's destiny."

There was no single, momentous, historic event, but articles that sustained the feminist analysis of gender were rejected for publication; grants for research based on this theory were denied (that's how the social control of knowledge works). Many Women's Studies programs – and there are some courageous holdouts – distanced themselves from most feminist activism. Inevitably, theory became divorced from politics; research narrowed itself to "objective science," which distanced itself from women's experiences. The defeminism of Women's Studies was under way.

Many programs (secure in having disconnected sex from gender) changed their names to "gender studies." Yet gender, we were warned, no longer included the concept of sex class, and was no longer a redefinition of what patriarchy called natural, inevitable "sex." Likewise, racism no longer included sexism (and the reverse). Turning away from feminism inevitably meant turning away from racism, or meant that racism was not an integral part of the oppression of women.

Meanwhile, radical feminists, exasperated, already had turned to the global community to build feminist connections, while academic feminism continued to fragment. Later, Women's Studies would include the international movement – but only *after* it was narrowed to "acceptable" issues.

What was acceptable? Well, sex discrimination, legal inequality. But not sex; not sexual categories, not sexual behaviour, desire, perception, acts, not sexual politics and power – no, all that was biology, a fixed and done thing. For example, many researchers and theorists were diverted from the study of sexual exploitation. When I was writing *Female Sexual Slavery*, more than one academic woman warned me that if I pursued that line of research, I would not have an academic career.

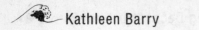

With defeminism, Women's Studies programs were legitimised, and they expanded. But as programs grew, gender ceased to be an analysis of sex as constructed by society. Gender and sex became two different things again: the physical, physiological, and biological were sex; everything else was gender. In fact, gender no longer had anything to do with being sexual. And sex no longer had anything to do with how we use sex and how sex is used to shape us.

Here are some examples of how defeminism works in academia (where feminists who do understand the radical connection between sex and gender are now outsiders – or harassed insiders – to the very Women's Studies programs we initiated twenty years ago).

- A student in my feminist theory seminar asks, "How come we have been studying feminist research for years and no feminists are writing about it in this way?" The question resonates for these politically conscious feminists and male supporters of feminism who feel betrayed by their education. I explain that radical feminists have continued to write this theory for twenty years. Yet a recent book declared that radical feminism died in 1975. No wonder radical feminist theory and research generally are not being taught or, worse, even *read* in most Women's Studies programs.
- Andrea Dworkin speaks at several colleges, and sometimes has to defend her and Catharine MacKinnon's feminist antipornography civil rights ordinance to hostile students who have read only the oppositions tracts and papers.
- Such African American feminist theorists as Michele Wallace and Ntozake Shange have never received the attention they deserve in US Women's Studies courses.
- "Women and development" courses are effectively segregated from concepts of feminism.

I don't want to leave the impression that radical feminists merely have been passive victims. Indeed, we edit book series and journals to ensure the continued publication of radical feminist work. We teach radical feminist works – photocopied when publishers let them go out of print. We watch our students become directors of wife-abuse and rape-crisis programs, as we continue connecting research to action, and theory to practice. Altogether, we go on behaving as if we were still alive – considering that we were said to have died in 1975.

Meanwhile, back in academic defeminism, the patriarchal meanings of sex returned. We began to hear about the "pleasure and danger in sexuality" (sado-masochism), as if that was in the nature of the sexuality of the person who pursued that pleasure and danger. Only when sex was renaturalised back into "innate biological drives" did it become a legitimate subject of Women's Studies. Conve-niently, the personal was no longer political. The "pleasure and danger in sexuality" was defended as a natural right of the not yet fertilised ovum – flows over the human rights of those who conceive it, carry it, birth it, and raise it.

Back in the real world these intellectual games are destroying young women's lives. The generation of women who are now teenagers face the sexual determinism of both sexual liberals and fundamentalist conservatives. Every year over one million US teenagers will get pregnant – one in ten between the ages of fifteen and nineteen; 34 per cent of girls age fourteen who become pregnant will give birth. These young women are disproportionately African American – because oppression always impacts the hardest on the least-protected classes. State parental consent laws are making abortion increasingly unavailable and the pregnancy rate is twice as high among teenagers of color as among Euro-Americans. Not only have lives been thwarted and health put in jeopardy, but the intense promotion of early sex combined with the increased denial of abortion to teenagers is effecting a major demographic shift in the female gender class. The next generation of women, having reared babies through their teenage and early adult years, will not inherit those few victories and emancipations won by women of my generation: although we opened educational and employment opportunities to women as never before, teen mothers will earn about half as much income as those giving birth for the first time in their twenties.

Isn't it all the more astonishing, then, that in the ivory tower sex has nothing to do with pregnancy, racism has come to mean only differences, and rights are only individual?

What's it all about?

Remember "the personal is political"? Well, first it's about making the personal unpolitical. It's about the use of feminism as a personal defence by some women of their private choices to submit to pornographically or reproductively mandated sex. It may seem harsh to pose this as women's choice. But in fact, the refusal of women of my generation to fully confront that very gender power now results in the *denial* of choice to today's teenagers – choice to be sexual and/or pregnant only when it will not jeopardise their health and well-being, when it is under their control and determination, if and when they want it.

It's also about "difference." That began with the appearance of socialist feminism, where theory separates women and emphasises their class oppositions to each other. I still remember an early Women's Studies conference in 1973, when working-class women were asked to sit on one side of the room and tell their complaints to middle-class women. Vitriolic charges were hurled and the real enemy was not even there. Difference ruled the day. But what I know from growing up poor myself is that the marginal are ultimately left to fend for themselves because *no politics of difference intends to include*. It is the making of the "other." When difference is our first recognition of each other it becomes the primary basis of separating women from each other. In an age no longer identified with the political consciousness that was developing in the 1960s, difference provides the first basis of racism, sexism, and class privilege.

"Difference" can mean that pregnant, black teenagers are a problem that only African American women – not all of us – need address.

"Difference" means that teenage pregnancy is a feminist reproductive issue disconnected from the sexualization of women and therefore from the feminist movement's protest against pornography. How teenagers got pregnant is separated from their *being* pregnant.

Difference. The word produces raptures in the ivory tower of feminist theory. It now goes under a new name: *deconstruction.* Many scholars have rushed to adopt this intentionally inaccessible theory recently imported to the US. Deconstruction tells us that everything, including our own selves, is about difference. Our selves are decentred selves; nothing has any inherent meaning. Therefore, not only is the personal not political; the personal and political are deconstructed in favor of their differences. (Don't worry about what that means because the meaning isn't always there, anyway. It's in the spaces between the differences. That doesn't make sense? Well, that's because we're not looking at the spaces in between.)

Take sex and gender. Remember how university feminism separated them. Well, deconstruction does not treat sex as innate; no, it goes a step further: it asks us to look at whatever is in "the spaces between" sex and gender. In other words, sex classes are false dichotomies because all dichotomies are false: male/female, white/black, oppressor/oppressed, rich/poor, and capitalist/proletariat. (Poof! Hierarchy disappears!) By a wondrous act of will, all dichotomies have been deferred. (Deferring is considered important because it is in the French meaning of difference.) All is about the spaces between, about nothing. Well, try telling that to the thirteen-year-old about to deliver the child she will rear until she is thirty-one.

Maybe you still don't understand? Just as well. These theorists like to think of theory as too complicated for ordinary folks. Deconstruction theories properly float only in the rarefied atmosphere of the ivory tower. (Sound classically male?) Or you understand but don't agree? Clearly you're a radical feminist stubbornly persisting with the "wrong analysis." Now that few remember what that analysis is, deconstructionists can make it up: "radical feminists tend to see the root of women's oppression in either women's biological capacity for motherhood or innate, biologically determined male aggression, as manifest in rape, which makes men dangerously different from women".

There you have it! It's *radical feminists* who make men "dangerously different" from women! And all the time I thought patriarchy had done that! But in all the emphasis on difference, deconstructionists are trying to tell us that men are actually no different from women? Well, that makes feminism vanish. Voilà: "postfeminism."

But feminism will not disappear by pseudo-intellectual fiat. Students may be the ones who will turn it around again. Along the hallways of academia, in muted tones, the questions are being asked: "What is this about, anyway?" "It doesn't sound right." There's something wrong here but I can't put my finger on it." Questioning leads to consciousness, to rage, to action. I wonder, as I hear these student utterances, didn't we begin that way over twenty years ago?

What I know from growing up poor is that no "politics of difference" intends to include..

---

* Originally published in *Ms. Magazine* (1991, January–February).

Deirdre Carraher, Sharon Cox, Elizabeth Daake,
Michele Gagne, Patricia Good, Jessie McManmon
and Marjorie O'Connor

"Generation X", The "Third Wave", or Just Plain Radical: Reviewing the Reviewers of Catharine MacKinnon's *Only Words*

As we stand on the library steps with other members of the college community, our candles burning bright, we remember the women killed in the Montreal Massacre. Each speaker reminds us of the many forms of violence against women that happen around the world. We know there are many who support us, but that some are sitting in the library, studying frantically for exams. Across the campus we see our supporters wearing the white ribbons distributed by the Women's Forum. The hours of work that went into preparing the ribbons and the mailing to which they were attached has made this vigil all the more important and personal for us. Each person sitting on these steps is a visible sign that there is an awareness that violence against women, the backlash against women, and the misogyny of our society are related. We recognize how wrong it is to blame the victims of violence, and we see the need to speak out and to demand change. We are here to remember, and to call for action.[1]

We're a group of undergraduate Women Studies concentrators at Holy Cross College, Worcester, Massachusetts who have spent many intense hours reading,

---

1. Elizabeth Daake, December 6, 1994. As co-chair of the Women's Forum, a feminist student organization at Holy Cross College, Daake has worked with her colleagues to draw attention to the extent of violence against women.

writing and discussing feminist theory and practice.[2] In terms of understanding the ways in which depictions of women shape behaviours and in particular the way in which pornography harms all women, we found that *Only Words* by Catharine MacKinnon (1993b) was one of the most shocking, yet empowering texts we read. With style, strength, courage, biting humor and impressive scholarship, she argues that pornography is not about the First Amendment protection of free speech. Rather she demonstrates that the harm pornography does to women is a civil rights issue that properly falls under the Fourteenth Amendment equal protection clause. Sexualizing violence and claiming it is protected as free speech needs to be challenged and MacKinnon has given us the resources to do just that. A rape that is packaged as pornography is neither speech nor free. It does not facilitate further speech: it silences.

Reading this material was for us a real jolt, an eye-opener. Most of us had no idea about the content of hard core pornography, no idea of the extent of the exploitation of women by this multi-million dollar industry. It was something that was hidden, perhaps in the bottom of a closet or under the bed. We now believe that it is something everyone should know about because the harm of pornography is not restricted to the women used in its production. As MacKinnon argues while it is considered entertaining to watch women being dismembered, abused, tortured, humiliated and treated as so many fragmented body parts, and while the women are depicted as enjoying the abuse, we are all harmed. Pornography, she argues, in not about thoughts, it is about behaviours. *Only Words* was not easy reading but our class was in agreement that issues such as rape, sexual harassment, prostitution and pornography need to be understood and written about.

Having worked hard to come to grips with her argument, we were shocked and angered when we realized how MacKinnon's work was attacked by supposedly objective reviewers in supposedly respectable publications. When we read the reviews of Carlin Romano (1993) in the *Nation*, Ronald Dworkin (1993) in the *New York Review of Books* and Susie Bright (1993) in *Express Books*, we wondered, "Did we read the same book?" Here were the same tactics that are used to silence us as undergraduates being used to silence, demean and threaten a senior

---

2. In the second semester of 1994, in our capstone course "Feminist Frames: Contemporary Social Issues", taught by Diane Bell, we studied Susan Faludi (1991), Catharine MacKinnon (1993b) Cynthia Enloe (1993), Joni Seager (1993) and Toni Morrison (1992). Our exercise for MacKinnon was to write (proposed) letters to the editors of three publications where particularly vicious reviews of MacKinnon had appeared. Patricia Good and Sharon Cox wrote in response to Ronald Dworkin's (1993) review in the *New York Review of Books*, Michele Gagne and Elizabeth Daake in response to Carlin Romano (1993) in the *Nation*, and Deirdre Carraher, Jessie McManmon and Marjorie O'Connor in response to Susie Bright (1993) in *Express Books*. This piece draws on those letters and retains individual voices in each section. Although we didn't always agree, the collaborative process has been fun and helped us clarify our own positions. We have read each other's papers, worked as a team and in sub-groups, and with some editorial assistance from Diane Bell, have drawn our ideas together. This has been quite an experience for women in their early twenties.

feminist who named an abuse against women that passes as free speech. What is so dangerous about setting out a well documented argument? Why were reviewers reluctant to take her ideas seriously? Why was she reviewed by persons known to be hostile to her position on pornography? In short why can the media not deal with a radical feminist analysis? We know that identifying as a feminist, especially a radical feminist can be dangerous. (On our campus such an identification provokes disdain, humor, and name calling: we are accused of male-bashing, of being frustrated, ill-tempered individuals.) But we also know that any woman who challenges male privilege is in danger. When Marc Lepine walked into the Engineering Department at Montreal, he singled out feminists as the cause of his problems. Certainly he killed fourteen women, but why did he assume they were all feminists? Was it because they were training in a field that had previously been all male? His act was not reported, nor is it widely understood as a sex based crime. Had he killed African American men while screaming a racist epithet, we would have had no trouble understanding the case as one of race hatred.

How we use words is important. Why is it so hard for society to name the abuse "hate speech" when it concerns women? Deirdre Carraher, for one, is highly suspicious of the labeling and the backlash:

Name calling trivializes your ideas, makes any substantive exchange impossible, and leaves you wondering how, when, where, it will ever be possible for women to enjoy the full benefits of citizenship, to walk safely through the streets at night, to be respected for ideas, to speak in your own voice, of your own experiences, to be a self-determining human being. Is it so much better for our generation? It seems that the backlash against feminism permeates our lives, but we do have foremothers and calling us "Generation X", as if we were lost and without moorings is not accurate. Similarly designating us the "Third Wave", must not be a way of driving a wedge between us and radical feminists such as Catharine MacKinnon.

"Intruder in the Lust" by Susie Bright

Why is Catharine MacKinnon trying to put the lid on sexuality? I'm one of the miserable group of book reviewers and legal scholars who forced ourselves to read every word of her rotten prose.... MacKinnon ... is the typical academic who must publish, but can't write (Bright: 1993, pp. 1, 11).

So what is Bright's expertise to review this book? She cites much anecdotal material and reveals that one of her books on sex was stopped at the Canadian border as a result of new obscenity legislation that incorporates some of MacKinnon's ideas (p. 12), but there is no evidence that she understands MacKinnon's legal analysis.[3]

---

3. Bright could have told us that she is the co-founder and editor of *On Our Backs*, a magazine for the adventurous lesbian; *Penthouse*'s first women's porn critic, and editor of the annual *Best America Erotica* series. She is hardly a disinterested critic.

Rather than spell out the feminist debate regarding pornography, Bright lumps MacKinnon with "the most right-wing fanatics in the country" (p. 12). There is no serious attention given to the argument of *Only Words*. Bright is bored by it. It is passé and, in her view, wildly out of step with the experience of "Generation X". She is much happier talking about MacKinnon's disposition, intentions and marriage, and confides that she sometimes wonders, "if MacKinnon has simply been driven mad by all the sick things that people do to one another" (p. 12). Apparently in addition to being boring, MacKinnon is also crazy!

Pointing out that she is a member of the so called "Third Wave", Deirdre Carraher writes:

I found numerous discrepancies in Bright's cliché laden character analysis of my feminist generation. Bright asserts that "Generation X" feminists (the use of this term alone is extremely limiting) are not able to and have no interest in relating to the Second Wave theorists such as MacKinnon. She goes on to say that a twenty-something feminist friend of hers regards MacKinnon "as if she were a pair of bell-bottom pants" (p. 12). The work of Catharine MacKinnon, Andrea Dworkin, Gloria Steinem and many others, form the theoretical base from which many radical feminists of my generation formulate their own questions and activism. These feminists are not stagnant women whose writings from the seventies are being read in Women's Studies classes as history: they are tackling urgent issues as they relate to women's lives today. Far from feeling distant from Catharine MacKinnon and her peers, I feel inspired by the possibilities for striking a powerful union between the second and third waves.

It is clear that for anyone interested in buttressing the institution of patriarchy, radical feminists must be stereotyped into one mold and it must be one that is at odds with mainstream society. If the impressive diversity amongst radical feminists was revealed, perhaps more and more women would feel they could relate to the movement. Someone from the right wing is having an apocalyptic nightmare as they read this: a world run by man-hating radicals. In order to prevent this radical coup d'état, the word feminist has been transformed into a negative and fear inducing label.

Marjorie O'Connor adds that:

Women of the so called Generation X are working hard to become powerful and successful, but they do not want to, nor should they have to sacrifice their female beauty. Bright attempts to turn Generation X women away from the Third Wave of feminism by presenting a harsh and unattractive image of a radical feminist. Feminism and feminist should not be dirty words, women should not be intimidated about being associated with them. If the Third Wave of feminism is going to gain momentum and fight the backlash, these must become acceptable words for women to believe in and use with comfort. It is important for future advancements that all women are empowered towards feminism and not persuaded to stay silent by misdirected reviewers such as Susie Bright.

Bright attacks Catharine MacKinnon in the same manner that feminists are so often stereotyped. Dominating the first page of the review is an "illustration" by Spain Rodriguez, of MacKinnon unattractively portrayed with baggy eyes, a stern countenance, and legs spread open. She sits atop of a strong box out of which naked men and women struggle and then race to video outlets. Andrea Dworkin, wearing worker's coveralls, sternly assists MacKinnon. The text of the review echoes the visual attack: MacKinnon's ideas, beliefs, or book for that matter are not really addressed. Instead, Bright attempts to trivialize the strength of MacKinnon's argument by presenting her as an overbearing, crazed feminist. By focusing on MacKinnon's physical appearance and attractiveness, Bright is guilty of exactly what MacKinnon seeks to expose in *Only Words*. MacKinnon's beauty should not be an issue, she is not an object to be looked at, rather she is a woman whose ideas and words must be heard. The *Express Books* attack perpetuates the damaging stereotype of radical feminists as ugly, mean and irrational women. The caricature is unflattering. What woman, feminist or not, would ever want to be depicted in such a manner?

Jessie McManmon is also angered by the use of labels:

"Femi-Nazi": is this a label that any young woman would want to be called or call herself? Surely not, but it is the latest in the ongoing bashing of Third Wave feminism. Offensive words such as these are being used by the media to disassociate the so-called "Generation X" from feminist causes such as the ones MacKinnon addresses in *Only Words*. Through subtle and blatant attacks, the media have been successful in pushing many of our generation away from identifying as feminists who are portrayed as anti-sex, man-hating, extremists. Their words are taken out of context and their message warped so that no woman can or would want to identify with a feminist cause.

Often book reviewers of feminist works so viciously misconstrue ideas and take quotations out of context so widely that the reader has no notion of what is being argued in the text. We are told by Ms. Bright that Professor MacKinnon is someone who is working to abolish sexuality. According to Bright, it is important to MacKinnon to shut women up: "Why do we have to keep our legs crossed for her?" demands Bright. As a member of the Third Wave, I would like to inform Bright: nobody asked you to. Analyses such as Bright's exemplify the underlying system working to keep our generation misinformed and keep women, as powerful and threatening to that system, as MacKinnon, under wraps.

"Between the Motion and the Act" by Carlin Romano

Suppose I decide to rape Catharine MacKinnon before reviewing her book. Because I'm uncertain whether she understands the difference between being raped and being exposed to pornography, I consider it required` research for my critique of her manifesto that pornography equals rape and should be banned. I plot and strategize, but at the last minute, I chicken out. People simply won't understand. Nonetheless, when I sit down to write, I still believe that understanding her support for censorship of pornography requires raping her, so I do the next best thing: I imagine the act (Romano: 1993, p. 563).

Thus begins Romano's review of *Only Words* in the *Nation* of November 15, 1993. Elizabeth Daake and Michele Gagne write:

While Mr Romano claims to be a rational, objective reader, he is not. Such a person does not exist, as we have discovered as we struggle to combine our different perspectives into a thoughtful, coherent response to his review. Although we both agree that Romano has an agenda that involves discrediting MacKinnon as a radical feminist, we strongly disagree about the actual focus of his review. Is he attacking MacKinnon's radical words, or MacKinnon as a radical feminist, and by extension all radical feminists?'

Michele believes it is MacKinnon's words that Romano seeks to discredit:

From the very first page of her book to her closing argument, Romano feels the need to disempower MacKinnon by silencing her. Catharine MacKinnon opens *Only Words* with a "thought experiment" that recounts three painful experiences that could have been very real experiences for any woman. The only problem is that woman's experiences of violence throughout history have been erased by those who choose not to see them as real experiences. The images MacKinnon evokes are shocking, and they obviously shocked Carlin Romano. He responds the only way he knows how. He responds by trying to silence the echoes of such images. Romano tries to discredit MacKinnon's "thought experiment" by first creating his own absurd and offensive scenario. When he chooses to use rape as a "thought experiment" in his review, in a sense, he normalizes the word rape. The contextual meaning of rape, which for many women is that they know the word through a painful experience that affects their lives violently, directly, and personally, is lost. For Romano, rape is truly only a word.

Romano then attempts to argue that MacKinnon is "trying to persuade us to believe that every actress in pornography works under the conditions of Linda Lovelace-like oppression that already constitute a punishable crime" (p. 563). In essence, Romano concludes that MacKinnon is merely bantering about the unjust treatment of the women who perform in these films. However, if Romano wasn't so concerned with silencing the words of MacKinnon before they had been written, he might have read them more carefully and realized that MacKinnon seeks to end the degradation of women, and that includes the humiliation that women undergo when solicited for porn films, and when these movies are viewed over and over again. More importantly MacKinnon wants to end the projection of negative images of women into a society where men and women are inequal. It is her argument that it is this inequality that is being exploited in sexually demeaning acts. If negative images of women, such as that of "vaginas being rammed" are kept in mainstream culture and displayed for entertainment purposes, then they will in turn be seen as possible roles for women to assume in everyday activities. Thus what MacKinnon wants to emphasize is that in order to make her anti-pornography campaign a success, there is a need to protect the rights of all women who are affected by pornography.

Elizabeth Daake sees:

The very images that MacKinnon wants to stop are the ones that Romano turns against her. Romano is not really addressing MacKinnon's book, but instead using the book to mount a personal attack on Professor MacKinnon. His vitriolic writing assaults MacKinnon as whining, irrational, man-hating, and overly sensitive, while he claims to be the rational reader. He is not. Romano reveals his true agenda and prejudices in his statement that MacKinnon's "slogans" will appear on "your banners" I can only assume that he is addressing radical feminists who are traditionally associated with speaking out and protesting violence against women. He reduces MacKinnon's complex argument about pornography violating women's human rights to a piece of feminist propaganda.

It is ironic that Romano's claims that MacKinnon's assertion that words can be actions is foolish, when in fact he proves its truth in his review. His vicious "thought experiment" rape of MacKinnon illustrates his own awareness of the power of words. Yet he sees no problem with his vivid mental rape of MacKinnon, because he says that this threat is only words, and therefore has no impact on women. He is wrong. As a woman reading this review, I felt physically ill at its violence. Not only is he using the act of rape in his book review, but he is blaming his victim for it because she dared to speak out. Since she has chosen to speak, she must be on a "star trip" and must be returned to her proper place.

The very hatred and ego that Romano claims MacKinnon promotes are exactly what he exhibits in his assault on her. She is constructed as the classic man-hating feminist: Hysterical, prudish, and whiny. He dismisses her argument by discrediting her personally. She is accused of having a dehumanizing attitude towards men and reducing them to penes, to body parts. Her view of sex is "insular", her argument "soaked in gender hatred". These combined charges sound very familiar to anyone who has read *Only Words* – they are MacKinnon's arguments about pornography if women are substituted for the poor, victimized men that Romano has apparently discovered. Romano is turning MacKinnon's words against her and attempting to silence her with them. He is far more guilty of gender hatred than she is, as his bitter refutation of her argument depends on dehumanizing her and constructing her in a way that is more convenient to his view of who should be heard.

This review is such a vicious personal assault, that I can not believe it was published. Somehow I doubt that if I wrote a letter beginning "Suppose I decide to castrate Carlin Romano before responding to his review", it would fare as well as his bitter attack. And it would be less threatening, because one in three men will not be castrated or be sexually assaulted in their lifetime.

Romano's review was published, and we (Elizabeth and Michele) felt compelled to respond, because he is not using only words, but he is mobilizing social resistance to radical feminists' analyses of existing power structures in order to silence MacKinnon. If we do not use our own voices to challenge outrageous attacks like those made by Romano, then he has succeeded in silencing us as well. Audre Lorde was right that our silence will not protect us, and by writing this response, we are not protecting Carlin Romano.

Many other people shared the outrage expressed by our class. In the December 27, 1993 edition of the *Nation*, an exchange was printed. Headed "Words are all I have," the editors noted that they had received "an unusually high volume of mail" in response to the Romano review and that "most of the mail was in spirited disagreement with Romano's method of reviewing MacKinnon's book". Still the editors believed publishing the review was consistent with their "commitment (not shared by all their readers) to untrammeled speech" (p. 786). Breaking with tradition Lindsay Waters of Harvard University Press, along with six co-signatures wrote that while "I believe firmly that publishers should not respond to the reviews of their books . . . Carlin Romano's piece is so vile I cannot refrain from telling you how horrified I am by it . . . there are limits. Romano has violated them" (p. 786). Romano, citing John Stuart Mill's *On Liberty* argues that responding to a text with only a "'portion of truth' . . . helps us refine some larger sounder truth" (p. 816). Romano accuses MacKinnon of lack of philosophical sophistication and Waters (1994, pp. 786, 816) calls Romano's argument "philosophically wrong". What disappears in these exchanges is the originality and clarity of MacKinnon's thesis. It is a point MacKinnon (1994b, p. 47) makes in responding to Ronald Dworkin.

"Women and Pornography" by Ronald Dworkin

> People once defended free speech to protect the rights of firebrands attacking governments, or dissenters resisting an established church, or radicals campaigning for unpopular political causes. Free speech was clearly worth fighting for, and still is in many parts of the world where these rights hardly exist. But in America now, free-speech partisans find themselves defending mainly racists shouting "nigger" or Nazis carrying swastikas or – most often – men looking at pictures of naked women with their legs spread open (Ronald Dworkin: 1993, p. 36).

Patricia Good and Sharon Cox see this review as located firmly within the political philosophical tradition of liberalism, and once again Mill is evoked. Professor Ronald Dworkin, a frequent contributor to the *New York Review of Books*, responds to MacKinnon's radical arguments in his customary liberal voice. His concern for individuals rights resonates with mainstream American political sentiment, yet disregards the consequences of the reality of majority rule. While pornography that is vile and degrading is hailed as "free speech", we would like to ask whose free speech are we talking about?

Dworkin's reluctance to deal with the topic is obvious in the opening paragraphs as he enumerates other more important, more liberal feminist issues such as "abortion and the fight for women's equality in employment and politics" that he suggests should be on a feminist agenda. Hoping to overshadow the influence of MacKinnon's analysis, Dworkin reveals his eagerness to turn his back on the harm of pornography and to silence the argument MacKinnon's is desperately trying to make heard. Moreover, there is room (and need) for discussion of all feminist issues, as well as different analyses of them.

Most of those who disagree with MacKinnon do so on the basis of their belief in the need to protect free speech and to make no exceptions. This absolutism asserts that protecting all speech, especially that which makes us uncomfortable, is in all our best interests. It is argued that once we start singling out particular classes of speech and restricting them, we begin on the "slippery slope" which can end in anything that offends those in power being banned. This would erode the very intent of the First Amendment. In explicating this position Dworkin evokes John Stuart Mill's theory that "truth is most likely to emerge from a 'marketplace' of ideas freely exchanged and debated" (1993, p. 36). We agree wholeheartedly with your statement, "It is preposterous to think that we are more likely to reach truth about anything at all because pornographic ideas are involved" (1993, p. 36). Furthermore we agree with you that this would still be no reason to ban hard-core pornography. What we ask you to look at in the marketplace of ideas, though, is not the ideas, so much as the market itself.

We know that women earn sixty-three cents in the male dollar. Pragmatically, in our world, this means that we are less than two-thirds as powerful, and when a less powerful group is subordinated, degraded, and abused repeatedly in films and magazines, it is no longer First Amendment territory. Similarly when African-Americans are treated more harshly, victimized and degraded more often in these films than whites, it is not merely coincidence: it is systemic. What it amounts to is a violation of civil rights – exactly what MacKinnon calls it.

Ronald Dworkin continues to display misunderstanding of MacKinnon's analysis by asserting that pornography is "deeply offensive" and thus misses the heart of MacKinnon's argument that pornography is not just "offensive" it is harmful. MacKinnon's radical approach demonstrates how pornography objectifies, exploits, and viciously reduces women, as a group, to the status of sexual devices rather than allowing them to be seen as human beings in their own right. She repeatedly focuses not on the harm of what pornography says, but on the harm of what it does through its acts, behaviours and expressions of violence as sexy. MacKinnon is referring to sex-based acts of discrimination that are achieved through manipulation, coercion, force, assault, intimidation, crime, humiliation, injury, torture and dehumanization. This is precisely what is harmful about pornography and is the key to her argument.

Ronald Dworkin claimed that MacKinnon's argument was a new one. MacKinnon, in her reply, has taken issue with this pointing out that as early as 1983 she and Andrea Dworkin advanced their equality approach to pornography through their civil rights ordinance that allowed "civil suits for sex discrimination by those who can prove harm through pornography" (MacKinnon: 1994, p. 47).

Further, Andrea Dworkin, in a debate with Ronald Dworkin in the mid 1980s at the University of California at Davis "even read to him about equality from his work. Are we to understand that it took him until now to hear it?" asks MacKinnon (1994, p. 47). He may continue to assert that she is pursuing a novel line but his argument for protecting free speech before equality certainly is not. It's been "business as usual" since Aristotle to assert that women (and minorities) are better off protected than equal.

On Silence and Speech
In this piece we have focused on the ways in which reviewers seek to silence radical feminist analyses. We know there are significant disagreements within feminist circles regarding pornography. Anti-censorship feminists argue that banning pornography won't eradicate violence against women, while pro-sex feminists argue that pornography liberates women. The former group has never understood that the Dworkin/MacKinnon ordinance (1988) is not censorship. We find it interesting that women of colour are now joining in the debate, especially with their critiques of misogynous rap (see hooks: 1994). We urge our generation to read and discuss *Only Words* and not be silenced by personal, ill informed and self-interested attacks. Along with MacKinnon (1993b, p. 109) we look forward to the time when "equality is a fact, not merely a word, [and] words of racial or sexual assault and humiliation will be nonsense syllables". Then silence will be something to celebrate.

> When this day comes, silence will be neither an act of power, as it is now for those who hide behind it, nor the experience of imposed powerlessness, as it is now for those who are submerged in it, but a context of repose into which thought can expand, an invitation that gives speech its shape, an opening to a new conversation (MacKinnon: 1993b, pp. 109–110).

Andrea Dworkin

Dworkin on Dworkin*

> *Andrea Dworkin talks about her work, her life and the future of feminism with Elizabeth Braeman and Carol Cox in this, the full version of an interview first published in the tenth birthday issue of* Off Our Backs.

Elisabeth Braeman: *The theme of* Letters from a War Zone Writings 1976–1989 *is that women do not have freedom of speech. What exactly do you mean by that?*

Andrea Dworkin: Well, I think that our restraint from being able to engage in speech operates on many levels. There's the superficial level of what's required to gain access to mainstream media; the answer is complete and total conformity, not just stylistically but in terms of content. You have to say what fits in their picture, what it is they want to hear. If you don't do that you will not be able to publish; you'll have a terrible time. That's across the board, for any political person. But it works in a much more ruthless way for feminists because men take feminist analysis as a sexual challenge and experience it that way, and therefore have a very visceral and vengeful reaction to pieces of "speech" that they don't like. They experience, I think, a lot of radical feminist writing actually as if it were a sexual assault on them; and since most of them don't know what a sexual assault is, they have the privilege of overreacting in that way.

    Then, on a deeper level, one of the things I've learned in the last fifteen years is how much women are silenced through sexual abuse. The simple experience of being abused, whether as a child or as an adult, has an incredible impact on everything about the way you see the world around you, so that either you don't feel you can speak because you're frightened of what the retaliation will be, or you don't trust your experience of reality enough to speak – that happens to a lot of incest victims. Or you are actually physically kept from being able to speak –

---

* Reprinted from *Trouble and Strife* (1990).

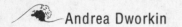

battered women do not have freedom of speech. So it operates on that level.

In *Letters from a War Zone,* I quoted Hannah Arendt, who was a brilliant woman but certainly no feminist, and her observation that without freedom of movement you can't have freedom of anything. And in fact most of us still live as quasi-prisoners in order to maintain some kind of safety. If you think about all the places we don't go, all the boundaries we have to accept in order to stay alive, then the extra boundaries that we put in there as a kind of buffer zone for ourselves so that we all feel safe whether we're safe or not, our freedom of movement is exceptionally restricted. And then also, I was referring to the restriction, the physical restriction of women's bodies in women's clothes, in things like high-heeled shoes, in girdles, in things that bind the body, where the object is to turn the woman into some kind of ornament and when turned into an ornament she then is deprived, literally, of the physical ability to move or it's severely impaired. So I think it operates on all those different levels and I think that any woman who thinks that she has freedom of speech or freedom of movement is absolutely denying reality.

EB: The argument used in defence of pornography is that it is freedom of speech and that women have freedom of speech and that we can combat pornography in the "marketplace of ideas". What you have said certainly has an impact on that idea that we can freely compete in the marketplace of ideas and that our words have equal impact as the words of pornographers do.

AD: I think that is a specific argument and it's very important to address it specifically. The First Amendment [to the US Constitution] only protects speech that has already been expressed and it only protects it from punishment by the state. It doesn't stop a man from punching you out for what you said. Supposedly there are other laws that do, but in fact they don't. It doesn't stop anybody from using economic recriminations against you for what you say. It doesn't stop anybody from deciding that you're an uppity bitch because of what you say and they're going to hurt you because you said something that they didn't like. In interpersonal relationships that women have with men, think about how often women are insulted verbally or are physically hurt because of what we say. We say something that is perceived as being not sufficiently compliant and then you take that and you put it out in the world in the sphere of social reality. There is no doubt that the First Amendment does not save women from all the kinds of punishment that women are consistently subjected to.

The second part is that the First Amendment protects people who have access to the media, and in our country that mostly means people with money. It doesn't protect anybody who doesn't have access and was never intended to. It was written by white men who owned white women and black slaves. A lot of them owned black slaves, none of whom ever got any First Amendment protection of any kind. In fact, if there's any kind of correlation between the First Amendment and the actual status quo, the keeping of wealth by those who have privilege, it specifically has to do with literacy. White men, who owned property, who owned women as chattels, who owned black slaves, also happened to be the people who could read and write; there were actually laws in the slave states saying that you could not teach a slave how to read, it was against the law. The First Amendment didn't do anything about it. Now, lawyers have all kinds of reasons why that's true. It doesn't matter. The point is that the First Amendment is now being used in an almost metaphoric way for freedom of speech as if the First Amendment protects everybody's right to speech and it doesn't. It's not a grant to individuals of a right to speak. If it were, you would be able to go to the government and you would be able to say, "I need four minutes on NBC. I have something I want to say." You can't do that [laughter]. I have found the arguments around the First Amendment incredibly naive, absolutely unwilling to deal with the reality of male power, the meaning of wealth in this society, and I've been deeply disappointed not to see feminists making an analysis that addresses the marginality of women's speech and the speech in particular of people of color, who also don't have that kind of access. Probably the worst liberal cop-out of the Women's Movement has been to accept this freedom of speech bullshit from white boys, who in fact do have freedom of speech, because they do have money and they do have access.

Carol Cox: You say in "Pornography and Grief" written in 1978, "Perhaps I have found the real source of my grief: we have not yet become a revolutionary movement." Are we closer or further away from forming a revolutionary movement?

AD: The honest answer is: I don't know. The movement has changed tremendously. On one hand, there has been an incredible global spread of feminism so that international feminism is tremendously vibrant and that is very hopeful for the future of women on the planet. But in the USA the epidemic of violence against women has intensified so greatly. The situation of women in my view is so much worse and so much of what was the Women's Movement twelve years ago has, in a sense, cut and run. They have taken what the Women's Movement has been able to give them, which is a kind of minimal economic advancement if you are middle-class and have certain skills, especially if you are an academic or a lawyer. A lot of women in the movement really are liberal democrats. Feminism has become more and more a lifestyle word.

On the other hand, I think there has been a deepening understanding of radical feminist ideas and more grassroots, radical activity now probably than there has ever been, even though it is not reflected in the media. There is also what I consider to be a relatively new development in that there are also men out there who have been at least partially formed by feminist ideas and who are, in some cases, activists against male violence against women.

At the same time, I see the solid middle, which every movement has to have, having kind of fallen apart. I am a radical but I'm a radical who believes that you have to have the whole spectrum of people. You need your mainstream

feminists, you need your reformists, you need the people who do all these different kinds of work, and I don't know what it means if you've got very brilliant, very resourceful feminists all over the country who are doing direct action, who are doing grassroots organising, but who are very poor and don't have access to mass media in a country where mass media makes up reality for so many people.

It is my impression that at the beginning of the women's movement – and I wasn't here for it, I was living in Europe at the time – people were very excited and thrilled and celebrational and all those words that I think are fairly good words: arrogant and pushy and brazen. However, they apparently didn't anticipate that people who had power were not going to be thrilled to give it up and might actually start fighting back. When they started fighting back some blood was going to flow because they have the means to hurt you very badly. We have lost that middle ground because the retaliation against feminists has been very serious and very systematic. Now women are making decisions for individual survival over political solidarity and political, what I would call, honour.

CC: When you say that you think a lot more radical, grassroots actions are going on, is that something you've seen by being around?

AD: You can't actually hear about most of it. It is not reported, even in the feminist press, which is much more shallow than it used to be and much less in touch with the women who are actually doing things. I know a lot of the women because I travel through the country all of the time and I see it. I see it happening. If I weren't there and I didn't see it, I wouldn't know it was happening.

Liberal feminism is the feminism that the media plays back to us. But through travelling I can tell you that there are women everywhere, in every part of the country, every small town, every rural by-way, who are doing something for women. Some of it is direct action, some of it is what is called social services, to do with battery and to do with rape. I think that there is a deeper understanding of the role of male violence in keeping women down now than there ever has been. How it is going to express itself in a way that's going to make the whole society have to deal with it on its own terms is another question. The Women's Movement in that sense has deepened, has reached more people, but one of the problems that we have is that some of us, in different ways and at different times, really are ghetto feminists. You know, we know ourselves and our five friends and that is how we see feminism.

But, in fact, any political movement that is really going to be successful is going to involve not just people that you don't know, but people that are very different from you. One of the interesting things about feminism now is that it is no longer the urban, middle-class movement that it started out being; is that you find feminists in Appalachia, you find feminists in Rock Springs, Wyoming, who are the strongest damn feminists you'll ever see in your lives and they are standing up to those men out there and that's sort of thrilling.

EB: Along those lines, what do you see as the changing role of lesbians in grassroots radical feminism?

AD: What I see disturbs me very much. I see women younger than myself, I'm forty-three, and I see women who are ten years younger than myself feeling, and maybe they're right because they're smart women, that they have to be closeted. Women who ten years ago would not have stood for being closeted now are exceptionally determined to have a very schizoid existence, a professional world in which they function another way. That upsets and depresses me beyond anything I can say to you. I think they have looked at the environment they live in and probably have judged it correctly but I hate it that they're doing that and a lot of lesbians are doing it.

In terms of the whole country, I see women in these grassroots groups taking stands for lesbians even if the lesbians are closeted. For instance, to go back to Rock Springs, Wyoming, for a minute, they include something about lesbians in everything they do and I think that a lot of women in the country consider it a moral imperative. Lesbians are still responsible for a lot of the leadership in whatever is happening all over the country, but there's much more hiding and secrecy and duplicity again and I find it very frightening.

EB: Do you think that has to do with the rise of the right wing?

AD: I haven't heard anybody have a different motive for anything that was done since Reagan was elected. That is too simple. I will tell you frankly: I think it is because of the pressure of the people around them and the people around them usually are liberal men. That's the point of contact, that's where the pressure hits home. You can blame it on a conservative environment but the fact of the matter is that those men, the ones who are close to you, the ones who are near you, the ones you work with, want to believe that you're there and they can fuck you. The pressure is coming from them.

Amerikans, by which I mean people who live in the United States, are incredibly juvenile about social change. Robin Morgan called it "ejaculatory politics": if it doesn't happen right away it doesn't happen. The Women's Movement in this country has all the same characteristics as the culture that we live in, short-term gratification, personal fulfilment, personal advancement, and yes, coming out as a lesbian can get in the way of that. Liberals and left-wing men have recolonised women around the fear of the right. This troubles me, it makes me feel like we're really suckers. We've always lived in a world that was right-wing. The world has always been right-wing to women. A lot of the reasons for the growth and the ascendancy of the right has to do with the status of women. Having some sort of bunker mentality about the right wing, as if you have to protect yourself from contamination by either this political philosophy or these terrible people, is not the right way to deal with it. The right way to deal with it is through confrontation and dialogue. I see women doing a lot of political purity trips that have no content

to them. They aren't doing anything except denouncing the right. If you ask them, what did you do for women yesterday, there isn't anything; and what they could have done they didn't do because they couldn't do everything. In other words, I have to get myself one hundred percent perfect before I dare do anything in the world around me to make it different. That's just nuts. You never will be perfect, we live with our limitations, we live with our failures and I think it's important to do whatever it is you can do and not have all of these very exquisite metaphysical excuses for not having done anything. I'm real old-fashioned that way.

EB: One of the recurring themes in Letters *is your isolation as a feminist woman writer writing about pornography. Do you think it's inherent in writing that you do it in isolation, or are there ways we can come up with new models to support each other and not write in isolation?*

AD: There is something inherent in writing that is very solitary and I think that writers come to such awful ends in life because it's almost a total abuse of the human system to use the mind the way you use your mind when you're a writer. But at the time I was writing *Pornography* which was from about 1977 through 1980, there wasn't the support that there would be now. It wasn't just lonely because writing is lonely. It was lonely because feminists did not want to deal with pornography. They wouldn't even consider that this was something that had to be done and that made it much worse. And, basically, I almost died from writing *Pornography*. I couldn't make a living. The book that I published is only one-third of the book that I planned to write, because there was no way that I could keep working on it. I often wonder what would have happened if I could have written more of it, because the next part of the book, the second third of the book, was specifically about how pornography socialises female sexuality. Since so much of the subsequent articles have been around that, it has always felt to me as if I have been operating sort of with an amputated leg. You know, where is that other leg I wanted this book to stand on? But I couldn't survive and continue writing this book. In that way I feel that the Women's Movement has failed many writers and many women and, yes, it could have been different.

EB: How could it be different if you were writing Pornography *today?*

AD: Partly the book has helped to create the kind of social support that would have made it easier. The politics around pornography have developed in such a way that there's a very solid social consensus about the importance of dealing with the issue. I think that the experience of actually looking at the pornography would always be upsetting and difficult and alienating, but when I was doing the initial work on *Pornography* women wouldn't look at it. The slide shows (put together by Women Against Pornography) have made a tremendous difference in women understanding what it is that we are talking about here. But when I wrote *Pornography* what I thought was, I have to write down everything in this because women will not look at it and, therefore, part of my job is to tell them what is in this, because if they knew they wouldn't be buying all these arguments that these men who use it tell them. It was an extraordinary experience for me. Year after year after year men told me there is no violence here, there is no violence here, there is no violence here, and I'd look at the picture and I'd say he is hitting her, what do you mean there is no violence? What I basically came to understand is that they were talking about their sexual reaction to the picture. They were never ever talking about what happened to the woman.

I had to go through it from beginning to end to try to figure out what people mean when they say this or that; how does this photograph operate in their sexual system, which is not my sexual system. It is not that I haven't been partially formed by it. I have been. But I also have resisted it and resisting it has changed the way I see these pictures. I think that now there is a whole lot more support out there for women who are taking all kinds of risks in relation to pornography. It is still not easy, but there isn't the same kind of isolation. Women have acted against it; women have made it part of an agenda of rebellion against male power. That makes a great difference.

CC: In "A Woman Writer and Pornography" you answer the question so many of us have wanted to ask you which is how you are affected by being immersed in pornography. Would you be willing to expand further on that question and tell us why you are willing to keep immersing yourself in this way?

AD: It's hard to explain. I see pornography as a kind of nerve centre of sexual abuse, of rape, of battery, of incest, of prostitution; and I see prostitution and rape as the fundamental realities for women. When I became a feminist, which was late compared to many women my age, I was very thrilled by feminist literature and I was very thrilled by feminism. It was enormously – that very misused word – , "liberating" for me. But I saw something missing from it too, and I felt that I had some of the missing pieces. If I could contribute my understanding of them, I would make feminism more whole and more living for more women, especially for poor women, especially for women in prostitution, especially for women who had experienced sexual torture of any kind, and so the commitment really came from that.

EB: Is that partly from you experience of your husband having battered you?

AD: That certainly is part of it. I haven't talked a lot about my whole life in public and the only thing I really have talked about is battery. I've written about it really only twice in non-fiction. There are two essays in *Letters*. I wrote the Hedda Nussbaum one which is at the end of *Letters from a War Zone* (US version) because I felt absolutely urgently that I had to for her sake and partly for my sake too because it brought back so much to me. I was married for three and a half years. That's a very small part of my life, but it had a big impact on me because I was tortured and no one who survives torture comes out of it unchanged. You either die or you find some way of using what it is that you know.

There are other things that have to do with it that I don't write about, that I've chosen not to write about. I'm very troubled by the fact that anything I say publicly about myself ends up in the pages of *Hustler*. I don't like my life being turned into pornography·for men. I can't stand it. Talk about the chilling effect – it's put a real chill on me, on what I'm willing to talk about and what I'm willing to write about.

EB: Carol Anne Douglas wrote a review of Intercourse *in* Off Our Backs, *June 1987. One of her main criticisms of the book was that you discuss no alternatives to intercourse, no alternative sexuality. She says, "Even criticising lesbianism would be better than ignoring it." How do you respond to that?*

AD: I don't agree with it. I decided to write a book about intercourse as an institution of sexual politics and to try and figure out the role of intercourse in the subordination of women. Intercourse has nothing to do with lesbians or lesbian sexuality *per se* and that's why it's not in the book. I remember when I was in England when *Pornography* was published, a woman from one of the radical lesbian groups questioned why I never used the word heterosexuality and in a funny way it was the same question. My answer to her was I'm not talking about heterosexuality, I'm talking about male supremacy. Heterosexuality implies that there's an equality within the relationship; and that obscures the reality of the man being on top.

Over the last fifteen years I've very much refined what my political targets are. My target in the broadest sense is male power. I made a decision about *Intercourse*. I wanted it to be a thoroughly rigorous book about this particular act. Second, I did not want it to have any shade, shadow or hint of "the happy ending". Or any implication that lesbianism was the answer to this particular set of problems because I don't think it is and if I ever did think it was, the lesbian sadomasochists have disabused me of that notion. I can't write about lesbianism that way. My view of what *Intercourse* is is politically different from Carol Anne's notion of what it should be.

CC: In "Pornography is a Civil Rights Issue", your 1986 testimony before the Attorney-General's Commission on Pornography, you discuss a definition of erotica articulated by Gloria Steinem. Do you believe that erotica exists and if so can it serve any kind of useful purpose for women?

AD: I don't know if it can exist in this world we live in. I don't think that much of it does exist. I think that the question itself is part of the male agenda around pornography and that's what troubles me so much about the question. There are deep political issues involved in discussing what it means to look at something and have a sexual response to it, especially for women. That question is always used to obscure what the political issues are, as if everything has to do with the product and nothing has to do with what drives a person to need the product. In that sense I would characterise it as a male question because the male question always is, is there gonna be something left for me? Part of male sexual response is this voyeurism, this objectification, as opposed to the way that women have practised sexuality, which has had more to do with being with someone who is actually alive, three-dimensional or, if you want to be mystical about it, four-dimensional, in that they also exist in time as well as in space.

I see nothing to preclude that erotica could exist. I have a question as to why people would need it, if they were indeed making love with each other and happy. Or are there people who have a right to have other people do things so that they can be sexually gratified, kind of servants in a sense? The fact of the matter is that right now there is not an "erotica" market. The pornography business is a $10 billion a year business and it is growing. It's based on sexualised inequality of women, whether expressed as dominance or expressed as violence against women. You couldn't sell diddly-squat of anything that had to do with equality. I see it as a question that has been a diversionary question for a long time. I don't have any objections to people devoting their lives to creating it, if that's what they want to do. But I think that the Women's Movement should stop pretending that it's some kind of essential bread and butter or even bread and roses kind of question, because it's not.

When I was working on *Pornography,* this "feminist" definition of erotica did not exist. In all the discourse about pornography, erotica simply means pornography for intellectuals. That's *all* it means. There is no difference in terms of the place of rape in the pornography, in terms of any kind of violence ranging from flagellation to mutilation. It's strictly a class difference.

Then feminists come along and say, "But we need erotica. We have to be able to say that we like sex. We have to be able to sign our loyalty oath to sexual activity. We have to be able to have these artefacts of sexuality." And I see that having to do a lot with male identification. In other words, we can be like men.

Gloria Steinem tried to do something basically very noble. She tried to use it as a vehicle for pushing forward an idea of sexuality based on equality. She means it. But most of the people using the word and most of the people who are making the material don't mean it. What they mean is simply pornography. The way that you tell what pornography is, frankly, you look at the status of women in the material. Is it filled with hatred of women or isn't it? Does it use and violate women or doesn't it? That is really not hard to figure out. We're all formed by this world that we live in. The fact that our sexuality participates in SM scenarios and is excited by hierarchy and differentials of power and that women are trained basically from birth to eroticise powerlessness and pain should not come as a surprise. The only thing that is a surprise is that a bunch of people would call it feminism and say it's good.

It seems to me that the great misunderstanding is that those of us in the anti-pornography movement have said we are pure, we have nothing to do with that stuff. We have never said that. None of us has ever said that. We've all said that we are fighting pornography because we know what it is. We are fighting for sexual equality because we've experienced inequality. We live in this world. We don't live twelve feet above it. None of us that I have ever heard or seen in my life have made claims of purity, let alone avowals of puritanism. These mischaracterisations have been really just propaganda tools. I see myself as living in this world. I know what sadomasochism is. I know what all those feelings are. I know what all the practices are. I don't think that I am different or better or above it. What I think is that it has to change and that we do not celebrate our powerlessness and call it freedom.

In the same way I have talked at different times about how mainstream media feminists have been corrupted really by the affluence that comes their way and the attention. It's a kind of social wealth even when it's not monetary wealth. It's a kind of identity that most women don't have any way of achieving. So if you're a professional media feminist then you get lots of identity which is a big gift and it's also a very corrupting gift. I often feel that in a funny way, parts of the lesbian community are equally corrupt in that they are totally self-referential. Their idea of feminism has to do only with each other and not with women who are different from them and not with women who are in different situations than they are. This tends to happen in New York, in Washington, in Philadelphia, in Los Angeles and in San Francisco. In the rest of the country there is much less of it. Whether by necessity or by choice I don't know, but lesbians in other parts of the country just simply have got to take the agenda of all women more seriously and I think that helps in diminishing the appeal of this clubhouse sexuality. It's very "we're special, we're different", which has always been a real problem in the Women's Movement around lesbianism. We are an elite. Somehow by virtue of being lesbians all this garbage does not have to do with us. I think it's manifested itself at different times in different ways but it's always been a refusal to take male identification among lesbians seriously. It is not just heterosexual women who identify with men. It's very hard, for instance, to want freedom or to have any desire to be someone in the world and not identify with men in some way or another. I think that lesbian feminists for a long time have refused to ask ourselves the questions that we've insisted other women ask themselves, as if we're exempt from it all because we're lesbians. We are not exempt from any of it; it just manifests itself differently. The sadomasochism and the lesbian pornography is a very logical expression of that.

EB: In "Women Lawyers and Pornography" (1980) you say, "whenever you secure for any woman – be she prostitute, wife, lesbian, or all of those and more – one shred of real justice, you have given her and the rest of us a little more time, a little more dignity: and time and dignity give us the chance to organise, to speak out, to fight back." What does this tell us about strategy?

AD: That goes to my concern about the Women's Movement losing what I keep calling its middle. That the women who are committed to achieving different kinds of reform and improvements in women's lives, as opposed to changing the complete structure, are very important and there are fewer and fewer of them. I think that what it means is that you can save a woman's life by doing something that helps her get past the problem that we have not been socially able to solve. Then she is there. She is somebody who has knowledge, has creativity and she can use those things. I have very strong political beliefs and I do things the way I believe in doing them, in ways from which other women have some kind of protection. But I also have a whole lot of respect for what people who do things differently can achieve. I think that people who work in what I would characterise as the reform part of the movement have very, very little tolerance for people who work in the radical part of it. In other words, they don't understand that we're necessary to them but I think a lot of us understand that they're necessary to us. Every time you help to prolong a woman's life in any way, shape or form you give all of us as well as her more of a chance.

CC: You consistently deal with issues of race and class in your work on violence against women. How does this analysis affect the strategies that could be put forth to combat violence against women which we might adopt as a movement?

AD: It's a really big question. The first thing is that simply acting on pornography and prostitution as urgent political issues includes women in the Women's Movement who have been excluded until now. All of the pejorative characterisations of the movement as a middle-class movement were in many ways not true. The Women's Movement always called on and involved women from all sectors of society. But, I would say that a lot of the women who have been involved in the Women's Movement are on a quest for respectability. They want to be acknowledged as decent, whole, honest human beings. This is right and fair, but there are enormous numbers of women who are living in what amounts to – slavery is not the right word, it's not slavery, it's a barely acknowledged kind of marginality. They too are human beings and they are being used, day in and day out, by men in ways from which other women have some kind of protection. The Women's Movement has never had anything to do with those women until we began to address pornography, which led to addressing prostitution in a real way, not in the liberal way of "Let's everybody have a good time and some of us want to be prostitutes."

In that sense, just dealing with the issue has changed the politics of the Women's Movement and I think a lot of what people call the split in the Women's Movement is basically a class split. I have seen it that way for years: the women who have used the Women's Movement to achieve some kind of respectability (which is not to say that they were necessarily born middle-class but they became middle-class because feminism conferred on them certain professional options that weren't there for them before) want to maintain that respectability above all else. You cannot maintain respectability and deal with the status of women in pornography and prostitution at the same time. It's as if women are saying, we don't want the stink on us, we just don't, we don't want to smell that way.

In addition, the reason that the Minneapolis civil rights law got passed and the reason that it was the kind of political event that it was, which nobody has ever written about correctly, is because it dealt with the reality of the impact of pornography on poor people and people of colour in cities, which is to say the zoning laws. The fact that politicians put the pornography where people of colour live. That is true in every city across the US. The ethnic or racial group may change, city to city. Minneapolis is extraordinary. It is 96 percent white and virtually all the pornography is dumped on 4 percent of the people, who are primarily American Indian – which is their term of preference; they don't like to be called Native Americans – and Black people. In Boston it's Asians and in Washington it's Blacks. You go across the country and that is the pattern that you see. We built, for the first time, a real coalition among all those people: people who were poor, people who had this happening to them and the very real violence around them increasing because of it and the economic deprivation becoming worse because of it. They all came together to deal with pornography and to deal with every issue of power around pornography, from real estate to corrupt local government to the woman-hating to the sexualised racism in pornography itself.

A lot of the battle around pornography has to do with the soul of the Women's Movement. Is it going to be a movement for women who just want better career chances, or is it really going to deal with the way that poor women and women of colour are truly exploited? Again, in Minneapolis, in the live shows in that town, virtually all the women in them are women of colour. I have never understood how people who claim to be leftist can ignore these facts around pornography; nevertheless they manage to brilliantly. What has happened is that we have broadened the base of the women's movement enormously, but we've broadened it to people who don't count. The horrible thing is that they don't count to these white women academics who have their lists of "isms" that they're against. They're full of correct left-wing politics: they deplore racism, they just won't do anything about it. They hate poverty – mostly they don't want to ever experience it. The fact that essentially the base of the Women's Movement has broadened because of this work on pornography is utterly meaningless to them because the women are meaningless to them. They don't care about them.

If you see an example of race hate that brings men to orgasm and is being sold for money, you do something about it. Are you going to live in the world of theory or are you going to live in the world? What has always been strongest about feminist theory is that supposedly it has something to do with the world. What we're seeing now is a kind of fracturing of the Women's Movement into people who live in the world and people who live in the academy. The academy has become the safe place for feminists to be. It's certainly safer than the streets.

EB: In "Nervous Interview" (1978) the fictional interviewer says, "If the personal is political . . . why aren't you more willing to talk about your personal life?" You give a paragraph answer basically saying that you need privacy to have a personal life and that the press "far exceeds its authentic right to know in pursuing the private lives of individuals . . ." Do you still feel this way and if so could you further explain?

AD: Since I wrote that, what has really had a tremendous impact on me personally has been the stuff that pornographers have done to me. I sued *Hustler* for some cartoons of me that essentially turned me into a piece of pornography and the courts said to me, you provoked it, if you want to open your big mouth what the hell do you expect? I went to court and I said I've been raped, these people raped me. They took me, they took my sexuality, they took my body and they made pornography out of it. The court said, well if you hadn't opened your big mouth it wouldn't have happened so it's your fault. I don't understand how anybody is supposed to live with that unless the accommodation that they come to is one of female silence. That you never open your big mouth again.

My understanding of "the personal is political" also is that what you have experienced in your personal life has a political dimension to it and you can use what you know in a way that has social value. It wasn't just a personal experience. It was something that has to do with women everywhere in one way or another. In a sense that is where my commitment is now. My commitment is to using what I know in a way that is political.

The issue of fame in this country is a very big one and is a very political one and it's one that I think feminists have been exceptionally mean and miserable about. A lot of women have been destroyed because they become famous in one way or another, usually for a very short period of time, and the burden that other feminists expect them to carry is one that nobody can carry. You can't carry a burden of purity. You can't carry a burden of being a symbol for other people. You have to continue to operate with respect to your own conscience. You can't be accountable to millions of people. You can't be. You can only be accountable to people that you really know. That is, in a sense, part of what the difference is. I have to draw a line of accountability and at the same time, increasingly, my behaviour does have an impact on other women that I don't know. Then there is some kind of accountability that I owe them, but what is it?

There are a lot of things I would like to talk about, and I do not want to read about them in *Hustler.* I don't want my life used against me, I want to use my life for women. That's the part I really do not know how to deal with. Where I think that there are personal experiences that it's appropriate for me to talk about now, I will not talk about them. I can't. People talk about freedom of speech, and all of these civil-liberties assholes go into court about what is going to chill speech somewhere for someone. I mean I want to tell you that my speech is fucking freezing to death and I am a writer. It does matter what has happened to me and it does matter how I learned what it is that I know and women do have a right to have some idea of what those things are and the pornographers in collusion with the courts have been successful in creating a social environment where I cannot survive having that discussion. My speech is as chilled as it can be.

CC: Do you find that talking about your life can be done more through fiction?

AD: I am working on a novel now and I wrote *Ice and Fire* and I think a lot of people choose to deal with things through fiction. Let me emphasise when I say that it is fiction. It's not documentary reality, but yes it's easier to deal with through fiction. Dealing with anything through fiction does not protect you from this kind of assault. For instance, some boys published a book this summer that said all kinds of horrible things about me including that I assaulted a particular woman. It had a quote from her saying that she said this. Now I have an affidavit from her saying that she didn't say it and that it never happened and in fact it never happened. What they use to buttress their arguments about what kind of person I am are largely quotes from my fiction. They quote from my short stories as if they are talking about me. What they are trying to say is that I'm a pornographer, I'm a dominatrix and they compare me to the Marquis de Sade. In doing so, all of their evidence is taken from the fiction.

EB: The question I wanted to ask you has to do with living with John Stoltenberg. Why have you chosen to do that?

AD: We've been living together now over fifteen years and we live together because we deeply love each other and that is the answer to the question. I have always felt that the way in which I was accountable to the Women's Movement was through my work: that if my work continued to be what it should be, then there was no question about it that I had to answer. In the early days when we lived together, it was very rough. I couldn't walk into a room without being called names because John and I lived together. Now people seem to have taken an attitude of benign indifference. I think that his work has been very important too. He has done a lot of organising against pornography and his book *Refusing to be a Man* is a brilliant and unique book. But that's not why we live together. He is a very kind person and we really love each other.

CC: One of the powerful statements in Letters *addresses the issue of censorship. You note in "Voyage in the Dark: Hers and Ours" (1987) that the work of Jean Rhys was obliterated. You go on to say, "I don't know why we now, we women writers, think our books are going to live." What do you suggest that women do so that the writings of women of this generation are not also obliterated?*

AD: That is a really important and hard question. *Sexual Politics* is out of print. *The Dialectic of Sex* is out of print. What women have to do is come to terms with the fact that we live in a society that simply censors better than state censorship. People have got to come to terms with the power of the publishing industry and the media in controlling thought and expression. They have to understand that it is an issue of power and money and people have to be less passive in relation to books. People have to take their money which they don't have much of and they have to buy books by feminist writers. They have to develop a much more sophisticated understanding of how the book industry works. A hard-cover book like *Letters from a War Zone* was virtually published dead. If it's still in bookstores in two months it will be a miracle. They have to understand that everything that they hear all the time about how everything can be published in this country is a lie and that part of the social function of the publishing industry is to buy up the rights to and then obliterate certain books so that nobody can get them. They have to stop thinking that they live in the liberal dreamworld of equality where fairness has already been achieved. It hasn't been achieved. You can be equal in your heart but it doesn't make you equal in the world. I think that the refusal to understand what happens to books by women goes along with this liberal refusal to acknowledge that power is a reality and we're not the ones who have it. What I'm saying is that women have got to start facing reality. You cannot build any kind of movement for change on wishful thinking. The wishful thinking is that we already have what it is we want and what it is we need. We don't have it. Women who want to write and communicate, which in a big country is hard to do – it's getting harder for them, not easier. There isn't more access, there is less access. People have got to take the economics of the publishing industry seriously and understand that very few writers will survive who do not write according to the demands of the marketplace, by which I mean essentially the demands of turning out books that you can consume as passively as a television show. That's sort of the standard.

EB: Is there anything else you want to say?

AD: I want to say more than anything that the Women's Movement has a chance to do something miraculous, which is to really tear down these hierarchies of sex and race and class. We can do it, but the way that you do it is not through rhetorical denunciations of injustice. You do it through attacking institutions of injustice through political action. That hasn't changed. That's what we have to do. The other thing I would like to say is, do something. You don't have to do everything. You don't have to be perfect, you don't have to be pure, do what you can do. Do it. Life is short and you don't know when it is going to end for you, so do it, do it now.

Catharine A. MacKinnon and Andrea Dworkin

Statement on Canadian Customs and Legal Approaches to Pornography

Untrue reports have been circulating that our feminist work against pornography is responsible for the repression of feminist, gay and lesbian materials in Canada. It is said that the anti-pornography civil rights law we co-authored was passed by the Canadians and that the first thing they did with it was censor gay books. It is said that Canada Customs recently seized feminist, gay and lesbian materials – including some books by Andrea Dworkin – under a 1992 Supreme Court decision called Butler that accepted our legal approach to pornography. It is said that in practice, Canadian court decisions using our anti-pornography legal theories are backfiring against liberating sexual literature. We want you to have real information about what has and has not happened.

The Anti-Pornography Civil Rights Law We Co-authored

Canada has not adopted our civil rights law against pornography. It has not adopted our statutory definition of pornography; it has not adopted our civil (as opposed to criminal) approach to pornography; nor has Canada adopted any of the five civil causes of action we proposed (coercion, assault, force, trafficking, defamation). No such legislation has as yet even been introduced in Canada.

The Canadian Supreme Court's Butler Decision

In 1992, the Supreme Court of Canada unanimously adopted an equality approach to pornography's harms to women. This approach was argued by the Women's Legal Education and Action Fund (LEAF), an organization of progressive Canadian women committed to advancing women's equality under the Charter of Rights and Freedoms, the new Canadian constitution. Unlike the US Constitution – which doesn't even have an Equal Rights Amendment – the Canadian Charter specifically guarantees sex equality and has been interpreted to require the government to promote it.

Donald Victor Butler, a pornographer, had been prosecuted by authorities under Canada's existing law against "obscenity", which is defined as "the undue exploitation of sex, or of sex and any one or more of the following subjects, namely, crime, horror, cruelty and violence". (This is very different from US and British obscenity definitions.) Butler argued that the obscenity law violated his rights to free speech under the new Charter. LEAF urged the Canadian Supreme Court to reject his argument and instead to reinterpret the existing obscenity law in "sex equality" terms.

Previously, in a case called Keegstra, LEAF had successfully argued before the Canadian Supreme Court that racist and anti-Semitic hate propaganda violates equality and multiculturalism rights under the new Charter, so criminalizing such expression is constitutional. LEAF sought to build on that argument, and other equality precedents, in Butler. Catharine MacKinnon, working with LEAF and LEAF counsel Kathleen Mahoney, participated in Keegstra and Butler. Andrea Dworkin, consulted by LEAF on the Butler case, opposed LEAF's position. Dworkin wrote a letter arguing that no criminal obscenity law should be supported. The Supreme Court of Canada, in its decision in Butler, accepted the essentials of LEAF's equality argument. The court held that the obscenity law was unconstitutional if used to restrict materials on a moral basis, but constitutional if used to promote sex equality. The court interpreted the criminal "obscenity" provision to prohibit materials that harm women.

Canadian Customs Procedures

For years Canada Customs has stopped material at the border under its own law and guidelines, which allow employees discretion to block the importation of obscenity. As a sovereign state, Canada has every right to control its borders especially given widespread resentment against what is often viewed there as US cultural imperialism.

None of Canada's customs policies or practices has been officially revised to reflect or incorporate the Butler sex-equality decision. A Canadian newspaper columnist found this out simply by asking Customs directly. Because customs officers are not using Butler, attempts to impugn the Butler decision by citing recent customs operations are sheer innuendo; no cause-and-effect link has been shown. Canadian customs employees have been doing what they have been authorized to do for years before Butler. For example, in 1993 some books by Andrea Dworkin were detained at the border for inspection, then released shortly thereafter. Those who cite this episode to show that Butler is being used against Dworkin misrepresent long-standing Canada Customs practices.

Reports that Canada Customs is using Butler to crack down on importation of explicitly gay and lesbian material are also fabricated. If this was actually happening, it would be illegal and could be opposed under Butler, which made the restriction of material on the basis of a moral objection (such as homosexuality) conclusively unconstitutional for the first time. The ruling clearly states that material that harms women can constitutionally be stopped (and this would include women harming women), but Butler does not mention anything about men harming men. Butler is silent on the subject of same-sex materials as such.

The Real Result of Butler

Canada Customs has a long record of homophobic seizures, producing an equally long record of loud and justifiable outrage from the Canadian lesbian and gay community. There is no evidence that whatever is happening at the border now is different from what happened before the Butler decision except that Butler has made moralizing, homophobic customs seizures illegal. For instance, when one court issued an outrageously homophobic decision against some gay male material, another court, citing Butler, specifically repudiated the moralism of that decision. To date one indictment under Butler has been brought against lesbian sadomasochistic material, a magazine published in the US with a Canadian circulation of forty. If this magazine is proven to harm women, including by producing civil inequality, the case should result in a conviction. Meanwhile various indictments brought against sexually explicit materials that do not show violence have been dismissed under Butler.

Canada's criminal obscenity law since Butler – like all prior laws that put power in the hands of government prosecutors rather than harmed plaintiffs – has not actually been used effectively to stop the pornography industry. This we predicted. The pornography industry in Canada has in fact been expanding massively, trafficking openly in materials that do not show explicit violence, including some of the exact materials prosecuted in Butler.

Analysis

In the United States, our Anti-Pornography Civil Rights Ordinance – together with related legislative initiatives against the harms of racist hate speech – has helped to trigger an escalating constitutional conflict between "speech" rights guaranteed by the First Amendment and "equality" rights in the principles underlying the Fourteenth Amendment. In our neighbor nation to the north, Canada's Supreme Court has determined that racist hate expression is unconstitutional (Keegstra) and that society's interest in sex equality outweighs pornographer's speech rights (Butler). Taken together, these two rulings are a breakthrough in equality jurisprudence, representing major victories for women and all people targeted for race hate. We wish that US constitutional consciousness were so far along.

Although we recognize that the equality test adopted by Butler is an improvement on Canada's criminal obscenity law, we still do not advocate criminal obscenity approaches to pornography. They empower the state rather than the victims, with the result that little is done against the pornography industry.

We are encouraged, however, that the Butler decision under Canada's new Charter makes it likely that our civil rights law against pornography would be found constitutional if passed there. And we are continuing our work to empower victims to fight back against harm committed by pornographers.

We hope that this statement helps you correct the published record – and deal with the attacks, rumors and disinformation – surrounding the relationship of our anti-pornography efforts to the Canadian Supreme Court's Butler decision.

Originally published in *Action Agenda* (1994, Fall).

Ellen Travis

Stranger than Fiction: The Backlash on Campus at the University of Victoria*

> *... when the moon was full and the river calm, I set out in a small craft for Hisland, the adventures hereinafter recounted being absolutely true*
> (Patricia J. Williams: 1993, p. 160).

On 15 April, 1993 four political science professors at the University of Victoria, British Columbia, filed a libel suit against the Canadian Broadcasting Corporation, following interviews with women about systemic discrimination at the university. The CBC broadcasts, alleged the professors, were defamatory because they "conveyed to the public affirmation of the imputation ... that female students and faculty members were being discriminated against by the male members of the University of Victoria's Political Science Department".

The suit against the CBC is one of the events in an academic battle taking place at the University of Victoria and other campuses in Canada, in which women's equality is being pitted against academic freedom. Known more commonly as the debate on "political correctness" or the backlash against the Women's Movement, the battle at the University of Victoria erupted after a nineteen-page report on discrimination against women was presented to the Political Science Department in the spring of 1993.

The professors allege that the CBC defamed them by broadcasting interviews with Somer Brodribb, chair of the committee that produced the report, and law professor Constance Backhouse, whose report on sexism at the University of Western Ontario in London was also negatively received by male faculty and administration when it was released in 1988.

---

* This article originally appeared in *Herizons* (1994, Fall).

The Chilly Climate Committee members (left to right): Sylvia Bardon, Theresa Newhouse, Somer Brodribb, Phyllis Foden, Denise McCabe and Nadia Kyba.   (photo: Jess Howard)

Day One. My arrival naturally having created quite a stir, I was nevertheless greeted with as much cordiality as curiosity and was pressed to tell, in every detail, of my long journey to this place (Williams: 1993, p. 160).

Well-known feminist theorist, Somer Brodribb, a professor in the Political Science Department, was chosen to chair the committee in the spring of 1992. Originally called The Committee to Make The Department More Supportive to Women, the committee was given a mandate to address the "climate" of learning for women in the department, with special emphasis on systemic barriers encountered by women students. Five female students – Theresa Newhouse, Nadia Kyba, and Denise McCabe and graduate students Sylvia Bardon and Phyllis Foden – joined Brodribb on the committee.

Among the students' complaints were reports that feminist scholarship was often marginalized or excluded from courses altogether; that professors did not interrupt men who dominated seminar discussions, but blocked discussions between women, especially when the discussion focused on feminism; that sexist humour was used as a classroom device; that male faculty members made sexual advances to female students at social gatherings; and that disparaging comments were made about feminists. For example, students heard professors referring to "feminist imperialists" and comments like "I'm not going to be evaluated by the feminist police."

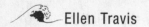

The committee presented its preliminary report in March 1993. The Chilly Climate Report, as it soon came to be known, was similar in its findings to those written by women on other Canadian campuses. Based on discussions with, and letters from, students in the department, the report recommended thirty-four changes to address systemic discrimination and create a more inclusive learning environment (see box). The report included recommendations on teaching practices, the hiring and promotion of faculty, curricula issues, and funding for women students.

> *Day Two* ... After much difficult translation, I came to understand that a man had alleged that he had been killed during the night. And only with the utmost patience did I come to understand further that he was accusing me of his murder (Williams: 1993, p. 160).

One week after the committee gave its report, all of the tenured faculty in the department, eight men, wrote a letter to the chair of the committee demanding that she provide "credible evidence" for references to sexual harassment contained in the report or else they would require "an unqualified apology".

If neither the evidence (names of students and professors involved) nor an apology were forthcoming, the letter warned, "It will be necessary for us to take further steps to protect our reputations."

Much has been made of this letter and for good reason: it reframes a discussion of systemic discrimination in apolitical terms, as though unrelated "incidents" happened, or perhaps didn't happen, to individuals who are all more or less equal in the power they wield in academia.

Importantly, the professors' letter ignores the bulk of the report, choosing to dwell on its most sensational aspect: sexual harassment. In their view, statements about sexual harassment are accusations that damage their own professional reputations, although no individual professors were mentioned and the report talks in general terms only about harassment experienced.

One wonders why the reports about harassment were felt to be more harmful to the men's reputations than, for example, excluding writing by women from required reading lists. The Chilly Climate Report doesn't accord special status to its section on harassment, which is appropriately called "Sexual Harassment and Everyday Hostility". However the men's fixation on the three hundred words that make up this section has succeeded in stalling the discussion of systemic discrimination in the department, turning it into a debate about whether false accusations were made against innocent men.

"Credible evidence", the letter further supposes, will lay blame on the proper culprits and presumably exonerate the rest who have never been sexist, and are therefore innocent. But the key point of systemic discrimination is that it doesn't scapegoat one or two people's "bad" behaviour, but looks at the whole picture: power and privilege in decision-making and in the acquisition of knowledge. The committee refused to apologize for or withdraw sections of their collectively written report.

After the impasse in the department became widely known, which took about a week, the university administration got involved. University vice-president Sam Scully appointed two investigators from outside the department to review what had happened and make suggestions about how to resolve the dispute. Marilyn Callahan from the School of Social Work and Andrew Pirie from the Faculty of Law wrote a brief summary of the events that occurred in the month following the release of the Chilly Climate Report. They made fourteen recom-

---

Highlights of the Chilly Climate Report

The Chilly Climate Report makes thirty-four recommendations dealing with discriminatory practices in the classroom, in curricula, and in hiring procedures. Ten of the recommendations are summarized below.

1. Courses at both the undergraduate and graduate level should include writing by women and feminist scholarship, regardless of the topic area.
2. Courses at both the undergraduate and graduate level should include writing that critically addresses sexism and racism and other inequities.
3. The department should take leadership in formulating a serious and unequivocal policy against sexual harassment.
4. Establish complaint procedures to deal with subtle differential treatment as well as overt discrimination. Discrimination should be a factor considered in reappointments, tenure and promotion, and merit pay increases.
5. Teaching evaluation forms should include a section for feedback on the course's attention to anti-sexist and anti-racist issues, as well as the instructor's attempts to create an equitable learning environment.
6. Guidelines for anti-sexist and anti-racist teaching should be developed. All new appointees, sessional, and visiting lecturers should be made aware of the department's commitment to an equitable learning environment.
7. Procedures are needed to assess courses' attention to all forms of discrimination, including classism and homophobia. A special committee to review curricula and vet new courses is needed. This committee should include female faculty and students who have a demonstrated commitment to feminist scholarship.
8. Feminist scholars should be aggressively sought out and encouraged to apply for positions in the department. Scholars should also be vigorously sought through minority networks.
9. Scholarships aimed specifically at financially disadvantaged women are needed; the department should request that the Faculty of Graduate Studies lobby funding sources in support of women students.
10. The department should create more work study positions for women students. As well, work study programs for women students should be arranged with women-oriented organizations, such as those providing services and research for women.

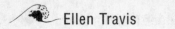

mendations that they thought would address the concerns of faculty, students, and staff within the Political Science department and on campus in general.

Callahan and Pirie's report is an attempt to address the interests of those in conflict, without denying the systemic inequalities that create differences in power among them. The first two recommendations state that the letter to Somer Brodribb was inappropriate and that it should be withdrawn. They go on to recommend that the Chilly Climate Committee should continue its work as originally planned and that the department should follow up with a mediator until it is "on an even keel".

Two weeks after Callahan and Pirie gave their review, Scully issued a vaguely-worded memo that seemed to suggest that he would not implement the Callahan–Pirie recommendations. At the end of the memo, he recommended that the male faculty withdraw the letter, but he also urged the committee first to withdraw the sections of the report the male professors objected to, not at all what Callahan and Pirie recommended.

> *Day Three* ... despite my poor amazement, my accuser then rose up again to insist that he had died, and was Not the Same Person he had been before my arrival on Hisland" (Williams: 1993, p. 161).

When shown the systemic power they have not recognized before, men often don't recognize themselves. Speaking specifically of sex discrimination from a male point of view, the problem doesn't exist until women complain about it. French writer Monique Wittig has said that, for men, "as long as there is no women's struggle, there is no conflict between men and women" (1992, p. 3).

Phyllis Foden, one of the committee members, has called it a "smoke and mirrors game". But the game itself is harassment as well. Jennifer Spencer, a committee supporter, puts it this way: "Their 'due process' processes women. It silences, isolates, and contains women's speech."

For women, the problem exists long before we finally speak of it. Before it exists in our consciousness, it exists in the jobs, scholarships, and grants not received; in the collegial respect not shown; in the loss of intellectual relationships with women whose work was never on assigned reading lists; in the inexorable certainty that conversations, no matter how academically they begin, commonly get around to the shape of one's legs and the colour of one's hair.

Feminist lawyer, Sheila McIntyre, was intimidated, harassed, and verbally attacked for her feminist perspectives during her first year teaching law at Queen's University in Kingston, Ontario. Hired in 1985 on a two-year contract, she wrote a sixteen-page memo to her colleagues at the end of her first year, documenting the harassment she experienced.

McIntyre reported that several male students told her that using inclusive language in lectures was "shoving my politics down students' throats". In one class, six male students planned "to take a run at Sheila". McIntyre said they "belligerently tried to prevent students who disagreed with their position from speaking, by a combination of insult, interruption, hostile gestures, and increasingly voluble but untenable argument". Afterwards, two feminist students in the class told McIntyre that they "no longer felt it safe to speak" and one of the women wanted to quit law school.

Over the course of the year, McIntyre had "at least two dozen visits from women students who found remarks (including dirty jokes) made in class by their professors to be sexist and offensive and/or who had been trivialized for raising gender issues. A total of nine colleagues were involved". McIntyre herself was pornographically depicted in the male students' washroom.

The memo also describes a visit she had from a male colleague, who told her that she was "coming on too strong around here" and that she was "non-collegial" for having disagreed with him in a faculty meeting. Other colleagues, McIntyre said, "repeatedly reinterpreted" her experiences for her, explaining them as having nothing to do with sexism.

Although McIntyre didn't make recommendations to eliminate systemic discrimination and harassment, her documentation is similar to the description of incidents outlined at the University of Victoria. So is the backlash she experienced.

Backlash at the University of Victoria came in many forms. It was argued that making non-discriminatory teaching practices one factor in awarding pay raises or promotions threatened professors' academic freedom. There were also personal attacks and accusations that the report amounted to McCarthyism and fascism. One of the professors, Warren Magnussen, described the Chilly Climate Report as "aimed at the creation of a religious cult, with its prophet and its goddess, and its mass of cult-followers doing their leaders' bidding".

Equity in the department will not be achieved by simply adding on courses on sex, race and other forms of discrimination, the Chilly Climate Report concluded. Discrimination should no longer be a "special topic" within political science, but should be acknowledged as a fundamental feature of a discipline dedicated to the study of power, which, after all, is what political science is all about. The more compelling reason is that there is no such thing as neutral knowledge. Knowledge reflects the distribution of social power in our society and institutions; the privilege of the white-skinned, heterosexual, and affluent man is pervasive in knowledge that wouldn't seem to him to have anything to do with race, sexuality, class, or sex.

Very few of the recommendations in the Chilly Climate Report would leave the choice to discriminate open and this is what makes them so controversial and threatening. Liberal-minded men, as a rule, don't mind being "challenged", but they get very upset when their choices are restricted. A "challenge" to change is relatively easy to swallow, since it presents you with an argument and lets you make up your own mind. The Chilly Climate Report is not a "challenge to change" in this sense; it seeks to alter the unstated yet accepted belief that choice and freedom have nothing to do with privilege or power.

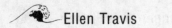

The Chilly Climate Committee maintain that their report is not defamatory and the CBC maintains that its broadcasts were not libellous. But what about the charge that the men have not been presented as they perceive themselves? This is true. The report presents the men as implicated in a context they deny the existence of. This becomes confusing. On the one hand, they acknowledge that sexism exists and, on the other hand, they want to identify which individuals are sexist. One minute we are talking about systemic patterns that shape male identities, regular guys and lechers alike, and the next minute we are talking about sexism as if it were an individual characteristic that some men "have" and some don't. This inability to hold on to the concept of systemic discrimination was eventually dubbed the Goldfish Memory Syndrome by committee member Theresa Newhouse. The shift occurs, producing a tiresome circularity, in roughly eight seconds, or the time it takes a goldfish to swim around the bowl.

> *Day Four* ... I was given to understand that one of the Menfolk elders would act as my counsel. "Dearest one," he said. "Dry your tears. If you are as you believe, innocent, rely on the justice of our laws, and the activity with which I shall prevent the slightest shadow of partiality" (Williams: 1993, p. 161).

In August 1993, university president, David Strong, appointed yet another team of investigators to review "the learning and working environment" in the Political Science Department. This time he chose Saskatchewan lawyer, Beth Bilson and former BC Supreme Court Judge Thomas Berger. Five months later, Berger and Bilson submitted a report which admonished the committee for using words like sexism, racism, and harassment. The report says these words have "flexible" meanings but cannot "be expanded or contracted according to taste", suggesting the committee chose its terms based on something as arbitrary as "taste". Berger and Bilson's report goes on to say that, "No one wishes to discount the collective experience of women."

After continued legal pressure from some of the tenured male professors, *The Globe and Mail* printed a retraction of its news stories about the Chilly Climate controversy. Scully had written to the paper to say that the Chilly Climate Committee was not an "official" committee, even though the precise terms under which the committee was created, by unanimous vote of the department, are reproduced for the record in the Callahan–Pirie review. The retraction appeared as students were demanding Strong's resignation for overturning an Equity Office decision on a harassment case.

These stranger-than-fiction events begin to take on the feel of Columbia University law professor, Patricia Williams' tale of a surreal journey to Hisland, quoted throughout this article. Williams' tale describes what happens when women and other marginalized groups make their experiences of discrimination public and it ends this way:

Day Five . . . I have been most brutally betrayed. I am to be burned at the stake in the morning along with those few brave souls who dared speak sympathetically of my unfortunate plight (Williams: 1993, p. 161).

The Chilly Climate Committee continues to reject the false promise Berger and Bilson, and others, have offered: that there is a way to say you are being discriminated against that will not produce anger, and that there is a way to take power without conflict. Committee members have answered demands and warnings to rephrase or to be silent by continually reasserting what they said in their original report.

Sylvia Bardon said she found it difficult to dispel the illusion that if she could "just say it the right way, everybody would get it". All of the members of the committee are angry about being told repeatedly that if only they would describe their experience differently, the response would not be hostile. Somer Brodribb says she is concerned about the possible results of this lesson in "patriarchal pedagogy". She says women are being encouraged to adopt a "politics of suppliancy" in which we speak provisionally, repeatedly reformulating our demands, as well as a "politics of flirtation" in which women are supposed to be ingratiating, and create a jovial and light-hearted atmosphere for discussions of discrimination.

The committee members continue to resist the pressure to make what they have to say appetising. Phyllis Foden says she has learned that "It doesn't matter how the hell you say it, they just don't want to hear it."

All eight of the tenured male professors in the department continue to teach Political Science at the University of Victoria. Six months after Berger and Bilson's report recommended that a woman from outside the university be appointed to chair the department, Rob Walker, one of the four men who brought the lawsuit, is the department's new interim chair. University president, Strong was reappointed for a new term by the university's Board of Governors on 20 June 1994. The libel suit filed by four faculty members against the CBC has not yet come to trial.

More than two and a half years after it began its work, the Chilly Climate Committee has now taken its sex discrimination complaint to the British Columbia Human Rights Commission. Phyllis Foden and Sylvia Bardon are working on master's degrees, but both say they have been unable to make progress during the last year because of the work generated by the Chilly Climate backlash. Nadia Kyba and Denise McCabe, who graduated just after the report came out, have both left Victoria, and Theresa Newhouse switched major programs, from Political Science to Women's Studies. Somer Brodribb is still on faculty at the university.

Meanwhile, no serious discussion, much less implementation, of the Chilly Climate Committee's recommendations has occurred, nor have the recommendations of other reports since issued been put into place.

Regular protests on the Victoria campus remind students, faculty, and administration that the conflict at the University of Victoria is clearly not over yet.

The committee continues to receive support from Women's Groups on the University of Victoria campus, across Canada and outside Canada.

Postscript
In spite of the Berger–Bilson report, Walker was reappointed Chair and his successor, another man, will take over the position in July 1996. Somer Brodribb has had to leave the Department of Social Science and is now in Women's Studies. Two female professors in the University of Manitoba Department of Political Science where another "inquiry" was held were not able to remain in that department. And at the University of British Colombia Department of Political Science, the 1995 McEwen report on systemic discrimination has been attacked as McCarthyism, with consequences for the Black and feminist "complainants". Silencing practises begin to take two forms: institutional/patriarchal threats including litigation, and the blaming, isolating and distancing behaviours of professional women and equity officers in particular.

Janice G. Raymond

Connecting Reproductive and Sexual Liberalism

Much of what I will discuss in this article applies to reproductive technologies.[1] However, it is important to understand that the critique is more far-reaching. The same principles have dominated pro-pornography and pro-prostitution theory and practice where an ideology of sexual liberalism is based on the demand for individual rights in which almost anything can be claimed as a right. These rights are increasingly defined as gender-neutral; a concept of choice that reduces choice to consumption; and a notion of privacy that more accurately translates into private privilege for men (and some women) and that fosters a private enterprise in women's bodies.

Reproductive abuse of women's bodies is accepted as normal, because sexual abuse has paved the way. Technological reproduction is not only part of the politics of reproduction, but of sexual politics too, for it is primarily about access to women and abuse of women's bodies – for medical research and experimentation, for financial gain, for clinical experience and adventure, for the manipulation of life. The connection between sexual and reproductive politics is material; that is, it is no mere metaphor. More and more, the old sexual roles within which women have been confined converge with the new reproductive roles women are offered. Men buying women for sex in prostitution bears striking resemblance to men buying women's reproductive services in surrogacy.

Reproductive liberalism has come to dominate the discourse and policy making of technological medicine in the industrialized countries, as sexual liberalism has come to pervade the media, the academy and, unfortunately, much of what passes for feminism. This liberal speak – the language of reproductive choice and sexual liberation – pervades not only the sex and reproductive industries but progressive and feminist theory and practice as well.

---

1. This article is an excerpt from my chapter, "A Critique of Reproductive Liberalism" from *Women as Wombs* (1993/1994b).

Reproductive liberalism underlies the work of a number of feminist proponents of surrogacy and technological reproduction. Much of the feminist advocacy of new reproductive arrangements has come from women who, in former times, might have been described as socialist feminists. More recently, however, much of their writing is more accurately described as postmodernist in theme and theory. I choose to describe them as reproductive liberals since, as with reproductive liberals in general, they endorse procreative liberty, gender neutrality, privacy, unlimited choice, and the promotion of the so-called liberating facets of reproductive technology for women.

Historically, many socialist feminists have espoused sexual liberalism. As Sheila Jeffreys (1985) has shown, socialist feminists advocated classic liberal positions during the nineteenth and twentieth centuries when they opposed the work of early radical feminists fighting against sexual assault, prostitution, and sexual slavery. More recently, some socialist feminists have promoted sexual liberalism, drawing from positions that permeated nineteenth- and twentieth-century socialist feminism (see Jackson: 1990). Over the last decade, socialist feminists have joined with other academic and professional sexual liberals to oppose the feminist antipornography campaign and have broadened their views to affirm sadomasochistic sexuality, man-boy "love", and prostitution.

We are now witnessing a liberalism that defines itself as feminism in the reproductive realm. This liberalism has opposed itself to the feminist resistance against new reproductive technologies and contracts. Like its sexual counterpart, which promoted male-dominant modes of sexuality as sexual liberation, feminist reproductive liberalism affirms surrogacy, in vitro fertilization, and many new reproductive procedures as reproductive freedom for women.

Feminist analysis and activism against the new reproductive technologies burgeoned in the early 1980s. Recognizing that technological developments were rapidly escalating on an international scale, women from First and Third World countries came together in 1984 to share information, shape analysis and response, and specifically name how these technologies harmed women. The challenge to this gathering of international feminists was to reorient the ethical and political discussion from a fetus-centered and gender-neutral view to a woman-centered perspective. That reorientation was largely due to the efforts and activism of FINRRAGE[2] members.

In the mid 1980s, however, another brand of feminist analysis of the new reproductive technologies took shape, emanating from the United States and, later, from Britain. It advanced a more "nuanced" and "sophisticated" assessment of these technologies, arguing that women could use them with benefit (while being abused by them). Some of this justification initially appeared in sections of the *Reproduc-*

---

2. FINRRAGE is the acronym for the Feminist International Network of Resistance to Reproductive and Genetic Engineering. Originally called FINNRET, it was organized in Groningen, the Netherlands, in 1984 and now consists of over 1000 members worldwide.

tive Laws for the 1990s: A Briefing Handbook (Taub and Cohen: 1988) associated with the Women's Rights Litigation Project at Rutgers University and in Michelle Stanworth's volume, *Reproductive Technologies* (1987/1988).

Reproductive liberalism is much broader than its feminist version. But it is important to examine the feminist liberal arguments advocating new reproductive procedures as a woman's choice, because reproductive liberals, especially in the United States and Britain, are seen as representing the feminist position on technological and contractual reproduction. Because of their institutional and professional hegemony, the so-called feminist debates about the new reproductive technologies in the United States are managed by the feminist reproductive liberals since it is they who dominate Women's Studies programs, the feminist media and journals, and the women's research institutes, and they serve as evaluators to granting agencies. Effectively, they have become the gatekeepers of feminist knowledge, presenting a more radical feminist politics as flawed and extremist. It is therefore important that feminist reproductive liberalism be critiqued and that radical feminism speak for itself.

The Balancing Act

Feminist reproductive liberals give priority to the question – which begs its answer – how do these technologies benefit women? This in itself is a peculiar chronology of inquiry since, one would assume, before deciding that such technologies can benefit women, one would have to prove the case. Yet the agenda is always framed by this initial question/answer. And following from this initial question/answer a second one: how do "we" ensure equal access to the technologies for everyone – poor, Black, and lesbian women, for example? Editor, Michelle Stanworth (1987/1988, p. 35), in the introductory essay to *Reproductive Technologies*, asks "whether we can create the political and cultural conditions in which such technologies can be employed by women to shape the experience of reproduction according to their own definitions."

Hilary Rose (1987/1988, p. 152) also argues that "the IVF cat is out of the bag, and – whatever else IVF does – it meets real needs for (some) real women, Consequently a feminism that accepts the diversity of women's needs must now work to limit IVF"s imperialistic claims over women's bodies, and its associated claim to consume even more of the health-care budget for high-tech, curative medicine." While pointing to the technological hegemony, nonetheless Rose seems to believe that IVF can be made available for some while restricting it for the many, in the interests of limiting high-tech and high-budget medicine.

As early as 1970, Shulamith Firestone suggested some supposed benefits of new reproductive technologies in *The Dialectic of Sex*. But she was page-lashed ruthlessly as naively optimistic by some of the same feminists who are now urging us to take a more balanced view of these technologies. As they critique much radical feminist writing, so they depicted Firestone's work as offering only facile solutions. In other words, she did not perform the recent balancing act of being both for and against. Having it both ways, in effect, sums up the more "nuanced" reproductive liberal critique. It poses as a sophisticated rational approach to both sides of the issue, encouraging women to recognize how these technologies not only abuse women but also how they can be used in women's own interests. Like the ways in which pain has been equated with pleasure for women, so too is abuse fused with use.

The Ontological Argument:
All Radical Feminists are Essentialists

Much of the feminist reproductive liberal critique caricatures radical feminist arguments against the technologies. Reproductive liberals fault critics of the new reproductive technologies for making motherhood naturalistic, biologistic, and almost atavistic – as radical feminism itself has been typed as essentialist and ontological. A mythical state of natural motherhood is conjured up from nowhere so that feminists who oppose technological and contractual reproduction can be attacked as dragging women back to the days of "anatomy is destiny" and as pitting nature against technology. For example, Michelle Stanworth (1987/1988, p. 34) cautions that "the attempt to reclaim motherhood as a female accomplishment should not mean giving the natural priority over the technological – that pregnancy is natural and good, technology unnatural and bad."

Radical feminist opponents of the new reproductive technologies do not pit nature against technology, nor do we extol a new version of biology is destiny for women. Opposition to these technologies is based on the more political feminist perspective that *women as a class have a stake in reclaiming the female body, not as female nature, but by refusing to yield control of it to men, to the state, and most recently to those liberals who advocate that women control our bodies by giving up control.*

Reducing radical feminism to the term cultural feminism, which they then set out to disparage, Juliette Zipper and Selma Sevenhuijsen (1988, p. 125) blame cultural feminists, especially in the United States, for returning women to "nurturance, naturalness and love" and for extolling "natural motherhood and natural procreation" as "the real values of feminism". They assert that feminist analysis must "shake free from the ideological inheritance of cultural feminism" and especially from the presupposition that the mother-child bond is sacrosanct (ibid, p. 126). Much of their criticism, however, is an artifact beginning with the term cultural feminism (see also Lienert, this volume pp. 155–68). As elaborated by Alice Echols (1983, pp. 64, 66), cultural feminism defines a potpourri of radical feminist simplifications, reductionisms, and distortions that run the gamut from invoking "biological explanations of gender differences" to a vilification of the left! Lynne Segal serves up a British variant on this theme of critiquing radical feminism as cultural feminism in her book, *Is the Future Female?* "Mostly from North America, where it is known as 'cultural feminism', it celebrates women's superior virtue and spirituality and decries 'male' violence and technology . . . Feminists . . .

like me recall that we joined the women's movement to challenge the myths of women's special nature" (Segal: 1987, p. 3).

Both Echols and Segal, for the most part, ignore the radical feminist critique of biological determinism and consistent emphasis on the social and political construction of women's lives. They quote selectively from radical feminist authors who have specified at great length and in great detail our own critiques of biological determinism and female essentialism, yet nowhere do they acknowledge these critiques. As feminist activist and writer Liz Kelly notes, the critique of biological determinism is one of the things that many radical and socialist feminists have always held in common. However, especially in their theories of sexuality, many socialist feminists ignore the dominant tendency in their own accounts of female and male socialization, which "are far more essentialist than their radical feminist counterparts. By drawing on revised Freudian categories, they offer a much more determined and limited view of change" (Kelly: 1987, pp. 23, 28).

As with sexuality, so too with reproduction. Liberal feminist writings on the new reproductive technologies portray women – especially women who are infertile – as needing these technologies. This conforms to the rationale of the medical and technological progenitors who constantly present these technologies as fulfilling the desperate needs of infertile women – not the researchers' own desperate needs for scientific advancement, status, and financial gain.

Feminists who oppose technological and contractual reproduction have recognized that motherhood is depicted increasingly as a need for women. Radical feminist opponents of the technologies have been extremely critical of the ways doctors and the media fit these technologies into their proposed vision of women's supposed natural motherhood and the ways in which women are channeled into trying yet one more invasive and debilitating medical procedure in order to become pregnant. Yet every time radical feminists cite the myth and manipulation of maternity – the revival of natural motherhood – by the medical and scientific progenitors, it is we who are faulted for perpetuating a naturalistic view of motherhood.

The "How Dare We Define Feminism" Approach

In a 1988 review of *Made to Order*, an anthology of writing opposed to new reproductive technologies, appearing in the *Women's Review of Books*[3] (see Spallone and Steinberg: 1987), Rayna Rapp criticizes the book for equating "feminism with opposition to the new reproductive technologies, as if there were a unified category called 'woman' whose natural ability to bear children now stands under the threat of total male, mechanical medical takeover ... Labelling a single oppositional stance

---

3. The *Women's Review of Books* is a US feminist publication whose coverage of both pornography and reproductive technologies has been almost totally authored by socialist liberals. Radical feminist work is unrelentingly assailed in the reviews and articles of this publication, which purports to be fair to all feminist viewpoints.

as 'feminist' and anything else as 'not' prematurely forecloses the strategies we need to develop" (Rapp: 1988, pp. 9–10). The equation is Rapp's, not that of the authors in *Made to Order*. But beyond this false equation is another more troubling concern. "Don't call your position feminist" has become one of the ten commandments of sexual and reproductive liberalism. This convoluted prohibition effectively says that feminists cannot dare to articulate what feminism means because if we do we are mouthing a single, correct-line, exclusionary feminist position. Articulating what feminism means, however, seems not exclusionary but honest. If we do not articulate what feminism means, what does feminism mean? And then we can debate what feminism means, rather than how dare we think we can say what feminism means! It would be much more fruitful to talk about the issues and the content of our differing positions than about relative postures of authority. The authority that anyone asserts in defining a position that is for or against or somewhere on the so-called more nuanced spectrum should come from an informed and reflective assessment, as well as her belief in the rightness of what she is saying. We must all take responsibility for our positions and argue the issues.

The Accusations of Absolutism Approach

Increasingly, opposition is translated as absolutism. Absolutism is an overused word to discredit the position of those who take a strong and often passionate stand. For example, Rebecca Albury (1987, p. 64) in *Australian Feminist Studies* attacks, among other things, the position of well-known Australian feminist critic, Robyn Rowland: "Rowland has tended to enter the public debate with an absolutist moral position . . ."

An oppositional stance is out of fashion in feminism, as is outrage, passion, and explicit political activism. Radical feminist writing is derided as reading "like a communique from the front lines."[4] Of course, one very well may be on the front lines, but that seems negligible. There was a time in this wave of feminism when it was honorable – not a cause for dismissal – to be on the front lines.

Many German FINRRAGE members experienced these front lines during the 1987 staging of thirty-three simultaneous raids by the Bundeskriminalamt (the German equivalent of the FBI) in the then West Germany. Files, research, radio and video recordings, address lists, and personal documents were seized by heavily armed police (two hundred in Essen alone), and during the raids women were forced to undress in order for police to note "non-changeable marks" on their bodies for future reference. Two women were jailed and one was kept in solitary confinement for two years, charged under the terrorist act (Corea and De Wit: 1988). The raids were directed overwhelmingly against feminist critics of genetic and reproductive technology.

Consistently, radical feminist critics of surrogacy and technological reproduction are faulted for their "absolutist" and oppositional approach and their

---

4. Rapp (1988, p. 9) uses this phrase to caricature the articles in *Made To Order*.

failure to ask the "more complex" question of under what conditions the new reproductive technologies might be useful to women. Rosalind Petschesky (1987, p. 280), for example, cautions feminist critics of the new reproductive technologies to recognize "complex elements" [that] cannot easily be generalized or, unfortunately, vested with privileged insight." Terms like absolutist, totalizing, universal conjure up images of simplemindedness and a lack of thinking on the part of those who oppose the new reproductive technologies. Supposedly, those who do more tough-minded thinking would emerge with a more balanced position. And presumably, those who are more attentive to race, culture, sexuality, and class will always take a provisional position on any women's issue. This critique is applied by liberals to women's issues but not, for instance, to progressive Central American or South African politics. If one is not a moral relativist on women's issues, one is by definition an absolutist.

Since the 1970s, socialist feminists have been accusing radical feminists of not having a class and cross-cultural analysis. They have consistently plied this line even in the face of evidence to the contrary. When the evidence could no longer be ignored, then the rhetoric changed. Radical feminists did not have the "right kind" of class and/or crosscultural analysis. For example, Rayna Rapp (1988, p. 9) also attacks *Made to Order* for "simply asserting solidarity with third world women and including essays that portray their condition." Being unable to chastise the collection for not including a cross-cultural analysis, she now finds the analysis merely "included". This is a patronizing and arrogant assumption; the essays of women from Brazil and Bangladesh are not "simply" included. They are an integral part of the analysis of the book, which offers an international spectrum of essays by women from France, Germany, Australia, the United States, England, Switzerland, and the Netherlands. Rapp's logic is all the more incongruous given her enthusiastic praise for the second volume under review, *Reproductive Technologies*, which is almost completely authored by Anglo and US women and includes little international analysis and no Third World perspective.

Academic and professional feminism in the United States today is permeated by sexual and reproductive liberalism, not by sexual and reproductive radicalism. Fortunately, feminism outside the academy and the professions is much more radical and vibrant. US sexual and reproductive liberalism has been narrowly focused on individual "rights," "needs," and "desires." In the surrogacy context, for example, the constant talk about rights has deceived many US women into thinking that we have more rights than we actually possess. One thing that I have found refreshing about working in an international context is that women from other countries, particularly in the developing world, have no illusions about their so-called rights.

Feminist liberalism has transformed women's reproductive abuse in technological and contractual reproduction into women's reproductive need, in the same way that the sexual liberals reconstructed the sexual abuse of women in pornography, prostitution, and sadomasochistic sexuality as women's sexual pleasure. There are also, however, important differences between sexual and reproductive liberal feminists. In feminist reproductive liberal circles, there is more opposition to surrogacy and more criticism of technological reproduction than was ever expressed about pornography.

One reason for this may be a visceral female identification with motherhood and children and with the importance of preserving this realm from abuse. Additionally, reproductive issues are seen as the domain of women, something women have the right to defend, especially in the name of children, whereas freedom from sexual abuse is something that women have to defend in their own name. Thus reproductive freedom is perceived as a broader issue that affects not only women, but children and men as well. It is not so singly identifiable as a woman's issue.

More instrumental has been the male history of support for reproductive rights. This comes especially from leftist and liberal men who have aligned themselves with campaigns for women's reproductive freedom, perceiving that their own interests are very much at stake. For example, Playboy magazine has consistently funded pro-choice abortion projects and supported pro-choice policy and legislation because it is in the best interests of progressively political, upwardly mobile men – playboys – not to be encumbered with the consequences of heterosex.

> It was the brake that pregnancy put on fucking that made abortion a high-priority political issue for men in the 1960s . . . The decriminalization of abortion – for that was the political goal – was seen as the final fillip: it would make women absolutely accessible, absolutely "free." The sexual revolution, in order to work, required that abortion be available to women on demand. If it were not, fucking would not be available to men on demand . . . The male-dominated Left agitated for and fought for and argued for and even organized for and even provided political and economic resources for abortion rights for women. The Left was militant on the issue (Andrea Dworkin: 1983, pp. 94-95).

Many so-called enlightened men promote reproductive rights for women, especially in areas such as contraception and abortion, whereas there is little male support for antipornography politics. Rather, the liberal establishment tries to malign women as prudes and puritans when they attack the sexual politics of a male-dominant culture. Liberals have also sought to discredit antipornography feminists by allying them with the politics of the right wing.

It appears far easier for feminist liberals to embrace reproductive freedom than to advocate for women's sexual freedom *from* the male-dominant modes of sexuality such as prostitution and pornography. Instead, liberals embrace women's sexual freedom *for* the male-dominant modes of sexuality. Their version of sexual freedom equals sexual pleasure, bracketed from any critique of women's sexual abuse.

Because many of the feminist reproductive liberals come from a socialist feminist background, they have regarded reproductive politics as more their terrain than sexual politics. Radical feminists have been more closely allied with issues of pornography, rape, sexual harassment, sexual abuse, woman battering, and other areas of sexual objectification and violence than have socialist feminists. The consistent historical tension between radical feminists and socialist feminists around issues of sexual abuse, dating back to the beginnings of this century, may provide one reason why some socialist feminists have taken a political stand against surrogacy and not against pornography.

Other socialist feminists, however, have come out in support of surrogacy. They uphold the liberal wedge argument that state interference with any so-called reproductive right will allow state repression of those few limited reproductive gains that women have won, mostly in the areas of contraception and abortion. Thus they find themselves in the position of having to play off one so-called reproductive right (the right to procreate by any means possible) against another – the right not to procreate (abortion). And they see any legal prohibitions on surrogacy as endangering the right to abortion. Furthermore, they subscribe to a superficial reasoning that the man's claim to the child is equal to the woman's. Accordingly, they argue that privileging the woman's claim is reverting to special protectionism that is reactionary toward women and fosters a maternal essentialism based upon a regressive notion of biological mother-right.

Socialist feminism has historically avoided the radical feminist emphasis on addressing how men – not only social or economic systems – oppress women. It has chosen to frame women's oppression largely in economic terms and has shunned any consistent analysis of sexuality as male-dominant power. Thus it pays little serious attention to how so called normal sexuality depends on women's oppression, since sexuality is not recognized as a male-dominant system in and of itself. For example, socialist feminist studies of women in the workplace have historically documented women's oppression through health hazards and economically dead-ended work, with little mention of sexual harassment as affecting women's work performance. Socialist feminists, with few exceptions, have not put much premium on the sexual abuse of women in pornography, prostitution, and the male-dominant modes of sexuality. Instead, their politics of sexuality reduces to a politics of desire magically sprung free from male sexual domination and abuse, a classic theme of laissez-faire liberalism. Their tendency has been to see any campaign against sexual abuse, pornography, and the male power modes of sexuality as a sideline, as a distraction from women's real oppression, whatever that may be, and indeed as a reactionary trap for women, equated with a conservative movement for social purity (Dubois and Gordon: 1984, pp. 31–49).

Further, socialist feminist critique of reproductive abuses has taken little note of the *connections* between the reproductive abuse of women and women's sexual oppression. Their reproductive politics has no sexual political foundation. For example, socialist feminists have focused on issues such as sterilization abuse, abortion rights, economic provisions for working mothers such as childcare, and

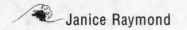

access to birth control for more women, without wanting to recognize that more is at stake They have emphasized *reproductive rights* and *reproductive access* for women to birth control and abortion and now, by extension, to the new reproductive technologies. But they include no analysis of women access to an independent sexuality freed from male definition and desire.

When a substantive reproductive freedom is not joined with a substantive sexual freedom, as it is not in a traditional socialist feminist calculus of reproductive rights, the result is a reproductive liberalism. The insistent refusal of many socialist feminists to admit the central importance of a radical feminist critique of the male power modes of sexuality is largely responsible for this liberalism and for the lack of connection between sexuality and reproduction.

Surrogacy's availability is the result of the conditions men establish among themselves to grant access to women and women's reproductive capacities. A critique of surrogacy that remains fixated at the level of providing workable economic options for women in the surrogate industry and tightening up the contract so as to remove some of the more extreme abuses to women never addresses the nature of surrogacy within the total context of the male access to women. Reproductive liberalism offers women no substantive vision of reproductive freedom or rights.

Women as Victims: The Social and Political Construction of Women's Reproductive Choices

The social and political construction of female reality is a basic tenet of modern feminism. The feminist saying, "the personal is political", reveals that women's choices have not only been socially, but politically, orchestrated as well. When men and women act in certain ways, they are more than mere products of their socialization. Social conditioning theories often lack a political framework. Male domination and female subordination are bound up with power. There are positive advantages in status, ego, and authority for men in the ways, for example, they exercise their sexuality. The male power modes of sexuality construct women's sexual and reproductive lives to conform to male dictates.

When radical feminists stress how women's reproductive choices are influenced by the social and political system and how women are channeled into having children at any cost to themselves, we are reproached for portraying women as victims. These reproaches have come mainly from feminist liberals but, increasingly, they are being echoed by liberal men. In the Baby M case, Gary Skoloff (Snyder: 1987), the lawyer for Bill Stern, summed up his court argument by stating, "If you prevent women from becoming surrogate mothers . . . you are saying that they do not have the ability to make their own decisions . . . It's being unfairly paternalistic and it's an insult to the female population of this nation." Skoloff probably learned this lingo from liberal lawyer Lori Andrews (1988, p. 293), who wrote, "Great care needs to be taken not to portray women as incapable of responsible decisions."

Choice occurs in the context of a society where, to put it mildly, there are fundamental differences of power between men and women. Yet feminists who oppose technological and contractual reproduction are vilified for supposedly claiming that "infertile women and, by implication, all women [are] incapable of rationally grounded and authentic choice" (Stanworth: 1987/1988, p. 17). Little is said about why women are willing to submit their bodies to the most invasive and harmful medical interventions – for example, because their lives are devalued without children, because of husband/family pressure, because there has been little research and few resources devoted to infertility, and because women are channeled into abusive technologies at any cost to themselves. There is the presumption that if women choose to treat their bodies in this way – as reproductive experiments, vehicles, or objects for another's use – this is not problematic. This argument is problematic, however, because it minimalizes the social and political contexts in which women's choices are made. Even the New Jersey Supreme Court decision, In the Matter of Baby M (1988), recognized that although many women make a choice to enter Surrogate arrangements and many others do not perceive surrogacy as exploitative, this "does not diminish its potential for devaluation to other women."

In addition to surrogacy and the new reproductive technologies, sexual and reproductive liberals have also claimed that women freely choose to enter pornography. This idea of pornography as a woman's unadulterated choice appeared most prominently in a document called the FACT (Feminist Anti-Censorship Taskforce) Brief. FACT organized for the sole purpose of defeating the Dworkin-MacKinnon feminist antipornography ordinance that makes pornography legally actionable as a violation of women's civil rights. Throughout the FACT Brief, the rhetoric of false victimization prevails. "The ordinance . . . reinforces sexist images of women as incapable of consent . . . In effect, the ordinance creates a strong presumption that women who participate in the creation of sexually explicit material [FACT's euphemism for pornography] are coerced" (FACT: 1985, p. 4). The FACT Brief went so far as to say that women have been stereotyped as victims by the statutory rape laws.

Radical feminists stress how male supremacy channels women into pornography and surrogacy as well as into other reproductive procedures, while liberals charge that radical feminists make women into victims. There is a mechanism of denial operating in these accusations. In saying that women are not victims of male dominance, the liberal critics absolve themselves of responsibility for the victims. They obscure the necessity to create social and political change for those who are victims and they disidentify with their own victimization.

The kind of choice that feminist critics of technological and contractual reproduction would defend is substantive, not a so-called woman's choice growing out of a context of powerlessness. Instead, the more substantive question is, Do such so-called choices as surrogacy foster the empowerment of women as a group and create a better world for women? What kind of choices do women have when subordination, poverty, and degrading work are the options available to many? The point is not to deny that women are capable of choosing within contexts of powerlessness, but to question how much real value, worth, and power these so-called choices have.

Women make choices about what they judge to be in their own self interest or survival, often in a desperate attempt to find safety or security, and often to give meaning to their existence. Andrea Dworkin, in *Right-Wing Women*, demonstrates that politically conservative as well as feminist women are aware of the ways in which women are subordinated to male dictates, yet the former make different choices than feminists do. They choose what they perceive to be in their own best interests. Like most women, they make survival choices in a context of restricted options. So are we then to anoint their choices merely because they freely choose? In a similar way, *because* some women choose to enter surrogate contracts or submit themselves to the bodily invasions of multiple IVF treatments does not validate those choices.

In one way, this discussion of the social and political construction of women's choices demonstrates the old philosophical debate between freedom and necessity. Necessity is imposed through the social forces that dictate the conditions of women's lives, conditions that women do not create. That women do not often create the social conditions within which they act does not abrogate their capacity to choose, but it does call for a more complex assessment of what we call women's choices, bidding us to focus less on choice and more on its constraints. What are the organized forces shaping women's choice of surrogacy and other reproductive techniques? For starters, the whole social context of sexual subordination in which women live their lives and which results, for many, in economic poverty, dead-ended jobs, and low self-esteem. In surrogate agencies, there is a conjunction of male medical, corporate, and legal interests promoting the reproductive management of women. The media put on a promotional show, as well.

This is not to say that women who sign surrogate contracts are simply passive victims. Women's victimization can be acknowledged without labeling women passive. *Passive* and *victim* do not necessarily go together. Jews were victims of the Nazis, but they were not passive, nor did the reality of victimization define the totality of their existence. Blacks were victims of slavery, yet no thoughtful commentator would ever portray slaves as passive. It seems obvious that women can be victims of pornography and technological reproduction without depriving women of some ability to act under oppressive conditions, else how could any woman extract herself from these conditions, as many have?

Feminists can move beyond a one-dimensional focus on women's oppression without *relinquishing the critique of women's oppression*. This is the most serious failure of sexual and reproductive liberalism – the relinquishing of the critique of the oppression of women. The end result of this abdication is that while lip service may be paid in minimal ways to the "possible" abuses of surrogacy and the new reproductive technologies, the present ways in which women do move beyond sexual and reproductive violence are never validated. For example, the sexual and reproductive liberal literature does not mention the exsurrogates and the expornography models who have organized to fight against surrogacy and pornography instead of promoting these as economic options for women. Many women who have been victims of pornography and surrogacy have become the systems' most powerful critics, but we are, instead, urged to examine the ways in which these systems of pornography and surrogacy, for example, are useful to women.

Finally, it seems obvious that one can recognize women's victimization by these institutions without shoring up the institutions themselves. When the sexual and reproductive liberals affirm that women are agents in a "culture" of pornography and technological reproduction, they sideline the agency of the institutions, thereby letting them off the hook. Why find evidence of women's agency within institutions of women's oppression and then use that agency to bolster these very systems? Why not locate women's agency in resistance to these institutions – for example, the agency of women who have courageously testified about their abuse in pornography and surrogacy, risking exposure and ridicule and often getting it; the exsurrogates who have fought for themselves and their children in court against the far greater advantages of the sperm source. Why locate women's agency primarily within the "culture" of male supremacy? And why shift attention from an analysis and activism aimed at destroying these systems to a justification of them? By romanticizing the victimization of women as liberating, sexual and reproductive liberalism leaves women in these systems at the mercy of them.

Sexual and reproductive liberalism has produced a new idealization of women's oppression; it defends the institution of surrogacy as providing the means for women's economic survival and the institution of pornography as freeing the expression of a repressed outlaw female sexuality[5] (Willis: 1983, p. 84). This idealization makes women's subordination and abuse honorable, much in the tradition of the nineteenth-century view of ennobling women's domestic confinement and "conservation of energy". If oppression produces sexually or reproductively "free" women, it is a grand case for more oppression – not for ending the sexual and reproductive subordination of women.

When pornography and surrogacy are idealized as choices, this defines a new range of conformity for women. Choice is not the same as self-determination. Choice can be conformity if women have little ability to determine the conditions of consent. A woman may consent to use the pill or the IUD as a contraceptive,

---

5. Willis writes, "A woman who enjoys pornography (even if that means enjoyng a rape fantasy) is in a sense a rebel, insisting on an aspect of her sexuality that has been defined as a male preserve. Insofar as pornography glorifies male supremacy and sexual alienation, it is deeply reactionary. But in rejecting sexual repression and hypocrisy – which have inflicted even more damage on women than on men – it expresses a radical impulse." Willis tries to have it both ways. In effect she is şaying to women, use it and be abused by it. But the two cannot be separated; there is not one kind of pornography that frees women and another that harms us.

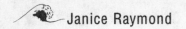

after having the risks explained to her, but she has no sexual and reproductive self-determination if she cannot say no to intercourse with her male partner. A woman who signs a surrogate contract, agreeing to bear a child for a contracting couple, consents to the arrangement, but she has little self-determination if she cannot find sustaining and dignified work and resorts to surrogacy as a final economic resort. Feminists must go beyond choice and consent as a standard for women's freedom. Before consent, there must be self-determination so that consent does not simply amount to acquiescing to the available options.

When technological reproduction perpetuates the role of women as breeders or encourages women to have children at any cost, this is not reproductive self-determination. It is conformity to old social roles garbed in new technologies and the new language of individual rights and choice. Under the guise of fostering procreative liberty, these reproductive arrangements help mold women to traditional reproductive roles. The fact that this compliance is ratified with the victim's consent only serves to emphasize how deeply conformity is entrenched and concealed in a gender-defined society.

Technological and contractual reproduction promotes the ideology that the problem of infertility cannot be confronted on an autonomous level but needs the intervention of medical and technical specialists to remedy the lack of biological children. Other options – an existence without children, an informed adoption – are not promoted as favorable alternatives. And thus women are left with the hollow rhetoric of choice – in reality, no choice at all.

Coercion and Complicity

Some critics of technological reproduction use the language of coercion to explain why women enter IVF programs or consent to surrogate contracts. Their attempt to show how choices are constrained for women under present social conditions is worthwhile, yet I do not find the language of coercion in the context of reproductive procedures particularly helpful. The degree and conditions of constraints on women are very different in the context of technological reproduction than, for example, in the context of pornography and prostitution. Most women in these latter systems have an extreme history of coercion, including rape, battery, incest, and child sexual abuse. Women are coerced into pornography and prostitution by pimps, lovers, husbands, fathers, as well as others:

> Pimps roam bus stations to entrap young girls who left incestuous homes – thinking nothing could be worse. Pornographers advertise for lingerie or art or acting models they then bind, assault, and photograph, demanding a smile as the price for sparing their life. Men roam the highways with penises and cameras in hand, raping women with both at once. Husbands force their wives to pose as part of coerced sex, often enforced by threats to the lives of their children. Women are abducted by pimps from shopping centers and streets at random, sometimes never to return. Young women are tricked or pressured into posing for boyfriends and

told that the pictures are just "for us", only to find themselves in this month's *Hustler* (Dworkin and MacKinnon: 1988, p. 43).

The political and social construction of women's options in systems of reproduction, however, is not the same degree of coercion to which women are subjected in systems of sexual subordination. Surrogacy comes closest in the instances where women have been deceived about their role or threatened after they have signed the contract. Women who undergo IVF procedures, however, are not coerced in this sense of extreme exploitation. In fact, women in IVF are complicitous to a certain extent that, nonetheless, does not deny the reality of the constraints or the ways in which women's choices are managed by the medical establishment.

Understanding women's complicity can help us to discern the different ways in which women come to accept what men want us to accept. This is neither to blame women, as the sexual and reproductive liberals do, nor to accept the institutions of women's reproductive oppression – the IVF mills and the systems of surrogacy – because women in these contexts are not outrightly coerced in the extreme. It is to say that pressure exists in many ways, not only at the level of coercion. It is also to make distinctions, reasserting the difference between social determinism and social constructionism. To affirm that women's choices and consent can be constructed, influenced, and pressured is not the same as to claim that women's choices are ruled by these social and political conditions. That reproductive arrangements are shaped by male power contextualizes but does not determine women's participation in these arrangements.

On the other hand, the language of coercion in the context of techno-logical reproduction says too little about the complexity of consent. As one woman doctor who had undergone infertility treatments explained, "Looking back over the events . . . I by no means consider myself a passive victim, but know that I actively subjected myself to this violation of my body" (Stens: 1989, p. 11). She then recounts a course of "violently enforced action" to conceive a child without letting her own subjectivity and agency off the hook. In retrospect, she realizes her own complicity in these reproductive manipulations.

Although women may participate in medical violations of their own bodies, many change and become resisters. The explanation of coercion flattens out the truth that women do act under conditions of oppression, but that their actions are qualified in significant ways. If surrogacy and IVF are violations of human dignity and bodily integrity, the violations occur whether they happen personally or to others. By participating in the exploitation of the self, one contributes to the exploitation of others. When women recognize their own complicity in their own oppression, often this recognition is a consciousness-raising event. For many, it enables them to get out from under the oppression.

Critiquing a theory of history that sees the self only as a product of socially constructed interactions with others and events, sociologist Kathleen Barry

(1990, p. 80) states, "Selves [in these theories] are not more than their material and social realities . . . With that, the future is rejected for women if they cannot project beyond the present and, therefore, beyond domination." Barry (p. 84) contends that "women usually know more about domination than they speak . . ." since women's subordination has been personalized and made private and intimate. The consciousness of oppression, spoken or not, creates a historical dynamism; theories about the social construction of women's choices, no matter how radical they are, cannot essentialize a woman's self, making social conditions determinative of her total reality. "With an interactive concept of the self in praxis, we can begin to study the social construction of women in a historical context and, thereby, discover that which enables and that which prevents any woman from becoming a 'woman unto herself'" (Barry: 1990, p. 87). Understanding the complexity of women's consent involves exposing the conditions of oppression that constrain women and their choices as well as attending to the ways in which women act and change – for good or for ill – as they gain or deny awareness and historical consciousness of what has been done to them. In some circumstances, it involves admitting women's complicity in our own oppression. Complicity has been women's stake in the system. Although the sexual and reproductive liberals lay claim to a nuanced view of women's oppression, they treat the social and political construction of women's consent as unproblematic. There is a constant pretension to complexity in their work, but it is as if, paying lip service to the rhetoric of complexity, they do not understand the reality of complexity in women's lives. Relying on a liberal theory of choice, they blame women and do not recognize the constraints on women's choices. Instead of looking at the complexity of women's agency under the conditions of oppression, they fault women for "getting themselves into these situations" or valorize the situations as liberating to women in ways "unintended by the patriarchs". They do not valorize women who resist, who bring suit against the surrogate brokers, who testify about their abuse in pornography, and who work for legislation to prosecute surrogate brokers, pimps, and pornographers. They simplify complexity. The sexual and reproductive liberals also reduce complexity to relativism. The fact that many women make different choices under conditions of oppression leads the liberals to an ethical and political relativism that claims it is impossible to make judgments about women's participation in prostitution and reproductive technologies and thus about the systems themselves. There is no right or wrong in their view, just simple difference. Surrogacy is neither good nor bad for women, they say. Different women make different choices. Different women do make different choices, and this suggests that we live in a world of ethical and political complexity rather than of moral relativity. Complexity demands that we search for moral and political answers to the various facets of reproductive trafficking instead of ignoring the search or reducing it to "everything is relative." Complexity demands moral discernment and the political courage to make judgments about what is oppressive or beneficial to women and then to act on these judgments.

Diane Bell

Speaking of Things that Shouldn't Be Written: Cross-cultural Excursions into the Land of Misrepresentations

Speaking out, speaking of, speaking with, speaking about, speaking for ... What did I say to bring the furies down on my feminist head? At the time it was really very simple. In collaboration with Topsy Napurrula Nelson, an Aboriginal woman from Central Australia with whom, over the past twenty years, I have worked, played, published, travelled, strategised, danced, sung, and painted (Bell: 1985; Bell and Nelson: 1989), we called attention to three facts: (1) Aboriginal men are raping Aboriginal women at a rate that qualifies as a human rights abuse and on a scale that constitutes a crisis; but (2) those whose voices one would expect to hear raised in outrage (i.e. Aboriginal Legal Aid and feminists) are, albeit for different reasons, silent on the nature and extent of the abuse; and (3) women's refuges and rape crisis centres that are modelled on Aboriginal women's traditional use of social space have been successful in providing safe places.

      For my part I contextualised these facts within a discussion of anthropological and legal modes of "representing" Aboriginal women and the transformation of gender relations in colonial and "post-colonial" Australia (Bell: 1993). Two case studies illustrated the complex dimensions and power plays that serve to privilege race over gender in the politics of Aboriginal self determination (Bell: 1992). On the issue of conceptualising rape, we cited a range of opinion on the awkward relationship of Aboriginal women to the women's movement (Bell: 1988; Fesl: 1984; O'Shane: 1976; Sykes: 1975; Watson: 1987). For her part, Topsy Napurrula Nelson spoke of the traditional modes of protecting women, of kin-based law, of women's sanctions against violent men, of safe spaces for women and girls, and of the increased vulnerability of Aboriginal women in the towns, fringe camps and on large reservations (Nelson: 1990a). These are ideas that I have heard expressed many times over by Aboriginal women in Central Australia. Often explanations

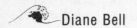

would be accompanied by drawings made onto a smoothed area of sand beside a speaker. Sketching quickly, women would illustrate traditional residential arrangements, then erase the clusters of lines that represented a variety of camps – some for extended families, some for women only, some for men – and sketch one arrangement, that of the nuclear family.

Topsy Nelson's and my attempt at a joint paper that reflected these ideas became an interplay of voices. In 1988, at a colloquium on the "Rights of Subordinated Peoples" at La Trobe University, Victoria, Australia, we took turns in explaining what was happening in Aboriginal communities in Central Australia (Bell: 1994). At that time we were made aware that raising the issue of intra-racial rape was going to be contentious. Interestingly it was not the Aboriginal men at the conference who objected. They were encouraging and stated that these were things that need to be talked about and that it was helpful to consider them in terms of the colonial relations. No, the opposition came from a conservative Muslim woman who argued these were private matters not to be discussed in public and a Pakeha woman who was involved in the Maori sovereignty struggle in New Zealand. Don't evoke tradition, she argued, and don't use gender as a wedge issue. However, both Topsy Nelson and myself felt that the incidence of violence against Aboriginal women was increasing; that the legal system needed to understand the complexity of violence against women in cross-cultural contexts; and that the voices of Aboriginal women living in the more traditional communities of Central and Northern Australia were not being heard.

The colonial encounter is inscribed differently on the lives of men and women, and in the locus of violence we have a clear example of how this difference registers: Aboriginal men are dying in police custody and the horror of this social fact has deeply scarred the Australian population (Elliot Johnson: 1991). While some Aboriginal women also die in custody, many more are being brutalised in their home communities (Atkinson: 1990a, b, c, d; Balendra: 1990; Bligh: 1993; O'Neill: 1994; O'Shane: 1988). Not to engage with the questions that intra-racial rape cases raise leaves rape shrouded in myth, the subject of spirited legal defences based on spurious anthropological evidence by lawyers, or the stuff of repressive law and order campaigns. But who may speak and in what voice?

In titling our piece "Speaking about rape is everyone's business" (Bell and Nelson: 1989), we were evoking an Aboriginal notion of there being a gendered etiquette when it comes to sensitive matters. The basis on which one speaks is always specified. What follows is a conversational pattern familiar to most who have probed such issues.

Question: "Who speaks for that one [a person or thing]?"
Answer: "I'm boss for that."
Question: "Who speaks for this one [place, ceremony, knowledge]?"
Answer: "That's man's business", or "That's woman's business."

Our title was an indication that we believed we could speak **to** each other and speak **out** to a wider audience. It was a defiant feminist statement that rape is about power and that silence about rape protects the abusers of power. So we were speaking **out,** not **for** other women.

    Women's Studies International Forum published a written version of the paper (Bell and Nelson: 1989) and all hell broke loose. In February 1990, a letter bearing no address and no signatures to validate the twelve names typed at the bottom of the second page was sent to colleagues and *WSIF*. It was not sent directly to me (although my address was on the article). It accused me of creating divisions within the "Aboriginal community", of appropriating Topsy Nelson's voice by citing her as "co-author" rather than "informant", of exhibiting white imperialism, and of exercising middle-class privilege. It concluded with the claim "sexism does not and will never prevail over racial domination in this country" (Huggins *et al:* 1990, p. 507). It was authored by twelve well-educated urban Aboriginal women, none of whom, to the best of my knowledge, had any in-depth fieldwork experience in the area of which we had written, but they all claimed to speak for Aboriginal women. Our title had enraged these women. I had no business to speak. Only Aboriginal women could speak for Aboriginal women. There was no need to specify any other basis.

    I sought advice from colleagues who said, "It will pass," but it didn't; it got worse. At conferences the rights of white women to work in Central Australia were discussed; journal articles appeared; I was called upon to defend myself on the ABC (Australian Broadcasting Corporation) and in letters to various journals. The issue became known as the "Bell debate" and many women offered support to the letter writers. After all, who wanted to be called a racist? Some women simply ducked the issue, and a few stood by what they knew and refused to be intimidated. Women were being raped and that issue had to be addressed. Our unspeakable article was the basis of many a talk but, I quickly learned, it was rarely read. Jumping on the bandwagon of "beat up a white feminist anthropologist who is now out of the country" (I had just taken up a position in the USA) was a popular pastime in 1990. Highly imaginative stories of conspiracies to silence the authors of the letter added an extra spice to the retellings. In reality *WSIF* took legal advice, sought signatures to the letter so that it could be published, and offered to publish a more detailed piece should the women wish to submit one (Rowland: 1991–92). They also sought a response from Topsy Nelson and myself. I tried to correspond with Jackie Huggins but she and her co-authors were not inclined to further discussion with a person such as myself, although they reserved the right to discuss the matters wherever, whenever, and with whomever they pleased, and they have at some length.

    Meantime, in the real world, gradually more and more Aboriginal women were speaking out and their stories were of unrelenting violence. Far from over-stating the case, we had only touched the surface (Atkinson: 1990a, b, c, d; Bolger: 1990; Carmody: 1990; O'Shane: 1988; Sculthorpe: 1990). Judy Atkinson (1990a; 1989, p. 11), an Aboriginal woman from Queensland, noted that "in one town no Aborig-inal girl over the age of ten had not been raped" and "rape is a daily occurrence but 88% go unreported, only pack rapes are reported" but, as our cases indicated, even they may not be reported (Bell and Nelson: 1989 pp. 411–12). Under-reporting

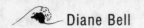

is a problem in all rape cases but there are particular reasons why, in small kin-based communities, where everyone knows everyone else, crimes go unreported: victims fear retribution, learn to protect themselves from further abuse by keeping quiet, and the power to intimidate is known to boys and men. Further, police are not always interested and may even be part of the abuse pattern. And, both Aboriginal men and women are reluctant to see offenders go to jails in distant cities (Atkinson: 1989, p. 21; 1990b, p. 14; 1990c, p. 20; Bligh: 1993; O'Shane: 1988).

Activists, Aboriginal and non-Aboriginal, who had long agitated for research on the issue of violence against women, wrote thanking me for opening the subject to a wider audience. Several began to tell me of the ways in which their projects and analyses were being threatened and deflected and of how they had been warned not to quote my work. I'd see a first draft that cited my work and then, when the published version appeared, it would disappear, although the ideas often remained. According to Huggins *et al.* (1990), it was right and proper to speak of inter-racial rape, but not intra-racial rape. You can't study "rape", one highly qualified Aboriginal woman researcher was told by a senior male Aboriginal bureaucrat. When she persisted another more compliant woman was appointed to take over the work. Jackie Huggins (June 1992b) in writing to say she had no interest in participating in an exchange with me stated that, on principle, she does not cite me. Others follow suit. Dialogue is difficult under these circumstances.

My file on the reception of our article is voluminous and it makes depressing reading. In all these exchanges and fora, the substantive issues raised by our piece were disappeared. There were post-modern discourses on difference, subjectivities, and representivity a plenty, but not a word on the issue of rape and, in the process, Topsy Nelson was also rendered voiceless. Huggins *et al.* (1990) demote her to the status of "informant" – a particularly offensive term in my opinion – and claim that because she cannot speak English, she can't have understood what was in the article! Here I would refer the reader to publications in which she speaks in perfectly intelligible English (Nelson: 1990a). Anna Yeatman, one of the self appointed non-Aboriginal academic chroniclers of the debate, refuses to cite our article as jointly authored and insists it is "Bell: 1989" (Yeatman: 1993). In rush to reverence difference and to heed the voices of certain Aboriginal women, it seems that Topsy Nelson cannot have a space. Her difference doesn't count. Or is it too difficult to hear, too destabilising of the race/gender hierarchy? It does after all promise a way out of the "no-speak" dilemma. Indignant that she was deemed a dupe of my anthropological pen, Topsy Nelson wrote to Jackie Huggins and *WSIF*:

> I had no Aborigine to write this down. Diane is like a sister; best friend. She wrote all this down for me. That's OK – women to women; it doesn't matter black or white. I want these things written down and read again later. I was telling Diane to write this story for me (Nelson: 1990b, p. 507).

This was not the first time that Topsy Nelson and I had worked together and in reviewing our several previous (and often memorable) interactions, I thought

I saw a way to build a more dynamic, less guilt-ridden appreciation of questions of gender and race. In "Intra-racial rape revisited: on forging a feminist future beyond factions and frightening politics" (Bell: 1991), I proposed we think seriously about the possibilities of actual, concrete friendship and personal trust as the context for dialogue. I sketched examples of positive, woman-affirming, cross-cultural collaborations. I argued that if we think of race as a given, all we can do is react. In such situations our modes of interaction are circumscribed by the construct "race" and the boundaries of the person become fixed. Before we can engage in dialogue, we have to breach these socially constructed boundaries. Whereas, if we emphasise relationality, and ground our analyses in the specificities of place and personal history, we can focus on connectedness and the rigidity of the bounded category of race gives way to permeable membranes. The shift in emphasis opens up the possibility of theorising issues of gender and race around particular relationships, and declares that our possibilities are not exhausted by our predicates (*white* woman, *Aboriginal* woman, *radical* feminist, *socialist* feminist). This shift from boundary maintenance to relationality is threatening if one has constructed a political identity on the basis of predicates. When the issue is rape, it is our vulnerability as women to rape that grounds the relationality and thus I am suggesting we begin with the issue (rape), not with the construct (race).

In my view, a feminism drawing on female friendship bespeaks a more robust feminist future than one cringing before socially constructed categories. If the cross-cultural politic is to be co-operative, the exchanges have to be two-way: we need to learn to be more sensitive to cultural difference, and Aboriginal women need to see there are women who are sensitive. We need not to be cowered by being told we are white and Aboriginal women need to acknowledge, as many have, that feminism has changed the environment in which they operate. In this I think white women have the major responsibility to create and foster the conditions under which dialogue might occur, but that does not mean we should suspend all critical faculties. We need to be able to talk and not be constrained by fear of being called racist. Aboriginal women need to be able to speak and not fear being dismissed as guilt tripping. It's not the end of the relationship to have a disagreement. If Aboriginal and white women can't argue and do so in a constructive way, then we need to consider whether the relationship is tinged by racism. In attempting to imagine safe spaces in which dialogue might occur, I would caution not all women are feminists and womanist politics are not necessarily part of Aboriginal female identity.

It seems I am now back to the issue of who may speak and in what voice. These issues are not unique to Australia. As African-American and Anglo-American feminists have argued, to adopt a right to speak based on biology, be it by reference to race or sex, denies the importance of the ways in which race and gender are socially constructed in different times and places. As Patricia Hill Collins (1990, p. 22) points out in exploring her working definition of "Black feminist thought" as encompassing "theoretical interpretations of Black women's reality by those who live it", that biological essentialism is dangerous and masks who produces knowledge and under what conditions. Patricia Hill Collins goes on to say (1990, p. 22),

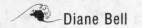

not all African-American women generate feminist thought and other groups may play a role in its production.[2] Working with a similar notion that it is the social construction of gender, not our biology that underlines women's experience of social inequality, Catharine MacKinnon (see this volume, pp. 45–54) asks "What is a white woman anyway?" and proceeds to build a theory in which Black women are central. Angela Harris (1990) who is not persuaded, accuses MacKinnon of false universalising, and calls for the telling of stories as a way of understanding difference. Two other Black women, e christi cunningham (1991) and Susan Christian (1991) find merit in MacKinnon's theorising. Clearly, the intertwining of race and gender narratives remains complex and controversial for African-American women.

Yet, when Larissa Behrendt surveys these debates from her standpoint as an urban Aboriginal woman (1993, p. 27), she endorses Harris' critique and argues that racism, not sexism, must be the basis of an Aboriginal jurisprudence. She too wants to hear the stories, but she only wants to hear those that privilege racism, particularly that of white women. Interestingly Behrendt (1993, p. 27) opens with the caveat that, "This is my perspective. I do not speak for all Aboriginal women" and then proceeds to generalise what Aboriginal women think, believe and have experienced. It seems that, in the mid-90s in Australia, we are witnessing a consolidation of an Aboriginal women's orthodoxy and that it is being attributed primarily to Jackie Huggins.[3] Sometimes, as in the case of Behrendt (1993), an earlier piece by Bobbi (Roberta) Sykes (1975) may be cited as the starting point, but the stories of women such as Vivien Bligh (1983), an Aboriginal woman writing in the early eighties of gendered justice and the needs of Aboriginal women who have been raped, are erased. In what has become known as the "Tiddas' Manifcsto"[4]

---

2. Recent feminist explorations of standpoint theories can illuminate this issue and do so without falling victim to essentialising. Arguing that oppression generates an epistemic privilege, feminist philosophers have built a powerful case for "starting thought with women's lives" (Harding: 1990). For a summary of some of the critical features of standpoint theory with reference to the knowledge of Aboriginal women, see (Bell: 1993, 281 ff).

3. Speaking on *The Coming Out Show* in September 1990, Huggins voiced her opinion that she was so disgusted with the racism of white women that she wanted no more to do with their politics, but she insisted that white women had to learn from Aboriginal women. In terminating her correspondence with me, she echoed the same sentiments (1992a). I am left wondering how one can learn when the party who insists that you listen refuses to speak to you. One can trace the development of Huggins' position on racism and sexism through a series of articles and interviews (Huggins: 1987; 1990a, b, c; 1991a, b; 1992b), but her position on feminist scholarship has been fleshed out more in written and oral commentaries on the debate over our article than in any sustained argument by Huggins. Nowhere have I seen Huggins identify herself as a feminist. Her bio-note usually says "historian and writer" (Huggins: 1992b, p. 70).

4. This was proclaimed by Liz Flannagan and Katrina Felton at the "Dealing with Difference: Women and ethnicity" conference of the *Lilith Feminist Journal*, and later broadcast, in part on *The Coming Out Show*, ABC Women's Broadcasting Unit, July 1993.

that racism trumps sexism, has come to be the story that Aboriginal women are said to tell. While "Tiddas" like Larissa Behrendt, Jackie Huggins and Eve Fesl call for the voices of Aboriginal women to be heard, many other accounts of the relationship of sexism and racism are ignored or dismissed (Atkinson: 1990a, b, c; Daylight and Johnstone: 1986; O'Shane: 1984; Payne: 1990; Sculthorpe: 1990; Watson: 1987). Where, then, is the richness of thought, the myriad responses to oppression and the particularised accounts of racism that American and Australian women of colour both demand and offer?

So, to return to the three facts with which I began. Frustrated with the defence oriented nature of existing services, the Aboriginal Women's Legal Group is moving to create separate services for women. In her award winning "Our shame: How Aboriginal women and children are bashed in their own community – then ignored", journalist Rosemary O'Neill (1994) retraces the ground we mapped five years earlier. There were no demands for her removal, no outcry at the mention of the intra-racial rape, instead O'Neill received the prestigious Walkeley Award for her report.[5] It seems our heresies have become received wisdom. At the national level there are Women's Initiatives Programs and the like but, the real action is at the local level, where women such as Topsy Nelson have authority. Out in the communities, away from the power struggles of the organisations that purport to speak for Aborigines, women are confronting the violence. In the Mutitjulu community Uluru (Ayer's Rock), Pitjantjatjara women like Kunbry Peipei, working with anthropologist Jane Lloyd, are achieving remarkable results on the issue of domestic violence (Finnane: 1995). These women are taking their message from one place to another. Aboriginal women are learning from each other. The media has caught up, the lawyers are paying attention, many Aboriginal women's voices are being heard, but too many academics are still writing commentaries on the commentaries and not engaging with the grim realities of gendered violence within Aboriginal comunities. In terms of service delivery, it is clear women from many different backgrounds are working together. However, the chilly environment engendered by the Huggins *et al.* attack persists. And, although it is now clear that Topsy Nelson and I spoke the truth, and that our analysis of the legal system was appropriate, I am still being abused, misrepresented, and misquoted in print and slandered by persons with little or no knowledge of the issues, or my background. It is more convenient to accuse feminists who speak out of being divisive than it is to address the conditions that give rise to violence against women.

5. This award by the Media, Entertainment and Arts Alliance, is for excellence in journalism.

Uta Enders-Dragässer and Brigitte Sellach

Feminist Educational Research De-radicalized: A Warning from Germany

This is the first time we have discussed publicly a 1991 attack on a radical feminist research project that one of us conducted in the mid-80s. This attack came from a male academic who published a polemic anti-feminist article in the well known German educational magazine *Pädextra* (Preuss-Lausitz: 1991). We describe why and how this attack happened and what the damage was to feminist educationalist theory and practice

Ulf Preuss-Lausitz's article was called "The empress' new clothes? Questions about feminist educational research with regard to boys." Its main target was a widely known feminist study on interactions in schools by feminist sociologist and educationalist, Uta Enders-Dragässer and feminist linguist, Claudia Fuchs (Enders-Dragässer and Fuchs: 1988a, 1989). The article was chosen as an example of the "narrow mindedness", "missing self-criticism" and lack of "scholarly work" of feminist educational research in general.

The interdisciplinary study of Enders-Dragässer and Claudia Fuchs – the first German research project on interactions between the sexes in schools – was funded through a political action program for women (1983/1984) in the state of Hesse, a result of a demand for such research by women active in the Women's Movement and the Green Party. Funding for feminist school research – by the government and otherwise – was practically nonexistent at that time, as well as later. Because of this situation, the project was a low budget study and drew considerably on the personal commitment of both researchers who could not draw on the resources of an academic institution. Nevertheless, the project was explicitly conceptualised within the context of already existing international feminist research in this topic (Frazier and Sadker: 1973; Oakley: 1982; Spender: 1984, 1985a; Spender and Sarah: 1980; Skinningsrud: 1984; etc.) It was also supported by a Women's Movement network "AG Frauen und Schule" (working group women and school), the only public forum for feminist school research at that time. Of special importance to this study was Norwegian psychologist Tone Skinningsrud's contention (1984) that the classroom is a social system with gender-specific norms that are open to change.

The research project, conducted from 1985 to 1987 focussed on two main questions: whether girls and women (in Hessian schools) were disadvantaged in school interactions and whether girls and women contributed competently to classroom interaction with as yet unrecognised interactional competences. The data were gathered in structured in-depth interviews with women teachers as well as through video recordings of classroom interaction. A linguistic evaluation of the videos was performed by Claudia Fuchs who had gained her academic credentials under the guidance of Luise F. Pusch and Senta Tröml-Plötz, two well-known feminist linguists in Germany with international reputations.

In 1987, Enders-Dragässer and Fuchs were in the middle of their research work when Hessian elected a conservative government which abruptly withdrew the funding. This meant that the data analysis and evaluation had to be cut short. After months of waiting and insisting on payment, a small final sum enabled both researchers to analyse and evaluate at least part of their data and to write a research report. Xeroxed copies of a preliminary report – which included findings from international feminist educational and linguistic research – (Enders-Dragässer, Schmidt *et al.*: 1986), and a final report (Enders-Dragässer and Fuchs: 1988a), were both very much in demand. The final report was published in a book in 1989 (Enders-Dragässer and Fuchs: 1989). As it happened, women, and especially female teachers from Germany, Austria and Switzerland, have repeatedly shown that women recognise and identify with the experiences of girls and women in schools as recorded on the videos or expressed in the interviews. They shared the views of the respondents and agreed with the researchers' contentions and interpretations and worked with them because they helped them to understand and to analyse their own daily practice in the classroom and in society at large.

What follows is a brief summary of some of the main findings of this study about interactions in schools. Some of the findings supported what international feminist educational research had already claimed for many years. Although it was assumed, generally, that girls and boys in schools were treated as equals, the study confirmed that this assumption was wrong. Girls and boys (as members of the group "girls" and the group "boys") behaved in gender-specific ways. They learned in gender-specific ways and even the contents of their learning were gender-specific. Boys got the bigger share of the teachers' attention and communication. If girls got more than their "normal" share of attention of about a third of the teacher's time (Spender: 1984; 1985a), boys immediately complained about the preference given to the girls. When that happened teachers of both sexes, as well as girls, showed a tendency to consider the boys' complaints as justified because they laboured under a perception distorted by sex-role stereotypes.

Within the unquestioned pervasive framework of gender hierarchy and sex-role stereotyping, boys as a group shunned cooperative interactions. Through male dominance in the classroom, a competitive mode of interaction and unruly and sexist behaviour, they created a competitive and disintegrative classroom atmosphere, thereby disadvantaging girls in many ways, especially by suppressing their classroom participation. These dynamics resulted in so-called "role conflicts" which the researchers analysed as a gender specific double bind, described by Tone Skinningsrud for the first time:

> Girls in the typical male discourse class are faced with a choice between two evils, being punished for being masculine/competitive or being looked down upon for being feminine/losers in the public competition. In face of this negative choice the resolution of non-action in public seems understandable (1984, p. 21).

Role conflicts of this kind also constrained the professional performance of women teachers: interviews and video recordings showed that they had to work hard, lesson after lesson to establish – and maintain – their expert status, since the boys as a group tended to deny their competence. This never ending power struggle led to enormous distress of girls and women in schools. It was expressed in interviews and evident during videotaped lessons – a finding which the researchers had not anticipated.

Shifting the lens from the issue of individual boys and girls (and teachers) to the issue of the classroom as a social system with gender-specific norms that can be changed, (Skinningsrud: 1984), a merit of this study later completely ignored because of the attack of Preuss-Lausitz, resulted in another main finding: the overall existence of gender-specific distortions of perception which made it difficult for teachers and students to see, to understand and eventually to change their gender-specific patterns of interaction. Their distorted perception made it difficult to perceive the distinct influence boys exerted in the classroom with their preferred competitive style of interaction, their ridicule of girls and women, their harassment and their violence, their norms of gender specific inequality and male dominance.

Using precise linguistic methods in school research for the first time by analysing videotapes with an linguistic methodology made it possible to describe various patterns of interactions as disintegrative and disadvantaging – or integrative and cooperative: another main finding of the study. One integrative pattern of interaction was the so called "open argument". It was based on consensus within the classroom which allowed an open development of the debate into various directions with the participation of all. If topics or texts on questions of gender and equality etc. were declared to be irrelevant – which boys often did in reaction to "open arguments" of girls or teachers (Enders-Dragässer and Fuchs: 1989, p. 119) – the integrative debate came to an end and immediately changed into a disintegrative one: girls and women now had to *defend* themselves and to "prove" that their arguments were altogether of "relevance" within the ongoing debate in the classroom. Thus they were deftly outmanoeuvred with whatever they said which was deemed "irrelevant". Claudia Fuchs called this frequent pattern of interaction the "argument of irrelevance".

These and other findings led to the conclusion that an overall double standard was at work in school interactions: girls and women were the quiet, self-disciplined and cooperative losers and the boys and men the noisy, unruly and destructive winners.

In their research report, Enders-Dragässer and Fuchs proposed that priority be given to the development of a cooperative style of interaction (as mostly shown by girls as a group) in order to change the classroom atmosphere for the better. The conclusion was that girls were disadvantaged in schools since their demonstrated interactional skills and achievements were not understood as learned skills but were perceived as "normal female behaviour" and thus devalued. The preferential treatment boys asked for and received in schools was perceived as "normal" and "fair". There was no understanding of the underlying interactional and educational deficiencies of boys. The competitive style of interaction (as mostly shown by boys as group) as well as conflicts with norms of masculinity were considered to be important causes of boys' deficiencies and frustration which significantly contributed to behavioural difficulties and underachieving. For these reasons, Enders-Dragässer and Fuchs strongly recommended that the male norms in schools, and especially in co-educative schools, needed to change – rather than the *girls* who, within a non-feminist framework, were seen as "placid" and "conformist" and needing to compensate for alleged "deficits".

After completion of the final report a Protestant church group engaged in gender work with men showed interest in the findings of the study and suggested some further research focussed on the situation of boys. A small grant made it possible for Uta Enders-Dragässer and Claudia Fuchs to conduct the first feminist research project in Germany on the situation of boys in schools. The idea was to record and analyse the consequences of male socialization and of norms of masculinity and to test their earlier findings about difficulties and deficits of boys, with a further emphasis on exploring the boys' distress and fear of failing as males. This research project, published by the church as a booklet (Enders-Dragässer and Fuchs: 1988b), was again very much in demand and since its publication has gained respect as a valuable contribution to questions of male socialization and gender sensitive practice work with boys, as do Spoden (1993, p. 34) and Böhnisch and Winter (1993, p. 105).

With both these publications on gender specific interactions available within the context of expanding feminist educational research and a growing public interest in the feminist debate on co-education in schools at the beginning of the 90s, it seemed feasible to attract more funding for further feminist school research and gender sensitive practice work in co-educative schools, especially with a focus on male violence in schools and further training of teachers. However, with the publication of his attack on Enders-Dragässer's and Fuchs' work in 1991, "progressive" educationalist Ulf Preuss-Lausitz made the crucial first public step that stymied feminist educational research and practice work. Moreover, although this was not obvious at first, his attack effectively split German feminist educationalists. How did he do it and how could this happen?

First of all, his five-page article in *Pädextra* was not written as a scholarly contribution to an intellectual debate but as an irascible and defamatory polemic. With the title "The empress' new clothes" – borrowed from fairy tale writer, Andersen – this self-appointed "supporter" and watchman of feminist research chose to express his opinion and to mobilize prejudices from asking "innocent questions" about the relevance of feminist educational research, thus suggesting in a sexist and not too subtle way that feminist educationalist research was a sham, was "naked" (and above all too foolish to notice). Suggesting that it was "daring as a man" to ask "questions", he was clever enough to side-step a scholarly debate of feminist research and its specific "answers", methodology and positions. For instance he "asked" whether the feminist debate might be mostly earmarked by dogma instead of facts; he wondered why feminist research rarely dealt with boys? Why the subjective experiences of boys and girls were rarely empirically analysed? Whether there was a danger that the qualitative feminist school research might abuse qualitative methodology? And whether quantitative research was altogether better than qualitative pilot studies etc. Of course he did *not* ask how feminist research was funded, whether it was institutionalized etc. In his view, feminist school research was narrow minded and lacked a critical dimension. Referring to the journal *Frauen und Schule*, conference documentations within the context of the AG Frauen und Schule network and a selective list of studies as the "mainstream" of feminist educational research, he considered it to be at a dead end and the research work not conducted properly. Furthermore, he maintained that the findings lacked empirical substance and evidence. But he did not even bother to refer to arguments and findings within the body of German and international feminist educational scholarship at large when asking his "critical questions" and stating his "critical" assumptions. And he was clever and careful enough not to state explicitly his own position within German educational doctrine, mainly that in co-educative schools girls were no longer disadvantaged.

Preuss-Lausitz' polemic was a classic example of how to effectively use the "argument of irrelevance" in order to change an open and integrative debate (of females and males) into a disintegrative one, fragmenting it into relevant and irrelevant topics and contributions, disintegrating persons in the debating group – one of the main findings of the study of Enders-Dragässer and Fuchs.

Having questioned the relevance and devalued the innovative potential of feminist research in general his next step was to "prove" his point by discussing a particularly "bad" example. His choice was the – in his words – "well known" and "often quoted" study on interactions of the sexes in schools by Uta Enders-Dragässer and Claudia Fuchs. Ulf Preuss-Lausitz complained about its "extremely meagre" empirical data base thus ignoring the study's explicitly chosen qualitative, rather than quantitative methodology. He also ignored the pioneering linguistic research part of the study and the financial problems the research suffered. Furthermore, there was no acknowledgment whatsoever of the exemplary international and interdisciplinary nature of this work. The final dismissal came with his assertion that the researchers had written up their study in a "journalistic" rather than scholarly way, thus denying the quality of a comprehensibly written research report and the evidence of qualitative data showing that and how girls and women are disadvantaged in school interactions, because of an overall double standard in school based on male norms, on male dominance, making use of sex stereotyped distortions of perception of actual interactional skills and achievements of girls and women.

Under the guise of asking "questions on behalf of the boys' situation" Preuss-Lausitz in fact advanced his own assumptions without, however, substantiating them: role conflicts of girls and boys as described by feminist educational research, he suggested, were outmoded. Today's girls and boys, he mused, have other problems. What these problems might be, however, he did not bother to tell us. And because not even he dared to ignore the internationally and beyond doubt established fact that boys get the bigger share of attention in schools, he introduced the catchphrase "pedagogical correctness" to justify this phenomenon. According to his own "quantitative empirical research of several years" about which he provided no details, "girls have the better social status in class", whatever this means. Anyhow, his research of "several years" seems to have left no traces in relevant bibliographies, because Böhnisch and Winter (1993), Frömelt (1994) and Spoden (1993) do not mention Preuss-Lausitz at all.

Preuss-Lausitz' concern is with the (poor) boys: disadvantaged by too many female teachers in elementary school and, in his view, utterly neglected by feminist educational researchers. Ironically, at the time his polemic was published, Enders-Dragässer's and Fuchs' research on boys was already in the third edition and acknowledged as a pioneering contribution to research into the situation of males (Spoden: 1993). Challenged by Uta Enders-Dragässer about his critique at a conference he told her that the study was all right, but that he didn't want the book to become a "cult book", in other words that he had problems with the reception of it.

It is quite understandable – though deplorable – that a male educationalist sides with the boys when feminist researchers irrefutably demonstrate the issue of male dominance and male deficits in the classroom and devise strategies aimed at reducing male privilege and influence. However, the use of defamatory polemics rather than scholarly debate is less than professional. It is not acceptable because it distorts and trivialises feminist research in the hope that others might dismiss it as well.

The attack, however, was not the only scandal. Anti-feminist attacks happen regularly and feminist researchers are used to dealing with them from time to time while continuing with their work anyway. In this case, unfortunately, we cannot report a happy feminist ending. In reaction to Preuss-Lausitz' article, the small German community of Feminist/Women's Studies' educationalists did not close rank against such an attack by either ignoring his polemic or refuting it. Sadly, rather than using it self-confidently and jointly as a chance to argue publicly for adequate funding and recognition of feminist educational research, they chose to fragment their own scholarly community and their own field of work by starting a debate on "correct" feminist research with the Preuss-Lausitz' polemic as reference text!

Pädextra had asked Enders-Dragässer and Fuchs as well as other feminist educationalists for a response to Preuss-Lausitz' article to be published in the same issue. The authors chose to ignore it. Others replied, however (Metz-Göckel and Kreienbaum: 1991; Nyssen: 1991). In both pieces the feminist academics who had not ever engaged in interactive classroom studies themselves lamented the polemic but in spite of revealing the unfounded and openly sexist nature of Preuss-Lausitz' snide comments, they nevertheless engaged with his assumptions. Elke Nyssen even took up Preuss-Lausitz' picture of the empress in no clothes, titling her response with a biblical quotation (Genesis: 2:3): "and they became aware that they were naked. Is the feminist school research a chimera?" They did not reject the assumptions of Preuss-Lausitz by directly supporting feminist researchers especially not Uta Enders-Dragässer and Claudia Fuchs and their research – the main object of Preuss-Lausitz' wrath. Elke Nyssen argued that the problem was that he had not taken into consideration the entire body of feminist educational research but only a small segment where, she added, some of his criticism might indeed be justified. Thus she gave credence to his attack in an underhand way without taking a stand herself. Sigrid Metz-Göckel and Anna Maria Kreienbaum defended feminist educational research against Preuss-Lausitz' polemic without, however, rejecting it as a polemic although it is a textbook example of hurt male ego and fret. Both responses did not mention the study of Uta Enders-Dragässer and Claudia Fuchs – to say nothing of voicing support for their work – and they did not include the attacked study in their bibliographies. Choosing between "objectively debating" a subjective male polemic by a member of the academic establishment and taking a stand in support of research from within their community, they let it happen that their own academic colleagues were discredited. They allowed a male academic to re-define "the standards" and the relevance of feminist research and to fragment it into "good" and "bad" research. They made this possible by letting him set limits to their own research work with polemic "questions", without even having to argue this point in a scholarly way.

According to Edith Glumpler (1995, pp. 8, 9) a change of positions, a new cutting of fields of research and influence is worked out within the still small community of Feminist/Women's Studies at the moment, with these debates about "problems" with the selective publication and reception of "certain research findings". Thus the study on interactions in schools of Enders-Dragässer and Fuchs is abused explicitly or implicitly as exemplary for feminist research work not meeting scientific standards, being "journalistic", "popularized" (because it was written comprehensibly and lectures were given to practitioners) and was critically questioned (because practitioners acknowledged it).

Glumpler describes the fragmentation of the feminist scientific community as a "change of paradigm" (1995, p. 9) and a mainstream reorientation of feminist school research giving up the interdisciplinary approaches and preferences of the earlier years. Annedore Prengel (1986) for instance, who earlier conceptualized the study on interactions in schools later done by Uta Enders-Dragässer and Claudia Fuchs recommended at that time a qualitative feminist methodology. She proposed to systematically observe and interpret using critical principles of feminist research: the interconnection of theory and practice, interdisciplinarity and partiality for women (Prengel: 1986, p. 41). Referring to the study she once conceptualized, she nowadays says, that studies into the different modes of behaviour of girls and boys are very problematic because of the binary construction of resulting data automatically furthering the binary construction of gender (Prengel: 1994, p. 145).

Glumpler (1995) explicitly deals with the attack of Preuss-Lausitz against the study on interactions in schools by Enders-Dragässer and Fuchs as a serious contribution to feminist discourse, when speaking about male colleagues already working with a critical focus on patriarchy. Consequently, the Preuss-Lausitz polemic is included in her bibliography whereas the Enders-Dragässer and Fuchs study on boys is missing.

A considerable loss of ground in feminist research has resulted because researchers and practitioners who aim for more radical and less heterosexist research and practice are becoming more and more marginalized. Besides, the new priority on "theory" alone, (post-modern or not) devalues the practical and political potential of Feminist/Women's Studies and ignores the growing demand for it in many fields of practice and politics.

And it gets worse: Jungwirth, when discussing educational research in the *Austrian National Report on Women* flatly states:

> . . . some studies, among them some studies frequently quoted and discussed by Spender (1985) and Enders-Dragässer and Fuchs (1989) do not comply with relevant scientific standards with regard to methodology or the presentation of findings (1995, p. 158).

Her bibliography of course contains the Preuss-Lausitz attack. Back to the boys, goodbye to feminist research methodology, international standards, international cooperation, international relevance?

Pauline Bart

The Banned Professor: or How Radical Feminism Saved Me from Men trapped in men's bodies and female impersonators, with a little help from My Friends

"Professor Loses Classes in Clash with Student"
Chicago Sun Times, 21 September 1992

"UIC firing feminist over discrimination"
Chicago Tribune, 24 September 1992

"Feminist Scholar Barred from Classroom"   *Chicago Flame, 25 August 1992*

"Pauline Bart: Victim of Feminist Backlash?"
Campus Chronicle, 19 November 1992

"Your penis envy finally got you."   *Anonymous mail*

"Ho. Ho. As a retired professor from the University of Chicago, I can say that I enjoyed seeing another Feminazi get a little comeuppance ... It is with great joy I see the balance being upheld from the male side also, after years of pummelling by the likes of you ... I would sign this: A Colleague, as I do most correspondence. But in this case I don't think so."
Anonymous mail, 23 October 1992

This is the story of how I told the truth, was thrown overboard by the Dean of Letters and Science of the University of Illinois with the collaboration of Sociology and Women's Studies, and how a radical feminist analysis helped me swim to survival.

"Radical Feminists look Medea in the eye" sociologist Barrie Thorne once said to me.[1] Some people admire that bravery, that telling it like it is. Some people think it is crazy, or, if they use psychological vocabularies of motive, self-destructive. Most people don't want to know what it is we see when we look at Medea, which explains why so many people, including feminists, don't want to hear or to teach about "the bloody footprints" (MacKinnon: 1987; Bart and Moran: 1993), about the endemic violence against women committed by normal men, and about the misogyny and male sense of entitlement that fuels it.

I wrote the following poem:

Agamemnon had it coming
Creon had it coming
Jason had it coming.
The Medea is the message.

History of a Radical Feminist as a Clear and Present Danger

Time Line: Born, 1930, Brooklyn NY; 1948 moved with parents to Santa Barbara California; 1949 married, had an illegal abortion; 1952 received MA and had first child; 1956 had second child; 1961 divorced, returned to school; 1967 received PhD; 1967–68 taught as Visiting Professor at University of Southern California; 1968–1970 taught at UC Berkeley as Lecturer – taught Women in Society and Literature, one of the first courses on women in the US, and a seminar on Women's Studies in my home since the campus was being tear-gassed; came as an Assistant Professor to University of Illinios at Chicago department of psychiatry and taught various sociology/Women's Studies classes at Chicago Circle Campus at University of Illinios; 1975 Head of psychiatry stopped me from teaching medical students, Visiting Professor at San Diego State, University of California Santa Barbara and University of California Los Angeles; 1992 Dean of Letters and Science stopped me from teaching sociology and Women's Studies or anything else in Letters and Science, taught in College of Nursing; 1995 retired.

In 1947–48, my second year of college, still living at home and commuting to Hunter College, a city college, by subway, I decided to allow myself the luxury of majoring in sociology, the field I loved, because I thought that some nice man would miraculously turn up, marry me, and support me in the way that my mother and her friends were financially supported by their husbands. In those days most married middle-class women with children did not work outside the home and were condemned as bad mothers if they did. If they voluntarily had no children, my mother called them "selfish" (so having children apparently was an act of

---

1. Cassandra was given the gift of prophecy and the curse of having no one believe what she said. Iphigenia was Agamemnon's daughter. He threw her overboard to persuade the wind to blow when his ship was becalmed during the Trojan War. If you tell the truth, as Cassandra did, they have to throw you overboard like Iphigenia.

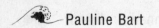

selflessness, a sacrifice). Therefore I didn't have to study anything practical such as high-school English teaching as some of my friends did "to have something to fall back on". As it turned out, ten years and two children later I separated from my children's father, and learned that I had no saleable skills. A master's degree in sociology and a token could get me on the subway but was worthless.

I received my MA in January 1952, one month before my twenty-second birthday, already having morning sickness as I took my MA exams. I wanted to get the socially necessary baby over as soon as possible. My husband had flunked out of his master's program in chemistry, and I thought it would be "castrating" to be two degrees ahead of him. The radical feminist critiques of Freud had not yet appeared (Weisstein: 1970; Chesler: 1972) and women who read too much knew from books and magazines that we could only achieve "true happiness" by subordinating ourselves to our husbands and children. Our husbands' masculinity rested on it. As Virginia Woolf said, we were to reflect them back at twice their size.

My Uncareer in Sociology

Yet, in spite of my love for sociology – the variables not necessarily the people – I have never held a regular position in a regular Department of Sociology and, in spite of my feminist scholarship and teaching in Women's Studies, I've always visited, sometimes with distinction, or lectured (as at UC Berkeley), or acted, or had a courtesy appointment. For the past twenty-five years I have been a member of a Department of Psychiatry, climbing the ladder from assistant to full professor. Each step upward was resisted by members of the administration and I had to fight for the promotion, supported by the secretaries and the administrative assistants who insisted that I appeal negative decisions because it was "just politics". They knew that the work I was doing on rape and rape avoidance was vital to their lives and those of their female kin and they were insulted by the then Head of Psychiatry who said it was "irrelevant to the mission of the Department". (I have since called it the seminal emission of the Department.)

I wrote "Cooptation is the sincerest form of flattery" (1971b, p. 734). But no department tried to coopt me. There are those who say that as a radical feminist I was always uncooptable. I don't know. Three jobs in the first four years after my PhD and shlepping my kids around does not make for an inner locus of control (sometimes I think an inner locus of control is another term for false consciousness). I was surprised with my difficulty in the job market – considered "good" at the time. I saw third-rate men being called for interviews while I waited for the mail – both morning and afternoon. I was, as a distinguished sociologist said, "Too old to be an assistant professor." After all, we were the same age, and look at how much he had accomplished, and look how little I had. And he was my friend. I knew it because he said he knew I needed a lover and a father, and he decided to be my father.

Progressive "hip" male sociologists were disappointed that I had studied depressed middle-aged women, "Portnoy's Mothers", for my dissertation – how uncool. It was bad enough in the "revolutionary" 60s to study women, but not depressed middle-aged women like their mothers. Rock star groupies who made plaster casts of their idols' penises would have been much more acceptable: to them; not to me.

The radical Berkeley Department of Sociology had not hired a woman in a tenure track position for fifty years, neither had the Department of Psychology. Women were not on the list of oppressed people for whose liberation they were fighting. That came later, when it was clear that the Women's Liberation Movement was not a fad like the hula hoop. My work suddenly became important, even publishable, and most important, saleable, since the burgeoning Women's Studies programs needed books.

To return to what C. Wright Mills calls the intersection of biography and history, I was married at nineteen. That was not unusual in 1949, the cusp of the frightful fifties, when Freudian hegemony was not yet challenged by feminists such as Chesler (1972) Weisstein (1970) and Millet (1970). I planned to transfer to UCLA to complete my senior year as a sociology major – following my husband who was going to graduate school in chemistry at USC – when I became pregnant. I had an illegal abortion because I didn't want to live if I couldn't go to school. I found this decision particularly ironic in light of my inability to obtain a tenure track job after my PhD: as a woman I was allegedly not serious about my career. How many men, I wonder, would have taken the risk and endured the pain I did, just so they could continue their study of sociology?

I divorced on my thirty-first birthday, as a birthday present to myself. I returned to UCLA – with two young children and erratic child support – to obtain my PhD. After six months I gained a National Institute of Mental Health fellowship to study the relationship between maternal role loss and depression in middle-aged women. Fortunately I could blend in with 60s students who were both politically and culturally radical: some called them "Flower Children" and others called them agents of communist countries bent upon destroying western civilization as we [sic] knew it. I twined star jasmine in my braids and people would ask me, "What's happening?"

In order to be able to support myself before I was awarded the fellowship, I substitute-taught in Los Angeles California junior high and high schools. I had obtained a California Teaching Credential when I decided to get a divorce and had problems as a student teacher because one day I didn't wear stockings. When I was teaching the Constitution I wanted to give out the Bill of Rights that was printed by the American Civil Liberties Union, my training teacher told me I couldn't because it was a controversial organization. She also told me that I was disturbing the children (eighth grade) because I was too negative. When I said I took as my model Socrates she replied, "Look what happened to him." As will be seen, my teaching has frequently been considered subversive.

I waited till I started getting called to substitute-teach and then insisted that my husband leave. I had left once before and allowed my husband to return

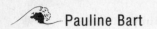

when he was waiting to kill me when I went on a date: this time I was prepared and told him I would call the police immediately when he called and threatened me. At that time none of us were as aware of violence against women – especially wives who leave – as we are now, but this experience helped radicalize me.

I learned more sociology teaching in South Central Los Angeles public schools one day and upper- middle- and lower-upper-class schools the next than I ever did in stratification courses. All the students were hostile since it was considered a victory to send the substitute teacher home in tears. But the middle- and upper-class students expressed their hostility verbally, which was easier for me to deal with than the more threatening hostility of the others. The exceptions were the "ghetto" students learning French, since that meant they were preparing to go to college and saw education as the way out. They gave me no problems.

Wedded Bliss

To return to my marital state, in 1954–55 my husband had a fellowship to the Harvard School of Public Health. I worked as a research assistant in a state mental hospital for Harvard, possible because there was good day-care in Boston for my two-year-old; my husband received a Master of Science. When I returned from the East Coast, I decided to go back to graduate school on the advice of the Harvard professors. Since this time my husband had an MS, a PhD would still leave me only one degree ahead of him. My parents wanted to send him to medical school, but were not interested in my post-graduate education, even though I was a better student. They believed, as did most people, that I was supposed to stay home and raise children. When I consulted the then Chair of Sociology whose research assistant I had been, he said I would never get a job if I were limited to the LA area where my husband was working, and suggested that since I was interested in mental health, I should try the School of Social Work. If, currently, a faculty member told a bright woman to get another master's in a traditional women's field rather than a PhD, she would know she was being discriminated against.

But, still a good girl, I duly trotted off to social work. When asked why I wanted to study social work, I said because I was curious. I also called the school Freudian. When that was questioned I said that a famous psychoanalyst was on their staff. They objected that one Freudian didn't make a department Freudian, to which I replied, "In good times social work is Freudian; in bad times Marxian." To my then surprise, because I didn't yet know that intelligent women who talked back were considered dangerous, I was not accepted.

I didn't know what else I could do. Since I couldn't go back to school, which at that time I considered my home, my safe place, I did what was expected of me. I had another baby. My husband did not want another child because he couldn't stand it when babies crawled on the floor. The floor was dirty, he said. I pointed out that he, as a physical scientist, should know the laws of gravity – where else could they crawl? But I still believed in the power of therapy to change people, so I told him he would get over it in therapy. And, because I had internalized the female sex role, I felt good that I was doing what was expected of me. I even bought a television set which I had resisted before.

It was only in the early Women's Movement that my way of being in the world was rewarded. I could talk about the personal. I could talk about the political. I could blend the two. I could and did say, "Our lives are our data," and "They cannot reduce our lives to 'mere anecdotes'." Personal disclosure was rewarded rather than punished, or seen as an indicator of weakness or what mental health mavens[2] called "inappropriate behavior".

Everything is Data

My personal and my sociological lives are joined at the hip, heart, and head, like Siamese twins. They cannot be separated. I turn my personal life into sociology and use sociological analysis to cope with my personal life. Everything is data (but data isn't everything) as I say; the statement was put on a fundraising T-shirt for Sociologists for Women in Society. I was able to analyze my misery as a trapped Culver City, California married housewife in the fifties, for whom the American Dream was the American Nightmare, oppressed by Freudian hegemony, the feminine mystique, what happened to Rosie the Riveter and so on. I counted my neighbors' interactions, with ethnicity and propinquity as the variables that emerged, sitting on my front porch while child-watching, just to keep my mind from rotting.

Conversely, I turned my mother's serious depression when she was fifty into my 700-page dissertation, "Depression in Middle-Aged Women" (Gornick and Moran: 1971) better known as Portnoy's Mother's Complaint (in part to prove it wasn't my fault, as my father had claimed). I studied rape, in part, because my students were raped and called me for help, and my first paper on rape resistance was inspired by a student who had been raped once and avoided rape once (Bart: 1987).

My interest in *Jane,* the feminist illegal abortion collective (Bart: 1987) was sparked by my own illegal abortion before Roe. It was performed by an MD in his office, without a nurse to wipe the vomit off my face when I threw up from the pain; paid for with my wedding presents; incomplete, such that I would have died had I not been at my mother's house two weeks later for the Jewish holidays when the pain started. My mother knew, as I did not, that the pain was from the abortion. The hospital would not treat me until I told them who had performed the procedure. That physicians qua physicians could mess up was not lost on me. Additionally, the physician who gave me a diaphragm without having me insert it, telling me to make sure it was covering my cervix and fit under my pubic bone, clearly was not aware that he could have said put it under Madagascar covering the Canary Islands. *Our Bodies, Ourselves* was not yet written. When it first came out in newsprint, published by the New England Free Press and selling for thirty-

---

2. In Yiddish, an ironic gloss for expert.

five cents, I brought copies to one of the first Sociologists for Women in Society meetings and had a woman demonstrate cervical self-examination in their room at the American Sociological Association meetings.

I continued to merge my personal and my academic life by having a seminar on pregnancy when my daughter was expecting a child and teaching Women and Aging when my father died, and my mother was being bounced among psychiatric units in hospitals, nursing homes, and board and care homes. I also survived that time period by thinking, "What does class mean for women?" It was clear to me that a man with all that money would not have been so docile, would not have been inhibited by a desire not to "make trouble". He would have stayed in his own home and demanded a full-time caretaker. It is true my mother has the "class privilege" of being in a nice nursing home ("nice nursing home" is of course an oxymoron, but compared to other nursing homes it's "nice"), and she receives extra care from private nurses' aides.[3]

On the other hand, it is possible that was there not a great deal of money involved, my sister would not have attempted to take control of my mother's life. And I think that there are working-class families where there is enough of a network to keep their elderly mothers out of nursing homes, although this may often be at the expense of her female kin's life plans. Yet gerontology tends to be taught in a gender neutral way in spite of the much larger number of old women compared with old men, and the women's greater economic vulnerability (see Dworkin: 1983).

Misogyny

I can also analyze my situation in the spring of 1992 when the Dean of Letters and Science banned me from teaching letters and science in "his" college. I was teaching "Gender and Society", an undergraduate course cross-listed in sociology and Women's Studies, a course I had taught many times before, but in Californian universities. When, as usual, I passed out anonymous questionnaires asking the students if they had been raped, if someone had tried to rape them, if they had been battered, sexually abused as children, sexually harassed and/or had been upset by having pornography forced on them, I discovered, to my dismay, that half the students (all women) had already been raped. This rate was higher than in similar classes in California, and I then understood why, in an earlier class survey, more students wanted to study violence against women than any other topic.

While the class was not required, one male social work major who took the class was argumentative from the beginning of the semester, and his disagreements with me ultimately led to my dismissal. He denied that women did more housework than men, the theme of one of the assigned readings, Arlie Hochschild's *The Second Shift* (1989). When a former student, who is a machinist, guest-lectured on sexual harassment on her construction sites, in the course of which she

---

3. See Bart: 1994, Introduction for a discussion of women and class.

mentioned that she was a lesbian, and that she was involved in a class-action lawsuit against the organization for whom the harassers worked, this same man said that women couldn't do construction work. In addition someone in the class, whose identity is unknown, reported the woman's sexuality to her employer. And, while my plane was fogged in at the Oakland California airport, the decision finding African-American heavyweight champion boxer Mike Tyson guilty of rape came down. My teaching assistant decided to discuss the decision in my absence, which led to this male student, "Jim" (a pseudonym), verbally abusing women in the class who defended the decision and reducing some to tears. He was so angry, the teaching assistant had to calm him down. Some students told me what had happened. Thus, when I next spoke to the class, I quoted Catharine MacKinnon, saying that I would not let women's experiences be invalidated in the class, particularly their experiences of violence, which are usually invalidated.

"Jim" came to my office asking if I were speaking about him, and complained that the class wasn't objective. I pointed out that no class was objective and he could transfer out of my class into one whose bias he agreed with. I offered to do the paperwork for him, since it was late to transfer. He refused to transfer, and said he wouldn't come to class when I spoke about rape. He informed his mentor, an older woman who was Head of the Chancellor's Committee on African-Americans, who apparently exacerbated the situation, and the tension in the class escalated. Some women were not coming to class and some of those who came were afraid to speak. When this student and his clique (I privately called them "The Gang of Four") came on the day I spoke about rape, one of his friends interrupted my lecture on the rape continuum shouting that the class was biased. What I thought was an interesting discussion followed, based in part on whether or not the class was "empowering", since the truths they read and heard about were not pleasant. Demystification rather than empowerment should be a criterion for judging discussions of violence against women. Catharine MacKinnon once said, "Since when is politics therapy?" (1987). Some women supported the men. When I asked if any men would support the women none did.

I said, "Heterosexual women support heterosexual men and lesbians support gay men" which I had written and spoken about several times in the past. (The original complaining student and his friends were gay but I was not specifically referring to them. I didn't know the woman was a lesbian.)

When the white gay man who had interrupted the class and the lesbian in a leather jacket who was part of "The Gang of Four" showed up, indignantly, in my office, I tried to explain that the first student, "Jim", was frightening some of the students. Not realizing I was being "set up", I then was interrogated by the white male student who asked why the women were so afraid. I said, "He's big." When asked what else, I said, "He's aggressive." And when asked what else, I naively told the sociological truth: "Maybe because he's Black."

The white male stormed out of my office, immediately told "Jim" who immediately complained to the Head of Sociology who immediately called the Dean who banned me from teaching in Letters and Science on the basis of alleged racism and sexism. There was a student support group for me headed by a male Chilean whose father had been tortured by Pinochet, and T-shirts reading, "Don't kill the messenger – keep Pauline teaching" were sold. Many support letters from distinguished feminists in the US and other countries were sent to the university, to sociology and to Women's Studies. Radical feminist faculty, especially law professors, wrote strong letters because I had experienced what one distinguished radical feminist law professor called star-chamber proceedings.

The local press and the Associated Press carried the story sympathetically and I was contacted by both Left and Right groups. I was even interviewed by a right-wing talk show host who called me a Feminazi and whose rhetoric about women not needing protection and about free speech resembled the Feminist Anti-Censorship Task Force brief opposing MacKinnon and Dworkin's proposed ordinance against pornography.

But for the support I received, almost all from outside the University of Illinois at Chicago, and much on e-mail which I would turn on every morning to keep me going, I don't think I would have survived. I didn't have a course of action (reason to sue) and so could not sue, but I hired a lawyer to protect me from being forced to retire, which was the university's plan. Allegedly they were threatened by a march of Black men on the administration if I were not fired. But African-American women faculty and students supported me and thought that "Jim" was being used by the administration to rid themselves of me because they disliked my politics and my style.

Catharine MacKinnon's 1987 theory of gender as hierarchy, not just difference, can explain why the complaint of a male undergraduate of a subordinated race, and a white male associate professor, could topple a tenured white, female full professor, who outranks them. Women frequently complain about male professors and rarely is redress granted. Since the university is hierarchical, and I am a full professor, some might have expected that I should have been given the benefit of the doubt, or at least due process. Since the university is racist, I should have had white skin privilege. Yet, I was accused of race and sex discrimination and found guilty, with no due process. If gender is hierarchy, if women are a class, then any male outranks me, and since gender is hierarchy, the support of a male, the Head of my Department (Psychiatry), kept my paychecks coming.

The woman Head of Affirmative Action, a "female impersonator" who opposed me, told me that I was over-involved with my students, therapeutic and maternal. You can put it on my tombstone! Such comments demonstrate how male values permeate teaching. I tried to protect the women in my class, half of whom had been raped and almost one-third of whom had been molested as children, from being additionally abused by aggressive misogyny in the classroom. A sociologist once told me that the reason I have been persecuted by the University of Illinois – since 1975, when a new Head was hired who was against anyone who was not an MD and who told me rape jokes [sic] – was because there was no powerful male protecting me. Not only was I terribly underpaid, but, when he left, the new acting Head forced me to stay in my office between 8:30 am and 4:30 pm every day, unless I could explain how my leaving, for fieldwork or lunch off campus, would help the department. I had to turn over weekly time-sheets in which I always said I discussed a possible grant over lunch. Such restrictions were harassment because of who I was and what I did, since they were not placed on other faculty members. University governance to whom I appealed said the restrictions were not a violation of my academic freedom, but the Committee on Freedom Research and Teaching of the American Sociological Association investigated the situation at my request and found discrimination. The Medical School didn't care but the new Head who was coming in was "embarrassed". He was born in New York and came from Yale, and said he had been around women like me all his life. He protected me as much as he could from the university's assault, promising to continue to pay my full salary if I tried to find classes to teach. He had previously substantially raised my salary in return for my promise to retire in four years.

The response to me has always been bimodal. Sometimes I am treated like a star, usually away from the University of Illinois, particularly in the many countries outside the USA where I am invited to speak and where it is assumed that sociologists are not value-free and are activists. Sometimes in Chicago I hear I am not a sociologist, "only political". Psychiatric vocabularies are used to discredit me, as they are with women generally. One lesbian anthropology graduate student took my class precisely because her advisor said I went "too far" although I was "supposed to be brilliant".

Fame

Fame came suddenly in the early 1970s because of Arlie Hochschild publishing my "Portnoy's Mother's Complaint" in the special women's issue of *Transaction* (Bart: 1970). The article was originally rejected by the other editors. One year later a somewhat different version appeared in one of the first feminist anthologies, *Woman in Sexist Society* (Gornick and Moran: 1971). I also edited two special issues of the previously conservative Mormon-flavored *Journal of Marriage and the Family* (1971b) which Jessie Bernard gave me to edit in the proverbial smoke-filled room: sociologist Alice Rossi's suite where the first Women's Caucus was organized (later called Sociologists for Women in Society). I didn't believe that I was famous, so that when I was asked to speak at the MIT graduation ceremony, I thought it was a joke, or that they had made a mistake. Why should a group primarily of men want to hear me and what could I say to them? Dick Gregory spoke instead.

I was asked to participate on the C. Wright Mills award committee in 1972 where I refused to vote for people who sexually harassed my students. The Chair of the committee said that just because I had been at the University of California and knew these things, it was unfair of me to use that as a criterion. I said that under their rules I hadn't made it. It was only because of the Women's Movement that they had to have me on the committee. I was using my own rules, and in those

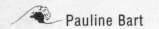

rules I did not reward men who exploited or tried to exploit women. I later heard that the committee Chair said that he had learned a great deal from me.

When a publisher.asked me to write *The Student Sociologist's Handbook* (1972) he suggested that a well-known male sociologist be listed as the author so it would sell better. Since I already knew that the academic world was corrupt, I was not shocked; merely taken aback. I am fortunate that my eastern European Jewish background enabled me to see them as the Cossacks early in my career and lack thereof. I felt sorry for my WASP upper-middle-class friend who expected justice from the University of Chicago because of affirmative action regulations.

My work on violence against women has made cocktail-party bantering difficult and has thrown a damper on my social life generally. As Andrea Dworkin said, "I'm a feminist. Not the fun kind!" I am controversial, make some students (as well as friends and lovers) uncomfortable, and have never been able to obtain a permanent job in Women's Studies or sociology. I have been a visiting professor, sometimes with distinction, but without permanency. The one department that offered me a real job was unpopular with their Dean, not coincidentally, and so could not get the position. One good friend of mine said that she couldn't recommend me for a position as Director of a Women's Studies program because I get angry. How can one be immersed in the study of violence against women, especially if one did not experience WASP socialization or Midwest socialization, and not be angry? In the former, one is supposed to act like an English lord with the gamut of emotions ranging from A to A–. In Midwest USA socialization one is supposed to always be nice. Since radical feminists study violence against women, that may explain the dearth of radical feminist perspectives in most Women's Studies programs. All that is traditionally said by people in such programs is that radical feminists don't talk about race or class. I stated at a National Women's Studies Association meeting that since I was a sociologist, anyone who said I didn't speak about race and class was guilty of either libel or slander, depending on whether such a statement was written or spoken (1986).

Men Trapped in Men's Bodies and Female Impersonators

You may be wondering what the title of this article has to do with its contents, aside from the fact that I am expected to produce clever titles. I have become tired of the post-modern clichés and liberal laissez-faire attitudes that one can choose one's gender(s) in the same way that one can choose one's breakfast. On the one hand any statistical difference between men and women that we point out is pejoratively called "essentialism", and yet cutting up one's genitals to be the other "gender" is not essentialist. Gender may be a continuum theoretically, but I will believe it de facto when men who gender-blend get women's salaries and women who gender-blend are free of rape and are paid men's wages. If gender is so socially constructed, who constructs it? Certainly not everyone. Why are men who become women, indeed girls, so aggressive about invading our space, for example at the all-women Michigan Women's Music Festival? That sounds like men trapped in men's bodies to me.

When I originally thought of men trapped in men's bodies I thought of the John Wayne types, the football players who battered men as part of their job description, and women at home as part of their male role description, of gang rapists in the hyper-masculine fraternity sub-culture, of pimps and pornographers, of incestors, of sexual harassers. In short I thought of men with a sense of entitlement to dominate other men and control women as a class, who believed that women owed them goods and services, and who punished women who did not gratify their perceived needs, to be smiled at in the street or to relieve their erections for example.

When I think of female impersonators I do not mean transvestites who imitate Judy Garland or Bette Davis. I think of those women who are biologically female but who have men in their heads, whose significant others are men, and who therefore are used by men to control other women. Putting down radical feminists such as Catharine MacKinnon has been the pathway to instant upward mobility for some female attorneys. It is no accident that some of the harshest criticism of the anti-pornography civil rights ordinance has come from women – for example from the woman Head of the American Civil Liberties Union and from groups such as "Feminists for Free Expression".

All radical feminist academics have stories of betrayal by women, especially women who label themselves feminists. Mine focuses not on the "good girl" in sociology who signed the letter from the executive committee of the department refusing me a position and did not protest about my not being able to teach sociology any more. Cowardice is gender-neutral rather than male. I think rather of the Head of Women's Studies, a former rape researcher, who asked me to write a blurb for her book, which I did, yet who supported the Dean's desire to fire me from teaching liberal arts and sciences, and then said "no" to my letter when I asked if I could at least have independent study students in Women's Studies. The Chancellor answered a lawyer who was a former Weather Underground[4] leader, Bernadine Dohrn, who protested my dismissal that the university made its decision in part because Women's Studies did not object. The Chair of Women's Studies distributed a memo stating that now Women's Studies had a problem of damage control. And, when I referred to her as "The Exxon Valdez Chair of Women's Studies", she showed people my note as an example of my alleged craziness.[5]

---

4. The Weather Underground was a radical activist group in the 1960s and Bernadine was underground for years.

5. The *Exxon Valdez* was an oil tanker owned by Exxon which seriously polluted Alaskan waters when it crashed. Exxon had a problem of damage control it was said.

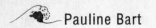
Pauline Bart

The Personal is the Political

My personal and political, my radical feminist and sociological selves are not separated. In addition to studying issues in which I had a personal stake and which were "good for the women" (I learned as a child to ask if it were good for the Jews), I find that I cannot enjoy reading works by people who treated women in their lives badly, whether they be saints like Tolstoy or sadists like Picasso. It is a gut feeling. I have not been able to buy any books by Adrienne Rich since she signed the brief against the MacKinnon–Dworkin anti-pornography civil rights ordinance, even though she said that the brief downplayed the problem of violence against women. I put out my hand to pick up the book, and it is as if an invisible thread pulls my hand back. This position is consistent with my never having slept with a Republican. Why should I give money or pleasure to people whose analysis and/or behavior harms women? I not only believe that the personal is the political, as we used to say when feminism was Women's Liberation, but I try to live my life that way. It makes for a lonely life.

However, I have the exquisite privilege of knowing that my research and teaching have made a difference, in depression, in abortion, in rape resistance. In my experience, everything I have put into the establishment has been money dropped down a well, and everything I have put into students has come back to me. Much of what I have put into women has also, but my recent experiences with the university and with the "sex wars" among feminists over pornography have made me re-evaluate my belief system. The "anti-censorship" [sic] pro-pornography women, many of whom have never read the MacKinnon–Dworkin ordinance, only read about it, and know little about our lives, say we are tools of the Right Wing; some of these women don't even know the difference between tear-gas and pepper-fog. I do, because the then Governor Reagan and California Attorney-General Meese ordered the Berkeley campus tear-gassed and pepper-fogged. Catharine MacKinnon was severely tear-gassed as part of her civil rights activism with the New Haven Black Panthers. When women who have never been arrested or jailed criticize Andrea Dworkin who has been jailed for protesting the Vietnam War, I am disgusted. I am compelled to say that everything men do, women do. But I also know that at least so far the differences are statistically significant.

The Beginning

Sandra Coney

The Last Post for Feminism

I am a post-feminist. I must be. According to a whole lot of people who must know better than me, we are now in a post-feminist era, experiencing postfeminism. I needed to go to the dictionary to sort this post bit out. I found out there are lots of post words. Some unfortunately don't give many signposts to the interpretation of post-feminist. For instance, post-Devonian, post-Carboniferous, post-Vedic and post-Permian. What were they?

I began to wonder if the post was a death sentence, a sign that whatever it was had been consigned to oblivion. Post-anal, I had trouble with too. What could be more post already than anal, I pondered.

Whether being post is good or bad wasn't solved by the dictionary. It varies with the circumstances. Obviously being post-war is better than being war, but is post-coital better than being coital? I doubt it.

Other words gave me more clues. Post-election, post-natal and post-menopausal were words I understood. So post is what comes after something distinct has happened, it's the period after something which has finished. And it's not important enough to get its own name.

I'm not clear who made the decision that the feminist task is completed and we can move on to the next stage. There were no resolutions that I know of passed through feminist conferences, no proclamations in women's bars. It comes as a bit of a shock to find that you're redundant, that you've been beavering away on something when it wasn't really necessary, like surfacing from the coalface with black lung only to find everyone's converted to natural gas.

I read about it first in magazines, those oracles of our time. Some journalist obviously spotted for us what we could not see, that the beachhead had been reached while we thought we were still pinned down in the trenches. I'm grateful. Without being told, I and hundreds of other protofeminists might still have been expending our energy on irrelevant subjects like whether women in Westport get abortions.

I'm glad we've arrived at post-feminism. I'm relieved we're in the post part now. Think of all the things feminists can stop doing.

They can start writing to their mothers and friends instead of newspapers and politicians. They can have parties and dinners instead of meetings in the front room. They'll be able to stop writing political tracts, submissions, pamphlets and magazines, and write post-feminist novels instead. For this they'll be able to get Literary Fund grants and university fellowships in letters.

They can quit working for shit wages in refuges, rape crisis and women's health centres, and get well-paid jobs instead. They can also find themselves a nice post-feminist man. Heterosexuality is back again; in fact, it's essential. Lesbianism is very un-post.

Post-feminism is not a political position, it's a style. There are no groups to belong to, there's no need to picket, to march, to lobby or work for women at all. All the barriers are down, it's every girl for herself and may the best girl win.

It's clear that post-feminists (the female ones) enjoy being girls. This is not sex-role stereotyping, but choice. The important thing about post-feminism is that women can do anything and some of them are choosing to be sex objects. Well, that's fine. In the post-feminist era anything goes: face lifts, teeth capping, hormone replacement therapy, collagen implants, diathermy, liposuction. Get your spare tyres shifted to your tits. Women used to feel pressured to do such things to compete. Not any more. Why put up with the bad bits when you can have them cut out? It's all just good clean post-feminist fun.

Post-feminists are into babies, designer babies, not the ordinary kind that projectile vomit and bite nipples. Designer babies don't have to cripple your career because there are nannies. It was really that simple. Why didn't someone think of it before? All that fuss about child care and getting daddies to share the load. Daft, weren't we. Post-feminist motherhood is very fulfilling.

Post-feminists have good jobs and they earn lots of money so they can get cleaning ladies to clean the loo . . . Protofeminists tried to get their men to do it, half the time. Griping at your man is very retro, very 70s, very pre-post. Post-feminists are more mature and go about it in a different way. Some of them are so perfect they've trained themselves not to go at all. Post-feminism is definitely post-anal as well.

Post-feminists spend lots of time at the gym (choice again) and have career paths. They service three mortgages and at least one man. They are super in bed. Post-feminists have no trouble getting their men.

Now I come to think about it, I'm not too sure I qualify as post. I'm too old, too flabby and I'm rude to men. What's worse, I'm not going to do anything about it.

---

* From Sandra Coney (1990). *Out of the Frying Pan: Inflammatory Writing 1972–89.*

III

RADICAL FEMINISTS

"INTERROGATE"

POST-MODERNISM

Susan Hawthorne

Deconstructing Fashion

You are standing in a crowd
                  moving sideway   crablike

I watch as you negotiate the spaces
                  reading an absence in the movement of your body

Your style is French
                  your dress too

I begin from the top:
        a bataille beret
                is set at a jaunty angle[1]
        your hair hangs forward
                splitting your forehead in two
        on your torso
                a derridean sweater and
        an irigarean jacket
                hanging loose
        a kristevan belt
                holds up
        faded foucault jeans
                from behind all I can see is
        a cape of lacanian obscurity
                and on your feet
        runners with deleuze
                inscribed on the heel

I turn and leave
                  doubting that we speak the same language

                                      (1990)

---

1. Some years after this was written, baseball caps with the names of Foucault, Derrida *et al.* appeared on the market!

Kristin Waters

(Re)Turning to the Modern: Radical Feminism and the Post-modern Turn

The struggle between post-modernism and feminism has been a particularly difficult one, dividing feminists and detracting energy from the practical work which has been a basis for the Women's Movement. On one side is the view that post-modernism provides a logical intellectual progression for feminism. This view holds that feminism as a modern intellectual discourse is either dead or *passé*, that its foundational and essentializing approaches are outmoded, and that its insights can be safely absorbed and transformed by post-modern theory. On the other side is the view that post-modern theory signals a treacherous diversion away from feminist ideals and goals. It holds that a gendered analysis is necessary for understanding our world, and that feminist theory can interactively illuminate analyses made from standpoints of race, class and culture.

Certain pieces of intellectual history become clear as one moves through the sound and fury of this dispute. Post-modernism gained currency in the USA in the 1980s and has influenced contemporary feminism, just as *earlier* and *ongoing* feminist challenges to hierarchy, polarity, modern meta-narratives, and traditional constructions both of individuals and social institutions, have been absorbed by post-modernism. So genealogically, feminist theory in the USA largely precedes and informs post-modernism, and not the reverse.

Feminist theory has, from the beginning, provided critiques of modern theories from the Enlightenment to the present. Feminism has also used both the theories and methods of modernism to further its goals. When this has been done self-consciously and self-critically it has proved to be enormously powerful. For many academic disciplines, feminism provides a major critical apparatus, and strong theoretical tools that make excellent use of, but are not limited to, gender analysis. So feminism has combined the exploration of new terrain and the creation of new approaches with a cautious but determined use of tradition. Much of academic feminism has accomplished this while remaining true to the political commitment which radical feminists count as essential. This often means scrutinizing the connections between theory and practice to ensure that they are strong, challenging theory which is too removed from the everyday, and seeking innovations to bridge the gap between colleges and communities. Making our own approaches vulnerable to challenges about the connections with practice, we count as a strength.

In the academic realm, during the last decade, post-modernism has moved forward and in some places supplanted feminism, posing as the smarter, more intellectual younger sister who will carry forward the baton. So while in the intellectual sphere, feminism and post-modernism continue to influence each other, what remains on a different but connected plane is the political struggle between the two, which will take place in the publishing houses, on journal editorial boards, on university hiring and tenure committees, and at conferences and meetings, but not, generally, in the streets, where feminists often find our bases of support, our sources of inspiration, our ground for theory, and our field of practice.

That is not to say that what goes on in the streets, in our communities, and at various governmental levels will not be affected because, as with (other) feminist struggles with patriarchy, the more time and energy absorbed in disputes about origins, legitimacy and power, the less time there is left over for action. In a sense then, this struggle, like many in the past, deflects feminists from forging alliances with communities and from putting our feminist currencies to work in practice.

My purpose is to set out some of the major criticisms of post-modern theory, and then to examine a few special cases of the general criticisms in order to construct an argument about what I see as some of the more nefarious connections between post-modern and modern theories. I suggest that the post-modern move to "destabilize the subject" is a reiteration of the modern argument against abstract ideas and I explore the *political* effect of this piece of high theory. I then argue that the post-modern move away from reason toward desire is a way of harnessing in the successes of feminist philosophy by once again confining women to the ghetto of desire and irrationality, as Enlightenment philosophy has done in the past. Finally, I claim that the post-modern emphasis on style is another way of putting the old-fashioned "feminine" back into feminism – by shifting attention away from substance that has concrete and material ramifications, toward a style which is elusive and obscure, ungrounded and apolitical. Indeed, each of these shifts, characterized as post-modernism and feminist post-modernism, has the effect, I will claim, of moving feminism away from its roots in politics and making feminism safer for the academy, but not safer for women.

Post-modern Theory Undefined

To what degree is post-modernism the rightful heiress of a moribund feminism, and to what degree is it something else in disguise? The effects of post-modernism on feminism are explored in Somer Brodribb's searing critique, *Nothing Mat(t)ers*, in

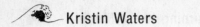

which, by directly engaging the texts of Foucault, Derrida, Lacan and others, she argues that post-modernism's "Dionysian delirium is another mask of masculinist reason", (Brodribb: 1992, p. xi). Her detailed survey of the terms "post-structuralist" and "post-modernist" reveals a stunning lack of agreement about meaning, appropriately enough, considering the slippery character of these terms. "Post-structuralism" is preferred by post-modern feminist Judith Butler (among others) whose assembled collection with Joan W. Scott, *Feminists Theorize the Political* (Butler and Scott: 1992), is largely an attempt to demonstrate post-modern contributions to contemporary feminism and to chastise feminisms that are not *au courant* in a post-modern way. But such is the confusion surrounding these theories that one of Brodribb's sources "describes how Jacques-Alain Miller (Lacan's son-in-law and literary executor) shocked an Ottawa conference ... "by saying that 'post-structuralism' was not a word used in France" (Brodribb: 1992, pp. 7–8). In other words, although the theories themselves originated in Europe, post-structuralism appears to be a US phenomenon. Adding to the state of confusion in which these theoretical phenomena seem to thrive, John Rajchman says, as to post-modernism:

> Foucault rejected the category; Guattari despises it, Derrida has no use for it: Lacan and Barthes did not live and Althusser was in no state, to learn about it; and Lyotard found it in America (Brodribb: 1992, p. 10).

Given the rejection of post-modern theory, even by its founders, why are the claims for feminism to be post-modern so insistent?

In particular, why is post-modern theory so attractive in the United States, while it is largely disclaimed even by those credited with inventing it, in its countries of origin? (see Delphy pp. 383–392 this volume). Just as designers look to Milan for high fashion, must American academics look to Paris and the rest of Europe for high theory? One senses that the critique of modern theory is only perceived to be valid when it has the stamp of approval from the home of the Enlightenment – like the child who rebels against a parent and then wishes for the parent to endorse the rebellion. Post-modernism, as a theory which looks to context and location for explanation, needs itself to be contextualized and located, historically and culturally.

Brodribb locates post-modern theory within the traditional mind/body dichotomy of modern metaphysics, and the patriarchal schemata of psychoanalysis. Writing in a creative and exploratory manner reminiscent of the exuberant feminist writing of Mary Daly, Brodribb explains :

> I define poststructuralism/postmodernism as a neurotic symptom and scene of repression of women's claims for truth and justice. Postmodernism is the attempted masculine ir/rationalization of feminism (1992, p. 20).

Brodribb sees post-modernism as an attempt to disassemble "feminine" matter traditionally and negatively associated with women, while reconstructing "masculine" form (1992, p. 147). In contrast, radical and socialist feminists have reclaimed and recast matter and women's bodies to provide a concrete, integrated analysis of the relations between mind and body. Borrowing the notion of praxis from Marxism, contemporary feminism draws a non-dichotomous view of mental and physical relations and rejects the polarizing approach of western traditions. For radical feminists, theory generates from women's unglamorous, embodied experiences and has emerged from grassroots accounts of rape, violence, displaced homemaking, childbirth, childrearing, unemployment, and also of love, work, friendship, mothering, and care. Making these concerns clear concomitantly makes obvious how post-modernism clashes with feminism. Post-modern theory is taken up with the Lacanian immaterial, the Derridean concern with structure and the silencing of women, or with Foucault's thanatical preoccupations (his obsession with death), with law, and with order.

Post-modern theory has been criticized by both traditional and feminist philosophers. In connection with these criticisms, which I shall briefly recount, related considerations arise. What is the genuine connection of post-modernism to various modernisms? Does post-modern theory deconstruct and move beyond the modern text or does it merely drape traditional modern theories, like empiricism and Freudianism, in a post-modern cloak as a manner of maintaining the modern biases against women and persons of color? Does the emphasis on desire reiterate the ancient and Enlightenment theories' denial of the attribute of reason to women – what Brodribb describes as "the irrationalization of feminism"? (1992, p. 20). And is this accomplished through the technique of producing a style which is so seductive, so cosy with the cutting edge of theory, and so enamored of new, if vague terminology, that the lure becomes irresistible? Is it possible that the so-called insights of post-modern theory are really insights produced by years of feminist theory and then appropriated by post-modernism? Can a rapprochement between feminism and post-modern theory be managed in a way that skirts the political dangers while taking advantage of theoretical insights? Raising these questions constitutes a first step in problematizing the relationship between these theories in a way that is sensitive to political as well as theoretical concerns.

Post-modern Theory Examined

The predominant philosophical criticisms can be distilled to three sorts: that post-modern theories are self-contradictory, that they are incoherent, and that they are nihilistic. The first type of criticism holds that these theories are contradictory because they deny the possibility of truth while at the same time proclaiming it. Post-modern discourses manage to wield a rigid authoritarian force about the indeterminacy of claims of all kinds, creating a kind of modern day Liar's Paradox, asserting the truth of the claim that there is no truth. In part this criticism generates from the post-modern dismissal of modern meta-narratives such as those

provided by Hegel, Marx, and Enlightenment Theory. In Lyotard's view, grand narratives are reduced to a rough equality with smaller, competing discourses which vie with each other for a kind of persuasive acceptance (Lyotard: 1984). Larger truth claims are to be substituted with smaller, more pragmatically-based ones. But the traditional epistemological knots seem to be irresistible:

> Thus, even as he argues explicitly against it, Lyotard posits the need for a genre of social criticism which transcends the local mini narrative. Despite his strictures against large, totalizing stories, he narrates a fairly tall tale about a large scale social trend (Fraser and Nicholson: 1990, p. 25).

Fraser and Nicholson identify one contradiction in post-modern theory: the simultaneous rejection and acceptance of meta-narrative discourse. Indeed for Lyotard, the rejection of old meta-narratives accompanies his creation of new ones. In the next section I explore the post-modern concept of "subject positions" to show the contradiction underlying assumptions about universes of discourse and what are deemed to be legitimate subjects. The sweeping stricture in post-modernism against truth claims is so broad that other examples of contradictions abound.

The second general criticism derives an incoherence from post-modern theory's negative character, primarily aimed at Derrida and deconstruction, but it can also be found in Lyotard's views on social criticism and in the antifoundational character of all post-modern theory. This criticism holds that the insistence on instability, indeterminacy, and reversal undermines the possibility of a positive construction of concepts. Theory-building itself becomes an impossibility as a result of the post-modern attack on philosophy. It is not only philosophy, but positive theoretical endeavor in any field which suffers under this approach. As a specific example of this criticism, I will show how the transformation of reason into desire by post-modern theory reiterates the modern attitude toward women and at the same time undermines access for feminism to powerful methodologies.

In a third and related mode, it has been widely argued that the lack of positive content and retreat from moral claims undermine all moral action, resulting in nihilism. As Fraser and Nicholson suggest:

> [Lyotard's] justice of multiplicities conception precludes one familiar, and arguably essential, genre of political theory: identification and critique of macrostructures of inequality and injustice . . . (1990, p. 23).

Moral theory, social theory, political theory, and one can argue, other philosophical theories as well, depend upon at least a bare-bones common normative ground of discourse on which discussion and dispute can be based. Erasure of this basis leads to a denial of the possibility of justifying moral judgments and to a nihilistic outcome, according to this criticism. The denial of a normative content, I shall argue, results in a movement away from substance and toward a focus on style which undermines the political basis of feminism. Further, by focussing on issues of style, post-modernism attempts to return feminism to the traditional realm of the "feminine" as defined by modern theory. The prevalent Enlightenment account of the proper sphere for the ideal lady, exemplified in the writings of Rousseau and Kant, is to attend to fashion and style, since the moral realm is not intellectually available to them.

These are condensed versions of philosophical formulations of the criticisms. Many of these criticisms have been originally articulated by feminist theorists as diverse as Linda Nicholson, Nancy Fraser, Somer Brodribb, bell hooks, and Nancy C. M. Hartsock, who have ascribed a specific gendered/feminist content to each. For instance, with regard to the alleged self-contradictory character of post-modernism, a feminist might ask what kinds of truths are denied – truths about women's experiences? Truths about sexualization, violence, oppression or wage discrimination? What kinds of positive constructions are lacking – the ideological structures of radical feminism that have allowed feminist criticisms to get under way? And crucially, a feminist must ask what kinds of moral arguments fail to get off the ground – at best ones about the failures of institutions to guarantee women's rights, and at worst ones about violent or inhumane conditions under which some women live?

We must explore some of the particular ways in which these general criticisms of post-modern theory are manifested. When and where is the transformation of concepts from feminist to post-modern beneficial and where it is detrimental? *In a post-modern world, theories become discourses, words become signifiers; both books and bodies become texts to be read, studied, and dissected, criticisms become deconstructions; and people and groups become fragmented selves, reason becomes desire, and substance become style.*

Women Become "Destabilized Subject Positions" or "Fragmented Selves"

Feminist criticisms of post-modern or post-structural theories focus on concerns that are specific to gender, race and class. Nancy Hartsock and a chorus of other voices argue that the deconstruction of the "subject" of discourse occurs at the historical moment when dominated and marginalized groups are gaining a voice and political momentum:

> First, rather than getting rid of subjectivity or notions of the subject, as Foucault does and substituting his notion of the individual as an effect of power relations, we need to engage in the historical, political, and theoretical process of constituting ourselves as subjects as well as objects of history (Hartsock: 1990, p. 170).

In post-modern theory agency and subjectivity both take the plunge. From this perspective, post-modernism amounts to a kind of theoretical subterfuge to undermine the newly acquired power of marginalized groups.

Butler's naming of Gayatri Spivak and Gloria Anzaldúa as feminist theorists using post-modern analysis to authorize the view that post-modernism is not bad for women of color is a remarkably unpost-modern appeal to authority (1992, p. 14). This is not to diminish the work of these feminists. Rather, if appeals to authority are to be invoked as the appropriate source for judgments about post-modernism, certainly many more women of color have expressed suspicion about the "deconstruction of the subject" and other post-modern moves, including bell hooks (1990), Barbara Christian (1987, see pp. 311–20 this volume), and Uma Naroyan (1989). Christian identifies post-modern theory as "hegemonic as the world it attacks and as particularly repressive of Black women's literature" (Anzaldúa: 1990, p. 338). hooks and Christian both assert the need to recognize Black involvement in theory production, but not at the expense of politics and clarity:

> The failure to recognize a critical Black presence in the culture and in most scholarship and writing on post-modernism compels a Black reader, particularly a Black female reader, to interrogate her interest in a subject where those who discuss and write about it seem not to know that Black women exist or even to consider the possibility that we might be somewhere writing or saying something that should be listened to, or producing art that should be seen, heard, approached with intellectual seriousness. This is especially the case with works that go on about the way in which post-modernist discourse has opened up a theoretical terrain where "difference and Otherness" can be considered legitimate issues in the academy (hooks: 1990, p. 24).

hooks well understands the usefulness of, and the problems with, the post-modern critique of identity, especially for Blacks and women, and as a feminist she never wavers from her insistence on the groundedness of theory in actual practice.

Naroyan is a non-western feminist who decries the political implications of a wholesale move away from modernism in a world where political structures are entrenched in modern concepts. She suggests that feminists in former colonial countries such as India, must sometimes frame challenges in the old-fashioned language of individual rights for women if they are to gain any political ground.

My view about the move to destabilize the unity of the subject is that it resonates of that quintessential modern epistemology, Berkeley's empiricism, for which he argues in his 1710 classic, *A Treatise Concerning the Principles of Human Knowledge*. Consider the parallel. Post-moderns hold that abstract general terms like "women," "men", "Blacks," and "Asians," wrongly attribute a single identity to widely diverse individuals. The singular forms of these terms likewise wrongly attribute a signifying and misleading identity to selves that are in fact fractured and fragmented. Hence, a methodology which argues in terms of women and men, and other identity groups is bound to fail, since these groups, and indeed the individuals who comprise them, cannot be meaningfully characterized in such ways.

More than two hundred and eighty years ago, George Berkeley, who became the Anglican Bishop of Cloyne, Ireland, argued against John Locke that there are no abstract ideas. His argument formed a central component of modern empiricism.

> But the unravelling of this matter leads me in some measure to anticipate my design by taking notice of what seems to have had a chief part in rendering speculation intricate and perplexed and to have occasioned innumerable errors and difficulties in almost all parts of knowledge. And that is the opinion that the mind has a power of framing abstract ideas or notions of things (Berkeley: 1710/1977, p. 558).

Berkeley provides a version of the 17th century argument for abstract ideas:

> For example, the mind, having observed that Peter, James and John resemble each other in certain common agreements of shape and other qualities, leaves out the complex or compounded idea it has of Peter, James, and any other particular man that which is peculiar to each, retaining only what is common to all, and so makes an abstract idea wherein all particulars equally partake — abstracting entirely from and cutting off all those circumstances and differences which might determine it to any particular existence. And after this manner it is said we come by the abstract idea of man or, if you please, humanity, or human nature . . . (1710/1977, pp. 558–59).

But Berkeley found himself in a modest position:

> Whether others have this wonderful faculty of abstracting their ideas, they best can tell; for myself I find indeed I have a faculty of imagining, or representing to myself, the ideas of those particular things I have perceived, and of variously compounding and dividing them . . . But I deny that I can abstract one from another, or conceive separately, those qualities which it is impossible should exist so separated . . . (1710/1977, p. 559).

Foucault and Lyotard have similar problems conceptualizing certain ideas. As Nicholson and Fraser point out (1990, p. 24), "[Lyotard] rules out the sort of critical social theory which employs general categories like gender, race, and class."

It fascinates me that although Berkeley's work purports not to be of a political nature, his argument against the abstract general ideas "man" and "humanity" were published shortly after the publication of Locke's *Two Treatises of Civil Government*, in 1689, just as political philosophers began arguing that the term "man" should include a wider scope of western European males and not just a select few property owners. Further, this Anglican Bishop was overseeing a ruling Protestant minority only a few years after the massive oppression of the Irish under the English monarch, William III. There were high political and economic stakes in ensuring that the term "man" referred to as small a universe of discourse as possible, one which certainly did not include working-class Irish, peasants, and Catholics. Since these groups constituted the great mass of humanity in Ireland, the notion that there was no such thing as "humanity" had great political value.

The term "man" was as politically charged in Berkeley's day as the term "woman" is today. Berkeley's purpose was to claim that the term "man," as an abstract idea, could have no meaningful reference. The post-modern turn makes the same claim about the term "woman." Clearly any political movement aimed at furthering the interests of men, or women, cannot do so without being able to meaningfully designate its constituency.

Enlightenment empiricists and post-modern theorists seem to share a kind of metaphysical nominalism, the view that there are no universal essences, either in reality or conceptually. How can ontological status be granted to such an obvious chimera, "woman" when no such thing exists? How can one identify as "Black" when to do so would require an essentialist and foundational claim? Like their modern forbears, post-moderns become ontological literalists in the face of political strategies and identity politics.

In contrast, radical feminists seem capable of embracing both abstract ideas (as politically powerful) and particular ones (as personally expressive). Since the personal is political these will often intersect. Many feminist philosophers express their disdain for metaphysics by ignoring it in favor of moral, social or political theory. One would be hard put to find a radical feminist of the 1990s ascribing necessary and sufficient conditions, essences if you will, for womanhood, or Blackness, or being Latin. This is partly because radical feminists tend to take a pragmatic and not a metaphysical approach to identity politics. It is also because they do not have to fear abstractions because they are so grounded in particulars. Personal stories, or narratives, form a basis for the Women's Movement and the notion of a grassroots epistemology has been one of the very first concepts to arise from feminism. This is what consciousness raising sessions were about. This is what the poetry and the prose are about. Honoring individual stories allows one to investigate both difference (particulars) and similarities (universal, general, or abstract claims). The irony is that in contrast, post-modern philosophers, by becoming deeply entwined in the arguments against philosophy and foundations, essences and metaphysics, give legitimacy to that which they are arguing against.

In Berkeley's world the fragmentation caused by the elimination of abstract general concepts was healed by the introduction of God – the glue that held the world together. What heals the fragmentation caused by post-modern theory, the loss of the concepts of Blackness, woman, of lesbian or mother? Or, since god is long dead, does the wound remain unhealed?

Conveniently Berkeley lived in a world (like ours) where the abstract generalization "men" was so invisibly omnipresent that one need not despair its "loss" amidst radical empiricism. In the fervor for political rights which charac-terized his period, the abstract concept "man" would persist as the cornerstone of

Enlightenment democratic theories. Woman, on the other hand, seems only present when actually named. The implied (that is, unstated) universe of discourse in our culture is men. Thus we must say, "woman doctor", "Black educator," "Asian store-owner" – any time men, or whites, are not the subject, the difference must be made clear by a qualifying term. Herein lies the contradiction: "Men" are the implied subjects of the universe of discourse. But because of the implied character of this position, "men" goes unmentioned. Women and persons of color, the named qualifiers, must be mentioned to signify a switch in the universe of discourse. But according to post-modern theory "woman" cannot be mentioned because we must destabilize the subject. We are fragmented. We cannot exist as a single abstract idea. So men are (powerfully and omnipresently implied) and women are not.

The present mystery is how philosophers claiming to be "post-modern" can reiterate the modern argument against abstract general terms and maintain the claim to have transcended modernism. How is it that post-modernism is frequently called "feminist" when the particular abstract general term under attack is not "men" or "western civilization," or "anglo-european tradition" or "literary canon" but "women", a term that found broad political resonance in the contemporary world perhaps as little as a decade before its "deconstruction"? The deconstruction of "woman" as "subject" becomes a kind of pornographic bondage by which the concept is first hogtied and then disassembled bit by bit like so many parts of a body in an s/m magazine, a fantasy, an act of ritual abuse. Thus, some of the "feminist" versions of post-modernism are merely another example of "token torturers", as described by Mary Daly, to describe the use of women who are supposedly in sympathy with other women to perform the sadistic tasks of excising female genitals. In this case, it is not the clitorises but the hard-earned theories resulting from years of radical and socialist, Black, Asian, Native and Latina feminist work, to name only a few, that are undergoing excision.[1]

Some post-modern feminists, while disavowing the use of the concept "woman," at the same time claim that criticism of this strategy is misguided. Butler (1992, p. 15) concedes, in one of her meeker moments, "it seems as if there is some political necessity to speak as and for women," as though "political necessity" were some minor, annoying addendum instead of the central pervasive activity of our lives that radical feminists posit. Butler accepts that the construction of subject positions can work to exclude women, and, as hooks asserts, Blacks, and that the category of "women", or Blacks, is indispensable for identity politics. But this is a conclusion feminists reached, and have long known, about all forms of identity politics. That which identifies us has long been a source of empowerment as well as a source of oppression.

---

1. Mary Daly (1978) counts the use of "token torturers", women in patriarchal culture serving as the immediate but relatively powerless instruments in torturing other women, e.g. in performing clitoridectomies, as one element of what she calls the "sado-ritual syndrome".

Reason Becomes Desire

What other theoretical permutations are suggested by post-modern theory from which feminism could benefit? Moving on from the concept of the subject, I propose to show how another concept, reason, becomes transformed by post-modernism. Numerous feminists have described how the attribute of reason, a useful and immensely powerful political concept, has been denied women since Aristotle and well into the present.[2] Legions of women over several millennia have lobbied for recognition of their share in the rational pie, and were generally subjected to a relentless sexualization and/or brutalization as punishment for their presumption.

Fourth century philosopher Hypatia personifies that odd historical character, a woman of reason, and provides a morality tale about what happens to women who presume to the mantle of rationality. She taught geometry and mathematics, and was considered an excellent astronomer. She was accorded the highest honor, unique for a woman of her day, directing the neo-platonic school of Plotinus, the highest academic position in Alexandria, then the center of intellectual activity in the hemisphere. Yet she was also dogged by sexual harassment when as Waithe recounts she was:

> . . . pursued by a student in whom her only interest was discussing philosophy. Hypatia finally ended the harassment by flinging the 5th century version of a sanitary napkin at him, exclaiming that the joys of sex rather than those of philosophy were what was on the student's mind (1987, p. 172).

Hypatia's womanly presumption was greater than most, rising as she did to the very pinnacle of the scientific world, and her downfall was particularly gruesome. Cyril, the Bishop of Alexandria "apparently hired/inspired a group of Nitrian monks" to punish her. According to a contemporary account they:

> . . . pull[ed] her out of her chariot; they hail[ed] her into the Church called caesarium; they stripped her stark naked; they raze[d] the skin and rend[ed] the flesh of her body with sharp shells, until the breath departed out of her body (Waithe: 1987, p. 172).

Hypatia's rise and fall presents an early allegory for what happens to a woman who aspires to reason and how she is reduced from a position of reason, first to desire, and then to blood and shards of bone. As sure as the Enlightenment conception of reason characterizes the modern masculinist world; and just as people of many aspiring groups reach for it, the post-modern *avant garde* makes reason *passé*, substituting desire as the key to power. Indeed, reason is enthymematically lurking for those in power, always there under the surface for use when needed. But reason

---

2. Several feminist assessments of reason come to mind, for instance, Ferguson (1993), Jagger (1989), and Lloyd (1984).

has never been attributed to those who are marginalized in our culture. Women and persons of color have long been characterized as creatures impelled by animal urges and lacking in rational capacity. For those denied both the attribution of reason and access to the means of developing and reshaping it, the usual realm of their long time ghetto, in this case "desire", is repackaged to appear as an appealing goal.

Aphra Behn, Mary Wollstonecraft, Maria W. Stewart, Harriet Taylor, Charlotte Perkins Gilman, and countless others, all lobbied, under various disguises, for *political* access to reason as the *metaphysical* key to power, the philosopher's stone of gender relations. Feminists have held for some time that notions of knowledge, reason and argumentation need to be reworked, noting that the separation of reason and emotion is artificial. Yet the feminist movement, to reclaim and reconfigure *reason* and *knowing*, becomes transformed by post-modernism, oddly enough in an indeterminist theory, into those ever-determined and deter-mining notions – *fantasy* and *desire,* so anti-rational, so "feminine", so "womanly", in a post-modern move that lands us squarely back into the throes of ever-so-modern Freudian psychoanalytic theory.

Another selection from Butler and Scott's *Feminists Theorize the Political* (1992) contains a reaction against feminist philosopher of science, Sandra Harding and others, who perform the highwire act of paying obeisance to post-modernism while getting about their important feminist work. Researcher and psychoanalyst, Jane Flax, claims that we need to rethink concepts of truth, justice, and so on, which surely most feminists believe, and she thinks we should:

> . . . let [concepts] float freely, and explore their differences . . . I would like to move the terms of discussion away from the relations between knowledge and truth to those between knowledge, desire, fantasy and power of various kinds. Epistemology should be conceived as genealogy and the study of the social and unconscious relations of the production of knowledge (1992, p. 457).

I can only think of Catharine MacKinnon, in her work with the rape victims of Bosnia/Hercegovina, letting her concepts of justice and emancipation "float freely" to explore a "radical shift of terrain". Certainly, we must continue to mount whatever conceptual challenges are needed to critique existing ideology, and feminists have not been shy about doing this. But to me desire means that which impels us and lacks free will. Fantasy means the realm of the psychoanalysts, those who dissect women's minds and impose a scheme which overdetermines childhood events instead of directing one to an empowering, future-looking, enabling path.

Carol Ann Douglas, who has for twenty-three years worked in con-temporary radical feminism, tirelessly writing, reviewing, and theorizing; the moving force behind the collective publication *Off Our Backs*, reviews a piece by bell hooks and Mary Childers:

> The most startling insight they presented was, to me, the suggestion that contemporary feminist theory has had to react to Freudianism and that Freud had failed to deal with class and race; perhaps white feminists [in the academy] have been reacting to an intellectual and political agenda set by white men. I was stunned by the thought that Freud's [Foucault's?] focus on sexuality [desire?] as the key to understanding all human interactions could have set the feminists' agenda, that it might be in reaction to the prevailing Freudian ideology that we focused on sex/gender as the central oppression rather than on sex, race and class simultaneously (1993, p. 17).

Economies of desire are precisely those that insist that men are hardwired for sex, and conclude that rape is a natural outcome of war and other "masculine" activities. Many theorists would be most happy to "include investigations into the philosopher's own desire and place within particular social locations and discourses," as Flax suggests (1992, p. 458), and as a former professor of mine did when he treated us to a Valentine's Day seminar on his sexual feelings toward his thirteen-year-old daughter.

Douglas' insight into the dominance of the Freudian agenda is not so stunning, nor even surprising to the many of us who have repeatedly noted and commented on it, but what is truly arresting is the sheer persistence of Freudian-styled theories, relentlessly sexualized, shamelessly substituting the mysterious for the material, miraculously transforming themselves into Jung and New Age, object relations – and post-modern. Given the distractions produced by a focus on among other things, fantasy and desire, it is small wonder that Douglas (1993a, p. 16, see this volume pp. 417–19) remarks about post-modernism, "You take the high road, baby, and I'll take the low road, and I'll be in Scotland, Peoria, Bangladesh, or any actual place before you."

Like the "destabilization of the subject," the transformation of reason into desire provides another example of a post-modern "contribution" to feminism. The contribution issues directly from modern Freudian theory, thereby substantiating my claim that post-modern theory is often a reconfigured modernism. The elevation of desire provides a substantial diversion away from "reason", a metaphysical concept centrally grounded in theories of political rights. In my view, women's struggle worldwide to be seen as rational individuals forms a fundamental stage in gaining political and civil rights. This is not because all cultures adopt the modern western notion of reason, but because western colonialism and imperialism have substantially exported our political systems and their intellectual detritus. Feminists, then, can and should explore reason and desire on their own terms wary of modern constructions which systematically exclude women, and Freudian and post-modern constructions which sexualize women according to masculine economies of desire.

This criticism of post-modernism – that reason becomes transformed by post-modern theory into desire – is an example of the second general criticism, that post-modernism is incoherent because it lacks the methodology for positive theory construction. The post-modern move away from reason toward desire is an important example of this criticism because reason represents the cornerstone for methodology in modern theory. As I claimed in the beginning, feminist theory draws, cautiously, critically and intentionally on modern theory, including its uses of reason, logic, empirical study, argumentation, and statistics. Most of these concepts and methodologies have been usefully analyzed and critiqued by feminism as part of an ongoing process. But they have not been wholly rejected. Without reason and with only desire as a guide, surely incoherence will follow.

Substance Becomes Style

Another post-modern contribution is its style. When I read the writings of Judith Butler and Patricia Williams the beauty of their prose seduces me, and I long (yearn) to be post-modern.[3] When a colleague remarks that a particular observation of mine is "very post-modern" I feel warm inside, smarter, like I belong in some academic version of *W* magazine. And when I accuse another colleague of having post-modern tendencies she smiles broadly and chirps happily, "no one has ever called me that before." Thus, a common response to post-modernism is that, "I was old enough to know that an attempt had been made to suborn me and young enough to have found the experience agreeable" (Waugh: 1977, p. 133).

It is instructive to compare styles and substance. Political scientist Cynthia Enloe has been providing both concrete and ideological feminist critiques of social institutions over several decades of writing on these subjects. Her style is direct and conversational and focuses without shame on women:

> . . . I had been taught by feminists over the last twenty years to be wary of presuming that the political actors with the most power – and the most media coverage – were the most useful starting points for figuring out exactly how politics work. I might get back to George Bush, and Francois Mitterand, King Fahd, and Saddam Hussein eventually. But coming to their ideological outlooks and uses of state power by way of particular groups of women, and the relationships of those women with other women, would prove more fruitful than taking the masculinist shortcut . . . (1993, p. 162).

Enloe argues that feminist analysis must include ideological critique, but not at the expense of looking concretely at individuals and institutions. Her work provides substantive analysis, empirically rich, although often using unconventional sources. It provides an excellent example of work that focuses on substance rather than

---

3. In contrast to the "yearning" to be post-modern, one finds hooks' (1990) critique of post-modern theory, in which she expresses a refreshingly retrograde and modern desire to make common cause with different people: "The shared space and feeling of 'yearning' opens up the possibility of common ground where all these differences might meet and engage one another" (p. 13).

style, where form follows function. The style is sensitive to personal narrative because Enloe is listening to women's stories. To use Sandra Harding's (1991) term, her work "starts from women's lives". Enloe holds that the examination of patriarchy must "build a bridge to what feminists are already revealing about the ingredients of actual women's lives in and around the military" (Enloe: 1983, p. 9).

But when Butler approaches the same subject – the US war with Iraq – she sings her Foucauldian analysis:

> The demigod of a US military subject which euphonically enacted the fantasy that it can achieve its aims with ease fails to understand that its actions have produced effects that far exceed its phantasmatic purview (1992, p. 12).

Prose like this can make me swoon. Butler concocts a Strangelove-like description of us all riding the television camera "Smart Bomb" into its ultimately bloodless target, euphoric with success and ignorant of the consequences, and I want to say "yes I said yes I will Yes" (Joyce: 1934, p. 777). But when she suggests "that we have been in the midst of a celebration on the part of the United States government and some of its allies of the phantasmatic subject" I wonder why the "phantasmatic subject" has replaced the admittedly more heavy-handed "masculinist ideology" or "murderous reality" that have served us so well, analytically, over recent years.

In the politics of style the stakes are particularly high, because so often in academe as well as in the popular press, what counts for salaries and prestige and position is what gets published, and what gets published and read depends on style. Feminist styles have not always sat well in academe. Thus, among our most illustrious feminist writers, Mary Daly, while situated in academe, has long been a pariah in her institution and Catharine MacKinnon wandered for many years without a tenured position. Kathleen Barry was denied tenure at Brandeis.[4] Audre Lorde, Dale Spender, Barbara Smith, Angela Davis, for long periods of time did not have secure institutional affiliations. So style, especially feminist style, along with gender, race and class, definitely affects location.

The post-modern style of high theory, dense discussion, and esoteric terminology partly issues from an embarrassment, especially in the humanities, of discussing concrete matters, e.g. so many women are raped, so many Latinas have been sterilized, so many children are abused, so many African-American women hold part-time jobs, and so on. This issues partly from an academic stricture against "empirical facts" that operates most assuredly in philosophy, but also in literature, and stretches even to the higher reaches of certain social sciences. Hence, feminist writers represent an embarrassment, with their grounded discussions of personal experiences and statistical data about violence and employment, and a myriad of other matters. Particularly in philosophy the mere suggestion that factual material

---

4. Barry was later tenured at the University of Pennsylvania.

may be relevant can be considered an indiscretion of the highest order, a violation of both method and style.

Legal scholar, Mary Joe Frug, realized the power of the post-modern style and expressed a kind of longing for it:

> I confess to having considerable performance anxiety about the post modern style myself. It may require more art, more creativity, and inspiration than I can manage (1992, p. 127).

Frug was another woman of reason who paid the ultimate price for her presumption. The law professor was murdered, stabbed to death, near her home in Cambridge, Massachusetts in 1991. Her work was an attempt to reconcile feminist and post-modern theory against the heavily masculinist legal tradition. A year to the day after her attack, she was "spirit murdered" in the *Harvard Law Review*'s annual "lampoon" edition which published a vile and hateful parody of her work, attributed to "Mary Doe, Rigor Mortis Professor of Law."[5] Thus Frug's fears about style were realized as hers was cruelly distorted for the pleasure of the nation's future elite. The reason for the spirit murder was not her post-modernism, but her feminism. The reason for her actual murder is still unknown.

While the post-modern style is tempting, there is so much work to be done in modernism that there is reason to resist the lure. True, we have uncovered, discovered, resurrected, reapplied, added and stirred, recounted and critiqued, but we still barely know what the implications of the many modernist theories are for feminism. For feminist theory to leap-frog over the modern period because it is, after all, masculinist, is unfruitful. To fail to selectively appropriate the powerful theoretical tools of multifaceted modern theories and readapt them for feminist analysis is a self-destructive move, especially if the reason is to pursue a more seductive style. But appropriations must be made self-consciously, as feminism does, and not in a state of denial and collusion, as is the post-modern way. To create a high style as an entrance requirement is contrary to everything for which feminism has always stood. Along with Douglas, we should be content to take the low road, and to reach our destinations.

Conclusion

Academic disciplines will long retain a core of practitioners who use traditional approaches. The "canon" is alive and well in our colleges and universities. Space on the margins is limited. During the 1970s and 80s marginal space was frequently occupied by feminists. If those spaces are replaced by post-modernists, will academic feminists then become an endangered species? In the United States this would mean that the connections between feminist politics and the academy would be lost. So the final product of the post-modernization of feminism would be the

---

5. Patricia J. Williams (1991) investigates the concept "spirit murder" as an alternative form of violence.

 Kristin Waters

depoliticization of academic feminism. Post-modernists (in league with their modernist colleagues) will have completed their task of refashioning an Enlightment-style role for women. Added to the denial of the subject (woman), the denial of reason, and the reassertion of a preoccupation with style would be the removal of politics from the represented "feminist" sphere. Women in the academy could become concerned with desire, not reason, with style, not substance, and with a domesticated rather than political realm.

The ability to posit a web of truth claims to which one can attribute objectivity is central to theoretical and practical endeavors, as Sandra Harding (1991) has argued. Further, to formulate positive constructs, concepts, and alternatives to traditional theories one needs a positive and not just a deconstructive mode of discourse. If terms are sometimes clumsy and over- or under-inclusive, it is still possible to proceed in ways which are sensitive to differences and nuances, something which the best feminist writing has done in an unparalleled way. Unlike the moral nihilism of post-modernism, feminism has consistently demanded that oppressive, exploitative and discriminatory practices are wrong, and that they destroy the credibility of the systems and theories which perpetuate them. Like the balance of mind and body posited by feminist theory, there is also a reintegration of fact and value, and an interaction of theory and practice which comprise a theory of harmonious balance and political engagement. It also leads to an insistence that we understand the politics of the theoretical move to absorb feminism into post-modern theory. If we are to resist enforced assimilation into post-modern theory, then feminists must politicize the theoretical.

Somer Brodribb

Nothing Mat(t)ers*

> *Dionysus, the "gentle-man", merry mind-poisoner, kills women softly. Male Approval Desire, under his direction, lacks a sense of distance from The Possessor. The Dionysian M-A-D-woman desires the approval of her god because she loves him as herself. She and he, after all, are two in one flesh. She and he are of one mind. She has lost her Self in his house of mirrors, and she does not know whose face she sees in her beatific visions.*
>
> *Thus Dionysus drives women mad with his femininity, which appears to be a relief from the stern masculinity of Apollo* (Daly: 1978, p. 69).

> *XIII*
>
> *we are unworthy your beauty,*
> *you are near beauty the sun,*
>
> *you are that Lord become woman.*
>> (H.D., "The Master")

In her poem, "The Master" (1981), H.D. evokes her relationship to Sigmund Freud, as patient and friend. Hilda Doolittle's *Tribute to Freud* (1956) expands upon her respect, admiration – indeed adoration – of Freud. The poem refers to "The Master's" revelation of the origin and significance of H.D.'s bisexuality, and her gratitude. What H.D. wishes then is that "the old man" will be rewarded by becoming woman, which he must have been close to being: how else could he possibly *know*. Or, as Mary Daly says, "she loves him as herself" (1978, p. 69). In "The Master," Freud/God gives the poet her self-understanding, "explaining" her bisexuality. But he forbids her "infantile" desires to prophesy and to meet the Mother. In some sense, she tries

---

* This is an excerpt entitled "The Labyrinth" from *Nothing Mat(t)ers* (1992).

to satisfy this desire by turning him into the Mother: Freud becomes the Goddess, the Lord becomes woman. Thus, H.D. attempts to master some part of her exploitation. Rachel Blau DuPlessis in "Romantic Thralldom in H.D." finds she "was vulnerable to the power of what she termed the 'héros fatal', a man whom she saw as her spiritual similar, an artist, a healer, a psychic. Again and again this figure that she conspired to create betrayed her; again and again she was reduced to fragments from which her identity had once more to be painfully reconstructed" (1979, p. 179). H.D. was a key figure in the Modernist school, and I am charging that the "romantic thralldom" she suffered is replicated in feminist encounters with post-modernism, post-structuralism, and deconstruction. H.D. tried to turn the Lord Freud into a woman, but not even her magic could pull that off. Pull off the phallus.[1]

Post-modernism is an addition to the masculinist repertoire of psychotic mind/body splitting and the peculiar arrangement of reality as Idea: timeless essence and universal form. When women appear in French philosophy as Sartrean holes and slime (Collins and Pierce: 1976) or Deleuzian bodies without organs (Guattari and Deleuze: 1983), the mind – and the matter – is masculine. Plato answered the question of Being by awarding true reality to the realm of ideas; the sensible world possesses only the appearance of reality. Post-modernism is no less metaphysical: here, too, the idea absorbs and denies all presence in the world. This particular trend in patriarchal thinking is neither new nor original: the Collége de France and the Freud school which created it have respectable traditions in Cartesian politics. Julia Penelope has uncovered the "patriarchal linguistic agenda" (1990, p. 17) of the Académie Française, founded by Cardinal Richelieu in 1635 with the purpose of creating a grammar that would correct women. The institutions as well as the texts which were patrons to post-modernism excluded and expelled women, including Simone de Beauvoir and Luce Irigaray. The rule is only man may appear as woman. Derrida creates Veronica – "true image" in medieval Latin, – woman as representation of the transparency of meaning. Then he deconstructs her while denouncing feminists for defining her: Veronica must be his and must be appearance only. She must be his (appearance) only. She may be summoned to appear, but shall not summon the College, to account; to politics, responsibility, justice. In any case, once at court, the jester Lacan rules that the law is the phallus and woman cannot speak; Lacan will speak in her place, however, since only man may represent woman.

Once satisfied to control her body and her movements, once pleased to create images of her and then order her body to conform, the Master of Discourse now aspires to the most divine of tasks: to create her in his image, which is ultimately to annihilate her. This is his narcissistic solution to his problem of the Other. But to do this, to create her in his image, he must be able to take her image, educating her to sameness and deference. Taking her body, taking her mind, and

---

1. Some of the best H.D. scholarship is represented by the works of Rachel Blau DuPlessis (1979, 1986); Du Plessis and Friedman (1981); Susan Stanford Friedman (1981, 1985); Deborah Kelly Kloepfer (1984) and Friedman and DuPlessis (1990).

now taking her image. But the task of taking women's image is ill-advised. In his narcissistic dreaming, he hallucinates, and even if we are called an illusion, he must ask: Where did the illusion of woman come from? What evil genius placed the idea of woman in man? In short, the New Age masculinity of self-deluded alchemists and shape-shifters is not going to be a successful strategy. There is something irreducible about Veronica after all, as they always suspected. She informs herself that women matter.

Foucault would have written on hysterical women, Lacan tried to write as an hysteric (Clément: 1983); Derrida (1978a) and Deleuze (Deleuze and Guattari: 1988) write of becoming-woman. In the section, "Memories of a Sorcerer, III", Deleuze and Guattari write "becoming-woman, more than any other becoming, possesses a special introductory power; it is not so much that women are witches, but that sorcery proceeds by way of this becoming-woman" (1988, p. 248). Is this male apprenticeship some sort of talisman to frighten contemporary feminists (previously known as "hysterics")?[2] Related to this is the curious omission of the sorceress in Foucault's history of sexuality, his intriguing point of departure. The *scientia sexualis* ignores but begins directly after the witch hunts. Yet is was the new printing press that enabled the dissemination of precise symptoms for inquisitors to extort as confessions. *The Malleus Maleficarum*, the first post-modern text, standardized patriarchal hysteria about female sources.[3]

What is the meaning of this particular ideology of masculine domination? Strange timing: the subject is now annulled by ungenerous and disingenuous white western wizards while women's and Third World liberation movements are claiming their voices (Hartsock: 1990; Christian: 1988; Barry: 1990; de Lauretis: 1989; Lazreg: 1988). Gallop (1988, p. 100) argues that post-modernism "dephallicizes modernism so men can claim to be current. If modernism . . . is itself a defense against feminism and the rise of women writers, post-modernism is a more subtle defense, erected when modernism would no longer hold."

We know we are in a world where politics is the separation of the public and the private, and man's,[4] western man's, image is everywhere. He is fascinated

---

2. One of the most studied of Freud's "cases" of hysteria was Anna O., who in reality was the Jewish feminist, Bertha Pappenheimer. Her experiences with male dominance and women's rights organizations are chronicled in a preliminary way by Marion A. Kaplan (1979), in Chapter 2 of *The Jewish Feminist Movement in Germany*. See also Dianne Hunter (1985) "Hysteria, Psychoanalysis and Feminism: The Case of Anna O.", in Shirley Nelson Garner *et al.* (Eds.)*The (M)other Tongue*.

3. Catherine Clément's sexist history of the sorceress in *The Newly Born Woman* (1975/1986) turns the persecution into a codependency relationship, a dysfunctional familial encounter. She hints at sado-masochism: "The hysteric must 'quit the show'" and be "done with the couple: perversion and hysteria, inquisitor and sorceress" (1975/1986, p. 56).

4. A note on usage: I use the masculine form only, as I argue that it is precisely the masculine which is meant by and in post-modern texts. Their positions and arguments cannot be uncritically extended to women – to do so would render women's experiences invisible. This book studies masculine ideology, and it points to the masculine referentiality of these concepts. *He*, *his* and *man* are therefore appropriate.

by this image and at the same time bored by it. His images, of himself and us, are before our eyes: this noxious narcissist has placed his body of knowledge across our desire to know. I reach for my body, but this "male-stream" (O'Brien: 1981, p. 5) corpus has imposed itself between my experience and my reflection. The access to formal knowledge is mediated by the Master (Le Doeuff: 1989, pp. 100–128; Lorde: 1981). The way to myself and other women is blocked by this male icon as a point of reference, for reverence. And I have to make arguments which sound extravagant to my ears, that women exist. That women are sensible. Only knowledge of the male body and male thought is considered essential, the female is unessential, the female is essentialist. And to contradict this, to speak against masculine culture, is so uncultured. The Masters of discourse have also said that it requires a great deal of sophistication to speak like a woman, clearly it's best left to men. Their texts play with and parade a hysterical femininity, in our best interests of course, to help us transcend the category of woman we somehow got into, and the neurotic idea that we can tell the truth. Or that we know when they're lying. Talking, writing, telling stories out of school: this is what we are forbidden. The Master wants to keep the narrative to himself, and he's willing to explode the whole structure of discourse if we start to talk. They don't want to hear our stories: listening to women's stories of incest and rape almost cost Sigmund Freud his career before he decided that these were simply female fantasies of desire for the father. He probed women's unconscious and denied our reality: his theory of human psyche and sexuality is an act of fear and betrayal. And he told us: it didn't happen, you made it up, you wanted it, you brought it on yourself. What is the Master Narrative? That we can't tell the truth, we can't tell the difference, between our rights and their wrongs. We can't tell.

The assertion that only sex is power and the arrogation of creativity to the masculine sex and the rendering of all creativity as sexual – this is patriarchal aesthetics.[5] Patriarchal passion sees violent sex as the essential creative act, even aesthetically, through a sort of metaphysical transubstantiation. This is their romantic belief that sex with the Master can produce the artistic spirit in the student. Male creativity is thus born in another, her work is given depth through the violent transgression of her boundaries. The Maestro's magic wand, the charismatic penis, is the conductor of true art. Great works of art can only be produced after a journey through violent and sordid sex which reveals and brings into being the true nature of the other: degradation. One can only create from pain, and sex. The superior Master of course, creates pain in another, makes his mark by leaving marks. What is central to the rape artist's ideology is that matter is worthless and must be given form. His. Matter must be recreated by man. Mother must be recreated by, and as, the masculine. Mother is dissociated from creativity and communication. Flesh is created by the word of god, not by the body of woman. Creation requires destruction, one is posed only in being opposed to another, consciousness is hostile to all

---

5. Fortunately, we have Audre Lorde's (1984) vision of the uses of the erotic for connection and community, work and joy.

others. Men are hostile and creative, women are sometimes good material.

For us, then, to speak is difficult, and it seems we must shift from amnesia to aphasia as parts of our consciousness appear unreal to us. Loss of memory, loss of speech: it is as though we cannot speak and cannot remember at the same time. Being fully conscious is dangerous. Women's memory, women's language, women's body and sexuality have been annulled in the patriarchal tradition which has feared the female sex. What we are permitted, encouraged, coerced into, and rewarded for, is loving the male sex and male sex: the bad girls are the ones who don't, and who thereby risk men's rage and women's fear.

Post-modernism exults female oblivion and disconnection; it has no model for the acquisition of knowledge, for making connections, for comm-unication, or for becoming global, which feminism has done and will continue to do.[6] You have to remember to be present for another, to be just, to create sense.

Feminists like Anne-Marie Dardigna (1981) and Andrea Nye (1988) have disclosed how psychoanalytic theory refuses to acknowledge the anguish of women's lives and stories of brutality which threaten the son's reconciliation with the Father necessary to his inheritance of privilege. As Nye argues, "the imaginary male self is threatened not by fusional maternal animality, but by the always-present possibility of renewed accusations from abused women, not by the nothingness of the intersub-jective, but by an empathy that will make him vulnerable to others' experiences" (1988, p. 161). The refusal to feel for or with women, the rejection of solidarity with women, assures the son's access to the Father's power. In fact, the Master from Vienna located the voice of the conscience in the Other – in the voice of the murdered father who becomes, with difficulty, the external internal voice – so that the ego is one's own but the conscience is founded only from an external threat of retaliation for murder (Freud, 1913). Indeed, ego and conscience are not connected here! According to Dardigna,[7] it is really the fascination for the all-powerful father that is at the centre of masculine desire (1981, p. 188). To desire a woman is in some sense to recognize her, and this threatens a loss of control over the divisions he has made in his life between his mind and his body, his reason and his emotion; between the women he uses for sex and the women he talks with about post-modernism. And the women writers he criticizes, not daring to confront the Father. As Wendy Holloway (1984) has shown, he withholds, withdraws, and does not meet her social,

---

6. This was the case in Nairobi, 1985. See Charlotte Bunch (1987), *Passionate Politics*, Section Five, "Global Feminism", pp. 269–362.

7. In her interpretation of the myth of Adam and Eve in the garden, Anne-Marie Dardigna recalls Eve's gesture of subversion: Eve senses the presence of the Tree of Knowledge, she tastes the fruit, and introduces new values of pleasure and perception. When she disrupts the pact of Father and Son, she is punished by male domination of her desire: "Thy desire shall be thy husband, and he shall rule over thee." In Genesis, the Father–Son alliance is reasserted: "the Father and the Son are reconciled by denying the desire of Eve as subject and transforming her into an object of their desire" (1981, p. 179). Men remain fearful of the dangers: knowing women, and knowing a woman threaten the Law of the Fathers.

sexual, emotional, political desires: too demanding, he will not satisfy her. Denying women's desire, politically or sexually, is a male power play. Andrea Nye's (1988) rewriting of the Freud creation story tells of male fears of the Father's revenge and disinheritance from patriarchal powers: getting close to women means losing economic and political power.

> Once there was a family headed by a brutal authoritarian father who in secret had a tendency to abuse his wife, his daughters and any women who came under his power. Sometimes he even abused his sons. His sons were uneasy about their father and about other men but they were men themselves. Therefore, they knew they were supposed to respect their father and learn to be like him. One son, however, listened to his mother, his nurse, and the talk of other women. He became very uneasy. The women told him of crimes that his father and other fathers had committed against women and about their suffering. But this son was also a man. He knew that he too had to become a father. Then he made his discovery. There was only one solution. The women were lying, they were in love with the father and wanted to be seduced. They had only fantasized the father's mistreatment. Now the son knew that he had been guilty also; he had suspected his father out of jealousy. And he repented. Now all the sons could come together, celebrating the father's memory and rejoicing that the father had committed no faults. Now they could follow in the father's footsteps and if accusations were made by the women or by any younger sons who happened to listen to women, the men would know what to say (1988, p. 159).

In this way, Freud felt he penetrated the mystery of female anguish: mysterious because women were unreal to him. Lacanian psychoanalysis also says we mean yes when we say no: "the tension of desire hidden in the most professed horror of incest" (Lacan: 1953, p. 12). In fact, the Freudian Oedipal myth warns men of the risks of loving the mother: death as a Father, death of the King.

Suzanne Blaise has argued that the current oppression of women would not have been possible without the death, the murder, of the mother. In *Le rapt des origines ou le meurtre de la mère: De la communication entre femmes*, Blaise (1988) shows how the male murder of the mother and the massacre of the value of the female and the maternal is continually re-enacted among women. Drawing from forty years of experience in the women's movement in France, she shows how the original murder of the mother by the sons has had serious repercussions for communication between women politically and personally. She reconsiders the current divisions, impasses, betrayals and violent denunciations among women in this light. Clearly, our relationship to other women, to our sex, symbolically and politically, is full of consequences for our sexuality. Blaise asks what it would mean for the personal and collective body of women to recognize that sexual politics is also the politics of matricide: "To possess the mother, man destroyed the woman; to possess the daughter, he destroyed the mother" (1988, pp. 10, 11).

Feminists have only begun to think through the effects for female sexuality of the wounding of the mother–daughter relationship. The mothers were also daughters, and this question has to be considered in generational as well as psychical time, as Luce Irigaray shows:

> But have I ever known you otherwise than gone? And the home of your disappearance was not in me . . . I received from you only your obliviousness of self, while my presence allowed you to forget this oblivion. So that with my tangible appearance I redoubled the lack of your presence (1981, p. 65).

> But forgetfulness remembers itself when its memorial disappears. And here you are, this very evening, facing a mourning with no remembrance. Invested with an emptiness that evokes no memories. That screams at its own rebounding echo. A materiality occupying a void that escapes its grasp.

Irigaray also argues that sameness and differences among women remain to be named. But we have to overcome our aphasia and our amnesia to *speak* our *minds* and live our time. Temporally, sex is *momentous*, while procreation is *duration*. Remedying aphasia, Irigaray (1985) wrote, "When our two lips speak together." Remembering birth, Mary O'Brien (1981) showed how biological reproduction is the substructure of human history, the unity of natural and cyclical time.

But such critiques of the misogyny of masculinist theory have been interrupted, arrested. Julia Kristeva, the self-styled "father of semiotics" has brought us the phallic mother: the phallus becomes the mother of us all in Kristeva's magical replacement of male supremacy. Her work is tied to the Lacanian formula of desire and/for female aphasia:

> On a deeper level, however, a woman cannot "be"; it is something which does not even belong in the order of being. It follows that a feminist practice can only be negative, at odds with what already exists so that we may say "that's not it" and "that's still not it". In "woman" I see something that cannot be represented, something that is not said, something above and beyond nomenclatures and ideologies. There are certain "men" who are familiar with this phenomenon; it is what some modern texts never stop signifying: testing the limits of language and sociality – the law and its transgression, mastery and (sexual) pleasure – without reserving one for males and the other for females, on the condition that it is never mentioned (Kristeva: 1974/1981, pp. 137, 138).

According to Kristeva, "women exist" is an essentialist statement, but nothing *is*, negation *is*, and is a higher form of being than woman.[8] More mundanely, this is the ideological practice of the organization of consent and deconstruction of dissent,

---

8. For an examination of critical approaches to Kristeva's work, see Eleanor Kuykendall (1989) who illustrates how Kristeva endorses Freudian paradigms and "leaves no place for a feminine conception of agency" (1989, p. 181).

necessary for professional practice. For Kristeva, woman is an attitude, not a sexual or political subject. As Ann Rosalind Jones (1981, p. 249) remarks, "'woman' to Kristeva represents not so much a sex as an attitude, any resistance to conventional culture and language; men, too, have access to the *jouissance* that opposes phallogocentrism". Woman represents the semiotic – an oceanic bliss/swamp of the mother – child dyad, a communication of rhythm, preverbal sound. "She" is an attitude best held by men: for Kristeva, it is in the work of male authors – Joyce, Artaud, Mallarmé, etc. – that this semiotic state of union with the maternal is best elaborated. This, I suspect, is why Kristeva forbids women to mention the game, to move to self-definition: it would block men's access to the primal maternal source of their verbal creativity, it would profane men's ancestral memories of Mother. If women claim and proclaim this matrix, it would be horrid. Then there would be real chaos. So women must be still and think of the linguistic empire. In Kristeva's view, "woman" or "women" by women is a bad attitude.

Let's be realistic, say some women. Do you really think that you can start from scratch and just leave theory out entirely, just because it's male? Don't you see that you can pick and choose from it all in order to make feminist theory? Or, as Elizabeth Grosz[9] puts it in introducing feminists to Jacques Lacan, "feminists may be able to subvert and/or harness strategically what is useful without being committed to its more problematic ontological, political and moral commitments" (1990, p. 7). This is based on her understanding of psychoanalysis as "a method of reading and interpreting (where questions of truth, bias and verification are not relevant)" (1990, p. 21). That rational – or irrational – science is pure methodology is an old ideology which feminist critiques of science have exposed (Keller: 1985; Harding *et al.*: 1983; Lloyd: 1984). These recent feminist analyses of masculine rationality show how subjective it is, how it masks and develops masculine domination. Such epistemological critiques warn against a dangerous and superficial neutrality.

The objection to "starting from scratch" suggests several objectives. First of all, women are punished who try to use unprocessed ingredients in their recipes in order to avoid preserving masculine categories and implications. As anyone who has ever done it knows, confronting patriarchy or critiquing "male-stream" (O'Brien: 1981, p. 5) knowledge is not "easy": it involves risk and there are consequences. There is so little support for radically feminist work; its costs are exorbitant politically, personally, economically, intimately, as Dale Spender's (1983) *Women of Ideas and What Men Have Done to Them* attests. It is not as though many women have been allowed to embark on and complete an enormous body of work which had then been judged to be a waste of time. Strange then, that this is so often raised and posed as a perilous, foolish course. "Immense political energy is devoted to seeing that alternatives are nipped in the bud, rendered ridiculous, and never adequately funded", charges Mary O'Brien with reference to women and health care

---

9. Grosz displays more inadvertent masculine supremacy with the statement: "Given the mother's (up to now) indispensable role in bearing children . . ." (1990, p. 146). Artificial wombs and placentas are still a fantasy. Even if Grosz is referring to "contract mothers", this negation of them as mothers participates in the patriarchal ideology which privileges genetic genealogy over birth (Brodribb, 1989a).

(1989, p. 213). All feminist work faces a reality of exceptional hostility masked by a self-satisfied ideology of acceptance by sexist institutions, some of which currently consume women's studies like a prestige item. Yet radical work is perceived as dangerous, and discomfits those who have made more stable arrangements within patriarchal systems. Rather than forbidding originality then, let us investigate the *scratching out* of women's writing as a historical and political process.

As for the idea that feminists should be ragpickers in the bins of male ideas, we are not as naked as that. The notion that we need to salvage for this junk suggests that it is not immediately available everywhere at all times. The very up-to-date products of male culture are abundant and cheap; it is one of life's truly affordable things. In fact, we can't pay not to get it, it's so free. So what we have is a problem of refusing, of *not* choosing masculine theoretical products.

The second difficulty here is the relationship of theory[10] to action implicit in the notion that feminist theory must be an arrangement of and selection from male theory, not female experiences. Underneath this notion lies the historically specific dualism of intellect vs act, theory vs practise, a masculine methodology and ideology which has trained and constrained us all. Even to the point where now some suggest (Weedon: 1987; Nicholson: 1990; Hekman: 1990) that male theory should be the vanguard for feminist practice, again reflecting a sense of inferiority and belief that all feminist thought will be and should be derivative of masculine texts not women's practice. Also, this approach does not recognize other feminists and other feminisms as alternatives to the male text. Are not the works of Women and Feminists: Black, lesbian, Jewish, working-class, Third World, Native – a more significant source for understanding difference and otherness than the writings of white, western men?

Barbara Christian's excellent article points to how womanist prose is being neglected. This new white western male[11] theory is a language that "mystifies

10. See Barbara Christian's (1987, this volume pp. 311–20) excellent article which points to how womanist prose is being neglected and how this new white western male theory is a language which "mystifies rather than clarifies our condition" (1988, p. 71). Barry (1990, p. 100) criticizes the racism of some feminist post-modernism.

11. See hooks (1990, 1991a) for a critical consideration of differences on race, sex and difference. Barry (1990, p. 100) criticizes the racism of some feminist post-modernism. Contrary to its claimed superiority on this issue, *Feminism/Postmodernism*, for example, contains no substantial engagement with the issue as Modleski points out (1991, p. 18). In "Postmodern Reductionisms: Diversity versus Specificity", Angela Miles argues that the "integrative politics of many feminists of colour and lesbian feminists are complex enough to be easily misread as both essentialist and deconstructionist by those who reject dialectical possibilities . . . Today, it is not hard to see diverse, heroic and exciting, practice among ever wider groups of women who are consciously and collectively claiming the right to define themselves/their identity, to speak for themselves, and to name their world; who are articulating their own values and visions; who are committed to building solidarity/sisterhood as they articulate their differences. Nevertheless, postmodern feminists choose not to see the new dialectical possibilities this practice creates and reveals. Their theory remains impervious to the lessons as well as the imperatives of practice."

rather than clarifies" the condition of Blacks and women (1988, p. 17). Related to the theory/action obfuscations of post-modernism, is the question of experience and what Hartsock (1983) and others have called a "standpoint". Responding to the charges that political feminism is "essentialist", Modleski points out: "But surely for many women the phrase 'women's experience' is shorthand for 'women's experience of political oppression', and it is around this experience that they have organized and out of this experience that they have developed a sense of solidarity, commonality and community" (1991, p. 17). Indeed, the writing of bell hooks is a profound examination of the obstacles to, but potentials for, female solidarity. It is grounded in black, female experience. hooks illuminates race differences and racist processes, and reconceptualizes female community and solidarity. She charges that essentialism is perpetuated by white hetero-patriarchy, while marginalized groups beginning from their own standpoint are targeted by an "apolitical" post-modernism. In a review of Diana Fuss' *Essentially Speaking*, she writes: "Identity politics emerges out of the struggles of . . . exploited groups to have a standpoint on which to critique dominant structures, a position that gives purpose . . . to struggle. Critical pedagogies of liberation . . . necessarily embrace experience, confession and testimony as relevant ways of knowing" (1991a, p. 180). Resisting the notion that race and experience do not matter, P. Gabrielle Foreman shows that "[r]ace, and the habits of surviving we've developed to resist its American deployment, *is* material in a racist culture which so staunchly refuses to admit it is so. This we know but find almost too obvious to write down. Yet our silent space is rapidly being filled with post-modern, post-Thurgood Marshall concepts of the declining significance of race" (1991, p. 13).

There *is* an identity politics to feminist post-structuralism: an identification with the male text. Elizabeth Meese, for example, writes: "when gender is the focus for examining difference, deconstructive criticism might even be said to be identical with the feminist project" (1986, p. xi). Or, we can spend our time cataloguing feminism's convergences with and divergences from this masculine point of reference, as Alice Jardine (1985) does in *Gynesis*,[12] or Hekman (1990) in *Gender and Knowledge*. In "The Discourse of Others: Feminists and Post-modernism," Craig Owens[13] mistakenly tries to improve the status of feminism by arguing that it is part of post-modernism:

> The absence of discussions of sexual difference in writings about post-modernism, as well as the fact that few women have engaged in the modernism/post-modernism debate, suggest that post-modernism may be another masculine invention engineered to exclude women. I would like to propose, however, that women's insistence on difference and incommensurability may not only be compatible with, but also an instance of post-modern thought (1983: pp. 61, 62).

12. See Toril Moi (1988) for a critique of Jardine's work as a post-feminism which never really had a feminist stage.
13. See Elspeth Probyn's (1987) critique of Craig Owens and Donna Haraway.

Linda Nicholson (1990, p. 6) holds that feminist theory "belongs in the terrain of post-modern philosophy." Jane Flax also absorbs feminism in post-modernism: "Feminist theorists enter into and echo post-modernist discourse . . ."; "feminists, like other post-modernists" (1990, p. 42). Flax (1990, p. 40) now believes that "The further development of feminist theory (and hence a better understanding of gender) also depends upon locating our theorizing within and drawing more self-consciously upon the wider philosophical contents of which it is both a part and a critique." Flax contradicts her earlier, radical position on female socio-symbolic practice: "If we deny our own experience, if we decide *a priori* to fit those experiences into categories which others have decided are politically correct, we lose the very possibility for comprehending and overcoming our oppression" (1977/1978, p. 22).

The Adam's rib approach is stated openly in Chris Weedon's *Feminist Practise and Post-Structuralist Theory*, and more implicitly in Nancy Fraser's *Unruly Practises*. In neither of these books do we get a clear sense of real struggle with or significant opposition to male theory, and so their value as critiques is also limited. Rather, the major situatedness of each writer is as expert bringing male theory to the women's movement. This suggests a new Aristotelian formula whereby theory is male and action is female, passive, there to be formed by the male seed or seminar. Female experiences are taken like tribute to be formed and informed by masculine theory.

What sort of kinship system is post-modernism? Certainly, it is not post-patriarchal. Who does the post-structuralist marketplace buy, sell, exchange, credit, legitimate?

In her introduction to *Feminism/Post-modernism*, Nicholson defines post-modernists as critical of objectivity and neutrality and this is, she claims, "even more radical" (1990, p. 3) than the work of scholars involved in "other" political movements, including feminism, Marxism, black and gay liberation. It is post-modernists, not feminists, who "have extended the field where power has traditionally been viewed as operating, for example, from the state and the economy to such domains as sexuality and mental health" (1990, p. 4). Thus, at least one century of feminist scholarship and practise is unrecognized, ignored, rewritten, trivialized. It appears that a certain authoritative consensus is being promoted and recirculated, a somewhat totalizing post-modern feminist metanarrative about the history and the potential of feminism. Curious how the critical practice is not situated in a study of the culture or the epistemology of post-modernism. Nicholson believes that post-modernism deconstructs the "God's eye view" (1990, pp. 2–3) bias of an Enlightenment methodology. I believe that Nicholson has *read* Derrida, but did not recognize him.

Gender and Knowledge: Elements of a Post-modern Feminism goes one step beyond the presentation of feminism as an aspect of post-modernism, and portrays post-modernism as the ultimate (post-) feminism. But then, "Consent", as Mary O'Brien ironizes, "relies on a perception by the public that, imperfect though a system may be, it is the only game in town" (1989, p. 213). And the game here is the absorption of all critical space by post-modernism. Hekman's project is to post-modernize feminism; hers is not a feminist critique of post-moderism, but a "post-modern approach to feminism" (1990, p. 3). It is no longer a question of extending post-modernism by adding gender; it is feminism which must be purged by post-modernism of Enlightenment, essentialist, absolutist and foundationalist tendencies. Cartesian epistemology, not class or heterosexuality, is the main enemy here, and Foucault, Derrida and Gadamer are brought forward to critique feminism. Indeed, Hekman's major target is not the sexism of social and political thought, but the "women's way of knowing" literature. Daly, Ruddick, Gilligan, Chodorow, Lorde, feminist standpoint theory, the "Marxist feminist camp" (1990, p. 40), the "contra-dictory" (1990, p. 30) radical feminists, the maternal thinkers, all are distinctly less perfect than Derrida and Foucault: "The strongest case for a post-modern feminism can be made through an examination of the work of Derrida and Foucault" (1990, p. 155). Hekman proposes a "conversation of mankind" [sic] (1990, pp. 9, 123) between feminism and post-modernism. In this *Taming of the Shrew* it seems that only man may speak of woman and not be a biological determinist. Hekman's assertion that life with men under the darkness of post-modernism would be different than under their "Enlightenment" is not convincing.

I reject both the theory/practice dichotomy as well as the male/theory use of female/practice as matter. (The child is usually matricidal anyway and has delusions of being self or Father-born.) Fraser (1989) and Weedon (1987), among others, suggest that if one is truly serious about social change, she must read and use the *male* bodies of work. Surely our activism must be something other than standing as experts bringing masculine formulations to movement matters? Bringing male theory to the women's movement is not feminist critique or intervention; it is a position of compromise within institutions and a form of quietism. It denies and hides the abusiveness of the ideology to which it reconciles itself and others. JoanScott sees theory as a way of ordering experience and determining political practice. We need, says Scott, theory that will enable us to think, analyze and articulate, "And we need theory that will be relevant for political practice. It seems to me that the body of theory referred to as post-modernism best meets all these requirements" (1988, p. 33). Instead, I argue the best methodology for evaluating the practice of theory that is put before us as what feminists must attend to if we are really serious about social change is whether it originates from women's experiences. We must be the origin, the source; not a tributary to masculine theory. This is what The Milan Women's Bookstore Collective suggests in their work, *Sexual Difference:*

> This book is about the need to make sense of, exalt, and represent in words and images the relationship of one woman to another. If putting a political practice into words is the same thing as theorizing, then this is a book of theory, because the relations between women are the subject matter of our politics and this book. It is a book of theory, then, but interspersed with stories. We believe that to write

theory is partly to tell about practice, since theoretical reasoning generally refers to things which already have names. Here we are dealing partly with things that had no names (1990, p. 25).

Certainly, bringing the women's movement and feminist theory to bear on male ideology and practice is a more risky position, and the Milan Collective takes those risks.

In *(Ex)Tensions*, Elizabeth Meese (1990c) reacts against the charges that feminist deconstructors are fathers', not mothers', daughters, and attacks the pioneers of feminist literary criticism as dominating, severe, austere, restrictive, controlling, orthodox. In particular, she targets the work of Showalter, Baym, Marcus, Robinson, and Auerbach in *Feminist Issues in Literary Scholarship* edited by Shari Benstock. Meese (1990c, p. 9) seems to be furious with Showalter[14] who "urges feminist critics to stick with theory received 'via the women's movement and women's studies'". Meese takes the position that Father Knows Best, or at least what mother does not, and that deconstruction will force Women's Studies' feminism to relinquish its power and "orthodoxy". Thus, Meese re-enacts the daughter's rage and rejection of the mother, and the turning towards the Father which ironically recreates her as the same. Luce Irigaray writes the daughter's process in "And One Doesn't Stir Without the Other":

> I'll leave you for someone who seems more alive than you. For someone who doesn't prepare anything for me to eat. For someone who leaves me empty of him, mouth gaping on his truth. I'll follow him with my eyes, I'll listen to what he says, I'll try to walk behind him (1981, p. 62).

Escape to the House of the Father is not one. It is the path to patriarchal wifehood. Jane Gallop puts the double-cross this way:

> Postmodernist thinkers are defending against the downfall of patriarchy by trying to be not male. In drag, they are aping the feminine rather than thinking their place as men in an obsolescent patriarchy. The female post-modernist thinker finds herself in the dilemma of trying to be like Daddy who is trying to be a woman. The double-cross is intriguing and even fun [*sic*], but also troubling if one suspects that it is the father's last ruse to seduce the daughter and retain her respect, the very respect that legitimized the father's rule (1988, p. 100).

The real absurdity of post-modernist feminism is its sexist context. For example, at a recent conference the male commentator[15] criticized Nancy Fraser for her sparse

---

14. See Modleski (1991, pp. 3–6) for an account of Elaine Showalter's switch to gender studies and "gynocidal feminism".

15. Tom Wartenberg, speaking at the special session on *Unruly Practices*, at the Society of Phenomenology and Existential Philosophy, 29th Annual Meeting, 11 October 1990, Valhalla, Pennsylvania.

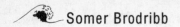

referencing of feminist work. But has he ever spoken against Foucault's or masculine theory's sexism? Those men who do take up feminist texts often only complain that the writer isn't feminist enough. He didn't complain that Foucault is not anti-sexist, which in any case does not involve him in the same political risk as it does Fraser.

The objections to radical feminism's break with tradition are particularly academic, because it is there, in the institution, that we must locate ourselves in the discourse in order to write credibly. For it is true that if we read/write/speak of women, very few will attend to what we say, even if the women referred to are not feminists. So that the objection to leaving male theory behind expresses a real fear of being silenced: unless you read/write/speak the boys, no one will listen to you. You will be outside the defined and policed arena of discourse. Now, in the academe, you cannot just say anything about male theory. You have to proceed with an immanent critique, that is to say, you have to expertly play the parts against the whole. You show, for example, how certain assumptions in the work actually defeat its stated purpose of human liberation, but once remedied, i.e. salvaged, the theory will work for women. An immanent critique can stay within the masculinist academic circle. In this position women become the technicians of male theory who have to reprogram the machine, turning it from a war machine against women into a gentler, kinder war machine. This is a very involving task and after years of playing this part it is understandable that there may be little desire to admit that the effort was virtually futile. An investment has been made, and the conformity is not wholly outer. What attitudes and feelings does this sexist context produce towards oppositional women who refuse this male material? Does a male-circled woman have the power and security to be generous? Having compromised her freedom, will she be less willing to compromise ours? Perhaps the most pernicious aspect of this arrangement, besides the ways it sets women against one another, is the fact that although the male academe values owning our freedom, it does not have to pay a lot for it. Masculine culture already controls gross amounts of female lives. Still, it seems to want more, but always at the same low price. The exploited are very affordable.

Barbara Christian

The Race for Theory*

I have seized this occasion to break the silence among those of us, critics, as we are now called, who have been intimidated, devalued by what I call the race for theory. I have become convinced that there has been a takeover in the literary world by western philosophers from the old literary elite, the neutral humanists. Philosophers have been able to effect such a takeover because so much of the literature of the west has become pallid, laden with despair, self-indulgent and disconnected. The New Philosophers, eager to understand a world that is today fast escaping their political control, have redefined literature so that the distinctions implied by that term, that is, the distinctions between everything written and those things written to evoke feeling as well as to express thought, have been blurred. They have changed literary critical language to suit their own purposes as philosophers, and the have reinvented the meaning of theory.

My first response to this realisation was to ignore it. Perhaps, in spite of the egocentrism of this trend, some good might come of it. I had, I felt, more pressing and interesting things to do, such as reading and studying the history and literature of Black women, a history that had been totally ignored, a contemporary literature bursting with originality, passion, insight and beauty. But unfortunately it is difficult to ignore this new takeover, since theory has become a commodity which helps determine whether we are hired or promoted in academic institutions – worse, whether we are heard at all. Due to this new orientation, works (a word which evokes labor) have become texts. Critics are no longer concerned with literature, but with other critics' texts, for the critic yearning for attention has displaced the writer and has conceived of himself as the centre. Interestingly in the first part of this century, at least in England and America, the critic was usually also a writer of poetry, plays or novels. But today, as a new generation of professionals develops, he or she is increasingly an academic. Activities such as teaching or writing one's response to specific works of literature have, among this

---

* Originally published in *Cultural Critique* (1987).

group, become subordinated to one primary thrust, that moment when one creates a theory, thus fixing a constellation of ideas for a time at least, a fixing which no doubt will be replaced in another month or so by somebody else's competing theory as the race accelerates. Perhaps because those who have effected the takeover have the power (although they deny it) first of all to be published, and thereby to determine the ideas which are deemed valuable, some of our most daring and potentially radical critics (and by our I mean Black, women, Third World) have been influenced, even co-opted, into speaking a language and defining their discussion in terms alien to and opposed to our needs and orientation. At least so far, the creative writers I study have resisted this language.

For people of color have always theorised – but in forms quite different from the western form of abstract logic. And I am inclined to say that our theorising (and I intentionally use the verb rather than the noun) is often in narrative forms, in the stories we create, in riddles and proverbs, in the play with language, since dynamic rather than fixed ideas seem more to our liking. How else have we managed to survive with such spiritedness the assault on our bodies, social institutions, countries, our very humanity? And women, at least the women I grew up around, continuously speculated about the nature of life through pithy language that masked the power relations of their world. It is this language, and the grace and pleasure with which they played with it, that I find celebrated, refined, critiqued in the works of writers like Morrison and Walker. My folk, in other words, have always been in a race for theory – though more in the form of the hieroglyph, a written figure which is both sensual and abstract, both beautiful and communicative. In my own work I try to illuminate and explain these hieroglyphs, which is, I think, an activity quite different from the creating of the hieroglyphs themselves. As the Buddhists would say, the finger pointing at the moon is not the moon.

In this discussion, however, I am more concerned with the issue raised by my first use of the term, *the race for theory*, in relation to its academic hegemony, and possibly of its inappropriateness to the energetic emerging literatures in the world today. The pervasiveness of this academic hegemony is an issue continually spoken about – but usually in hidden groups, lest we, who are disturbed by it, appear ignorant to the reigning academic elite. Among the folk who speak in muted tones are people of color, feminists, radical critics, creative writers, who have struggled for much longer than a decade to make their voices, their various voices, heard, and for whom literature is not an occasion for discourse among critics but is necessary nourishment for their people and one way by which they come to understand their lives better. Cliched though this may be, it bears, I think, repeating here.

The race for theory, with its linguistic jargon, its emphasis on quoting its prophets, its tendency towards "Biblical" exegesis, its refusal even to mention specific works of creative writers, far less contemporary ones, its preoccupations with mechanical analyses of language, graphs, algebraic equations, its gross generalisations about culture, has silenced many of us to the extent that some of us feel we can no longer discuss our own literature, while others have developed intense writing blocks and are puzzled by the incomprehensibility of the language set adrift in literary circles. There have been, in the last year, any number of occasions on which I had to convince literary critics who have pioneered entire new areas of critical inquiry that they did have something to say. Some of us are continually harassed to invent wholesale theories regardless of the complexity of the literature we study. I, for one, am tired of being asked to produce a Black feminist literary theory as if I were a mechanical man. For I believe such theory is prescriptive – it ought to have some relationship to practice. Since I can count on one hand the number of people attempting to be Black feminist literary critics in the world today, I consider it presumptuous of me to invent a theory of how we ought to read. Instead, I think we need to read the works of our writers in our various ways and remain open to the intricacies of the intersection of language, class, race and gender in the literature. And it would help if we share our process, that is, our practice, as much as possible since, finally, our work is a collective endeavour.

The insidious quality of this race for theory is symbolised for me by the very name of the special issue of the journal in which this article originally appeared – *Minority Discourse* – a label which is borrowed from the reigning theory of the day and is untrue to the literatures being produced by our writers, for many of our literatures (certainly Afro-American literature) are central, not minor, and by the titles of many of the articles, which illuminate language as an assault on the other, rather than as possible communication, and play with, or even affirmation of another. I have used the passive voice in my last sentence construction, contrary to the rules of Black English, which like all languages has a particular value system, since I have not placed responsibility on any particular person or group. But that is precisely because this new ideology has become so prevalent among us that it behaves like so many of the other ideologies with which we have had to contend. It appears to have neither head nor centre. At the least, though, we can say that the terms "minority" and "discourse" are located firmly in a western dualistic or "binary" frame which sees the rest of the world as minor, and tries to convince the rest of the world that it is major, usually through force and then through language, even as it claims many of the ideas that we, its "historical" other, have known and spoken about for so long. For many of us have never conceived of ourselves only as somebody's other.

Let me not give the impression that by objecting to the race for theory I ally myself with or agree with the neutral humanists who see literature as pure expression and will not admit to the obvious control of its production, value and distribution by those who have power, who deny, in other words, that literature is, of necessity, *political.* I am studying an entire body of literature that has been denigrated for centuries by such terms as political. For an entire century, Afro-American writers, from Charles Chesnutt in the nineteenth century through

Richard Wright in the 1930s, Imamu Baraka in the 1960s, Alice Walker in the 1970s, have protested the literary hierarchy of dominance which declares when literature is literature, when literature is great, depending on what it thinks is to its advantage. The Black Arts Movement of the 1960s, out of which Black Studies, the Feminist Literary Movement of the 1970s and Women's Studies grew, articulated precisely those issues, which came not from the declarations of the New Western Philosophers but from these groups' reflections on their own lives. That Western scholars have long believed their ideas to be universal has been strongly opposed by many such groups. Some of my colleagues do not see Black critical writers of previous decades as eloquent enough. Clearly they have not read Wright's "Blueprint for Negro Writing," Ellison's *Shadow and Act*, Chesnutt's resignation from being a writer, or Alice Walker's "Search for Zora Neale Hurston". There are two reasons for this general ignorance of what our writer-critics have said. One is that Black writing has been generally ignored in this country. Since we, as Toni Morrison has put it, are seen as a discredited people, it is no surprise, then, that until recently dominant critics in the western world have also been creative writers who have had access to the upper middle-class institutions of education and until recently our writers have decidedly been excluded from these institutions and in fact have often been opposed to them. Because of the academic world's general ignorance about the literature of Black people and of women, whose work too has been discredited, it is not surprising that so many of our critics think that the position arguing that literature is political begins with the New Philosophers. Unfortunately, many of our young critics do not investigate the reasons why that statement – literature is political – is now acceptable when before it was not; nor do we look to our own antecedents for the sophisticated arguments upon which we can build in order to change the tendency of any established western idea to become hegemonic.

For I feel that the new emphasis on literary critical theory is as hegemonic as the world which it attacks. I see the language it creates as one which mystifies rather than clarifies our condition, making it possible for a few people who know that particular language to control the critical scene – that language surfaced, interestingly enough, just when the literature of peoples of color, of Black women, of Latin Americans, of Africans began to move to "the centre." Such words as *centre* and *periphery* are themselves instructive. *Discourse, anon, texts*, words as latinate as the tradition from which they come, are quite familiar to me. Because I went to a Catholic Mission school in the West Indies I must confess that I cannot hear the word "canon" without smelling incense, that the word "text" immediately brings back agonising memories of Biblical exegesis, the "discourse" reeks for me of metaphysics forced down my throat in those courses that traced *world* philosophy from Aristotle through Thomas Aquinas to Heidegger. "Periphery" too is a word I heard throughout my childhood, for if anything was seen as being at the periphery, it was those small Caribbean islands which had neither land mass nor military power. Still I noted how intensely important this periphery was, for US troops were continually invading one island or another if any change in political control even seemed to be occurring. As I lived among folk for whom language was an absolutely necessary way of validating our existence, I was told that the minds of the world lived only in the small continent of Europe. The metaphysical language of the New Philosophy, then, I must admit, is repulsive to me and is one reason why I raced from philosophy to literature, since the latter seemed to me to have the possibilities of rendering the world as large and as complicated as I experienced it, as sensual as I knew it was. In literature I sensed the possibility of the integration of feeling/ knowledge, rather than the split between the abstract and the emotional in which western philosophy inevitably indulged.

Now I am being told that philosophers are the ones who write literature, that authors are dead, irrelevant, mere vessels through which their narratives ooze, that they do not work nor have they the faintest idea what they are doing; rather they produce texts as disembodied as the angels. I am frankly astonished that scholars who call themselves Marxists or post-Marxists could seriously use such metaphysical language even as they attempt to reconstruct the philosophical tradition from which their language comes. And as a student of literature, I am appalled by the sheer ugliness of the language, its lack of clarity, its unnecessarily complicated sentence constructions, its lack of pleasurableness, its alienating quality. It is the kind of writing for which composition teachers would give a freshman a resounding F.

Because I am a curious person, however, I postponed readings of Black women writers I was working on and read some of the prophets of this new literary orientation. These writers did announce their dissatisfaction with some of the cornerstone ideas of their own tradition, a dissatisfaction with which I was born. But in their attempt to change the orientation of western scholarship, they, as usual, concentrated on themselves and were not in the slightest interested in the worlds they had ignored or controlled. Again I was supposed to know them, while they were not at all interested in knowing me. Instead they sought to "deconstruct" the tradition to which they belonged even as they used the same forms, style, language of that tradition, forms which necessarily embody its values. And increasingly as I read them and saw their substitution of their philosophical writings for literary ones, I began to have the uneasy feeling that their folk were not producing any literature worth mentioning. For they always harkened back to the masterpieces of the past, again reifying the very texts they said they were deconstructing. Increasingly, as their way, their terms, their approaches remained central and became the means by which one defined literary critics, many of my own peers who had previously been concentrating on dealing with the other side of the equation, the reclamation and discussion of past and present Third World literatures, were diverted into continually discussing the new literary theory.

From my point of view as a critic of contemporary Afro-American women's writing, this orientation is extremely problematic. In attempting to find the deep structures in the literary tradition, a major preoccupation of the new New Criticism, many of us have become obsessed with the nature of reading itself to the extent that we have stopped writing about literature being written today. Since I am slightly paranoid, it has begun to appear to me that the literature being produced is precisely one of the reasons why this new philosophical-literary-critical theory of relativity is so prominent. In other words, the literature of Blacks, women of South America and Africa, etc., as overtly "political" literature was being pre-empted by a new western concept which proclaimed that reality does not exist, that everything is relative and that every text is silent about something – which indeed it must necessarily be.

There is, of course, much to be learned from exploring how we know what we know, how we read what we read, an exploration which, of necessity, can have no end. But there also has to be a "what," and the "what," when it is even mentioned by the New Philosophers, are texts of the past, primarily western male texts, whose norms are again being transferred onto Third World, female texts as theories of reading proliferate. Inevitably a hierarchy has now developed between what is called theoretical criticism and practical criticism, as mind is deemed superior to matter. I have no quarrel with those who wish to philosophise about how we know what we know. But I do resent the fact that this particular orientation is so privileged and has diverted so many of us from doing the first readings of the literature being written today as well as of past works about which nothing has been written. I note, for example, that there is little work done on Gloria Naylor, that most of Alice Walker's works have not been commented on – despite the rage around *The Color Purple* – that there has yet to be an in-depth study of Frances Harper, the nineteenth-century abolitionist poet and novelist. If our emphasis on theoretical criticism continues, critics of the future may have to reclaim the writers we are now ignoring, that is, if they are even aware these artists exist.

I am particularly perturbed by the movement to exalt theory, as well, because of my own adult history, I was an active member of the Black Arts Movement of the sixties and know how dangerous theory can become. Many today may not be aware of this, but the Black Arts Movement tried to create Black Literary Theory and in doing so became prescriptive. My fear is that when theory is not rooted in practice, it becomes prescriptive, exclusive, elitist.

An example of this prescriptiveness is the approach the Black Arts Movement took towards language. For it, blackness resided in the use of Black talk which they defined as hip urban language. So that when Nikki Giovanni reviewed Paule Marshall's *Chosen Place, Timeless People*, she criticised the novel on the grounds that it was not Black, for the language was too elegant, too white. Blacks, she said, did not speak that ways. Having come from the West Indies where we do some of the time, speak that way, I was amazed by the narrowness of her vision. The emphasis on one way to Black resulted in the works of Southern writers being seen as non-black since the Black talk of Georgia does not sound like the Black talk of Philadelphia. Because the ideologues, like Baraka, come from the urban centres they tended to privilege their way of speaking, thinking, writing, and to condemn other kinds of writing as not being Black enough. Whole areas of the canon were assessed according to the dictum of the Black Arts Nationalist point of view, as in Addison Gayle's *The Way of the New World*, while other works were ignored because they did not fit the scheme of cultural nationalism. Older writers like Ellison and Baldwin were condemned because they saw that the intersection of western and African influences resulted in a new Afro-American culture, a position with which many of the Black Nationalist ideologues disagreed. Writers were told that writing love poems was not being Black. Further examples abound.

It is true that the Black Arts Movements resulted in a necessary and important critique both of previous Afro-American literature and of the white-established literary world. But in attempting to take over power, it, as Ishmael Reed satirises so well in *Mumbo Jumbo*, became much like its opponent, monolithic and downright repressive.

It is this tendency towards the monolithic, monotheistic, etc., which worries me about the race for theory. Constructs like the *centre* and the *periphery* reveal that tendency to want to make the world less complex by organising it according to one principle, to fix it through an idea which is really an ideal. Many of us are particularly sensitive to monolithism since one major element of ideologies of dominance, such as sexism and racism, is to dehumanise people by stereotyping them, by denying them their variousness and complexity. Inevitably, monolithism becomes a metasystem, in which there is a controlling ideal, especially in relation to pleasure. Language as one form of pleasure is immediately restricted, and becomes heavy, abstract, prescriptive, monotonous.

Variety, multiplicity, eroticism are difficult to control. And it may very well be that these are the reasons why writers are often seen *as persona non grata* by political states, whatever form they take, since writers/artists have a tendency to refuse to give up their way of seeing the world and of playing with possibilities; in fact, their very expression relies on that insistence. Perhaps that is why creative literature, even when written by politically reactionary people, can be so freeing, for in having to embody ideas and recreate the world, writers cannot merely produce "one way".

The characteristics of the Black Arts Movement are, I am afraid, being repeated again today, certainly in the other area to which I am especially tuned. In the race for theory, feminists, eager to enter the halls of power, have attempted their own prescriptions. So often have I read books on feminist literary theory that restrict the definition of what *feminist* means and overgeneralize about so much of the world that most women as well as men are excluded. Nor seldom do feminist theorists take into account the complexity of life – that women are of many races and ethnic backgrounds with different histories and cultures and that as a rule women belong to different classes that have different concerns. Seldom do they note these distinctions, because if they did they could not articulate a theory. Often as a way of clearing themselves, they do acknowledge that women of color, for example, do exist, then go on to do what they were going to do anyway, which is to invent a theory that has little relevance for us.

That tendency towards monolithism is precisely how I see the French feminist theorists. They concentrate on the female body as the means to creating a female language, since language, they say, is male and necessarily conceives of woman as other. Clearly many of them have been irritated by the theories of Lacan for whom language is phallic. But suppose there are peoples in the world whose language was invented primarily in relation to women, who after all are the ones who relate to children and teach language. Some Native American languages, for example, use female pronouns when speaking about non-gender specific activity. Who knows who, according to gender, created languages. Further, by positing the body as the source of everything, French feminists return to the old myth that biology determines everything and ignore the fact that gender is a social rather than biological construct (see also Delphy, pp. 383–92 this volume).

I could go on critiquing the positions of French feminists who are themselves more various in their points of view than the label which is used to describe them, but that is not my point. What I am concerned about is the authority this school now has in feminist scholarship – the way it has become *authoritative discourse,* monologic, which occurs precisely because it does have access to the means of promulgating its ideas. The Black Arts Movement was able to do this for a time because of the political movements of the 1960s – so too with the French feminists who could not be inventing "theory" if a space had not been created by the Women's Movement. In both cases, both groups posited a theory that excluded many of the people who made that space possible. Hence one of the reasons for the surge of Afro-American women's writing during the 1970s and its emphasis on sexism in the Black community is precisely that when the ideologues of the 1960s said Black, they meant *Black male.*

I and many of my sisters do not see the world as being so simple. And perhaps that is why we have not rushed to create abstract theories. For we know there are countless women of color, both in America and in the rest of the world to whom our singular ideas would be applied. There is, therefore, a caution we feel about pronouncing Black feminist theory that might be seen as a decisive statement about Third World women. This is not to say we are not theorising. Certainly our literature is an indication of the ways in which our theorizing, of necessity, is based on our multiplicity of experiences.

There is at least one other lesson I learned from the Black Arts Movement. One reason for its monolithic approach had to do with its desire to destroy the power which controlled Black people, but it was a power which many of its ideologues wished to achieve. The nature of our context today is such that an approach which desires power single-mindedly must of necessity become like that which it wished to destroy. Rather than wanting to change the whole model, many of us want to be at the centre. It is this point of view that writers like June Jordan and Audre Lorde continually critique even as they call for empowerment, as they emphasise the fear of difference among us and our need for leaders rather than a reliance on ourselves.

For one must distinguish the desire for power from the need to become empowered – that is, seeing oneself as capable of and having the right to determine one's life. Such empowerment is partially derived from a knowledge of history. The Black Arts Movement did result in the creation of Afro-American Studies as a concept, thus giving it a place in the university where one might engage in the reclamation of Afro-American history and culture and pass it on to others. I am particularly concerned that institutions such as Black Studies and Women's Studies, fought for with such vigour and at some sacrifice, are not often seen as important by many of our Black or women scholars precisely because the old hierarchy of traditional departments is seen as superior to these "marginal" groups. Yet, it is in this context that many others of us are discovering the extent of our complexity, the interrelationships of different areas of knowledge in relation to a distinctly Afro-American or female experience. Rather than having to view our world as subordinate to others, or rather than having to work as if we were hybrids, we can pursue ourselves as subjects.

My major objection to the race for theory, as some readers have probably guessed by now, really hinges on the question, "for whom are we doing what we are doing when we do literary criticism?" It is, I think, the central question today especially for the few of us who have infiltrated the academy enough to be wooed by it. The answer to that question determines what orientation we take in our work, the language we use, the purposes for which it is intended.

I can only speak for myself. But what I write and how I write is done in order to save my own life. And I mean that literally. For me literature is a way of knowing that I am not hallucinating, that whatever I feel/know is. It is an affirmation that sensuality is intelligence, that sensual language is language that makes sense. My response, then, is directed to those who write what I read and those who read what I read – put concretely – to Toni Morrison and to people who read Toni Morrison (among whom I would count few academics). That number is increasing, as is the readership of Walker and Marshall. But in no way is the literature that Morrison, Marshall or Walker create supported by the academic world. Nor given the political context of our society, do I expect that to change soon. For there is no reason, given who controls these institutions, for them to be anything other than threatened by these writers.

My readings do presuppose a need, a desire among folk who like me also want to save their own lives. My concern, then, is a passionate one, for the literature of people who are not in power has always been in danger of extinction of co-optation, not because we do not theorise, but because what we can even imagine, far less who we can reach, is constantly limited by societal structures. For me, literary criticism is promotion as well as understanding, a response to the writer to whom there is often no response, to folk who need the writing as much as they need anything. I know, from literary history, that writing disappears unless there is a response to it. Because I write about writers who are now writing, I hope to help ensure that their tradition has continuity and survives.

So my "method", to use a new "lit.crit." word, is not fixed but relates to what I read and to the historical context of the writers I read and to the many critical activities in which I am engaged, which may or may not involve writing. It is a learning from the language of creative writers, which is one of surprise, so that I might discover what language I might use. For my language is very much based on what I read and how it affects me, that is, on the surprise that comes from reading something that compels you to read differently, as I believe literature does. I, therefore, have no set method, another prerequisite of the new theory, since for me every work suggests a new approach. As risky as that might seem, it is, I believe, what intelligence means – a tuned sensitivity to that which is alive and therefore cannot be known until it is known. Audre Lorde puts it in a far more succinct and sensual way in her essay "Poetry is not a Luxury":

> As they become known to and accepted by us, our feelings and the honest exploration of them become sanctuaries and spawning grounds for the most radical and daring of ideas. They become a safe-house for that difference so necessary to change and the conceptualization of any meaningful action. Right now, I could name at least ten ideas I would have found intolerable or incomprehensible and frightening, except as they came after dreams and poems. This is not idle fantasy, but a disciplined attention to the true meaning of "it feels right to me." We can train ourselves to respect our feelings and to transpose them into a language so they can be shared. And where that language does not yet exist, it is our poetry which helps to fashion it. Poetry is not only dream and vision; it is the skeleton architecture of our lives. It lays the foundations for a future of change, a bridge across our fears of what has never been before (1984, p. 37).

Charlene Spretnak

The Disembodied Worldview of Deconstructive Post-modernism*

What is particularly worrisome about many current expressions of deconstructive post-modernism, especially in analyses of contemporary culture and politics, is the utter glee at citing evidence of violation and cultural dismemberment of all sorts. Many post-modernists' observations about the effects of commodification and mass media are telling (although quite a few of the more extreme conclusions would be justified only if each of us passed our days with a small television set strapped in front of our faces so that mass media constituted our *sole* reality). I find it eerie that one rarely encounters an (apolitical) deconstructive-post-modern analyst who is the least bit wistful over what has been lost. Instead, the attitude is one of triumph at naming the perceived disempowerment of everyone and everything (except the corporations running the mass media, as political post-modernists note) and a "sophisticated" passivity that mocks any attempt to change the situation. A deconstructive-post-modern "advanced" attitude in a recent anthology is typical of the syndrome: "Why then be sad as the body is unplugged from the planet? What is this if not the more ancient philosophical movement of immanence to transcendence as the body is on its way to being exteriorized again?" (Kroker: 1987, p. 3). Indeed, it is the ancient patriarchal dream: transcendence beyond the body.

Obsessive subjectivity has finally folded in on itself until it has devoured the (language-based) sense of self and destroyed the logic of subjectivity altogether. But, of course, there is a subject acting here. It is Man the Autonomous Destroyer, a painfully distorted and alienated caricature of the human embedded in the unfolding universe. The contemporary forms of subjective idealism that assure the individual that nothing outside one's constructing mind has any claim on one are initially experienced as liberating for anyone who has suffered domination. Such idealism and hypersubjectivity are particularly alluring to those most severely damaged by

---

* Excerpt from Charlene Spretnak (1991). *States of Grace: The Recovery of Meaning in the Post-modern Age.*

patriarchal socialization: they who experience all relationships as oppressive. The aggressive surge of denial called for by deconstructionism, however, leads to a flattened valuelessness in which nothing is left but the will to power. The preferences of an individual or a group can then carry the day only through political manipulations and displays of power, control, and forceful domination. Hence some observers conclude that the extreme relativism of deconstructive post-modernism leads to a societal model of ruthless power plays and perhaps even fascism. The causal dynamics underlying such behavior were not invented only twenty-some years ago in Paris. Their long history has its origins in patriarchal culture's brutal and self-destructive divorce from the body – the Earthbody, the female body, the body of the mother. Inculcated perceptions of profound separateness yield alienation, deep-seated rage, and reactive cravings for autonomy and control. In every era their presence seeks lofty philosophical justification.

Denial, even systemically elaborated, cannot lessen our existential dependence on the complex ways of the Earthbody. Now even those elemental processes are besieged, degraded, and unreliable. Tragically, the nihilism implicit in deconstructive post-modernism is simpatico with the larger dynamics of disintegration and loss of meaning in our time: the death of the planetary Grand Subject, the ruin of the majestic ecosphere that gives us life and is our greater body. What is needed is not a lock-step ecocentric "foundationalism", so feared by deconstructionists, but a creative orientation of *attentive and respectful engage-ment* with the natural world, from our own body to the unfolding presence of the entire cosmos. After all, what is human culture but an extension of the dynamic physicality of the planet?

Effects of Deconstructionism on Feminism

Post-modern feminism seeks to protect women from "metanarratives", which, it maintains, are always oppressive to the individual. Toward that end, commonsense warnings that white, middle-class feminists must be careful not to project our experience onto women of color and working-class women have now been transformed into deconstructionist assertions that feminism can be *nothing but* "a politics of difference". (Beyond the realm of theory, of course, commonalities, often quirky and unpredictable, become apparent whenever women of color and white women – whenever persons – actually work together over time on shared goals.) To speak of any commonality among women is to commit the deconstructive-post-modern sin of "essentialism", the "failure" to perceive that every single aspect of human existence is supposedly "socially produced" and determined in particular, localized circumstances about which no generalizations can be made. Hence some white post-modernist feminist academics criticize their African-American peers for speaking of "the African-American experience", which post-modernists judge a false commonality, and they are skeptical of the very concept of gender-based analysis in feminist theory.[1] Even to speak of common dynamics involving women in

---

1. Objections to the deconstructive-post-modern "defense" of the "margin" have come from supposedly marginalized people themselves. See, for example, Barbara Christian (pp. 311–20 this volume).

cont. next page

cultures that are patriarchal is rejected as "totalizing". Some post-modern French feminists are adamant in insisting that naming the political subject of feminism the female sex reproduces the biological essentialism and the binary logic that have relegated women to an inferior role.[2] Their acceptance of the patriarchal formula that "necessarily" ranks the biological female as inferior unfortunately reflects the influence of the post-modern psychoanalyst Jacques Lacan and the legacy of Simone de Beauvoir's assimilation of so much of Sartre's expressed revulsion toward the "immanence" of the female body and his preference for "masculine" transcendence via projects of rationalist consciousness.

That deconstructive post-modernism disallows speaking of commonalities renders much analysis and activist theory impossible, a conservative aspect that has been addressed by a number of political deconstructionist feminists who seek a modified version suitable for activists (Fraser and Nicholson: 1988; Kipnis: 1988; Diamond and Quinby: 1988; Alcoff: 1990). Even more promising is the movement of some deconstructive-post-modern, post-Marxist feminists toward ecofeminism because they have come to appreciate its view of the world "as active subject, not as resource" and its linking of "meaning and bodies", which was inherited from cultural feminism.[3] Certainly the somewhat amazing insistence by some feminists that race and class each have a "material base" that gender lacks can be seen as participation in the patriarchal and post-modern project of "erasure" and denial of the elemental power of the female body. No matter what kinds of "social production" shape gender within a culture, the physicality of the female body with its elemental capabilities (to grow people of either sex from one's flesh, to bleed in rhythm with the moon, to transform food into milk for infants) is a core reality to which culture responds, usually with considerable elaboration, in negative or positive modes.

---

1. *cont. from previous page*
For a critique of gender-skepticism among post-modernists, see Susan Bordo (1990). Bordo critically examines the "recent academic marriage which has brought indigenous feminist concerns over the ethnocentrisms and unconscious racial biases of gender theory into a theoretical alliance with (a highly programmatic appropriation of) the more historicist, politically oriented wing of post-structuralist thought (e.g. Foucault, Lyotard)" (p. 135). Bordo identifies a new feminist "methodologism" emerging from this union that lays claim to an authoritative critical framework that "often implicitly (and mistakenly) supposes that the adoption of a 'correct' theoretical approach makes it possible to avoid ethnocentrism". She also discusses the result of certain feminist appropriations of deconstructionism that are animated by "fantasies" of replacing the "view from nowhere" but arrive only in a "dream of everywhere".
2. See Laura Kipnis (1988, p. 159). Kipnis also notes, "Whereas 'American feminism' is a discourse whose political subject is biological women, 'continental feminism' is a political discourse whose subject is a structural position – variously occupied by the feminine, the body, the Other". Articles by several of the French post-modernist feminists have been gathered in Elaine Marks and Isabelle de Courtivron (1981) and Toril Moi (1987). Also see the special issue on French Feminism of *Signs* (1981). *7* (1).
3. See Donna Haraway (1988, p. 586). Haraway's observation that what must pass for "objectivity" is partial connection between the two selves who are ever in process is *simpatico* not only with ecofeminist attention to connectedness but also with the ancient teachings of Dhamma on the ever-changing "self".

On balance, the work of some deconstructive post-modernists, such as Foucault, has added to the process – which in feminism pre-dates deconstruct-ionism – of revealing the oppressive concepts and socialized behavior that consti-tute modern, patriarchal society, yet the effect of deconstructionism goes far beyond that contribution. When young feminist intellectuals emerge from our decon-influenced colleges intent on "subverting all [feminist] theory", whose purposes are served? When a woman accepts the deconstructionist insistence that she can have no experience of her body/mind that is not mere social construction, has she not been disempowered at a profound level? When women are told by deconstruc-tionists that they cannot refer to *any* commonality among *any* women for purposes of activist analysis, has not feminism been silenced and women atomized? It is a mystery to me why this reinforcing of the patriarchal status quo has been championed by so many women who carry a torch for "liberating", "radical" deconstructive post-modernism. The popularity of its disembodied, hypersubjective world view is not a victory for women.

Denise Thompson

The Self-Contradiction of "Post-modernist" Feminism

The concept of a "post-modernist" feminism is a contradiction in terms because, while feminism is a politics, post-modernism renders its adherents incapable of political commitment. There are a number of reasons for this inability. In this paper, I will be addressing only one of these in detail – post-modernism's inability to challenge structures of domination. While feminism needs to be able to identify domination in general, and male domination in particular, in order to challenge it, post-modernism refuses to identify, and hence cannot contest, relations of domination and subordination.

The term "post-modernism" refers to a vast body of work, not only within the category "post-modernism" itself, but also within the categories of thought which post-modernism sees itself as challenging, i.e. the Enlightenment, "modernity" and western philosophy in general. Since the rigorous examination of such an enormous field is impossible, I will confine my investigation to a number of texts which are explicitly self-identified as feminist and as favourably disposed, although not uncritically, towards post-modernism (or post-structuralism – the terms are inter-changeable for most purposes. But see Huyssen: 1990 for a distinction between them).

The chief problem with "post-modernist" feminism is its inability to name forms of domination, and in particular in a feminist context, to identify male domination as the adversary challenged by feminism. This inability is a result of its refusal to engage with grand structures of oppression, which in turn is a result of its reluctance to engage in what is variously called "grand theory", "grand synthesis", "meta" or "master-narratives". Since there is no identifiable structure of domination within "post-modernist" feminist terms, neither are there any identifiable common interests among women, either to ending male domination however it is manifested wherever women are situated, or to creating forms of mutual recognition and love between and among women.

Prevarications on questions of domination are endemic to post-modernism. The terms "domination" and "power" are endlessly reiterated, but in senses which, at best, contribute nothing to any political enterprise committed to challenging domination, and at worst, actively undermine it. Sometimes the only domination allowed is that of "language", although it is a "language" which occupies the whole terrain of the social (not to mention the real). Either resistance is futile because the phallus is the essential and inescapable definer of the symbolic, and hence, of all meaning and reality (Mitchell and Rose: 1982; Rose: 1989); or the only resistance permitted is incoherence, incomprehensibility, absurdity or madness. (I am referring here to the work of Jacques Derrida, and to arguments about language by Julia Kristeva and Luce Irigaray.) At other times, resistance is futile because domination is so multiple, capillary and mindless. Either resistance is a nothing but a mirror image of its adversary, or there is no adversary at all because power is merely something happening (Foucault: 1976; Foucault: 1978; Foucault: 1980; Morris and Patton: 1979). Somer Brodribb puts it thus: "Foucault's only answer to 'what is power' is 'it moves'" (Brodribb: 1992, p. 46). And Nancy Hartsock points out that, in Foucault's account, "[p]ower is everywhere, and so ultimately nowhere" (Hartsock: 1990, p. 170) "Postmodernist" feminism's obligatory token gestures towards "race, class and gender" remain focused on the categories of the oppressed, and rarely name the ruling class interests involved.

Susan Bordo gives us one reason why "post-modernist" feminism might be reluctant to name male domination, when she refers to "intellectual boredom with stale, old talk about male dominance and female subordination" (Bordo: 1990, p. 151). This remark occurs in a list of suggested reasons why what she calls "feminist gender-scepticism" might be enticed into "operating in the service of the reproduction of white, male knowledge/power". Whether or not she herself is too bored to talk about feminism's central problematic, she does not say, although the context implies that she is. However, boredom is hardly an adequate or appropriate response to the feminist need to keep naming the enemy.

Another reason why "post-modernist" feminism might be reluctant to focus on male domination concerns the risk of characterising women as "victims". Focusing on male domination, so the argument goes, makes men out to be more powerful than they are, and can only make women feel trapped and helpless. But to acknowledge that women are victims of male violence and constraint is not to define women only as victims. Those fearful of confining women to perpetual victimhood seem to have forgotten (or never to have known) the relief of hearing one's oppression named as oppression, rather than merely as a personal, idiosyncratic failing. "The personal is political" means just that. It is a liberation all in itself to have the enemy clearly identified as such. To realise that the fault lies, not in one's flawed self, but in a reality to which one can say "no", is a vital step in the process of extricating oneself from oppressive conditions. Recognising the constraints to which one is subjected is an intrinsic aspect of acknowledging one's own moral agency under oppression (to use Sarah Hoagland's phrase: "Of course, to locate the fault only 'out there' is to become trapped in the other half of the 'internal/external', 'personal/political' dichotomy". [1988]). Moral agency requires an ability to decide not only the scope but also the limits of one's own responsibility, the extent to which one is not responsible as well as the extent to which one is, to what extent one can act as well as the extent to which one cannot. But to refrain from naming victimisation is a failure to name oppression.

The most explicit reason given for post-modernism's reluctance to name the dominators, however, is its denunciation of "meta-narrative". "Post-modernist" feminism sees its primary task as the avoidance of what Jane Flax has called "linear, teleological, hierarchical, holistic, or binary ways of thinking" (Flax: 1990, p. 15). Flax also warns us that:

> Any episteme requires the suppression of discourses that differ with or threaten to undermine the authority of the dominant one. Hence within feminist theories a search for a "defining theme of the whole" or "a feminist standpoint" may require suppressing the important and discomforting voices of persons with experiences unlike our own (1990, p. 28).

Or as Nancy Fraser and Linda J. Nicholson put it:

> Practical imperatives have led some feminists to adopt modes of theorising which resemble the sorts of philosophical meta-narratives rightly criticised by post-modernists . . . [These modes of theorising] are very large social theories – theories of history, society, culture, and psychology – which claim, for example, to identify causes and constitutive features of sexism that operate cross-culturally (1990, pp. 26–7).

Or as another devotee of post-modernism put it:

> Postmodern feminists worry that because feminism purports to be an explanatory theory, it . . . is in danger of trying to provide the explanation for why woman is oppressed or the ten steps all women must take in order to achieve true liberation . . . Although postmodern feminists' refusal to construct one explanatory theory may threaten the unity of the feminist movement, and pose theoretical problems for those feminists hoping to provide us with an overarching explanation and solution for women's oppression, this refusal adds fuel to the feminist fires of plurality, multiplicity and difference (Yeatman: 1989, p. 217).

And again:

> . . . feminist theorists must abandon their own versions of the modernist meta-narratives which have inspired the great general theories of modernity (Yeatman: 1990, p. 290).

These kinds of denunciations are not explicitly used against the postulation of male domination as the central problematic of feminism (although they are used against Marxism). Indeed, for Jane Flax, it is not the feminist *identification* of male domination which constitutes "linear", etc. thinking, but the search for "*a cause or 'root'* of gender relations or, more narrowly, male domination" (p. 28, emphasis added). Presumably, then, feminist theory which did not look for "causes", or which characterised male domination as its own "cause" and raison d'être, would not be denounced in the above terms. Nonetheless, feminism, usually designated radical or "cultural" feminism, is frequently denounced as "essentialist" and "falsely universalising" by other feminists. And the feminism which is so denounced is invariably the feminism which is most explicit in its identification of male domination. (See Thompson: 1991 for a detailed account of such denunciations and the chief target of their attack, "cultural" feminism; also Lienert this volume pp. 155–68.)

Hence, it is the feminist identification of male domination which is dismissed as a "totalising" concept, as a unifying device finessing the problems of differences among women, as yet another "grand synthesis" no different in kind from the "phallologocentric" theories of the modernist, Enlightenment past. But to the extent that male domination is as multifarious and all pervasive as everyday life, and to the extent that "human" existence continues to be defined in terms of the male, feminism cannot afford not to reserve for itself the right in principle to challenge the whole domain, however that is characterised in practice. In that sense, feminism must be "totalising", must lay claims to the entire terrain, must grasp the possibility at least of challenging any and everything. That does not mean that feminism is not therefore multifarious. Indeed, once again, it must be, at least as multifarious as the enemy it is struggling against, and probably more so, as women attempt to create new forms of being or transformed versions of the old. To name the social problem challenged by feminism, "male domination", is not to set up yet one more "master narrative" no different in kind from the old but still current phallocentric ones. Feminism is in no danger of "mastery" for the foreseeable future. It is too threatening, too subversive of the phallocratic status quo, as long, that is, as it is not seduced into an ancillary relationship to the still powerful boys' narratives, a temptation which "post-modernist" feminism has not so far managed to resist. Feminism has no need to limit itself to Foucault's "local theory", or Lyotard's "petits récits", and to drop out of the "grand theory" stakes. Feminism cannot drop out because it has never been in.

It is not as though "post-modernist" feminism never mentions male domination. It does. But the term is used in a curious way, either as a secondary political concern to "gender", "gender relations" or "women", or as one among a number of disparate phenomena none of which has any political priority or significance over any other. (For an example of the latter, see the discussion below of Chris Weedon's treatment of "interests").

For Jane Flax, the political and theoretical priority for feminism is "gender": "The single most important advance in and result of feminist theories and practices is that the existence of gender has been problematized" (Flax: 1990, p. 21). It is this privileging of "gender" that prevents her from recognising male domination as the primary challenge for feminism. She sees "male dominance" as merely one form of "gender relations", and as a hindrance to the adequate investigation of those relations. In a section headed "Male Dominance" (pp. 22–4), she says that the nature of "gender relations" has been "obscured" by the existence of male dominance. In societies where men dominate, she says (implying that there are societies where men do not dominate), men are not seen as a part of "gender relations", and so they are not defined as a "gender". This creates an asymmetry in any account of "gender relations". Whereas what women "are" can be endlessly investigated, what men are is rarely the subject of investigation. So the problem with the male dominance of "gender relations" is not the oppression of women by men, but the fact that what those relations "really are" is obscured from us as long as men dominate. She appears to be unaware that "gender relations" would not pose a problem for feminist political analysis and action if there were no question of male power involved. Neither is she aware of the absurdity of any attempt to find a "really Real" of "gender relations" outside the social relations of male supremacy within which "gender" is currently structured.

The obscurity is not dispersed by Flax's own account of the problems with "gender relations". She tells us that there are "at least three dimensions" to "gender". The first dimension is that "gender" is "a social relationship" and "a form of power . . . [which] affects our theories and practices of justice". But the only social categories she mentions in this context of justice are "race and economic status". Women are not mentioned. Throughout her discussion of the other two dimensions of "gender" – as "a category of thought", and as "a central constituting element in each person's sense of self and . . . of what it means to be a person" – there is no mention of the two sexes, women and men. It is not until the very end of the discussion, when she criticises the idea of "sex roles", that we are given any hint that "gender" might be connected to the existence of two sexes (pp. 25–6). She makes no mention of the fact that feminism's concern with justice involves justice for women, including women located within the dominating hierarchies of race and class, but primarily women as women assigned the subordinate role in the dominating hierarchy of sex. Hence, Flax's insistence on "gender relations" as the central problematic of feminism itself obscures feminism's challenge to male domination.

In their paper, "Social Criticism Without Philosophy", Nancy Fraser and Linda J. Nicholson also mention male domination without giving it central importance in feminist politics (Fraser and Nicholson: 1990). In their criticism of Jean-François Lyotard's *The Postmodern Condition* (1984), Fraser and Nicholson point out the limitations of Lyotard's starting point, Philosophy. "Suppose", they say, that "one began, not with the condition of Philosophy, but with the nature of the social object one wished to criticise. Suppose, further, that one defined that object as the subordination of women to and by men" (p. 26). But instead of leaving the criticism there, with Lyotard's failure to recognise the subordination of women by men (a not unsurprising failure, of course, on the part of any malestream theorist), they go on to identify the chief problem with Lyotard's thesis as a "rejection" of "many of the genres . . . necessary for social criticism". On Fraser's and Nicholson's account, then, the problem with Lyotard's thesis is that it is not multifarious enough to deal with "a phenomenon as pervasive and multifaceted as male dominance". And the problem with male dominance is not basically the subordination of women, but the fact that it is "pervasive and multifaceted". As of course it is. But male dominance could be homogeneous, monolithic, or confined to restricted areas of social life, and still be a problem. The problem with male dominance is male dominance. Finding it a problem needs no extra justification.

Instead of overtly identifying the feminist challenge to male domination as a "master narrative", "post-modernist" feminism accuses that challenge of "essentialism" and "universalism". The charge of "essentialism" is usually levelled against radical feminism, which is in fact the only feminist standpoint which explicitly identifies male domination as the enemy. In the case of Jane Flax, however, the accusation is directed, not towards radical feminism, but towards Marxism and, because of its continuing commitment to a Marxist framework, towards socialist feminism:

> Marxists (including socialist feminists) uncritically apply the concepts Marx should have used to describe a particular form of the production of commodities to all areas of human life at all historical periods . . . Marx and subsequent Marxists replicate rather than deconstruct the capitalist mentality by essentializing what is in fact a product of a particular historical and variable set of social relations (Flax: 1990, p. 154).

But Marx did not apply the concepts he developed to "all areas of human life at all historical periods". On the contrary, the Marxist concepts of "ideology" and "modes of production" point quite clearly to the historical specificity of "life", and to changes in consciousness with changing historical eras. Flax's charge of "essentialism" against Marxism is an oddity amongst "post-modernist" feminists (although not among malestream post-modernist theorists – see Lyotard: 1984), most of whom are still tied to their socialist feminist origins. Chris Weedon, for example, sees (Althusserian) Marxism as an ally in her "post-modernist" feminist enterprise (Weedon: 1987, pp. 27–32). The point to be noted here, however, is that Marxism, like radical feminism, clearly names domination, in the Marxist case, capitalist domination and class relations.

For Chris Weedon, in *Feminist Practice and Poststructuralist Theory* (1987), the problem with so-called "essentialist" theories is their fixity, and hence their inability to deal with change:

> In a separatist move some feminist discourse has sought to offer . . . an alternative version of the truth of femininity [to the patriarchal one] . . . in allying meaning to

true essential non-patriarchal femininity, such discourse inevitably attempts to fix femininity once and for all (1987, p. 99).

This sense of fixity . . . in dominant, liberal-humanist assumptions about subjectivity . . . seems to rule out change (1987, p. 105).

Among the discourses which she identifies as "essentialist" are liberal humanism, radical feminism and sociobiology. Not all of these are "essentialist" in Weedon's terms because they appeal to "biology". Sociobiology does, of course, but the fixity of liberal humanism stems from its commitment to "a conscious, knowing, unified, rational subject" (p. 21), while the fixity of radical feminism relies on its appeal to "a humanist essence of womanhood" (p. 81). According to Weedon, the chief benefit of "a feminist post-structuralist framework" is its ability to evade fixity, and hence its commitment to change:

A post-structuralist feminism . . . committed as it is to the principles of difference and deferral, never fixes meaning once and for all. For post-structuralism femininity and masculinity are constantly in process and subjectivity, which most discourses seek to fix, is constantly subject to dispersal (1987, p. 99).

But Weedon does not ask, much less answer, any of the hard questions about "change", because her framework precludes it. She does not ask why we (whoever we are) need to change, nor what we need to change from, nor what we need to change to and why. Her account valorises change for change's sake, and devalues fixity merely because it is fixed. Although she refers frequently throughout her text to "relations of power", she is indecisive about the nature and locus of domination, about whose interests are maintained and enforced, and whose interests are elided, trivialised or denied. Although she makes frequent references to a concept of "interests", the question of whose interests are involved is not coherently addressed.

For example, in her section, "Language as Discourse" (pp. 35–42), she presents us with a proliferation of "interests", some specific, some so vague as to be meaningless for political purposes, i.e. for the purposes of identifying particular forms of relations of domination and subordination. A sample of those "interests" as they appear sequentially in the text are: "the status quo", "selective interests", "some professionals and social groups", "some groups and individuals", "legal discourses", "interest group", "class, gender and racial interests", "the interests of men in reproducing and legitimizing dominant forms of femininity and masculinity", "particular values and interests", "interest groups like women and Blacks" (Does that exclude Black women?), "the family", "patriarchal familial oppression", "male privilege and domination", etc.

Such a disparate multiplicity may be necessary in the interests of non-fixity. But it is no help at all in identifying either the enemy feminism is opposing or what feminism is struggling for. Neither is it any help in identifying the enemy challenged by class politics, i.e. the capitalist ruling class, nor the enemy challenged by anti-racism, i.e. white supremacy, Anglo cultural hegemony, imperialism, and colonisation and its aftermath. Her mentions of "gender, race and class" are tokenistic because their reference is largely confined to the categories of the subordinated – women, the working-class, Blacks – rather than being directed towards challenging the ruling class interests involved in the maintenance of subordination. Once, she mentions "capitalist, racial and patriarchal interests" (p. 150; oddly enough in a discussion of psychoanalysis), but she does not say what those interests are. And she makes a number of references to "gender power relations", "the interests of men", and "patriarchal power relations", and defines the latter in terms of "power relations in which women's interests are subordinated to the interests of men" (p. 2). But the political import of these references is lost in a welter of vague, undefined and unlocated concepts like "power", "interests", "social groups", "social relations", "social and historical specificity", "historical process and change", etc.

"Post-modernist" feminism's reluctance to name domination, and to specify the nature and identity of the dominators, forces it unwittingly into positions which it does not want to adopt. On the one hand, "post-modernist" feminism is explicit in its resistance to the dominations of "race, class and gender" (as is feminism in general). On the other hand, by locating the political and theoretical problematic in invidious and hierarchical distinctions between women, "post-modernist" feminism reproduces the same paternalistic and patronising attitudes it is supposedly challenging.

One example of this unwitting reproduction of elitism is Linda J. Nicholson's argument confining "feminist theory" to the privileged space of the academy. The first sentence of the Introduction to *Feminism/Postmodernism* reads: "From the late 1960s to the mid-1980s, feminist theory exhibited a recurrent pattern: Its analyses tended to reflect the viewpoints of white, middle-class women of North America and western Europe" (Nicholson: 1990, p. 1). If the feminist theory referred to here is confined to what is published and what comes out of academic institutions, then the implication is that feminists who have no access to publishing or to academic institutions are not doing feminist theory. But feminists are theorising wherever we are situated. Some of us may be doing it more rigorously, more consistently, more thoroughly, or with more public recognition, than others. But all of us are doing it, because feminism entails a theoretical approach to the world, a generalising from experience, an explaining of problems by generalising about the way the world is. We theorise when we read, engaging with the texts, arguing with them, working out what they mean. We theorise in conversations, discussing and debating with each other, clarifying agreements and disagreements. We theorise in response to day to day problems and the innumerable examples of male supremacist values, practices and meanings which surround us. To assert that it is predominantly "white, middle-class" women who do feminist theory is an elitist exclusion which denies feminism's origins in the lived experiences of women. Indeed, in the light of the problems with academic feminist theorising – its obscurity and hence, elitism, its ancillary status in relation to malestream theory, and, most important of all, its inability to adequately identify and locate male domination – it could be argued that academic feminist theory is less feminist in its commitment than the theorising of women struggling to make sense of their own lives.

Another example can be found in the following advice by Susan Bordo, in her paper "Feminism, Post-modernism and Gender Scepticism":

> ... the agents of critical insight into the biases of gender theory [i.e. of feminism] were those excluded and marginalized: women of color, lesbians, and others who found their history and culture ignored in the prevailing [feminist] discussions of gender ... as new narratives began to be produced, telling the story of the diversity of women's experiences, the chief imperative was to *listen*, to become aware of one's biases, prejudices, and ignorance, to stretch the borders of what Minnie Bruce Pratt calls "the narrow circle of the self". For academics, this required, too, that we stretch the established borders of required curriculum [etc.] ... all ideas ... are condemned to be haunted by a voice from the margins ... awakening us to what has been excluded, effaced, damaged (1990, p. 138 – emphasis in the original).

To whom is this advice being given? Obviously to those who are in the privileged position of not having to listen, and who need to be reminded of their duties and obligations. Obviously, too, it is not advice for "the excluded and marginalised", who are once again excluded and marginalised from the category of those being addressed. So the "excluded" are not "us", and neither are "we" among the "excluded". Who, then, are "we"? Partly, "we" are academics, although not "women of colour", not "lesbians", and not "others".[1] Whoever and whatever else "we" are, "we" are among the privileged who can magnanimously bestow or withhold "our" favours, bound by a noblesse oblige graciously to turn "our" attention to those less favourably situated than "our" own advantaged selves. Such an elitist position sits uncomfortably within a feminism committed to challenging those very attitudes.

It also sits uncomfortably within a feminism committed to challenging the exclusion, effacing and damaging of women under conditions of male supremacy, of *all* women including the relatively privileged. If we take seriously the feminist insight that the personal is political, we will not be tempted to turn away from our own damage and effacement. If we take seriously the feminist identi-

---

1. This inclusion of "lesbians" as just one category among the plurality of categories of women, neatly depoliticises a lesbianism which was all politics in the early days of "second wave" feminism (and still is in the embattled enclaves of radical feminism). Lesbians are not simply one kind of woman, but women who have said "no" to heterosexuality in the interests of creating loving relationships among women. In that sense, lesbianism, unlike class, race, ethnicity, etc., is relevant to all women because any woman can say "no" to heterosexuality and love women.

fication of male domination as the main enemy, we will not be tempted to reinforce hateful hierarchies between women. And if we take seriously the feminist project of creating connections of love and identification among women, we will not be tempted to ignore the invidious distinctions of race, class, etc., which do exist, and which must be abolished if women are to claim a human status uncontaminated by male supremacist interests and values.

The tendency on the part of "post-modernist" feminism to slide unknowingly into assertions which, in its own terms, it does not want to make, is nowhere more evident than in the usage of that central defining concept of "post-modernist" feminism: "essentialism". Although "post-modernist" feminism explicitly rejects "essentialism", and indeed chiefly defines itself through that rejection, "essentialism" nevertheless re-emerges within "post-modernist" feminism's own ranks, erupting very like a "return of the repressed", in the postmodernist accusations of "essentialism" levelled against radical feminist texts.[2]

"Essentialism" is the nemesis of "post-modernist" feminism. It is its chief target of attack, and yet the critique of "essentialism" relies on the very framework post-modernism is at such pains to reject. The meaning of "essentialism" depends on a master narrative of truth. "Essentialism" is to be avoided because it is false, and it is judged to be false from a position which is outside all positions, on criteria which would be everywhere and always the same. Its falsity needs no justification. No specific cultural and historical context, no particular political interests, no identifiable position of the speaker, is appealed to in order to demonstrate the falsity of "essentialism". "Biology" does not determine "society" – full stop. This is asserted as a self-evident fact which anyone can know. Such knowledge would not vary according to the knower's sex ("gender"), race or class – to reiterate the three great loci of oppression. It is a knowledge which sits outside all positions, objective, disinterested, disengaged.

At the same time, there is also usually an implicitly moral and political justification given for the post-modernist dismissal of "essentialism" – the criterion of historical change. This criterion is moral in the sense that it is assumed, although never overtly stated, that certain aspects of present conditions, are bad and must be changed for the better. And it is political in the sense that historical change would require the challenging of current relations of power. But this moral and political justification for the falsity of "essentialism" is subsidiary to the primary one – the appeal to the "truth" of the non-determination of history by "biology" rests in the first place on the transparent rightness of the assertion. On this criterion of "change", it must not be true that "biology" determines history, because that would

<hr>

2. For a detailed treatment of accusations of "essentialism" and "biologism" levelled against certain radical feminist writings, and the unfounded nature of those accusations, see: Thompson (1991, chapter 10). At the time I was writing this book, the mid-1980s, the "essentialism" accusations emanated from socialist feminism. The locus has now shifted to "postmodernist" feminism, as have many of those individual theorists who previously identified as socialist feminists.

mean that present historical conditions could not be changed. However, questions of why those conditions might need to be changed, what is wrong with them, what is to be abolished, what retained and what transformed, in whose interests and against the interests of whom are the changes to be effected, are rarely addressed. And they never are addressed adequately because post-modernism's commitment to undecidability debars it from explicitly and unequivocally identifying the location of domination.

I would not want it to be assumed that, in this argument against the "essentialism" accusation, I am asserting that "biology" does in fact influence history. All I am asserting is that whether it does or not is irrelevant. Feminism is a politics and a morality, and not a natural science like biology (to the extent, that is, that the "biology" alluded to in the "essentialism" accusation is the natural science, and not just a trigger word to elicit a knee-jerk reaction of contemptuous dismissal on the part of the audience). As a consequence, all the questions addressed by feminism are moral and political ones, questions of what ought and ought not to be so, and questions about the ways in which male power ensures that male interests prevail and female interests are excluded, trivialised or co-opted, and what is to be done about that in specific cases. Empirical facts are always important in a political enterprise, either to substantiate an argument or to demolish an antagonist. (And those facts must be true if they are to be useful as substantiation or demolition). But feminism is not an empirical enterprise per se, uncovering facts, biological or otherwise. Feminism is a politics devoted to the cause of Women's Liberation whatever the facts. And given that feminist politics takes place within a social order determined by phallocratic reality, the "facts" will frequently be against us anyway.

An example of the dilemma of post-modernism's commitment to a truth-telling position outside all positions, is to be found in Jane Flax's book, *Thinking Fragments* (1990). Although Flax sees her book as a "conversation" between post-modernism, feminism and psychoanalysis, her primary and preferred standpoint is post-modernist rather than feminist or psychoanalytic. Although she has criticisms of post-modernism from both feminist and psychoanalytic perspective's, the one she falls back on in the last analysis is post-modernism – she refers to herself as "a post-modernist theorist" (rather than a feminist or a psychoanalyst), and characterises the book as her "attempt to find a post-modern voice" (p. 4).

She sees her project as a refusal "to synthesize ... conflict and irresolvable differences ... into a unitary, uni-vocal whole", and as an attempt to "provide more or less space for a variety of voices" (p. 4). And yet, she herself gives priority to the post-modernist "voice". True, this is a "voice" which speaks from no one ethical and political position, and hence a paradox in that it is a position which explicitly defines itself as no position at all. But although Flax admits to "feelings of unease" about "being without a secure ground or point of reference" (p. 5), she does not appear to be aware of the full extent of the paradox entailed by the enterprise she is engaged upon. Without a speaking position, the speaker represents herself as speaking from a position outside all positions, i.e. from a universal position appealing to a "truth" unlocatable in any terms other than its own self-evidence. Flax does locate herself variously as "therapist, philosopher, feminist, and political theorist" (p. 3), and "white, female, materially comfortable, . . . citizen of a rich and powerful First World country, . . . teacher of political theory in a predominantly Black university, writer, and mother" (p. 43). She also locates herself as a participant in, variously, "contemporary western thought", "western culture", "philosophy", "contemporary social transformations", etc. Yet none of these frameworks identifies the moral and political location of her own account, the values she espouses and those she rejects, the relations of domination she intends to challenge. Indeed, in identifying her account as an aspect of "contemporary western thought", etc., she inadvertently aligns herself with the dominators. Despite her expressed intention not "to speak as a disembodied, impersonal truth teller or critic" (p. 43), that is exactly what she does.

Another example of a contradiction post-modernism falls into as a result of its commitment to anti-"essentialism" appears in a paper by Linda Alcoff, "Cultural Feminism Vs Post-structuralism: The Identity Crisis in Feminist Theory" (Alcoff: 1988). Alcoff criticises what she calls "cultural" feminism for its "essentialism", and "post-structuralism" for its "nominalism". "Nominalism" she defines as "the idea that the category "woman" is a fiction and that feminist efforts must be directed toward dismantling this fiction" (p. 417). The reason why "the category of 'woman' is regarded as 'a fiction' within a post-structuralist framework is because the category 'woman' is constructed via social discourse" (p. 419). Such a position is worrisome for feminism, she argues, because (among other reasons):

> If gender is simply a social construct, the need and even the possibility of a feminist politics becomes immediately problematic. What can we demand in the name of women if "women" do not exist and demands in their name simply reinforce the myth that they do? . . . For the post-structuralist, race, class, and gender are constructs and, therefore, incapable of decisively validating conceptions of justice and truth because underneath there lies no natural core to build on or liberate or maximise (1988, pp. 420–1).

Both in her identification of "essentialism" within "cultural" feminist ranks, and in her critique of the "nominalism" of post-structuralism, it is Alcoff's own commitment to "essentialism" which shows through. In the case of "cultural" feminism, specifically the work of Mary Daly and Adrienne Rich, Alcoff sees "essentialism" where none exists. She finds it, not because it is in the work she cites, but because her own viewpoint is so intrinsically tied up with "essentialism". She sees "essentialism" because she wants to see it, not because it is there. In the case of post-structuralism, specifically the work of Derrida, Foucault and Kristeva, she is justifiably worried about the political implications of scepticism about the category of women. But her response at least partly reproduces the very problem she purported to discover in the work of Daly and Rich. Why does the assertion that what women "are" is socially constructed (and, not incidentally, men too) entail the assertion that women do not exist? (Do men not exist either?) If women do not exist in "society", where then do they exist? Her conclusion is that women exist as a multiplicity of "identities". But what are those "identities" if they are not "social constructs" like the general category "women" itself? Although she clearly eschews a "natural core", her account nonetheless leaves us with no other alternative. Hence, the "essentialism" which formed the ground of Alcoff's complaint against "cultural" feminism returned with a vengeance in her criticism of post-structuralism, and in her postulation of "identity politics" as the feminist way forward.[3]

Although in this paper I have concentrated on "post-modernist" feminism's refusal to name domination through its eschewal of "master narratives", and some of the contradictions it falls into as a consequence, there are a number of other reasons why "post-modernist" feminism is incapable of political engagement. With its anti-humanism, "post-modernist" feminism is unable to make an explicit commitment to an ethical vision of a human condition unfettered by hierarchies of domination. With its rejection of "truth", it is incapable of distinguishing truth from lies, deceptions and distortions. With its "anti-moralism", libertarianism and "non-judgementalism", it is able neither to make its own values explicit, nor to oppose the male supremacist values which give meaning and reality to the oppression of women. Hence it is unable to acknowledge and condemn the evils of domination, to decide between right and wrong, or to commit itself to the cause of justice for women. Nonetheless, feminism, even one coupled with the modifier "post-modernist", requires judgement. Feminism is a political and moral[4] commitment. Post-modernism is antithetical to political and ethical engagement. To place them

3. Alcoff's chief concern in this paper is the question of individual agency. She is concerned that feminism not embrace a theory which disallows the possibility of action by individuals to change oppressive circumstances. This concern is clearly spelled out in her final section, on "Positionality". However, too often throughout the paper, it is secondary to the conundrum of the category of women, and the wrongness of "essentialism" and "nominalism", all of which are problems in themselves, and not because of their deterministic implications.

4. I use the terms "ethical" and "moral" interchangeably, as synonyms. Both refer to questions of value, to judgements of what ought and what ought not to be the case, to what we are for and what we are against in the process of creating the good and challenging the bad in our own lives. "Ethics" and "ethical" is the preferred term in radical lesbian feminist writings, (e.g. Hoagland, 1988, and the journal *Lesbian Ethics*), while the term "moral" is usually reserved for the moralism of the male supremacist Right. But I want to retain the term "moral" for our own purposes, because it is a word in common usage, unlike "ethics" which has a more esoteric ring to it. It is true that the common usage has implications of moral imposition and invidious exclusion. This is especially the case for lesbians who have many experiences of being labelled "bad women". Nonetheless, the making of moral judgements is not a prerogative of the right wing. To substitute "ethics" for "morality" within a feminist context implies that only the Right is "moral". But feminists are moral beings with a standpoint from which we judge the moralism of the Right as immoral because of its functions in controlling women in the interests of male supremacy.

together in the same substantive phrase is a contradiction in terms. As Somer Brodribb succinctly put it: "mostly, deconstruction means never having to say you're wrong. Or a feminist" (Brodribb: 1992, p. 9).

The dilemma of "post-modernist" feminism is compounded by the male supremacist nature of the master texts cited as the "seminal" works of the post-modern canon, (Braidotti: 1991, pp. 132–46;[5] Brodribb: 1992) works whose authors authoritatively deny their own authority, and hence their own responsibility as agents within the privileged locations where those works are produced. As well, texts identified as "post-modern" are frequently characterised by a cryptic inscrutability which demands investments of time and energy unjustifiable in feminist terms. Post-modernism is committed to epistemological indeterminacy, and is avowedly resistant to definitional consistency in the name of a challenge to "the western intellectual tradition". It insists on the inherently shifting nature, and hence undecidability, of meaning. and rejects outright the logic of assertion and the possibility of truth (and falsity). As a consequence, it is often impossible to pin its assertions down long enough to decide on their meaning, much less their truth or falsity and the values being espoused or rejected. Within post-modernist terms, the question of "what is wrong?" is excluded a priori.

It is for all these reasons that I have included "post-modernist" within quotation marks when it is coupled with feminism. But because the contradictions are not readily apparent, and because "post-modernist" feminism occupies a hegemonic place in the domain of academic feminist theory, there is a great deal of work still to be done to expose the contradictions.[6]

---

5. Although Braidotti has a quite devastating critique of the work of Foucault, Deleuze and Derrida, she nevertheless spends an inordinate amount of time, space and energy on a detailed exegesis of their writings. Not only does the lengthy exegesis make no reference to her eventual critique, the critique itself – that the "crisis in Western subjectivity" is a crisis of masculinity – renders such an exegesis irrelevant in feminist terms.

6. For two recent works exposing the contradiction, see: Modleski (1991); Brodribb (1992). Both of these authors are concerned about the ways in which postmodernism permits a male take over of feminism, because of its scepticism, in the name of feminism, towards the category "women". If it cannot be decided who belongs to the category of "women", then nobody does. And if there are no "women", then feminism has no identifiable constituency and anyone can join in. As I argue in this paper, however, the deeper problem is the post-modernist refusal to acknowledge male domination, and the still pervasive tendency for men to dominate whatever terrain they occupy.

Katja Mikhailovich

Post-modernism and its "Contribution" to Ending Violence Against Women

> *... be ever mindful of the hundreds of women who may never see their children again because ... after taking as much abuse as they could ... they've protected themselves by killing their husbands and are now serving prison terms.*
>
> *And don't forget the countless women who have died at their own hands, rather than live in fear of death at the hands of their spouse.*
>
> *Also keep in mind the endless women going in and out of mental institutions because they just can't deal with the reality of having an abusive husband so they relinquish their rights to reality.*
>
> Susan Schechter (1982: p. 53)

For three years I had the luxury of devoting my time to the scholarly pursuit of studying for a PhD. I see this time as somewhat privileged, as prior to this I worked in refuges for homeless young people, rape crisis and incest centres and refuges for women escaping domestic violence. Returning to full-time study seemed like a momentary reprieve from a hidden war zone in which women and children were the main casualties. I had come to this work through my own experiences of male violence and became part of the Women's Movement and feminism because they offered me the most compelling and meaningful understandings of what had happened in my life, and to those women and children with whom I work.

Whilst being involved with these areas of service delivery, I learnt a great deal about working collectively with women. In particular, I learnt to value and trust personal experience and at a more general level, to see my experience in terms of a broader feminist politic. In addition to this, I had the chance to do a great deal of listening and talking and I began to read, a real luxury. I read books about feminism and specifically radical feminism. These books and articles gave me a framework within which to make sense of male violence against women. Through them I began to question, challenge and be critical of the misconceptions, myths and false-truth claims made about women and the nature of violence in our lives. And because I understood radical feminism to be inextricably linked to action, this required a commitment to action for change – change to the inequitable or oppressive conditions in many women's and children's lives, and a change to all structures and conditions of injustice across class, race or gender.

I began to see myself as part of a collective group called "women". This did not mean that we always agreed, that we were all the same, or that we didn't sometimes argue bitterly about our differences. I certainly came to recognise and appreciate the strengths of our diversity. However, it did mean on some level, over some issues, we could come together to find solidarity and strength. When the issue was male violence against women, and in particular rape, we came together in large numbers. If not literally, then we found solidarity through women's writing, and it was radical feminist writing that spoke most powerfully to me about violence against women. In the writings of Susan Brownmiller (*Against Our Will*, 1975), Kathleen Barry (*Female Sexual Slavery*, 1979), Mary Daly (*Gyn/Ecology*, 1978/1979), Susan Griffin (*Pornography and Silence*, 1981), I found feminists theorising and naming male violence against women. In the work of Elizabeth Ward (*Father-Daughter Rape*, 1983), Jocelynne A. Scutt (*Even in the Best of Homes*, 1983), and Elizabeth A. Stanko (*Intimate Intrusions*, 1985) I found accounts of women's experiences of violence, rather than stories of violence disguised as excuses to protect men who were violent. Andrea Dworkin (*Letters from a War Zone*, 1988), Catharine A. MacKinnon ("Pornography: Not a Moral Issue", 1989b), Pauline Bart ("Rape as a Paradigm of Sexism in Society: Victimisation and its Discontents", 1989) and Marilyn French (*War Against Women*, 1992) continued to elaborate and develop the broader social and political understandings about violence in women's lives, without losing the reality of women's everyday experience. These were a few of the radical feminist texts, which were significant in developing my understandings of violence against women.

After years of working with women and children who had been subjected to violence and of being involved in political action devoted to seeking change, I needed time to reflect on those experiences and to submerge myself in theory. I hoped to explore new strategies and actions, and perhaps to find different ways to conceptualise and understand the problems faced by women opposing male violence. Postgraduate study offered just such an opportunity, but it was not as straight forward as I expected. During my undergraduate degree in Health Education, I had been introduced to a range of post-modern theories. These had certainly *captured* my attention and I embarked upon a study that would give me the opportunity to examine how feminist post-modern theory could assist in the conceptualisation of violence against women. Specifically, my study considered the ways in which women have been constituted as "victims" of male violence this century, and the implications for women's identity. I wanted to explore the links between post—modern theory and practice and was particularly interested in strategies and practices which might emerge that could make a change in this area. After three years of searching, I have to say I came up with very little. Not only do I no longer wish to devote my time or energy to the post-modern pursuit, I have grave concerns about its usefulness as a tool for feminism, particularly for those concerned with violence against women. It is these concerns that are the focus of my discussion here.

In Pursuit of the Post-modern

In order to understand something about this phenomenon called post-modernism, and before we can evaluate its contribution or value to a field, it is helpful to know what post-modernism claims to be. Although this question is itself squarely grounded in modernity, as it attempts to ground meaning to a concrete knowable, perhaps even universal meaning, this is where I began.

I turned to texts by authors contributing to post-modern theory revered within certain academic circles, including Julia Kristeva, Jacques Derrida, Luce Irigaray, Jacques Lacan, Hélène Cixous and Michel Foucault. I discovered that their works had been influenced by authors such as Sigmund Freud, Friedrich Nietzsche, Louis Althusser, Martin Heidegger and Ferdinand de Saussure, and I found myself taken deeper and deeper into a post-modern labyrinth. I attempted to read these primary sources but found them convoluted and vague in their applicability to my area of interest. I soon turned to any interpretations of these *classics* that could help me negotiate my way through the texts. (Unfortunately my first response, and the response of many women I have talked with since, was to doubt my own intellect and ability to make meaning of these texts. Fortunately, I abandoned this lapse of reasoning before too much damage was done.) It was not that I was "theory shy", but that I failed to see why concepts should not be conveyed with simplicity and clarity. Ideas that claim to be enlightening or liberatory surely ought to be made available to the greatest possible range of readers. It perturbed me somewhat, to read that years later Foucault had remarked, "What is post-modernism? I'm not up to date" (Brodribb: 1992, p. ix). Rosenau (1992, p. 17) suggests "the term post-modern is employed so broadly that it seems to apply to everything and nothing all at once". On the basis of my experience I would suggest that confusion is to be expected when engaging with post-modernism. It could even be argued that post-modernism deliberately aims to throw everything into confusion, using a particularly obfuscatory style.

According to Rosenau (1992, p. 178) extreme post-modernists are dubious about the possibility of communicating altogether, and therefore see little reason to communicate exactly what they mean. Ambiguous presentations which invite an infinity of interpretations are seen as an asset from the post-modern point of view, as is jargon, which is supposedly interesting in itself. How long we subject students, friends or ourselves to this confusion is of pressing concern to me. I have not been able to share these texts with my sisters within women's services. As far as I am aware, these texts have not found their way onto the library shelves of rape crisis centres or refuges. However, this is not to say that women are not exploring in similar ways to myself, how to use these ideas to empower women's lives outside of academia.

In trying to negotiate my way through this post-modern maze, I was relieved to find feminist interpretations of post-modern thought. For example, Irene Diamond and Lee Quinby's *Feminism and Foucault* (1988), Chris Weedon's *Feminist Practice and Postructuralist Theory* (1987), Elizabeth Grosz' Contemporary Theories of Power and Subjectivity (1990a), Allison Jaggar and Susan Bordo's *Gender/Body/Knowledge* (1989), Linda Nicholson's *Feminism/Postmodernism (1990)*, or Judith Butler's *Gender Trouble* (1990), offered some very interesting accounts of post-modern thought and theory within a feminist context. Some of these writers focussed their work upon specific issues such as sexuality or the body, others engage theoretically with notions of power and knowledge, also significant in radical feminist theorising. For some time post-modern feminist writings sustained my interest, particularly texts concerned with notions of power. However, this is not to say these texts were any more accessible than non-feminist post-modern writing, and my friends and colleagues rightly criticised these texts for their dense, elitist and incomprehensible jargon. Students and friends would tell me that it left their heads in a spin; or that they threw it across the room in frustration, or gave up. The experience was disempowering or silencing. One student commented to me that reading the mass of post-modern masculine discourse was like *forced oral sex.* I could no longer continue to dismiss my own and others discontent and sometimes pain. This was not a theory evolving from women's everyday lives and experiences in all its diversity, but an academic intellectualising that can only be described as hegemonic. Radical feminism can be distinguished by its attempts to create theory from women's experiences, whilst I have found that post-modern feminism appears to be distinguished by its separation and distance from those without access to a limited sphere of formal education. This is not to say that radical feminist writings speak for all women, rather that they allow for women to write of their specific experiences in the world as they know it.

Post-modern Feminism and Violence Against Women

I spent years reading post-modern texts seeking alternative interpretations and conceptualisations of male violence against women, which would hopefully generate liberatory practices and strategies. In order to do this I spent months at a time considering critical ideas within post-modern thought. For example, deconstruction is a primary post-modern method of analysis. I spent considerable time questioning whether deconstruction inevitably leads to relativism or nihilism (basically the end point of which is, nothing exists, nothing really matters, and anything goes), and if not, then when, and where do we stop deconstructing? This type of questioning has led to a debate within feminism about whether categories such as "woman", "gender", or "oppression" can be shown to exist, let alone survive. Do we also begin to contest meaning within the context of interpersonal violence? In fact, the contestation of women's experience of rape and the male perceptions of the sexual act, have long been played out in courts of law and were part of the feminist agenda well before the rhetoric of post-modernism. Given that within a post-modern world truth no longer exists, how then can we argue for a validation of women's experiences of violence? This is not to say that feminists have ignored issues concerning patriarchal truth claims. Challenging *truths* is not new to feminism. Radical feminists have contested and resisted the dominant patriarchal meanings given to these experiences historically, through the process of re-naming and re-creating the stories and meanings given to women's experiences of rape, incest and domestic violence.

Similarly, the notion of the human subject or the self is significant within post-modern theory, and is particularly pertinent to women subjected to male violence. To post-modernists the subject (human being, individual, person) is fictitious, or a mere construction (Rosenau: 1992, p. 42). Carvetta describes the subject as "a mask, a role, a victim, at worst an ideological construct", whilst Flax argues that the self is only a "position in language, a mere effect of discourse" (cited in Rosenau: 1992, pp. 42–3). Are we all merely linguistic constructs located within a set of cultural and historically specific discourses, and if so, how do we go about transforming the self, at the level of the individual? Is it by having privileged access to the production of discourse alone? This seems a dubious and somewhat sinister idea. Need I remind you of who has had control of the production of meaning historically? Put simply, it has been a male generational struggle between older men with younger men over the ownership of knowledge. Post-modernism as a theory rests firmly on the foundation of a long line of patriarchal practice. How productive is it for women to philosophically dissolve the self in a culture in which we are continually being annihilated physically, sexually, emotionally and spiritually? Violence has as its consequence the subordination, conquest and ultimately the extermination of the *self*. Currently, the discourse about healing from violence is saturated with concepts such as gaining a sense of self, reclaiming the self, building self-esteem, or trusting the self, with the aim of empowering women. Whether or not the concept of self should, or can be shown to exist becomes irrelevant, when the consequence for thousands of women survivors of violence, embarking either collectively or individually, on a journey of "self affirmation" is proving useful. We can hardly afford to deconstruct the very categories by which we have made meaning, without offering a viable vision of the future.

Can any of us afford a dialogue of *disconnection, discontinuity or fragmentation* and the erasure of words like oppression, exploitation and domination? In the post-modern project these terms are described as outmoded. I would also question for whom is post-modernism a *politics of difference*.[1] Could it be that

---

1. The phrase "politics of difference" in the post-modern context cannot be understood completely outside of its French origins. In the writings of French post-modernists the use of *differend* and *differance* do not adequately translate into the English meaning of difference. For example Rosenau (1992, p. xi) uses Lyotard's concept of differend as "*difference* in the sense of dispute, conflict or disagreement about the meaning of language"; and Derrida's definition of differance as "a structuring principle that suggests definition rests not on the entity itself but in its positive and negative references to other texts. Meaning changes over time, and ultimately the attribution of meaning is put off, postponed, deferred, forever".

white, middle-class privilege has finally discovered *difference* and it now needs to create a language within which this can be expressed; a language which is exclusive to a group with access to a particular level of education? Difference is not a discovery of post-modernism. Women of colour have spoken of differences with White, middle-class, heterosexual, First World feminists long before post-modernism became fashionable. The expression of difference has been made painfully clear to me through listening to Aboriginal women's experiences in white feminist collectives, or to women's accounts of violence at the hands of fathers and husbands. Equally so are men's accounts of being provoked or their stories of women "asking for it", or of women being to blame for violence perpetrated against them. How useful is it for women in this context to argue that "there is no truth". It takes more than an intellectual idea to convince a rapist, the judiciary, and a misogynistic and racist culture that there is more than one view. In a world where inequalities of power exist across race, class, gender, age, and sexuality, we should proceed cautiously with the heralding of the era of "multiplicities". We must be at least aware of the potential consequences for women. It is primarily from a position of privilege and power that one can discover difference, or at least allow difference to be articulated. Difference is both a part of the texture of lived experience, as well as the basis of unity and connection. Here, I am asserting that White male western discourse can no longer withstand the critiques made against it, and must now find a way to talk about power, injustice and oppression without losing control of that discourse. What a wonderful strategy to obliterate the accumulated knowledge and strength gained by social movements opposing oppression, to divert energy and to make the most significant question between us; whether we can claim anything at all by calling ourselves "Woman", "Black", "Lesbian", or any other category signifying unity and alliance.

Generally post-modernism sits most comfortably in the realm of philosophy, within which there exists a long standing debate about whether philosophy has a practice. This theory emerges from the practice of intellectualising or thinking, without the necessity to include experience or intuition. Although post-modernism is said to challenge a whole epoch or paradigm for making sense of the world (known as the Enlightenment Project of Modernity), it nonetheless replaces this paradigm with one, no less masculinist than its predecessor. Whether it be through quantum physics, eastern philosophies or post-modern deconstruction, the voice of masculine discourse continues to occupy this new territory. It is primarily the voices of men that create the metaphors for meaning that are given space in post-modern discourse. Even in this *epoch of change*, the dominant words and ideas that create the meanings by which we make sense of the world, come from a masculine discourse. In both the modern and post-modern era it is primarily men who make the metaphors for meaning. For example James Jean replaced the image of the world as a machine in saying, "the universe begins to look more like a great thought than a great machine" (cited in Capra: 1982, p. 76).

Friedrich Nietzsche said:

> ... there are many kinds of "truths," and consequently there is no truth ... "Truth" is therefore not something there, that might be found or discovered, but something that must be created (1990, p. 55).

The Buddha thousands of years previously said:

> We are what we think. All that we are, arises from our thoughts. With our thoughts we make our world.

Notwithstanding the potential for liberation to be found in such ideas, history has shown us that good ideas alone do not make a significant difference to the oppressed, the dispossessed or suffering. To work for change in the lives of women who have experienced violence and to decrease the use of violence against women in the future, I embrace the words and meanings arising from women's experiences. I will continue to create and work with radical feminist theory that names the violence committed against us, and seeks to change the structures that perpetuate it. As Elizabeth Ward states in *Father – Daughter Rape*:

> In the development of the feminist movement, women have seized the power of naming. This is a revolutionary power because in naming (describing) what is done to us (and inevitably to children and men as well), we are also naming what must change. The act of naming creates a new world view. The power of naming resides in the fact that we name what we see from the basis of our own experience: within and outside patriarchal culture, simultaneously (1984, p. 212).

I believe a good measure to apply to theories, and specifically post-modern theory, is to ask the following questions: Whose interests do they serve; do they have a liberatory purpose and who will benefit from them; how useful are they and to whom, and what direct actions and strategies emerge from these theories? Then we will see the real threat that the radical feminist pursuit of truth, grounded in the gritty reality of women's lives constitutes, and then we can begin to name the backlash, on the streets and in the academy.

Renate Klein

(Dead) Bodies Floating in Cyberspace: Post-modernism and the Dismemberment of Women*

When the Women's Liberation Movement burst on the scene again with rage and passion internationally in the late 60s and early 70s, one of its first demands in western countries was for women to be "Our Bodies – Ourselves". This slogan, soon to become the title of an influential book on women's health (Boston Women's Health Collective 1969/1973/1992), reflected women's anger that our sexuality, reproduction and health was defined and controlled by different "experts": male doctors and scientists who personally and politically had constructed women's social inferiority as based in women's biology. Outraged at this reduction of real live women to (hetero)sex objects, "breeders" and women-as-walking-diseases in dire need of (male) control, radical feminists responded with books such as: *The Hidden Malpractice. How American Medicine Mistreats Women* (Corea: 1977/1985); *Men Who Control Women's Health* (Scully: 1980/1994); *How to Stay Out of the Gynecologist's Office* (LA Feminist Women's Health Center: 1981). Women's health centres were established and became places where women taught each other holistic care about our bodies/ our lives. Together with Phyllis Chesler's groundbreaking *Women and Madness* (1972), the radical feminist agenda canvassed in consciousness raising groups (and not just in the west, see Bhate *et al.* on women's health in India, 1987) was unambivalently clear: women, individually and collectively, were fed up with domination of our lives – bodies/souls/spirits/minds – and demanded an end to all social and individual violence including sexual, medical and psychological abuse.

The hard work of radical feminists to put theory into practice in the 70s and 80s enabled many women to shake off male-defined patriarchal notions of (hetero)sexuality, stereotypical "feminine" beauty, illness and health, and encouraged

* I gratefully acknowledge Susan Hawthorne's spirited feeling/thinking body/mind who not only contributed much to this piece but even more to my life. And I thank Sheila Jeffreys for commenting on a draft
and Tania Lienert for good conversations.

us to become self-confident persons in our own right with a strong identity and feminist-defined sense of Self (thereby disavowing psychoanalysis). Indeed it was argued by many writers (e.g. Mary Daly, 1978/1979) that to develop a strong Self was as crucial for individual women as for the collectivity of women in order to stand up to patriarchy and get rid of the mindbinders as much as the footbinders. Each woman was encouraged to become *Woman Herself* (Rowland: 1988) but also to develop "gynaffection" (Raymond: 1986/1991). "Sisterhood is Powerful" thus became synonymous with alliances of strong, determined women whose diversity (e.g. class, race, sexuality, culture, etc.) was one of their strengths, and whose vision and determination to be free individually and collectively would end women's oppression.

Given the emphasis on "Our Bodies – Ourselves" – the expressed importance for women to conceptualise themselves as holistic persons – it was not surprising that radical feminists responded swiftly and loudly when the age of test-tube baby technology arrived with Louise Brown in 1978. We exposed the technodocs' new/old claims of selfless service to (infertile) women's desires for babies as dehumanising medical violence (and Big Business) aimed at reducing women to their body parts, and the new/old attempt to control (infertile) women as a social group via their bodies, specifically their dismembered fertility, as "the exploitation of a desire" (Klein: 1984; 1989a). Books such as *Test-Tube Women* (Arditti *et al.*: 1984), *The Mother Machine* (Corea: 1985) and *Man-Made Women* (Corea *et al.*: 1985) became internationally known classics (followed by, among others, Spallone and Steinberg: 1987; Klein: 1989a and b; Rowland: 1992; and Raymond: 1994). Concurrently, FINRRAGE (The Feminist International Network of Resistance to Reproductive and Genetic Engineering) established itself as an international lobby group. Its aim was to stop the "new" pro-natalist technologies in the west as well as the "old" anti-natalist population control technologies in the so-called Third World which were spreading rapidly with more and more provider-controlled contraceptives such as Norplant, RU 486 (the abortion pill), and the development of the anti-fertility vaccine (Akhter: 1992; 1995; Richter: 1996; Klein *et al.*: 1991). This double emphasis is important: not only are *individual* women in the west (and elites elsewhere) split into body parts by reproductive medicine but the *collective bodies* of Third World women (and poor women in all countries) are treated as sheer numbers and manipulated according to the imperialist and eugenic ideology of the population control establishment (see Declaration of Peoples Perspectives: 1993; also this volume pp. 519–24). Radical feminists continue to oppose this reductionism in reproductive medicine and population control and ask to remember that women are *people* and that as 52 percent of the world's population, they remain the world's poor, illiterate and continue to serve the other half: men.[1]

---

1. With this comment I state the obvious: women continue to be victims wherever one looks. This does not deny that women have agency and in fact are not only survivors against all odds of many of the inequalities/injustices/atrocities/tortures, but can be found at the forefront of all groups which work for a better future. But it *does* say that the hegemonic nature of hetero-techno-patriarchy which radical feminism defines as *inclusive* of diversity (based on race/ethnicity, class, age, sexuality etc.) remains unbroken in its global dominance over women as a social group.

As was to be expected, radical feminists' exposure of their divide-and-recombine game was resisted by gynecologists and scientists (who feared losing their new lucrative playground), but also by liberal and socialist feminists. Their accusations varied from saying we limited women's "choices" to accusations of "male conspiracy theories", alleged unkindness to infertile women and "throwing out the baby with the bath water"; in other words going too far in our rejection of these technologies (see in particular the collection by Michelle Stanworth: 1987/1988). And of course there were the usual accusations against radical feminist work that we are "essentialist" and condemned these technologies because they were "unnatural" *in spite of* radical feminism's first and foremost commitment to social change (see Lienert; Raymond; and Rowland and Klein; pp. 9–36 this volume for further discussion on this hapless theme). Nevertheless, these debates, whilst at times fierce, were still focused on women: Is reproductive medicine in women's interest? Against women? Or both/and? In fact some socialist feminists argued for access to these expensive technologies for poor women. And liberal feminists, using the equality argument, pleaded for non-discriminatory access by de-facto couples and lesbian women and the right to sell one's body as a commodity (e.g. in surrogacy; see Lori Andrews, 1986).

However, while liberal, radical and socialist feminists were engaged in their debates on these technologies, the late 80s and 90s saw a rapid proliferation of post-modern and queer "feminisms" within literature, philosophy, cultural studies, and sociology[2] – increasingly embraced by many (ex-)socialist[3] and some liberal feminists.[4] Interestingly, bodies, previously avoided by all except radical feminists for fear of being called "essentialist" – that ultimate sin which seems to confer an express ticket to hell – began featuring prominently in post-modern feminist writings. Was this veritable explosion of body writings reason for joy?[5] Are radical feminists about to get new allies in our critique of cut-and-paste science? Is "Our Bodies – Ourselves" returning as the catchcry for the next millennium?

After pondering this question through much (torturous) reading of post-modern texts, my (short) state of innocence – to speak in true post-modernist

2. Since the mid-80s feminist contributions to the sociology of the body have gained much prominence, possibly in part because of sociology's previous lack of consideration given to women (Eckermann: 1994, p. 93; Stacey and Thorne: 1985). I'm grateful to Liz Eckermann for pointing this out to me.

3. See, for example Michèle Barrett's new introduction to the 1988 re-publication of *Women's Oppression Today* where she predicts the imminent surge – and importance – of post-modern body writings for feminist theory (pp.xxviii and xxxiv).

4. I want to point out, however, that judging from books about post-modernism (Rosenau: 1992; Bertens: 1995), the overwhelming majority of post-modern writers appear to be men who rarely even acknowledge feminism.

5. *Bodies that Matter* (Butler: 1993); *Volatile Bodies* (Grosz: 1994); *Reading, Writing & Rewriting the Prostitute Body* (Bell: 1994); *Sexy Bodies* (Grosz and Probyn: 1995); and *Imaginary Bodies* (Gatens: 1996), are just a few of many recent post-modern feminist texts.

jargon – has turned shocked disbelief. How is it possible to theorise "bodies" in thousands of pages, yet invisibilise women? Post-modern feminist writing on the body dismembers real live women "out there" as much as reproductive medicine. In fact I have come to believe that post-modern body writers are "cutters with words" whose tools are similar to the ones of "cutters with knives". In what follows I will discuss some of the themes in post-modern body writings and elaborate on why I believe that they not only undermine the radical feminist quest for women's liberation but constitute a dangerous collusion with anti-feminist foes that must be passionately resisted. The point I am making is not that (all) post-modern body feminists have come out in support of reproductive medicine/genetic engineering. (I don't know if they are even concerned about these developments.) Rather, I believe that post-modernism itself mirrors these technologies. Hence their *implicit* legitimisation by post-modern body feminists. As for my (innocent) moment of hope to have found new allies, post-modernism's insistence on multiple positions would not, of course, allow the endorsement of radical feminists who have identified reproductive medicine as violence against women. But endorsing multiple subject positions leads to a libertarian position of "anything goes" which is precisely what reproductive technologists want – flexible bodies, pliable bodies, techno-bodies – cervixes with "hostile" mucus are circumvented by using fallopian tubes as the site for embryo injections; old eggs can be combined with young wombs.[6] The *women* whose bodies are thus dissected and recombined are absent, they do not matter.

Bodies Without Women: Objects and Texts

The bodies I have been reading about in post-modern feminist writings do not breathe, do not laugh, and have no heart. They are "constructed" and "refigured". They are written about in the third person: ". . . human bodies have the wonderful ability to . . . produce fragmentation, fracturings, dislocations . . ." (Grosz: 1994, p. 13). Women are absent and although speaking of "embodiment" and "corporeality", much of the post-modern feminist discussion perceives a body as a "thing" that can be used by its "owner" and others, as a ". . . political, social, and cultural *object* par excellence . . . (Grosz: 1994, p. 18, my emphasis). Dehumanisation at work here; the "embodiment" feels cold/I feel cold. Bodies are seen as texts. As Dorothy Broom writes, ". . . the social meaning of 'a woman's body' *is discursively produced* by (among others) medical texts and practices (1991, p. 46, my emphasis). This then is writing *about* women's bodies – or body parts – writing about *representation* only.[7] In post-modern writings real live women (who do not exist) have been reduced to bodies which in turn have become texts.

As texts, bodies are objects, (thinking) fragments, or surfaces, to be inscribed, marked, written on, written. Corporeality may be described as fluid and

---

6. For fictional, poetic and dramatic renditions of these practices see *Angels of Power* (Hawthorne and Klein: 1991).

7. Curiously, the absence of real-life women in post-modern feminist body texts reproduces the absence of women in pre-feminist (male) scholarship!

transgressing boundaries but I can't share the excitement. I am worried because I can't find the women amongst/in/above/around their body parts. Similar to the way in which women are (literally and metaphorically) cut up into a series of body parts in reproductive medicine – "bad eggs", "diseased tubes", "hostile wombs" – that can be dissected, poked, prodded and recombined at will – post-modernism dismembers woman. By revelling in multiple subjectivities, decrying entities such as "self" and "identity" as "essentialist and "universalist", celebrating "de-stabilisation" and "otherness" – now called "alterity" – often put forward violently and nihilistically, post-modern body writing legitimises – and indeed hails as potentiality – disruption, displacement and discontinuity (see also Klein: 1990 and Klein and Hawthorne 1995 and 1996; Brodribb: 1992). At its most extreme, post-modernism disappears women. Here too, reproductive medicine shows many parallels: the pregnant woman is disappeared in favour of that part of her body which develops into the foetus/child: at best she is an "uterine environment"; the menopausal woman is disappeared: what remains are "decayed ovaries".

Gendered Bodies: Triumphant Hetero-reality[8]

Although post-modern feminist body writers insist that they are talking about "gendered" bodies, much of their work has remained within a framework that reveres "the fathers" of these womenless bodies/dismembered body parts as *authorities*: almost always the same assembly of pale men. (*Question:* Are post-modernists allowed to have authorities?) From Freud to Foucault (a veritable cult hero), Nietzsche to Merleau-Ponty, Deleuze to Derrida, Lacan to Lyotard, Barthes to de Man (no order or affiliation implied) and many many more, it is *MEN* who colonise the pages of supposedly feminist writers. Their ubiquitous presence tries to invade the reader's self – mySelf – I feel assaulted. But within the context of the academy that has never stopped resisting the development of strong women-centred Women's Studies that *discusses women qua women*, such (resurrected) prominence of men is understandable; it might well be one of the reasons why feminist post-modernism, so utterly unthreatening to male hegemony, is allowed into the academy and even seen as the only legitimate feminist theorising in many places. Indeed, Liz Grosz, one of the most acclaimed body theorists, but also a long-time feminist, comments that "feminist theory is necessarily implicated in a series of complex negotiations between tense and antagonistic forces" which she defines as "the overwhelming masculinity of historical privileged knowledges" and "the broad political aims and objectives of feminist struggle" (1995: p. 45). Describing this as an uneasy and problematic relationship, she continues:

---

8. This is Janice Raymond's (1986) term. It is much broader than heterosexuality and denotes the prevailing world view in which the relations between men as a group and women as a group are centre-stage and ". . . woman exists always in relation to man" (p. 3). This world view continues to be adhered to by women (and men) of all sexualities including lesbians in post-modern body writings.

This tension means that feminists have had to tread a fine line either between intellectual rigor (as it has been defined in male terms) and political commitment (as feminists see it) – that is, between the risks posed by patriarchal recuperation and those posed by a conceptual sloppiness inadequate to the long-term needs of feminist struggles – the tension between seeking acceptance in male terms and retaining commitment to women's struggles (pp. 45–46).

This quote reveals much about Grosz herself and explains why her work is one big invocation of the male masters even if she is critical of them and even when she discusses women (see her introduction, 1989, to Julia Kristeva, Luce Irigaray and Michèle Le Doeuff). She has obviously made the decision to beat the boys at their own game – and good luck! However, her words are reaffirming patriarchy, likening "conceptual sloppiness" to "commitment to women's struggles". She thereby not only agrees with the masters' superior (if flawed) theorising, but by implication, seems to equate the (radical) feminist project of developing women-centred theory and practice with "conceptual sloppiness"![9]

Yet other body writers, such as philosopher Moira Gatens (1996) seem to take the hetero-relational framework not only for granted but see it as an absolute necessity: ". . . many recent developments in contemporary feminist theory explicitly stress the necessity to engage with dominant or 'malestream' theories of social and political life . . . Such engagement is active and critical" (p. 61). Gatens follows her own advice and theorises "imaginary" bodies by invoking the same list of men as cited above with a few additions such as Spinoza (also mentioned in Grosz: 1994). Thus her writing on corporeality, bodies and difference remains firmly within a hetero-relational framework: these are theories about women's bodies in a man's world. Similarly, Judith Butler, theorises the "lesbian phallus". (Unsurprisingly) she draws heavily on Freud and Lacan and, believing that the phallus is transferable, suggests that we need "the critical release of alternative imaginary schemas for constituting sites of erotogenic pleasure" (1993, p. 91). My radical lesbian feminist Self cringes: I know, I know, Butler is talking about the "imaginary" – and it's all performance anyway – but *why* thirty-four pages on the lesbian phallus? What is "alternative" about this as a site of erotogenic pleasure for lesbians? Earlier, in 1990, Butler had already written: "Lesbianism that defines itself in radical exclusion from heterosexuality deprives itself of the capacity to resignify the very heterosexual constructs by which it is partially and *inevitably* constituted" (p. 128; my emphasis). (How defeatist! My radical lesbian feminist Self by now needs lots of chocolate.)

---

9. From a radical feminist point of view such reified hetero-reality is rather outdated as it does nothing to enhance theorising of differences – and indeed similarities – among women where women are centre-stage, thus displacing man-as-the-norm. As I have argued elsewhere (1990), the critique of androcentric scholarship is a neccessary step in feminist scholarship. However, critiquing can only go so far: we need original creative thinking that constructs women-centred knowledge by daring to build on feminist work.

Although supposedly at the cutting edge of feminist theorising, I have come to understand that post-modern body writers reproduce outdated and unproductive (sexual) sameness/difference discourses.[10] *Even if sexuality, gender and sex are deconstructed, hetero-reality remains at the centre of their writing* (for another example see Grosz, 1994, on body fluids of women *and* men, pp. 192–210). Joan Hoff could not have put it more succinctly when she said that post-modernism is "phallic drift" – and *paralysis* (1994b). And I think of Audre Lorde: "The master's tools will never dismantle the master's house" (1981).

No doubt the masters' tools of hetero-reality rule supreme in reproductive medicine. Here the (allegedly) universal *raison d'être* for woman to give man "his" child (from "his" genes), or to remain "feminine for ever" with hormone replacement therapy, is used as the justification for these technologies – whatever the price to a woman's health/life. Combined with the post-modern framework of dissecting and reassembling, "surrogates" are dismembered rent-a-wombs; egg "donors" are ovaries blown up with hormones to yield multiple egg cells: womenless body parts here too, all in the name of producing the commodity "baby". And as an increasing number of women move into reproductive medicine, they too mimic the fathers: the pioneers in white.

Question: Why is the man in the (lesbian) (feminist) head so difficult to displace? Why, when there are already thousands and thousands of pages of feminist theories to discuss, is it men that get reinvoked?[11] The desire to gain male approval and be admitted to the boys' club? The excitement of rewriting/ imitating/being better than men? (Real) fear of punishment for disobedience to the masters? The decision that to be part of the dominant group makes for an easier life? All of the above? But at what price to the soul?

"Reshaped" Bodies and Cyborgs: Post-modern Disembodiment

In the face of persisting – and indeed worsening – media and fashion images of "beautiful" women as needle thin and in child-like frocks, women continue to battle to love (or at least like) our bodies – ourselves and to develop self-confidence and an identity of our own. Alarmingly, dieting is now found to be a necessity for girls as young as four years old (Wigg: 1995), resulting for many in debilitating eating

---

10. See Catharine MacKinnon (1989a, p. 216) for a discussion of the futility of arguing that women are similar to, or different from, men (in either analysis men remain at the centre), and Sheila Jeffreys, pp. 359–74 this volume, for problematising post-modernists' return to gender.

11. Whilst admitting that her discussion of male body theorists offers neither a "new nonpatriarchal or feminist framework", Liz Grosz justifies her focus: "No one yet knows what the conditions are for developing knowledges, representations, models, programs, which provide women with nonpatriarchal terms for representing themselves and the world from women's point of view" (p. 188). Published in 1994 I find this revelation staggering. It invisibilises feminists who have theorised, invented, laughed and acted not just for the past twenty-five years, but for centuries. Indeed, if we were all to wait for the *conditions* to be right, feminist practice would be impossible!

disorders and long-term health problems. Self-inflicted body mutilations are on the increase. Meanwhile, post-modern feminist body theorists are fascinated with "bodily inscriptions" and suggest (referring back to Nietzsche one more time) that ". . . pain [in S/M] serves as a mode of corporeal intensification" (Grosz: 1995, p. 199). The body is described as "the inscribed surface of events" (Butler: 1990, p. 129 this time drawing on Foucault). She is intent that the aim of inscription is to render ". . . 'identity' . . . in whatever form, permanently problematic" (p. 128). Good advice for women who struggle to withstand losing the last bit of respect for themselves as they go through recurring phases of bingeing, dieting, cutting themselves up?

Both Butler (1990) and Grosz (1994) discuss Franz Kafka's horrific story *The Penal Settlement* where a mutilation machine, the Harrow, inscribes the punishment on a prisoner's body. Reinvoking Foucault (who draws on Nietzsche), yet again, Butler suggests that the body "as the medium" . . . must be destroyed and transfigured in order for "culture to emerge" (p. 130). Indeed it is only just before the prisoner dies that the inscription of his body has produced knowledge – he now knows/has become conscious of the sentence for his crime. Grosz, describing Kafka's instrument of torture as "an ingenious device" and "a system which has exquisite appropriateness", goes on to say that "Consciousness is a by-product, perhaps even an epiphenomenon, of the inscription of the body" and, "For that split second before death, the prisoner knows, and indeed accepts and *embodies*, law" (1994, pp. 134–37, my emphasis). While I certainly would not want to infer that Butler and Grosz condone Kafka's brutal fantasy of "becoming", their invocation of this story, supposedly to show that bodies are always inscribed and that ". . . processes of body inscriptions must be understood as literal and constitutive" (Grosz, p. 137), makes my own blood curdle. Indeed, when I take this theorising "literally" (no doubt I will be accused of taking it too literally!) it provides a justification not only for bodily mutilation as self-loathing, but for (celebratory?) body piercing, branding and S/M practices.

In the name of post-modern feminist theory, is anything that extends surfaces, by inscribing them – or indeed turning the inside of the body out – "performative subversion" (Butler: 1990, p. 128) and ". . . anti-essentialist decentring of identity" (Grosz: 1994, p. 21)? Supposedly this is empowering. Such "cultural seepage" (*idem*) also suggests that extended corporeality can be achieved not just through seminal fluid (hetero-reality invoked again!) but through acknowledging that ". . . women's corporeality is inscribed as a mode of seepage" (Grosz p. 203), for example the "fluidity" of pregnant women's bodies. Reproductive technologists might want to borrow this concept. It parallels their argument that visualising the growing foetus via ultrasound is empowering for women. Indeed, removing immature eggs and maturing them in the lab so they can be fertilised with sperm to form an embryo – in theory possible without the knowledge of the women from whose bodies the eggs were extracted – could be described as (empowering) seepage. The human genome project too can be justified in this light: mapping people's genes and in future removing "bad" bits and adding "good" bits is simply extending women's (and men's) corporeality. What's more, it's just a bit of performative fun! If you think that nipple piercing adds to *your* sexual enjoyment, perhaps adding on that extra bit to *your* X chromosome might do an even better trick! Such facile thinking, of course, negates the dangerous politics implicit in reproductive medicine and genetic engineering; who has the power to decide which genes are desirable and who is allowed to live? It is indicative of the rampant liberalism inherent in post-modernism which (inadvertently?) justifies the most woman/people-hating theories and practices in the name of refusing to take a stand and instead climaxes at the excitement of inscribing bodies.

The point that the "flesh-and-blood female body" is conceptualised as an object – "the referent" – has been taken up by pro-prostitute post-modern writer Shannon Bell (1994). Her project "rewriting the prostitute body" consists of putting a positive construction on prostitution by discussing prostituted women ". . . inscrib[ing] their own bodies in diverse and contradictory ways . . ." (p. 4). It is the "wordflesh" of prostitutes and the "fragmented politics" of performance artists such as "Post Porn Modernist" Annie Sprinkle that, Bell believes, rewrite the prostitute "body" as a transgressor, an ". . . open, protruding, extended, *secreting* body, the body of becoming, process and change" (p. 141, my emphasis, "seepage" again!). Through "parody, play, displacement, tracing and overwriting" – all post-modernist techniques, Bell explains, Sprinkle, the pornographic woman (with 150 feature porn movies and 20 feature videos, we are told) occupies the space denied to her by feminists (pp. 148–152). Her "prostitute body" has "no inherent meaning" (p. 4). It is not the exploitation, violence and humiliation perpetrated against prostituted women by customers and pimps that inscribes itself on her body/herSelf. Rather, she "chooses" to feel empowered by her role. Pain turned pleasure; degradation turned empowerment, the reduction of woman to body (parts) – all legitimised through post-modern body writing.[12]

Given the post-modern obsession with disruption and displacement and the notion of "empowerment" through transgressing boundaries, the fact that even cosmetic surgery has been vindicated by feminist post-modernists as empowering should not come as too great a shock. Indeed one could argue that cosmetic surgery is an excellent example of "inscribing surfaces". In her interesting study of Dutch women's experiences with cosmetic surgery, *Reshaping the Female Body* (1995), Kathy Davis, in typically post-modern fashion, cannot decide whether she should condemn cosmetic surgery – her initial reaction – or whether "The desire for cosmetic surgery can be situated in women's struggle to become *embodied* female subjects . . ." (p. 173, my emphasis).[13] Davis decides to adopt a "having-your-cake-and-eating-it-too" strategy (her term) and suggests cosmetic surgery is both: ". . .

12. See Evelina Giobbe, pp. 479–80 and Kathy Barry, pp. 448–55 this volume, for very different analyses of prostitution.
13. In spite of my criticisms of Kathy Davis' work (which include that she too, refers to the usual group of learned men), her framework does include real live women and in that way differs from other writers quoted earlier.

profoundly disempowering and a road to empowerment at the same time" (p. 153). I sympathise with her dilemma in adopting this position – and it does remind me of my own research with involuntarily childless women whose pain and desire for a child, no matter how socially conditioned or otherwise determined, can indeed be heart wrenching. But to endorse technologies that are highly unsuccessful, can have serious long-term health effects and indeed kill – true for both cosmetic surgery and reproductive medicine – can never be in women's interest. It's like endorsing masochism, or encouraging a woman to stay with her batterer – surely this is not feminist. An even greater problem I have with Davis' analysis concerns her inability to see that cosmetic surgery is the epitome of a technological fix of body parts: the nose, chin, breast job, always one bit that is perceived as lacking, never any satisfaction with the whole, not even post-operation. This is in fact confirmed in the women's own stories. "Diana" muses after a reconstruction of her face: "This face in the mirror, you just don't recognize it any more . . . I just couldn't (pause) yeah, couldn't bring it *together*. It – it wasn't a whole any more . . ." (p. 104, her emphasis).

It is in her definition of "embodiment" as whether a particular woman's body parts are what she desires them to be, that Davis concurs with the earlier mentioned post-modernist body writers who see inscriptions on and extensions of isolated body parts as "embodiment".[14] Importantly, changes to this artificial embodiment – which might also include internal bits such as ovaries of menopausal women artificially booted up with estrogen – are only achieved with the help of experts: cosmetic surgeons, gynaecologists, implant makers.[15] This disjointed, reductionist rendition of a real live woman's embodiment – her body/herSelf/her soul/her spirit – according to Davis then becomes the basis for a woman's "identity": ". . . to make sense of herself *vis-à-vis* her body" (p. 168). So "the woman" – whatever that means – and her body are accepted as two separate entities. Is this the old pre-feminist mind/matter distinction, but this time taking place *within* a woman? With the "matter" – the body – without inherent meaning yet again: inscribable, extendable, malleable? If from this one infers that the split-off mind is superior – why on earth do post-modern body feminists spend so much time (helped by their prestigious fathers) on these devalued body bits that are so wanting, so inferior?[16] Merging post-modernism and reproductive technologies, could reimagined tech-nologised bodies be our future?

---

14. Post-modern feminist definitions of embodiment at times are plain bizarre. Australian academic, Zoë Sofia, writes: "In driving a car . . . we are in embodiment relations when we identify our body with the car's body, making allowances for its proportions as though they were our own" (Sofia: 1995, p. 156). I call this displacement embodiment!

15. As I have remarked throughout this article, post-modern feminist body writers too rely on male experts for their theories!

16. What a retrograde un-post-modern question! I should know by now that post-modernists delight in paradoxes and contradictions.

And, sure enough, enter the new post-modern feminist icon: the "cyborg" – part machine/part human – which, according to US historian of science, Donna Haraway, by the end of the 20th century is all of us. "The cyborg is our ontology; it gives us our politics . . . not afraid of permanently partial identities and contradictory standpoints" (1991, pp. 150, 154). Such cut-and-paste bodies, Haraway suggests, fight the good fight against unity and indeed ". . . *all* claims for an organic or natural standpoint (p. 157, her emphasis). Whilst harshly criticising Catharine McKinnon for her "totalising" radical feminist theory "of experience", she seems oblivious to her own (and other post-modernists') "totalising" theory of declaring real live women redundant, and instead, glorifyies fractured, disassembling and reassembling cyborg identities which, thirteen times she tells us, are not "innocent". Cyborg feminism is a celebration of disembodiment in a grand way. But Haraway boldly admonishes, "This is the self feminists must code" (p. 163). (*Question:* do cyborgs ever smell roses? feel angry? passionate? do they laugh? have they a soul?). She states further, "It is time to write *The Death of the Clinic*. The clinic's methods required bodies and works; *we have text and surfaces*" (p. 245, my emphasis). The women in India whose "texts and surfaces" hurt and bleed from injected anti-pregnancy vaccines and implanted contraceptive rods (as in Norplant), and indeed, the women in IVF programs whose ovaries just burst because of hyperstimulation through fertility drugs, might have a problem understanding this post-modern cyborg world. Apart from its insensitivity to human suffering caused *precisely* by these technological feats, Donna Haraway's Cyborg fantasies, sadly, collude with those of the biotechnology establishment who for a long time have fantasised about the total manipulation of reproduction without women.

Bodies in Cyberspace: Built-in Obsolescence?

So the cyborg roams cyberspace, has virtual net sex and its self ". . . is a multiple distributed system" (Turkle: 1996, p. 149). Mind downloaded, transcendence achieved. A post-modern feminist body writer's apocalypse come true: the body destroyed so that culture can emerge (to paraphrase Judith Butler (1990), as quoted earlier)? "Net chicks" along with many many more "netheads" (see Spender: 1995c)[17] happily playing in MUDs (Multi-User Dungeons), ". . . become authors not only of text but of themselves, constructing new selves through interaction" (Turkle, p. 151). Great, says the post-modern girl, I'll try out a few new selves, thank you, and I don't even need to go under the knife? Indeed, MUD-ing – and playing cyberspace games – is much easier than cosmetic surgery. The bodies of women finally become immaterial: body loathing, so ubiquitous in post-modern feminist writings, is overcome.

---

17. Presumably, terms such as "nethead" and "geek" are neutral. Yet as Spender (1995c) and others have convincingly pointed out, they really mean boys by default. One of the first magazines for women interested in cyberculture is named *Geek Girl*: so much for the presumed "neutrality" of cyberspace/virtual reality which remains as gendered – and (hetero)sexist – as *real* reality!

Strange then that virtual reality remains so eminently more of the same: it's a very white and *female* Virtual Valerie that invites players to have sex/rape/ dismember/reassemble her, and it is undoubtedly very *male* players that embark on this task. (Or could this be an example of the "alternative imaginary schemas for constituting sites of erotogenic pleasures" for women? [Butler: 1993a, p. 91].) It is a 21-year-old *male* student who defends the violent characters he plays on MUDs with it's "something in me; but quite frankly I'd rather rape on MUDs where no harm is done" (in Turkle, p. 152). So hetero-reality and violence survive with the same ease with which body/texts can be dismembered. And the "harm done" survives as well, but it's clean harm, without the messiness of blood, guts and gore of *real* bodies of *real* women in *real* life. It's just so much fun. And if you're fed up with one of your own multiple selves – or one of your players – just flame it, kill it. With the click of a button dead bodies are floating in cyberspace: the ultimate bodily obsolescence; mind rules supreme. And people are saying, just as they do with pre-virtual reality pornography, that this has no impact whatsoever on what you do in "real" life – who are they kidding?

In sum then, far from changing sexist and racist reality, virtual travel in cyberspace – although blessed with post-modern fantasies and desires of dispensing with unruly women's bodies and selves – is the latest fad and with its twin, repro- ductive medicine and genetic engineering, the cyber industry is laughing all the way to the stock exchange. Meanwhile of course, far away from such elitist mind games, the world's majority continues to live *real* lives, with *real* bodies and *real* selves.

Our Bodies – Our Selves: Radical Revolt

The plethora of post-modern body writings and the hype of supposedly non- gendered cyberspace, if successful among today's young women, could substantially contribute to their (further) alienation from their own bodies and by implication could alienate them from (radical) feminism with its focus on developing a strong self-sufficient Self based on a holistic concept of body-and-soul. Together with mind/body invaders parading as health experts (and a booming cosmetic surgery industry), the medicalisation – and indeed geneticisation – of women's lives, takes hold of girls/young women at an increasingly younger age: they get used to seeing their body composed of (wanting) pieces which all need different experts to fix them up.[18]

Maintaining that women *are* Our bodies – Ourselves, that being human equals integrity of mind/body/spirit, that we *have* a humanity that must not be

---

18. Best documented for Germany (Schüssler and Bode: 1992), there is an increasing trend to urge girls from as young as seven years to see a gynaecologist once a year for a check-up including a vaginal exam. The girl gets a passbook with her picture and is encouraged to trust "Uncle Doctor" as her friend. The subtext, of course is that she learns early to see her "reproductive" health separate from herself: not part and parcel of her physical and mental well being but a separate entity which is quality-checked as to its later sexual and reproductive usefulness.

violated, is feminism's heresy of the 90s. But it is crucial for survival. Conceptualising our bodies as ourselves is *not* static; it is *not* romaticising, it does *not* presume a homogenised "natural" body – whatever that might be: there are as many "bodies" as there are women, and they are constantly changing. (But despite their differences there are enough biological/social similarities to warrant attribution to the social group women.) Being critical of the hetero-relational post-modern project of objectification, fragmentation and alienation – as well as its fling with "techno-bodies" – I reject the equation, "modern-equals-old-hat". (And I'm not even a technophobe: I enjoy nattering on the net!) I am asking to perceive women *in their diversity* as whole human beings in their own right: not an assembly of body parts that need fixing up; not an appendage to any man, religion or state that can be "owned"; not a gender – or a sex – which has no meaning unless it is compared to the "other" sex/gender. In spite of post-modern nihilism, women do exist (with messy bodies and irreverent minds). They/we merely want to live and let live: free from injustice and dominance, particularly in relation to our geographical locations, ethnicities, sexualities, social class. It seems so simple, so easy, the bare minimum of being human. Yet it is so insidiously resisted, just at a time when women around the world urgently need solidarity to prevent their annihilation in the name of elite (white) men's population-panic of losing power and privilege. It almost breaks my heart to see so many post-modern feminists buying into the dissect-and-fragment plot. And it makes me angry when I hear young women regurgitate such life-hating rhetoric. But then, with true radical feminist optimism, I observe the waves rolling in, one after the other, eternally. And I am absolutely certain that the next wave of radical women who will revolt (one more time) and reclaim their bodies/their lives/their Selves with passion, will arrive. Do I feel the earth move?

Sheila Jeffreys

Return to Gender: Post-modernism and Lesbianandgay Theory*

There has been a sudden enthusiasm for and incorporation of the work of the Masters of post-modernism, Lacan, Foucault, Derrida into feminist theory in the eighties. Feminist critics have argued that this has led to a depoliticising of feminism (see Brodribb: 1992). In the area of lesbian and gay theory the work of post-modernist male icons and of theorists inspired by them has been greeted with even more enthusiasm. This is not surprising since that which is called lesbianandgay theory, i.e. theory which homogenises lesbians and gay men, must be palatable to gay men. Anything which smacks too outrightly of feminism is regarded with suspicion. The project of creating independent lesbian feminist theory is now seen by many as bizarrely separatist. The stars of the new lesbianandgay theory, Judith Butler and Diana Fuss, are women but involved in recycling a feminism founded on post-modernist mainly gay Masters, which does not irritate male gay sensibilities. This is not an easy task. How, for instance, is the phenomenon of drag to be made not just acceptable but even seen as revolutionary in lesbianandgay theory when it has stuck in the craw of feminist theory ever since lesbians dissented from gay liberation? It is to be accomplished by a return to gender, an invention of a harmless version of gender as an idea which lesbians and gay men can endlessly play with and be revolutionary at the same time.

The version of gender the lesbianandgay theorists are presenting is a far cry from the understanding of gender which other feminist theorists might have. It is gender depoliticised, sanitised and something difficult to associate with sexual violence, economic inequality, women dying from backstreet abortions. It is gender reinvented as play for those who see themselves far removed from the nitty gritty of women's oppression. It goes down well in the world of lesbianandgay theory because it is feminism as fun instead of feminism as irritatingly challenging.

---

* Extract from *The Lesbian Heresy* (1993).

Let us first look at who the new lesbianandgay theorists are since this might help to understand why they have chosen their particular politics. Whilst the heavy feminist politicos of the seventies are likely to have had backgrounds in politics, history and sociology, the new variety come from literary and cultural studies and film studies. Let us take as an example the book, *Inside/Out. Lesbian Theories, Gay Theories,* edited by Diana Fuss (1991). Judith Butler teaches in a Humanities Center and is therefore not necessarily in the area of cultural criticism. The other eighteen authors are and cover literature, media, film, photography, art history. There is no reason why a literary critic should not make a valuable contribution to the development of political theory but when all that is seen as "theory" by a whole new generation of lesbian and gay students and teachers emanates from the arts rather than the social sciences then there may be reason for alarm. This might help to explain why this new theory has little time for old-fashioned talk of material power relations, for economics, for power that does not just play around but resides in the hands of particular classes and elites. Post-modernist theory elevated language to a pre-eminent place in the political, the word became reality, the cultural critic became the political activist by wielding a pen and the housewife who gets beaten up by her husband because she leaves one cobweb in a corner becomes strangely invisible.

Let us now look at the authorities cited by the new lesbianandgay theorists. The notes to Diana Fuss' (1991) introduction cite Judith Butler, Lacan, Derrida more than once, Foucault, nine more men and two more women. You might feel that this was truly surprising since such a huge body of original lesbian feminist theory exists which could be an inspiration, but this theory does not exist for the new lesbianandgays. There are no references to Mary Daly, Audre Lorde, Janice Raymond, Julia Penelope, Sarah Hoagland, Charlotte Bunch. These separatists of the intellect who posit a lesbian theory into which gay men are not easily assimilated have been disappeared.

At the root of the gender problem in the new lesbianandgay theory lies the idea of the dominance of language and of binary oppositions therein which comes from Lacan and Derrida. Language is seen as overwhelmingly important. Whilst other feminists might see language as important in a landscape of other oppressive forces in maintaining the oppression of women, such as economic constraints, male violence, the institution of heterosexuality, the new post-modernist lesbianandgay theorists see language as primary. Language operates through the construction of false binary oppositions which, by some mysterious process, control the way people are able to think and therefore act. Masculinity/femininity is supposed to be one of these binaries, the one which is most fundamental to the oppression of women and lesbians and gays.

The post-modernist feminist drops men out of the analysis. Power becomes, in a Foucauldian sense, something that just floats about constantly reconstituting itself for no real purpose and with no real connection with real human beings. Thus, Judith Butler ascribes power to "regimes" as in "the power regimes of heterosexism and phallogocentrism seek to augment themselves through a constant repetition of their logic . . ." (1990, p. 32). Elsewhere she continues to anthropomorphise heterosexuality.

> That heterosexuality is always in the act of elaborating itself is evidence that it is perpetually at risk, that is, that it "knows" its own possibility of becoming undone (1991, p. 23).

This is a "heterosexuality" with a postgraduate degree! A feminist analysis might generally ask in whose interests these regimes were set up and operate, a *cui bono* question might not seem out of place. Then men might pop into the picture.

Butler's understanding of gender is similarly removed from a context of power relations.

> Gender is the repeated stylization of the body, a set of repeated acts within a highly rigid regulatory frame that congeal over time to produce the appearance of substance, of a natural sort of being (1990, p. 33).

She says elsewhere that "gender is drag". Gender then becomes a way of holding the body, clothing, appearance and it is not surprising that Butler is able to come to the conclusion that all forms of swapping gender about, such as drag and lesbian roleplaying, are revolutionary. But it is unclear where the actual vulgar oppression of women fits into all this. When a woman is being beaten by the brutal man she lives with is this because she has adopted the feminine gender in her appearance. Would it be a solution for her to adopt a masculine gender for the day and strut about in a work shirt or leather chaps? When gender is seen as an idea, or a form of appearance, then the oppression of women does disappear. The tendency of the idea of gender to invisibilise the power relations of male supremacy has been commented upon by radical feminist theorists.[1] Gender as a concept has always been more popular amongst liberal and socialist feminist theorists and now post-modernists.

When feminist theorists of any political persuasion have written about gender in the past they have seen it as something which might be overcome, superceded. Feminists, whether heterosexual or lesbian, have been quite reasonably insulted by being called either feminine or masculine. They have seen themselves, as most still do, as conscientious objectors to gender who were refusing to have any truck with it and refusing to act it out. Some pursued the track of androgyny but the limitations of this approach have also been pointed out by radical feminist theorists.[2] Androgyny, as an idea, has been seen as depending on a continued notion of masculinity and femininity, since it is supposed to combine traits associated with

---

1. For a good exposition of radical feminist politics and the idea of gender see Denise Thompson (1991).
2. On the idea of androgyny see Janice G. Raymond (1986/1991) p. 12.

both these concepts and therefore to reify them rather than leaving them behind. This project that feminists and lesbian feminists have been engaged in for up to twenty years or more of exploding gender by refusing to behave according to the laws of gender, has now been declared not just ill-conceived but impossible by some post-modernist feminists. Butler identifies the "pro-sexuality" movement within feminist theory as saying that sexuality is "always constructed within the terms of discourse and power, where power is partially understood in terms of heterosexual and phallic cultural conventions". She agrees with this and states that it is impossible to construct a sexuality which is outside these conventions.

> If sexuality is culturally constructed within existing power relations, then the postulation of a normative sexuality that is "before", "outside", or "beyond" power is a cultural impossibility and a politically impracticable dream, one that postpones the concrete and contemporary task of rethinking subversive possibilities for sexuality and identity within the terms of power itself (1990, p. 30).

Feminism as it has been generally understood has been declared impossible. Post-modern theory has been enlisted to support the sexual libertarian and specifically sadomasochist project.

Most feminists of the 70s and 80s will probably have seen themselves as engaged in the task of eliminating gender and phallocentric sexuality. We have been involved in the creation of something new and different. Now we discover that we were trying to do something impossible. I have young lesbian students who will say to me "Surely you have gender in your relationship." They do not know that they are being insulting by discounting more than twenty years of struggle by lesbian feminists to have no such thing. It is nearly as frustrating as when men used to tell me as an embryo feminist, that there was such a thing as "natural" femininity and masculinity. Men don't tend to tell me that any more, only post-modernists of both sexes. Such students accept, as a result of high ingestion of post-modernist theory, that it is impossible to sidestep gender. You cannot break out of a binary opposition, according to Derrida, you can only give more weight to the weaker half of the binary and cause it stress and strain.

To imagine that you can sidestep it is said to be essentialist. A quite new meaning of the word essentialist has been invented so that it can be used against all those who maintain some belief in the possibility of social action to create social change. Once upon a time we might have known where we were with essentialism. It represented the belief that men and women were naturally and biologically different. This was not a belief of radical feminists who have always been mission-aries of social constructionism, though it has suited feminist theorists of other faiths to pretend to the contrary. Chris Weedon (1987) is one post-modern feminist who reiterates in her work the puzzling assertion that radical feminists who want to transform male sexuality in the interests of women's freedom are really biological determinists who believe it cannot be changed! What is now called essentialism is the belief that a lesbian can eschew gender, or the belief that it is possible to practise a sexuality not organised around the penis or power imbalance. Such beliefs are said to be essentialist by post-modernists because they rely on the existence of an unknowable essence of lesbianism. All that is known or that can be thought is gendered and phallocentric, and only playing within the rules of this system can alter it. It would be possible to reverse the game and accuse those who tell lesbians that they cannot get out of gender or phallogocentrism of essentialism with rather more justification one might think. But inventing and hurling around new versions of essentialism is something I would like to avoid. Suffice it to say that the idea of the inevitability of gender and phallogocentrism is brutally determinist, pessimistic, and manages to wipe the feminist project of the last twenty years off the map. It fits into the general post-modernist tendency to regard political activism and the belief that political change is possible as suspicious, derisory and somehow vulgar.

Let us look more closely at what Butler sees as the revolutionary possibilities of drag. The social construction of gender is a very old and basic tenet of feminism. But to post-modernists, this, like other traditional and very well worn feminist insights are seen to be new and exciting. And indeed it may well be that they are seeming exciting to a whole new generation of young women who don't have any access to feminist literature of the 60s and 70s because that literature does not appear on their courses and is nowhere referenced. The revolutionary potential of drag and roleplaying, Butler asserts, lies in the ability of such practices to illuminate the fact that gender is socially constructed. They reveal that gender has no essence or ideal form but is all just drag whether put on by feminine heterosexual women or masculine heterosexual men or roleplaying lesbians or male gay drag artists or clones.

> Drag constitutes the mundane way in which genders are appropriated, theatricalized, worn, and done; it implies that all gendering is a kind of impersonation and approximation. If this is true, it seems, there is no original or primary gender that drag imitates, but gender is a kind of imitation for which there is no original . . . (1991, p. 21).

Gender, inasmuch as it comprises only gestures, costume and appearance, can indeed be seen as drag, or as Butler also calls it "performance". The "performance" is supposed to show up the fact that there is no "inner sex or essence or psychic gender core." If this is to be a revolutionary strategy then how would it effect change? This is not very clear.

> How then to . . . engage gender itself as an inevitable fabrication, to fabricate gender in terms which reveal every claim to the origin, the inner, the true, and the real as nothing other than the effects of drag, whose subversive possibilities ought to be played and replayed to make the "sex" of gender into a site of insistent political play? (1991, p. 29).

Apparently the audience of the gender as drag performance is to realise gender is not "real" or "true". But what do they do having made this realisation? Will heterosexual women and men witnessing drag shows rush home and throw off gender, proclaiming to their spouses that there is no such thing as masculinity and femininity? This doesn't seem terribly likely. If gender were indeed an idea, if male supremacy only managed to carry on because little lightbulbs of realisation of the falsity of gender were failing to be illuminated in the heads of men and women, then Butler's strategy might be destined for success. But she has a liberal and idealist understanding of the oppression of women. Male supremacy does not carry on just because people don't realise gender is socially constructed, because of an unfortunate misapprehension that we must somehow learn how to shift. It carries on because men's interests are served thereby. There is no reason why men should give up all the real advantages, economic, sexual, emotional, that male supremacy offers them because they see that men can wear skirts. Similarly the oppression of women does not just consist of having to wear make-up. Seeing a man in a skirt or a woman wearing a tie will not be sufficient to extricate a woman from a heterosexual relationship when she will suffer socially, financially and quite likely physically, in some cases with the loss of her life, if she decides to slough off her oppression.

According to those who celebrate playing with gender it is not just the assumption of a gender that might seem incongruous, i.e. femininity by a man or masculinity by a woman, that is potentially revolutionary. Apparently the performance of the expected gender role can be too. This idea has been around in gay male theory for some time. Gay male commentators on the development of the 70s phenomenon of the masculine clone, leather man, have disagreed over the revolutionary potential of this development. Many gay theorists have been understandably dismayed. They have seen gay masculinity as a betrayal of the principle of gay liberation which sought to break down gender stereotypes and saw masculinity as a concept that was oppressive to women (see Humphries: 1985; Kleinberg: 1987). Others have argued that the masculine gay man is revolutionary because he questions the effeminate gay male stereotype. It has been pointed out that the revolutionary potential of the masculine gay man might well not be realised because the unsuspecting passer-by would not realise the man was gay and might just think he was masculine. How after all was anyone to know? The argument that masculinity donned by gay men could be politically progressive seems in the end simply to be a way of seeking to justify what some gay men wanted to do, or were attracted to. The right-on-ness was invented after the fact, perhaps because some gay men realised the retrogressive nature of the masculinity they adopted to "pass", to feel powerful or to be sexually attractive, and needed to reassure themselves.

The return to gender which has been taking place in the gay male community since the late 70s in terms of a renewed enthusiasm for drag shows and a newly masculine style has had its analogue rather later in the lesbian community. It was not until the 80s that the return to gender became obvious in the lesbian community with the phenomenon of a rehabilitated roleplaying and lipstick lesbianism. It was convenient that there were ideas in the works of the post-modern Masters which would provide an intellectual justification and allow feminist objections to be overridden and derided in the academy. Judith Butler demonstrates in *Gender Trouble* (1990) that old fashioned psychoanalysis in the form of a Joan Riviere paper from 1929 plus Lacanian utterances on femininity as masquerade and parody can be deployed by the new lesbianandgay theorists of cultural studies to support the performance of femininity by lesbians as a political strategy. This strategy is elsewhere called "mimicry" although that is a word not well suited to Butler's analysis since it would suggest that some original exists which can be mimicked and indeed she does not use it. Carol-Anne Tyler explains the idea of mimicry using Luce Irigaray.

> To be a mimic, according to Irigaray, is to "assume the feminine role deliberately ... so as to make 'visible', by an effect of playful repetition, what was supposed to remain invisible ..." To play the feminine is to "speak" it ironically, to italicize it ... to hyperbolize it ... or to parody it ... In mimicry, as in camp, one "does" ideology in order to undo it, producing knowledge about it: that gender and the heterosexual orientation presumed to anchor it are unnatural an even oppressive (1991, p. 53).

But Tyler is critical of this idea. She points out that if all gender is masquerade then it must surely be impossible to distinguish the parody from the "real". There is no real. Thus, the revolutionary potential must be lost.

It is the idea of mimicry which lies behind some of the acclaim by cultural critics of Madonna. Madonna is supposed to undermine ideas of the fixity and reliability of gender by assuming femininity as performance. Mimicry requires that the femininity to be assumed be exaggerated. This is apparently how innocent observers are to know that a revolutionary strategy is being engaged in. The over-the-top degree of make-up or height of shoe heel would reveal that gender as performance was being undertaken. Cherry Smyth, exponent of "queer" politics, tells us that traditional female clothing can be revolutionary when discussing the work of lesbian photographer Della Grace:

> Some of the iconography is indeed robbed from women sex-trade workers and post-punk fashion, which injects a violent autonomy into femme chic, making it trashy and threatening, rather than vulnerable and submissive, to wear a mini-skirt and revealing bodice (1992, p. 44)

This style is best personified, she says, in "Madonna herself, who is probably one of the most famous examples of queer transgression" (1992, p. 44). Feminist theorists who are neither "queer" nor post-modern have a great deal of difficulty in seeing Madonna as transgressing against anything but feminism, anti-racism and progressive politics in general. bell hooks, the Black American feminist theorist, explains that Madonna obeys and exploits the rules of white male supremacy rather than challenging them. She says that Black women cannot see Madonna's change of hair colour to blonde as "merely a question of aesthetic choice" but arising from white supremacy and racism. In *Truth or Dare: In Bed With Madonna* she sees her using the "position of outsider" to "colonize and appropriate black experience for her own opportunistic ends even as she attempts to mask her acts of racist aggression as affirmation" (hooks: 1992, p. 159). She points out that Madonna, in using the motif of innocent female daring to be bad, "relies on the continued production of the racist/sexist sexual myth that black women are not innocent and never can be" (hooks: 1992, p. 160).

hooks quotes Susan Bordo at the head of her article as saying that the "'destabilizing' potential of texts" can only be determined in relation to "actual social practice" (hooks: 1992, p. 157). If we look at the "destabilizing potential" of mimicry in this way then we are forced to recognise that there are many examples around us all the time, on public transport, at office parties, in restaurants, of women assuming exaggerated femininity. It is hard to know how to tell the difference between thoughtless, common or garden femininity and sophisticated femininity as masquerade. There is snobbery involved here too. There is clearly a distinction of value being made between women's choices to wear precisely similar clothes according to whether they are ignorant and unenlightened or whether they have done cultural studies and read Lacan and made a deliberate and revolutionary choice to wear lacy lowcut bodices.

Why is there such excitement about all this? It is difficult to believe that the post-modernist lesbian theorists are serious in seeing mimicry or roleplaying generally as a revolutionary strategy. But the theory does allow women who want to use gender fetishism for their own purposes, whether erotic or just traditional, to do so with a smug sense of political self-righteousness. Playing with gender and all the traditional paraphernalia of dominance and submission, power and power-lessness that male supremacy has ever produced, seems like fun. Whereas to a generation of women who grew up in the 60s make-up and high heels meant pain, expense, vulnerability, and a poor sense of self, a new young generation are telling us that these things are wonderful because they are choosing them. There is a new generation who seem to puzzle about how we manage to have fun without plucking our eyebrows and shaving our legs. Meanwhile the construction of gender seems unthreatened. We simply have the phenomenon of lesbians joining in to help shore up the façade of femininity. There was a time when lesbian feminists saw it as consciousness raising to appear in public or on television in a guise which delib-erately eschewed femininity. We believed that this would show women that an alternative to femininity was available. Now we are told by the parodists, mimics, performance artists, that for a lesbian to appear dressed up in the way that might be expected of an extremely feminine heterosexual woman is more unsettling to male supremacy. It's hard to see why. Those most likely to be unsettled are surely the feminists and lesbians who feel completely undermined and even humiliated by having a lesbian show and tell the world that she wants to be feminine too.

Apart from the return to gender there is another aspect of the post-modernist approach to lesbian and gay studies that does not appear to be an obviously useful revolutionary strategy. This is the radical uncertainty about lesbian and gay identity. Both male and female theorists are adopting radical political tasks for the emergent lesbian and gay movements of the 70s. Naming was particularly important to lesbian feminists who were well aware of the many ways in which women generally were disappeared from history, scholarship, from the records as soon as they married and lost their names. We knew it was important to place ourselves on the map and struggle to remain there. It was crucially necessary to adopt and promote the word lesbian because it established for lesbians a separate identity from gay men. Lesbian feminists in the western world then sought to flesh out this identity. We were constructing for ourselves a conscious political identity. Lesbian feminists have always been radical social constructionists in their approach to lesbianism. A lesbian identity which would defeat hostile and controlling stereotypes of lesbians and form the basis of our political work was constructed through poetry, works of theory, our conferences, collectives and everyday political work. It is an historically specific identity. The lesbian identity currently being constructed by sexual libertarians, queer nation theorists is quite different. The identity which is chosen and constructed will fit the political strategies undertaken.

Post-modernist lesbianandgay theorists seek to throw overboard any concept of even temporarily stable identity. Three political concerns seem to underlie this endeavour. One is a concern to avoid essentialism. This is a concern which does not seem particularly relevant to lesbian feminists who are pretty well aware that their lesbian identity is a deliberate and clearly intentional social construction. But it is a concern in particular for gay male theorists who are faced with a gay male culture far more anchored in ideas of essential identity than that of lesbians. The gay male concern with essentialism has dictated that lesbianandgay theorists in general should be very absorbed in this issue. As Richard Dyer expresses this in *Inside/Out*, the "notion of the homosexual":

> . . . seemed to sail too close to the wind of the kind of biological etiologies of homosexuality that had been used against same-sex relations and, by holding up a model of what we inexorably are, to deprive us of the political practice of determining what we wanted to be (1991, p. 186).

The other political concern underlying the desire for radical uncertainty is that of avoiding ethnocentrism. It was felt by the radically uncertain that a stable concept of what a lesbian or gay man is would be bound to reflect the ideas of the dominant racial or ethnic group and fail to allow for the considerable differences in experience and practice of those of other cultures. As Dyer writes:

Work that sought to establish the continuity of lesbian/gay identity across time and culture seemed to be imposing the way lesbian/gay sexuality is for "us" now upon the diversity and radical differences of both the past and "other" (non-white, Third World) cultures and often eliding the differences between lesbians and gay men (1991, p. 186).

Within Women's Liberation, and lesbian feminism in general, considerable work has been done by Black and ethnic minority women to assert their own different identities without radically destabilising the idea that there is such a thing as a lesbian. This work has been done by Black lesbians, Jewish lesbians, Chicana lesbians, Asian and Indigenous lesbians, all of whom have been asserting a lesbian identity. This common identity does probably arise from western urban culture and would not necessarily transfer outside of that arena. Indigenous lesbians in Australia, for instance, have questioned the relevance of a word based upon a Greek island for their identity, and have pointed out that woman-loving in traditional indigenous culture does not allow room for an urban lesbian identity. But the importance for lesbian organising in urban western culture of a recognisable identity has seemed important to political lesbians across the board. The fact that the identity might make no sense to Indigenous peoples or non-urban peoples in general does not negate its importance as an organising tool in its own context.[3]

Another reason for suspicion of the lesbian or gay identity was based upon Foucauldian notions of "the very operation of power through the regulation of desire that lesbian/gay politics and theory were supposed to be against" (Dyer: p. 186). If the categories of homosexuality were invented as tools of social control then, Dyer suggests, we should be careful of the ways in which our use of them could contribute to this regulation. It is good and useful to be reminded of how we should interrogate our political practice and even what we take for granted politically, such as that we call ourselves lesbians, to check that we have not slid into politically unhelpful or even damaging ways. But when we look at the way that radical uncertainty is practised in lesbian writing then we might wonder if this spring-cleaning has gone too far. Post-modernist writers are keen on the importance of making their subject position known lest they should be seen as pretending to universality or objectivity. Lesbian feminists quite unaware of post-modernist theory developed their own version of this in newsletters in the 80s where they would identify themselves in biographical notes as "Ex-het. middle class, fat-oppressed, fem, Libran" and so forth, but they tended to be certain of all these aspects of their identities. Elizabeth Meese gives us an example of the post-modernist version of radical uncertainty:

Why is it that the lesbian seems like a shadow – a shadow with/in woman, with/in writing? A contrastive shape in a shadow play, slightly formless, the edges blurred

---

3. Comment made by Aboriginal lesbian Marie Andrews.

by the turns of the field, the sheets on which a drama is projected. The lesbian subject is not all I am and it is in all I am. A shadow of who I am that attests to my being there, I am never with/out this lesbian. And we are always turning, this way and that, in one place and another. The shadows alone, never mind the body, make such a complex choreography in our struggle to make sense (1990b, p. 70).

Many pieces of post-modernist writing on lesbian themes begin with several pages of this kind of introspection on the writer's lesbian identity. Similarly when post-modernist academics give speeches they tend to spend the first twenty minutes interrogating their own subject position, leaving little space for the content that the audience is patiently waiting for. It may well be that many lesbian readers have never felt like a shadow or felt that they had a huge struggle to make sense, but in post-modernist feminist writing there is much agonising on how hard it is to speak or to write. There is an anguished agony of the artist here which many of us who simply seek to express ourselves as simply and frequently as we can, just cannot afford in ordinary political struggle. Judith Butler begins her piece in *Inside/Out* with just such anguished introspection on who she is being when she is asked to go and give a speech as a lesbian.

At first I considered writing a different sort of essay, one with a philosophical tone: the "being" of being homosexual. The prospect of being anything, even for pay, has always produced in me a certain anxiety, for "to be" lesbian seems to be more than a simple injunction to become who or what I already am. And in no way does it settle the anxiety for me to say that this is "part" of what I am. To write or speak as a lesbian appears a paradoxical appearance of this "I", one which feels neither true nor false. For it is a production, usually in response to a request, to come out or write in the name of an identity which, once produced, sometimes functions as a politically efficacious phantasm. I'm not at ease with "lesbian theories, gay theories," for . . . identity categories tend to be instruments of regulatory regimes . . . This is not to say that I will not appear at political occasions under the sign of lesbian, but that I would like to have it permanently unclear what precisely that sign signifies (1991, pp. 113–14).

I find this kind of writing politically worrying. Butler uses the word homosexual in the first sentence in application to herself which is not something that the average lesbian feminist would feel able to do. The word homosexual has even more specifically male connotations than the word gay for most lesbians who became political in the 70s and who would not see themselves as being in an identical category with gay men which could be covered by such a single word. This suggests that Butler is one of the new lesbianandgay theorists who has chosen to abandon a separate lesbian politics. The use of particular words may help us to place Butler politically but it is her great angst about where she places herself which forms a problem for lesbian or gay politics. It's not exciting or inspiring to be faced with radical uncertainty but that's not sufficient as a criticism. What needs to be asked, and many heterosexual feminists, Black writers as well as lesbians are beginning to ask, is whether it is politically useful to become so doubtful about the word lesbian or other political categories such as woman or Black when the oppressed groups making use of these identity categories are only just beginning to make space for themselves historically, culturally, and in the academy.

The point of post-modernist questioning of subject positions was that members of dominant groups should acknowledge their biases so that readers could more easily recognise certain writing as being part of regulatory systems. This is all fine and good but it is not the members of dominant groups who have taken up this opportunity to be radically uncertain and there is no good reason to expect that they would wish to. It is not the vice-chancellors of traditional universities who begin orations with twenty minutes of agonising over their subject positions and their right to be saying what they are about to say. Male, heterosexual, white academics are not taking up the opportunity in droves either. It seems to be mainly women, lesbians, gays and members of ethnic minority groups in general who are feeling under pressure to be radically uncertain. Whilst the certainties of regulatory regimes remain in place it may be that the best political way to fight them is to have some certainty ourselves about who we are and what we are doing. It could be that the requirement to be uncertain is simply feeding into the general difficulty the oppressed have with feeling confident and assertive in opposition to the dominant myth-making machinery. It could be helping us to feel powerless.

Diana Fuss devotes a whole chapter to the question of lesbian and gay identity politics in her book, *Essentially Speaking*. She suggests that lesbian theorists have been more committed than gay men to the idea of an essentialist identity.

> In general, current lesbian theory is less willing to question or to part with the idea of a "lesbian essence" and an identity politics based on this shared essence. Gay male theorists, on the other hand, following the lead of Foucault, have been quick to endorse the social constructionist hypothesis and to develop more detailed analyses of the historical construction of sexualities (1990, p. 98).

Now this will be a surprise to lesbian feminist readers. The opposite has been our common experience. As a teacher I have discovered over and over again that the idea that male homosexuality is socially constructed is anathema to some male gay students and difficult to accept for many more, but not difficult for lesbians. Many lesbians, after all, have chosen to love women for political reasons, very often after half a lifetime of wifehood and motherhood in which they never thought of being attracted to women. Gay men do not often have this experience. It is difficult to find any who will say that their sexual preference is political and the result of consciously choosing to leave women or heterosexuality. Maybe, then, Fuss means that lesbian writers have not promoted the idea of social construction even though most lesbians at the level of experience have accepted it. But this seems an unreasonable suggestion too. There is a quite massive literature on political lesbianism and the idea that heterosexuality is a political institution, constructed as the foundation of women's oppression. But Fuss ignores this literature apart from mentioning Adrienne Rich on several pages, perhaps she has never seen it, though much is actually taught on Women's Studies courses. She explains that lesbians subscribe to essentialism more enthusiastically than gay men because as women we are more marginal and the certainty of an essentialist identity therefore seems more important to our security. This really seems like the opposite of the question that is really interesting to ask, which is why gay men who have less need of an essentialist identity in terms of their security subscribe so much more tenaciously to such.

According to Fuss, and other post-modernist lesbianandgay theorists, it is Foucault who has taught the world that sexuality is socially constructed. Particularly it is he who has taught us that sexual identities are differently experienced in different historical periods. So, Fuss speculates, it might be because of lesbians' greater need to adhere politically to essentialism that there has been a "scarcity of Foucauldian analyses on lesbian sexuality compared to the plethora of such studies on the gay male subject" (Fuss: 1990, p. 99). This is a distinctly surprising statement. Quite apart from the inaccuracy of attributing essentialism to lesbian theory, there is another problem here. Why should lesbians do Foucauldian analysis? Why should they use the work of a gay man who did not really notice women let alone lesbians in his theory, to describe their experience, and one whose insights were antedated considerably by lesbian feminism? Lesbian feminists, in particular Lillian Faderman (1984, 1991), have done their own excellent and groundbreaking work on the changing forms and development of woman-loving in history. But Fuss does not reference Faderman.

How can she manage to overlook lesbian feminism and believe that lesbians cannot do theory if they are not striving to fit themselves into the unsuitable concepts of a gay man? This must be because Fuss's starting point is not in lesbian theory or lesbian feminism. She does realise that male gay theory cannot entirely encompass lesbianism. For instance, when talking about the importance of social constructionist theories of lesbian and gay identity she suggests that these will help in theorising the differences between lesbians and gay men but does not seem to regard these as large.

> ... invention theories allow us to make important distinctions between male homosexuals and lesbians, two groups which are frequently conflated in the research on sexual minorities (research noticeably skewed in the direction of the gay male subject) but which, in fact, are not constructed in precisely the same ways (1990, pp. 108–9).

One might even wish to be a little stronger than that and say that lesbians and gay men were actually constructed in very different ways but Fuss, being resolutely lesbianandgay in her approach, prefers to be much more mild and tentative. It is interesting considering that post-modernist theorists see themselves as unmatched in their attention to "difference" that they sometimes reveal themselves as very timid in acknowledging such differences as those that are politically constructed between men and women. Fuss' starting point is in gay male theory, and in post-modernist men in general. At the same time as not referencing Faderman she has nineteen works by Derrida in the bibliography.

It does seem to be his work which has sent some lesbian and feminist theorists into a tizzy over essentialism. She tells us of his "recent efforts to deconstruct 'essence'" (1990, p. 102). It is clear that the word essentialism is not being used in the traditional ways in these post-modernist writings. Many detractors of radical feminist theory do, with little evidence, accuse it of being essentialist in its old-fashioned sense of biological determinist. Anti-pornography campaigners are accused, for instance, of believing that male and female sexuality are essentially different. But Fuss does not use the word in the same way. She, like other post-modernist theorists, tends to use the word to describe any politics based upon any concept of identity, constructed or otherwise, or any politics which believes that there is any similarity amongst a class of people on which political theorising or action can be based. It is a concept of essentialism so often directed against anyone who believes in or suggests political action that some feminists and other activists have come to believe that the word is just a way of saying that political action is vulgar. It may be that post-modernists have committed verbicide on this term and that it can no longer be used usefully.

The struggles which theorists like Butler and Fuss are having with concepts like gender, identity and essence arise from the works of their male authorities. These lesbian theorists are not situated within lesbian or feminist politics but are seeking to forge a unified lesbianandgay politics based on male gay theory. They criticise lesbian feminist politics, when they mention it at all, for its failure to measure up in terms of their post-modernist male masters, and wrestle to fit lesbian politics seamlessly into the pockets of gay post-modernists. Meanwhile lesbian feminist theorists are engaged in a strange shadow play of seeking to criticise these intrusions of what is clearly a rather inappropriate theory onto the stage without being familiar with its origins. Not many of us have read nineteen works of Derrida and many will not want to, but we are expected to struggle to answer his questions, introduced by his women followers.

I would like to suggest that however daring post-modern theorists see themselves to be they are actually simply placing a fashionable intellectual gloss on old-fashioned liberalism and individualism. A good example of this is the effect that exposure to post-modern theory can have on straightforward political analysis in respect of pornography. Kobena Mercer is a former member of the Gay Black Group in London and is now teaching art history at the University of California, Santa Cruz. Whilst in the Gay Black Group he used the insights of feminist anti-pornography activists to critique the work of the white gay American photographer, Robert Mapplethorpe. Much of Mapplethorpe's work focused on black male nudes. Mercer interpreted the photo entitled "Man in a Polyester Suit" which showed "the profile of a black man whose head was cropped – or 'decapitated', so to speak – holding his semi-tumescent penis through the Y-fronts of his under-pants" as perpetuating "the racist stereotype that, essentially, the black man is nothing more than his penis" (Mercer: 1992, p. 96). He saw such photos as perpetu-ating "racial fetishism" an "aesthetic idealization of racial difference that merely inverts and reverses the binary axis of colonial discourse" (Mercer: 1992, p. 99). Then, he says, he became aware of conflicting readings of Mapplethorpe's work as a result of becoming familiar with post-structuralist theory. Indeed once in the academy, and he is now an academic, it is not easy to hold on to positions which can be seen as vulgarly political. The ideas of post-modernist cultural studies made him realise:

> The variety of conflicting interpretations of the value of Mapplethorpe's work would imply that the text does not bear one, singular and unequivocal meaning, but is open to a number of competing readings (1992, p. 102).

He decides that the question of whether Mapplethorpe's black male nudes "reinforce or undermine racist myths about black sexuality" is "unan-swerable" because of the "death of the author" argument in post-structuralist theory. He now interrogates his own subject position as he views the photographs and wonders whether "my anger was also mingled with feelings of jealousy, rivalry or envy" the "anger and envy" being the effects of his "identification with both object and subject of the look." Cultural criticism of this variety depends on the individual. It is just opinion and people have different ones. "A great deal depends on the reader and the social identity she or he brings to the text" (1992, p. 105). Mercer has become radically uncertain and is now as apologetic about his earlier clear anti-racist stand on Mapplethorpe as we have seen many lesbians become about their earlier embarrassing feminism.

Another example of the way in which post-modernist-speak serves to leach out political meaning is the blurb for a conference entitled "Forces of Desire" at the prestigious Humanities Research Centre at the Australian National Uni-versity in Canberra in June 1993 on sexualities and culture.

> The key issues here will be the examination of sexuality without the dominance of a master model, and the structuring and restructuring of desire. Speakers will be invited to address a range of topics, such as: multiple sexualities as practices and life-styles beyond the dominant models with investment in reproductive sexuality; the costs of sustaining such models; the varieties of sexuality – masochism, sadism, perversions, heterosexualities, gay sexualities; sexuality as normative and the possibilities and purposes of resistance to and transformation of these norms; knowledges as implicated in sexual practices – the erotics of knowledge production, the desire for knowledges; the interactions of sexuality, knowledge, power and violence.[4]

---

4. Publicity material about visiting fellowships for the Humanities Research Centre at ANU's 1993 theme "Sexualities and Culture".

It may be that lesbian feminist readers are already feeling rather puzzled about how their analysis would fit in here. In fact lesbians are not mentioned. They seem to have been disappeared into "gay sexualities". How many are there of these? The varieties of sexuality start off with masochism and sadism and nowhere seem to include anything specifically egalitarian. The lesbian feminist critique of heterosexuality as an institution does not seem welcome since in this "model" we only have "heterosexualities", this plural form somehow not lending itself to such an analysis. "S's" have appeared on all sorts of things as we might expect with a certain post-modern approach which seeks to cover all eventualities with plurals which end up excluding lesbians and feminists and much that could be called political analysis. In favour of "difference" everything has been homogenised here. I always wonder how the plurals and singulars are decided upon. For instance there are singulars of masochism, sadism, desire and power but plurals of everything else. There is a politics here of course, even a "master model" perhaps. I suspect that the politics is a sexual libertarian one of sexual minorities, mainstream gay male politics of the moment. It could be that the "gay sexualities" are supposed to include pedophilia, transsexualism and so on, all represented as somehow equal to "lesbianism" if that fits anywhere here at all. There do not seem to be any radical or revolutionary feminists on the list of research fellows or speakers invited. But they do include Gayle Rubin, proponent of lesbian sadomasochism and butch lesbian transsexualism, Jeffrey Weeks, Foucauldian gay historian, Carol Vance, a leading libertarian lesbianandgay theorist and Cindy Patton, who has bemoaned the amount of seriousness given by feminists to the issue of sexual abuse. Surely it must be difficult for sado-masochists, dwellers on the "sexual fringe" such as Rubin, to maintain that they are really daring, when they are invited, and financially supported, by a prestigious institution in this way.

Post-modernist lesbian and gay theory performs the useful function of permitting those who simply wish to employ the tools and trappings of sexism and racism to feel not only justified but even revolutionary. Lesbian roleplaying, sado-masochism, male gay masculinity, drag, Madonna's mimicry, her use of black men and black iconography, Mapplethorpe's racist sexual stereotyping, can be milked for all the pleasure and profit that they offer in a male supremacist culture in which inequality of power is seen as all that sex is or could be. The enjoyment of the status quo is then called "parody" so that it can be retrieved by intellectuals who might otherwise feel anxious about the excitement they experience. For those post-modern lesbianandgay theorists who have no interest in taking their pleasures in these ways, the ideas of radical uncertainty, of the utopian or essentialist nature of any project for social change, provide a theoretical support for a gentlemanly liberalism and individualism.

Sue Wilkinson and Celia Kitzinger

The Queer Backlash*

In recent years, the word "queer", long used as a term of insult and self-loathing, has been reclaimed by lesbians, gay men, bisexuals, transvestites, transsexuals – and even (some) heterosexuals – as a proud declaration of nonconformist sexualities: "we're here, we're queer; get used to it!". In place of the medicopsychiatric "homosexual", or the euphemistic and self-justificatory "gay", the word "queer" is seen as confrontational and as underscoring the fact that we are "queer" ("deviant" and "abnormal") to a world in which normality is defined in rigid and suffocating terms. In what follows, we present the theoretical and political strategies of the queer movement, with particular reference to its key strategy, "fucking with gender", and we try to account for the apparent popularity of queer, both within and beyond the academy. Finally, we present a radical feminist critique of queer theory, and show that queer is centrally antagonistic to radical feminism.

What is Queer?

Influenced by, and in many ways an offshoot of post-modernism, queer theory aims to deconstruct and confound normative categories of gender and sexuality, exposing their fundamental unnaturalness. There are no "true" gender identities or "natural" sexes: rather maleness and femaleness are "performances" or "simulations". According to Butler maleness and femaleness are:

> . . . *performative* in the sense that the essence or identity that they otherwise purport to express are *fabrications* manufactured and sustained through corporeal signs and other discursive means . . . an illusion discursively maintained for the purposes of the regulation of sexuality within the obligatory frame of reproductive heterosexuality (1990, p. 136).

---

* Some of the material in this article first appeared in Celia Kitzinger and Sue Wilkinson (1994). *Gender and Society*.

"Simulation" means not a replica of something that actually exists, but an identical copy for which there has never been an original. Disneyland, for example, has been described as a simulation whose function in proclaiming its status as "unreal" is precisely to make the rest of the USA look "real" (Baudrillard: 1988). Gender, too, is conceived as an exact copy of something that never really existed in the first place: there is no "real", underlying maleness or femaleness on which we base our performances. The post-modern body "is the body of the mythological Trickster, the shape-shifter of indeterminate sex and changeable gender ... who continually alters her/his body, creates and recreates a personality ... and floats across time from period to period, place to place" (Bordo: 1993, p. 144, paraphrasing Smith-Rosenberg: 1985). This is, in the language of post-modernism, indicative of an identity in flux, a protean fantasy, an intricate textual dance, a narrative hetero-glossia, a choreography of multiplicity, and a celebration of a transcendent polyvocal self at a time when "the rigid demarcations of the clear and distinct Cartesian universe are crumbling, and the notion of the unified 'subject' is no longer tenable" (Bordo: 1993, p. 144). In this theory of fluctuating and continually altering selves, "sex" is an area "of fashion and style rather than biology and identity" (Chapkis: 1986, p. 138). "Being" man or woman is conceptualised not as core identity, but rather as "a put-on, a sex toy" (Schwichtenberg: 1993a, p. 135) or as a "temporary positioning" (Gergen: 1993, p. 64).

In conceptualising what have previously been seen as "core" identities (man/woman; hetero-/homosexual) as no more than fluctuating fashions or perfor-mances, queer theory, like post-modernism more generally, embodies a hope for the future abolition of these divisive patriarchal binarisms, ushering in the age of the post-lesbian and, of course, the post-heterosexual. In this imagined world, man does not exist, nor woman either; hence the concepts of heterosexuality, homosexuality and bisexuality are literally unthinkable. The "sex" of the person you have sex with is not only irrelevant in terms of social meaning and identity: it is also unspeci-fiable, because "sex-as-gender" is no longer a meaningful concept. Such a vision of the future is not, of course, specific to post-modernist and queer theory: it has a long history within the gay, lesbian and feminist liberation movements (e.g. Radicalesbians: 1970; Piercy: 1979). What is distinctive about post-modern and queer (as opposed to lesbian feminist) theory is the strategy envisioned for getting "there" from "here".

The notion of "queer heterosexuality" is one component of the post-modern strategy for transition into the brave new world of the future. Such a world would have no use for the concept of "queer heterosexuality" because there would be no such "thing" as heterosexuality, no "men" and "women" to perform it, nor any heteronormativity against which to be positioned as "queer". But in the interim, queer theorists give "queer heterosexuals" a walk-on role. "There are times," says queer theorist Cherry Smyth (1992), "when queers may choose to call themselves heterosexual, bisexual, lesbian or gay, or none of the above". According to Cathy Schwichtenberg (1993a, p. 141), one could "come out" and participate in a range of identities "such as a lesbian heterosexual, a heterosexual lesbian, a male lesbian, a female gay man, or even a feminist sex-radical". Another writer offers this list: "There are straight queers, biqueers, tranny queers, lez queers, fag queers, SM queers, fisting queers" (Anonymous leaflet: 1991, cited in Smyth: 1992, p. 17). Queer celebrates its own "inclusiveness".

Fucking with Gender

If all is artifice, simulation and performance, if "sex" is only a passing fashion, there is no point in opposing this by looking for some underlying reality or truth about "men" and "women"; rather the strategy becomes actively to participate in the artifice precisely in order to underscore the fragility of "sex" and "gender" *as artifice*. This strategy is described as "gender play" (Schwichtenberg: 1993b), "gender bending" (Braidotti: 1991), or, most popularly, as "genderfuck" (Reich: 1992) or "fucking with gender". The gender-fuck is supposed to "deprive the naturalizing narratives of compulsory heterosexuality of their central protagonists: 'man' and 'woman'" (Butler: 1990, p. 146) and to illustrate the social constructedness of "sex", in all its multiple meanings.

This key queer strategy, the gender-fuck, is about parody, pastiche and exaggeration. It replaces *resistance* to dominant cultural meanings of "sex" with carnivalesque reversals and transgressions of traditional gender roles and sexualities, which revel in their own artificiality. Media figures like Prince, Boy George and Annie Lennox have been cited as gender benders (Braidotti: 1991, pp. 122-3), but the most famous example of contemporary gender-fucking is undoubtedly Madonna:

> Madonna, too, puts forth a disguise but less as a concealment than as a brash revelation of artifice. It is the essence of camp – cracking the mirror, dressing up and acting out to *expose* the constructedness of what in other settings passes as 'natural' male, female, or heterosexual (Henderson: 1993, p. 122).

This celebration of denaturalisation is typical of the gender-fuck, and Madonna has been described both as a "post-modern feminist heroine" (Kaplan: 1987 in Mandzuick: 1993, p. 169; Schwichtenberg: 1993, p. 132) and as a "queer icon" (Henderson: 1993, pp. 108, 119, 122).

Lesbian photographers often claimed as "queer" include Jean Fraser and Tessa Boffin (1991) whose controversial collection of lesbian photography, *Stolen Glances* (Beloff: 1993), was compiled, they say, not in the "attempt to naturalize a 'lesbian aesthetic' . . . but rather to celebrate that there is no natural sexuality at all", and out of an interest in "subversive strategies of representation" (1991, pp. 20–1). *Love Bites*, a collection of photographs by Della Grace, is also cited as an example of gender-fucking: one photograph, "Lesbian Cock", shows two lesbians dressed in leather and biker caps, both sporting moustaches, and one holding a life-like dildo protruding from her crotch:

> Lesbian feminists think things like lesbians giving blow-jobs to dildos should be kept quiet . . . [F]or women to indulge in gender-fuck somehow isn't acceptable. But lesbians do. Lesbians even have 'gay male sex' (Grace, quoted in Smyth: 1992, p. 44).

A varied cast of characters has claimed (or been ascribed) the "queer" label and lauded for its gender-fucking prowess. In the name of "queer", some lesbians reclaim butch femme roles (as "changeable costuming", MacCowan: 1992, p. 300), and some gay men reclaim camp ("the pervert's revenge on authenticity", Dollimore: 1991). Transvestism and cross-dressing "draws the binary logic of sexual identity into question" (Bristow: 1992) and for just $25 you can attend a four-hour intensive "Cross-Dressing Workshop" with "genderbending Justin 'Glam' Bond, and Drag King Elvis Herselvis", with movement direction, cross-gender make-up technique, costume advice and hairstyling demonstrations all included (Advertising flyer: 1992). Transsexuals have a part to play because "the surgical removal and implantation of body parts reveals that one's flesh can be cut, so to speak, like a suit" (Bristow: 1992) and because, symbolically speaking, "we are all transsexuals" (Baudrillard: 1988). Hermaphrodites, too, are "a pornotopian escape from . . . rigid binarism" (Williams: 1992, p. 261) and Annie Sprinkle, "post-Porn Post-Modernist" and "bi-girl" (Sprinkle: 1992), sometimes bracketed with Madonna as a queer performance artist (e.g. Williams: 1992, p. 234), delights in the gender-fucking ambiguity of her "first time with a F2M-transsexual-surgically-made hermaphrodite".

Queer Attractions

With "queer" support for such a dazzling variety of "perversions", and given that the biological sex of sexual partners is dismissed in favour of gender as performance, it is hardly surprising that "many queer activists are wondering what's stopping gay men and lesbians from developing a sexual politics that also embraces bi- and heterosexuals" (Pickering: 1992). Within the academy, there are, indeed, some signs of this, with the lauding of queer theory both for its "inclusivity" and its "discursive opposition":

> . . . above all, the deployment of the term 'queer' promise[s] to incorporate as well as create a whole range of sexual identities – including dissident heterosexual ones – within its political project (Bristow and Wilson: 1993, p. 9).

In this vision, all those who are similarly "transgressive" share an affinity and equality; "sexual minorities" organising together can constitute a revolutionary potential.

For feminists, queer theory's attractions include a powerful sense of possibility and of the power to change. Feminists have spent more than a century challenging concepts of the "natural" which relegate women to the kitchen and the bedroom, and justify and condone their subjugation by men, and now see the potential of queer theory to denaturalise – and subvert – essentialist links between "sex" and "gender" as considerable. For lesbian feminists, queer's comprehensive deconstruction of heteronormativity also particularly appeals. Sheila Jeffreys (1993, chapter 6) has pointed to the lesbian – and lesbian feminist – romance with "out-lawry", and the "outsider" element of queer may feed into this, particularly when combined with the "bad girl" frisson provided by queer notions of "transgression".

For the jaded academic palate, sated with high seriousness, dalliance with queer promises "fun"; and celebrations of "pleasure" may seem more enticing than concerns of "political correctness". It is not difficult to be seduced by queer theory's "wit", "ingenuity" and "panache" (Beloff: 1993). Outside the academy, too, queer has caught the public imagination in a way feminism never has. Queer notions have seeped into everyday contemporary culture – especially fashion and advertising. Queer is a designer label for the latest consumer accessory. The British national newspaper, the *Guardian* (22 Oct 1994), tells us that the "must-have accessories" of 1994 (watch, sunglasses, pencil case) are "gender benders", "the ones that know no bounds". The women's magazine, *Elle*, carries a feature entitled "The New Unisex" (Briscoe: 1994, pp. 91-6) "a style and mode of behaviour that befits both sexes, and in so doing, transcends sex itself . . . calculated sexual ambivalence". The feature is strikingly illustrated by fashion advertisements (Dolce and Gabbana, Armani, Oliver) in which male and female models are "so close in look and spirit they are like incestuous twins". The 1994 Paris fashion shows incorporate "the new unisex" and the gender-bending haute couture of Jean Paul Gaultier (Patton: 1993, p. 95) and include a collection entitled "Transcending gender: The presentiment of femininity in the play of its disappearance", with models wearing "austerely tailored jackets, from under the hems of which exploded huge skirts made up of a mass of tiered organza and chiffon ruffles" (Brampton: 1994, p. 2). The enthusiastic appropriation of queer in both academic and popular contexts might lead one to be suspicious as to its longer-term value as a source of change.

What's Wrong With Queer?

While superficially attractive for its vigour, wit, sense of possibility and trans-formative potential, the move towards queer is, in fact, a conservative one – and one that is deeply dangerous for radical feminism. Within queer, radical feminist analyses are ignored or marginalised at best, subverted or derided at worst. Despite its "denaturalising" potential, queer theory is centrally antagonistic to feminism. This is partly because queer theorists see feminism as a totalising "grand narrative", whose meanings and values must be subverted and thrown into question, along with the other explanatory frameworks in politics, science and philosophy – mere fodder for deconstruction in the post-modern age. More than this, however, queer politics is often expressed in terms explicitly oppositional to feminism – especially radical feminism, characterised as "moralistic feminist separatism" (Smyth: 1992, p. 36). Lyndall MacCowan (1992, p. 323) wants to "reclaim the right to fuck around with gender" but also insists that "we need to take back 'lesbian' as a sexual definition disburdened of any political justification". Within queer theory, there is no attempt to problematise pleasure, much less to engage with radical feminists' attempts to do so (see Jeffreys: 1990; Kitzinger and Wilkinson: 1993; Kitzinger: 1994), other than to characterise these as repressive, restrictive and totalitarian in effect or intent. Queer functions as apologia or justification for much behaviour seen by radical feminism as damaging to women and – especially – to lesbians. The queer critique not only ignores, but sometimes reverses, key feminist critiques, particularly radical feminist critiques: of sadomasochism; of gay male culture; of transsexuality/transvestism; of bisexuality; and of heterosexuality.

Queer implicitly – and often explicitly – supports and encourages sado-masochism (both heterosexual and lesbian/gay). The queer movement displays a continuing fascination with violence and degradation, including claiming as its own – and, if necessary, as queer "avant la lettre" (Merck: 1993, pp. 1, 9) supporters of pornography and sadomasochism. Such preoccupations were epitomised by the Operation Spanner campaign, which, in seeking to decriminalise "consensual" sado-masochistic sex between gay men, became a *cause célèbre* for the British queer movement. Radical feminist analyses of lesbian sadomasochism as modelled on heterosexual practice (e.g. Linden *et al.*: 1982) are explicitly opposed to the queer valorisation of sadomasochism as "transgressive" sexual practice:

> It is important to highlight the SM sex battle as it signifies why so many dykes developed a dissatisfaction and disaffection for 'lesbian feminism' and consequently feel attracted to the transgressive elements putatively offered by queer (Smyth: 1992, p. 38).

Cherry Smyth (1992, p. 36) even raises as a possibility (and leaves unanswered) the question: "is straight SM automatically queer, while a mono-gamous 'vanilla' lesbian couple living in suburbia isn't?" This explicit endorsement and validation of sadomasochism at the expense of lesbianism is a worrying development of queer theory.

Also particularly striking is queer theory's valorisation of gay male culture. Gay male concerns (notably the traditions of camp and drag and a preoccupation with anal eroticism) predominate, even for female writers (e.g. Butler: 1993b; Sedgwick: 1993); and lesbian emulation of gay men ("Learning from the boys", as one subtitle puts it [Smyth: 1992, p. 42]) is frequently advocated. Lesbian queers endorse as progressive "alliances between pro-sex anti-censorship lesbians and like-minded gay men . . . so opening up the possibility of new models for the expansion of lesbian erotic possibilities" while "equal nurturing" sex is characterised as "prepubescent" (Smyth: 1992, p. 37). Not only does this dominance of gay male interests serve comprehensively to "disappear" lesbians from the queer agenda (Jeffreys: 1993; 1994), it also runs directly counter to a long history of radical lesbian feminist political work separate from gay men (e.g. Stanley: 1982; Hoagland and Penelope: 1988).

Radical feminist critiques from the 1970s on (e.g. Raymond: 1979/1982/1994a) which have argued that transsexual surgery and treatment serves only to *reinforce* gender conformity. The "transsexual fabrication process" serves simply to substitute one sex-role stereotype for another, posing no challenge to the prevailing stereotypes of a role-defined society. Men are turned into artefactual women, into (hetero)patriarchal stereotypes of femininity. Fifteen years on from the original publication of *The Transsexual Empire*, Raymond (1979/1982/1994a) contends that contemporary developments in "transgenderism" (including "a plethora of terms such as 'transgendered', 're-gendered', 'gender-blending', 'gender-bending', 'gender fucking' and 'transhomosexuality'") do no more than extend the lexicon of so-called gender-dissonant behaviour. There may now be "a continuum of gendered expression", but there is still no sign of a transformative sexual politics (see Janice Raymond's 1994 Introduction).

Queer politics are "bi-friendly" (Weise: 1993, p. xiv). Under the queer banner, "transgressive marriages" (i.e. heterosexually-married women having "lesbian" sex. French: 1992) are proposed as a "validation" of bisexuality (Eadie: 1993, pp. 148-9); and specific heterosexual acts are considered "transgressive": "When I strap on a dildo and fuck my male partner, we are engaging in 'heterosexual behaviour, but . . . it feels *queer*" (unnamed woman, cited in Wilson: 1993, p. 113). "Queer straights" are billed as "more fun for bisexuals to hang out with" than "straight queers" (Eridani: 1992, p. 180), and the University of California at Berkeley's gay student society (the "Multicultural Bisexual Lesbian Gay Association") recently gave a "Queerest Couple" award to "a bisexual woman and her straight boyfriend" (Trnka: 1992, pp. 110-11). All of these examples provide implicit support for "lesbians" (or lesbian-identified bisexuals) engaging in heterosex. Sex with men is presented as especially exciting or "transgressive" because "forbidden" by lesbian feminists (e.g. Terris: 1991), who are widely castigated for "political correctness" (e.g. Elliott: 1992, p. 234) or "judgemental moralism" (George: 1993, p. 57). Whether celebrating the joys of bisexual sex, or promoting bisexuality with explicitly anti-lesbian arguments, these queer-inspired proponents of a "new" bisexual politics completely fail to engage with radical feminist analyses (see Wilkinson: 1995, for an extended discussion).

In a similar way, queer theory also ignores radical feminist analyses of *hetero*sexuality. There is no representation of heterosex as eroticised dominance and submission (e.g. Dworkin: 1976/1982, 1987; Jeffreys: 1990), or of heterosexuality as an oppressive and compulsory institution (e.g. Rich: 1980; Wilkinson and Kitzinger: 1993). Rather, queer reclaims as "feminist" the female dominatrix scenes of male pornography (with even the British newspaper colour magazines offering chilling examples of fashion trends and films which combine "a vision of kitsch art and kinky sex" [e.g. McDowell: 1994, p. 9]). Queer theory provides renewed justification for heterosexual feminists' refusal to notice that they *are* heterosexual – or for their tendency to dismiss their heterosexuality as unimportant, based on transitory and provisional attributions. Asked to identify themselves as heterosexual, many feminists react with defensive anger (Kitzinger and Wilkinson: 1993, p. 5).

The queer elision of heterosexuality and homosexuality as sexually – and hence politically – equivalent or interchangeable is not as radical as queer theorists would have us believe. It was Kinsey's (1948) famous invention of the "heterosexual-homosexual continuum" (borrowed in part from Freud's theories of innate bisexuality and polymorphous perversity) which set the stage for a wide-spread dissolution within psychology of any specific differences between lesbians and heterosexual women (see Kitzinger: 1987). The presentation of lesbianism and heterosexuality as equivalent betrays the underlying liberalism of queer theory – a liberalism which negates both the political force of lesbianism as a refusal of the heteropatriarchal order, and the radical feminist analysis of heterosexuality as the key site of women's oppressions. As the meanings of heterosexuality and homosexuality become blurred within a fantasy world of ambiguity, indeterminacy and charade, the material realities of oppression and the feminist politics of resistance are forgotten:

> It is difficult . . . to acknowledge the divided self and engage the pleasure of masquerade while at the same time fighting a strikingly antagonistic legal and social system for your health, your safety, your job, your place to live, or the right to raise your children (Henderson: 1993, p. 123).

In sum, then, the "transgressive" impulse of queer theory manifests itself at least as much against feminism as against heteropatriarchy. Such aspects of the queer movement render it less a symptom of the "defeat" of, and more an indication of the growing "backlash" against, feminism, particularly radical feminism (see also Parnaby: 1993; Miller and Harne: 1995). Pleasure is prioritised over political analysis, and lesbian concerns, in particular, are frequently rendered invisible. As radical feminists, we need to resist the incorporation and depoliticisation of our agenda by the queer movement. We must not become part of the queer backlash.

Christine Delphy

French Feminism: An Imperialist Invention

"French feminism" is a baffling topic for everybody: and it is no less so for feminists from France than for feminists from the USA, Britain and any other Anglo culture.

From the outset it needs to be understood that feminists in France don't need to call their feminism a particular name, any more than American feminists call theirs "American feminism". So – first of all: what is "French feminism"? "French feminism" is not feminism in France. So, why has it been deemed necessary by Anglo-American feminists to specify in ideological terms the actions and the writings of feminists from France? And, why give a *national* label to a particular set of ideas or brand of feminism? How relevant are national boundaries to feminism – or indeed to other social and ideological movements – and how relevant *should* they be? Finally: how was what is now known as "French feminism" constructed? In whose interests was it so construed? Who decided what it was and what it was not? *What went into the bag and what did not?*

In constructing "French feminism", Anglo-American authors favoured a certain political trend, overtly anti-feminist, called Psych et Po, to the detriment of what is considered, by Anglo-American as well as French feminist historians (Picq: 1993), to be the core of the feminist movement; and their bias has contributed to weakening the French movement (Moses: 1992a). More and more protests are being heard about the voluntary or involuntary distortions and omissions of the Anglo-American version of "French feminism". The aim of this article is not, however, to set the record straight: that work is already under way (see Moses: 1992a and b).

Anglo-American proponents of "French feminism" have also consistently conflated "women writers" with the "Women's Movement" (Moses: 1992a), thus eliminating the activist dimension of that movement. They promoted as "Major French feminist theorists" (Moi: 1987, p. 5), a "Holy Trinity" made up of three women who have become household names in the Anglo-American world of Women's Studies, which itself is increasingly divorced from the social movement: Hélène Cixous, Julia

Kristeva, Luce Irigaray. This was in spite of the fact, never revealed to the non-French public, that the first two are completely outside feminist debate in France, and not being considered feminist theorists, can hardly be considered "major feminist theorists". It was also in spite of the well-known fact that has been dealt with diversely by Anglo-American exporters, that at least the first two not only do not call themselves feminist, but they have been known to actually denounce feminism.

Although these facts are well known, they are not seen as a problem. Why? "Never would Americans proclaim nonfeminists to be the figureheads of their own movement" (Ezekiel: 1992). What do you call doing to somebody else what you would not have done unto you? The term "imperialism" springs to the lips. And that is indeed the conclusion reached by both Moses and Ezekiel. They see imperialism at work in the Anglo-American construction of "French feminism". Moreover, they see this imperialism as related to domestic agendas: "opponents have taken as their targets, not its American agents, but the French themselves" (Ezekiel: 1992); and "the French . . . are blamed for aspects of ourselves that we do not like but do not take responsibility for (like our racism and our classism)" (Moses: 1992a).

"French feminism", as an American and more widely English-speaking fabrication, was created by a series of distortions and voluntary or involuntary errors about what was happening in France from the mid-1970s on. These distortions have a pattern. We do not have several competing views or definitions – which shows that the distortions are not random. On the other hand, if we did (have competing views), then we would not have "French feminism". "French feminism" is thus a highly consensual object in the sense that the only debates about it focus on its relevance to Anglo-American concerns – there are no debates about what it is. Everybody seems to know what "French feminism" is – at the same time that it is never really defined and remains elusive. It is therefore impossible to give, in any objective way, an ideological definition to what is an ideological current, and is perceived as such, in feminism.

The only objective way to define it is to say that it is a body of comments by Anglo-American writers on a selection of French – and non-French – writers: Lacan, Freud, Kristeva, Cixous, Derrida and Irigaray are the core group. But there are others. "French feminism" then is an Anglo-American strand of intellectual production within an Anglo-American context. From now on, when I speak of French feminism without quotation marks, I am referring exclusively to this Anglo-American body of writings, and when I speak of French feminists, I am referring to its Anglo-American authors.

Destabilizing Feminism

The main reason its inventors invented their brand of feminism as "French" was that they did not want to take responsibility for what they were saying. And in particular for their attempt to rescue psychoanalysis from the discredit it had incurred in feminism – but not only in feminism, as this discredit is general throughout the social sciences. They pretended that *another* feminist movement thought it was great – that in fact it was all the other, admittedly strange, movement was interested in.

That took some doing and it is excellently related and analysed by Claire Moses in "French Feminism in US Academic Discourse" (Moses: 1992a). Moses points out that at the time of the famous 1978 *Signs* issue on feminist theory, "the Prefaces always identified Cixous, Kristeva and Irigaray as French 'writers' or 'intellectuals', never as 'feminists'." She goes on to note that the French movement was consistently presented by Marks and De Courtivron as "in discontinuity with historical feminism"; that Domna Stanton (in the 1978 *Signs* issue) "identifies language as the site of feminist struggle in France". She gives many examples of the way the French movement was misrepresented. The fact that it was a movement that shared many traits with other movements, in terms of preoccupations, analyses, campaigns, demands, activism, was not only ignored, but denied. It was said that there was a movement – but a movement of writers who "problematized the words 'feminist' and 'feminism'" (Marks and De Courtivron, quoted by Moses: 1992a, p. 223).

Here I want to focus on one point in particular, and that is the closeness – both personal and ideological – to psychoanalysis, of the women selected by French feminists and their equal distance from feminism. As has been noted by Moses, French feminism was equated with "women writers". If it is mentioned at all that they are Lacanian, nowhere does it ever appear that two of them – Irigaray and Kristeva – are practising psychoanalysts. In the way that Cixous' and Kristeva's anti-feminist declarations are, variously, treated as non-relevant, the fact that they are not part of the feminist debate in France is considered so irrelevant as to be not even worth mentioning. It is implied that actual feminists from France look up to these writers – which is necessary in order to make them look significant to the domestic reader. Their real importance in France is never evaluated - for instance by the number of times they are quoted or appear in feminist discussions, which is almost non-existent!

What is implied by portraying these women as important in feminism is that whether one calls oneself a feminist or not is not relevant; what is further implied by asserting that they are important for feminists in France is that feminists in France do not consider that relevant either. The message is that in order to speak in or of feminism, one does not need to be a self-defined feminist. The impact this had on domestic feminism is to blur the frontiers between feminists and non-feminists. However, this is not a consistent policy. At other times, Kristeva and Cixous are on the contrary reclaimed as feminists, in spite of themselves. This is a spectacular manifestation of imperialism. Kristeva's or Cixous' outspoken anti-feminism can be dismissed: "despite their disclaimers, it is difficult not to classify Kristeva and Cixous as feminists" (Tong: 1989, p. 223). It is suggested that they do not know their own minds. There is a level of contempt here that is truly unbearable – but if one manages to forget and forgive the condescension, what is the message to the Anglo-American reader? That writings that are meant as anti-feminist are just as important to feminism as feminist writings. Again, the line is blurred, and the feminist debate opens up to welcome anti-feminist opinions, which are to be treated on *a par with* feminist opinions.

That was opening the way for things yet to come such as the introduction into feminism of Freud and Lacan – first as "French feminists", then as feminist *"tout court"*, and finally as "founding fathers". Proponents of French feminism were able to use this opening to offer the real hard stuff – unreconstructed Continental psychoanalysis. And the Anglo-American scene has been transformed to the extent that a book on psychoanalysis is seen as intrinsically part of feminist theory, in spite of the total absence of any discussion of feminism (Gallop: 1982). That is something that could not have happened before the invention of French feminism, and which could still not happen in France, whoever the author.

But the most interesting feature of French feminism is the underhand way it deals with essentialism. French feminists do not dare – yet – to hold up essentialism as "A Good Thing". But they promote it by saying that it is not essentialism. A good deal of their time is taken up "defending" Irigaray against accusations of essentialism (Schor: 1989, pp. 38–58; Fuss: 1990, especially pp. 55–83). But why exactly? Is it because they are convinced that Irigaray is not essentialist? They cannot be, as Irigaray makes no bones about it, and never tries to defend herself against something she does not see as an indictment. Anglo-American essentialists are in a more delicate position: they want the thing without the sting. And since of course this is not possible, what they are accomplishing on their domestic scene is a regression. Everybody talks about essentialism, but nobody knows what it is any more, as essentialist theories are presented as non-essentialist. Even Freud and Lacan, whose essentialism was established a long time ago in *all* quarters, not only in feminist circles, are now being "revalued" and absolved.

Moreover, in an apparently contradictory, but really coherent movement, essentialism is increasingly presented as something which, although it cannot be endorsed outright, might not be "the damning criticism it is supposed to be" (Smith: 1988, p. 144). Paul Smith and Diana Fuss credit Irigaray with such sophistication that, it is implied, she can only "seem" essentialist; on the other hand, if she were found to be – and not just to seem – essentialist, then, it is implied, might she not have a good reason? Although they cannot decide on the matter – Fuss even writes that "Irigaray both *is and is not* an essentialist" (Fuss: 1990, p. 70) – they agree that if she is, it is a strategy, even "a key strategy . . . not an oversight" (Fuss: 1990, p. 72). Thus, under the guise of trying to understand complex European thinking, Anglo-American authors are working their way towards a rehabilitation of essentialism.

Imperialism as a Strategy for Disappearing at One Stroke Feminism . . . and Women

The invention of French feminism happened at the same time as the invention of "French theory". Monique Wittig for instance, is cited early on in the same breath as Hélène Cixous – and sometimes she is defined as belonging to the same strand – *écriture féminine*. There is more than sheer ignorance at work here. Even when it is recognized that she cannot be in the same strand since she is herself very vocal about repudiating *écriture féminine* and all that strand stands for, she is still always quoted in conjunction with the "Holy Three", very seldom by herself or in conjunction with Anglo-American feminists who are theoretically close to her. The same of course holds true of Cixous – her plight is exactly symmetrical, although for reasons that should be clear, by now, it is for Wittig that I feel. Michèle Le Doeuff, who is not particularly bashful about her theoretical stand, is also lumped together with the essentialists, "despite her disclaimers" as Tong would put it (Tong: 1989, p. 223).

Do the stars of "French theory" – who are also the master-minds behind the women, according to French feminists, fare better? No. Lacan, Derrida, Foucault, Barthes, they're all one to the Anglo-American compulsion to unify the "French", to homogenize them, and to deny them any individuality. How is it possible to treat in the same article, never mind in the same sentence, writers such as Foucault and Lacan, who come from totally opposite traditions, and who furthermore are very open about their disagreements?

Anglo-Americans have created whole new schools of thought – or at least academic trends – by comparing French writers who cannot be compared, by "putting in dialogue" people who have nothing to say to each other, and by giving this ready mix names like "post-structuralism" and "post-modernism". How will that improbable mixture withstand the test of time? Not very well: Foucault's social constructionism will not, even with the help of the Marines, ever blend with Lacan's essentialism.

And why are French authors – male or female, feminist or not – almost never compared to Anglo-American counterparts, however similar, but only to other French writers, however different? Because that would show that there are differences among them on the one hand, and similarities between them and their commentators and translators in the Anglo-American world on the other. Internal homogenization and external differentiation: this is how groups – national, ethnic, sex groups – are constituted. In exactly the same way, French authors are seen as a group which is defined by – and only by – its difference to the group which has the power to name. They are constituted as an Other.

If one has to admit that the work of writers can be interpreted, and that the word of the author on her/his own work need not be the last, or the only one, it is an entirely different kettle of fish to pretend that these works can be totally abstracted from their objective, historical contexts. And this is precisely what is being done, to female and male writers who had the bad luck to be born in France. Moreover, if Anglo-Americans have the right to "take their good where they find it", as the French say, and to use quotations from France – or any other part of the world – to create their own theories, the line must be drawn at calling that creative endeavour "French theory". Nobody owns their own writing; but everybody deserves a fair hearing, and that is what the French do not get. They are entitled to be understood and appreciated, or dismissed, for what they did or said, not hailed or damned for what some other French person did or said: *"tout se passe comme si la désignation de 'français' effaçait ou rendait secondaires les tensions sérieuses entre les oeuvres de Cixous et d'Irigaray (ou celles de Lyotard et de Derrida)"*[1] (Varikas: 1993, p. 64). Interestingly, Anglo-American commentators who do try to put Foucault or de Beauvoir (or others) in perspective, and to understand why they said what they said when they did, do not call that "French theory" (Kruks: 1992, pp. 89–110).

But does the fact that the French – and other nations which are not imperial *powers* – also use national stereotyping to exorcize their home problems make it less imperialist? We are talking here of an attitude: its relation to actual power is, in all cases, based more on representations than on reality. I have argued above that French feminism was invented in order to legitimate the introduction on the Anglo-American feminist scene of a brand of essentialism, and in particular a rehabilitation of psychoanalysis, which goes further than the native kind expressed by Nancy Chodorow, Carol Gilligan and Sara Ruddick.

The other feature of this intellectual current, which is definitely not exhibited by the native essentialists (Chodorow, Gilligan, Ruddick) is that it questions the very basis of what defines a feminist theoretical approach. In the usual definition, a feminist theoretical approach is tied to a political movement, a movement aimed at effecting actual change in actual society and in actual women's – and men's – lives; the main feature of this tie resides in the questions that are asked of the objects under study. That necessary tie does not mean that some abstract activist instance dictates the topics to be studied, but that any feminist – scholar or not – should be able to argue the relevance of the questions she raises to the feminist movement as a whole. In order to demonstrate that hypothesis, I will turn to a case-study of one of the key moments of the whole operation – Alice Jardine's *Gynesis* (1985).

In this work, "French theory" is constituted as a "whole", by a series of rhetorical manoeuvres that use distortion and generalization, imperialism and orientalism. First the feminist movement in France is cast as D.O.A. in the "socialist" era, after a series of murderous struggles, from which it is supposed not to have recovered. So, exit French feminism in the usual sense of "feminist". Feminists are still there, however. How is Jardine going to dispose of them? We have already been told that feminism, "that word", "poses some serious problems". It does, indeed, if, like Jardine one can think of only one place to look for it . . . the dictionaries! She then dismisses the feminists "who qualify themselves as feminists in their life and work" (Jardine: 1985, p. 20) – because that would be too simple – and Goddess forbid!

---

1. It all happens as if the label French erased or diminished the serious tension between the works of Cixous and Irigaray (or those of Lyotard and Derrida).

But here plain factual distortion, counting on the normal ignorance of the American reader, gives way to imperialism: what counts is only what I say counts. It is not only because it would be too simple that actual feminists from France will not be discussed, but because: "When in the United States, one refers to . . . 'French feminisms', it is not those women one has in mind." There is something circular, or tautological, in the argument: "I will not interest myself in those women because they are not of interest to me." But circularity and tautology, as exemplary expressions of *self-centredness*, are essential components of the arrogant beauty of imperialist thinking.

In the next sentence, American interest is what constitutes feminists from France as important or not important in an objective, real way: these women are said to "have a major impact on theories of writing and reading". The place where that "major impact" is supposed to have happened is not specified: it may be the USA, it may be the whole world – isn't it the same thing? And Jardine lists: Cixous, Kofman, Kristeva, Lemoine-Luccioni, Montrelay.[2] Then she moves on to say that "the major new directions in French theory over the past two decades . . . have . . . posited themselves as profoundly . . . anti- and/or post-feminist" (Jardine: 1985, p. 20). This is a strategic move, which overturns all previous understandings about what kind of thinking is useful for feminism. But the best is yet to come: this said, she proceeds to explain that she will deal with the men, because "the women theorists in France whose names have been mentioned here are . . . in the best

_____

2. At the time Alice Jardine's book was published, Women's Studies and Feminist Studies were undergoing the only time of expansion they have ever known in France. A research program had been launched at the National Centre for Scientific Research in 1983 which lasted till 1989. At the time it was under way Jardine was in France writing about the "Parisian scene". It was extremely varied in its ideological and theoretical orientations, as it regrouped on its board the Who's Who of Women's Studies in France. Over a period of six years it examined more than three hundred research projects and funded eighty, in all disciplines and on all topics – including, of course, literary criticism. Why is it that most of the names Jardine lists never appear in the bibliographies of any of these projects, even of the few that were psychoanalytically oriented, if they made such a "major impact"? And why is it that Jardine does not mention this research program, which was the talk of the – admittedly provincial – town of Paris and which she could not have helped hearing about?

Similar tactics are used by Toril Moi: "The publishing history of French feminism in English-speaking countries confirms the overwhelming impact of the three names of Cixous, Irigaray and Kristeva" (1987). This is a somewhat disingenuous and even perverse statement on two accounts: first, the publishing history of these three writers in English is supposed to prove their popularity *in France!* And, secondly, that publishing history is not so external to Moi as she, pretending to "discover" it, would have us think. By all acounts, her *Sexual/Textual Politics* (1985) was decisive in starting that trend. And what was the thrust of that book? To pit "Anglo-American feminist criticism", which she finds disappointing, against what she calls – coining the phrase – "French feminist theory", and whose first chapter is entitled "From Simone de Beauvoir to Jacques Lacan" – thus establishing Lacan as a "feminist theorist", a paradox not even the most psychoanalytically oriented feminists in France would have dreamt of defending.

French tradition . . . direct disciples of those men" (p. 21). And although she does "not mean this as a criticism", she comments that these women's works consist of "rewritings of the men . . . repetitions and dissidences from those men" (Jardine: 1985, p. 21).

We are thus given to understand that these anti-feminist women are not only the producers of the most important work for feminist thinking; but that their thinking derives from men, to the extent that they need not be considered themselves. The reader may be surprised. But this is where the orientalism comes in to confuse and guilt-trip us: this is the French brand of feminism, and even though it may seem strange, what if feminists from France like it? As in all colonialist discourses, there's a mixture of both fake respect and condescension for the culture. Enough respect to warrant the attention of the American reader: "French feminism" is important, we must listen to what it has to say. But that respect is really condescension: for what sort of feminists can feminists from France be if they take as their major theorists women who not only are anti-feminist but are men's parrots? On what sort of clichés in the reader's mind is Jardine counting? What sort of stereotypes are necessary to believe in this scenario of French feminists, indeed of any *feminists?*

But Jardine insists it is "in the best French tradition". So subservience to the men is seen as both unique to the French[3] – and not so damnable as it might seem: from the moment it has been deemed "French", and since the French are an interesting culture, it cannot be condemned as easily as all that – Jardine extends the cultural relativist wing to protect it. Could she have sent the same message using a US example? Could she have decided that So-and-So is an important writer for feminist issues even though that person does not address the topic, or worse, is against feminism? Could she say that today the most important US writers for feminism are Katie Roiphe or Camille Paglia, or even Philip Wylie? And if she did, where would it place her? But why could she not? After all, opponents are important. They do need to be discussed. But is it the same thing to say that Patrick Moynihan's theses must be discussed and to say that he is the main theorist of and for feminism?

There are three points that need to be made here. It is true that, since there exists a continuum of feminists and anti-feminists, this creates particular problems which have been noted by Judith Stacey (1986, p. 243), for "drawing the line" especially when writers with clearly anti-feminist views, such as Paglia, call themselves feminist, as they increasingly do in the USA today. The point has been raised regarding Irigaray by Maryse Guerlais (Guerlais: 1991) and Eléni Varikas (Varikas: 1993) in France. It is a difficult one because, although Irigaray's work is not used in Women's Studies in France, her arguments are very popular with

---

3. Again, Moi uses the same tactics: "French feminists on the whole have been eager to appropriate dominant intellectual trends for feminist puposes, as for instance in the case of the theories of Jacques Derrida and Jacques Lacan" (Moi: 1987, p. 1).

important parts of the Women's Movement in Italy, and smaller but still significant audiences in France and Holland. However, inasmuch as there are, in feminism as elsewhere, definitional problems about borderline cases, these problems are always situated at the margins: they do not touch on the core.

Writers who situate themselves *vis-à-vis* feminist questions are part of the feminist debate – including those who *oppose* feminism; but even though the latter are discussed, they are not treated in the same category as writers who define themselves as feminist. Feminists have always discussed anti-feminists: one could even say that this constitutes a major part of feminist writing. Exposing and analysing patriarchal ideology has been on the feminist agenda from the very beginnings of feminism. But anti-feminists and feminists have distinct places in feminist analysis. Patriarchy and its intellectual productions are an *object* of study, they are not and cannot be a *means or a tool* of feminist analysis.

The case is quite different with writers who are not necessarily hostile to feminism but who *do not* address feminist issues. The question is not "friend or foe?" but "what do they bring to the discussion?" This is the case in France, of Kristeva, who does not address the questions raised by feminists because she does not know what they are. Her only information about feminism is the kind of caricatures circulated by the media. This is the case also of women like Michelle Montrelay or Eugénie Lemoine-Luccioni, who are traditional psychoanalysts and cannot even be described as "anti-feminist", since that implies engaging with feminist ideas, which they do not. Their position is best described as a traditional "male-supremacist" or "pre-feminist" view. It is so widely held in France by psychoanalysts that feminists have never felt the need to discuss those three in particular.[4] So here the point is rather: could Jardine, or any other supposedly feminist writer, decide that an English or American author, whose work is not considered relevant and is not discussed by English and American feminists because *she/he does not discuss feminist questions*, represent what is most interesting in the feminist scene of those countries?

This is precisely what Jardine, and with her, the other French feminists are saying: on the one hand, that there is no difference between feminist thinking and patriarchal thinking from the point of view of their use for feminist analysis: and on the other hand, that addressing questions that are relevant for feminism is irrelevant for participating in the feminist debate. That makes feminism itself an irrelevant position.

This could not be argued from a domestic position, using domestic examples: straw-women had to be invented who, supposedly from *within* feminism, were questioning and invalidating a feminist approach; but it had to be a feminism

---

4. This is why Cixous and Irigaray, who know what feminism is, must be distinguished one from the other, the first being anti-feminist, and the second feminist by her own definition. They must, furthermore, both be sharply distinguished from the second group, Kristeva, Montrelay and Lemoine-Luccioni, who do not know what feminism is, and who are neither feminist nor anti-feminist, but *pre-feminist*.

so strange, so foreign that this would be as credible as it was improbable. It had to be French feminism. The second part of the message is: If the French can do it, why can't we? And they did.

Feminism could not be invalidated from within the French feminists' own culture, i.e. Anglo-American culture; men could not be reinstated as the main interlocutors, as the arbiters of all knowledge, including feminist knowledge, from a domestic position. But introducing "French women" was the way to introduce the idea that to be anti-feminist and to still be part of the feminist debate was acceptable; the next step was to do away with the women and to reveal the men behind them, according to the purported native women's wishes, so that men could be, once more, *centre*-stage, in feminism as well as everywhere else.

Promoting essentialism was the main motive behind the creation of French feminism; but there was a further and, when one thinks about it, not vastly different, reason, for that invention: and that was putting Women's Studies scholars "in dialogue" again with male authors.

Joanna Russ, commenting on a review of Joan Scott's *Gender and the Politics of History* (1988a) in *The Women's Review of Books,* put it so well:

> . . . my undergraduate students assure me that feminism is no longer necessary because we've solved all that and various female colleagues and graduate students derive it from two white gentlemen, ignoring twenty years of extra-academic and other academic feminist work and writing. I would say that we've been betrayed, were not such a remark one of the banalities of history. And so heartbreaking (1989, p. 4).

I want to add: and academic.

The price paid by resistant women is literally incalculable – that is I know of no currency in which its cost can be counted. It is thus not at all surprising that the temptation to "dilute" the challenge is not always resistible, or indeed resisted (Smyth: 1993).

Joan Hoff

The Pernicious Effects of Poststructuralism on Women's History*

While spending the better part of two academic years out of the United States in the early 1990s, I became increasingly perplexed by the current emphasis on post-structural theory in the writing of women's history. I say this because such theory may not only isolate this highly successful new subfield from the on-going Second Women's Movement in the United States and from history teachers trying to integrate material on women into their classes, but also, most sadly, isolate American historians of women from their counterparts in eastern European and Third World countries who are only beginning to write about their past.

The potentially paralyzing consequences of this theory upon the writing of women's history in the United States arose innocuously enough in the mid-1980 as many scholars in women's history sought to find concepts in French post-modernist theory that would enhance the emphasis already being placed on gender. Unfortunately, most began with Michel Foucault who in his work on sexuality talked extensively about gender, but largely neglected to focus on women. Moving on to other male post-structuralists whose theories were equally insensitive or hostile to half the human population, a male-defined definition of gender that erased woman as a category of analysis, emerged as a major component of American post-structuralism.

* This piece was originally based on remarks given at a plenary sessions of the British American Studies Association (BAAS) annual meeting on April 19, 1993, in Sunderland, England and at the Teaching Women's Studies Conference on May 20, 1993, in Lódz, Poland while I held the Mary Ball Washington Chair in American History at University College Dublin during the 1992–1993 academic year. I would like to thank Karen Offen, Karen Winkler, and Marian Yeates for reading and commenting on earlier drafts. Two shorter versions of it appeared in *The Chronicle of Higher Education* (1993) and *Women's Studies International Forum* (1994); and a similar version to this one appeared in *Women's History Review* (June 1994), entitled "Gender as a post-modern category of paralysis."

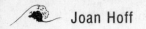

From the beginning, therefore, post-structuralism in the United States threatened to sever the field of women's history from its political roots by insisting that "there is no experience outside of the ways that language constructs it." Valid as such an assertion may be in linguistic terms, it is enraging to feminist activists, especially those representing racial minorities, and unintelligible to the vast majority of history teachers trying to integrate material on women into their classes because it denies retrievable historical "reality", substituting instead the "linguistic turn", meaning historical analysis based on analysis of representation.[1] Like all post-modern theories, post-structuralism casts into doubt stable meanings and sees language as so slippery that it compromises historians' ability to identify facts and chronological narratives, and uses gender as a category of analysis to reduce the experiences of women struggling to define themselves and control their lives in particular historical contexts to mere subjective stories.

This line of argument is perplexing, because leading historians of women have been defining gender as the socially conditioned behavior of both sexes, in their research since the late-1970s. Gender as a category of analysis did not need to be reinvented using a special linguistic jargon, except to eliminate the category of woman in the much touted new field of gender history. Moreover, this original use of gender, in the hands of early practitioners, did not cut academic analysis off from the realities women face in their daily lives. Instead of promoting women's history into the mainstream, as predicted by some advocates of gender history (Rose: 1993 and Canning: 1993), post-structuralism leaves activists without generalizations about the commonly shared experiences of women as a basis for activism. It also leaves most historians in the United States and abroad, floundering as they try to convert facts into chronological narratives despite the "linguistic turn."

Ironically, French post-modernism (of which American post-structuralism and post-feminism appear to be watered-down versions) is either being ignored or subjected to rigorous questioning, by feminists activists and scholars abroad (Brobribb: 1992, pp. 7–8, 20). For example, Margaret MacCurtain and Mary O'Dowd, two Irish historians of women, noted in 1991 that "there are signs of a European reaction against" this distinction between women's and gender history, and "a recognition" that its origins have more to do with the "way in which women's history has developed in North America", than in any inherent supremacy of the post-structural gender history. They concluded that it "may not necessarily be

---

1. See Sonya O. Rose (1993, p. 90; paraphrasing Joan Wallach Scott). It is not the purpose of this piece to discuss the linguistic technicalities of the current debate in the United States over post-structural literary criticism, semiotics, new historicism, new cultural history, or cultural and symbolic anthropology. My concern is with the possible motivations for, and the practical implications of, the "linguistic turn" in terms of feminist politics, public policy, and the writing and teaching of women's history in the United States and in countries where this field is only beginning to develop. For those interested in these complicated linguistic debates as they apply to history, a good place to start is: Gabrielle M. Spiegel (1990); Kathleen Canning (1994) and the dialogue on Women's History/Gender History cited above in Rose: 1993, pp. 89–128.

helpful in studying the history of women in other countries where, as in Ireland, much basic research still need to be done" (MacCurtain and O'Dowd: 1992, p. 2). Moreover, I believe that certain characteristics of post-modern theory make it more difficult and more dangerous for historians of women to adopt than for those scholars in such disciplines as film criticism, semiotics, or literature. They have always emphasized textual analysis without, as is the case with history, threatening to destroy the discipline itself, or a subfield such as women's history. Post-modern theory disadvantages the field of women's history in three ways. First, it is hostile to the basic concept of linear time and of cause and effect assumptions which most professionally trained historians continue to honor in their teaching and writings. Second, post-modern theory's misogynist and very specific historical origins among post-World War II Parisian intellectuals – from Lévi-Strauss and Lacan to Foucault and Derrida – require excessive intellectual modification and machinations to include women. Third, its stress on diversity through the technique of *différance* has led some historians to commit the anachronistic crime of applying the fragmentation of contemporary American society indiscriminately to the past. Finally, post-modern theory, again given its origins, is designed to be politically and legally paralyzing. Let me explain why all of these characteristics threaten the very existence of not only the field of women's history, but also of traditionally conceived history in general.

Post-modernism is No Friend of History

Post-modernism cannot under any circumstances be considered "history-friendly". For post-modernists, "history has no reality" because "it [history] assumes a material world, an external reality unappropriated by the cultural and aesthetic" (Rosenau: 1992, pp. 63–6). Most historians, as teachers and writers, traditionally organize facts into some kind of chronological narrative rather than fit them into a theoretical framework. Since World War II with few exceptions – such as economic and labor history – the discipline of history generally has not been distinguished by its adherence to macro-models or theoretical, especially linguistic, debates but, rather, by its empiricism. For post-modernists, historical epistemology falsely assumes the existence of a real, material world and linear change over time based on causality. All that can be described using post-structuralist methodology is the moment of observation that has no past, present, or future. Therefore, historical agency – real people having an impact on real events – is both impossible and irrelevant. For post-structuralists, each historical moment is unique and does not necessarily relate to any other one, except that perhaps a series of random possibilities could indirectly shape the next random possibility, but not in a historically causal way. Therefore, history as an unbroken continuum cannot survive the scrutiny of deconstructionist methodology because to see history as linear not only is essentialist, but also requires the interposition of that which post-modernists must deny: that is, praxis, which by definition "demands commitment and change." (Hoffman: 1975, pp. 16–17).

Memory, another important ingredient of traditional history (and oral history when studying women), is viewed by post-structuralists as a most suspect representation of the past. They contend that memory does not allow one to relive experience because the past cannot be duplicated in the present or future. In Derrida's famous example, Rousseau's memory of his mother's love forever stands between him and adult love, making him a "aged child" (to say nothing of a misogynist). According to post-modernists, in remembering the past, Rousseau creates an interaction with the present that prevents him from knowing the present as whole and complete, because this interaction between the past and present never ends, although it is not causal in the traditional use of that word (Derrida: 1974). It is simply an on going process with no beginning or end in a series of unrelated, random memories. If historical moments and individual memories of them seem to have no connection with one another, then their relationship is totally random as in Heisenberg's scientific principle of indeterminacy which describes the chaotic reaction that exists at the center of each atom. History, according to post-modern theory, is at best chaos and, at worst, does not exist at all in the sense that there is no "truth" about human actions, human thought, or human experience to be revealed through research (Rosenau: 1992).

Let me add parenthetically that traditional historical concepts are currently under simultaneous attacks from post-modernists and from neoconservatives in the United States. The latter are trying to undermine the entire field of history with their theories about post-history. By the term post-history neoconservatives mean the "death" of history in the modern period, at least as we have known it during the Cold War, because of the apparent triumph of capitalism over communism at the end of the 1980s. Thus, post-structural historians of women have joined the ranks of all the other trendy "post-isms" or "end-isms" and largely neoconservative theories of our time such as post-God, post-death, post-feminism, post-women's history, and post-nature (Rosenau: 1992; Hoff and Farnham: 1990; Brodribb: 1992). I call these the "end of everything" theories and believe they are all profoundly influenced by contemporary concern over the increasing socio-economic divisions in American society, to say nothing of the impending millennium.

Contrary to the claim of post-structural historians that women's history has lost its identity, or their predictions that women's history is about to "dissolve", it is their deliberate depoliticization of power through representations of the female self as totally diffuse and decentered that has created the current sense of lack of agency that they now attribute to women of past (Kruks: 1993). If women's history is "dissolving," it is only doing so in a sea of relativity created on the head of a semiotic pin by deconstructionists, not because the field itself has nothing to offer contemporary feminism except post-feminism. I simply don't know what to make of the terms post-feminist or post-feminism, because I think a more accurate, albeit oxymoronic, term would be post-structural feminist and post-structural feminism. This distinction conveys the existence of definite difference between kinetic, activist feminism and the more contemplative, linguist approach of post-structural feminism. In the United States the term post-feminism is most often used by neoconservatives and antifeminists in an attempt to indicate that feminism is dead. Such attacks are usually accompanied by a barrage of New Age psychobabble.

For feminist historians of women (as opposed to post-feminist or post-structural historians of women), if gender analysis does not include women as a discrete category, it is meaningless both as a methodology and as a material underpinning for political action. By taking women out of the definition of gender, there is also no need to use confrontational political language to describe their past or present historical condition in society; instead, through linguistic gymnastics the political becomes the impersonal – with potentially deadly results for radical feminism, as I discuss below. Likewise, Sonia Kruks has concluded that:

> ... hyperconstructivisme implicite du post-modernisme ... risque de transfomer la subjectivité elle-même en pure fiction et de détruire jusqu'à la catégorie de femmes ... Car, a moins d'admettre que les "femmes historiques réeles" vivent et meurent, qu'elles décident et agissent et qu'elles peuvent être plus ou moins opprimées ou libre, nous risquons devenir nos propres fossouyeuses (1993, p. 21).[2]

While no apocalyptic claims about the "death" of women's history were made during the 1993 Ninth Berkshire Conference on the History of Women, as had been the case at the 1990 meeting, the current influence of post-structuralism among historians of women could be found in the titles of the sessions at both conferences: "Reifying otherness," or "Boundaries of difference," or "Woman as discursive terrain," or "Medicalization, discourse, and representation," or "Consumption, nationalism, and the female body," or "Inscribing, crossing, and transforming boundaries," and the "Feminization of the American subject". Such titles need to be translated to be understood by rank and file historians and, like so many post-structural terms, can mean anything or nothing. Their use threatens to undo the success of early practitioners of US women's history in the 1970s, who gained the attention of historians in other fields with their straight-forward language and compelling chronological narratives.

But obfuscation is not the only, perhaps not even the major, danger post-structural theory poses for women's history. Too often, post-structuralism has assumed peculiarly ethnocentric characteristics in the United States. The debate over women's or feminist history versus gender history that has emerged is not completely unique to North America because similar ones arose in other English-speaking countries such as Australia, New Zealand, Canada, England, and even

---

2. Translation: "The excessive constructionism implicit in post-modernism . . . threatens to transform female subjectivity into pure fiction and to destroy even the category of woman . . . Because unless it is admitted that an 'historical female reality' lives and dies, that women decide and act and that they can be more or less oppressed or free, we risk becomming our own grave diggers".

India. In the United States, however, this debate is associated with the fact that the revival of the field of women's history was completely intertwined with the development of the Second Woman's Movement beginning in the late 1960s. Therefore, the controversy over women's history versus gender history represents a form of ethnocentricism complicated by political overtones – often confounding to those outside the country (Hoff: 1992; MacCurtain and O'Dowd: 1992; Kruks: 1993). American historians of gender thus adapted those post-structural ideas denying any collective concept of woman or women in a peculiarly ethnocentric way, in part because they were uncomfortable with obvious political origins of US women's history as it emerged early 1970s co-terminus with the Second Women's Movement. As I suggest below, this enthnocentricism also arose because neocon-servatives began to praise and reward post-structural gender studies within American academic circles.

Post-structural historians in United States thus pride themselves on the scientific, intellectual, and apolitical superiority of gender history over women's history. Historians of gender specifically criticize historians of women for concen-trating too much on identifying "woman" as a discrete category, rather than stressing multiple female identities. Post-structural scholars also argue that gender history is in line with today's new theories of how science operates, because it critiques the Enlightenment tradition and denies the possibility of any objective truth. Within several academic disciplines they further claim that post-struct-uralism is more intellectually satisfying, because it represents an elite, cutting edge of theoretical interpretation, which requires a very specialized type of academic training to understand. As with any complicated theory that becomes *au courant* within in intellectual circles (as well as superficially popularized within mass culture) many academics now use post-structural rhetoric without understanding its origins or implications for their own areas of study. This is particularly true among historians because the discipline of history in the United States has not been customarily based on any theory, let alone a difficult to comprehend linguistic one.

Few American historians, regardless of field of specialization, understand the sophisticated linguistic and ahistorical concepts on which post-structuralist is based. Thus, when historian Joan W. Scott said that post-modern gender analysis represented a "methodology and theoretical reformulation . . . especially in the areas of symbolic representation and theories of language", that would change the organization of knowledge in the humanities and social sciences, most historians in the United States were impressed, but not sure what it all meant (Scott: 1988a, p. 36; 1987a, p. 22). Scott was also sincerely concerned about the "relatively limited impact women's history was having on historical studies generally". She apparently concluded that this lack of influence was due to the fact that historical studies of women were simply confirming, rather than challenging stereotypical views of females in history based on "inherent characteristics and objective identities consistently and predictably different from men's". That is, women's history up to that point often confirmed reductionist stereotyped views of women as oppressed by patriarchy (Scott: 1988a, pp. 3–4). So a more "radical epistemology" seemed in order to satisfy both needs: 1) her desire for more theoretical sophistication, and 2) her activist desire to exercise more impact on the field of history in general. Her solution, followed with less intellectual integrity by many, turned out to be the post-structuralism associated in the United States primarily with Jacques Derrida, whose misogynist views did not bode well for the study of women *qua* women.

Post-structuralism is No Friend of Women

My second concern about the impact of post-structuralism on women's history, therefore, has to do with the inherent sexism of post-modern theory. Here Somer Brodribb's book, has made my task much easier because she has presented a compendium of radical feminist criticism that demystifies post-modernism, revealing it as "the cultural capital of late patriarchy" (Brodribb: 1992, p. 21; see also this volume pp. 297–310). In other words, it is the patriarchal ideology of preference for the end of the twentieth century. It is clear that both women's history historians and gender historians agree that there can be no objective historical or scientific truth in any timeless, context free way that western society has assumed since the Enlightenment. (In fact historians of women initiated this attack on essentialism, or the presumed "truth" of Enlightenment concepts, when they first began to place women at the heart of gender analysis in the late 1970s.) Both also agree that all such claims to objectivity and neutrality in the past have been masks for asserting male power. As noted below, they disagree over whether there can be a gender-neutral historical discourse that does not, like traditional history, make women invisible and politically inviable.

In the same way that Carole Pateman's book, *The Sexual Contract* (1988) exposed the androcentric and misogynistic qualities of modern liberalism present in the political theories of John Locke and other Enlightenment writers,[3] Brodribb's *Nothing Mat(t)ers* (1992) similarly critiques the "fathers" of post-structuralism. Using feminist, not post-modern language (except when quoting others), Brodribb analyzes and dissects the evolution of various definitions and examples of post-modern, post-structural, deconstruction, and semiotic theory demonstrating that the misogynist message of post-modernism is even more subtle than Locke's because instead of substituting a new political vision for an old one, male post-modernists since the 1960s have been disguising their failure as revolutionaries to

---

3. See Carole Pateman (1988, pp. 19–117, especially 82–100). In offering the social contract as a substitute for the classical patriarchal theories of Robert Filmer, for example, Pateman definitively shows that John Locke did not refute previous masculinist notions about political rights. Instead, more subtly and insidiously than ever before he reinforced patriarchy by separating paternal power from political power, relegating the former (along with women) to a status outside the boundaries of civil society and politics. Thus, Pateman argues that the "emancipatory potential of contract doctrine" contained a basic gendered contradiction – namely that all men but not all women were born equal and, hence, only men were capable under liberalism of giving their consent to be governed.

change the post World War II world by devising an ideology in which, to use Simone de Beauvoir's words, "appearances are everything . . . [and] the whole real world disappears into thin air" (de Beauvoir: 1968, p. 636).

How does this disappearing act manifest itself as misogynist? Based on the "massaging" of "privileged" texts deconstructionist methodology has been described as an intellectual form of "masturbation" that results in an "endless deferral of sense" (Brodribb: 1992, p. 8). American post-structuralism specifically defers feminism in two primary ways. First, it defers radical feminism in the same way that violent pornography objectifies women—it dismembers and disconnects women from any material experiential base. By disconnecting women from their factual context, females are annihilated through disassociation and physical violence, just as radical feminism is destroyed by dispossession from its political roots through the phallologocentric theories of post-modernism. This way of deferring radical feminism uses the same methods as violent pornographic representations of women and, not surprisingly, has the same impact on women: it silences or co-opts them with the implicit threat of violence, or in everyday life, with threat of not being acceptable to the men with whom they associate. The result is female silence, fear or, at the very least, anxiety (Hoff: 1989). In the latest "academencia" game, to use Mary Daly's term, male and female post-feminists now tell academic women that they can avoid being silenced by writing and talking (and reading texts) like the post-modern boys. This process inevitably results in denying that women's experiences can be used to create feminist theory and, as I noted above, accounts for some of the ethnocentricism of American post-structuralism.

Post-structuralism thus defers not only radical, but also mainstream, feminism through the cooptive, infiltrative practices of "Tootsie" men. Drawing on the movie in which Dustin Hoffman dressed up as a woman and became a better friend of a real (meaning physiologically) woman than a real woman, sociologist Kathleen Barry has called this phenomenon the "Tootsie syndrome," whereby "Tootsie" men become better and more authentic representations of women than real women – better mothers than real women, better feminists than real women, and finally, better women than real women (Barry: 1989; Brodribb: 1992).[4] As a result, male post-structuralists (and their female followers) are becoming part of the backlash movement against both radical and mainstream feminism in the United States. It is not surprising that this has happened since some of the French intellectuals, who were the "fathers" of post-modernism, exhibited such misogynist views that at times they seemed to claim that only men could speak for women.

The irony of all this, according to Tania Modleski, is that various post-modern theories are being "carried out not against feminism but in its very name", and undermining the political effectiveness of the Second Women's Movement. After all, how effective can female post-feminists be as political activists, Jane Gallop has

---

4. In l983 Elaine Showalter first coined the term "Tootsie" to refer to men (other than transvestites) who pretend to *be* women. Tania Modleski (1991, pp. 3–6).

asked, "wearing the hand-me-downs of men-in-drag, [and] writing a feminine which has become a male transvestite style?" This "Tootsie syndrome" in all of its various manifestations is curiously deceptive, especially as practiced by academic men. Many post-structuralists use feminism as a pretense to enter the field of gender studies, where their fascination with masculinity is leading to more emphasis on men than women, and more emphasis on difference or diversity among women, rather than on commonalities they may share (Modleski: 1991, p. x; Gallop: 1988, p. 100).

Modleski has noted that many post-structuralists use feminism simply as a "conduit to the more comprehensive field of gender studies" (Modleski, 1991, p. 5) because they are primarily interested in deconstructing masculinity. Thus, feminist critics of post-structural historians who employ gender as a *post-modern* category of analysis focus so much on "male sensitivity and male persecution" and "multiple masculinities" that they downplay male privilege. Often, they are also "implicitly denying the existence of patriarchy" and espousing theories about the predominance of differences among women in which "the voice of gender risks being lost entirely" (Banner: 1989, p. 104; Dinnerstein: 1989, p. 13; Dalton: 1987–88, p. 11).

As a sophisticated linguistic technique, post-modernism is a very useful methodology for purely textual analysis, but as French feminist Christine Delphy has pointed out, it is irrelevant for analyzing the material reality of gendered relationships because as a linguistic tool it was not designed to discern the existence of socio-economic hierarchies that give meaning to gender differences (Delphy: 1993 and this volume pp. 383–92). When this pitfall is not recognized, it can lead post-structuralists to deconstruct gender relations in a socio-economic void. In this way gender can become a *post-modern category of paralysis*, destroying any collective concept of woman or women through the fragmentation of female subjects. By ignoring that difference and dominance go hand-in-hand and clouding dominance with rhetoric about multiple and indeterminate identities or consciousness, post-structuralists can deny or mask that gender analysis is, after all, about the authority of men over women.

It is fairly evident why male post-structuralists want to use post-modern theories to hide male dominance, but why should post-structural feminists (assuming this is not a contradiction in terms as I have suggested above), especially in the United States, be so obsessed with showing diversity at the expense of gender identity? Obviously *différance* is an important linguistic tool of deconstruction because it is a linguistic way of showing how meaning arises out of implicit or explicit contracts (binary opposition) which, while represented in opposition, are in fact interdependent on one another, and derive their meaning from their unstable relational positioning in space and time, rather than from their apparent antithesis. This highly useful linguistic technique for analyzing texts was developed primarily by the French beginning with Saussure and continuing through Lévi-Strauss to Derrida. When simplistically applied to society (or women's history) the results are often as mystifying and misleading as when social scientists at the turn of the century similarly tried to apply Darwin's ideas on evolution theories.

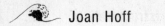 Joan Hoff

Poststructuralism is No Friend of Women's Rights

My third concern is about diversity and its deleterious impact is most obvious in my own field of specialization – women's legal history. Critical race theory offers an extreme, alternative deconstruction of what is called "rights talk", compared to feminist jurisprudence and critical legal theory. The latter have maintained since the 1970s that obtaining formal legal rights does not end discrimination for disadvantaged groups, such as women and minorities, because they do not take into consideration structural and attitudinal inequalities that pervade mainstream society. So rights talk, according to feminists and critical legal theorists, often gives the illusion of equality and creates exaggerated expectations (and ultimately disappointment) among civil right advocates. Feminist jurisprudence is particularly critical of the individual male rights approach that offers symbolic, but little substantive equality to women and minorities, unless they act like white men. Likewise, critical legal theorists maintain that the pursuit of antidiscrimination law has not come close to ending racial inequality because of the inequality that continues to exist based on class and race (Hoff: 1991; Freeman: 1988; Unger: 1986; Tushnet: 1984.).

Critical race theorists, in contrast, positing an excessive post-structural view of diversity, now argue that "rights discourse" is "the most effective of the insurrectionist discourses utilized in the struggles of people of color". (R. Williams: 1989, p. 104) because "rights are islands of empowerment". (P. Williams: 1991, p. 233). According to critical race theory, rights talk about multiple identities and consciousness based on endless diversities among people is a way for outsiders to be heard and to pursue equality (Boris: 1994), *even though it is next to impossible under American law at the moment to make such arguments successfully in court.* "In principle, therefore", according to Patricia Williams, "the more dizzyingly diverse the images [of rights] that are propagated, the more empowered we will be as a society" (Williams: 1991, p. 234). In principle – maybe, but in practical terms – this is not grounds for proving individual or group discrimination in US courts of law. In particular, such arguments do not advance the cause of civil rights in its most proven potent form: class action suits based on the shared physically or socially constructed characteristics of groups of people who have been discriminated against (Chateauvert: 1994).

If racial, gender, and identity differences are made the basis for equality before the juridical battle for traditional equal rights has been won, poststructuralism in the form of critical race theory will not advance the cause for civil rights, and may even set back the cause for justice in the United States. This is not to say that the courts have not sometimes granted "false" equality to women and minorities in certain civil rights decisions. An appalling recent example of "false" equality can be in seen in "no fault" divorce case statistics showing that women are more often than not impoverished by these so-called equal settlements. In their pursuit of traditional male equality, women and minorities must be ever mindful that it can backfire. Nonetheless, these groups should acquire as many civil rights based on male standards as possible, in the hope that the real ones will outweigh the false ones in their struggle for justice and equality in the United States.[5]

Multiple identities and rights talk based on an excessively diverse view of American society are simply no threat to the legal or political establishment in the United States as of the 1990s. If rights began to be granted under American law on such an extremely particularlist or individualistically based premise, they would not result in full equality for members of disadvantage groups. Such groups, including women, remain second-class citizens because they share common group liabilities that cannot be alleviated through the idiosyncratic granting of rights to individuals who do not identify with each other. To create exaggerated expectations about the empowerment of diversity is to repeat the mistake made by those who maintained during the height of the civil rights movement in the 1960s that affirmative action laws would end racial injustice in the United States. False hope placed in largely white, male post-structural definitions of diversity is no better than false hope placed in equality based white, male standards.

One of the worst examples of this multiple identity and diversity approach at work can be found in post-structural interpretations of the infamous class action suit, *EEOC v. Sears, Roebuck and Co.*, 504 F. Supp. 241; 628 F. Supp. 1264 (31 January 1986). A number of non-lawyer post-structuralists have asserted that the case, on behalf of Sears' female workers in lower paying and less prestigious jobs than male workers, should have been argued on the basis of female differences and consciousness (Scott: 1988b). In fact, the only way a *prima facie* claim for sex discrimination can currently be made is through establishing (often with aggregate statistics) that women *as a group* shared legally and socially constructed characteristics that resulted in Sears' systematic discrimination against them over the years (Hall: 1986). The fact that the EEOC under Clarence Thomas woefully mishandled the case is usually not noted by those who argue that the case could have been won by emphasizing extreme differences among Sears women workers (Hoff: 1991). They also ignore the way in which the Reagan-Bush administrations throughout the 1980s, with similarly conservative appointments like Thomas', contributed to the general juridical backlash against affirmative action of that decade.[6]

---

5. Most American post-structuralists, especially non-lawyers, are also confusing equity with equality when they advocate replacing the latter with difference because under the US legal system equality is almost exclusively based on comparisons between similarly situated individuals; it cannot be based on differences among them – only equity jurisprudence provides for this distinction. When post-structuralists advocate "an equality that rests on difference", or that "difference constitutes the meaning of equality" as both Zillah Eisenstein and Joan Scott have, I have difficulty distinguishing their position from the "radical individualism" of classical liberalism which they both renounce. See Hoff (1991, pp. 31–6, 257–62, 356–64).

6. The Sears decision was largely the result of the district court judges showing both greater hostility and sophistication about the quantitative methodology involved in affirmation action statistics purporting to show discrimination; wanting more anecdotal (personal) testimony from the female plaintiffs that EEOC inexplicably failed to provide; being overly impressed with the fact that Sears had already initiated an

cont. next page

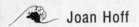

Initially, when US historians of gender began to emphasize differences and diversity among women, it sounded innocuous and familiar to historians of women – nothing more than diversity within a commonly shared set of socially constructed female characteristics. Instead, post-structuralism has become a way for historians of gender in the United States to impose supposedly benign, and neutral diversity on the past because of their legitimate concern with the fragmentation and increasing socioeconomic inequities of contemporary American society. Previous societies were probably not as systemically diverse as contemporary ones and so this is an anachronistic way of looking at the past. Yet it is the gender historians who accuse the women's history or feminist historians of being anachronistic by projecting present political concerns or values on the past (Bock: 1989)! What could be more anachronistic than imposing contemporary concern over fragmentation, i.e. diversity, of the present on the past so that no sources of patriarchal power or hierarchy can be held responsible for collective oppression in any time period? By replacing historical reality (meaning socially constructed gender, race, and class differences) with a thousand points of power, difference, and identities, post-structural historians of gender do not threaten mainstream society as some of them claim. To the contrary, established power in the United States welcomes diversity arguments because at the end of the twentieth century, it serves as a form of social control by keeping individuals and groups at odds with one another. All the government and courts have to do is grant them diversity in order to ensure that they do not notice that country and the world is moving on to global economic interdependence (meaning more lower paying jobs in most advanced, industrial countries) and popular cultural conformity.

Post-structuralism is No Friend of Feminist Politics

It was not until historians of gender began to redefine gender based on a male-defined post-structuralism, which denied the existence of female culture and female experience, that historians of women began to become concerned about where it would all lead. So my fourth and final concern is about politics because it soon became evident that for some deconstructionists, *différence* came to mean that "the female subject of feminism" consists of "each woman's consciousness and subjective limits." Thus, according to Teresa de Lauretis (1986), women are defined by their differences rather than any commonality derived from subordination under patriarchy over time. Differences among women, de Lauretis has asserted, will prevent feminism from ever again being represented as a "coherent ideology". In this sense, deconstruction represents an attack on radical political feminism in the United States. Yet this point of view is what Scott has praised in reviewing de

---

6. *cont. from previous page*

internal affirmative action program; and finally insisting that EEOC had not proven "discriminatory intent" on the part of the company. These attitudes were characteristic of the juridical backlash in the 1980s and can be found in other affirmative action cases of that decade of Reagan-Bush conservatism.

Lauretis' work as a "crucial breakthrough for feminist theorizing" apparently because of its commitment to anti-essential particularism (de Lauretis: 1986, p. 14; Scott: 1987, p. 17).

While anti-essential particularism can be applied to textual analysis without destroying the discipline of English or film criticism, it denies to historians the possibility of asking (and attempting to answer) certain painful political questions of great importance when studying half the female population such as, what is it about the complicitous experiences of women that have contributed for so long to their own subordination over time? In a 1991 essay, Joan Scott went so far in the direction of particularism as to emphatically reject any "appeal to experience as uncontestable evidence" in historical research, because experience makes ideological systems in any time period appear fixed rather than in a constant state of change of mutable identities. Although Scott insists that "experience is not a word we [historians] can do without", she is never quite able to define it. Instead, using a circular thought process she concludes enigmatically that one-dimensional "discourses produce experiences" which, in turn, "position subjects and produce their experiences" (Scott: 1991, pp. 777–79, 797).

By denying female experience, female and male post-structuralists are "engaged in a process of disengagement". This means they do not think that it is possible "to reclaim or rehabilitate post-modernism for feminist uses." According to Somer Brodribb, for post-feminists "to simply add woman to the recipe for the 'death of man' and the 'end of meaning' would be Sophie's choice" (Brodribb: 1992, p. 20). Such a folding in of woman makes no difference, has no meaning, and no political significance, despite the claims of some post-feminists to the contrary. For this reason, post-modernism and its compatriot in arms in the never-ending patriarchal war against women, violent pornography, cannot escape their masculinist, exclusionary origins anymore than they can claim to be post-patriarchal. They are simply still two more patriarchal ways to assert male dominance over women by literally and figuratively silencing them by deconstructing (or hacking) them up into smaller fragmented pieces.

In post-modern theory and literature women are more often expelled or excluded than included on the assumption that man can represent woman. This is evident as in Derrida's creation of Veronica and Lacan's obsession with silencing women through his phallogocentrism, hence his fascination with women who attempted to kill other women, like Aimeé, the subject of his 1932 thesis. By claiming only men can speak for women, male post-modernists appropriate not only women's bodies and minds, as earlier misogynists have done, but also their images. Thus, these post-modern "men in drag" defer feminism by endorsing Dionysus or the androgynous Tootsie male who offers himself as a mediator "between the feminine world and the world of the Father" (Gallop: 1988, p. 100; Brodribb: 1992, p. 138). We know from the attempts at androgyny of the turn of the century through the 1930s and again since the 1960s, that it usually ends up being co-opted by masculine discourse and imagery that it purports to transform with a male-defined version of feminism. Ronni Sandroff, editor of *On The Issues: The Progressive Women's Quarterly*, captured the essence of this process with her term Phallic Drift. "Like a compass needle that drifts North, no matter how you turn the instrument", she said, "Phallic Drift is the powerful tendency for public discussion of gender issues to drift, inexorably, back to the male point of view" (Sandroff: 1994, p. 2).

The increasing emphasis on masculinity in the study of gender have led Kathleen B. Jones and Anna G. Jónasdóttir (1988) to conclude that post-structuralism prides itself on asserting that neither feminism nor female culture constitutes a coherent philosophy or ideology. It therefore follows that feminist politics (and the female experiences that drive it) is no more meaningful than any other kind of constructed politics. Feminism no longer can be used to alleviate conditions of female oppression, because "identity is not an objectively determined sense of self defined by needs, any more than politics is ... the collective coming to consciousness of similarly situated individual subjects" (Jones and Jónasdóttir: 1988; Scott: 1988a, p. 5). In a word, post-modernism depoliticizes gender.

If experience can not be based on socio-economic categories and on the diversity and variability of common gender identities in different time periods, then there can be no political or visionary (I prefer this word to utopian) history from which contemporary feminist activists can draw sustenance and insight for opposing and critiquing the obvious discrimination against women in the United States and other countries. Instead of remaining simply another useful method-ological innovation for studying women's history and keeping that history relevant to the Second Women's Movement – as gender analysis was in the 1970s and early 1980s – in the hands of post-structuralists, it has become a potentially politically paralyzing and intellectually irrelevant exercise for endlessly deconstructing binary oppositions and analyzing myriad representations of cultural forms, relational identities, and discourses – disconnected from material reality. As a result, gender history in the United States is becoming more and more removed from political and legal activism. As historian Linda Gordon has noted, the current emphasis among historians of women on "'difference' is becoming a substitute ... for opposition", before the political battle has been won (1986, p. 25).

Using post-structural jargon to support gender as a category of analy-sis, historians of gender attempted to go beyond the definition of gender employed by historians and those in other disciplines since the mid-1970s. It was in that decade when many women scholars in the United States began to move toward "the self conscious study of gender" without the aid of post-structuralism. Initially employed by those feminists writing the new social history in the last half of the 1970s, gender simply meant "the cultural definition of behavior appropriate to both sexes" (Pleck: 1983, p. 54). This early definition of gender, which the new social historians began to employ, allowed feminists historians of women to reject biological essentialism as the rationale for women's subordination by concentrating on the ways in which different societies over time interpreted and attached values to the conditioned behavior and perceptions of women and men. Most importantly, in the hands of feminist social historians gender analysis from the 1970s also carried with it a promise of change, self-determination, and ultimately emancipation from patriarchal bondage (Canning: 1993; Hoff: 1992; Barry: 1991).

This earlier understanding of gender and the use of a sex/gender class or a "prism of sex" analysis (Jones and Jónasdóttir: 1988, p. 5; Barry: 1991) in historical research is quite different from the post-structural one that emerged in the United States in the 1980s. Gender analysis moved beyond the material and cultural representation of sex (biological differences), to a totally abstract representation of sexual and all other kinds of differences between women and men created by society. Thus, material experiences become abstract representations drawn almost exclusively from textual analysis; personal identities and all human agency become obsolete, and disembodied subjects are constructed by discourses. Flesh-and-blood women, of course, also become social constructs, according to post-structuralists, with no "natural" or physiological context except as a set of symbolic meanings constructing sexual difference.[7]

The theoretical result of this new post-structural definition of gender is to reduce sex/gender analysis to some other social structure. Rather than to "preserve gender as an independent analytic category in its own right," it is reduced to "a signifier of other relationships or power, or as primarily a constitutive of power" (Jones and Jónasdóttir: 1988, p. 7). The negative significance of this loss of gender as an *independent* category of analysis is also not always appreciated by post-feminist historians caught up in the Phallic Drift.

The apolitical origins of post-modernism have been commented upon by a number of feminist scholars (di Stefano: 1990; Bordo: 1990). Even though some post-structural feminists have expressed concern about modifying post-modernism so it can address feminist political issues (Rose: 1993, p. 99, Note 23), they usually have not discussed why it wasn't more difficult for historians of women to be seduced in the first place by a theory that did not provide any basis for feminist politics. Most simply put, post-modern theories are politically paralyzing because they arose out of a situation that male intellectuals found political paralyzing in post-war Europe – especially in France and Germany. Germans scholars developed critical theory and the French, post-modern linguistic theory, to rationalize their own disillusionment. With respect to the latter, Simone de Beauvoir noted as early as 1963: "It is a dead world they [the post-structuralists] are building" based on "defeatism" and lacking any "historical dimension". Because "the Revolution had failed [and] the future [was] slipping from [their] grasp", French novelists and

---

7. For more details see Hoff (1991, pp. 352–56 and 1992, pp. 16–17, 25–29). Instead of biological differences giving rise to societal views of women and men, according to the 1970s definition of gender, the opposite becomes true in the post-modern definition whereby physical differences are "created" and given meaning only by their representation, not because of their existence. Thus gender is viewed as preceding sex. See Delphy (1993, pp. 1–9).

scholars of the 1960s first attempted to use structural linguistics to accomplish a scientific conversion of the humanities (not unlike a similar attempt by scholars at the end of the nineteenth century to apply the science of their day to the newly emerging social sciences). When this failed "linguistics provided the critics of the scientific approach with the conceptual weapons" with which to continue to voice their discontent, but this time they attacked all forms of structuralism, especially Enlightenment ideas about truth, laws of nature, and progress through linear thinking (de Beauvoir: 1968, pp. 636–67; Pavel: 1990, p. vii; Brodribb: 1992).

As I noted at the beginning of this article, I think that this same political and disciplinary danger exists for women in other countries who are still in the process of constructing authentic female voices from the past. It must also be remembered that US historians of gender have had the luxury of turning to any and all theory *because*, beginning in the late 1960s, a pioneer generation of historians of women produced a number of monographic narratives. This is a luxury female historians in most other countries, who want to document their own history, do not enjoy. To skip the traditional stage of chronological fact-finding by writing about the experiential histories and memories of various races and classes of women and instead to adopt deconstructionist methodology would mean ignoring the material and psychological oppression of women's past and present lives. Female scholars attending international conferences, especially from non-English-speaking countries often express anxiety about the apolitical character of post-modernism, especially in recently liberated countries like Poland, where women constituted such an important component of Solidarity in the 1980s. For example, I heard Polish women at the Teaching Women's Studies Conferences held in May 1993 in Lódz say that they could not afford to abandon politics for linguistics, especially when their rights were being curtailed by the democratically elected parties in their Parliament. Instead of remaining simply another useful methodological approach for the study of women, post-modern gender analysis, in contrast to women's history, with its original female-centered definition of gender, has retreated from the political and legal arenas in which the battle for rights of women continues all over the world.

Post-structuralism is a Friend of Generational and Racial Conflict

If, indeed, post-modernism is ahistorical and misogynist, as well as politically paralyzing, why has it been taken up by historians of gender in the United States and given such attention in academic journals? A number of reasons come to mind. One I have already mentioned: the impulse among some historians in the 1980s to impose anxiety about the fragmentation of the present on the past. A related reason can be referred to as the "delayed disillusionment syndrome" among American academic leftists – not unlike that experienced earlier by French and German intellectuals after World War II. Already familiar with both German critical theory and French post-modernism, older Marxist-Leninist academics in the United States during the 1980s seemed increasingly susceptible to the nihilism present in such theories (be it through re-reading Nietzsche or Foucault and Derrida). They feared becoming irrelevant or unsuccessfully liberal in the age of conservatism represented by the Reagan and Bush administrations.

If some older historians succumbed to the bewildering splintering of American life and general disillusionment with conservative politics and embraced post-modernism, what attracted the younger ones? Most new or revisionist theories in any discipline usually start out as correctives of old ones by a new generation. In women's history in the United States, I am calling the group of women who began to revive and revitalize women's history in the early 1970s – the pioneer generation of historians of women (Hoff: 1992) in which I include myself. This was the same generation that participated in the formation of the Second Women's Movement in the United States. That these two historical experiences are represented in one or two age cohorts in the United States, is not a plot or conspiracy on the part of women of my generation and older. But it does give us a formidable collective memory that presents a number of problems for younger scholars. It is not without significance that in asserting their professional identity and right to career advancement in a tighter and more demanding marketplace, many of them chose a methodology and theory that rejected both our experiences and memories of those experiences.

Such generational conflict within history and other disciplines is common. Although this is the first time it has occurred primarily among women who are historians of women, because until the last twenty-five years there weren't enough of us to constitute a separate subfield over which to disagree. Of the various phases and generations that the writing of women's history in the United States has passed through since the 1960s, each one was more methodologically and theoretically sophisticated than previous ones. As a result, the subfield of women's history emerged on the cutting edge of theory in the discipline of history in general. It was almost inevitable that there would be more experimentation with interdisciplinary approaches beyond the social/cultural, ethnographic, and sex/gender analysis stage that women's history had already reached by the mid-1980s (Hoff: 1992; Canning: 1994).

Was it that some older, as well as many younger, historians of gender were simply captivated by the elitist idea of keeping women's history in the theoretical limelight? Possibly. By privileging the text, post-structuralism is elitist by definition. Also, post-modernism, in its purest form, asserts that such existing texts should only be analyzed (reconstructed) by "readers", regardless of authorial intent or socio-economic setting in which it was written.

If this were simply an academic debate over methodology and theory, I would not be so concerned. However, post-structuralism reared its relativistic head in the United States at a *crucial political moment:* just as women and minorities were beginning to find their voices and speak out with a collective identity. It told them that there could not be such commonality of purpose and that their texts did not mean what they said, because they had no reality or purpose outside of being reconstructed by post-structuralism. This privileging of texts has led groups, already marginalized by color or ethnicity, or sexual preference, or geographical location (such as minority and western women), who have not produced many texts, to fear that post-structuralism could result in silencing them by denying the presence of real women (and men) as political agents. It is perhaps not coincidental that American post-structuralism and neo-conservatism emerged at the very moment when it looked as though certain marginal groups in the United States were on the verge of obtaining more civil liberties and the long-sought-after (however problematic) equality with white men (Jones and Jónasdóttir: 1988).

For all these reasons, academic and activists women of color in the United States have expressed justifiable apprehension over the possibility that post-structuralism may become the dominant mode for interpreting women of the past and present (e.g. Christian: 1987 and this volume pp. 311–20; Hill Collins: 1990). The concern of women of color about deconstructionist methodology is threefold. First, they suspect that it may be established as a hegemonic practice in elite academic circles, thereby displacing the collective understanding of racism that women of color have struggled to obtain by using African or nationalist modes of analysis and an Afrocentric feminist epistemology rooted in both experience and action. Second, they suspect that post-feminists who use deconstructionist methodology may be unintentionally racist because it prompts them to suggest that race, like gender, is a discursively constructed concept. Finally, they fear that political opportunities in the post-Cold War world will be irrevocably lost if not realized in the 1990s.[8]

Post-structuralism is a Friend of Phallic Drift

As if the misogynist, ahistoricism, apoliticalness and possible racism of post-modernism were not enough, I believe that female post-structuralist in the United States, regardless of discipline, are repeating a serious mistake made by another generation of women in the 1920s and 1930s. Historian Carroll Smith-Rosenberg has pointed out that during those decades American women stopped speaking to each other in a common language. A younger generation of women began adopting the trendy male scientific and literary language of the interwar years, particularly Freudian and medical terminology (Smith-Rosenberg: 1985, 1989). Initially, many literary figures such as H. D. and Djuna Barnes and a variety of professional women, especially psychologists and psychiatrists, intended, *I repeat intended*, to give female or feminist interpretations to these avant-garde terms and concepts, but in the long term *they were co-opted or silenced by them.*

---

8. *Daedalus* (1987, Fall) addresses the problems when United States feminists adapt French deconstructionist methodology academic and political purposes. For a discussion of the Afro-feminist analytical model, see Rosalyn Terborg-Penn, Sharon Harley, and Andrea Benton Rushing (1988); Gloria I. Joseph and Jill Lewis (1981/1986); Chandra Talpade Mohante (1984, pp. 333–59); and Maxine Molyneux (1985, pp. 227–254).

In this process of Phallic Drift, these elite, well-educated women *unintentionally* lost the ability to communicate with other women, especially across class lines about public feminist issues. In contrast, an earlier generation of female Progressive Reformers at the turn of the century retained a common "womanly" language in their efforts to unite women of all classes. The communication gap, which developed during the interwar years, gradually became worse in the decades following the Second World War until it became painfully evident during the futile struggle for ratification of the Equal Rights Amendment in the United States between 1972 and 1982 (Hoff: 1991; Brodribb: 1992).

Post-structuralism also intervened, therefore at a *crucial intellectual moment:* just as activists of the Second Women's Movement by the late 1970s and early 1980s were again beginning to be able to communicate across both class and race lines by developing a unifying language so effectively used by women reformers during the Progressive Era; just as historians of women were using the new social history and definition of gender as social constructed behaviour to show greater class and race diversity – without deconstructionism – in addition to the shared commonality of subordinated and oppressed female experiences across class and race lines. Once again, as in the interwar years, a younger generation began to say that they would transform the defects of women's history using, not feminist but masculinist, theories. "The master's tools," as Audre Lorde remarked, "will never dismantle the master's house" (1984).

Like their predecessors in the 1920s and 1930s, today's female post-structuralists and post-feminists seem likely to be co-opted by those very male theories that have already turned Tootsie men into representations and spokes*men* for real women. The Phallic Drift of the 1980s and 1990s is much more subtle and seductive than the educated women of the interwar years ever encountered in their attempts to turn Freud and Marx into women-friendly theorists, because the latter never pretended they were women. However, the "fathers" of post-modernism insist on "aping the feminine . . . [and women who follow in their footsteps often end up] trying to be like Daddy who is trying to be a woman" (Gallop: 1988, p. 100).

As a stubborn relic from the 1960s and tenured guerilla to boot, I write these words more in sadness than anger, because I regard the current divisions among historians of women over women's versus gender history as counterproductive. While I hope for some intellectual accommodation between the two by the end of this century, if post-structuralism prevails, it could effectively sever the connection between women academics and women activists in the United States, harm the teaching of women's history at all educational levels, and hamper the study of women in countries where such scholarship is just beginning. Such is the insidiousness of the Phallic Drift of post-structuralism.

This is not the first time that theories from Europe have disrupted certain American academic disciplines. In fact, this has happened so often since World War II, that it is said European theories come to the United States to die – meaning that they are not adopted across the Atlantic until they are on their way

out abroad. While I believe that deconstruction will remain a useful methodology for textual analysis, I think that the claims of post-structuralism to destroy history or to resolve, or remove, all past contractions and dichotomies from history are being exaggerated at the moment. Like so many other useful theories and methodologies since the 1960s such as structural functionalism, cliometrics, critical legal and race theory, and now post-structuralism, they usually do not live up to their advance billing; go though an unintelligible, elitist stage; and finally after demystification, become one of many serviceable tools upon which historians draw depending upon the type of sources they encounter on any given research project.

One of the original goals actually achieved by early American practitioners of women's history in the 1960s and 1970s was to write so as to encourage the integration of the new material into general history classes and to provide facts and figures that would be useful in the struggle for women's rights in the United States and abroad. Until recently, that goal was being met. However, the various paralyzing aspects of post-modern theory make it, and especially its use of gender analysis to deny the category woman, a very "dangerous supplement" for the future of women all over the world who are still struggling for their rights – to say nothing of the future of women's history in the United States, and the future of the Women's Movement in the last decade of the twentieth century.

Somer Brodribb

Withdrawing Her Energy

why don't women just withdraw their energies she sniffed.

i thought you must be kidding
but okay i'm desperate and exhausted

and so i decided to Withdraw My Energy and see.
maybe patriarchy
would just retreat too
is that how it works?
i've been smashing and smashing and all i really had to do
was just walk away??

why do women just give it so much time? she rolled her eyes.
uh huh. yeah right. but okay, i'll try
because i know they take my time my life
and i have to take time out to recreate my humanity
but that's not what she means
she means it's my fault

sure i'll pretend i can
and i'll pretend it's mine
and i'll stop wasting my time
fighting it
i'll just go to Salt Spring.

anyway i walked to the bus station
so far no domination but it was early
and waited an hour in the schwartz bay terminal cafeteria
it was empty so no problem

for a while
until this stupid shit sits as close as possible to me
staring in my face in a cafeteria of fifty empty tables
sucking on candies and leering.

jesus christ doesn't he KNOW that i've Withdrawn My Energies???
clearly i must not be doing this right
and then his friend comes over and they speak about women and advance
heh heh heh
you goin to Salt Spring?

i withdraw to the cement steps behind the cafeteria and read my book *(How to Disengage in the post-bourgeois post-feminist post-colonial Year of Bennetton)*

Christ don't these assholes know i'm not only disengaged but 38 and a professor??

okay so i go up to the very top of the ferry in the corner, up and up the stairs,
stupid assholes could never find me up here anyway who cares no big deal not
like i'm not used to it but TODAY I'VE WITHDRAWN for chrissake

to forget also about when the boy student who burns flags said
at least she's okay to look at man how old do you think she is don't tell me you
don't get a hard on . . .

at least. anyway, clearly i had not withdrawn my sexual energy enough. so. i'm
going to try it today.
whatever it takes, after all.
whatever it takes.

and at the top of the ferry a red-haired high school student simply must sit at
my bloody table.
oh relax it's just a boy.
i put on my sunglasses and stare out the window.

so, you live on salt spring?
no.
you have friends there?
no.
just going for a visit then?
yes.
do you have a car?
NO! i'm just going over there for a WALK!
you been there before?

yes.
stay long?
no!
see much of the island?
just a bit.
where do you work?

trying to draw me out. a woman must always be easy to locate.

The cafeteria man is staring angrily a few tables away.

I leave the ferry
race ahead pick a street and walk.
the red-haired boy seems to live on this of all streets. for a while he is walking
behind me before he comes to his house.
don't they realize women can be anti-social?

the road is now empty and rambled with little streams and dark
forests and sudden hills i'm alone, at last—but a pick up truck
women know the true meaning of that
swerves by and the men in it turn and look and i know i have to withdraw back
to the public marina
i fight with the darkness among the trees for a while because it is mine it should
be mine but there is not even a space open in my own silence

this morning i read about bosnia and that look is like the rape camps and that
look is everywhere and no one admits it
no one burns ITS flag

i find a fucking picnic table from which i can see the sea and the boats but still
be in view in case i am withdrawn.

i go for a coffee and wait for the ferry there's no where else i can go it seems
without a car and a private fucking boy escort

so i sit again at the top of the ferry in a corner table and four hockey watchers
are next
hehe heh heh wouldn't it be great if you could just take the 45 second break and
hump hump give it to her eh?
yeah but go back in and play after it man?

so i stand on the car deck watch women and children in old cars

at the bus stop parking lot
the spa tanned ticket clerk tells me he doesn't take the bus so he doesn't know
when it comes
how they withdraw my energy.

with a large dog and a pick up truck a man comes over and says really sweetly
have you missed your bus?
he wants to give me a ride. god he looks normal. even the dog looks normal. after
all it will be an hour ride on the local Pat Bay 70 bus
why after all this is probably a nice man it's just that i've never been able to tell
the difference between a jagged edge slasher and a suburban jogger
it's just that there hasn't been a difference
for about 5,000 years or more
depending on the literature you read

and what you've withdrawn from yourself and other women.

and how come anyway
no one said to the marxists
oh why don't you just withdraw your energies from capitalism?
or why don't you just stop giving apartheid your time?

why don't you just get in the truck?
it's no good to fight you'll see
you're making too much out of it
you think too much

Avoid confrontation. Don't disturb.
Don't get involved.
Life on the sidelines:
profit from neutrality (at first)
Become a mediator
and cover things up.
Give up on
women
liberation
movement

I said no, I've been encouraged
and i live this way

Carol Anne Douglas

I'll Take the Low Road:
A Look at Contemporary Feminist Theory

How do we picture the world? Do we use broad, bold brush-strokes to depict an outline or pattern that sharply conveys a particular image, or do we fill in thousands of details inside the outline, and outside it, too, to keep from dichotomizing between inside and outside? Once we have filled in all of the intricate patterns inside and outside, is the outline still there? I am trying to convey my impression of the state of feminist theory. Is the outline still there, and what does it mean?

Roasting The Post

In reading some post-modern feminist theory,[1] I made the shocking discovery that some academic feminists think that there are two kinds of feminist theory. Apparently, feminist theory that directly tries to discuss specific subjects such as violence against women is "low" theory, while theory that is about other theory and that draws on ideas of men such as Michel Foucault is "high" theory. If that's the case, then you take the high road, baby, and I'll take the low road, and I'll be in Scotland, Peoria, Bangladesh, or any actual place before you.

Apparently, the works of Adrienne Rich, Mary Daly, Audre Lorde, Barbara Smith, Catharine A. MacKinnon, Andrea Dworkin, and virtually everybody else who has ever moved women are "low theory". What I thought was feminist theory is much too close to how ordinary women think, no matter how elegant its language, to be the most serious kind of theory.

I admit that I have written theory about theory, but I try to use low-tech rather than high-tech theoretical words.

When I read this new theory, I am rather pleased by the tolerance it

---

1. Post-modernists suggest that little is certain about the world – Marxists, materialists, etc. are modernists.

displays, but I am dumbfounded by the lack of passion. Would any of this theory ever move anyone to do anything?

Although I was already a radical feminist, I studied Marxist theory in graduate school; it seemed to be the closest thing to feminist theory that was then (in a conservative university in the early 70s) available, since it dealt with empowering ordinary people and ending class domination. Initially, I was quite interested in learning about a class-based theory. Then, I was very interested in the development of Marxist humanism, which tried to consider simultaneously the need for self-expression and an end to class-based oppression. Eventually, however, the theories about theories and the abstractions about abstractions bored me; I didn't care how many dialectics could be balanced on the head of a pin. At some point, language can become so dense and dull that almost nobody wants to read it.

I think that something similar is happening to academic feminist theory. I don't care how many discourses can balance on the head of a pin.

I think that many academic feminist theorists, even quite a few of the kind I find boring, care deeply about developing a theory that takes into account the situations of all women, or that at least is aware of its limitations when it does not do that. However, as well as discussing women, it is important to reach women, to move women. I get the impression that some of these academic women have become so careful about language, so careful not to make any assertions, that they feel blocked themselves, thus are unable to move anyone else.

In criticizing some academic feminists, I absolutely do not intend to criticize women because of their location in academia. As an adjunct professor, I teach a course in feminist theory at a nearby university. Theorists such as bell hooks, Catharine A. MacKinnon, Marilyn Frye, Gloria Anzaldúa, Sarah Hoagland, Barbara Smith, Maria Lugones, and Mary Daly are writing courageous, outstanding, moving theory while working at universities. What distresses me is theory that seems to move further and further from nonacademic women, theory that seems to be written with the expectation that only academic women will read it.

Keep The Passion

It is important for feminist theorists to be caring and careful, but it is equally important that we not lose our passion, and qualify and distance ourselves from everything we say. Caution, scholasticism, and abstraction are definitely not the messages that feminist theorists of color are conveying to white feminist theorists, and are not the best response that white feminists can give. Let's do the most passionate, most daring, most outrageous work we can, and that has at least a chance of being an appropriate response. Most of the feminist theory written by feminists of color in the past few years has been much better written than the theory done by white feminists (with some exceptions, such as Sarah Hoagland

and Marilyn Frye), and that's not because white feminists can't do it; it's because many have become too cautious and too academic, in the bad sense of the word. We all need to be both more careful and thoughtful and more daring, which is a difficult trick, but let's get on with caring and daring.

Fun With Theory

The more I read of turgid theory or theory that has good points but appears to be written only for academic women, the more I want to look at my own language and break out of it. As I look back at my feminist writing, I agree with most of what I have written, but I think that perhaps my language has been somewhat formally constrained. No doubt some of the post-modern feminists, although I hate to admit it, have partly influenced this feeling. Although just a few post-modern feminists, at their best, have styles that blend complexity with interesting language and moving personal reflections (if you think of Gloria Anzaldúa and Maria Lugones as somewhat post-modernist), most post-modernists have gone in the other direction and influenced me by negative example, especially in their writing styles.

When I say I am tired of writing as though I were copying model sentences into copybooks, I do not mean that I want to give up words such as "radical feminist", "lesbian feminist", or "woman". Never! I mean that I want to be a little more colorful. Why should Mary Daly have all the fun?

I want to write feminist theory like a love song, movement I love you, movement I love you, movement I love you. You've given me so much, you've shown me so many new ways of thinking. I want to shout with exaltation when another exciting feminist book comes out – there's a new bell hooks book, how can she write so many; hurray, a new book by Marilyn Frye; oh, I can't believe it, there's a new Mary Daly book, I want to shut myself away for days and read it. Again and again there are women coming forth for a demonstration, marching again and again, hurray for the old faces, hurray for the new faces, hurray for the new old faces, we were marching twenty years ago and we'll march twenty years from now with women who are now girls or not even born yet.

Movement, you scare me with all of your moods, your fights, your stubbornness, why can't you get it right? Why do we keep messing it up? Why do we have to keep discovering that we have let somebody down? I love you, why can't you get it right? I love you, why can't I get it right?

Meadowtations

Last summer, I walked in a meadow in Yellowstone National Park. The meadow covered sloping hillsides with wildflowers and dipped into a valley with a pond that generally seems to be surrounded by bison.

The meadow has so many meanings. For the grizzly, it is a larder full of yampah roots.[2] For the butterflies, it is the place of nectar-bearing flowers, and

---

2. A carrot-like plant.

Carol Anne Douglas

each butterfly species I watched seemed to visit only one species of flower. The coyote, the mountain bluebird, the meadow vole (mouse), the mule deer and the many grasshoppers all have their own perceptions of the meadow.

A developer, a park ranger, a photographer, a painter, a poet, a tourist who drives by and does not stop, and a hiker all have their own impressions of the meadow. Realize that these different people have different genders, races, ages, and physical abilities, and the meadow is still more different. An Asian-American woman ranger, a Jewish male tourist in a wheelchair, a Chicana hiker who has been raped and never feels quite safe, will all have different perceptions of the meadow. (I am of course indebted to Judy Grahn's book *Mundane's World* for its perspectives of animals for thinking of some of this imagery.)

I love the meadow – its butterflies, its deep blue gentians, its red-tailed hawks, the thrill of seeing the bison when I reach the top of the hill and the slightly scary thought that they might move across the meadow and block my path behind me (one does not just go marching through a herd of bison) while I walk on further. While cherishing my own experience, I want to have some sense of the many meanings it has for others, not to think my meadow is the only meadow. I want to remember what the meadow has been, and imagine how the Crow, the Shoshone, and other nations feel about losing it to the whites. I want to remember that the valley was created by volcanoes, and that the earth there is still volcanic and may someday erupt again.

I want to walk as thoughtfully everyplace I go, although I know that I will not always do so. I want to read city streets as carefully as I read a meadow, or a feminist theory book. I want my feminist theory to hum like the meadow. If we want to be aware of everything and everybody at all times, perhaps we are setting ourselves an impossible task, but a nevertheless important one.

* Originally published in *Off Our Backs* (February 1993).

420

IV

REFUSING TO BE SILENCED

Yenlin Ku

Selling a Feminist Agenda on a Conservative Market: The *Awakening* Experience in Taiwan

The feminist movement in Taiwan, as it emerged in the early 1970s, generated impressive social change.[1] Over the last two decades feminists have been remarkably productive despite operating with limited social and economic resources and within a highly restrictive cultural and political environment. The movement has been, by necessity, innovative and flexible. The complex experience of Taiwanese feminists and the dynamic nature of the movement is worth recording and analyzing not only in itself, but because it also adds a new dimension to contemporary feminist discourse, which has been rooted in the heritage of the west and articulated by western authors, or Third World women trained in western academia.[2] With its non-white, non-western tradition, Taiwan has never been part of the first world, nor does it share the collective memory of most Third World nations of having been colonized by a western power for hundreds of years. Its old heritage of Chinese culture and recent history of fast economic growth and political liberalization also place it outside the Third World experience. Owing its ideological origin to western feminism, the movement has diverged notably in its priority and strategies, taking into consideration the tradition of communal collectivism and Confucian ethics of social harmony. Yet it has been faced with similiar issues that may have or still confound feminists in other parts of the world: women's changing roles in the public and private spheres, the choice between ideological purity and

1. In Ku (forthcoming), I trace the contemporary feminist movement in Taiwan back to the mid 1970s and try to give a historical and sociological account of the issues and strategies involved.
2. I use "west" and "western" as a short hand for Dahlerup (1986), Katzenstein and Mueller (1987), Jayawardena (1986), Mohanty, Russo and Torres (1991), Andreasen *et al.* (1991), Backhouse (1992), Ryan (1992), and so on. All these works are grounded in either the First or the Third World experience.

pragmatic gains for women on issues like abortion, more equality or protection for women in the labor market and at home, recognition of sexual violence as a social issue in a more feminist world, the uneasy partnership of the feminist movement and political formations already in place, and the interrelationship of the feminist movement and Women's Studies, and so on.

My personal growth has been closely tied to feminist movements and feminist studies since the early 1970s, when an American friend lent me a copy of Robin Morgan's *Sisterhood is Powerful* in Claremont, California,[3] which provoked me to think about women's status. Margery Wolf's *Women and the Family in Rural Taiwan* (1972) was another book that taught me to rethink what I thought was the familiar. Returning to Taiwan in the mid-1970s, I taught at National Chio Tung University and volunteered to work for the Pioneer Press, a short-lived feminist press, which exuded the idealism and passion for social reform of the 70s and was ambitious in organizing large-scale activities. On my first visit to the Pioneeer Press, I met Li Yuan-chen, a young lecturer of Chinese literature, who was there for the same purpose and later became the pivotal visioner and movement organizer in the 80s. We started a life-long friendship and comradeship then and there.[4]

Li's perseverance convinced a small group of women to start the first feminist magazine, press, and movement organization, *Awakening*, in 1982. At a time when feminist ideas were considered too radical to be accepted by the mainstream media, it provided a forum for the supressed voices and a ground for mutual support. For many of us, *Awakening* was the major source of friendship and strength for daily struggle in a gloomily anti-feminist society.

To answer the questions raised by the movement as well as those by the critics of the movement, we felt the pressing need for acquiring new knowledge, keeping records, and learning from the feminist experience in other parts of the world. In 1985, I had chances to attend the Asian Women's Conference in Davao, the Philippines, the NGO World Women's Conference in Nairobi, Kenya, and to visit women's organizations in New York City. Exhilarated by the world-wide feminist struggle, and informed by the newly sprung academic field of Women's Studies, I co-founded the Women's Research Program (WRP), which was the first inter-collegiate Women's Studies center (sponsored by the Asia Foundation) in Taiwan, and offered

---

3. I was a graduate student in linguistics at Claremont Graduate School. Most of the early feminists in Taiwan have studied abroad at some point of their lives.

4. Ten years of selfless dedication to the feminist cause and organization work cost Li her health, opportunties of promotion, and time to pursue her own interest. She burned with the desire to express herself through creative writing, but other women's suffering always seemed more impending and needed immediate attention. Finally in the summers of 1991 and 1993, when younger women could share the burden of the Movement, she took refuge in a Buddhist temple to finish her novels *Intimate Talks about Love* and its sequel *Intimate Talks about Marriage*, the first books ever published in Taiwan looking at women's sexuality from women's point of view. They were well-received by "virtuous women from good families". The first one even won the Good Book Award from the Taipei City Government in 1993.

the first Women's Studies course in that year.[5]

In 1987, as political liberalization accelerated on the island and social movements gathered momentum, *Awakening* registered itself as a foundation, enhancing its ability for fund raising. It was also in 1987 that I was invited to deliver a paper on the feminist movement in Taiwan in a conference on "Female intellectuals and the development of Taiwan society", organized by the all-male editorial board of *China Forum*, a journal for social and cultural discussion, to celebrate the International Women's Day. For the first time, the feminist movement was formally recognized and discussed in an academic meeting, but many attending the conference (mostly female university instructors) argued that a feminist movement did not exit, and, citing the constitutional guarantee of gender equality argued it was not needed, and would not be accepted by women in Taiwan. They criticized *Awakening* for being too radical for a women's group, too small to have social impact, and so on. Some asserted that the correct approach to the Women's Movement was demonstrated by the newly founded New Environment Housewives League, which tried to win social respect by cleaning the environment instead of subverting gender roles or antagonizing the sexes. At the Women's Research Program, I was also constantly reminded to heed our images as scholars, not feminists, by my colleagues. Feeling unable to bridge the gap between academia and activism, or to live up to their level of "respectability", I left the Women's Research Program in 1987. It was Li Yuan-chen and other feminists' moral support that sustained me through the struggle during this period.

In spite of the unfavorable social atmosphere, a handful of core members at the *Awakening* kept the movement alive and vigorous until it generated wider social support in the 90s. Within the last decade it has successfully pushed for legalization of abortion; drafted the Equal Employment Bill and Revision of the Family Law; institutionalized protection for teenage prostitutes; pressured the government to revise its gender-biased primary school textbooks; and changed government hiring policy for banks and credit unions, training policy for insurance workers, and retirement policy for female employees in socio-educational institutes. We saw these legal reforms and policy matters as critical steps in generating the conditions under which women could be safe at work, at home and at study.

Besides its planned, annual activities, *Awakening* also responded quickly to the fast changing social environment and women's new social needs. For example,

---

5. The first such course was not easily accepted by the administration. First of all, I had to conduct a survey on campus to prove there was such a need. Then, because National Chiao Tung University with its emphasis on science and engneering had a sex ratio of 4,000 (40 male : 1 female), I had to name the course "gender relations" to arouse student interest and to invite well-known guest speakers who were sympathetic to feminism but not necessarily feminists themselves. Students were encouraged to bring their own experiences into classroom discussion. A national newspaper, *Min Sheng Daily* (1987), surveyed the major college campuses and named it one of the three most popular courses on our campus. Now I teach Women's Studies courses regularly and openly discuss feminism in class. Women's Studies are also established on other campuses now.

in 1987, *Awakening* and Rainbow, a rehabilitation program for teenage prostitutes, organized a coalition of thirty-one women's, human rights, native people's rights, and religious groups to march on the red-light district in Taipei, and to launch an island-wide signature campaign against the inhumane traffic in under-age women. By making prostitution a human rights issue, it immediately captured the attention of the media and the public. As a result, the coalition was transformed into the more permanent Taiwan Women's Rescue Association, and the police set up a special project to regulate the trade. In 1988, a Mr Taipei Beauty Pageant was staged as a parody of the Miss World Beauty Pageant when the latter was held in Taipei. The absurdity of a beauty contest was instantly noticable as the gender role was reversed. In the 1989 national election, *Awakening* drew up a joint women's platform with several other women's groups, organized a women's policy promotion team to speak at campaign rallies, hosted a debate on women's policies between the candidates of the ruling and the opposition party, and invited Ethel Klein from Columbia University to give talks on women's leadership training and election strategies. Before the 1992 election, it publicly evaluated the past performances of sitting legislators, and invited candidates to present their views on women's issues and make commitment to related policies. In 1994, it orchestrated a successful anti-sexual harassment demonstration in Taipei, preceded by public hearings in large cities and lecture tours on campuses to bring out over 1,000 women and men. For the first time, women in Taiwan marched for a women's issue *per se*, that did not have to be justified by other causes such as human rights, religion and so on. By the mid-90s our campaigns and strategies have come to resemble those of the western radical feminists more closely than twenty years ago.

Since the mid-80s, *Awakening* members have worked behind the scene to organize new women's groups for specific purposes. It helped to deliver the Taipei Women's Development Center for the rehabilitation of women surviving a family trauma in 1983; the first Women's Studies Conference, and the first Women's Research Program, in 1985; the Rainbow Project in 1986; the New Environment Housewives' League, the Warm Life Association, a mutual support group for divorced women, and the Taipei Women's Rescue Association in 1987; Angels Askew, a loosely organized study group of young women, in 1989; Between Us, the first lesbian group, in 1990; Women's Studies groups on campuses in the early 90s; and the Feminist Studies Association in 1994, which, made up mainly of female university teachers and cultural workers, considered itself the academic arm of the feminist movement. Proliferation of these grassroots groups helped to draw together women, some of whom were reluctant to be identified with feminists, to work for diverse and common causes. *Awakening* also assisted and subsidized women outside Taipei to organize their own Awakening, sisterly but independent groupings of local women. In 1993, it began to issue a quarterly newsletter in English, edited by its foreign volunteers. In 1994, more than thirty *Awakening* members and friends pooled together their savings to open the first women's bookstore and coffee shop called "fembooks" in Taipei, which also offers regular lecture series. When these groups were newly formed, their memberships greatly overlapped and the resources seemed to be stretched thin. But over the years, each developed its own characteristics and focused attention, while the *Awakening* remained the leading group tackling a broad spectrum of issues and continued to open up new fronts of struggle after the late 80s. The turn of events in 1994 signaled a new phase of the movement, which has won greater support and paid more attention to the cultural arena.

Compared with movements elsewhere, the Taiwan experience bears some unique features. Firstly, on this densely populated small island, most political, economic and cultural activities take place in Taipei, the capital.[6] The concentration of activities gives the movement organizers easier access to the ruling apparatus: the central government, the legislature and the media, as well as more frequent interaction with other social movement groups to speed up feminist reform. Secondly, the fast economic growth in the 1970s–1980s and rapid political liberalization since the 1980s provided for the acceleration of social and political events. Taking advantage of the political opportunites of this period, movement organizers agitated for changes in favor of women which would have been considered too radical in a previous era. Nevertheless, Confucianists' emphasis on social harmony and hierarchical order hampered the development of individualism and the notion of equal rights.[7] Colonial rule under Japan in the early twentieth century further fortified patriarchal practice. Moreover, as Taiwan has been excluded from the international community since the 1970s by the People's Republic of China, the status of women in Taiwan is not monitored by the UN and its agencies,[8] and we do not enjoy the legal protection and institutional support to which women of most UN member nations are entitled. By firmly upholding feminist goals while remaining flexible in its tactics, *Awakening* patiently cultivated women's consciousness in

---

6. Taiwan, with an area of about 36,000 square kilometers (roughly the size of the Netherlands and West Virginia, USA) is the second most populated state in the world, next to Bangladesh. At the end of 1992 the total population was 20,752,494, with 10,044,213 females and 10,708,281 males (sex ratio: 107). Nine years of primary through junior high school education is compulsory. In 1992, female enrolment in primary schools was 1,065,735 and male 1,135,233, in junior high schools female 574,079 and male 604,949, in senior high schools female 107,858 and male 122,018, in vocational schools female 268,425 and male 232,296, and in colleges female 303,359 and male 349,803. Birth rate for women was 16.16% and for men 16.6%, death rate 4.24% for women and 6.34% for men. Infant mortality rate was 4.87% for female and 6.33% for male. Life expectancy at age 0 for female was 77.22 and for male 71.79 (Directorate-General of Budget, Accounting and Statistics, Executive Yuan, Republic of China, 1993).

7. Today's feminists often hold Confucianism, especially Neo-Confucianism, responsible for the constraint imposed on women's autonomy and development. Yet Confucian teachings on the rules of propriety and restriction of one's desires could have lessened overt display of misogyny and thus gives women a safer public space once they have managed to move to certain social positions. This aspect of Confucianism remains to be studied.

8. Nevertheless, Hong Kong and Macau, which the PRC also claims to be its territory, are listed in UN statistics.

every affordable way, took every political opportunity to act, and waited until a sizable number of women were ready to make demands for themselves. What a small group of women have achieved under adverse cultural and political circumstances in the past decade manifests the strength of women's collective energy and determination. We expect more women will be empowered as feminism becomes more accepted in Taiwan so that more permanent and radical changes will be produced in the next decade.

Diana E. H. Russell

US Pornography Invades South Africa: A Content Analysis of *Playboy* and *Penthouse*

> *What would it say about one's status if the society permits one to be hung from trees and calls it entertainment – calls it what it is to those who enjoy it, rather than what it is to those to whom it is done?*[1] (Andrea Dworkin and Catharine MacKinnon: 1988).

I focus on pornography rather than on the eroticized violence in mainstream media, because I believe it plays a significant role in the occurrence of rape and sexual assault in countries where it has been allowed to proliferate, and because it promotes and reinforces sexism. These common concerns of feminists differentiate us from conservatives who see sex and nudity in themselves as sinful, dirty, and immoral.

Most western countries have embraced the view "that freedom of expression is more vital to democracy than the risk of harm arising from the widespread dissemination of pornography" (Court: 1979, p. 237). The South African government, in contrast, implemented severe restrictions on pornography in keeping with its endorsement of the International Convention for the suppression of the circulation of, and traffic in, obscene publications (Court: 1979, p. 237). While many western nations are also signatories to this convention, several of them simply ignored it, or, in the case of Denmark, renounced it. The Danish government decided to condone pornography in 1969 in the belief that this would result in a decrease of sex crimes (Court: 1979, p. 237).

Like South Africa, the governments in some western-influenced countries like Singapore and Japan decided to take an anti-pornography stance. The leaders of independent African nations have, to my knowledge, also chosen to restrict

---

1. A young girl was shown hanging from a tree in a series of photographs of bound and dead-looking Asian girls in *Penthouse* magazine.

pornography, which they perceive as an undesirable and immoral western import.

When analyzing the relationship between the availability of pornography and the increase in rape rates in several countries, researcher John Court noted that in South Africa, "the desire for pornography appears to be much more pronounced among Whites" (Court: 1979, p. 239). UCT Political Studies lecturer Mary Simons remarked that when she was an honours student at UCT, her Black male colleagues "found that one of the most difficult things about coming to res [residence] was their exposure to blue movies, which they had never seen before" (Dunlop: 1993, p. 9). Further research is needed to find out if White and African men in South Africa do indeed have significantly divergent opinions about pornography and its effects. Could it be that a small minority of white South African males will seek to impose their desire for access to more hardcore pornography on the majority of South Africans (women from all ethnic groups and African men) who are not interested in this material? Because pornography has harmful effects, this would indeed be a tragic occurrence because disinterested men can be socialized into becoming interested in it.

Pornography was first banned in South Africa in 1931 by the Entertainments [Censorships] Act.[2] After several amendments, this Act was repealed by the Publications and Entertainments Act.[3] The Publications and Entertainments Act was amended twice before being repealed by the Publications Act.[4] The Indecent or Obscene Photographic Matter Act,[5] which banned photographic pornography, was amended by Act #72 of 1983, and is still in force today.

Also banned were movies and literature that were considered to be too sexually explicit by the Censorship Board of the Nationalist government, as well as materials considered politically threatening to their monopoly of power and privilege. In this era of the so-called new South Africa, however, the Nationalist government has lightened up on the kinds of materials they ban.

For example, the government permitted Ralph Boffard, a Texas businessman who secured the rights to publish *Penthouse* in South Africa, to start publishing a special edition of the United States-based *Penthouse* magazine in February 1991.[6] In order to make it acceptable to the government, and perhaps to South African citizens as well, most of the sexually explicit materials published in *Penthouse* everywhere else in the world, have been – and continue to be – omitted from the South African edition. By January 1993, *Penthouse* sales in South Africa had reached about 70,000 copies a month.[7] Impressed by the success of *Penthouse*,

---

2. Act 28 of 1931.

3. Act 26 of 1963.

4. Act 42 of 1974.

5. Act 37 of 1967.

6. Progressive people in the United States avoid using the terms "America/n" – which have become the colloquial terms for that country and its citizens – since they also apply to Latin America as well as North America. Hence, its usage is seen as yet another example of US imperialism.

7. "*Playboy* in South Africa". (1993).

Times Media Limited planned to produce the first South African edition of *Playboy* Magazine towards the end of 1993.[8]

The publication of these magazines in South Africa is one of many manifestations of US cultural imperialism that I consider to be a serious problem for South Africa to deal with. The importation, both legal and illegal, of pornographic and non-pornographic videos, films, and TV programmes that reflect the violence, materialism, racism, misogyny, and homophobia prevalent in US culture, is having deleterious effects on South Africa. These damaging, violence-promoting effects are likely to increase the more such materials are embraced by South Africans.[9] It is vital that South Africans decide before it is too late how they want to deal with this realitvely newly-born South African industry.

Playboy and *Penthouse* in the United States

In the United States, *Penthouse* Magazine has 4,600,000 paid subscribers and *Playboy* Magazine has 3,600,000 – making these the two best-selling pornographic magazines in the country.[10] Studies conducted by many magazines indicate a pass-along readership of between two and five copies. Probably this number is closer to five copies for pornographic magazines because many people are embarrassed to buy their own copies, while minors may not be permitted to purchase copies by their families or by the sellers. Assuming five copies per magazine, the estimated readership of both *Penthouse* and *Playboy* is approximately forty-one million people.

The launching of *Penthouse* and a South African edition of *Playboy* has caused little public controversy or protest. Instead, these magazines appear to be welcomed by White liberals and leftists. *Weekly Mail* reporter Mark Grevisser, for example wrote a lengthy article about the publication in South Africa of *Penthouse* – "the worlds best selling porn mag" – claiming incorrectly that: "There is no substantial evidence linking sexual violence to pornography" (Grevisser: 1991). However, he did at least attempt to represent different sides of this controversy in this article by quoting the views of feminists opposed to pornography. Only two years later, another *Weekly Mail* reporter chose as an example of "the good news" in 1992 that "*Playboy* gears up for publication in South Africa" (Forrest: 1992, p. 6).

In a much more seriously pro-pornography article, *Weekly Mail* reporter Heidi Kriz declares, "The censors see dirty pictures. The new feminists see liberation" (Kriz: 1992, p. 1 at 5). She goes on to characterize as new feminists Madonna, the international pornographic icon, and Jane Raphaely, editor-in-chief of *Cosmopolitan* and *Femina*. Raphaely lauds what she sees as Madonna's liberated behaviour as reflected in her best-selling book, *Sex* (Madonna: 1992). "She [Madonna] takes every form of pornography and systematically demystifies it by putting it in her

---

8. "*Playboy* in South Africa". (1993).

9. For example, see Mabaso's statements about the contribution of foreign media products to sexual violence in Soweto in Russell (1991).

10. The National Research Bureau, 1992.

control", Raphaely enthuses, after publishing several of the pictures from *Sex* in *Cosmopolitan* (Kriz: 1992). "She is sending pornography up and so reduces its power to hurt women", Raphaely proclaims. And: "Above all, she is in control and that is what separates the women of the 90s from the girls", she eulogises (Raphaely: 1992, p. 12).

But while Madonna appears to be acting out of positive choice, many of the images she has concocted celebrate the merger of sex and violence. Hence, far from being a "relentless attack" on patriarchal power, as *New York Times Book Review* critic Caryn James proclaims, Madonna reinforces such power. Elaine Hawkins puts it this way:

> It must be acknowledged that Madonna herself has been active in the creation of her own image, but that creation has been allowed precisely because she projects a version of femininity which, despite its apparent radicalism, is not ultimately a challenge to the system. With immense perception, Madonna has keyed into the discontent of many young women and offered a way out. But it is no way out: the image reeks of conservative individualism (1992, p. 26).

There is a picture in *Sex* in which a woman places the blade of a knife on Madonna's crotch. In another photograph a woman kisses Madonna, who is tied to a chair, while holding open scissors to her jugular vein. Madonna has her mouth open, her tongue out, reciprocating the kiss. In a third picture, Madonna smiles while two skinheads of ambiguous gender attack her. One is holding her arms above her head while the other pulls up her skirt and gazes at her genitals. It appears as if she is about to be raped. In general, *Sex* is a macabre parody of mostly-lesbian S/M. These pictures do not demystify sexual violence. Nor does the portrayal of rape as a pleasurable act for men and women reduce its power to hurt women. Instead, these images reinforce the widespread myth that women are masochistic and enjoy the dangerous combination of weapons and sex, as well as being raped. Madonna's decision to reinforce these dangerous myths is irresponsible, all the more so because she is a role model for millions of young girls. Reporter Janine di Giovanni asks:

> Are those teens who *jol* to Madonna videos at birthday parties or in discos, and who emulate her numerous reinventions of self, now going to be influenced by *Sex*, to be instructed that being in touch with your body means having your nipples pierced, playing with knives and whips and keeping an open mind about bondage and sado-masochism? (1992, p. 198).

Madonna has chosen to become a pornographer, not just a "porn star". There is nothing liberating for women about this.

One wonders how Kriz can possibly argue that the following statements by Jane Raphaely, then Madonna, are examples of the "new" or "revisionist feminist line":

Lust and even domination and submission in the sex act are all part of nature's plan. "If you watch animals mating there is a strong element of domination and submission", says Raphaely. "There is a tendency on the part of one of the partners, mainly the male, to be dominant and insistent. It's very logical for women to go along with that" (Kriz quoting Raphaely: 1992, p. 5).

Generally I don't think pornography degrades women. The women who are doing it want to do it. No one is holding a gun to their head (Madonna: 1992).

Some women want to be slapped around . . . I think for the most part if women are in an abusive relationship and they know it and they stay in it, they must be digging it (Madonna: 1992).

Only the one who hurts you can comfort you. Only the one who inflicts the pain can take it away (Madonna: 1992).

Sex with the young can be fun if you're in the mood . . . One of the best experiences I have had was with a teenage boy . . . He was just a baby (Madonna: 1992).

There is something comforting about being tied up (Madonna, 1992).

Describing the holders of such thoughtless sexist nonsense as representatives of new feminism is like describing F. W. de Klerk as representing the new form of liberation philosophy. Perhaps it reveals the wishes of the white men who run the *Weekly Mail* that the real feminists would just disappear, or be goaded into silence. Simply because it is written by a woman does not contradict this possibility, since she would be likely to jeopardize her job if she wrote a real feminist attack on pornography.[11]

Kriz contrasts her notion of the new feminist pro-pornography stance with the so-called "traditional" feminist view articulated by Sheila Meintjies[12] that "anything that perpetuates the objectification of women is wrong and regressive" (Kriz: 1992, p. 5). Feminists have long objected that heterosexual pornography, as well as many images of women in mainstream media, portrays women as sex objects – tits, cunts, asses – not as whole human beings with intelligence, ambition, and creativity. Dehumanizing women in this way makes it easier for men to rape them. Men are portrayed very differently in all media, albeit in destructive stereotypic ways that reinforce notions of manhood that also contribute to violence against

11. I made considerable efforts to get the *Weekly Mail* and the *Argus* to permit their readers to read a critique of Jane Raphaely's well-publicized views on Madonna as a liberated woman, but they refused. This is but one of thousands of examples of the consequences of these and other South African newspapers being written by men for men, often at women's expense.
12. Sheila Meintjies – University of Whitwatersand Gender Forum.

women. Later in Kriz' article she appears to deliberately obfuscate the so-called traditional feminists' critique of pornography with the right-wing sex-is-sin approach to this issue. This manipulative and pejorative association is frequently used by leftists in western countries.

It is understandable that South Africans who have fought for democracy against an authoritarian racist government for so long would be tempted to support whatever this government has opposed, including pornography. But just because it is understandable doesn't make it right. On the contrary, it is vital that progressive South Africans educate themselves about the impact of pornography rather than mindlessly embracing this material because western nations have done so, or because the Nationalist government has suppressed it for so long. It is also important that more Black South Africans express their views on this subject before their younger generation gets hooked on this pernicious White western form of sexism and, in some cases, racism.[13]

Conclusion

Assessing the consequences of pornography is one thing; deciding what to do about it is another. Since an assessment of the consequences *does* reveal many extremely destructive effects, the logical next question becomes how it should best be dealt with.

It is argued that despite its harmful consequences, the censorship of pornography would undermine freedom of speech. The fallacy here lies in assuming that censorship is the only effective way to try to combat pornography. There are many ways to oppose pornography that do not involve censorship, for example, writing letters, editorials, and articles in newspapers, magazines or books, public education about the detrimental effects of pornography, speak-outs by pornography survivors, demonstrations, marches, confrontations with pornographers and their defenders, graffiti protests of pornographic ads, window displays, porn stores, etc., sabotage against the property of pornographers and their commercial outlets, tearing up pornography and other acts of civil disobedience.

It is also fallacious to think that all legal actions constitute censorship. For example, restricting pornography in the US in ways that are consistent with the First Amendment is not censorship, even if it is done by government action.[14]

Many feminists in the United States support the idea that pornography constitutes a civil rights violation by virtue of the fact that it discriminates against women. Viewing pornography in this way rather than as obscenity allows it to be handled legally, like other civil rights violations. There are many advantages to this

---

13. According to two "coloured" women informants, many "coloured" males are already hooked on pornography.

14. Catharine MacKinnon, personal communication, January 1990.
The final section of my book *Making Violence Sexy: Feminist Views on Pornography* (1993) includes a section on feminist actions against pornography, none of which can be considered pro-censorship.

approach (see, for example, Dworkin and MacKinnon: 1988). However, I believe there is a more appropriate and effective way to deal with pornography in South Africa.

The African National Congress has proposed dealing with racist hate speech by criminalizing it in recognition of the harm that can be caused by such overt expressions of bigotry. Racist hate speech presumably includes racist advertisements, racist literature, racist cartoons and pictures, as well as public statements that are racist. An equally valid case can be made for criminalizing sexist hate speech, including sexist advertisements, literature, cartoons, pictures, and public statements. The same holds true for homophobic hate speech. Clearly, pornography qualifies as a form of hate speech. Legislation that is devised to deal with racist hate speech should be equally suitable for dealing with sexist and homophobic hate speech.

Viewing pornography as a manifestation of hate speech rather than as a form of obscenity or a violation of women's civil rights, shifts the focus away from the issue of censorship and the common cause claimed by both pornographers and those in defence of freedom of speech. It also reduces the likelihood that charges of being pro-censorship will be manipulatively used to defend pornography – as has happened in the United States. Significant inconsistencies in the ways that racist hate speech and sexist hate speech are handled would be more obvious if the same laws apply to both. Hence, if the government and/or the public do not consider the criminalizing of racist pictures and cartoons as unacceptable instances of censorship, it would make it more difficult for people to argue that outlawing equally abusive sexist pictures and cartoons does represent an unacceptable form of censorship.

It is imperative that South Africans tackle the issue of pornography now, before it has become so deeply entrenched in this country, and before men have become so dependent on having it at their disposal, that it becomes virtually impossible to eradicate.

Acknowledgments

I am very grateful to the following people for their assistance with this article: to Desiree Hansson, for her substantive editorial suggestions, Angela Harraway and Lyn Turner for word processing assistance, Melissa Farley for supplying some of the original pornographic photographs, and Dennis Bell for photographing some of them.

Teboho Maitse

The Past is the Present:
Thoughts from the New South Africa*

The theme of my paper is the past is the present, just to give an indication of how the past often influences the present, particularly in newly liberated countries, because the more things change, the more they remain the same, especially with regard to women's lives. Today in a newly liberated South Africa men have a claim to the past, present and future, while women are confined to the mythic past of African culture that promotes, condones and glorifies gender inequality.

The ability of Black South Africans as a people to pick up the threads of their lives together even after suffering unimaginable atrocities under the injustice of apartheid is remarkable. Their practical commitment for reconciliation has both negative and positive implications for the future. There has been a pact of forgetting, and the peace process has been geared towards the achievement of national unity at all cost. Thus women who have borne the suffering of both racial and gender oppression are bound by this pact, and they have been denied the opportunity to relate their own personal experiences of sexual, physical and emotional violence by the police, comrades, as well as known and unknown men, in the interest of maintaining national unity. *Reconciliation* and *forgiveness* have become buzz words within the South African communities.

While I do appreciate the fact that people of different beliefs and outlook in life are prepared to forgive each other and live together as a people, I do have a problem with the fact that this forgiveness and reconciliation business only means forgiving visible crimes which were carried out by the apartheid regime.

It does not include crimes which were committed by men against women. Some men are not even aware that they have wronged us.

I argue that there is a misuse of the words *forgiveness* and *reconciliation.* I know that this may sound too Catholic (I am one), but how can there be

---

* Paper presented at the International Women's Day event organised by Women Against Fundamentalism. Leeds Civic Hall, March 4, 1995.

436

any forgiveness without remorse? How can a rapist be expected to be remorseful because he raped you when you denied him his conjugal rights or you were wearing short and revealing clothes? He beat you when supper was late after he'd had a rotten day at work and his boss was really horrible to him? How can women be expected to reconcile with people who have been dehumanised and who in turn have dehumanised others? How can we reconcile with people who have turned us into objects of pleasure, manipulation, humiliation, shame and pain? How can women reconcile with people who sterilised them without their consent? Lastly, how can we reconcile with people who injected us with Depo Provera or inserted the Dalkon Shield in our wombs because they were obeying the government which was bent on curbing the Black population? Listen, how can we expect him to be remorseful when all he did was exercise his right or he was doing his job? And above all, how can you expect him to be remorseful because you are only a woman and you have to obey and cherish your master at all times?

Anyway what does reconciliation mean to the average person on the street who is not religious? I sincerely think that the church ought to redefine the meaning of reconciliation in relation to men's attitudes towards women, as well as those men who are violent towards women. Otherwise this pact of forgiveness, just like everything else in the world, will benefit the brotherhood of men. Women need the space to articulate the pain they suffered through the years of apartheid in South Africa, war in the former Yugoslavia and the troubles of Northern Ireland: to let men know that they did not only kill and beat each other senseless, but that they have also maimed, raped and killed innocent women just because they happened to be women they were married to, lived with or were out on the streets on their own. Therefore, to have meaningful change in the world, particularly between men and women, there should be a forum, another Nuremberg if you like, where women can relate their own personal experiences without any intimidation. "A number of survivors of the Nazi concentration camps and Stalin's gulag enriched humanity by telling their stories as they were – ordinary human experiences of suffering without any ideological masks" (Ramphele: 1990, p. 13). Women need this too.

Nationalism

As I've already mentioned the pact for forgiveness is based on the desire to achieve national unity, which we acquired through the national liberation struggles and the April 1994 elections: a fulfillment of the African National Congress' promise of a democratic non-racist and non-sexist society. Therefore, it is important to briefly discuss what is nationalism and its implications for women. Nationalism refers to a human grouping which can identify itself as a historically evolved community of people, with a common culture and common descent (Davis: 1978, p. 8).

However, nationalism can be a very elastic concept of identification by the oppressor and the oppressed. It can be both progressive and reactionary, because it implies a unity and identification of different classes and genders to which individuals belong. Nationalism fails to acknowledge that within the nation there are two categories of people: men and women whose relationship with each other is that of the dominator and the dominated (Thiam: 1986, p. 22). Therefore, nationalism allows us to bring into its fold both our perceived and lived experiences as gendered beings. Hence it does not offer women any protection from various forms of male violence; instead, rape, battering, harassment, molestation and sexist jokes continue within the umbrella of nationalism to keep women in their place (Mies: 1982, p. 27).

Do not get me wrong, nationalism as a concept of identification is a very powerful tool. However, it has its shortcomings with regard to women. As a result, some women have not had an easy relationship with it, because nationalist movements have rarely taken seriously women's experiences of how women become colonised or how we can throw off the shackles of that material and psychological domination. Rather, nationalism typically has sprung from men's feelings of disempowerment, men's humiliation and their hopes for war, as well as from the anger at being denied power or turned into a nation of "boys" (Enloe: 1989, pp. 122–66).

In South Africa the emergence of nationalism amongst the oppressed people paved the way for women's entry into the "nationalist political family". Women identified with men as the oppressed and exploited nation. However, this political family, like the domestic, remained under patriarchal domination. There was no indication that women's entry might unsettle the male-dominated national liberation movement, because while women shared a common goal with men of toppling the apartheid regime, women were not expected to fight these struggles as natural beings, but as gendered beings (Beall and Toades.: 1989, pp. 30–56). In my view this is the crux of women's domination and subordination: we have failed to realise that the term nationalism has a double meaning and men can double-speak, because in times of crisis our biological attributes are overlooked and yet at the same time they are subtly exploited to boost the numbers and morale of the nation, as I will explain later on.

My theory is that nationalism brings into relief its own deployment of new and old forms of patriarchal control over women. Nationalism equips the new nation with a clear strategy of reshaping men's language by adopting very subtle ways of retaining their power and control. This is done by merging traditional values of the old with the new society, particularly the promotion of motherhood and of the idea of women as naturally suited to this role because of their supposed spiritual, moral and physical needs (Gaitskell and Unterhalter: 1989, p. 60). In reality nationalism denies women individual identity, because women have to be so-and-so's wife and so-and-so's mother. If women concur with this idea, in my view this indicates women's myopic views on nationalism. Although being members of nationalist movements offers us a temporary respite from the harsh brutality of state oppression with a promise of a glorious future, nationalism also blunts our perceptions about what that change may mean to us as women. I say this because we have failed to question why all popular images of members of the national liberation struggles are typically male, and if they show women at all it is normally a picture of a woman soldier with an AK47 in her hands and a baby on her back (Wallace: 1979, pp. 21–2). This is a clear indication that our participation in this political family is only a temporary one because once it's over we have to pick up the baby.

Violence

Today in a new South Africa, African women are urged to observe African tradition and culture which existed prior to colonisation and apartheid. Some men are advancing theories that using violence against a woman is not a crime because it is part and parcel of African culture. I will list just two examples of violence as well as the prevailing attitudes in society and the police force.[1]

A female student in the Western Cape was raped by a fellow student. When this boy was asked why he raped this woman, he said that in African culture if a woman refused to have sexual intercourse with you, a man had a right to do it by force. In the townships of Johannesburg there is a new phenomenon: a group of young men use undisguised sexual violence against women: they abduct a woman and gang rape her, sometimes holding her hostage for days (Russell: 1991, pp. 62–83); they are also known to insert objects in women's vaginas (Maitse: forthcoming).[2] A young woman who had been raped by these men said:

> I had just got into my car when suddenly two men wielding knives uninvitedly joined me. They made me drive to a quiet place while they were drinking. When we reached this place they took turns in raping me, they were laughing all the time and enjoying themselves. They forced their private parts into every opening I have. They then left me half-naked, covered in blood. I got into my car and drove to the hospital where I was told to go and report the case to the police first. At the police station I walked in front of all those people naked. The police interrogated me as if I was the perpetrator, they were shouting at me and asking me why I didn't lock my doors. They kept on saying: Were you hitch-hiking at the time? Were you wearing a short skirt? Were you drinking? (Maitse: forthcoming).

I have to say that while this phenomenon of gang rape is going on uncurbed by the police, it has not elicited any form of condemnation from the government and church bodies. No one wants to get involved because it is perceived as the woman's problem, so these men continue raping women with impunity.

Conclusion

South Africa is a liberated country and it is supposedly a democratic, non-sexist and non-racist society. However, in my understanding non-sexism cannot be

1. Research data obtained in South Africa during December 1993 and April 1994 through semi-structured interviews and questionnaires.

2. See my unpublished PhD dissertation, entitled: *For Better For Worse: Women Battering in South Africa.*

achieved through the laying down of arms and liberation from racist oppression. Non-sexism can only be realised through a complete social change in gender relations. It needs a willingness by men to change their attitudes towards women, as well as men's acknowledgment that a woman has the dignity and worth of a human person (Pietila and Vickers: 1990). This change of attitudes also requires an intensive dissection of all the aspects of our cultures which have for years maintained our hierarchical and patriarchal structures both in the family and in society. Thus while the struggle for racial equality has ended, women in my country have entered a new phase of struggle. It is a struggle against violence, be it private or public, against every woman young and old, a struggle for equality, a struggle to change perceived cultural norms and values which dehumanise us as a people. Lastly, it is a struggle for a country where all its people are aware that if they do not stop the violence, they condone it, and that in our view they are also guilty of having violated our basic human rights.

Tatyana Mamonova

Freedom and Democracy –
Russian Male Style

En route during my last trip to Europe, I was reading *Stern* on the plane. Under the heading "Die Russen – Mafia in Deutschland, Mädchenhandel, Prostitution, Killerkommandos" (Eissele and Müller: 1994, p. 19), I found that 50,000 very young women from eastern Europe came to Germany in the 1990s, only to become prostitutes, 10,000 of them against their will. Some teenagers were sold to the west for 500 Deutschmarks. Several of them were killed while trying to escape. Marina Aristova, my colleague in St Petersburg who directs the Center for Abused Women and Children, told me recently that these matters are taken lightly by the Commonwealth of Independent States (CIS) media, especially the television broadcasters. She told me a story about the amusement of three rapists who had practised "Kama Sutra" on their female victims. Alas, this kind of representation of the new freedoms in Russia is not an exception.

A post-perestroika traveller, a certain Vitali Vitaliev, decided to experience the joys of western life in Australia. Connoisseurs had recommended that he begin with the red light district of King's Cross in Sydney, something like Saint Denis or Pigalle in Paris, or 42nd Street and Broadway in New York. Our traveller, however, was disappointed and wrote about his experiences in the Melbourne newspaper the *Age*. He complained that the Chinese girl on stage had stripped without any inspiration at all. As he put it, "The girl reminded me of a self-peeling potato, if such a thing can exist" (Vitaliev: 1990). And she was so lazy that she didn't even try to feign embarrassment at being naked in front of clothed men. Vitali, on the other hand, was unable to experience the promised sexual excitement for which he'd paid Aus$8 (negotiated down from Aus$25): "No matter how hard I tried I was not aroused". When he touched her, he found that "her skin was cold and wettish, like that of a snake. Or a frog. She did not feel human at all" (p. 10).

The same Vitali Vitaliev had spoken out earlier (1987, pp. 4–5) in the magazine *Krokodil* and argued that contemporary prostitution had no social roots and that it all stemmed from greed. Greed and not need at all. Of course he meant the greed of women selling themselves, not the pimps. As Elena Leonoff, my young Australian friend who unlike many of her contemporaries in Russia grew up with feminist ideas, retorted, Vitali did not face the prospect of having to strip in public to earn a living. Instead he could judge "fallen" women from his comfortable chair on patriarchy's Olympus. In her letter to the Editor of the *Age* Elena Leonoff noted: "It's too bad Vitali didn't save some of his revulsion for the men who run and profit from these strip joints" and commented that since he was paid more than Aus$8 for writing his article, ". . . there is no danger that we'll see Vitali dancing in a G-string for a living" (Leonoff: 1990, p. 12).

Unfortunately, Russian women have not had the opportunities to acquaint themselves with the feminism that Elena has enjoyed. Choking on glasnost, the CIS woman now rushes between trying to get lipstick and trying to get married, preferably to a foreigner. More than fifteen hundred CIS women have paid about US$80 each to the "Grooms by Mail Agency at Nakhodka", set up in the early 1990s. Each of them is hoping to land in the USA, where they are certain that men know women better than in Russia and won't saddle them with a double burden. Galina, thirty-six years old, sent three photographs and went to great lengths about how she dislikes cooking and cleaning but is willing to do it for a sweetheart in the United States (Grooms By Mail Agency: 1990).

These types of businesses are developing fast. For example, the brochure for "European Connexions 94" distributed in Atlanta in 1994 had the following text: "Russian ladies, truly beautiful, want to meet you". For a fee of US$8–15 per name, an American man can order the address of any woman in the two-hundred name catalogue. And why are Russian ladies so desirable? As the brochure text spells out: "Unlike Americans, they understand the realities of life all too well and their expectations are far more reasonable. They are unpretentious and down-to-earth, and their view of relationships has not been ruined by feminism."

The film *Little Vera* was one of the first signs of "sexual freedom" in Russia. *Playboy* immediately seized the initiative and Natalia Negoda, its star, was asked to pose nude for the magazine. The financial reward, as the actress confirmed, played an important part in her decision to offer herself as a cover girl (Collins: 1989, p. 17). In 1995, the first Russian-language edition of *Playboy* was launched in Russia. Art Troitsky, its editor, has high hopes for the venture: ". . . our literary tradition is among the best". And, "We are hoping it will reverse the decline in the tradition of thick literary journals in Russia". But, as taxi driver Sasha, thirty, who displays the Playboy symbol prominently on the dashboard of his car says, when asked "What does *Playboy* symbolise to Russians?" "Sex" – so the aspiring editor will have to contend with *Playboy's* global image (MacKenzie: 1995, p. 25). The current outpouring of pornographic publications in Russia demonstrates how far the male-ocracy has gone: young women learn to be sex objects for profit. Larisa Kuznetsova's (1990) column "Open Tribune" in the Russian magazine *Working Woman* calls on women to rebel and unite against the "pornos" and she talks about the rise in prostitution in Russia, including that pornography which is exchanged for hard currency. Her analysis echoes that of western feminists (see MacKinnon and Dworkin: 1994b), a man who buys a woman is buying power, not sex, and it is a primitive, crude vulgar power of one person over another. She explores the relationship between the problem of prostitution and the problem of power as a working instrument in the struggle against rape and prostitution.

There are others who are also trying to reverse the trend. In 1990 the magazine *Abroad*, amongst others, published research findings that revealed a direct correlation between pornography and rape (Baxter: 1990, p. 19). On average, for every two percent increase in pornographic press circulation, there was a one percent increase in the number of rapes. But the pornographic press makes it acceptable for men to be tolerant of those who commit these crimes. The conclusion is clear: pornography generates the conditions under which sexual crimes are deemed less important than other violent crime.

On November 30, 1989, the St Petersburg television show *600 Seconds* reported the multiple rapes of one woman in the course of a single day by four different men. And the newspaper *Evening St Petersburg News* (August 1994) carried a report indicating that the number of rapes and attempted rapes rose by thirty-four percent between 1990 and 1994. Although there is ample evidence that violence against women is on the increase, Soviet women are starved for information that would empower them with knowledge of their rights. The spectre of patriarchal taboos has alienated them from the goddess of justice – jurisprudence. And, despite the fact that male terrorism has pursued all women without exception, only a very small percentage of them has resorted to the judicial process in the event of rape. Thus, the five to eight years of prison for a convicted rapist still constitutes nothing more than a legal text.

Despite the opening of several centers for female victims of rape and battering, trade in the female body is flourishing. Slippery, sticky "mass culture" offers a rich assortment of "new goods". Imported and CIS-made pornographic tapes spew forth in profusion from thousands of recently opened video studios. Video syndicates, offering illegal foreign films, have popped up in Moscow, St Petersburg, Tbilisi, Odessa, and Voronezh. Hitherto provincial Voronezh had not made this list of cities by accident. It is the center of the Russian state video industry. For roughly US$10, anyone can acquire the most graphic pornography. Now, television and film are trying to catch up with this "progress".

All this began long before perestroika. In the 1980s I was writing and speaking out about these practices in *Women and Russia* (Mamonova: 1984) and I later gave speeches in many different countries about sexism in Russian culture (Mamonova: 1992). What seemed to most people to be "harmless amusement" for the male half of the population, has led to a catastrophic spread of pornography. Scribblings from male bathroom walls have made the "happy" transition to the free market of the pornographic press. In 1990 the "Prose of Life" column in *Ogonyok*, a well-known weekly illustrated literary-artistic magazine, finally began a discussion of this issue when they revealed that in Moscow there were about thirty open markets for pornography. There they distribute "literature" like "Sex Glasnost", "Brezhnev's Lovers", "12 Verbal Portraits", "Love in Prison" with detailed descriptions of all kinds of rapes, and selections from the *Kama Sutra* including recommendations regarding the application of sharp and heavy instruments to intensify the sex act (Barykin: 1990, pp. 18–19). Too bad the passages do not include that while entertaining himself in this manner, Prince Kuntalasa killed his well-known wife Malaiavati with scissors. Another, Prince Panshalasa, ended the life of his beautiful courtesan, Madkhavazena when, during sexual intercourse, he hit her too hard with an iron.

Raging "progress" isn't easy to stop. Little has changed since I first spoke out. Few are prepared to listen. The antagonism between Russians and Americans, repeated like a broken record, keep us from taking a good look at each other. Both women and men have remained victims of the cold war. They barely notice the similarities of patriarchal structures and relations under communism and capitalism. Since the very first days of my exile from the USSR and throughout the following fourteen-year period, I have been continually asked at press conferences and symposia about the difference between Russian and American women. I answer ironically that in Russia women's consciousness lags behind the laws, and in America the laws lag behind women's consciousness.

I see both societies as maleocentric structures where the consequences for women are nearly analogous. Much to the consternation of journalists in the east and west, I have pointed to the similiarities for women. These similarities are becoming more and more obvious. Emphasizing the so-called differences between people amounts to the well-known colonial strategy of "divide and rule". I have encountered much hostility and arrogant indifference both in the USA and Russia. Even liberals, male and female, have resisted my calls to co-operate. Lacking USA "know how" about seeking funds, I held on precariously at the margins of society. I was thwarted in my attempts to bring my knowledge of both systems to the broader public, both in Russia and the USA.

In the late 1980s and early 1990s scandal mongers were writing articles and books, dreaming up shocking "differences" and "distinctions", as if to satisfy the curiosity of the uninformed. The American novelist Francine du Plessix Gray in *Soviet Women*, for example, proclaimed Russian women "matriarchs" whom she labelled "superwomen":

> After dozens of evenings spent with distraught, henpecked men and with a dismaying abundance of superwomen, I reached the conclusion that the Soviet Union might be as much in need of a men's movement as of a women's movement. (1990, p. 48).

Fortunately serious researchers and feminists such as Rochelle Ruthchild of Norwich University and Charlotte Rosenthal of the University of Southern Maine, have critiqued Gray's oversimplified formula and identified the dangers behind such positions:

> Women have little economic or political power . . . Women's double burden on the job and at home often prevents them from advancing in their careers . . . [The state's] birth control policy with its heavy reliance on abortion shows that women have for all intents and purposes been put off from participation in the decisions of government. If women had real power over birth control policy, the picture would be quite different (1990, personal communication to TM).

Bonnie Marshall, Professor of Russian Literature, Pedagogical Institute, St Petersburg, expresses it even more crisply.

> As second-class citizens in a patriarchy [Russian] women have become accustomed to bad treatment. They have learned to deal with oppression and to thrive under it. Their spirits fail to wither. Men, on the other hand, are accustomed to being treated as privileged members of the patriarchy. They cannot cope with their wounded dignity under Communism (1991, personal communication to TM).

Now, as perestroika and glasnost turn Russian society inside out, sexism has moved on to more blatant, visual forms. Beauty contests – or shows to be more precise – are excellent testimony of this move. The budget for the contest finals at the Rossiya Cinema came to around one-and-a-half million roubles. The organizers were counting on a substantial return. They planned to use the winners of the show to earn hard currency. The female body had been transformed into immovable, or "movable" property. Kersten Gustafsson, a Swedish correspondent, writing in the *Moscow News*, provided her own commentary on this phenomenon:

> All the girls in the finals had to answer one question from the TV audience. In this way they were given a chance to demonstrate their ability to speak and think: As for the rest, the whole contest reminded you of the cat exhibition recently shown on the *Vremya* (Time) *Evening News Program* (1989, p. 13).

In the west the liberalism of the 1960s did not lead to women's liberation. Rather it was women who paid the price for the "pleasure" of the "sexual revolution". In the CIS of the 90s, beauty shows have become the new image of Russia, not the space flights of Valentina Tereshkova or Svetlana Savitskaya. And what is happening in the backwoods? It appears sexism is alive and well there too. A news report about the city of Togliatti showed that organized crime, prostitution, and pimping are on the rise, as if they'd been leavened with yeast. The information in the following paragraphs has been taken from this report published in *Volga Komsomol* (1988). The information was drawn from police reports.

From an explanatory note written by a girl born in 1973 we hear: "I was sold for 130 rubles today". Another girl, an eighth grader reported, "I've been sold lots of times. The first time was in July 1987, they paid the guys [pimps] fifty to one-hundred rubles". She serviced ten to twenty clients, from a dormitory for foreigners. The pimps pick out the "weak ones", who are on bad terms with their parents and teachers. Sometimes they drag them right out of school. They get eyeliner and electronic watches.

Natalia Ivaniuk, a criminal investigation officer, is disturbed by the current situation. In six months twenty-six girls have been detained. Pimps catch them everywhere, drive right up to the dermatology-venereal disease clinics where the girls are being treated and carry them off to the men's dormitory. It is mostly teens who fall into the trap, girls aged thirteen to nineteen.

Vladimir, twenty years old, a professional pimp, sold three girls in one night for 170, 60, and 130 rubles. He kept the money. The girls accepted everything from cosmetics to faded jeans. Another pimp raped a teenage girl and then decided to sell her. He made a deal for her in the men's dormitory for 117 rubles. They started dragging the girl from room to room. When she saw a police car, she threw herself out of a window. She was hospitalized for a month.

On the morning of August 27, 1987, we learn from the operations report, how Olga was discovered. She had strangulation marks on her neck, puncture wounds on her body and bruises. The pimps had attempted to drown her, then had beaten and tortured her for three hours but she wouldn't confess to having filed a complaint with the police. Towards evening they abandoned her in the dormitory. Then once again they beat her, tied her up and dragged her around. One threw his belt around her neck but it broke, so he used his tie to strangle her. The girl beat him off when he started striking her with scissors.

Sveta recounts how she was sold at the age of twelve The pimp's conversation was harsh, "You're coming to the dorm. Period. And just try not to come". Right now they were ordering one girl who is thirteen, afraid and staying home, but she will have to come out. "She used to 'sniff' before," explains Sveta. Many of them "sniff" starting in the sixth or seventh grade. A guy gives you the solution, a narcotic substance, for free, then you owe him.

Olya, a ninth-grader, told her story, "I was walking down the street. Two guys came up to me. 'Hey, get Sveta from the fourth floor, apartment one.' Why not help? I went up the stairs and rang the doorbell. A guy opened up. Before I could blink those two behind me had pushed me into the apartment. They raped me. If they hadn't given me gonorrhea I wouldn't have filed a complaint with the police. It's mortifying".

Attempting to deal with the exploitation of women in prostitution is not new. Few probably remember that in the 1920s Alexandra Kollontai's argument was widely known; patriarchal marriage differs from prostitution only in that the woman sells herself to one man rather than many. There used to be a slogan, "Fight prostitution, not prostitutes". A law was passed punishing owners of bordellos, dens, and pimps, not the women they discriminated against. In the 1930s Stalin dealt with the problem expeditiously by sending all prostitutes to Siberia and proclaiming the curse banished from Soviet society. Brezhnev evidently didn't believe Stalin had solved the problem and repeated this act in 1980 before the Moscow Olympic Games.

During my return to Russia in 1994, after fourteen years of exile, having finally received my documents through six lawyers, I gave interviews to the media and found audiences who wanted my words and who I had missed all these years. Two thousand copies of the *Woman and Earth Almanac* which I publish in the USA and distributed free of charge in eastern Europe rapidly disappeared into the hands of women hungry for intellectual food. Recently, our fifteenth anniversary issue came out. This issue carried a symbolic publication date, 8 March 1995, lauding women's rights. It has doubled the numbers of our international subscribers who support the *Almanac*'s endeavour towards raising consciousness in Russian society – the society where women are anxious to fight for real democracy and real freedom.

Editors' Note: Some of the references cited in this article were lost in a fire at the author's home. Despite all efforts, we have been unable to complete the bibliography for this article. Our thanks to Janet Zmroczek, The British Library, London, for her invaluable help in trying to locate missing references.

Kathleen Barry

Pornography and the Global Sexual Exploitation of Women

Pornography, traditionally defined as the visual representation of prostitutes in the sex trade, is both the practice of sexual exploitation and the ideology of cultural sadism. As a practice of sexual exploitation, women perform in pornography and they perform pornography in their personal relationships. This has led to a normalization of the prostitution of sexuality (Barry: 1995). But that is not all. Pornography is at once a practice of sexual exploitation and the ideology for it. The function of ideology is to justify, legitimize and normalize power relations that produce oppression. I have called this the ideology of cultural sadism – a set of ideas that culturally promotes asymmetrical gendered relations through promotion of sadistic sex in the use of women. As a media of sexual objectification, pornography is the cornerstone of women's oppression, particularly in western, economically developed countries.

Pornography is violence against women. But it is also more and other than that. Feminists forced onto the defensive have justified the movement against pornography because it is violence against women. But that narrows the range of its real-world impact; the violation that is produced in and through pornography is not limited to violent acts. Pornography may or may not be violent, it may be more or less violent, but it is always a sexual objectification, an act of power by which women are reduced to things, treated as not human. As pornography is both acts of sexual objectification and a media-driven ideology, it reduces sex from a human interactive experience to an objectified thing, a thing to be gotten, had, taken. The foundation of all sexual exploitation is in the objectification of women and of sex which is a reduction of woman to sex. Pornography promotes the idea that woman is sex, a thing, to be purchased for sex, married for sex, dated for sex, used for sex, seized for sex.

Sexual Exploitation and the Oppression Of Women

Feminist action against pornography is confrontation against sexual *oppression*, the condition of inferiorizing women as a class through the use of sex and sexuality. Sexual exploitation is not only specifically sexual but it sustains reproductive control over women and promotes their economic marginalization in the labor force. Women's oppression operates through power structures of gender hierarchies, sustaining women's inferior status in economic, political and social life. Sexual objectification is a core dimension of the oppression of women, operationalized through the public sexualization of women, particularly in pornography.

The oppression of women through gender hierarchies of patriarchal power does not operate as a separate system of domination as if it were distinct from other modes of domination and conditions of exploitation. Nor is it simply a matter of defining "isms" and attaching them together to identify oppression. Pornography and prostitution are capitalized market institutions of sexual exploitation wherein female is not only equated with and sold as sex, she is also sold as color, culture, as child, and as lesbian. Market characteristics that consumers demand and buy are Black female, or Asian female, or children or women who act like children, or girls who act like adult women. They buy women who act like children, or girls who act like adult women. They buy pornographic versions of lesbian sex. All are objectification, all are dehumanizations. If in addition to that the sex is violent, there is another level of violation.

Massive global industries market sex, where woman is the sex that is portrayed and enacted, bought and sold, in pornography and in prostitution. Prostitution, which is increasingly accepted as merely "sex between consenting adults", is only one aspect of sexual exploitation globally, and an instrument of western – particularly US – hegemony in its control over market economies in the developing world. Therefore sexual exploitation, particularly through pornography and in prostitution, is marketed and traded, in world economies through western markets of business and military men and western-originated sex industries massively deployed in newly industrializing economies until they become self-sustaining there.

In *The Prostitution of Sexuality* (1995) I have identified four general conditions of sexual exploitation in relation to marketing conditions which prevail in different stages of economic and social development.

1. Trafficking in women predominates especially in the least economically developed, poorest countries of the world where women have almost no place in the public sector. With women's exclusion from the public sector, their labor is marginalized in the informal economy and sexual exploitation is rendered into a public/private duality to service men in marriage or in prostitution. But considering the privatization of women in marriage and the family, prostitution most frequently is the result of brutal force and kidnapping by traffickers.

2. Military prostitution is organized and develops with the massive deployment of military troops in war-ravaged regions. Both trafficking and sex industries are

organized to meet male market demand from the military presence, usually procuring women and girls who are often displaced during war, or through trafficking. War produces the market commodities for military sexual exploitation of women, as women are over two-thirds of the world's refugees.

3. In the developing world, with the intensification of economic development comes a population shift from rural to urban, from domestic-oriented production to export-oriented production. With the migration of women to cities as they are displaced from their traditional (informal sector) labor in rural areas, sex industrialization develops, buying off women who are then marginalized in or excluded from the developing labor force. In the first phases of sex industrialization, sex industries of prostitution and pornography in the west establish markets and business operations in the newly industrialising countries (NICs). This, like military prostitution, is an acute phase in which western hegemonic control of world markets facilitates deployment and growth of new sex industries. This is the transition phase in sexual oppression as women's privatized sexual exploitation in the home, marriage and the family is made public, institutional and economic in ways that it had not been when social life was private, primarily rural and women's lives were confined within the household and the informal economic sector.

4. In advanced, economically developed countries where the private sector of marriage and family is no longer the primary or only domain of women, sexual oppression configures around women as a public fact. Public sexual exploitation takes place particularly through the normalization of prostitution and pornography, producing what I have called the prostitution of sexuality. As women cannot be contained and confined by oppression that has previously and in earlier forms of economic development operated through the family and in marriage, their potential economic and emotional independence from patriarchal domination is thwarted by the configuration of oppression as specifically and publicly sexual. Pornography becomes a central tool for the subordination of women. Liberalized laws and attitudes facilitate its widespread dissemination [sic!] through ideological and institutional reduction of woman to sex. Sexual exploitation follows women to work and down the streets in sexual harassment and rape, in dating and at parties, in personal relationships that are increasingly influenced by the pornographic sexualization of society.

Not only does sexual exploitation as a marketed fact of women's oppression vary by the stages of economic development and according to the public and private conditions of women as I have identified here: it also serves as an instrument of western hegemony over the developing world. Therefore the production of sex industries in the west is not only the problem of US or European or Australian women: through the marketing of those industries to the developing world, they are part of the facts of western hegemony. For example, the pornography and prostitution expected by American men stationed in US bases in the developing world that leads to massive sexual exploitation of women in those regions develops from those men's access to pornography at home. Their sexual contempt for American women is extended to and against women of the region to which they are assigned, women who, because of their race or culture, are taken as whores before anything else.

In the USA the social institutions of pornography and prostitution are embedded in the liberal state, the state that elevates individualism for the sake of promoting market exchange above all other values. I am not speaking of the superficial, relatively meaningless political party distinctions between liberal and conservative. Rather, I am referring to liberalism as a state ideology of capitalist market economies in advanced, economically developed countries. Central to the perpetuation of those market economies is the ideology of liberal individualism is the foundation for promoting market exchange and a competitive labor market.

In the 1990s, "debates" over pornography, particularly in the United States, reflect reactive responses that come from the capitalist market economy and its supporting ideology of liberal individualism – "debate" being a construct that suggests freedom of expression and acceptance of varying points of view. But in liberal individualism *anything* that is produced is marketable, and therefore the market defines and controls the "debates". By contrast, in liberation struggles, oppression is not debatable. There are not two or many pluralistic viewpoints from the standpoint of the oppressed. Liberal ideology of the western market economy, by elevating "choice" and "speech" over all other human actions and socio-political conditions, renders oppression invisible. Consequently, the years of censorship that those of us who have confronted sexual exploitation have been subjected to is excluded from the liberal, market-driven discourse of freedom, speech and choice as that discourse excludes oppression as a fact, as a thought, therefore as a condition and as an analysis.

It is in this context – the liberal and patriarchal state, the production of pornography and the promotion of it as a patriarchal ideology – that sexual exploitation has been confined within a discourse of liberal individualism where speech is reified into a quintessential act. Speech has been made into a central defining feature of freedom because liberal individualism in its promotion of market economies reduces freedom to that which services markets. (This is what liberal individualism did to the feminist issue of abortion, reducing it from an issue of a woman's right to control her own body only to a matter of "choice".) Analysis and debates over whether or not pornography is speech, whether or not that speech is harmful and hateful, is founded in a discourse of liberal individualism that is intended to obscure the fundamental power relations of both the liberal market economy and of patriarchy.

Oppression is what is missing in the debates and formulations regarding pornography. Oppression is missing because sexual power which involves naming agency – men as exploiters of women – is obscured. Oppression is missing because pornography, along with women's bodies, is that which is marketed.

As liberalism attempts to colonize feminist action against sexual exploitation, reducing it to its terms, we witness the return of blaming the victim.

From right wing spokespersons such as Rush Limbaugh to women such as Katie Roiphe and Naomi Wolf, oppression is rejected when women's victimization is denied and male agency in the sexual exploitation of women is obscured. With agency obscured, the harm to women from sexual exploitation can only be their own fault; similarly, new conservative officials now treat drug abuse as the fault of the abuser, taking attention away from tracking down the traffickers.

Feminist Struggle against Oppression

Invariably, feminist action must confront sexual oppression within the ideological and material conditions of its society. In the USA and the west in general, radical feminist action that confronts pornography must struggle both *within* and against liberal individualism to do so. Invariably the dominant patriarchal discourse imposes the terms of the debate, and in the case of feminist anti-pornography action those terms are increasingly framed as "speech". This is not the language of a struggle for liberation from sexual exploitation. Hence debates about speech, about whether speech is speech or speech is an act, are meant to constrain the movement and deflect attention from the fact that from a sociological standpoint all speech is human action. It is the acts of sexual exploitation that oppress women, acts sustained and promoted by the ideology of cultural sadism.

Consequently, feminist struggle for liberation from sexual oppression must fight both from within the dominant discourse against its definition of speech, and from outside that discourse, pushing beyond the limits of national ideology and state interests in market relations. That means addressing the global condition of women not only from particular challenges to any of these ideologies, but from global norms that transcend all state ideologies.

Consciousness destroys ideology: it breaks through non-conscious patterned thinking that embeds within it the assumptions of the dominant power relations. Global feminist consciousness searches beyond liberal or socialist or any other state ideology in order to identify the common dimensions of women's oppression, the conditions of oppression that women experience and struggle against across cultures and beyond national boundaries. In that sense, pornography is not the central issue of sexual oppression globally. Nor is free speech the dominant issue in confronting sexual oppression. Yet, at the same time, because pornography and sex industries are the core of normalized sexual exploitation in the USA and in the west in general, and because the USA still controls the dominant interests in the global economy, pornography, like the US military and like almost everything the USA deploys to the Third World, will be implicated in women's oppression everywhere. It is part of what is exported to the developing and war-ravaged parts of the world, both informally through US, European, Australian and Japanese men in their sexual colonization of women as soldiers and as businessmen, and through specific sex industries from pornography to prostitution to mail-order brides.

To cast sexual oppression in a global context, I have drawn from United Nations human rights principles which protect both individual rights of human beings and collective rights to self-determination of peoples, and I have analyzed the material conditions of sexual exploitation as they vary from developing to developed regions. There are no international or national laws that are not patriarchal and certainly international human rights law, as it is codified in United Nations Conventions, bears the stamp of liberal individualism with its focus on individual rights. But in its protections of human rights, it has been significantly shaped by 1960s state revolutions and, from the 1970s, by Indigenous peoples' attempts to establish their rights as peoples within nation-states against colonization in the Third World. This has led to the codification of economic, social and cultural rights of self-determination of peoples and responds to conditions of oppression as well as individual protections.

New international activism is needed that is feminist. The Coalition Against Trafficking in Women, working internationally with UNESCO and globally in the development of feminist networks in each world region against sexual exploitation, has developed new international human rights law against sexual exploitation.

In defining sexual exploitation in the Convention Against Sexual Exploitation, we have cast the widest possible net to encompass the range of conditions of sexual oppression and have defined sexual exploitation as a form of power:

> . . . a practice by which person(s) achieve sexual gratification or financial gain or advancement through the abuse of a person's sexuality by abrogating that person's human right to dignity, equality, autonomy, and physical and mental well-being.[1]

Accordingly, following from the universal principles of human rights, the Convention Against Sexual Exploitation declares that "it is a fundamental human right to be free from sexual exploitation in all of its forms".[2] Its forms include battering, pornography, prostitution, genital mutilation, female seclusion, dowry and bride price, forced sterilization and forced child-bearing, sexual harassment, rape, incest, sexual abuse and trafficking in women. Although we are aware that these forms of sexual exploitation do not all pertain to every culture, or to each country equally, we believe it is crucial to name them as they are all part of women's oppression in a global context.

In transcending the liberal-individualistic discourse of advanced developed states, the Convention identifies sexual exploitation *as oppression* by specifically rejecting the distinction between so-called "free" and forced prostitution. Turning to the act of sexual exploitation by which exploiters gain and those who are exploited are harmed, the issue of consent is neither the primary nor

---

1. See Appendix "Convention Against Sexual Exploitation". In Barry (1995, p. 326).
2. The Penn State Report: International Meeting on Sexual Exploitation, Violence and and Prostitution. UNESCO and Coalition against Trafficking in Women. State College, Pennsylvania (1991, p. 7).

the only defining characteristic of human rights violations. Therefore, in the Convention, in relation to prostitution, a woman's body is understood to always be bought and sold as a commodity or exchanged, but not always for money. The Convention calls upon state governments to reject any policy or law that legitimizes prostitution of any person, male or female, adult or child, so-called "First or Third World", that distinguishes between free and forced prostitution, or that legalizes or regulates prostitution in any way as a profession or occupation. Instead state governments are called upon to adopt appropriate legislation that recognizes prostitution as an acute form of sexual exploitation and penalizes the customers, recognizing them as perpetrators to be criminalized while rejecting any form of penalization for the prostitute.

The Convention calls upon state governments to enact regulations that hold pornographers liable for the violation of women's human rights through sexual exploitation. And it calls upon states that are currently undergoing industrialization processes to reject policies and practices of economic development that channel women into conditions of sexual exploitation by eroding their traditional economic base where it has existed and preventing them from access to new opportunities in economic development. Therefore, this Convention introduces the human right of women to full integration into economic development with dignified paid labor at a decent standard of living, following the already existing United Nations human rights protection of everyone to the right to meaningful and dignified labor. This protection requires prohibiting sex tourism and the market in mail-order brides that has already been prohibited in the Philippines (see Barry: 1995, p. 158). Furthermore, this convention recognizes the need for women in the migrating process to be protected from sexual exploitation, particularly as domestic labor in private homes as they migrate from rural to urban areas, or from one country to another. Both migration and this type of labor make women particularly vulnerable to rape and to being trafficked into prostitution. Employers who sexually exploit women in the migrating process will be held criminally liable.

For all these reasons the Convention recognizes sexual exploitation as a political condition of oppression. Accordingly it requires that states recognize escaped victims of sexual exploitation as politically persecuted and provide them with asylum as well as according them refugee status. Protection from fraudulent contracts used by traffickers, as well the recognition of women's right to retain their own passports, are fundamental human rights included in the Convention.

The Convention recognizes that as a human rights violation, all forms of sexual exploitation are injurious to women's physical and mental health and well-being. Therefore it calls upon state governments to provide a wide range of supportive services upon request, including HIV and STD testing, substance abuse rehabilitation, counseling, day-care, housing, income support, preferential access to credit loans to start small businesses, and skills training programs.

Notably, the Convention establishes the groundwork for national legislation appropriate to the condition of sexual exploitation which prevails in each region. And it goes beyond confining sanctions against sexual exploitation within civil remedies to be initiated by victims. Daringly, because it recognizes sexual exploitation as a human rights violation and therefore real harm, it requires criminal sanctions to alleviate the conditions.

No new law will end oppression. Patriarchy, like every other form of domination, will not make itself illegal. However, in the struggle for liberation, in the case of sexual exploitation, law is recognized as a force that can generate new norms and standards. Feminist activism that introduces new legal norms and standards opens the way for supportive programming and policy changes. The Convention builds upon global work against sexual exploitation as much as it simultaneously encourages the development of it.

A global feminist network has developed which, along with human rights organzations, is proposing this Convention to the United Nations. The Convention is a product of international activism and consultation in each of the world regions that involved this network in its development. Therefore in its development it has been modified and reformulated to fit the particular needs of women in different world regions, cultures and conditions. In that sense, it is an international grass-roots feminist action. Internationally, it has been developed in collaboration with UNESCO in relation to international human rights law.

At the same time, a 1994 United Nations Declaration to Eliminate Violence Against Women has been adopted. While seeming to be an advance in international human rights, it actually is a major setback for work against pornography and prostitution – both of which are excluded, intentionally, from the Declaration because neither are considered violence or sexual exploitation. Furthermore, now that the UN has been convinced to adopt a Declaration which is a statement of principles with no enforcement, resistance is strong against a Convention which would require action against all sexual exploitation, including pornography and prostitution. Liberal individualism once more has coopted women's issues and found the least effective way to address women's issues. Furthermore, with the Declaration US hegemony once again sets the terms.

In developing the new Convention it has been obvious that one must struggle at every level of patriarchy – international and grassroots. This struggle, based on the radical feminist commitment to address the commonality of women's condition, is global in scope and force. Ultimately law, neither civil nor criminal, neither national nor international, can replace struggle against sexual exploitation. Feminist consciousness is the foundation of that struggle and it must continually be expanding into developing new strategies and actions against the conditions of sexual exploitation that both confine and connect women globally. Such a struggle begins and is sustained in the conviction that a world without sexual exploitation is possible.

Natalie Nenadic

Femicide: A Framework
for Understanding Genocide[1]

The current genocide in Europe is historically unprecedented. It is a Femicide. This makes it unique not only in the sense that each genocide is unique but because none has been so characterized by sexual atrocities as is the one in Bosnia Hercegovina and Croatia.

I

The technology of genocide changes every time genocide appears in history. How to carry one out develops and evolves over time. The central ways perpetrators deploy a genocide and what distinguishes one genocide from another depends on its circumstances and historical period: what its perpetrators have at hand at a given time to make it happen in what they deem the most efficient and economical way.

We owe our modern understanding of genocide to the legacy of the Shoah (the specific assault against the Jews). Under the category of "crimes against humanity",[2] genocide was tried and punished for the first time in history at the

---

1. This article is an attempt to begin transcribing and theoretically cohering some of the work with and by survivors of the Kareta Feminist Group. Kareta is the first feminist organization that formed in Croatia after the fall of communist totalitarianism in 1990 and the first, in November of 1991, to discern a pattern of sexual atrocities as genocide through work it began with survivors during the height of Serbia's attack against Croatia and when Serbia was preparing the assault it would launch against Bosnia-Hercegovina six months later. Kareta co-founder, Asja Armanda (1992), named the atrocity she was seeing around her a "Femicide". Jill Radford and Diana E. H. Russell have named and written about "femicide" as the killing of women by men because they are women. See Radford and Russell (1992). Andrea Dworkin named the systematic destruction of women in ways that are specific to how women are destroyed, including but not limited to killing, "gynocide." See Dworkin (1974).
2. "Crimes against humanity" are genocidal crimes *during war*. "Genocide", as recognized by the Genocide Convention, are genocidal crimes perpetrated in peacetime as well as by means of war.

Nuremberg Trials. A precedent established in response to this assault against the Jews *specifically* was an expansion of the definition of who and what constituted the *totality* of humanity. Crimes against humanity now officially recognize that humanity is comprised of diverse ethnic, racial, national, and religious components and that the destruction of any such *part* of it is an attack on the *whole* of it (Finkielkraut: 1992, pp. 29, 35–6). Humanity finally officially included diverse ethnic, racial, national, and religious groups, as defined by the particularity of men's experiences of them, but stopped there. *They* became synonymous with humanity, which they are, and *their* destruction meant genocide, which it is, and *genocide* became crimes against humanity, which it is. But genocide targets yet another group and humanity is even bigger still.

II

Since the Shoah, the practice of genocide in Europe has expanded and evolved to include more visible and pronounced attacks on women as a group, employing ways men use to destroy women in daily life. Today, on the Serbian-occupied territories of Bosnia-Hercegovina and Croatia, every sexual atrocity against women in what is called "peacetime" is directed into the service of the Serbian genocidal policy of "ethnic cleansing" of non-Serbs – predominantly Bosnian Moslems and Croatians[3] – and exploded in frequency by war. This genocide targets women and girls of these national and religious groups in specific and additional ways. Sexual atrocities are a central technology of it. Rape is an efficient and economical tool of genocide.

One legacy of the Shoah is that it enhanced awareness of certain aspects of genocide. At least it has enabled some, though too few, to know what to call some of what the world is gawking at in Bosnia-Hercegovina and Croatia. What has occasionally became visible are the national and religious components of this genocide.[4] Even this recognition might be considered a remarkable, if tragically slow breakthrough given that this genocide is not, and cannot, be happening in the exact pattern of the last genocide in Europe.

Unlike the Nazis, Serbian fascists are not using the technologically sophisticated extermination centers characterized by gas chambers and crematoria

---

3. Victims are targeted by Serbian forces because they are not Serb and in further ways because they are women who are not Serb. In Croatia and in Bosnia-Hercegovina the Serbian minority is targeting the Bosnian Moslem and Croatian majority populations as well as non-Serb minorities such as Hungarians, Albanians, Jews, Italians, Czechs, and Ruthenes. See Kostovic and Judas (1992); Schwartz (1992); War Crimes Investigation Bureau (1992); Gutman (1993).

4. It took nearly a year and a half of lobbying, from fall 1991 to winter/spring of 1992–1993, by Indigenous women's organizations and survivors for the media, human rights groups, and the international women's community to respond to the sexual atrocities in this genocide. When they finally did, they responded in that order, with those who were informed first, recognizing them last. As with every aspect of this genocide which finally managed to attain some visibility, it has been followed by a backlash of whitewashing and denial.

to carry out their mass killings.[5] The Omarska death camp in Serb–occupied Bosnia-Hercegovina and the Samarica death camp in Serb-occupied Croatia are *not* Treblinka and Auschwitz. Among other genocidal methods, Serbian fascists are employing the modern genocidal innovation of rapes and rape/death camps to destroy the Croatian and Bosnian Moslem people.

Serbian fascists are committing genocide through mass rape and serial rape ending in death and mass rape and serial rape to produce what they consider Serbian babies to populate and maintain the Greater Serbian state.[6] Corpses are also raped. Women's breasts are sliced off and their wombs ripped out[7]. Sometimes the women and children are burned alive.[8] These rapes are committed on the Serb-occupied territories of Croatia and Bosnia-Hercegovina, in different types of concentration camps, and in rape/death camps,[9] in which the victims who survive the initial massacres and deportations are interned.[10] If women are already pregnant prior to this assault, their bellies are ripped open since those fetuses are not Serb. Birthing women are left to die in ditches (see Omerdic: 1992, June 29, p. 5). In her

---

5. In the Bosnian port city of Brcko, Serbian fascists employed a crematorium to burn the bodies of their victims to hide traces of their crimes. However, this *exception* cannot be compared with a Nazi *system*. They also used Brcko port's concrete mixer to destroy the deformed bodies once the mass graves had filled up. See Omerdic: 1992, June 29, p. 8. Most of the supporting sources I cite are Bosnian and document genocide against both Moslems and Croats, the most numerous of the non-Serb victims.

6. The outlined pattern of sexual atrocities as genocide has emerged from Kareta Feminist Group's work with survivors and with their work with other Indigenous women's and survivor groups and from my work with them. These groups include the Bosnia-Hercegovina Refugee Women's Group "Zena BiH", International Initiative of Women of Bosnia and Hercegovina "Biser," Mothers for Peace, SOS Battered Women's Hotline. Some of this research has been used as the basis of and is cited in MacKinnon (1993a). It is a standard content of survivor testimonies.

7. For example, in Bratunac Bosnian resistance forces found "many dead young women and girls on whom the Chetniks (Serbian fascists) unleashed sexual atrocities: they would rape them, slice off their breasts . . ." In Odzak they found 600 slaughtered bodies all over the streets. "The dead women were naked, propped up on fence spikes." (Omerdic: June 1, 1992, pp. 3, 11).

8. For example, Serbian fascists burned 150 Bosnian Moslem and Croat women and children alive in the Sivci basement concentration camp. See *SDA* (1992b).

9. For example, there is a rape/death camp in Visegrad Banji for Bosnian Croat and Moslem girls and women who are subject to sexual terror and executions. "This is the fate for 400 girls taken away in Cekovici". See Center for Anti-War Activities (1992, pp. 3–4). Serbian fascists have used some settlements as special camps for raping Bosnian Moslem and Croat women and girls. In the Vestfalija rape/death camp in Brcko they sexually torture, rape, and mutilate female children. See Omerdic (1992, June 29, pp. 6–8).

10. Deportations are often carried out in trains, cattle cars, forced marches, and buses. "On the railroad tracks from Prijedor to Doboj there are 23 'O' wagons with 4,000 women and children, which never reach their destinations. In those 'wagons of death' as the banished call them 2–4 children die daily". See *SDA* (1992a); Jewish Community Relations Council (1992). Roy Gutman's Pulitzer prize winning articles for *Newsday* have covered deportations and Serbian death camps extensively. See Gutman (1993).

work with rape/death camp survivors of the Bosnia-Hercegovina Refugee Women's Group "Zena BiH", Asja Armanda (1992–1993) has discerned that the majority of women and girls who survive the various types of Serbian concentration camps and rape/death camps have been interned in them for at least 21–28 days to ensure pregnancy.[11]

Serbian fascists also use rape as a public spectacle to induce women to leave their homes and never return. These sexual atrocities are done "for Serbia." Sometimes they are filmed as they are taking place. The film footage of genocidal sexual atrocities – the pornography of genocide – is used as propaganda in which the ethnicities of the victims and the aggressor are switched. This propaganda serves to create an alibi for Serbia's policy of territorial conquest and genocide. Presenting the victims as the aggressor is meant to obscure, justify, and excuse genocide, as if anything can, and to rally Serbs even further against the groups they are destroying.[12]

The fact that sexual atrocities characterize this genocide does not mean that this is the only genocide in which rapes have been committed or that women have not been targetted in specific and additional ways in other genocides. Nor does it mean that this genocide is being carried out through sexual atrocities exclusively. There were Jewish women victims of sexual atrocities in the Nazi extermination centers, and they were targeted in other ways specific to their being women such as being immediately gassed if pregnant (See Lengyel: 1947; Perl: 1948; Rittner and Roth: 1993). There are however differences between the gender-based crimes in the Shoah and those in this genocide. Those of today are happening fifty years *after* those during the Shoah, in a different location, under different conditions and with different technological methods at hand for exterminating a group. The genocidal rapes of today confirm that the destruction of women as women lends itself to every politics, every time period, and every place.

It also appears that the sexual atrocities during the Shoah did not occur with the same breadth and frequency as in this genocide, in which almost every survivor reports being a witness to, or a victim of, sexual atrocities and in which almost every woman who entered one of a variety of Serbian concentration camps or a rape/death camp was a victim of sexual atrocities whether or not she, herself, lived to tell about it. Moreover, Nazi policy against Jews did not conceptualize rape for forced impregnation and forced childbirth as a method of *genocide* as does Serbian genocidal policy. The fact that women and girls are the primary victims of Serbian genocidal rapes, also does not mean there are no male victims of sexual atrocities in this genocide.[13]

---

11. Observations made during conversations with survivors 1992–1993.

12. The Nazis also created excuses for territorial conquest and genocide such as staging and filming "attacks" by Poles against Germans, complete with Polish uniforms, to justify Nazi overrunning of Poland. The minutes from the planning of these staged events were part of the evidence at Nuremberg. See Jackson (1946, pp. viii–ix). But these films, of course, are not pornography.

13. Serbian forces have also raped Croatian and Bosnian men and have forced victims to rape each other in sadistic performances for concentration camp guards. Dr Mladen Loncar (1993) of the Medical Center

cont. next page

Serbian "ethnic cleansing" has introduced the innovation of mass sexual atrocities and rape/death camps as a central way of carrying out genocide. We can be sure that all present and future fascists and misogynists of the world are watching and taking note about how to do it and how to get away with it. It is Serbia's unique contribution to the history and method of genocide.

Of the *wide* range of Nazi genocidal atrocities, the *specific* assault against the *Jews* stood out in the intensity and scope of its horror. It became known as the Shoah. Of the *wide* range of Serbian genocidal atrocities, the *specific* assault against *women* in Croatia and Bosnia-Hercegovina through sexual atrocities stands out in the intensity and scope of its horror. We can call it Femicide. Like the Shoah, this Femicide is a concentrated, distinctive, and distinguishing part of a unique and wider genocidal system.

The destruction of Bosnian Moslem and Croatian women in this Femicide has made clear that genocide is the destruction of an ethnic, racial, national, religious, *and gender* group. Being awake to this Femicide builds on knowledge acquired from the legacy of the Shoah – grasping genocide as an assault on racial, ethnic, national, and religious groups through the particularity of men's experiences of them and women's overlap with that – and combining it with the knowledge we are acquiring by listening to the female survivors of this one. This femicidal assault against these *specific* women in this genocide also makes clear that the destruction of *any* women, *any* group of women, anywhere and anytime is a crime in and of itself and on its own, and that when women are destroyed, *all* of humanity is irreparably violated. Women are targetted as women in every genocide whereas genocidal sexual atrocities constitute one part, albeit the most heinous, of a larger continuum of global and historical crimes against women. Femicide contains genocide, and in addition something more.

III

What will it take for women to recognize that globally, as women, we are targetted for destruction? What specific cataclysm in the history of our social subordination will forge in us, as a fundamental element of our identity, an awareness of the fact and the means by which our specific social group is being destroyed? Which

---

13. *cont. from previous page*

for Human Rights, himself a concentration camp survivor, has collected these testimonies and works with the survivors. Sterilization is a common policy of genocide. Dr Loncar's report includes survivor accounts of systematic sterilization by Serb forces through medical radiation, complete and partial castrations and beatings on the genitals in different types of Serbian concentration camps – accompanied by verbal taunts that they will not make any more Croatians. This is something like the opposite of what they tell their female victims, saying, as they are raping them, that they *will* give birth to a Chetnik child.

Fred Pelka (1995), founder of the Boston-based group "Men to End Sexual Assault" and counsellor under the auspices of the Boston Area Rape Crisis Center to male survivors of male sexual violence, has written on Dr Loncar's work with male survivors of sexual atrocities in genocide. On the policy and practice of sterilization in the Nazi death çamps see Robert Jay Lifton (1986, pp. 270–284).

outrage against us will so shake the conscience of the world that it will force us to acquire a preparedness for dealing with our own possible demise?[14]

Woman-hating has had intense moments in history that characterize distinct periods and underlie rich cultures. For example – citing primarily western experiences – there was the mass sexual slavery of ancient Greece, the burning of millions of women in Europe as witches, mass rape and forced pregnancy of African women in the United States under slavery, nineteenth century medical and psychiatric experimentation on women, crimes against women during the Shoah, and sexual atrocities against Korean and other Asian women by Japanese soldiers during World War II. In addition to these historical and culturally specific assaults on women, there are the daily systematic ways women and girls are discriminated against and destroyed through sexual abuse. They include such violations as sexual harassment, objectification, rape, battery, incest and child sexual abuse, denied and forced abortions, denied and forced motherhood, forced sterilization, prostitution, sexual murder, and pornography – a modern filmed entertainment version of most of these.[15]

These and other historical atrocities against women were not perceived as systematic assaults on women as a people during the time they were taking place. They went unnoticed to almost all but their victims and re-emerged in history in different forms and as politically unintelligible and unconnected events. Women, as a group, have had no history of the atrocities against us that could leave an indelible mark on our group memory, that we could vigilantly guard against forgetting, so as not to allow them to happen again. Men have been the primary authors of history and have been careful about which parts of it they would reveal. Significantly, they hid and were silent over their crimes against women. Femicide, in the sense of monumental crimes against women, happened before, but has not been registered and historicized, as such, while it was taking place, and in a way that would endure. Then, there wasn't a coherent theoretical framework that could recognize crimes against women as politically motivated. The closest that exists to one is feminism, but feminism – the practice of creating a cogent analysis of social life and subordination, with an associated Women's Movement – is modern and is still largely inchoate. It did not intersect historically with these events. Today we are closer to having an understanding of women's subordination that is capable of registering the existence and occurrence of daily and monumental crimes against women, their political function in male supremacy, and their further implications. The Femicide in Croatia and Bosnia-Hercegovina is the first Femicide to be grasped

---

14. In 1976 Andrea Dworkin posed a similar question responding to Susan B. Anthony's question of 100 years earlier in 1870 about what event will "startle the women of this nation into a self-respect". Dworkin asks of "peacetime" rape: "Isn't rape the outrage that will do this, sisters, and isn't it time?" See Dworkin: 1976, pp. 48–49.

15. Andrea Dworkin (1974) introduced this historical approach in her book *Woman Hating* and named the atrocity "gynocide". She elaborates on it further in "The Coming Gynocide" in *Right-Wing Women* (1983).

and documented as such, while it is taking place, because it is happening during a time when feminism exists to recognize it.[16]

The genocide in Bosnia-Hercegovina and Croatia is an assault on women. Croatian and Bosnian Moslem women and girls are being systematically destroyed in Serbian rape/death camps. Now is the time, and this is the event against women that should shake the conscience of the world. The outrage that is happening to these women specifically, here and now, should also bring visibility to the sexual abuse and subordination of women everywhere.

IV

Count IV, "crimes against humanity", charged genocide as a separate category of crime within the rest of the Nuremberg War Crimes Tribunal. The specific events at Nuremberg had global resonance. The international precedent established in response to the Shoah, *specifically*, told the world "Never Again", to no ethnic, national, racial or religious group, nowhere, in any shape or form, for no reason ever. It enhanced global awakeness to anti-Semitism and lent legitimacy to other struggles to end subordinations based on ethnicity, nationality, race, and religion (Finkielkraut: 1992, p. 36). It effected the formation of a Genocide Convention by the United Nations in 1948 that recognized genocide as a crime that could be perpetrated in peacetime as well as by means of war.

Charging the crime of Femicide – genocidal sexual atrocities – as a separate category of crime within the rest of the Hague War Crimes Tribunal can do for women what Nuremberg did for subordinated racial, national, ethnic, and religious groups.[17] An international precedent in response to the destruction of Bosnian Moslem and Croatian women, *specifically*, can tell the world "Never Again" – to no women, no group of women, nowhere, in any shape or form, for no reason ever. It could prevent another Femicide from happening again somewhere else. It can also lend legitimacy to global struggles to end the sexual abuse and subordination of women everywhere. Just as the Nuremberg War Crimes Tribunal had an ethical obligation to charge perpetrators of the crime of the Shoah, the Hague War Crimes Tribunal has the same obligation to charge perpetrators of the crime of Femicide.

The recognition and understanding Nuremberg brought to genocide did not include the specific and additional ways women of the targetted racial, ethnic, national, and religious groups were being destroyed. Unlike Nuremberg, if the Hague War Crimes Tribunal charges perpetrators of this Femicide, it necessarily brings

---

16. Catharine MacKinnon (1993a, 1994a) is the first major theorist of modern feminism who understood that Femicide is happening in Bosnia-Hercegovina and Croatia and has been theoretically accountable. Survivors sought her to represent them as their lawyer in international legal proceedings. See also Dworkin: 1993.

17. Indigenous women's and survivor groups are pushing for this recognition. Some of these groups include Kareta, International Initiative of Women of Bosnia and Hercegovina "Biser", Bosnia-Hercegovina Refugee Women's Group "Zena BiH", Mothers for Peace, and NONA.

with it visibility to the destruction of national and religious groups through the women who are part of them. Recognition of Femicide brings with it recognition of the other components of genocide which was not the case at Nuremberg.

V

Survivors chose to speak out and let the world know about genocidal sexual atrocities so that they could thereby stop them and maybe save the women who were left behind *and* so that this would never happen again. Not only did they choose to speak, they also filed their own lawsuit in New York charging the head of the Bosnian Serbs with sexual atrocities and other acts of genocide (see K. v. Karadzic). On October 2, 1992, just days after coming out of Prijedor,[18] Bosnia-Hercegovina, Jadranka Cigelj, a survivor of the Omarska rape/death camp and the first woman to let the world know about the genocidal sexual atrocities there, told an international feminist and women's forum: "I want to say this because of the women who were left behind".[19] Her sentence encapsulates the obligation of all women who are not "left behind". An international legal forum and precedent that will hear the experiences of these women, recognize them, and serve some form of justice can return some of the dignity that was taken away from them. Legal justice facilitates and is part of the continuous process of survival and healing. The international visibility of such a forum can also draw others to assist survivors in that process as well. It will make it more possible to guard the memory of what they suffered from the slander and revisionism which silences survivors' speech and lessens chances for survival.[20] It can give women, as a group, something to remember.

VI

This Femicide shows women that the world is even more dangerous for us than we ever imagined. By not intervening to stop the Femicide in Croatia and Bosnia-

---

18. Prijedor is a city in Northwestern Bosnia-Hercegovina that suffered some of the worst and most efficient ethnic cleansing. It is also site to the most notorious Serbian death camps.

19. "Women in War" international feminist and women's conference and survivor speak-out held in Zagreb on October 1–4, 1992 and organized by Kareta Feminist Group and Women's Help Now. I attended this conference and heard these words.

20 Genocide revisionism is not simply an abstract concept but constitutes very real acts. It means permitting and encouraging genocide to continue and not doing anything to stop it. Revisionism has had an especially active presence in this Femicide and has ranged from such acts as obstruction of information from reaching the international feminist media and contacts, suppression of information, public denial of events, and alteration of testimonies, to whitewashing the reality of Femicide once it finally became known, and rape and genocide war profiteerism. See, for example, Armanda and Nenadic (1994), p. 2 about the revisionism of Slavenka Drakulic; Kareta Feminist Group and International Initiative of Women of Bosnia and Hercegovina – "Biser" 1994 about the revisionism of Vesna Kesic. There have been numerous responses to these and other figures by survivors and Indigenous women's groups. Revisionism in this Femicide warrants a study of its own.

Hercegovina the governments of the world have failed women everywhere. They have sent women the message that the fact that women are being destroyed in rape/death camps is not a domestic or foreign policy concern and interest of theirs. The possibility also exists that the Hague will not charge genocidal sexual atrocities. This would tell us that the world is even less ours than we thought.

We know what Serbian fascists have learned from men, but what will the world's men learn from Serbian fascists? Now that they have crossed a threshold and set a precedent in woman-hating, how can we be sure that our governments will not follow suit and do this to us one day through their domestic or foreign policies? How can we believe that they will not round us up in rape/death camps? No one ever believed that places like Auschwitz or Serbian rape/death camps could ever come into existence. Now rape/death camps are an innovation of this genocide. What will they think of doing to women next?

Evelyne Accad

Truth versus Loyalty

> *I only arrived at the savage, primitive truths of life after years of life after years of struggle.*
>
> Nawal El Saadawi (1982)

An event which triggered great emotions in my life, which marked the development of my career, a point of fixation or crystallization which determined the focus and aims of my writing, was when I read about excision and infibulation, the cruel practice of sexual mutilations millions of women suffer from all over the world – most specifically in some countries in Africa and in the Arab Gulf. At the time I was preparing a doctoral thesis at Indiana University (Accad: 1978). It was the first time I had heard about it. I was already aware of many practices of oppression afflicting women, since it was some of them which had motivated me to leave my country of birth, Lebanon, but excision was the summum of anything I could have imagined. I was sick for several weeks, my thesis took a different turn, and the title of my first novel, *L'Excisée* (1988), was already determined.

I used the word excision because I saw it as reflecting both the physical and psychological aspects of the mutilation. The two seemed to me closely connected and part of the same oppression. But when speaking about Sudan, I chose to use the word infibulation, rather than genital mutilation, or circumcision, or excision, because, even though it describes only one form of the operation, it is the form which is used ninety percent of the time in the Sudan and it is thus the practice women's struggles concentrate against. Infibulation is the most severe form of genital mutilation. On the wedding night, the woman undergoes a double defloration: the opening of the sewn-up vulva with a sharp object or the male penis, and the rupture of the virginal membrane.[1] It should be stressed here that female

---

1. Hosken's (1982) pioneering research on the practice of genital mutilation names three kinds of operation: (i) Circumcision (Sunna) is the removal of the clitoral prepuce and the tip of the clitoris. Sunna means tradition in Arabic. (ii) Excision/Clitoridectomy is the removal of the entire clitoris, usually with the

cont. next page

genital mutilation is not an Islamic or religious practice as such, even though both Moslems and Christians practise it in Egypt and other parts of Africa and the Arab Gulf. The practice antedates the Monotheistic religions and was observed on the Mummies in Egypt (Hosken: 1994).

My struggle to include the topic of genital mutilation in my discussion of Arab women's problems had drawn strong responses from a member of my doctoral committee. At the time I presumed the issue was too emotionally charged, and too controversial and new, to be dealt with in an academic environment. It was 1975, declared the International Women's Year by the United Nations, which mobilized feminists around the globe on this issue, and stirred much controversy, debate, and resentment on the part of some African women who saw European and American interference as reductionist and ethnocentric, representing them in racist, misogynist, backward, inhuman terms thus reinforcing the stereotypes. Now, many books and articles have come out, inside and outside academia, in the west as well as in the east, and from many different angles, perspectives and commitments (see Bennett: 1993; Cloudsley: 1981; El Dareer: 1982; Erlich: 1986; Hosken: 1982/1994; Lightfoot-Klein: 1989; Lionnet: 1989; Ogunyemi: forthcoming; Saadawi: 1982; Saurel: 1985; Thiam: 1978; Walker: 1992).

I remember being torn apart in this conflict at a meeting of the African Literature Association in Madison, Wisconsin, where I had presented a paper and used the term mutilation. I was immediately attacked by one of my African male colleagues for not using the word tradition.[2] The plenary session split in a heated debate along race rather than gender lines. I was very depressed to see the African women siding with the African men. But in the evening, I discovered the reasons behind this apparent division, when I sang one of my compositions on genital mutilation and the pain it causes in women. Some of the African women present had tears in their eyes and came to thank me after the performance. They told me the reason they had sided with their men in the morning was because they had to be loyal to them. In front of the West, loyalty was more important than truth, but I was right in denouncing the practice. In public, race was what mattered, in private the women could voice their concerns. With time, I have become more aware of the issue of truth versus loyalty and how it causes women to be split when they should be uniting on crucial issues (Accad: 1990).

---

1. *cont. from previous page*
labia minora, and sometimes all of the external genitalia, except parts of the labia majora. (iii) Infibulation or Pharaonic circumcision is the removal of the entire clitoris, the labia minora and parts of the labia majora, the two sides of the vulva are scraped raw and then sewn together, the entrance to the vagina is obliterated except for a tiny opening to allow urine and menstrual flow to drain. More recently, by defining genital mutilation as "tradition", the topic is removed from public discourse and becomes an issue of religious reflection (Hoskens: 1982/1994).
2. *The Encyclopedia of Islam* (1975–76, p. 946) mentions Ghazali reporting the Prophet's words addressed to Um'Attya, Mukatti'at al-Buzur (the Clitoris Cutter) telling her "to cut it but not overcut it, the face will be embellished and the husband will be pleased".

Being an Arab Lebanese Christian, with a Swiss mother and a Lebanese father born in Egypt, myself born and raised in Beirut – one of the most cosmopolitan places in the world at the time – presently teaching in the United States, gives me a perspective I might not have otherwise. It allows me to see problems from many angles, to identify or distance myself when necessary. It gave me courage to leave when I felt life was closing in on me, and strength to return when I thought I might be effective in bringing about some necessary changes.

In 1978 and in 1983, I travelled to Egypt, the Arab Gulf (specifically Bahrain and the United Arab Emirates), the Sudan, the Ivory Coast, and Senegal. And more recently, in 1993, I went back to Cairo, Egypt. On these trips, I met women from all levels of society. Over this period, it has become clear to me that I am perceived as "different" by both eastern and western men and women. I wondered, for example, why one of the western midwives, who spoke Arab fluently, having lived in the area longer than I, nevertheless delegated me to talk to one of her patients and try to find out why she had taken the decision she had. Did she think I was perceived by her Arab patient as an Arab, therefore better able to get her trust and confidence? On the other hand, some of the intellectual feminist women in Tunisia refused to talk to me because of my US connection. They perceived me as a spy, someone they could not trust. Later I realized that this was not the real reason for their rejection, but a pretext in hiding their own feelings of insecurity, jealousy and resentment (Accad: 1993). It became clear to me that my métissage was both an advantage and a handicap.[3] I did not experience rejection by women when travelling and researching throughout the Gulf or in the rural areas of North Africa and the Arab world. The uneasiness came mainly from the intellectuals, probably because they are more likely to have sublimated or reinterpreted their experience of oppression in terms of patriarchal ways of thinking (such as Marxist, nationalist, capitalist, and so on).

It also became clear to me that, contrary to the perspective of many intellectuals and political women and men involved either in the United States or the Middle East, rural and urban women from the lower strata of society are very outspoken on the subject of sex, love, and their relationships to their husbands and family. Contrary to what some intellectuals have expressed, they see the need for change in these areas of their lives (Kader: 1988). This assessment is reinforced by the Sudanese woman leader I interviewed, who says that it is much easier to work – struggling against female circumcision – with rural rather than educated people, because they are more simple and direct; they look at things practically and accept advice and help when they see it.

Some of the reasons given in the interviews I carried out were that excision was for: embellishment, tradition, purification, reduction of sexual desire to render women more controllable, more accepting of their main role in life, the

---

3. See Lionnet (1989) who defines *métissage* as a dialogical hybrid that fuses together heterogenous elements". See also Chedid (1985).

production of children. "An excised girl will protect herself," said one of the patients in an Egyptian hospital, meaning that it will help her keep her virginity. The aesthetic reasons given seemed connected to the notion of purification, itself connected to religion. Many nurses claimed the labia looked ugly and needed trimming. Sometimes they performed the operation on a woman during delivery in order to embellish her. Purification and embellishment are connected to notions of identity themselves connected to religious prescriptions. People often express their differences from other cultures through such marks inscribed by rites of passage.

In the Sudan, women who had been subjected to circumcision or who had witnessed the worst form of excision – infibulation – done on relatives or friends, not only voiced their opinion against it, but they are involved in a wide campaign and actions aimed at struggling to eradicate the practice. The struggle they described to me seemed quite remarkable. They go to the countryside with programs of hygiene and development. They explain the connection between diseases and infibulation which the people have no effort in making. They stage plays and have radio programs to teach the people about the disastrous consequences linked to the practice, and they also educate the midwives and lead them to other means of earning a living than performing these operations. I believe this is where hope really lies: in these courageous women and men, living in their own culture, who have organized with the various groups they are surrounded with, struggling to eradicate dangerous and harmful practices, who work with and for the people, trying to bring better conditions on all levels of their lives.

At the time of writing I am faced with the prospect of a mastectomy or lumpectomy. These two "ectomies", like clitoridectomy, are lived by an increasing number of women all over the world, and particularly in the United States. It is the price we pay for modern civilization. The pollution, pesticides, depletion of the ozone layer, nuclear disasters, estrogen induced cancers, and mistreatment of nature are finally catching up with us. As Chikwenye Okonjo Ogunyemi (forthcoming) states:

> Cultural determinism becomes the focal point of the politics of ectomy: to cut or not to cut? The mind boggles at Western culture's playing on women's bodies: hysterectomies, oophorectomies or ovariectomies, salpingestomies, episiotomies, mastectomies . . . I envision ectomy as a trope to express the excision, the cutting off, the exclusion attached to woman's destiny.

I am too overwhelmed by emotions, fears, anguish, rage, but also a renewed sense of the urgency, beauty and cruelty of life to be able to express what I am going through right now, except in my journal. Someday, I hope to write it down for another publication. The link that ties me to all the women around the world is being reinforced in this tribulation and sorrow.

Epilogue

When I woke up, June 16, 1994, on the operating table and put my hand to my left chest which was completely bandaged, I immediately realized my breast was gone. I did not cry like I had three months earlier when I woke up from the biopsy, and had found out it was cancer. From now on, I told myself, I belonged to all my sisters who had been mutilated, all the amazons crossing Amazonia, one breast cut, the other flowing freely in the wind! I was in physical pain. They gave me pain "killers." I noticed how all of my treatment had aggressive warlike names and connotations – chemotherapy was discovered during World War II experiments with nerve gas. I wished there were different, softer cures for cancer. My whole body, mind and spirit rebelled against this aspect of the disease – as well as others – but particularly this one, since I am a pacifist and hate violence. One of my friends noticed how barbarian these practices of cancer treatment are. Future centuries will look upon us as we look upon the way past centuries treated some disease: with contempt and horror!

I plan to write a book on my personal experience with breast cancer based on the diary I kept and – substantiated with bibliographical research, personal observations and analysis of cultural differences – related through interviews with women and doctors in France, Tunisia, Lebanon and the US. I need to do it for myself: to exorcise the pain; and for other women: those going through the same Calvary, or those who will in the future; all those who need to be made aware of the dangers we are living in in this century: the post-modern era. I plan to approach this difficult topic on both emotional and intellectual levels.

Marjorie Agosin

Amidst the Smoke We Remember: Mothers of the Plaza de Mayo

> *Censorship has various masks and forms. It may be imposed indirectly by the ruling power, or may be self-imposed by the writer in anticipation of reaction. In the latter case clandestine publications may become the vehicle for expression, or the writer may seek to veil her message under elaborate metaphors understandable only to an elite few who communicate with each other through such "double-talk". In either case, the effect is the same: to limit one's readers and thus, severely restrict the impact of one's message.*
>
> *Censorship attacks not only the woman who writes but also the woman who reads. Friends have told me that, during the years of repression in Argentina, carrying a book under one's arm was a mark of subversion. Also, the imposition by the government of which books we can or cannot read makes us muzzled beings, prisoners of decrees based on the values of caution, repression and torture.*
>
> Marjorie Agosin: *Women of Smoke*, pp. 11–12.

Historically, the movement of the Mothers of the Plaza de Mayo constituted the first political response to the disappearance of Argentine citizens, a policy implemented by the military government in March of 1976 (Jelin: 1976, p. 48; Bousquet: 1982, p. 91; Simpson and Bennet: 1985). The group originated in a modest fashion, starting with fourteen women who met each other through the long, formal procedures and pilgrimages in search of their missing loved ones. From this, the movement was born, motivated by a concrete circumstance: the loss of loved ones. Partisan ideology was not an issue for this group of women; they were motivated by a common pain. From its birth, this group stimulated the social movement towards the transition to democracy in Argentina. These women were the only ones to publicly protest the repression in Argentina. Later, they would be followed by other women in Chile, El Salvador, Guatemala and Uruguay.[1]

The metaphor of the plaza and the silent and solitary march was converted into an essential symbolic aspect of their fight. They chose a place where women had traditionally been prohibited from gathering: the plaza. Within Argentine society, the plaza is a public space dominated by patriarchy, just as all of the buildings that surround the plaza – the banks, businesses and government offices – are dominated by that same masculine power. The women added their presence to this male domain, leaving their private and traditional settings, their homes, and their daily battle for bread to feed their families.

The women united in a collective action of solidarity that sprang from their biological roles as mothers. It is precisely this role that made them develop a uniquely female set of images within the political sphere. The mothers constituted a group of women that, without worrying about the ideology of changing their sex roles, produced an enormous change in the female consciousness.[2] The collective nature of the protest challenged the stereotype that characterizes women as not being able to organize. It also demonstrated that the resignation, weakness and passivity considered to be typical female characteristics are also false.

The white kerchiefs worn by the Mothers of the Plaza de Mayo came to be recognized by the entire world as an example of the metaphors of female political symbology. The white kerchief represents the female role. Nevertheless, the kerchief worn by the Mothers of the Plaza de Mayo has been changed, revised and elaborated under a new canon: the kerchief is embroidered with the name of the child who has disappeared.

The kerchief is an object that covers the hair, keeping it invisible. When the name of a lost child is embroidered onto the kerchief, that name becomes visible, and gives a new symbolic meaning to the kerchief. The fact that the child's name is embroidered by hand reflects the connection between the hand that creates the name and the bearer of that name. That is to say, the two bodies, the one identified on the head of the woman and the woman herself, are united.

The embroidered name has a more profound significance within the female symbology. Throughout history, women have been characterized by the activity of embroidering. For women, sewing has been a form of writing a text. To link sewing with the kerchief is a way to expose this text; when exhibited on a woman's head, it becomes a metaphor of the private and public.

For the Mothers of the Plaza de Mayo, the symbol of the white kerchief has the following connotation: "We began using this colour because it is the symbol of peace, something that unites us with all mothers." (Jelin: 1976, p. 50). Also, when referring to their belief in non-violence and to their marches, they point out the following:

---

1. The literature that treats the theme of the transition to democracy is varied, although very little has been written about the fundamental role of women in this process. See O'Donnell (1986); Vicuña (1985).
2. Kaplan (1982) has a very interesting article about the phenomenon of women's collective action in periods of crisis.

We tried not to be aggressive with words, thinking that our children were hostages. Non-violence was also a way of defending ourselves; we knew that if we created violence, it could generate a reaction that was contrary to what we were trying to achieve (Jelin: 1976, p. 50).

The white kerchiefs and the slow, silent, circular march around the pyramid in the plaza de Mayo create a female political character. The silence reflects the silence imposed on the female gender for centuries, which relegated women to waiting, to resignation. But here, silence holds a new significance. It is a silence that accuses, a silence that asks, "Where are our children?"

The activity that takes place every Thursday in the Plaza de Mayo was born from a break with the dominant ideology. Here, there are no slogans or pamphlets. The action is separate from all partisan activities and separates itself from the male political ideology. The mothers define themselves as defenders of life, and as a movement that is not passive, but pacifist. This is crucial for understanding female political activity under authoritarian governments, where death becomes a gratuitous instrument of the torturer. In societies ruled by dictatorships, the ideology of death is the prevailing force that dominates and contrasts with the ideology of life and, above all, with the right to protect life.

In addition, the symbology of photography has also been an important instrument in the female protest movements. Photographs are associated with the metaphor of embroidering the name on the kerchief, that is to say, with memory and remembering. The Mothers of the Plaza de Mayo and, later, members of other movements in Latin America such as the Group of Mutual Support formed in Guatemala in 1983, and the Association of the Detained and Disappeared formed in Chile in 1979, carry photographs of their missing relatives during the protests.

The symbolism of the photograph rises to various levels. In the first place, the photograph is tied to the chest of the person who carries it, emphasizing the link between the body of the living person and the search for the missing individual or dead body. Also, it produces a strong visual image. The photograph is tied to a woman who in reality is saying, *"This face is mine, it is part of my body and I have the right to find it"*.

The action in the Plaza, the silent march, the white kerchiefs with the embroidered names and the photographs that stare out at the passers by emphasize the symbolic, metaphoric act of the Mothers of the Plaza de Mayo. This semiotic of dress reflects non-violence and peacefulness as well as public suffering. The persistence of these rituals of continual protest, which have taken place since 1977, helps to create a powerful image of repetition and familiarity. Now the general public, from the generals who observe these women from their balconies to the passers-by, becomes part of this collective vigil. The pain becomes public.

The strategies and rules for carrying out political action observed in the Mothers of the Plaza de Mayo, motivated by a moral, but not moralizing, doctrine, are also utilized by the women of Chile today. The techniques they use include the appeal to other groups within the country and the communal search for truth and justice. It is very possible that the Mothers of the Plaza de Mayo have influenced their Chilean compañeras. Perhaps the future will show profound connections between these movements of female resistance.

In 1983, a critical year for political activity against Pinochet's government, women were an essential element of protest and were visible in the fight against authoritarianism. In Chile that year, a unique movement was formed called "Women for Life".[3] The name gives an indication of the nature of the movement, showing a clear parallel to the movement of the Mothers of the Plaza de Mayo whose slogan is "In search of life; we want them to be alive".

Unlike the movements in Argentina, El Salvador and Guatemala, Women for Life is not exclusively a movement of mothers, but rather a collective initially formed by twenty-six women of different political leanings and social classes. These women resolved to fight against the dictatorship and its principal strategy was to assemble large groups of women that lived in Santiago and mobilize them in the struggle against the dictatorship. In a theatre in Santiago, El Caupolicán, ten thousand women of all social and economic classes met. The theme of the meeting was "Freedom's Name is Woman".

The structure of Women for Life and its strategies for carrying out political tasks are clearly different from the techniques employed by men. The members of Women for Life, like the Mothers of the Plaza de Mayo, are not motivated or directed by political parties. Obviously, individual members belong to different parties, but they are all motivated by a common belief in the power of dialogue. They practice democratic political encounters in an open fashion. That is to say, the collective, Women for Life, has been able to draw from other movements of women throughout the country, such as the movement of working-class women and the feminist movement. It is through this dialogue that ideological differences are resolved and non-violent protest and solidarity are practiced.

Women for Life is an example of a movement whose operation is based on a series of symbolic gestures and actions. For example, at times, groups of women march in the plazas of Santiago, carrying photographs of the missing and detained, invoking their names, demonstrating that their loved ones are present and alive through their voices and memories.

The insistence that this movement is "for life" creates an ideology tied to rebirth and hope. The emphasis on life contrasts with the death to which the country submits on a daily basis. The rituals of collective marches, support for human rights organizations, fasts for political prisoners, and protests on International Women's Day can be attributed to the constant labour and shared participation of Women for Life with other groups working for social and political reform within the country.

Among the actions of public protest carried out by Women for Life are the peaceful marches in central parts of the city. The marches usually begin in

3. Valdés, Teresa. For a copy, write to Flacso, Leopoldo Urrutia 1950, Santiago, Chile.

three different places. The women carry colored ribbons and join the ribbons together in one spot. Some of the slogans used in these demonstrations are: "Freedom's Name is Woman", "Let's go, woman", "No more because we are more", and "1986 is ours. Women's Word".

The group, Women for Life, has performed many, varied activities in its short life and has implemented vast changes in a society dominated by patriarchy and violence. The most prominent metaphors of this movement allude to the visibility of women in public areas of the city: in plazas, gardens, and in the different sectors, including the popular sectors and upper-class neighbourhoods. One of the group's most important contributions has been the implementation of non-violent strategies throughout a city and country that are dominated by violence.

Photographs also occupy a fundamental place in the set of symbols created by Women for Life. In addition to attempting to save their loved ones from oblivion, Women for Life uses the photographs to appeal to a moral, collective consciousness that embraces the entire country. The organization put up posters throughout the country, particularly in Santiago, of Loreta Castillo, a young student who was tortured in August 1984. After torturing her, the secret police dynamited her body and publicly denounced her as being a terrorist. The photograph of Loreta Castillo acts as a reminder of this tragedy. She appears smiling, full of life, and rejecting death.

The occupation of various public spaces and the covering of walls with the faces of the victims of the dictatorship are part of the metaphorization and daily activity of these women in cities oppressed by dictatorship, hatred, and continual hunger. Women for Life's activities are always open and visible. In general, the protests are carried out during the day and in clearly visible spaces, reinforcing the fact that these women do not have anything to hide, as opposed to the torture, disappearances and clandestine prisons that are hidden in Chile by the government.

The women wear their hair out, loose, and they wear light-coloured clothing. Their steps defy fear, and their hands are always open to reflect another of their slogans, "We Have Clean Hands". Their hands have never burned or tortured anyone. This metaphorical ritual of openness contrasts with the police in Chile, who wander through the streets after sunset with their faces painted black and their uniforms full of weapons. The women project an image of life, opposing the image of death projected by the police.

Among Women for Life's common strategies for carrying out political action are constant attempts to initiate dialogue with the opposition. Overcoming their fear, the women pass out pamphlets to educate members of the opposition. Other techniques are direct observation of the police and face-to-face confrontation. In this way, the women defeat terror. During the marches, we observe the participants as they attempt to speak with the police who line the streets, preventing the columns of women from moving on.[4] Posters that read "We Are

---

4. This information about tactics useful to dominate fear appears in pamphlets that circulated throughout the city. See also Kirkwood (1984).

More" and "Soldier, Chile Needs You" are ways of saying, "We are here, meet us face to face". This tactic is typical of non-violent movements, and accentuates Women for Life's desire for solidarity and collective mobilization in Chile (see Sharp: 1980).

On Wednesday, 30 October 1985, Women for Life sponsored a general march of approximately five thousand women. The following statement was read aloud: "We are more for justice, we are more for democracy, we are more for solidarity, we are more for life, we are more". For Women for Life, there are no more partisan ideologies, but instead, a globalization of the collective desires of women who are dominated by the wish for the restoration of a free, just and dignified country.

The cases of the Mothers of the Plaza de Mayo and Women for Life are examples of political movements formed by women that continue to grow and develop. They are primarily movements that were born from practice and through practice, not theory. Both the Mothers of the Plaza de Mayo and Women for Life arose in response to a drastic necessity that affected women of every social class. The disappearance of loved ones and social injustice, especially hunger, forced women to unite and organize.

In response to authoritarianism, the private becomes public. Food and the lack of food become social and political issues of fundamental importance. The women, conscious of their role as providers of basic necessities and as guardians of the family, organize themselves around these domestic issues and fight. In the case of the Mothers of the Plaza de Mayo, contact with jails was of fundamental importance in motivating the women. In the case of Women for Life, everything began with a group of friends who saw the need to present an alternative to fascism. They resorted to grouping women in different communal kitchens, and in this way, groups of women were born, formed from the politics of necessity and in search of a public voice.

Politics and rebellion were born from daily experience. These movements of women still do not concern themselves with hierarchies, power and order, but rather function more from similarities than from differences. The attitudes of solidarity, togetherness, and democratic decision-making are the foundations of these two groups that are attempting to create a system of harmony and peace in order to fight against the dominant systems of violence and repression.

The negation of authoritarianism and the establishment of democracy in the country as well as in the home are the goals of female political activity in these two countries of the Southern Cone. These manifestations of non-violence have, or are beginning to have, great repercussions. We can see how the Mothers of the Plaza de Mayo was at first a movement exclusively of the mothers of individuals who had disappeared. Now, the organization has begun to include other groups, not only of mothers but of all citizens interested in human rights and the freedom of human beings. The same happened with Women for Life, which has been able to convene all sectors of Chilean society more successfully than the opposition groups that are dominated by men.

The institutionalized hierarchy of political values has disappeared in the two movements cited. The central concerns of these women are the right to life and the right to exist in peace in a patriarchal culture where death and fear are daily strategies used by the government to terrorize the public.

The politicization of these groups of women does not follow established theories concerning collective mobilization. In the first place, these women made their original decision to go out in search of the truth without the intervention of political parties or male leaders. For this reason, the mothers' actions force a re-examination of preconceived theories about social movements, where women's movements are always considered to be passive and irrelevant to the general political situation. In the cases examined in this article, the opposite is shown. The division between the personal and the political disappears, especially in the case of the Mothers of the Plaza de Mayo. The mothers are the only ones who publicly protested the Falkland War; for this reason, the Mothers are an important force in the restoration or, better said, the maintenance of democracy at an ethical and ideological level in Argentina today.

In Chile, the women's protests against the military dictatorship have given a new air of legitimacy to Women's Movements. Notwithstanding the Chilean suffragists of the 1930s and 1940s who fought to secure women's right to vote, women always worked for and through political parties. Beginning in 1983, Chilean women proposed an answer to authoritarianism that came from within. One of the essential contributions of Women for Life has been the affirmation and estab-lishment of feminism as a pacifist movement in complete opposition to the ruling authoritarianism.[5] Another contribution has been the negation of violence in public and official spaces and within the home. One of the slogans utilized in the protests is "Democracy in the country and in the home".

Mothers of the Plaza de Mayo

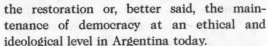

5. For a basic bibliography on women and non-violence, see *Piecing it Together: Feminism and Non-Violence* published by the Feminism and Non-Violence Study Group, 2 College Close, Buchleigh Westward Devon, 1983. See also Jaggar (1983); McAllister (1982).

Cuando me enseñó su fotografía
   me dijo
ésta es mi hija
aún no llega a casa
hace diez años que no llega
pero ésta es su fotografía
¿Es muy linda no es cierto?
es una estudiante de filosofía
y aquí está cuando teniá
catorce años
e hizo su primera
comunión
almidonada, sagrada.
ésta es mi hija
es tan bella
todos los días converso con ella
ya nunca llega tarde a casa, yo por
   eso la reprocho
   mucho menos
pero la quiero tantísimo
ésta es mi hija
todas las noches me despido de ella
la beso
y me cuesta no llorar
aunque sé que no llegará
   tarde a casa
porque tú sabes, hace años que
   no regresa a casa
yo quiero mucho a esta foto
la miro todos los días
me parece ayer cuando
era un angelito de plumas en mis
   manos
y aquí está toda hecha una dama
una estudiante de filosofía
una desaparecida
pero ¿no es cierto que es tan linda,
que tiene un rostro de angel,
que parece que estuviera viva?
Aquí están nuestros álbumes
éstas son las fotografías
de los rostros
acérquese, no tenga

When she showed me her photograph
   she said,
This is my daughter.
She still hasn't come home.
She hasn't come home in ten years.
But this is her photograph.
Isn't it true that she is very pretty?
She is a philosophy student
and here she is when she was
fourteen years old
and had her first
communion,
starched, sacred.
This is my daughter.
She is so pretty. I talk to her every
   day.
She no longer comes home late, and
   this is why I reproach her
   much less.
But I love her so much.
This is my daughter.
Every night I say goodbye to her.
I kiss her
and it's hard for me not to cry
even though I know she will not come
   home late
because as you know, she has not come
   home for years.
I love this photo very much.
I look at it every day.
It seems that only yesterday
she was a little feathered angel in my
   arms
and here she looks like a young lady,
a philosophy student,
another disappeared.
But isn't it true that she is so pretty,
that she has an angel's face,
that it seems as if she were alive?
Here are our albums,
these are the photographs
of their faces.
Come closer, do not be

miedo
¿es verdad que son muy jóvenes?
   es mi hija,
ire ésta
Andrea y ésta
es mi hija Paola
somos las madres de los
desaparecidos.
Coleccionamos
sus rostros
en estas fotografías
muchas veces hablamos con ellos,
y nos preguntamos
¿quién acariciará
el pelo de la Graciela?
¿qué habrán hecho con el
   cuerpecito de Andrés?
Fíjese que tenián nombres,
les gustaba leer
eran muy jóvenes
ninguno de ellos alcanzó a celebrar
sus dieciocho años,
aquí están sus fotografías,
estos inmensos álbumes
acérquese,
ayúdeme
a lo mejor usted
lo ha visto
y cuando se vaya al extranjero
lleve una de estas fotografías.

afraid.
Isn't it true they're very young?
She is my daughter.
Look at this one.
She is Andrea and this
is my daughter Paola.
We are the mothers of the
disappeared.
We collect
their faces
 in these photographs
and we often talk with them
and ask ourselves
Who will caress
Graciela's hair?
What have they done with Andres'
   little body?
Notice that they had names,
they liked to read,
they were very young.
None of them ever got to celebrate
their eighteenth birthday.
Here are their photographs,
these immense albums.
Come close,
help me.
Maybe you
have seen him,
and when you travel outside the
   country
take one of these photographs
   with you.

Evelina Giobbe

The Marketplace of Ideas

Recently I've been thinking about numerous conferences and public hearings that I've attended on the issue of pornography. As I reflected on the community forums, the panel discussions, the endless debates, one theme kept recurring in my mind: the concept of the "marketplace of ideas". Within the context of intellectual discourse, the marketplace of ideas is a figure of speech, if you'll pardon the pun, which we use to frame discussions about where, how and with whom we have discussions. It is a metaphorical place in time where the democratic exchange of ideas occurs. But for many women, women like myself in particular, the marketplace of ideas is a very concrete space where we are walled into a compound built on the illusion of a slippery slope; where brick upon brick is mortared with the specious rhetoric of free expression and the door is bolted shut with the First Amendment.

In the bargain basement of the marketplace, men's fantasies are projected onto the blank screens of women's lives. In the bargain basement of the market-place of ideas, women's experiences are captured in camcorders, frozen on rolls of 35 millimeter film, trapped in the tangle of yards and yards and yards of videotape. In the bargain basement of the marketplace of ideas human beings are magically transformed into mere pictures and words, sealed in the plastic shrink wrap of the constitution, carried away in unmarked graves of plain brown paper bags.

I live in the bargain basement of the marketplace of ideas: a red tag special, tossed on a sale rack picked up and picked over by countless sweaty palms, the pages of my life thumbed through by anonymous hands and sticky fingers. I am a woman whose youth is frozen in time, frame by frame, in the technological recycling bin of prostitution: I am a woman who has been used in pornography.

If you peruse the racks of this very real marketplace, you will find me sandwiched somewhere between my sisters in the video section among such titles as *Abused Runaway, Teen Street Slut* and *Call Girl.* You can buy us, rent us, or if you don't want to take us home, you can stroll over to the peepshow booth, drop a quarter in the coin box, and watch us caught in an endless pornographic loop of sexual humiliation and abuse. With a pocket full of change you can see us bend, twist, turn and spread our legs for your pleasure. Drop in another coin, and watch us lay with any manner of man or beast, and if there is no living thing within reach, any common household object will do. Another coin and you can hear us beg for more. Reach in your pants for just one more quarter, quickly though, before the metal curtain snaps shut on the object of your desire, a tortured smile captured in a freeze frame, dead eyes staring out at you. Or . . . Walk back to the magazine section and you can see me as a child, painted and dressed in a garish pornographic parody of a woman. Pick up a later edition, and you can see the woman I'd become, genitals shaved and exposed, hair in pigtails, a grotesque parody of the nymph child. One of a thousand pseudo-Lolitas whose market appeal declined before her twenty-first birthday.

I was raised in a brothel by pimps and johns; pornography is my family photo album. If you lay the pictures end to end, you can track the deconstruction of a human being, the death of a woman, reconstructed and resurrected as a "whore": desired, despised, discarded.

I've been out of the sex industry for about two decades. I've survived the prostitution; outlived a good many of the johns, but the pornography that was made of me still exists. Somewhere some pimp masquerading as a publisher is packing up a shipment of magazines, while some other pimp, somewhere else, who's masquerading as a film distributor is filling a truck with pornographic video cassettes. Waiting for these deliveries on the other end, is some sticky-fingered john, with a pocket full of quarters, waiting to buy yet another piece of my youth, in the bargain basement of the marketplace of ideas. I want them to stop. I want us to stop them.

Originally published in *Action Agenda* (1994).

V

FEMINISM RECLAIMED

Susan Hawthorne

From Theories of
Indifference to a Wild Politics*

What is the velocity of a falling body? a body moving through space sensing
neither the relative time nor the relative motion of its fall?

How long does a body falling into a seizure take to fall?

Which is the time?
Which is the space?

If a body is senseless to the motion the time the space the pull of gravity as
she falls can she be a sentient body?

Which is the body?
Which is the mind?

(Hawthorne: 1993b, p. 86)

This paper arises both out of my experience of epilepsy and a history of twenty years of activism in the lesbian feminist movement. These are the facts.

Both experiences have melded together because in my life, by an almost strange coincidence, their manifestation was simultaneous. This is my personal history. This is my political history.

With the arrival of feminism in my life came, finally, a language, words with which to understand one another, shared talk in consciousness raising groups that allowed us all to arrange the patterns of our lives into political shapes. In the same year came the biggest seizure of my life that left me without memory and without words for three days.

---

* This paper was first presented at the Politics and Poetics of the Body Conference, University of California, Santa Barbara, USA, April 30, 1994.

> If a body only notices that she has fallen   (now face down on the ground)   that it happened some time before this moment   (her eyes open to her position but not to any memory)   that gravity has pulled her down   – how can she know she has fallen?   that time itself has been seized?   that memory has not encoded the moment or the actualization of the fall?   What then? (Hawthorne: 1993b, p. 88).

Feminism gave me a politics of engagement. A politics that ensured I looked at my life, that I measured it by how much I was able to effect change. Feminism made sense of the world – a world that had been an uncomfortable place until then; a world that rejected me on the basis of something that could not be seen. And although I knew I was not the only person with epilepsy in the world, I had never met anyone who acknowledged this label. Apparently there were hundreds of thousands like me, but where? Feminism allowed me to speak of this.

I came to feminism with an awareness of my own separation from the world. And I found others, who, through different experiences, had reached similar conclusions.

Part of my history was about erasure, absence, invisibility, and a kind of death.

> If memory has for a moment   (or for several unquantifiable moments)   been erased scrubbed clean by the fall through time through space what proof has she that she exists? (Hawthorne: 1993b, p. 88).

Until feminism I had no proof of my existence. Woman hidden behind man. Epilepsy hidden by silence. Lesbianism hidden by ignorance. Ignorance of my self. I had no memory of the history of women. It had been scrubbed clean by its fall through time. I had no memory of seizures. My own body/mind had scrubbed that one. And I had no knowledge of the history and culture of lesbians in this world.

> Only later, when she says   What happened?   (assuming something did)   can she call on her existence.   But when she fell sensing none of the things essential to conscious existence   did she exist as anything more than an object falling? (Hawthorne: 1993b, p. 88).

The pre-conscious state is one of confusion; is one of lacking the right words to say what you feel. The pre-conscious state is what many of us were living until we engaged in feminist politics: both theory and practice. At some point each of us said, What happened? How did this happen? And as we searched our memories we found the words and worlds of women that made sense of our lives. This was politics. We laughed, we danced and we loved one another. We wrote poetry. Some of these poems drew threats of legal action from executors of other poets.[1]

---

1. Robin Morgan wrote two poems, "Arraignment (I)" and "Arraignment (II)" in which she says, "I accuse/ Ted Hughes" (I) (Morgan: ND, p. 76) and "How can/I accuse/Ted Hughes/of what the entire British and

cont. next page

She can know only that she has fallen through space into another time but only as an object.   At the moment of non-existence she cannot be a subject (except that she is subject to the laws of gravity and the continuous flow of space/time) (Hawthorne: 1993b, p. 88).

We claimed our right to be the subject of sentences. Sentences that began:

Chloë liked Olivia (Woolf: 1929/1974).

The two women were alone in the London flat (Lessing: 1976, p. 25).

I am a monster.
And I am proud (Morgan: ND, p. 86).

Until then we had been like the invisible woman in another of Robin Morgan's poems, pulling on our bodies to make the men around us feel better (Morgan: ND, p. 46). We were not the subjects of our own bodies, of our own selves. We had to consciously claim them. Through the women's health movement, through the establishment of rape crisis centres, refuges and a host of other movements around sexuality, women and madness, women and disability, women and reproductive autonomy, we became subjects of our bodies, to some extent. Also, we set up courses in Women's Studies; many of us wrote books, composed music, painted and sculpted, invented new words and new ways of living. Through this we gained control of our minds, to some extent.

At the moment of non-existence during the fall she (like any particle) could move along two paths a tendency to non-existence (death) in which case the subjectless state would have persisted or she could resonate towards the tendency to exist (which she did) and move back towards the possibility of subjectivity (1993b, pp. 88–89).

In the late 70s and early 80s post-modernism, primarily through the work of French and North American feminists, began to be read by feminists. This

---

American/literary and critical establishment/has been at great lengths to deny/(without ever saying it in so many words, of course): the murder of Sylvia Plath" (Morgan: ND, pp. 78). Arraignment (I) was not permitted publication, but appeared nevertheless in pirate editions in Australia and Canada which were speedily distributed throughout the Women's Movement. "Not that it isn't enough to condemn him/of mind-rape and body rape" (Morgan: ND, p. 76) (I) becomes: "her accusation of rape could be conceived as metaphor/and besides, it is permissable by law for a man to rape/his wife, in body and mind." (II) (Morgan: ND, p. 78). After detailing the circumstantial "coincidence" of two wives suiciding, the poet ends her poem with the lines: "Meanwhile,/Hughes/has married again." (Morgan: ND, p. 78b). This poem and its publishing history remind us of the power of words when formed, spoken, placed on the page. And of the dangers of whistleblowing.

was the point of choice – non-existence through the erasure of post-modernism, because of the death of the author; because of the reverberations of "woman does not exist"; because of an examination of the absences within the work.

The other choice was radical feminism. Have you ever noticed the persistent creativity of radical feminists? There are poets, novelists, artists in every medium, musicians, composers, film-makers, builders and craftswomen.

> She leaves a frail trail of light burning brighter as consciousness returns to her eyes.
> She lives!
> (Hawthorne: 1993b, p. 89).

It became fashionable during these years to deny being a radical feminist. Essentialist! they cried. Universalist! Radical feminism may have suffered an absence, may even have lost consciousness for a moment, but it has not died. Radical feminism is burning brighter today than it has for the past decade. Unlike post-modernism, it is a theory of engagement; a theory that engenders meaning; a theory that is here and now.

The Problem with Post-modernism

Post-modernism is a politics of indifference. For post-modernists, women are indifferent. Difference and differánce are credited with power, with being, with masculinity. The indifferent, as Luce Irigaray points out, is the one who "lacks", the one with "deficiencies", the one who attracts "negative" attributes, the feminine (Irigaray: 1985b, p. 207). (The indifferent is, above all, boring.)

It is hardly surprising that this should be so, post-modernism is a masculine theory that posits difference as a foil for its own indifference to the world and to others.

The Other is also valorised. Disconnected as post-modern theorists are from the Other, the Other is capitalised to show its otherness, that is, says the post-modernist, not me; I'm not one of them.

The Other (anybody outside the peer group of post-modernists) and the indifferent (women), should, according to post-modern theory, stay out there, should not exist. Nor should they write books that claim centrality for the author (the author is dead, remember), or for the class of woman (woman does not exist, remember). Nor should they speak of solidarity, sameness, connectedness. The different, the differánt, the masculine, will prevail. And through this valorising of difference comes an overwhelming indifference.

How does post-modern theory change our lives? If we become so differentiated that we fear to speak up on behalf of one another, how will we ever effect political change? If we seek out absences, what then of consciousness? If we seek the gaps without paying attention to what is there in reality (whether in the real mind, the real body, the real world), we will fail to see that the world is becoming more violent, more masculinised, more indifferent each day. If we disengage then we will fail to hear the words of real women from all around the world who are working to change their daily conditions.

Through differentiation and the power of difference, come old powers (cross)dressed in new clothes. There is the old power of heterosexuality, crossdressed in queer sexual practice: sado-masochism, transvestivism, transsexuality, straight queers, lesbian queers, lesbian boys, butch and femme and paedophilia. There is the old power of sexual domination based on difference, so that radical feminist sexuality can be proclaimed: boring, prudish, all the same.

Other old powers dressed up by post-modernism include: Eurocentrism: you can't be a post-modernist if you haven't read Nietzsche, Freud, Lacan, Derrida, Foucault, Baudrillard, Deleuze, Bataille. For all the talk of margins, it's strange how these names congregate in western Europe; Androcentrism: you can't be a post-modernist if you haven't read Nietzsche, Freud, Lacan, Derrida, Foucault, Baudrillard, Deleuze, Bataille. You *can* be a post-modernist if you haven't read Kristeva, Cixous, Irigaray; but if that's all you've read, you're probably not a proper post-modernist. As a radical feminist, I prioritise books by women, because I want to find out more about my culture, my history, the history of fifty-one percent of the world's population. But if I quote only women in my scholarship, I'm called essentialist. If they quote only men? If I were from an endangered ethnic group, would I be accused of essentialism, if I read only works by my compatriots? Women are an endangered cultural group, and have been for the past 2000–5000 years.

The words and works of women through the ages give meaning to my life. (And I should point out that the fluidity of perspective granted by post-modern theory has been practised by writers for thousands of years. Think of the different points of view in the work of poets as ancients as Sappho; think of Virginia Woolf's technique in *The Waves* – and there are many others.) Post-modern writers, men and women, quote predominantly men. Any of the above list will do. To erase, once again, the words of women, so soon after we've found them, is to eradicate that sense of meaning; it is to scrub our memory clean; it is like burning the words of Sappho again; it is a return to indifference.

> In post-modernism the real absences are:
> the absence of real women
> the absence of a politics that will change the world
> the absence of challenge to domination and oppression
> the absence of commitment
> the absence of women's voices
> the absence of meaning
> the absence of wildness

The Problem with Epilepsy
Epilepsy is one of those difficult to classify examples of the body/mind self: it is and isn't a disability; it is and isn't invisible; it is and isn't the body; it is and isn't the

mind. In this regard it challenges our assumptions about ourselves, and it extends our need for theory. For theory that is not caught in an absence since, anyone familiar with this experience will confirm, absence and epileptic indifference are static conditions. They produce conservative and reactionary responses. They are states of dullness.

(a) It is and isn't a disability

Is
• It is temporarily disabling in various degrees from mildly to severely. For some, the frequency of these temporary disablings means that they are life-disabled, that is, they cannot live in ways others take for granted. There are prohibitions on: driving, some forms of employment, scuba diving and other sports and activities.

> Patience, they all say –
> Insensitive to your needs. Don't
> Learn to drive, don't
>
> Ever fly, or
> Parachute, or scuba dive
> Since each could mean the end of
>
> You. But what of life?
> (Hawthorne: 1993a, p. 120).

Isn't
• In between seizures, the epilepsy may be totally invisible. For some this means an apparently normal life and almost normal lifestyle, although "apparently" is a key word: they may have to avoid alcohol, watching television, long periods of sleeplessness. Photosensitive fits build up in different ways from other fits.

> It can take
> a different amount of time
> depending
> on the element triggering the fit
> for the seizure
> to actually happen.
> The aura
> could be anterior
> as much as a day,
> an hour, a minute
> or
> just a few seconds.

ALTERNATIVELY,
THERE CAN BE
A TOTAL LACK OF AURA
AND THE ACTUAL SEIZURE CAN SEEM,
FOR A WITNESS,
INSTANTANEOUS.
RED AND BLACK
(Delmotte: 1993).

Is

•   The social stigma is still a major factor for many people – few grasp the political nature of coming out due to "normalised" environments and expectations. That is, there are no lesbian epileptics, at least that is the assumption. Like lesbians, those with epilepsy may not know anyone else with whom they can share their feelings and experiences. The formation of community is not easy.

Isn't

•   Some of these prohibitions may have little or no impact. Not many people want to go parachuting; others, such as driving, may be lifted after fit free periods.

Is

•   The internalisation of the stigma can make some people very timid and frightened. My voice and body shook the first time I spoke the word. I have had other people come and talk to me, after a reading, and I have seen them shake too; and I have had to lean closer to hear the whispered words.

Isn't

•   The social stigma has shifted slightly in recent years as some begin to see the parallels with other oppressions. For example, both lesbians and those with epilepsy may be the only members of their families in these communities; they may also have to decide whether or not to come out. The most recent thesaurus prompted this poem:

Epilepsy

> see *spasm*
>   *frenzy*
>   *nervous disorders*

> Embedded near *spasm* are: convulsion and orgasm
>   fit and seizure
> *Under the general head of **Agitation***

> *I find* frenzy *under the general heading of* **Insanity**
>> only a semi-colon or two separates me from
>>> *alcoholism*
>>> *unintelligibilty*
>>> *hysteria*
> and a variety of manias
> And this is the New Edition!
> (Hawthorne: 1993a, p. 181).

(b) It is and isn't visible

Is

• When it is visible, for example in the case of "grand mal" seizures, it is highly visible. There is no escaping it. The body falls, jerks; the person may groan, vomit, urinate, defecate. This is visibility in its most vulnerable and embarrassing form.

> I dance
>> She waves her arms about.
>> She falls.
>> Her pupils dilate.
>> Her teeth bite into the tongue.
> I am dancing.
>> Her face is blue.
>> Like the blue of cyanide.
> I rampage.
> I rage.
> (Hawthorne: 1993a, p. 123).

Isn't

• Between seizures, epilepsy is invisible. I have a sense of being an "imposter" when I speak of epilepsy as a disability. It is not the word we need, as it is a fluctuating state. Also its visibility may depend on the people around. It may not be visible to the one having the seizures.

> Still not believing
> I stand in front
> of the mirror
> stretching to see
> the teeths' marks.
>
> Unconvinced, I
> want a witness,
> though the body

shows its experience
I am no witness to it.
(Hawthorne: 1994b).

(c) It is and isn't the body

Is

· The body is visibly affected in manifestations of epilepsy (even mild absences, which others might not notice, affect the eyes). Muscles convulse, teeth bite into the tongue, the body may go rigid, or fall and be bruised. The after-effects include sore muscles; bitten tongues, bruises and it may result in secondary injuries such as burns, cracked or broken bones. Sometimes people die as the result of fits, either as a direct result of the fit, or because the person was driving, climbing, walking beside a cliff, crossing a road.

> Death shoves me from behind,
> I turn but cannot see death's
> face in this dark corner.
>
> It hauls me across the room,
> head banging against the tiled
> floor, there is the dull thud
> of a body falling.
>
> Legs kick against kitchen
> cupboards. Like a fish out
> of water, the mouth gasps
> in an agony of helplessness.
> (Hawthorne: 1993a, p. 173).

(d) It is and isn't the mind

Is

· During some kinds of seizures, the person is unconscious; others describe heightened senses of fear, or joy.

> You say that in your dream
>   in some kind of fit or seizure
>   you were entrusted with language.
> (Hawthorne: 1993a, p. 156).

Or as Dostoyevsky writes:

> If in that second – that is to say, at the last conscious moment before the fit – he had time to say to himself, consciously and clearly, "Yes, I could give my whole life for this moment," then this moment by itself was, of course, worth the whole of life. (Dostoyevsky: 1968, p. 244).

Isn't
· The body is the site of the effects. And although the brain may be attributed as causing seizures, not all can be physically traced. This is described as idiopathic.

Is
· In a post-epileptic state the mind is conscious, thoughts are present, but there are no words.

> I have no words to answer with
> words
>   fall
>   into the void
> echoes
>   empty
>   of meaning
> simple
>   sounds
>   stroking my waxy ears
>
> I have no words to answer with
> (Hawthorne: 1993a, p. 139).

If the mind is unconscious, to what extent is the mind involved? Is it totally physical? To what extent is language a sign of consciousness? If consciousness is present, and language isn't, is the person a "subject"? Is there will?

> Mother, help me!
> Return to me the words they've taken.
> Colour my memory with images.
> Invent a history for me.
> Mother, help me!
>
> Help me relearn the language
> caught inside my tongue.
> (Hawthorne: 1993a, p. 175).

Wild Rage

As someone who publicly names my disability, epilepsy, I do not fit the assumptions of normality. Similarly as a lesbian I do not fit easily into the dull economy of patriarchy. What is important is the invisibility of my status as a lesbian and as someone with epilepsy. Until they are publicly named, I can pass. But I don't want to pass in the dominant paradigm. I don't want to be a part of dominant culture stupidities. My status gives me another kind of intelligence – intelligence about exclusions once a sexuality or a condition is named. As a white middle-class woman I can enter the domain of dominant culture – that is, until my body gives me away and I have a seizure in public. My body in the epileptic state is untamed. Uncivilised. Wild.

If you've ever been present at a seizure, it can be a frightening experience. And the spectators' terror determines their outlook afterwards. This is changing slowly – thanks to the effort of some individuals – but buckets of water, accusations of drunkenness, mistaken diagnoses of madness, do still occur out there in the public world. This makes me wild.

I don't know whether my epilepsy is genetic or caused by some injury. If it were genetic and genetic screening had been available, would I have been eliminated? Would my mother have succumbed to social and scientific pressure? Would the wild child be eliminated? And if she had refused would she be denied social and medical support if it were required? Similarly, would that support be denied if it were the result of injury? Certainly I'd have been eliminated for both reasons in Nazi Germany, as were other wild elements in the population.

Uncivilised. Wild. Passion. Rage. I am wild. Wild for me brings together the "wild" of wilderness, the "wild" of rage, the "wild" of untamed – whether it be women or culture. The current push to eliminate genetic disorders through screening is to eliminate the wild elements in society. Wild children, wild women need to exist in order to maintain a culture of diversity.

Radical Feminism

In coming out, very publicly, as someone with epilepsy[2] I have been fortunate in having had the parallel experience of coming out as a lesbian. And, depending on the context, one or other is an easier event. In feminist circles it is easier to be a lesbian; in mainstream circles it is easier to be a person with epilepsy. In some contexts, it is better to remain silent about both.

My awareness of radical politics has come through careful thought about the consequences of "the personal is political". It has taken me twenty years to begin to develop the theoretical connections in this area of my personal and political discourse. Without radical feminism, it would have taken longer.

---

2. I do not use the word epileptic, except as an adjective, since it is not a defining characteristic; and in general the only illnesses used in these ways are those considered as having an overwhelming mental element and having negative overtones: cf. an epileptic, a schizophrenic, a paraplegic, a manic depressive, a spastic, a nymphomaniac, a kleptomaniac etc. as against: an arthritic, a peptic, an anginic, a canceric – as you can see I'm having to make up words.

Connectedness, the importance of shared experience, of solidarity in a wilderness where sometimes yours is the only voice have been important in coming to grips with a range of very personal experiences among women of diverse cultural and personal backgrounds. I have not experienced sexual abuse as a child, but that does not mean that I cannot understand that sense of separation, of alienation from the self that sometimes results; and my reaching out to try to understand experiences I have not had are important paths on the way to changing ourselves. I know that only one in a hundred of you will have any personal experience of having epilepsy, nevertheless I hope that you can get an inkling of understanding from my words. Why else talk? Storytelling is the thing that makes us human. We need to tell and to listen to stories, if the world is to become a better place.

During most of the last 2000 years we have heard only a few stories of women's achievements. Mainly they have been men's stories of war, heroism, conquest and all the terrible things that go with these. There are women's stories, old ones and new ones, that we will hear if we have the patience and are not indifferent. Storytelling involves engagement, responsiveness between teller and listener; it presupposes community.

Storytelling is also about the production of meaning. In reading hundreds of books by women over the last twenty years (no I have not read that list of men I mentioned earlier, although, not being a proper post-modernist, I have read the women) I have looked for stories that empower me as a woman, as a lesbian and as someone who has epilepsy (amongst other things). I have found a poem by Sappho, that I read, not simply as a description of desire, but in addition as an account of how it feels to have a seizure,[3] and I have responded with my own rewriting of this poem

---

3. *Sappho. Fragment 31.* Translated by Gillian Spraggs (Spraggs: 1991, p. 55) Of all the translations I have read of this poem, Gillian Spraggs' translation seems to pick up the subtleties best. Here is her version.

He seems to me the peer of gods, that man
who sits and faces you,
close by you hearing
your sweet voice speaking,

and your sexy laugh, which just this moment
    makes
the heart quake in my breast: for every time
I briefly glance towards you, then I lose
all power of further speech.

My tongue is smashed; at once a film of fire
runs underneath my skin; no image shapes
before my eyes;
my ears are whining like a whirling top;

cold sweat pours down me, and in every part
shuddering grips me;
I am paler than summer grass,
and seem to myself to be at the point of death.

based on the experience of seizures.[4] I have read articles that interpret the voices heard by Joan of Arc, as an account of another kind of epilepsy (Foote-Smith and Byrne: 1991). I have read much the same story about Hildegarde of Bingen. And the prophecies of the Delphic oracle have also been described as utterances of post-epileptic priestesses. It doesn't much matter to me whether any of these can be proved. That is not the point. Rather, radical feminism gave me a way to come to understand and draw together different parts of my separated selves. Those separations were, I believe, due to our masculinised culture that taught me to hate the

---

4. Susan Hawthorne (1994). Variations. Unpublished.

i

To me you are divine
as you play your role–
speaking, listening,
laughing that laugh

that runs through me
like an electric current.
The shock, the jolt as I
watch. My voice

dries up; it is hot like sand
in a desert creekbed
and it slides slowly away
from me. My eyes die,

I hear nothing as
lava flows under
my skin. Seized,
my mind flees–

down, down into the
underworld, into a
kind of death.

ii

I watch her, your public face;
I hear her speak the expected words
of coupling love.

Her smile eats at me like acid;
my ribs are scorched and the
heart jolts inside its cage.
When I look at you, heart
emptied, voice hollowed,
now meaningless

I speak empty breath.
My tongue fallow, no
harvest of words

only froth, a dead-eyed
gaze and muscles that
cringe convulsively.

My mind quivers, retreats
toward death, and I know
that only death is an end.

iii

Fortune has deserted me today
as I watch the one sitting
face to face with you

Across the room I listen as
words and laughter fall
from your lips

My heart becomes a
jolting carriage and my
tongue is electrified by

fear. Fire runs through
my veins and I can no longer
hear your words, your laughter,

for the humming in my ears.
I convulse, and sweat
runs cool down my face,

drained of colour–
death would be better
than this jealousy.

different parts; taught me and many others to cover it with a veneer of self-protective indifference; taught us all to disengage and to eradicate meaning from our lives.

Post-modernism is intent on all these things, in particular in disengagement from the self (so that we will enjoy abuse of the body and not object to sado-masochism in all its forms); in a denial of our shared experience (so that we will not experience the joy of solidarity, of sisterhood, of community – all of which are enhanced by diversity); in disengagement from political practice (so that we will become fragmented communities, committed to nothing but violence and the same old abusive uses of power, crossdressed or not); to the fragmentation of society (so that we will not assume any commonality with women from other countries or cultures or other times; again we will lose our history); to the silencing of all peoples because of the erection of artificial centres (so that we in the southern hemisphere, on the rim of the Pacific or anywhere not deemed the centre, will never be able to assume others know anything about us at all; or those of us called epileptic, schizophrenic, or whatever newly invented label, will feel the same).

What is lacking in these theories of indifference is the wild joy of existence. The most pervasive thing about the post-seizure state is that you couldn't care less about who you are, where you are, or what is going on around you. So indifferent are you to your surroundings that names for people become interchangeable. One can easily be "dragged" from one place to another and it has little impact on the psyche. In this corpse-like state you believe anything – literally.

On the other hand once the mind is awake again and has shrugged off that oppressive dullness, a kind of wild joy is possible. The body, the mind is stimulated, seeking, wild with energy and possibilities. Remember the wildness of consciousness-raising groups (the wild anger, the wild fun of graffiti, the wild dancing at the first women's dances, the thoroughly wild ideas each of us had about history, about art and culture, about nature and about ourselves, the wild possibilities we had to work towards.)

I would like to propose a wild politics that knocks theories of indifference off their feet. Wild politics incorporates a range of ideas about economics, people, poetry and the land. I know it will make some people wild with rage, but for those of you who are tired of dullness, indifference, and strangled imaginations I suggest a daring strategy, one that produces new worlds and new theories to live by based on wild politics.

Wild Politics – A Manifesto[5]
The New Economic World Order is the last of a long line of coercive methods of control. The process of industrialisation has been a process of ever-increasing

---

5. At the Peoples' Perspectives on "Population" conference held in Comilla, Bangladesh, December 12–15, 1993. See Hawthorne: 1993c. Many thanks to all the women there whose ideas and discussions were central to the writing of this piece. See also UBINIG, this volume, pp. 519–24.

interference in the lives of people – from structured and alienated work for wages to the medicalisation of women's bodies and souls, now extended to interference with life processes. The New Economic World Order is very like the New Intellectual World Order of Post-structuralism, Post-colonialism, Post-feminism. It is about controlling the ideas of uppity wild people, amongst them women, Indigenous peoples, the disabled, lesbians and anyone marginalised by limited access to the resources of wealth, power and information.

Patriarchal capitalism seeks to control the wild elements that have, up until now, resisted control. We need to develop a wild politics to resist control over these wild elements including: wild seeds, wild land, wild farming, wild peoples, wild women, wild reproduction, wild sexuality and wild markets. Patriarchal intellectualism seeks to control the imaginative construction of wild ideas through poetry, outrageous acts of artistic invention, outrageous and wild political acts (e.g the Guerilla Girls), and the inventions of a world so new that it is only a shimmer at the edge of consciousness.

Wild Types

Wild types is a term used in genetics that identifies unregulated genetic structures. Wild types occur in all living organisms and are not the result of human interference through breeding or hybridisation. Wild types are the source of genetic diversity and critical to the continuing biological diversity of the planet. Wild types include all kinds of people who add imagination and diversity to the world, who challenge the stale and the dull, who engage with life and politics, who rage and who are wild.

Wild Seeds

Wild seeds are the seeds of plants that remain in the hands of people who use them for subsistence or a self-sustaining lifestyle. Wild seeds are in evidence in every country, culture and geographical region of the world. Traditional Aborigines use wild seeds and their products to produce food, medicines, resin, implements, decoration and cultural products. The people of India use the Neem tree for over 200 different purposes. The Amazonian peoples use wild plants to sustain their lives. Traditional healers use wild products – seeds, herbs, roots – to heal the body. Indigenous peoples and peasants from all over the world used wild seeds and wild plants. These seeds and plants are under threat from the TRIPS policy of the latest round of GATT, which threatens to control this source of diversity through a universal application of the US patent law.

Wild seeds are also the kernel of a new thought, a new insight that grows and spreads wildly across the planet (Hawthorne: 1992, p. 65). Feminism is such a seed. In spite of the forces ranged against it feminism has taken off around the world like wild fire. The forces ranged against such seeds of thought, in the guise of intellectual prowess, include: the prowess of obscurity, the luxury of theory divorced from action and political change; the security of indifference, and the accumulative power of commercialisation.

Wild Land

Wilderness regions and commons are lands that remain untamed and outside the ambit of private ownership. Wilderness areas are harvested through collecting and hunting by their traditional collective owners for medicinal and food stuffs. Wilderness is land not subjected to invasive methods of cultivation. A wilderness is minimally affected by human intervention in its ecosystems and it sustains a wide range of wild seeds, wild plants and wild animals.

The foundation of diversity through commonality comes about through wild theory. Anecdote, storytelling and reflection on experience produce insights which sustain the psyche and move one to action. These ideas are not subjected to comparison with the dominant paradigm that tends to co-opt imagination for commercial purposes, then destroys the imaginative seed of the idea through intellectual R&D. Nor are they checked for commercial usefulness and profit. Rather the production of meaning and purpose is integral to their growth. Wild theories are dynamic and flexible, instead of being pursued in museums of indifferent learning, maintained to uphold the dominant paradigm. Wild theory allows for diversity and disagreement, but it does not allow intellectual abuse or violence.

Wild Farming

Wild farming is productive work done for the purpose of subsistence. Wild farming depends on a detailed knowledge of local conditions and of the environment. Wild farming is self-sustaining, non-invasive and regenerative. Examples include mosaic burning patterns developed by Aborigines, use of medicinal substances extracted from plants and animals, irrigation based on natural cycles of flooding, hunting and herding small numbers of animals.

Wild farming is related to wild thinking, which depends on a detailed knowledge of oneself and one's social and cultural context. Wild thinking is productive and leads to exchanges with other thinkers.

Wild Peoples

Minority populations, indigenous and tribal peoples are considered "wild" peoples by bodies such as the Genome Project. They are subjected to many kinds of tests, such as scraping from the inside of cheeks as a method of collecting banks of genetic information on human gene pools. Having suffered genocidal policies through murder, environmental destruction, removal from their lands and cultural and linguistic annihilation, this is just one more policy threatening the existences of these peoples. They are regarded by multinational institutions as wild peoples because they resist being drawn into the capitalist market economy, as they adhere to a politics rooted in reverence for the land, its resources and its ecology.

The removal from cultural and linguistic traditions that has accompanied the dispossession of the majority of the world's people has led to cultural imperialism on a scale never before encountered. This imperialism includes Coca Cola,

McDonalds, the spread of communications networks (in particular CNN television) and the spread of dominant paradigm theories such as racism, sexism and post-industrial post-theories. At precisely the time when indigenous peoples are speaking out against the system and writing it, suddenly the author is dead! There is no longer anything but absences and text. There is little more than the dullness of a blank page or the pseudo-liberation of electronic bulletin boards and virtual realities.

Wild Women

Women are regarded as wild types because they too, until recently, have remained a small part of the market economy, and in large numbers they still produce what is regarded as unproductive work connected to the household, rearing, caring and cultivating. There are many wild women writing books, creating theory and imagining new kinds of worlds. A new history of the world is being written, new approaches to economics and science, new ways of writing. But wild women are rarely quoted on the TV screens that flicker in every living room or hut in the world. Women are also wild because again, until recently, reproduction has remained an untamed and uncontrolled aspect of existence. Women's wildness is under threat from coercive population control policies, from the new reproductive and contraceptive technologies and from a host of other medicalisations of our lives.

With so-called assisted reproduction methods there are increasing levels of control over all aspects of life. Children are also prevented by more and more invasive means including the pill, IUDs, Norplant, Depo-Provera, and sterilisation. Assisted reproduction includes: IVF, GIFT, microinjection, amniocentesis, chorionic villi sampling, ultrasound and the mechanisations of birth (Klein: 1989). All of these procedures control who is born and add value to the resulting child through R&D, labour and technical interference. The intended result is that no wild children – no children with visible or hidden disabilities – be born. Such children, because of their disabilities, are regarded as expendable because they too cannot easily be drawn into the market economy and productive waged labour.

Wild Reproduction

This is still the norm, but with increasing interference and intervention in reproduction, wild reproduction will become a rebellion and a resistance. Refusal to subject oneself to genetic screening for "unwanted" or "undesirable" genes such as femaleness will result in sanctions. In particular, where such refusal is followed by the birth of a wild disabled child, no social services will be provided. Wild reproduction means not knowing and refusing to know the sex or genetic characteristics of a child. Wild reproduction allows for wild types.

Wild children and wild adults use direct language to describe themselves. They describe themselves with words that make others wild, words that are not euphemisms or which erase them. They use words like crippled (Mairs: 1990; Mairs: 1992) or mad (Jeffs: 1993), words that do not allow for silence or for the luxury of ignoring the experience. They use words like torture. Wild people name unequivocally the world they experience.

Wild Sexuality

Wild sexuality is sexuality that refuses to conform to the model of eroticisation of differences. This means a refusal to play the power games expected of women and men, or refusal to imitate these models. Wild sexuality refuses patriarchal definitions of institutions such as marriage, heterosexuality, dominance/submission sexualities and sexualities that commodify others – amongst them prostitution, sex tourism, pornography and marketed sex commodities such as the "toys" and implements of sado-masochism.

Those who engage in wild sexuality also speak directly. They use words like lesbian. They don't mince words about the equation of torture with sado-masochism and other dominance/submission sexualities. They resist and name the luxury of saying no during sexual torture and equate it with the appropriation of torture unwillingly experienced under repressive political regimes (Hawthorne: 1991). They compare it with the luxury of indifferent theories that ignore the painful realities of daily life. They do not seek to separate sexuality and daily life through the performance of titilating rituals which commodify intimacy. Wild sexuality is joyful and each engages with the other on a range of levels including the body, the mind, the history and memory, the present and the future.

Wild Markets

Some economies exist outside the mainstream. Wild markets are markets not based on monetary exchange. They include reciprocal arrangements between people or donated labour or goods, donated not on the basis of tax deductibility or on self-serving notions of "aid". Wild markets include the exchange of information between wild women and/or wild peoples engaging in wild politics. Wild markets include exchanges between communities engaging in wild farming.

Wild markets are analogous to wild conversation that may emerge as the result of wild thinking or as a part of wild sexuality. These are exchanges that are not carried on to get the better of someone, that are not "negotiations" between the powerless and the powerful, that are not about consenting to another's viewpoint against one's will. They are free interchanges that create energy. Wild conversations can occur in a range of settings and they emerge when each person is accorded the respect of the listener or group. There are no hidden agendas in wild conversation, and the variation in power is minimised.

Wild Politics

Wild politics embraces a wild philosophy and refuses co-option into patriarchal and capitalist institutions as outlined above. It resists the backlash and the silencing of wild women in every quarter, including in academia. It resists the eradication of meaning through the creation of stories and taking political stances seriously. Wild politics is life affirming, values diversity, self-reliance, creativity, and the sustaining of cultural traditions that support equality. Wild politics is rooted in the earth and in knowledge of local conditions and environments, and encourages respect. Wild politics encourages productivity and exchange that gives as much (or more) as it takes, and is not based on growth and accumulation of property or power. Wild politics is feminist and in keeping with the resistances of Indigenous peoples, the poor and the marginalised. It resists Coca Cola colonisation and accumulation, over consumption, fundamentalist and repressive ideologies, mass communications, the military and interference by international scientific, monetary and cultural elites. Wild politics is a politics of joy.

Santa Barbara
Rape Crisis Centre

Mission Statement*

We, the women and men of the
Santa Barbara Rape Crisis Center,
believe sexual assault is destructive
to the lives of survivors, their
families and friends, and to our
society. Sexual assault is an
unacceptable, unconscionable form
of oppression which must be
eradicated from our culture and
from all cultures where it exists.

     The Santa Barbara Rape
Crisis Center is dedicated to helping
people survive the trauma of sexual
assault and to eliminating this
brutal crime from our society.

     To fulfill this mission, the
Santa Barbara Rape Crisis Center
provides:

1. crisis intervention, counselling,
   advocacy and support for sexual
   assault survivors and their family
   members and friends in order to
   assist in their healing process.
2. community education and
   prevention programs to increase

El Centro
Contra la Violación

Declaración de Propósito

Nosotros, las mujeres y hombres del
Centro Contra la Violación, creemos que
el asalto sexual destruye la vida: la vida
de personas que han sobrevivido un asalto,
la vida de familiares y amiga/os de la
(del) sobreviviente, y la vida de nuestra
sociedad. El asalto sexual es una forma de
opresión inaceptable, y por lo tanto tiene
que ser eliminado de nuestra cultura y de
todas las culturas en donde existe.

     El Centro Contra la Violación se
dedica a dar apoyo a mujeres y hombres
para que puedan sobrevivir el trauma de
un asalto sexual y trabaja para eliminar
este crimen brutal de nuestra sociedad.

     Para llevar a cabo estos
propósitos, el Centro Contra la Violación
provee:

1. ayuda durante una crisis, servicios
   de consejeras y consejeros, terapia,
   abogacía y apoyo para sobrevivientes,
   sus familiares y amiga/os.
2. programas de educación. Estos
   programas incrementan el
   conocimiento y el entendimiento del

---

* Originally published in *Outcry* (1994, Mayo/May).

the awareness, empathy and understanding necessary to effect the attitudinal and behavioral changes which are essential to the elimination of sexual assault.

Our Commitment to Diversity

Daily, the Santa Barbara Rape Crisis Center witnesses violence resulting from the oppression of women, children, and others who are denied power in our culture. We recognize sexual assault is a form of violence in which sexual acts are used as weapons to terrorize and dominate people, particularly women. Sexual assault thus perpetuates male power and control over women and those with less power. Our mission in the community is to oppose and eliminate sexual oppression.

We also recognize that all forms of oppression are inherently violent in that they create and maintain inequitable power structures. Thus we affirm that our activities in the community at large and the internal structure of our organization must not promote or condone any form of oppression. Our internal policies must reflect respect for diversity. We must make it possible for all kinds of women to be included and empowered. We welcome the participation of men who share a commitment to these goals. Within our organization, we strive to model a society free of violence and oppression.

asalto sexual y ayudan a crear los cambios de actitud y de comportamiento esenciales para eliminar el asalto sexual.

Nuestro compromiso hacia la diversidad

El Centro Contra la Violación Sexual es testigo diario de la violencia resultante de la opresión de mujeres, niños, y otros grupos a los que se les niega poder en nuestra cultura. Reconocemos el asalto sexual como una forma de violencia en la cual los actos sexuales se emplean como armas para aterrorizar y dominar principalmente a las mujeres. De esta manera, el asalto sexual perpetua el poder masculino y el control sobre mujeres y todos aquellos con menos poder. Nuestra misión en la comunidad es combatir y eliminar la opresión sexual.

Reconocemos también que toda forma de opresión es inherentemente violenta tanto en cuanto crea y mantiene estructuras de poder injustas. Por tanto, afirmamos que no solo nuestras actividades en el conjunto de la comunidad sino también la estructura interna de nuestra organización no debe promover ni acoger ninguna forma de opresión. Nuestro reglamento interno debe reflejar este respeto hacia la diversidad. Debemos hacer posible que toda la diversidad de mujeres sean incluidas y dotadas de poder. Aceptamos con agrado la participación de hombres que comparten estos objetivos. Dentro de nuestra organización, luchamos por modelar una sociedad libre de violencia y opresión.

To this end:

- SBRCC will develop policies which assure the safety, freedom and empowerment of all people.
- SBRCC will work to eliminate oppression in the form of stereotypes, myths, name-calling, blaming, violence, and all expressions of oppression which prevent people from achieving their potential in society and isolate them from each other.
- SBRCC will strive to hear, understand, and validate the lives of all women, including: victims and survivors, lesbians, women of color, women of all ages and physical appearances, differently abled women, women of all religions and spiritual beliefs, women from diverse cultural and economic backgrounds.
- SBRCC endorses an inclusive concept of family which goes beyond the traditional nuclear family. We recognize family as any two or more people bonded by affection and committed to their mutual welfare.

       Working toward these goals will further the rights of all people and insure safety, empowerment and freedom in our daily lives.

Con este fin:

- El Centro Contra la Violación Sexual desarrollara reglamentos que garantizan la seguridad, libertad e igualdad de poder a todos los individuos.
- El Centro Contra la Violación Sexual trabajara por eliminar la opresión en forma de estereotipos, mitos, palabras derogatorias, violencia y todas aquellas expresiones de opresión que impiden que la gente alcance su potencial en la sociedad y que los aísla de los demás.
- El Centro Contra la Violación Sexual luchara por escuchar, entender, y validar la vida de toda mujer, incluyendo: victimas y sobrevivientes, lesbianas, mujeres de color, mujeres de cualquier edad y apariencia física, mujeres capacitadas diferentemente, mujeres de cualquier religión y credo espiritual, mujeres que proceden de diversos marcos económicos y culturales.
- El Centro Contra la Violación Sexual apoya un concepto inclusivo de familia que va más allá del concepto tradicional de familia nuclear. Reconocemos como familia cualquier relación de dos o mas personas unidas por su afecto y su cometido hacia un mutuo bienestar.

       Nuestros esfuerzos hacia estos objetivos refuerzan los derechos de toda la gente y nos proporcionan seguridad, poder y libertad en nuestra vida diaria.

Powhiri Rika-Heke/Sigrid Markmann

Common Language – Different Cultures: True or False?

We have a story or three to tell – hers, hers, and ours. These are stories of disjoint but parallel pathways, which have led to a common and integrated journey. We don't know where this journey will end but we're determined to enjoy ourselves getting there.

Powhiri

My story began before my birth in the Chinese year of the monkey. I am a child of Ngatihine, Ngapuhi, Te Rarawa, Te Aupouri, Ngatikahu. I must also admit to a few white sheep which I shall keep, for this article, firmly in the closet. The founding ancestor of Ngatihine, the iwi I feel most connected to because of its female beginnings, was a beautiful, strong and powerful woman called Hineamaru. Her blood flows through my veins and the veins of all her people. Through her, the women of my iwi are also beautiful, strong and powerful.

While it may be true that many other iwi actively prevent the female members of their respective nations from having a public voice, it is not my experience of my iwi. We speak, as our men do, on occasions of importance or when the need arises. However, this is not to say that some of our men, who have been seduced by the patriarchy of pakeha society, do not proceed to relegate Maori women to a position of subjugation and servitude – a position which western patriarchy has forced many of its female members to endure. It cannot be denied that our world has been greatly affected by these notions of superiority which some people, of the male persuasion, who possess a rather troublesome appendage, feel is their god-given right.

Because of the notions created by pakeha socialization, which some of my people have adopted with a passion, we continue to try to rectify the results of these processes which have been imposed over the past one hundred and seventy years or more. While the roles of the Maori men and women of my iwi are not equal or the same, they are complementary and neither is more important than the other. Though I, not so secretly, believe that women are more important to the survival and strength of my people because we bear, raise, nurture and educate the children and matrilineage is always easier to prove. Now I have a story within this story.

Daddy is waiting at the back door. He stands, with hobnail-booted feet, astride. His Al Capone hat, with holes – made by a machine-gun during the war Daddy says – hugs his head. It must be hard for Daddy – he's really my grandfather – trying to raise me by himself. Not that I'm any bother. At least I don't think I am.

"Are you day-dreaming again?" He hitches his trousers. "I'll go without you," he adds, moving off to the front gate.

I struggle to get my gumboots on, tripping and tropping along so I don't get left behind.

"Taihoa, Daddy! Wait for me! I can't get my hoha boots on!"

Daddy strides along the road to the hall. I reach his side after a short sprint, slip my hand into his, and enjoy the sound of a new morning. Even the sun peeping over Te Tarai o Rahiri is noisy with its brightness. We don't talk. We just scuff and clip along, kicking at stones because they're there. The clump clump of our boots on the road fills my ears. Daddy whistles. I'm sooo happy . . .

. . . Daddy moves off to where the men are standing against the fence. They're laughing at some joke, punching each other on the arm, smoke curling into the crisp moring air. The women shuffle near the hall door, yarning, laughing, slapping at tangi-weto kids and smoking too . . . They move off to Aunty Mere's where kai will be prepared. The kids are trailing behind, giggling and laughing, chasing each other into the teatree. They'll be crying soon, those hupe kids. They always end up fighting and running off to tell tales. Tell-tale-tits! Wouldn't catch me telling tales – I like to sort things out myself.

I follow Daddy over to Archie and Uncle Mane. Our "beanpole" teacher has gone off to grease up to Aunty Mere and the other women. Shet! There's that cheeky Johnny Poto. What's he doing here? He should be with those little kids. Don't poke your tongue out at me, Johnny Poto, you tiko heihei.

"Well, Pussynose, you'd better go with Aunty Mere. The workers will be pretty hungry by smoko." Daddy's words interrupt my eye-fight with Johnny.

"But they're doing cooking and stuff and I want to work in the barn with . . ." my voice trembles. I take a deep breath. "Daddy, the other boys are going to be working and Johnny Poto's going, see! And, I'm stronger than him AND I can give him a hiding too!"

"I know, Baby, but I want you to make me some scones for smoko. You make better scones than those other women and I only like to eat yours. So, you run along and make me some beaut scones so those other fullas will be jealous."

"Oh, Daddy," I almost cry, clutching at his arm, "please . . ."

"Look, when we do our place you can help then, but not this time, okay?"

"You promise, Daddy? You not telling tekas?" He shakes his head, turns, and walks off toward the other men who are moving to the first paddock. The sun is already hot and sweat glistens on faces and shoulders. That purari paka, Johnny Poto, is poking out his tongue again and making his face ugly. I hope the wind changes. Kaitoa then!

"Okay, Daddy. See You."

"Hooray, Baby. You make those scones nice and fluffy." His voice fades as I break into a run to catch up with my aunties and those hoha kids.

"When I grow up I'm going to be a man and then I won't have to do the cooking!" I don't know why the women laugh as I walk briskly, head held high, amongst them. "And just you wait 'til I'm big, Johnny Poto, just you wait!"

It didn't really happen like that but I did have a grandfather who raised me and taught me that I could be anything and do anything I wanted to do. He was also protective of me around people who were hooked into socially constructed roles based on gender. He tried to ensure that I wasn't hurt by the narrow views of others, by creating situations like the one described in the story . . ."You make better scones than those other women and I only like to eat yours".

The truth was that I actually made terrible scones as a kid and they're not much improved now. My Daddy was the cook in our family and made beautiful fluffy scones. He tried to teach me how to make these wonderful creations by setting up two lots of ingredients on our kitchen bench. Everything he did I would do. His scones were soft, light delicacies while mine were like little briquettes, and sometimes even the same colour. In his retirement he was often surrounded by his other grandchildren and was a regular baby-sitter to infants of less than a year old. He was not a man who didn't know how to bath, feed, burp and change a baby.

I saw all these things my cow-cocky, conservative-voting grandfather did. I also saw my aunts taking their rightful places beside their husbands when cows needed to be rounded up for milking, when fences had to be built or mended, when the tractors or the trucks had to be used around the farm. I listened to the women in my family making major decisions about the purchase or sale of the livestock, the new farm machinery, the modernization of the milking machines, the construction of the new pigsty, whether or not to drain the paddocks near the orchards, and I learned that there were roles for men and women other than those prescribed by the state and its social engineers. I learned to question power structures and to actively challenge them, not only in the pakeha world but also within my own iwi. I've learned to work on two fronts. Challenging the male-dominated power structures as well as power structures which are monocultural and inherently racist.

As one of the few Maori woman who was able to indulge herself in pakeha feminist groups, such as the Women's Studies Association of New Zealand, I often found myself in inenviable situations. Very few Maori women could afford the luxury of going off to a conference for a weekend because they were concerned with the real-life struggles often associated with the under-class of many societies.

Will the children be able to take any lunch to school today? Will we be evicted because we're behind with our rent? Will my partner beat me because he's frustrated? How can I ask the family for more money when we haven't paid the last lot back? How can I take the baby to a doctor if I can't pay – again? These are questions which many feminists have never considered because of the privileged positions they have within society. So, it often caused a dilemma for me at such conferences when feminist issues, which I wanted to hear about or discuss, were scheduled at the same time as issues pertinent to me as a Maori woman. It was even worse when I had to choose between going to a seminar for lesbians or a seminar for Maori women. On such occasions I would opt for the Maori group. This was the group I perceived to be the least empowered.

International conferences caused me the same problems. My seminar choices were also determined by race rather than, necessarily, by issues. I've always thought it more important to show my support for the most disadvantged group. In feminist circles I experienced this group to be women of colour/Black/First Nations. It would be wonderful not to have to face these dilemmas, but until all feminists deal with the issues of racism, not only within society as a whole, but also within the feminist movement in particular, this will be a source of constant irritation and frustration for many feminists.

Black German

Look at me
I'm a black woman
This is my country too

Hear me
This language is my mother tongue
My mothering tongue

See my daughter
She is black
Her language is of this country
She is of this country
People
White people
White people born in this country
If they talk to me
Talk to me as a stranger
A foreigner
A visitor
A tourist
To their country

They do not see
Nor do they want to see
That there are black people
Who are of their country
Whose parentage
At least some of it
Is as white as their own

Some people
Some white people
Some white people who do not know me
Who do not know my family tree
Who do not see my white mother in me
They
They want to kill me
Or those who look like me

They want to kill me because
My hair is crinkly
My eyes are brown
My skin is black

These people do not care
That the language they speak
Is my first language
The language of my mother
My grandmother
My grandfather

These people do not care
That this is my country
That this is the only country I know
The country I have worked for
The country I love
But it is not a country I would die for

These people do not know
These people do not care
It's as simple as that

I totally support the notion of global sisterhood and have worked, in my own way, to bridge the gaps between my white sisters and my sisters of colour. It's been a precarious path to tread, trying to see both sides of an issue unclouded by preconceived prejudices and biased generalizations. Though I've not always been able to maintain an impartiality, being a Gemini has probably helped me to do this but at other times has caused me to become even further confused. I also see that much of our oppression as women can be directly attributed to men who maintain their power through the institutions, ideologies, systems and structures which they have constructed for the precise purpose of sustaining their powerful positions in the world and keeping women subordinate. I've also been able to make choices about the way I live my life so that men disturb my existence as little a possible.

I'm not anti-white but I am pro-Maori, pro-First Nations. While I'm not anti-men, I am pro-women. I am prepared to work with the men in my family so that they become pro-feminist. I don't put up with sexist remarks from any men and am not afraid to openly and publically challenge them. I am unconcerned by how men see me. I figure that if my National-voting, dairy farmer grandfather could love me and support me in my life convictions then everyone else can go jump. I've never been a "good" public servant because hierarchies and people in positions of power have never intimidated me. My grandfather pointed out to me, when I was quite young, that even the Queen's shit stinks. A bit crude for some, I'm sure, but he did have a point. That's my story.

Sigrid

I was born in Germany during World War II. My parents showed much civil courage during the time of the Third Reich which resulted in my father living in exile for the duration of the war and for several years afterwards. My mother, who endured the war in the land of her birth, with a small child to care for by herself, was only able to be with my father on a few occasions. My father had to move in and out of Germany, during the war years, like a thief in the night. His refusal to join the Nazi Party or to work with them in any way marked him as a traitor.

My mother showed her defiance in more subtle, but equally dangerous, ways. We lived in an apartment building in the coal mining city of Dortmund. During the time of the Third Reich the people were "encouraged" to celebrate Adolph Hitler's birthday and other similar occasions, by flying the Swastika – that very public symbol of Nazism – from their windows, balconies, roof-tops, anywhere which was appropriate. In the apartment, where we lived, was a woman, a friend of my parents, who was a senior member of the local Nazi Party. One of her jobs was to ensure that the apartment occupants observed the occasions of Nazi pride by displaying the Swastika. On one such occasion my mother's friend paid her a visit to tell her that she must observe the Führer's birthday by flying the national flag. My mother replied that she was "flying" the flag and proceeded to show her friend a tiny, no bigger than 40 sq.cm., Swastika which she had placed in the corner of her window. Of course, both women knew that this "show" of patriotism was more of an insult than a celebration. My mother was able to point out, quite truthfully, though both women knew it was not the real reason, that she did not have the financial means to honour the Führer with a bigger flag. I think that, had it not been for the friendship between these two women, my mother may very well have suffered for her defiance.

My family was finally reunited in 1949 and my development as "a bit of a rebel" was, if not encouraged by my parents, at least supported by their convictions that I should think for myself and believe in my own individuality. I played football with the boys in our street. Mutti didn't like that I often came home with torn dresses and skinned knees but she never said I shouldn't or couldn't play football. My father was proud of my athletic abilities and encouraged me to throw and catch, as well as to run and jump, and kick a football.

During my last year at high school I was appointed as Speaker for the School. This was to be my undoing as far as my high school career went. At a very public occasion I made an impassioned speech about the corruptness of some of the teachers who abused their positions and actively worked against students they disliked by marking exam papers in a non-objective way. During that same speech I also challenged the system which continued to ignore – even in a mining district – the lives of working-class people, perpetuating the myth that middle class was the only valid class. I also spoke out against the narrow conservatism of the curriculum which did little to validate the aspirations of students who were more technically inclined. After that speech I realized that too many of my teachers would make the rest of my time at school difficult and, after leaving the stage I continued walking right out the door. I haven't been back to that school since.

My mother received a big bouquet of flowers that afternoon and my father came home from work early to be with his daughter, who had left school without a high school qualification. Both my parents were, understandably, disappointed but agreed to support me in my decision to leave school. However, they were also quite determined that I would have to live with the consequences of my decisions and encouraged me to get a job.

The next few years found me working in Belgium, France and England, during which time I attended classes, as an adult student, and studied for my Abitur, the qualification for admittance to university. I attended university during which time I secured a scholarship which took me, among other places, to a Navajo Reservation in Arizona. That time offered me an intimate insight into the struggles of peoples torn from their heritages by all-powerful, self-righteous, blatantly racist authorities – both the state government of Arizona and the federal government of the United States of America.

What I saw on that reservation, what I learned from the friends I had made there, enabled me to see, even more clearly than I had previously, the history that I had to live with as a German – the history of the Third Reich. This strengthened the growing convictions I was developing that I, as a German, would strive to ensure that the voices of marginalized peoples would never again be silenced.

My first real oportunity to do something positively constructive in order to realize my commitment to empower peoples disadvantaged by power cultures occured not long after I had left primary and secondary teaching to take up a position at the university, I was invited, along with another collegue, to develop a state supported curriculum on non-sexist education. I was also working with a small group of women in our city to establish the first home for abused women. My theoretical politics were becoming my lived politics.

Several years ago I realized that the English literature taught in our university, and probably in most universities throughout the world was deficient in that the selection of material deemed suitable for university study was too narrow. I saw that the literature selected continued the myth that white US/European middle-class male was the only valid and worthy literature. Because our university was one of the new "reform" universities of the 70s, it was easier for my colleagues and I, in the English Department, to introduce the literatures which had been, thus far, absent from most university programmes. We were aware of the fact that it was Europeans, in the main, who were and are still, to some extent, responsible for the atrocities perpetrated against Indigenous peoples. Racism is a European export. We, therefore, felt it not only necessary but also an obligation for us, as Europeans to participate in an education of our own peoples so that we could end the violations ourselves.

For me, as a European, the terms "radical feminism" and "decolonization" don't only mean ridding ourselves of the trappings of dominant power structures; they mean, above all, shifting the focus of perception and seeking non-repressive ways to the dominant discourse. As white European women and feminists we have to learn to listen and to respect; to learn our own history so that our Black sisters no longer have to explain what has been done to them. Thus began the Women's Studies courses and the new English literature courses which eventually led me to the literature of Aotearoa/New Zealand and, in particular, to Maori literature in English.

So begins our story. How have we, women from completely disjoint cultures, with unrelated languages, nurtured in different hemispheres, living in each others' antipodes, managed to build a coalition across these boundaries? In a practical sense it has required an enormous amount of energy and adjustment. It has meant that one of us left her place of origin, her land, her family, her country and lives, for some time at least, in a foreign land. It has meant, for both of us, being open to the cultural differences which each brings to our working relationship.

The German concern about rules, regulations, formalities, inflexible time-frames, the "man"-made strictures of living in a densely populated country, has been tempered by an Aotearoa-Maori attitude of nothing is infallible, rules are meant to be bent, time is relative, authorities are not always right and, what does it matter a hundred years from now anyway? At the same time, this seemingly more casual approach has also undergone subtle change whereby goals set are more determinedly sought, the focus sharper, more intense, and actions are fuelled by a need to be successful in an alien land in order to help others achieve success at home. We admit that these "characteristics" of a German woman, and a Maori woman are over-simplified and smack of generalizations, to some degree, however, there is a certain "truth" in them.

While we have these differences and learn to adjust to and accept them, we also have common meeting places which we both arrived at, on our individual journeys, by following different paths. One of these places is our identity as women focussed women and the knowledge that, while we are both relatively "successful" in terms of the positions we occupy within the institutionalized patriarchy, we are also painfully aware that other women are not so positioned simply because they *are* women.

Male Academics I Know

An academic gown
DPhil, History
Maketh the man

Without these trappings
Including the honorific prefixing his name
on his office door
He, is just a boy

Faculty meetings
He quotes, chapter and verse
Regulations for this nothingness
or that nothingness

Some people
admire his ability to
KNOW THE SYSTEM

He is uncompromising
in the interpreting and implementing
of rule this-and-that
paragraph such-and-such
line so-and-so

But,
as I said before
Without his rule books
Regulations
and a "resting-on-his-laurels" doctorate
He,
is just a boy
full of his own self-importance

Powhiri Rika-Heke/Sigrid Markmann

With the limited power we have taken for ourselves, from the institutions which both sustains us and tries to bridle us with the restraints it imposes by way of cumbersome regulations, near-sighted administrators, and gate-keepers who fear the unknown and want to relegate all power to themselves, we will continue to challenge the systems which imprison women, which inhibit their progress, which stifle their development as whole, fulfilled persons. Until every woman's potential is reached and until that state is supported and valued by the patriarchy we, as women, as feminists, as radical feminists must never give up the struggle to free ourselves and our sisters from that oppression.

Sisters

Tuahine,
we are not of the same blood.
Though we both have seafarers in our past
Your line comes from Vikinger times
Mine from Hawaiki.

While I acknowledge the white sheep in my family
that ancestry is of far less significance
in the land I call Aotearoa
and which latterly, you do too.

In acknowledgement of your sensitivity,
to me and my people
I call your country Deutschland,
Munich München, Cologne Köln.

I was asked once, by my black sisters,
"Why do you give so much energy
to those white girls?"
I did not tell them that my kuia, my grandmothers,
had told me I must be a bridge,
a bridge between our people and white people.
I did not tell them that my first thought had been
"But bridges get walked on and worn out".
No, I did not tell them, though I wanted to.
I had to claim my own actions, to live with them,
and to make any adversity my strength.

I've seen the white, middle-class, privileged women
and where they come from.
I've seen the advantages they enjoy,
simply because they're white

I've seen that their struggles are often different from mine
but I've also seen the commonalities we share
as women
as sisters
as mothers
as daughters
as a gendered underclass
to patriarchies all over the world.

And so I say,
do not be afraid
to link arms with me
brown and white together
sisters in spirit and soul
white and brown
complementary
sister mine.

Nganampa Health Council and the Ngaayatjarra, Pitjantjatjara and Yankunytjatjara Women's Council Women's Health Project

Our Health Project

- The Women's Health Project is about improving women's health on the Anangu Pitjantjatjara lands.
- Project workers are working with women as they think about their health issues.
- We have women's health meetings.
- We are interviewing all the women health workers and nurses. We listen to their ideas, their problems and the things they say that they need to learn.
- Older women in communities tell us they want to teach Women's Law to younger women.
- Project workers want to help them to carry out their ideas and to get funding to pay for their work.
- Younger women are interested in learning more about their Law.

> I'm a young woman and I'm only learning about the way of women. Because of the work I was doing I have been in the company of older women and we have travelled around, looked at women's sites and blocked them – through meetings – from mining interests. The women have taught me about our Law and so I collect information and become knowledgeable. I was travelling around and working with senior women for three years.

> I'm really glad now that I appreciate the fact that women hold so much knowledge. I am learning it and in return will be able to teach the children coming on, and in turn they will teach. Yes, I want this Women's Project to go for a long time so that I can continue to learn and so that other women who are young will learn and the generation after us and the one after that will learn.

I want our senior women to teach us and our children. The way things are now we are in danger of losing our culture. I'm looking ahead, and writing this so that in the future our kids will be well and strong. I want our culture to stay strong and the Women's Project is a way to help us to achieve this.

My name is Sandra Lewis and my daughter is Sonya.

- The Health workers want to learn more about Women's Law. They say they need this traditional knowledge as they make progress with clinical skills.
- The nurses want to learn more about *anangu* way from the senior women.
- Evaluation is very important in our work. We evaluate as we go.

Tjikilyi learnt about Action Research. She found the model easy to understand and she was able to draw it, teach it to Suzy and Cyndi and apply it to a particular problem. As she worked she began to use Pitjantjatjara words which describe the process very well:

Kulilkatinyi - thinking whilst going along

Nyakukatinyi - looking around whilst going along

Palyalkatinyi - doing whilst going along.

We can see that the Action Research process is a good one to follow for the Women's Project.

Pitjantjatjara and Yankunytjatjara Women's Council

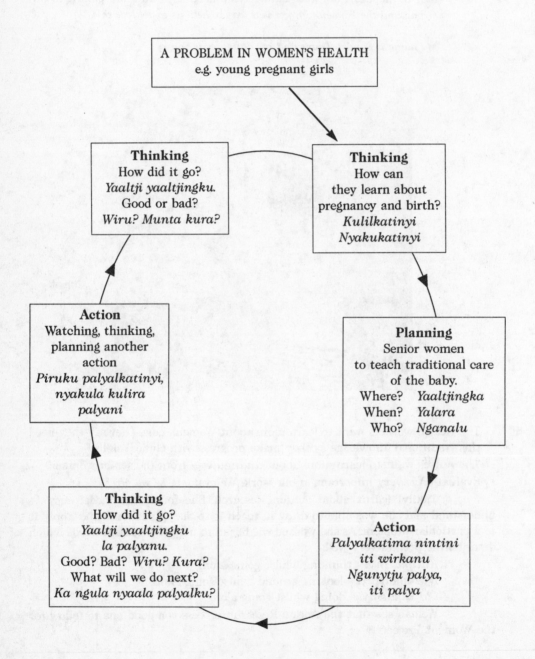

ACTION RESEARCH MODEL
by Tjikilyi

A PROBLEM IN WOMEN'S HEALTH
e.g. young pregnant girls

Thinking
How did it go?
Yaaltji yaaltjingku.
Good or bad?
Wiru? Munta kura?

Thinking
How can
they learn about
pregnancy and birth?
*Kulilkatinyi
Nyakukatinyi*

Action
Watching, thinking,
planning another
action
*Piruku palyalkatinyi,
nyakula kulira
palyani*

Planning
Senior women
to teach traditional care
of the baby.
Where? *Yaaltjingka*
When?   *Yalara*
Who?   *Nganalu*

Thinking
How did it go?
*Yaaltji yaaltjingku
la palyanu.*
Good? Bad? *Wiru? Kura?*
What will we do next?
Ka ngula nyaala palyalku?

Action
*Palyalkatima nintini
iti wirkanu
Ngunytju palya,
iti palya*

UBINIG

Declaration of People's Perspectives on "Population" Symposium

Introduction

Between December 12 and 15 of 1993, sixty-one women from twenty-three countries from around the world met in Comilla, Bangladesh, to build and ratify a collective position on population control programmes and policies. The international symposium People's Perspectives on "Population", explored a wide range of related issues such as environmental degradation, the New Economic World Order, emergent policies (especially the upcoming International Conference on Population and Development, Cairo, 1994), science and reproductive technologies, genetic engineering and language.

This declaration is a feminist critique of the logic of domination that underlies population control policies. In most countries population-control policy is hidden behind terms and programmes such as family planning, mother-child-care and safe motherhood.

We Oppose Population Control

- Population policies are designed to control the bodies, the fertility and the lives of women: because it is women who bear children.
- Population policies have inbuilt racist and eugenic ideologies through the process of selection of the ones who have the right to survive and dismissing everyone else, such as the Indigenous, the disabled and the Black. They have the goal to eliminate the poor instead of poverty.
- Population policies represent the interests of the privileged elites and a lifestyle of over consumption in the countries of the north as well as of the elites in the Third World.
- There cannot be any feminist population policy because it violates and contradicts the basic premise of feminism.

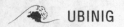

Population control programmes are based on international collaboration between organizations such as the United States Agency for International Development, the Population Council, Rockefeller and Ford Foundation, United Nations Fund for Population Activities, and pharmaceutical multinationals. The World Health Organization's Human Reproduction Programme facilitates such collaborations.

These agencies are now attempting to set the agenda for Women's Movements and organizations by co-opting their language and individual women to legitimize population-control policies. Although this co-optation plays a very divisive role and confuses issues, many women around the world are resisting this.

Language and Representation

Population-control programmes were devised already in the 1950s in the name of "poverty eradication" and containment of communism. Today they are used, supposedly, to curb environmental destruction and to ensure "sustainable growth". In fact, however, over all the years these programmes have subjected women in the south to a whole range of coercive technologies and methods which have often ruined their health and their lives.

The population establishment attempts to hide these horrors by cloaking them in words hijacked from the Women's Liberation Movement, and thus try to convey the message that they fall within an ethic of care and human rights; and that they expand "reproductive choice", especially for women.

Language is meant to reflect people's reality and history. Therefore we reclaim words and phrases that have been appropriated because they are part of our Movement's history. It is part of our resistance to create a language which expresses our visions as well as women's reality.

Our resistance to population control policies must never be confused with the opposition of the religious and political right to the same policies.

We reject the term "poor" as it is usually applied to Third World countries as they have wealth which is exploited by industrial and capitalist concerns. We reject the term "carrying capacity" as a tool which enables the objectification of people and nature. We reject the term "population": people are not demographic variables. That's why our critical reflection on "population" starts with putting the word in inverted commas.

In the present global discourse the term "democracy" usually stands for capitalism and gives false hopes and expectations to people namely, access for all to the global supermarket.

We demand respect for the integrity of women's bodies, outside the confines of compulsory heterosexuality, while the religious right and fundamentalists give primacy to the lives of fetuses, compulsory heterosexuality and motherhood.

The media have consistently equated economic and political crises in the Third World to "population explosions". We reject such media images which maintain the domination by the north and southern collaborators, of the south.

We will demystify these terms and see to it that the interests camouflaged by this language will be brought into the open.

The New Economic World Order

We are now living in a neo-colonial period despite the fact that the colonizing powers were forced by people's resistance and national liberation movements to allow so-called "political" independence in Latin America, Africa, the Caribbean, Asia and the Pacific. Economic dependence and external and internal colonialism continue. The new colonial institutions such as IMF and World Bank have maintained the colonisers' power.

After the oil crisis, credit based development was promoted in the south. To solve this crisis the World Bank introduced so called Structural Adjustment Programmes (SAPs). In the name of SAPs, the World Bank and the International Monetary Fund dictated prescriptions in which Third World countries have to sacrifice health and food subsidies. Their public health and welfare infrastructure are systematically dismantled and privatized. These diminished health-delivery services are technologized and virtually reduced to instruments of population control. The poor, and particularly poor women, are the main victims of this global policy everywhere.

Another aspect of this new world order is the further globalization of the world market system. The General Agreement of Tariff and Trade (GATT) signed in December 1993, intends to open up the economies of the south, particularly their agricultural sector, to multinationals and to biotechnology. Through the regime of Intellectual Property Right the privatization and commodification of all lives is intended.

With the ecological and economic crisis deepening the old colonial methods of naked violence and repression are used when needed, such as the Gulf war, to ensure control of resources. It is clear that population control policies are central to this strategy. They are a continuation of war in disguise.

This remilitarization of the world has also reinforced patriarchal structures and attitudes such as violence against women, mass rapes in wars and general brutalization of every day life. Commodification and trafficking of women are increasing.

The globalization of the world market economy has shifted and blurred boundaries between the north and the Thirld World. What we used to understand as the Third World (under-developed, poor) is no longer concentrated only in the south of the planet. Poverty is also increasing and becoming a permanent feature in northern and industrialized countries.

The globalization of the world market economy also leads to a concentration of wealth in the hands of ever fewer people and to a polarization of the societies, particularly of the south. But in many parts of the world, people are actively resisting this destruction of the basis of their lives. In this process they often develop visions which go beyond the capitalist-patriarchal growth model.

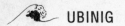

Environment

The growth oriented development model has led to severe environmental degradation in most parts of the world, which have, in turn, undermined peoples' security and livelihoods. We reject the prevalent notion that "overpopulation" has a causal connection with environmental degradation.

The north, with twenty percent of the world's people, consumes eighty percent of the total resources. One of the key factors causing environmental destruction is the excessive use of energy in production and consumption. This energy is based on non-sustainable resources such as petrochemical, coal and nuclear energies. These resources are depletable and the extraction processes themselves destroy the environment. The use of such forms of energy is essential to the development of high technology which perpetuates the growth oriented development. Overconsumption in the north cannot be isolated from production patterns and technological processes, nor from the forces creating "consumer demands".

Migration

The growth oriented development model has increased the number of poverty, environmental and political migrants and refugees. Interference of world powers with the active collaboration of the lucrative and growing armaments industry has led to war, while low intensity conflict has led to further displacement of people as war refugees. The demands of capitalism also direct the movement of low-wage labourers.

The phobia of overpopulation has not only distracted policies from the actual causes of migration, but has further victimized the victims. Sixty-five per cent of migrants and ninety percent of refugees are women and children. The northern countries, in response to migration issues, are making stricter laws to close the borders, while in the new free market economy, resources and capital are flowing freely from the south to the north, dragging migrant and low wage workers with them. Double standards are practised when it comes to the movement of the world's citizens between those who are welcome and can afford to move freely and those who are shunned or exploited for their labour. With the signing of GATT, goods can move without restriction whereas migration remains constrained.

Reproductive Science and Reproductive Technologies

Reproductive technology has been developed to control women's procreative capacity. For women in the south, population controllers promote longer acting injectable or implantable contraceptives that leave women as little room as possible to resist contraception should they want to bear a child. A woman can "forget" to take the Pill but once Norplant is inside her body, she cannot remove it herself. These maximum control contraceptives manipulate women's hormonal and immune systems effecting long-term changes in their bodies.

Ever since the "Pill" – originally placed on the market on the basis of tests on a tiny number of young Puerto Rican women, five of whom died during the testing – population controllers' attention to contraceptive safety has been minimal. There is an extensive literature critiquing the shoddy science used to show the alleged safety of various contraceptives, particularly Depo-Provera, Norplant, the anti-pregnancy vaccine, and RU-486.

In the north, reproductive technologies serve a pro-natalist, rather than an anti-natalist goal. For example, in Japan, Quebec (Canada) and elsewhere, where the fertility rate has fallen, governments and media are conducting a scare campaign that the "population" is endangered by this fall. This campaign, along with the notion that motherhood must be central to women's lives, places pressure on women to have a child. Many women turn to technologies such as in vitro fertilization, promoted as highly effective though its failure rate is in fact still ninety percent.

Increasingly technologies are invented that are controlled by the provider, that is, the physicians, the drug companies, the state. Formerly, contraceptives, like the diaphragm, were more under the control of women (user-controlled.) Whether in relation to curbing or enhancing fertility, these provider-controlled technologies effectively undermine women's control over their own lives while burdening them with full responsibility for fertility and absolving men of their responsibility.

Therefore, long-acting contraceptives such as Norplant are not an advance in contraceptive technology but an advance in control. They are purposeful instruments inspirited by eugenicists whose programs of population control were designed explicitly to curtail the number of Black, Indigenous, disabled and poor white peoples.

We note with special concern the situation of Indigenous peoples in various countries who are subjected to coercive methods of fertility control in order to appropriate their land, their commons, their resources, their culture. Their traditional family planning and health practices are discarded in favor of modern technology and practices that result in their extermination.

We are deeply concerned about the plight of people with disabilities who are often subjected to physical abuse and are being used for experimentation and implementation for contraceptive drugs and devices such as Depo-Provera and Norplant. Prenatal testing and embryo biopsy are aimed at determining who is worthy of being born.

Therefore we say no to amniocentesis; not to sex predetermination; no to embryo biopsy and the in vitro fertilization technology that makes human embryos available for manipulation.

We further oppose the industrialization and commercialization of reproduction through "surrogate mothers", in vitro fertilization, and sex pre-determination clinics opened by new entrepreneurs.

UN Conference on Population and Development (ICPD)

In September 1994, the International Conference in Population and Development (ICPD), which is largely funded by the UN Fund for Population Activities (UNFPA),

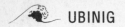

will take place in Cairo, Egypt. This conference will pave the way for more population control policies in the coming decade, based on the false assumption that population growth threatens the survival of the planet.

We must reveal the underlying aims being set for the ICPD, which include the myth that the population growth of the south is the problem, while obscuring over-consumption and the wasteful life style of the rich and the elites of the world.

Women's Needs

Women's basic needs of food, education, health, work, social and political participation, a life free of violence and oppression should be addressed on their own merit. Meeting women's needs should be delinked from population policy including those expressed as apparent humanitarian concerns for women. Women should have access to safe contraception and legal abortion under broader health care. These needs can only be met if all life is respected and accorded dignity. We demand an end to exploitation of people and the earth.

For all these reasons we state again that we oppose population control policies in all forms. Also there cannot be a feminist population control policy. Our voices cannot be used to legitimize an anti-women, anti-poor, anti-nature population policy.

People are not "population". Population control: NO!

Mahnaz Afkhami

Towards Global Feminism:*
A Muslim Perspective

Waging their struggle in the colonial environment, Third World feminist thinkers have achieved a multicultural ethical and intellectual formation and a plethora of experience relevant to the development of an internationally valid and effective discourse addressing women's condition on a global scale. The question is whether this foundation can become a springboard for a global discourse. By definition, such a discourse must transcend the boundaries of Christian, Jewish, Muslim, Buddhist, socialist, capitalist, or any other particular culture. It will be feminist rather than patriarchal, humane rather than ideological, balanced rather than extremist, critical as well as exhortatory.[1] The global feminist discourse recognizes that the problem of women constitutes an issue in its own right, not as a subsidiary of other ideologies, no matter how structurally comprehensive or textually promising they might seem to be. It insists in relating concepts to the historical contexts in which they are embedded (see Delphy: 1987, pp. 80–109). Since "traditional" concepts are by definition founded in patriarchal discourse, global feminism must be skeptical of propositions that present them as liberating. This feminism is not anti-man; rather, it sees the world in humane terms, that is, it seeks a redefinition of social, economic, and political principles of societal organization on the basis of non-paternalistic models. Realizing that such a feat cannot be accomplished without or against men's participation, it does not hesitate to engage men politically in favor of the feminist cause. On the other hand, given the present effects of the historical process, feminism will be critically aware of and fight against patriarchal structures and institutions.[2]

---

* This article is taken from the introduction to Afkhami and Friedl (1994).

1. I realize that these terms are problematic. The function of a global discourse is to define and clarify the concepts invoked by these terms in a way that is suitable to the requirements of an equitable system of gender relations in the twenty-first century, if not earlier in the so-called "new world order" (see Kandiyoti: 1991, pp. 23–42).

2. For some possibilities of what might constitute a discourse that has a chance of transcending fixed sexual polarities see Kristeva (1989, pp. 198–217).

The global feminist discourse rejects the notion that "east" and "west" constitute mutually exclusive paradigms; rather, it looks at life as evolving for all, and believes that certain humane and morally defensible principles can and should be applied in the west and in the east equally. The point is not that, for example, Iranian women should forget the problems that are obviously "Iranian" and intensely present. It is, rather, that unless Iranian feminists think globally, they will neither be able to mobilize world opinion for their cause, nor succeed in breaking out of the boundaries of patriarchal discourse on their own; and, therefore, they will likely fail to address their problems in a way that will lead to their solution.[3]

At present, of course, reality belies the potential. The disparity in physical and material power between the developed and less-developed countries forces Third World women to withdraw to reactive positions, formulating their discourse in response to the west and its challenge. Consequently, they fail to think globally, that is, to move beyond the Indigenous culture they have objectively outgrown. Their discourse remains nationalistic, parochial, fearful, tradition-bound, and rooted in the soil of patriarchy. The world, however, is undergoing a qualitative change, an important aspect of which may be the tumbling of nation states qua culture boundaries. In the process, women may gain a chance to promote on a world scale the kinds of ideas that are applicable to women everywhere. If they do, Third World women will be able to critique women's condition in the west from a vantage point that transcends the cultures of Abraham, Buddha, and Confucius and thus will help the women of all "worlds of development", including Iran.

I am not suggesting therefore that the west be taken as the standard for the evaluation of women's conditions in Iran. On the contrary, it seems to me that there are significant issues of commission and omission in the western discourse that can be addressed profitably only from the global feminist position. The virtue of the global position is that it partakes of the wisdom of all cultures and that it accommodates differences in the levels of economic and social development without succumbing to either the normlessness of cultural relativism or the self-righteous parochialism of any particular culture.

The heightened awareness of female human rights that exists today throughout the world makes possible a more unified and effective approach to the global feminist movement. Western feminists can help this process but only to an extent, because they are burdened by two severe handicaps. First, they carry the onus of historical western hegemony, even though they themselves are the victims of a taxing patriarchal order (Chaudhuri and Strobel: 1992). Second, their problems

---

3. What appear as obstacles to the development of a global approach to a feminist social and literary criticism – namely, the contemporary emphasis in universities on cultural relativism, on one hand, and on textual and deconstructionist analysis, on the other – may prove a positive force for the future involvement of Third World women in the construction of a global discourse. The transition from parochial/relativistic to a global approach is already taking place as more and more feminist positions are advanced mutually through intellectual representatives of western and non-western cultures.

as women are often of a different order than the problems of women in Third World countries. Consequently, they appear alternately as self-righteous promoters of their own western culture, when they advocate principles and rights that differ from the tenets of Third World societies, or as self-deprecating defenders of atrociously anti-feminist conditions, when they explain away oppressive behavior in the developing world on the grounds of cultural relativism.

Non-western feminists can be instrumental in the development of a viable global feminism, despite their historical handicap. As the world moves from a disjointed society of nation-states to an increasingly interconnected economic and technological system, and as the symmetry of the enclaves of poverty and backwardness in the developed and developing countries is increasingly apparent, it becomes easier for Third World feminists to develop a sense of empathy with their sisters in other parts of the globe. Indeed, unless such empathy is effected and expanded, patriarchal norms, for all practical purposes, will not be transcended and feminism, global or otherwise, will not fully succeed.

It is from this vantage point that the originary myth in the Shii lore[4] may be successfully engaged. Here is a chance for Iranian women to transcend the parochial discourse. By showing at once the similarity in the historical treatment of women in all societies and the need for women to deny the legitimacy of the patriarchal order in all cultures, Iranian women can challenge the claim that there is something unique in Islam that separates it from other human experiences. The goal is to contest the right and legitimacy of Iran's patriarchal clerical order to be the sole interpreters of the values, norms, and aesthetic standards of Shii Islam – a religion that lies at the core of Iranian culture. The truth is that there is nothing sacred about a limited and highly protected discourse, developed over centuries by a society of zealous men in order to produce and maintain a regime of control, a major function of which is to keep women in bondage – for ever.

---

4. By "originary myth in the Shii lore" I mean the liberating impulse to stand for right and challenge abusive authority. This is said to be the essence of the Shii movement and is symbolized by both men (Husayan, Prophet's grandson martyred in Karbala) and women (Zynab, Hysayn's sister and courageous defender). It should be noted that the primeval impulse to freedom is present in all lasting human movements, religious or secular. It is the patriarchal form and content that deny it to women and historically corrupt it everywhere.

Cathie Dunsford, Beryl Fletcher, Susan Sayer

Surfing the Edge of the Alphabet

> *They were nothing more than people, by themselves. Even paired, any pairing, they would have been nothing more than people by themselves. But all together, they have become the heart and muscles and mind of something perilous and new, something strange and growing and great.*
>
> *Together, all together, they are the instruments of change.*
> Keri Hulme *the bone people* (1985, p. 4).

We are a group of feminist writers living in Aotearoa/New Zealand who are challenging the tradition of writers working in isolation. We pool our resources and work together in order to maintain as much control as possible over our creative productions before submitting them for publication. In this paper, we talk about our feminist politics and how we deal with patriarchal reactions and subsequent issues that have emerged from our collective work.

Susan: The collaborative process of editing that we have developed has produced good results. Through editing other women's work, I have learned how to be self-critical. We have become very familiar with each other's strengths and weaknesses, and where we would once take a great deal of time explaining, we now simply signal in one of our many coded responses.

Beryl: Some people have said to me that they could not bear to work collaboratively because they could not cope with other writers telling them what to say, or being forced into so-called political correctness. They've got the wrong end of the stick. This is how it works. The writer writes the text and she has the final say on content and style. The editors work on the text paragraph by paragraph, noting any sections that do not work and ask the writer, is this really what you wanted to say here? Or we point out repetitive phrases or clichés or continuity problems.

We also do an authenticity check. We ask, does this ring true to our New Zealand experience? This is particularly important to me because I always have lesbian characters in my novels and Susan and Cathie give me invaluable insights into lesbian life that I would otherwise miss out on.

Susan: As well as editing Beryl's novels, we have worked together on the last two anthologies of new writing by New Zealand women that Cathie has edited. On the occasions that I have challenged Beryl over the politics of her characters, I have asked: is this the point-of-view of your character or your own politics? A problem inherent in writing is getting what you want to say on the page. How a text can be read is a constant issue for us as feminists. While we are not interested in promoting the idea that every woman is a good woman, neither do we wish to add fuel to existing woman-hating fires. The multiple readings possible in our process help to iron out such problems.

Cathie: I edited New Zealand's first feminist collection, *New Women's Fiction* (1986), in isolation when I was in the USA on a Post-Doctoral Fulbright Scholarship at the University of California, Berkeley. Although it was difficult doing this work away from my homeland, I established some principles that I kept to with my next three books, *The Exploding Frangipani* (1990), *Subversive Acts* (1991) and *Me and Marilyn Monroe* (1993). I was determined to tap into new writers who might not be involved with established literary circles. We advertised for stories in women's centres, marae[1] and other places where women gather. I did not want to do a "best of" anthology, where the same pool of writers is published over and over again. This practice tends to operate as a gate-keeping device that makes it very difficult for new writers to break into publishing. However, it is important to publish established writers with new writers, so that the book will be commercially viable. *New Women's Fiction* sold out very quickly, so it obviously hit a nerve. Now there is a greater variety of writing styles and more sophisticated and confident experimentation with new techniques. New feminist writers have emerged in Aotearoa whose voices were not being heard before. Their work is continually challenging mainstream notions of literary technique and the idea that we should necessarily keep politics, especially feminist politics, out of literature. *Me and Marilyn Monroe* is a logical development from *Subversive Acts*. The brief was to write about any aspect or theme pertaining to the body. Issues and theories about the body are very important in feminist theory at the moment. One interesting thing that happened was that the Maori writers gave a very different interpretation of the body theme compared with the Pakeha writers. Some saw the body as a metaphor for the land.

Reaction to the books has been, on the whole, very positive, but there has been some critical attack. Some of these have been the predictable type of review where the critic wants to read another sort of book rather than the one under

---

1. Marae refers to the complex of meeting ground and meeting house where public events take place in Maori society.

review. In my first collection, New Women's Fiction, one reviewer did not want to read so-called narrative realism and more or less said that until women writers moved towards post-modern techniques, they would not succeed in the literary world. Later, reviewers complained because Subversive Acts was too subversive in tech-nique and approach. I have also been attacked publicly and in print for being gay, for being too colourful, too large, too happy – in short, too everything. Yes, and too successful! We're writing and publishing for a feminist audience and as yet we don't have many reviewers in New Zealand who are familiar with the issues we are raising. We are also held back by a traditionalist industry that has only just begun to discover what lies beyond our boring old colonial roots. We simply have to believe passionately in what we do, write and act with integrity, and have a strong network.

Beryl: To me the important thing is that these feminist voices get published. I remember how difficult it was when I was young to find any other woman writer except for Katherine Mansfield. I honestly believed that you had to be male to be a fiction writer. Later, when I became a radical feminist, I learned that this had happened all over the world and that women's history and fiction and art had been systematically silenced for centuries. I know that radical feminists are often accused of a "false universalism" that states that women form an oppressed class the world over, but I really believe that the similarities of women's experience across time and culture are enormous. Male violence, silencing, poverty, control of fertility, enforced sexual codes, these are the universal problems of women living in the confines of patriarchy. Having said this, I also believe that differences between women, both cross-culturally and in terms of power relations between groups of women, must be acknowledged. This is why it is so important that a variety of women's writing is constantly being published and is readily available.

Susan: Our work has provoked extreme responses. On the one hand some reviewers are furious at our nerve in challenging genre conventions and that we claim space that they feel should be exclusive to "real" literature. For them, women's writing is self-indulgent and when we dare to call ourselves intellectual, it is almost as if the idea of a feminist intellectual is a joke. On the other hand, some reviewers respond with enthusiasm to the feminist imperatives inherent in these collections. Thank-fully, we aren't trying to please everybody.

Beryl: I find the type of review where the perceived genre or style of the book is attacked rather than the book itself particularly annoying. And I do see it as sexist because in New Zealand there is a perception that women writers write bleeding-heart narrative realism which is often seen as so-called confessional or autobio-graphical writing. Part of the decolonising process of writing is to do away with these absurd hierarchies of worth, most of which, despite fervent protestations to the contrary, do have a recognisable gender dimension. Some critics of my novels decry my traditional use of narrative techniques and imply that I should go in for magic realism or some other contemporary technique. I don't mind this. What I do mind is their sub-text informing me that I write like a woman and if I don't change, my work will never be classified as literature. This is a more subtle version of the warning, don't label yourself a feminist writer.

Cathie: That happened with *Me and Marilyn Monroe* where a powerful metaphor, the body as battlefield, was a recurring theme. One critic, a university lecturer in English, chose to interpret this metaphor literally and said that "I would personally far rather worry about the size of my tits than be blown to pieces in the Battle of the Somme." This statement was later taken up by other commentators. One critic stated that the metaphor, body as battlefield, was both "silly and offensive".

Beryl: Offensive to whom? The hundreds of thousands of women who have died of anorexia or who have died at the hands of rapists in war?

Cathie: These are very emotional issues. We are in the middle of a revolution about the representation of women's bodies and there is a lot at stake, not the least of which are the huge financial interests involved in the dieting, medical and sex industries. We have to keep asking who benefits from the extreme forms of control of women's bodies that are constantly being promoted?

Susan: I think we forget how radical we are, or are perceived to be. All kinds of anxieties came into print. One reviewer openly panicked about being "the only man [not true] at a Cathie Dunsford book launch" as if his body was under threat. Another reviewer pleaded, "We can't all hate our bodies, surely sometimes our bodies enable us to experience great joy."

Beryl: There is also the controversy over the introduction that Cathie wrote for the book. Some critics complained that she provided a feminist analysis of the text when she should have presented the stories without comment.

Cathie: For me, it is a given that any reading of a text is coming from a subjective place. It's a mixture of experience, theory, critical skills, emotional responses, cultural conditioning and so on. It's crucial to be honest and ethical about where we are coming from. At Dunsford Publishing Consultants, we deal with clients with a wide range of experiences. We have to consider every voice carefully, weigh up the skills of the writer in terms of what s/he sets out to do, rather than imposing our own belief systems onto a text. What really scares me are the critics who purport to be objective but have clearly identifiable prejudices, who suppress and deny new writing on the grounds that it is simply "not good enough". Let's remember that Keri Hulme's prize-winning novel *the bone people* (1985) was refused by major New Zealand publishers who considered it "too feminist" with "too many Maori words". This is still happening to writers in Aotearoa and overseas.

Susan: This criticism is part of the myth that literature stands on its own merits, that it is an apolitical universal. Feminism is just one of many stances taken against oppressive structures. The same gate-keeping tactics are applied to other activists;

the judgement that what is represented can at best be relegated to a sub-genre outside mainstream concerns.

Beryl: I find it highly ironic that the same people who criticised Cathie's feminist introduction as not objective enough, (i.e. that Cathie gave a "false" reading of the stories), pay lip-service to the post-modern notion that meaning is derived contextually through subjective process and that there can never be one definitive reading of a text. Cathie's introduction is her reading of the text, not an objective fact, and she clearly states this in all her work. Yet the critics claim that there should be a definitive reading. Why is there such a fear of difference?

Cathie: Good question! I think it's part of growing up in a colonised country where we are taught to revere Britain and the northern hemisphere as the authority figures.

Susan: We have been fortunate in that the political challenges that have faced the three of us living in Aotearoa have increased our respect for difference. The South African rugby tour of 1981 ended the myth of a racially egalitarian New Zealand. Feminists, amongst others, have had to re-evaluate their politics according to the specific features of colonial rule. Fear of difference is enacted through denial. If we deny difference, we don't have to reveal what we uphold as the standard.

Beryl: This is the challenge of group work. We have to respect difference, but we also have to develop political principles and contexts that make our work clearly definable as feminist. To me, one of the most important features of radical feminist practice is collaborative action.

Susan: Collaborative action is what makes feminism radical. The meanings attributed to radical feminism are many and I would not agree with them all. Lesbian experience is central to my particular needs and actions as a feminist radical.

Cathie: For me, radical feminism is having a belief system matched by activism. Consequently, I am always stressing the context of my/our work. We must keep questioning our goals and using theory to complement our actions, instead of theory becoming a tool distinct in its own right. One of the major ideas from radical feminism is that theory must be grounded and that personal experience always exists within a political framework. My writing classes are essentially practical workshops and are run through various organising bodies, including continuing education departments, polytechs, local arts councils, women's centres and marae. One of the functions of the classes is the distribution of information to people who find the publishing industry mysterious and difficult to understand. Information about forthcoming publications and how to get published is very seldom shared with writers. Each year I work with hundreds of writers and I ask them to share the information with others. I attend the New Zealand Book Publishers' and Book Editors' conferences and distribute all the relevant information back to the writers.

Susan: The radical feminist politics inherent in your workshops demystifies the publishing industry and this challenges the competitive model. Our belief that there is room enough for all our work enables us to support each other and all the women writers that we meet. One of the good things that happens is that community writing groups have evolved from your classes, like Over The Fence which has two self-published anthologies to its credit and the lesbian writers' group I have worked with in Hamilton, Scratching the Surface. Writing groups produce confident writers, well-edited manuscripts. The more the better.

Cathie: People sometimes don't understand that writing is like any other profession where skill and expertise have to be learned. The emphasis is on working with the writer, empowering the writer, rather than slashing red pens through their work as some editors do. Then the writer returns the manuscript and we look it over and offer fine-tuning and publishing advice, which ranges from advice on how to approach a publisher to using individual contacts within the industry. Often we simply send the text directly to a publisher we know will give it fair consideration.

Susan: Now we are beginning to work with women on a wider level encompassing other arts and politics. I think it is very important to branch into as many areas as we can. Writing academic work can be as creative and challenging as writing fiction. Indeed I wonder why we make such a distinction. While writing academic work, I became fascinated with feminist theories of power in language. Mary Daly was a strong influence on my thinking and writing in the mid 1980s. I found the combination of intellect and play inherent in her writing compelling. My fiction project became one of exploring these ideas, getting under the skin of everyday usage, for example, "La Ngu Age" in *The Exploding Frangipani* (1990) which Cathie co-edited with Australian author, Susan Hawthorne. Once the question of point-of-view or where we are speaking from is opened up, the idea of fiction falls away. The main quest in my fiction at the moment is to ask: how can lesbians articulate love in a patriarchal language? I think this kind of deconstruction holds great potential for radical theorising.

Cathie: I agree. I enjoyed working with Susan Hawthorne because we started examining these ideas in co-editing *The Exploding Frangipani*. It was wonderful after the isolation of editing the first book. This began a long and fruitful working relationship and friendship. My first novel *Cowrie* (1994) represents the collaborative process that we three have developed, but it has involved a wider group, including invaluable editorial advice given by Audre Lorde, Spinifex editors, Daphne Brasell and others. I think it's significant, and reflective of our breaking down traditional boundaries, that several different publishers, editors, and writers from a range of cultural perspectives have given feedback in the editing process. Our cross-cultural support network keeps me going. I'm currently working with British literary critic Sara Fuller-Sessions on ways we can break down the colonial barriers that separate our literatures. It's deeply exciting. I feel very positive about the future both for myself and for other women writers. For me, the old system of divide and rule, the fragmented communication between writers and editors and publishers, is on the way out. I see all our collaborative work as the crossing of borders, cultural, physical, metaphorical. And I know that once these borders are crossed, there will be an outpouring of brilliant women's writing. It's happening already.

Berit Ås

A Feminist University: The Thrill and Challenges, Conflicts and Rewards of Trying to Establish an Alternative Education

Setbacks in the form of patriarchal resistance to change in Women's Liberation struggles are not new. And yet, my deep concern about a new threat to feminism did not surface until a large group of Norwegian women social scientists gathered in 1976 to discuss their work and their future. It suddenly occurred to me that we would be completely lacking in historical sense if we did not foresee a backlash. I presented this argument and proposed that we should build an Archive or a Women's University. The intention was to save and conserve all the findings about important women artists, academics and philosophers, so that it would not be necessary for future feminists to search for and establish these facts again.

More than one hundred women turned this suggestion down and accused me of being separatist. Their optimism was enormous: never again would a backlash occur! I, however, was faithful to my intent and decided to try to build this place. I had support from only two women – one American and one Swedish born – both of whom were nearer to my own age than the majority of the young optimists.[1] From this experience I wrote up a theory about how to organize women who lack time and money to be involved. Its main message was: "never organize women for anything else than success!" (Ås: 1985b).

While intended success was a trigger for our activity, the time period between the first organizational efforts and the purchase of a house was remarkably fruitful. Prior to the official opening of the university in 1985 we had engaged in some hard thinking and strategizing:

---

1. The report on how ideas and plans were developed, how the organizing of fourteen working groups took place, and how we finally found a motherhouse in which we started our activity has been published in *Storming the Tower* (Ås: 1990; see also Ås 1985a/1989).

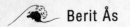

- Classroom research established how girls and female students were often harassed, overlooked and silenced in co-education. We needed to create a place where women could study/work without male influence.
- Since most conventional universities in Norway resisted offering Women's Studies, teaching Women's Studies resulted in a benefit for all students by providing access to materials. Female students in particular needed this resource.
- Since the results of Women's Studies were of such tremendous importance to large groups of women in their *everyday* lives, research results should reach further than groups of young students. Our students would have to be admitted irrespective of age and former educational background.
- This would demand a very special pedagogy and the development of teaching material for those different groups.
- Since we were influenced by the Women's Movement, we wanted to develop the planning groups, the funding organization and the administration as a flat structure, enshrining sound democratic principles.

The Name: A Stumbling Block

The choice of the name "The Women's University" was immediately followed by protests. Two persons wanted to take us to court for using "University" without paying attention to common rules about the quality of the students. In their view students had to be of a certain quality and had to show that they had graduated from colleges or other higher schools to apply. We responded by denying such elitist thinking. The original meaning of "university" pointed both in the direction of "for all" and towards a "holistic" view. But the conclusions of a series of people, women scholars included, was that they were afraid it could result in a devaluation or degrading of universities. The two protesters who had applied to the Ministry of Justice and the Ministry of Education were not permitted to take up the question for further evaluation. The Minister of Justice, the conservative Mona Røkke, was the woman Norwegians can be grateful to for changing the Conservative Party's view on women's rights regarding abortion. The Minister of Education was the Labor member, Kjersti Kolle Grøndahl, now the president of the Parliament. On entering her job as a minister she decided to appoint at least sixty competent (and probably discriminated against) female professors during her time as minister. Years ago, a "People's University" had been built in Norway on arguments similar to ours, mainly the right to education for all citizens interested, so our name was not without support.

Building effective strategies takes a long time, but the hard work by women to obtain high representation in politics created a long-term effect. The criticism that we were arrogant and impertinent women became louder. "Why could we not, like other women, be a little modest?" our detractors asked. "Why could we not be content with 'a study organization'?" Again a split occurred in our own ranks. For women to "pretend" that they are worth something, is quite unacceptable in an authoritarian country like Norway where patriarchal values continue to permeate the culture. Fortunately I have an intelligent mother, a stern, strong and outspoken suffragette, and she was the one who warned us not to be fooled: "When men build," she said "they label their houses with fine and high-status names. Take on the discussion! Show them your independence and importance."

What Should be Taught?

I had attempted to visualize a female culture with respect to five strong dimensions: language, organizational life, money and technology as well as time use and self-reliance. But it soon became obvious that research in Women's Studies did not naturally fall into categories similar to those that organized the conventional faculties of the universities of the world. This had often brought forward the critique that women's research can not be appropriately evaluated within a single discipline, and that it is "disorderly" and badly designed. I had taken for granted that for the most part we would make visible *additional* information to research already undertaken and that since universities had been constructed *by* men, *for* men, the most useful work we could do was "to cure the blind eye of a patriarchal institution" (Ås: 1985a/1989, pp. 393, 193).

As the Curriculum Group for our university worked on this issue, it quickly became clear that the world of women was not, indeed, an *additional* world. As Jessie Bernard put it: "Because of our social circumstances, male and female are really two cultures and their life experiences are utterly different" (Bernard: 1981). Thus the Curriculum Group had to consider an alternative arrangement of the faculties for a future Women's University. At the First Interdisciplinary Women's Studies Conference, in Haifa in 1980, we began to sense an underlying structuring of knowledge to which women scholars related their findings. From then on the seriousness of searching for this "other knowledge base" relevant for groups of people which are oppressed but at the same time responsible for people's health, survival and the environment's (re)productivity, became obvious to us. The Board of the Feminist Foundation agreed that these issues should be the interconnecting areas from which we would teach, do research, and develop our philosophy in the years to come (see Fig. 1). My own visits to some Indigenous groups around the world, as well as to some religious congregations, revealed that their holistic perceptions of the world were, in many ways, congruent with our cognitive map.

Organization and Leadership

It is a common political understanding that the end product is strongly dependent upon the instrument used for its construction. If a final dual leadership or a troika were to administer the university, it would be necessary to try out this organizational structure in the planning group.

A flat structure is a very complicated structure indeed. It is vulnerable to hidden agendas and influence from strong personalities. These problems can rarely be avoided, but they can be counteracted with strong by-laws and clear working rules for every unit involved in the work. The special conditions which supported a

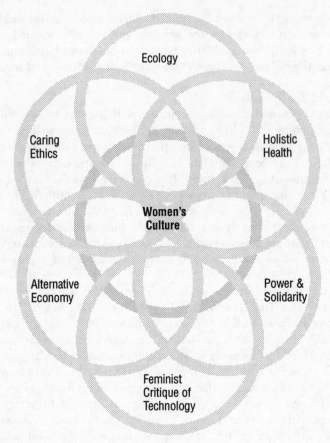

Figure 1:
Arrangement of Faculties developed by Curriculum Group.

flat structure in our planning group stemmed from the fact that communication had to be oral. Neither time nor money was available to the sub-group members and the board had to consist of one reporting member from each group.

The first group became the Feminist University Fund. Its main function was to use a small sum earned from one of my publications to pay for paper, stamps, short travels and office space. The second group was to develop the curriculum. They had to formulate their goals and the strategies for reaching them. An economy group and a group for information and public relations worked closely with the office group and the group for finding used furniture and office machines. We all knew that each group should develop a program, set their time limits, election rules for members, and working schemes. We all knew, too, that democratic procedures take time and that one has to work hard to avoid misunderstanding and conflicts.

To function as a Foundation we had to rely on a lawyer who had been recommended to us as a feminist. She was employed in one of the most respected and conservative firms in town. When she took on the job of constructing our by-laws, she asked us to tell her exactly what we wanted her to do. We wanted no men on the board: this was against Norway's representation laws for both sexes. She wrote the election rules to fit our wishes. At that point we asked her if the rule that only women should be elected to the board would be in place before signing. Her answer surprised us, but we understood immediately that she was right. "Nobody will complain," she said, "because a complaint will reveal that there is not a sufficient number of women on the boards of any of the other universities in Norway. And men don't want them either. So please relax." "In addition," she said, "Nothing from my august firm will ever be controlled."

The strategy was that the Board of The Women's University Foundation should consist of women from every political party in Norway. This was to ensure that, irrespective of what kind of government we had, there would always be a direct line to that government via one Board member. Another strategy was to try

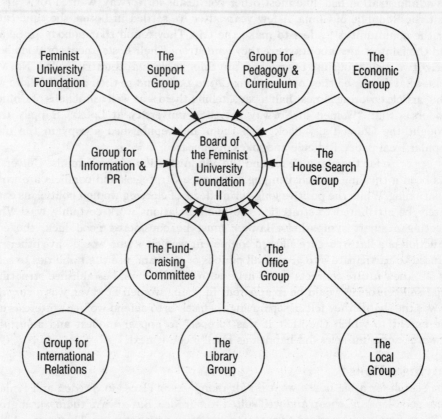

Figure 2. The organizational structure of the Feminist University Planning Group

to encourage one of the right-wing parties to adopt a program for supporting the project. A fine woman from the Christian People's Party agreed to that and, since we usually could rely on Labor and another party to the left in the political left/ right dimension, much work backed by political authorities could be accomplished.

Public Relations

To sell our ideas, an English journalist who wrote for thirty papers around the world was asked to write a piece about us. He did. The first copy I received was from a daily in the Arab Emirates. The article was very well placed on the second page of the paper. The moment I saw it I knew that it would end up in the Norwegian Embassy in that region, and from there it would be mailed to our Department of Foreign Affairs, at which time people would start to wonder whether this project was really that interesting.

I don't know in how many places this original article was published, but one particular occasion did serve us well. We had finally been able to purchase a house situated in Løten, a small community of 7500 inhabitants. The mayor and his administration had, like most other politicians in Norway, wanted for years to visit the Republic of China. A few years after we settled in Løten, the time came for the community's leaders to make the trip. They found that nobody in Beijing had the faintest idea about where they came from. Their hosts knew nothing about their two neighbouring towns nor anything about a country called Norway. Somewhat depressed they opened their *China Daily* and to their surprise there was a big article covering almost half a page, telling them – as well as millions of Chinese readers – that: "Women in Norway get their university at Løten." Happily they brought the China Daily back with them and republished a copy in the most popular local paper. Ridicule and jokes disappeared.

So far the planning for and the administration of the Feminist University has been a thrilling and challenging experience. Strategies and conflicts are worth mentioning. While the positive long-term effects of electing women politicians could barely be attributed to strategies, the public relations work certainly was. While meeting a smart sympathetic lawyer must be considered good luck, the construction of a flat structure allowed competent women – who would have otherwise refused to participate – to give small periods of time and use their abilities to serve us. We knew future conflicts would arise with older men and established structures. That self-censoring would be so apparent in young women however, was a surprise, as was the shame they felt in separating themselves to defend women's interests and the extent to which they felt it was "proper" to appear modest and adjustable. However, some miracles did happen as I will recount next.

Buying a House

The search for a big house went on for many years. Places in Sweden and Finland were good-looking, cheap and well suited to our idea. But always there was a group of Pentecostals who arrived to compete and offer a higher price. They were able to outbid us on four occasions. Finally, on the fifth attempt we found the place: a marvellous old wooden hotel in one of the fjords of Norway. It was a site which Kaiser Wilhelm from Germany, lords and barons from Great Britain, and the King of Norway, visited to fish salmon in the summer. It was in bad shape, but extremely interesting for those women who had formed a Nordic group of architects, planners and historians. When they heard of it they immediately raised 40,000 Norwegian crowns (US $5000) towards the purchase price of 700,000 N. crowns. We were all in high spirits. The community's forty-one women's organizations were contacted and we started, once more, to feel hopeful. Unfortunately one of the greatest lay ministers in Norway heard about it. He immediately contacted the press to tell the journalists that God had spoken to him in a dream. God had told him that he wanted him to buy the hotel, not radical feminists. It made a good story and mobilized hidden aggression and spite towards those of us who had been vigorous feminists during the 1970s. Again we had misfortune. The Norwegian Missionary Association owned the old "castle". They had observed that some of us had been drinking beer while working. So suddenly, they found that against us sinners, our competitor, known as "God's happy glamour-boy", was a better customer. It seemed they were dreaming about large gatherings of religious groups and good business for small shop owners. Our case was lost. The fifth house was now out of reach too. Anti-feminists and patriarchy cheered. My family and my friends encouraged me to quit: "You will then find out if the other women in the groups are as motivated as you have been," they said. "If the work only depends on your commitment then you should rather give up!"

That year I left Norway and visited a previously Catholic Women's University in Halifax: Mount Saint Vincent University. I was inspired by the president, Margaret Fulton, who emphasized: "Keep it small." She promised to come and help out in the initial phase if we succeeded in purchasing a house. Meeting this woman was a good omen. Returning in December, I found that "the house searchers' group" had been offered three abandoned buildings: a big timber school in a mountain community, a governor's house in a southern town and an old people's home in the green and rich farming area in the middle of Norway. We settled for the old people's house. Witty tongues claimed that we were moving from senility to university!

How to Pay and How to (Re-)build?

Our most successful strategy was developed by a female economist who had returned from the US and who had learned fundraising. She insisted on gathering signatures about the need for a Women's University from women representing many different social and political groups: a woman banker, a leader in the Farmers' Party, women union leaders, nurses and housewives, scientists and well-known feminists. From that base she approached a series of financial backers: publishers and small firms, women's groups and unions. The original University Fund had used its 16,000 N. crowns (US $2000) to finance its fundraising activities. In daily papers,

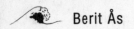

where our Public Relations Group had referred to this fund, it must have induced a false belief that the money we had amounted to thousands of dollars. Several firms and individuals offered us their services for large fees. We didn't know whether to cry or laugh. However, for many people this misunderstanding created greater confidence in our ability to succeed. They thought we had money!

A series of methods was used to raise money. "Pass the lists on for The Women's University: 10 N. crowns per female student." In the county where we had lost the fine hotel to the lay minister, women were so mad that they gathered 100 N. crowns (US $13) per woman. Some women scientists offered to lend us money. We did not dare to accept their offers, but asked them if we could use their money in such a way that we could harvest the interest from their savings. A special arrangement was made with a bank, and a few women lent us sums which amounted to 75,000 N. crowns (US $10,000). Publishers and a few small industries allocated sums ranging from 5000 to 10,000 crowns.

Then an older woman, a cunning politician from the Labor Party, decided to use her connections. She wrote a letter to all the 450 community councils in Norway, asking them what kind of initiatives they had taken to support their own women during the women's decade. "If you have not thought about it and feel that you should have done something," she wrote, "you now have the opportunity to donate 1 N. crown for every woman above sixteen years in your community." She had used official statistics to calculate the exact number of female inhabitants in the appropriate age category.

It was with money from the eighty community councils which responded positively to this approach that our motherhouse was bought. Stories were told about how the politicians had laughed when they read the letter but hundreds of thousands of N. crowns were collected in this way. Similar letters went to the counties; seven of the nineteen approached responded positively. The old people's house in Løten was ours when every community council member had agreed to the sale. We had learned that women's projects are so vulnerable that we could not risk a debate about prices, activities and owners.

Problem Solving

One person in each community has absolute power to decide on housing matters. In Løten the fire chief had that power. We thought the house was in perfect order. Old and bed-ridden people had lived in the multi-storey building. We knew how far away the escape ladders should be and there were three staircases on each level, never more than six meters from a bedroom. Thus, nobody understood when the fire chief suddenly declared that no more than nine people were to stay over on the first floor until the house had been totally rebuilt. In desperation we paid a local architect to produce the drawings for re-building. The visits to banks started. We were usually given a smile and a "no". All our plans to start teaching seemed to vanish into thin air, until I remembered one special signature on the list of signatures the professional fundraiser had gathered: Karin Loekhuag, banker. I called her and we met for lunch. She made one phone call and within four days I was asked to contact one of her banking colleagues.

We entered his office and shook hands with the group of bankers. There were sandwiches and cakes on the table. Since we had experienced so many bad trips I asked if the cakes were leftovers from the last meeting. The men laughed and said they had set the table for us. The architect was asked how much she needed. She explained with some reluctance that a re-building would amount to at least 1,800,000 N. crowns (US$248,000). They smiled again and the bank director said that we should agree on 2 million N. crowns. We were taken aback and asked them why they wanted to invest in us. "Well," they answered "a university is something we may be asked to fund once in a lifetime. Small shopkeepers are people we meet every day!"

On my way home I cried and laughed. Only many years later did it occur to me that what I had experienced as a miracle, may be the way men make business with each other all the time: great sums of money, relaxed feelings, handshakes and big smiles.

Victories and New Crises

The education program was received with much enthusiasm. Adult women who had been without a chance to finish their continuation exams were especially happy. Carpenters took their theory classes and their exams after having built the small dormitories which we needed. Higher education was planned. Seminars were attended. Because we did not fit into any category, allocating funds from the state budget became difficult. The Department for Education shook its head and insisted that we would have to abandon the idea that an institution could teach all kinds of people in the same place. Old men of the Parliamentary Committee of Education considered our intended procedures – and deemed them impossible. Fortunately, the majority of the committee members were women. Accustomed to problem-solving, one of them suggested that the problem could be fixed by constructing a new category and labelling it "The Women's University". When this was done, the committee allocated twice as much money as we had asked for.

But the interest on loans had to be paid; bills ran high; repairs were more expensive than expected. Sleepless nights came and finally, I became sick from worry. In bed one morning I thought we finally had to declare ourselves bankrupt. Then I heard a voice say: "Whenever you get into trouble, call me!" I tried to remember whose voice this was, and I suddenly realized it was a woman I had met, only once, at a fundraising party. She spoke English. She had given me her address and phone numbers. When I contacted her, she answered my call.

"I am in trouble," I said. I am sure I did not identify myself. There was a short pause. "How much?" she asked. She must have recognised me. I calculated rapidly how many US dollars one million N. crowns was, and said "$137,000." A new silence in my ears. "I think I can make it," said the voice, "but not immediately."

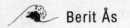

The Opening of The Women's University

The Women's University opened in August 1985. The building had been refurbished. The mayor, ministers and the Ombudsman for Women's Rights were guests. Miracles were obviously working in our interests. From studying the successes and failures of small institutions, it had become clear to us earlier that state and county authorities usually wait for about three years before they decide whether a project has a chance of survival. For that reason the Board at The Women's University never told anybody about the million N. crowns we received as a gift during our time of crisis. Since 1985 the sum from the Parliamentary Committee has been increased each year, and professionals have visited from Japan, China, Australia, Thailand, the US and the Nordic countries. The present Prime Minister, Gro Harlem-Brundtland, as well as teachers and women's groups from other towns have stayed and enquired about teaching methods, the organization, and the dual leadership. The former Prime Minister, Oddvar Nordli, explained and argued for women's universities in an educational video. He predicted that they will be established everywhere.

Three years ago we established a second Women's University in Norway. While the first one specialized in teaching organizational theories and leadership from women's perspectives, the second is developing curricula for teaching women to plan communities and counties with a focus on women's interests. The first unit is located in the middle of Norway, the second in the north.

During the fall of 1994, a Women's University in Sweden began to operate. The planners had visited both Norwegian universities and had spent almost three years planning their school. In January 1995, a second decentralized unit extended their activities in the most northern part of Sweden. The mayor of a small town, Kiruna, in Sweden has visited the mayor at Løten and discussed with him what an institution like ours means to the local environment. Very openly we can claim that it means quite a bit in financial terms. Twenty-five people on the salary list and 100 employed in more limited jobs during the year is important for a small community. Culturally it plays a fine role. In the fall of 1994 the Norwegian Queen visited the place and participated as a student in two classes. One was for adult women in the community who finally had an opportunity to take their high school education. The second was a course in women's rights and human rights. When she was told that women's rights in Norway have been weakened she encouraged the other students to protest!

When we were finally established and well into our second year of functioning, a high official remarked that he felt we had truly done "the impossible". "In my opinion," he said, "it is impossible to function for such a long time without more permanent funding! It is as impossible as to walk on water!" "Impossible?" I said, while looking around and observing how the other women smiled. "You see: if you have learned to take the first two or three steps, the rest of the walk – on water – is not that difficult."

The next day a Christian daily informed the public that now Mrs Ås, too, had been walking on water! In 1995 we celebrated our tenth anniversary. We insist that we live well and develop a series of studies on all levels in the years to come.

Epilogue

In this article the name "The Women's University" and "The Feminist University" have been used interchangeably. Three years ago we decided on the latter and we retain that title in English. During the ten years of our existence we have constantly grown. From a budget of 400,000 N. crowns in 1985, we now have a budget of 7 million. The state, which allocated 300,000 N. crowns for the first year, was contributing 2 million by 1995. The student population has increased from a few hundred to more than a thousand in 1995. The variety and number of courses offered have also increased. We provide education at all levels and we are pleased that our experience shows that students who started with continuing education and high school studies proceeded with lectures at the college level and are now in the "other" university system.

Education for women leaders has been offered by "a flying team" to eight locations around the country. The Women's University North plans to use a similar decentralized model for its teaching program and is building on the same organizational and knowledge base as the motherhouse at Løten.

The curriculum will continue to grow: a university course on women's history and experimental teaching on holistic health from a feminist perspective, as well as a new pedagogy course for adult education are planned. The "convent model" of teaching, doing research and producing may finally take a step forward when this year, we start to grow medicinal plants.

Because of our stressed financial situation, our steps have been taken one at a time. All the contributions above 50,000 N. crowns – from private donors and firms – have been given by women. This year we asked the twenty firms in Norway with profits above a billion N. crowns to sponsor the celebration of our first decade. *If* such firms contribute, it will be with sums from 5,000 to 10,000 N. crowns. However, most of them didn't care to reply, and one of the wealthiest – the Norwegian oil company Statoil – answered that they were not interested in this activity. The answer arrived on the same day that Statoil allocated nine million N. crowns to widen the top sector within Norwegian sport.

The Feminist University is characterized by continual struggles, a steady growth, ongoing discussions about feminist views and practice, and constant agitation for money. The rewards are many: grown-up women have just delivered their personal comments on how the years at the motherhouse at Løten have changed their lives and given them new energy, a better self image and encouragement. Can we ask for more?

Jalna Hanmer

Taking Ourselves Seriously

To know the future is to know the past. To know the current moment is not enough.

Several years ago I realised I am rapidly becoming the only woman left amongst staff and students at the University of Bradford to know how and when Women's Liberation Movement newsletters, bulletins and other regular publications of the 1970s and early 1980s developed and, frequently, which of these are British. With such a dismal lack of basic information, a knowledge of when, in a longish run, various publications provided the leading theoretical edge of the Women's Liberation Movement could not even be formulated as a question. Further, without some basic knowledge, women did not know where to begin a search for material relevant to their interests or how to understand whatever they did find in the archival collection on the Women's Liberation Movement held at the Bradford branch of the Feminist Archive.[1] Problems experienced by women in using the Archive drove home how the recent past – my living memory – is not shared by increasing numbers of women. This wave of women's political struggle is becoming as opaque and ill-understood as that of the nineteenth century.

Early on in the MA Women's Studies (Applied) course on Feminisms and Sexual Divisions the question arises, what knowledge do each of us have of 19th century feminism in Britain? I give my own pre-Women's Liberation Movement knowledge, "some crazy women chained themselves to the railings outside Parliament". This brief, but total knowledge statement is echoed by those of other

---

1. There are two branches of the Feminist Archive, in Bradford (21 Claremont, Bradford BD7 1DP) and in Bristol (Trinity Road Library, Trinity Road, St Philips, Bristol BS2 ONW). Bristol has a particularly good collection of locally based Women's Liberation Movement newsletters and bulletins, while the Bradford branch is focusing on Women's Liberation Movement material 1969-1979. Donations are gratefully received and donors individually acknowledged in the cataloguing system.

women. Only those with access to more recent education in Women's Studies or some other disciplinary area with work on women and gendered social relations know more. In *Women of Ideas and What Men Have Done To Them* (1982), Dale Spender explores what it means to lose our heritage and how losing both herstory and history are major ways of securing the subordination of women. It is not an accident that we do not know our past. People without a past do not have a future. They remain subordinated, the onlookers in the history of the socially dominant and, at best, honorary members of the privileged caste, group, or class.

When we discovered violence against women in Britain, we thought we were the first women to do so. We believed no one previously knew about violence to women from men with whom they lived or had lived or were related to in some other way. It was with some surprise that we discovered a small part of the past. It helped to know that someone had written an influential article with a title we did not think we could get away with today, *Wife Torture in England* (Cobbe: 1878). It helped to read historical accounts of activism on violence against women as this began a process of connection with the past (for example, May: 1978; Tomes: 1978). It helped to engage in a struggle to save the Fawcett Library collection from being broken up and culled for "important" books which were to be placed – within the Dewey decimal system of library classification – at the London School of Economics. We experienced a moment of living heritage when at the Fawcett Society meeting in 1976 (an organisation that many of us from the Women's Liberation Movement had rushed to join in order to be able to vote), we were confronted by women in their 80s and even 90s speaking of their and their mothers likely reaction to the possibility that the collection might be dismembered. "My mother would be appalled", said one elderly trustee of some ninety books housed in the Fawcett collection, succinctly summing up the personal position of the most elderly and prestigious members of the Society.[2] Those of us who had recently joined the society began to relax, recognising political allies from the so-called "moderate" suffragist movement of the nineteenth and early twentieth centuries. To know the past is to connect with the present.

Saving our knowledge and finding ways of passing it on involves more than attacking revisionist history, important as that is. The aim is to create a map, a guide, for future generations of women so that women who did not share a particular moment in time may have access to it. In Britain the early years of the Women's Liberation Movement, 1969–1979, saw a proliferation of ephemeral publications, so-called "grey material". Those original ideas, turned out on the duplicator, often indistinct or blurred, and circulated to small numbers through women-only publications, were major source material and remain so for the future. Because political activists in this decade utilised multi-media, there are songs,

---

2. The alternative offer, to keep the collection together and to add to it, was accepted by the members at this meeting. The Fawcett Library is now located at London Guildhall University (Calcutta House, Old Castle Street, London E1 7NT).

photographs, posters and film as well as a multiplicity of forms of written work. Organisations and struggles around specific issues had special relationships with particular songs as well as specific visual representations, for example Gloria Gaynor's, *I Will Survive*, was described at the time as the national anthem of the National Women's Aid Federation.[3] In some future time, say fifty to 100 years from now, these multi-media source data will be needed for women to be able to assess the development of ideas, actions and times in which we lived and live. They also will enable other women to discover, if it is not possible to maintain conscious continuity, a feminist past, just as we did.

The ten year period, 1969–1979, preceded and provides the basis for the subsequent widespread publication of feminist academic work in books and other publicly available sources. To achieve accessibility to the core ideas of the British Women's Liberation Movement these ephemeral materials need collecting and ordering in relation to the Women's Liberation Conferences held between 1970–1978, women's organisations, demonstrations, campaigns, meetings, and local regional and national group activities and publications. The first part of the project consists of listing the above activities by date, followed by collecting and cataloguing the relevant newsletters, journals, single publications, conference hand-outs, minutes and other notes on meetings, flyers, posters, and any other materials that relate to each of these. Oral history interviews then run alongside specific occasions or organisations or locally based activities.[4]

There is a sense of urgency about this project as complete sets of some publications are yet to be collected by at least one of the existing archives in the UK. Twenty five years is not that long ago, but it may be too far away to ensure everything is collectable. Further, while the collection of ephemera is being under-taken by women in many locations in Europe, in Britain these poorly funded or unfunded archives are constantly threatened with closure and, as a result, the loss of material.[5] Unfortunately, disagreements amongst women who assume responsi-bility for collections may also lead to losses. At its best when all else fails, storage in damp garages, sometimes dry attics, provides a slender thread of continuity. This

---

3. The National Women's Aid Federation was the original title of the refuge movement for women and children leaving home because of violent men. This organisation subsequently devolved into Northern Ireland Women's Aid (129 University Street, Belfast BT7 1HP), Scottish Women's Aid (12 Torphichen Street, Edinburgh EH3 8JQ), Welsh Women's Aid (3848 Crwys Road, Cardiff DF2 4NN), and National Women's Aid England (PO Box 391, Bristol DS99 7WS).

4. During the 1994–1995 academic year, Elizabeth Arledge-Ross, as part of the mapping project, began to interview women in Leeds and Bradford about their involvement in the Women's Liberation Movement during the 1970s and, with the help of Karen Boyle, to greatly improve the organisation of the Archive and the cataloguing of its material.

5. A partial listing of these archives and other sources for information on women can be found in a study carried out by IIAV (Internationaal Informateicentrum en Archief Voor de Vrouwenbeweging) and KVINFO for the Commission of the European Communities (Kramer and Larsen: 1992).

replicates in a material way the retention and loss of conscious knowledge of the past referred to earlier. Because retention and loss of knowledge is about power and whose ideas are to prevail, securing the feminist past in all its diversity is a future oriented radical feminist activity.

So what of the future? If we cannot be sanguine about retaining knowledge of the Women's Liberation Movement and our radical feminist past then to secure the future, the present must include work to retain consciousness of the past. To keep alive knowledge of women's struggles with each other and with men; their efforts to understand and organise against their oppression and exploitation, means passing it on from woman to woman from mother to daughter through the generations. There have been bigger waves of women's protest and activism than that which began at the end of the 1960s and there may be even larger, or perhaps smaller, ones to come. We cannot know this with certainty, but we can point to recurring patterns of high and low mobilisation of women to resist and transform their social situations in countries around the world. If we had full access to this knowledge, our heritage, think how empowered our social and collective identity would be.

Working to retain the past is also a radical feminist activity – in an activist and intellectual sense – in the here and now. Women's Liberation Movement publications and activities were usually women-only in Britain. To respect the woman-only distribution policy of these publications makes it even more difficult to obtain funding and therefore, secure the future of these sources, but remaining loyal to the intentions and thereby the politics of its authors and editors, is a way to maintain an herstorical organisational tradition. Seeking to secure women-only anything is as subversive now as it was in the 1970s, as a consequence, something of the feelings and meanings attached to women-only activities and publications is conveyed to women today. This simple action, this experience, creates a present connected to the past.

Respecting the diversity of Women's Liberation Movement material is another aspect of radical feminist activity today. This requires coming to terms with emotionally charged beliefs and actions and accepting that sisterhood was, and is, about disagreements as well as agreements. While at the time disagreements could be responded to in intensely personal ways, on another level, disagreements are not unfortunate occurrences linked to personal inadequacies, but central to the development of ideas and understanding. The Women's Liberation Movement in Britain was diverse with multiple connections from the student movement, to sexual libertarianism, to the anti-imperialist struggles, to the political left via various forms of Anarchism and Marxism, to gay liberation. To seek to deny the relevance of any source or connection is to create revisionist history.

Because radical feminism is about social transformation in the interests of all women, multiple positions are to be respected. This is of course, easier for women who were not activists during the 1970s as all of us involved in those times have views on what was important and what remains crucial. To move forward each of us should vigorously argue our position, but to secure the future it is up to us to leave as complete an account as possible so that women who come later may make their own judgements, building on our work and achievements just as we have built on those of women who came before us. Taking ourselves seriously is to recognise and value a diverse heritage of our own making and to act to preserve it for future generations of women.

Mary Daly

The Witches Return: Patriarchy on Trial*

Throughout that academic year (1988–1989) countless gynocidal/biocidal atrocities had been reported locally and around the United States. I had continually stressed with my students that since patriarchal scholarship and professions commonly present interrelated events as if they were not connected with each other, they should constantly attempt to See and to Name the connections. That year presented us with an abundance of material to analyze. It was evident that many crimes against women were happening, that the war against women and nature was escalating.[1]

      During that year I had, as usual, spoken at a number of universities. Of particular significance was my visit to Virginia Tech in Blacksburg, Virginia, where I gave the Keynote address for Women's Week on April 6. There I met Evelyn Wight, a Feminist activist whose sister, Rebecca, had been murdered almost one year before (on May 13, 1988) on the Appalachian Trail in Pennsylvania while hiking with her lover, Claudia Brenner. When Evelyn introduced me at Virginia Tech. that

---

* Excerpt from *Outercourse: The Bedazzling Voyage containing recollections from my* Logbook of a Radical Feminist Philosopher *(Be-ing an Account of my Time/Space Travels and Ideas—Then, Again, Now and How)* (1993).

1. Indeed many of my friends were making files of newspaper clippings about atrocities. Many of these occurred in March and/or April 1989: A twenty-eight-year-old woman who was a Wall Street investment banker was gang raped by eight youths, aged 14 to 17, in April. Her skull was fractured by the youths, who used a pipe and a brick. They showed no remorse, sang a rap song, bragged about what they had done, and called their actions "fun". The body of the eighth woman victim of serial killings in the area of New Bedford, Massachusetts, was found that April. Within that time period, two women (Lesbians) from the Boston area who went on vacation together to a small Caribbean island were murdered on the beach there. The Exxon Valdez oil spill that spoiled Prince William Sound in Alaska occurred in late March. The two nuclear reactors close to Boston – the Seabrook, New Hampshire, reactor and "Pilgrim" in Plymouth, Massachusetts – were getting back into operation. The list can go on, and on.

evening she spoke of the murder of her sister by a man "whose only motive was to destroy the image before him: Two strong women . . . together." Evelyn explained:

> Claudia Brenner's incredible physical strength and mental determination enabled her to hike four miles to the nearest road after being shot five times and still carrying three bullets in her body, and then hitchhike to the nearest police station. She refused attention to her wounds until she was certain the search for Rebecca had begun. They found Rebecca's body where Claudia had left her, covered with a sleeping bag to keep her warm.

> Rebecca was dead and the man who killed her was gone. He has since been found and sentenced. Claudia is alive and well today. But this is an unforgettable tragedy. I urge you never to forget it.

I went on and gave my Keynote address, but I could not forget Evelyn's words. Afterward without fully understanding why I was doing it, or how I could make my invitation become Realized, I asked Evelyn if she would come to Boston to speak if we could make it possible. I took her address and phone number, as if I could really make such an event happen. I Now Realize, of course, that the idea of "The Witches Return" was already brewing . . . subliminally.

Soon after that it became clear that it was Time to put patriarchy on trial. I envisioned an Event that would expose the gynocidal/biocidal atrocities and the connections among them, that would publicly bring the criminals to trial, and that would Conjure Nemesis. Women would have an opportunity to Hex the killers of women and nature and to experience and celebrate Ecstasy.

Together with Cronies and students I Brewed the Event which would be called "The Witches Return". We decided that it would be a women-only multi-media production and that it would be held in Sanders Theatre at Harvard University. The best date that we could arrange for the use of Sanders was Sunday, May 14, 1989, which happened to be Mother's Day.

"The Witches Return" was brought into be-ing through the creative work of strong Witches.[2] We planned the Event rapidly. In this Witch Trial the Witches would be the Judges and the Jury. The accused would be:

> Larry Flynt, figurehead for the pornographers
> Jack the Ripper, figurehead for serial killers
> Exxon, figurehead for Earth-rapers of every kind
> The Moronizing Media, figurehead for the Wit Dimmers of the world
> Sigmund Freud, figurehead for all professional Mind-fuckers
> Boss-town College, figurehead for the Brain-drainers of academia
> His Nothingness of Rome and His Arrogance, Cardinal Flaw, figureheads for the Soul-killers of women.

---

2. These include Mary Stockton, Producer, and Carole Tillis, Director.

We plotted the construction ... and destruction of eight wooden dummies representing the accused, each of which would wear appropriate attire and have a suitable balloon head. For example, Larry Flynt would have a suit of $10,000 bills, and Boss-town College would be dressed as a football wearing a roman collar.[3] Gifted women were assigned to make the costumes and props for the cast. We also planned to have music and electrifying sound effects. Together with Joyce Contrucci I wrote the script. We had time for only two rehearsals.

On May 14 hundreds of women poured into Sanders Theatre. The opening address was given by Evelyn Wight, who Stunned the audience as she spoke calmly and movingly of the murder of her sister. At the conclusion of her speech I Pronounced a Nemesis Hex.[4]

After Conjuring the Elemental Powers – Earth, Air, Fire, Water – I Conjured also the Presence of Foresisters – Joan of Arc, Harriet Tubman, Matilda Joslyn Gage, Sojourner Truth, Charlotte Perkins Gilman, Virginia Woolf, Andrée Collard – while pointing to the large beautiful portraits of them on the backdrop of the stage. Then the lights were turned off.

When the lights were turned on again Melissa Fletcher danced to the Spooking refrains of "The Witching Hour", while fierce jailors carrying large Labryses took their positions on stage. Thus the scene was set for "The Witches Return".

Brief Lunar Interruption

At this point in my typing of the *Logbook* entry I am interrupted by the clumping of Catherine's hooves. I turn around and find her dancing. The reference to "The Witching Hour" has set her off, apparently. Getting into the mood, so to speak, I read the refrain for her. That does it! She swings her body and sways her head, kicking her hooves to the words I have read. Wild Cat thumps her tail in Time with every line. She uses that appendage as a kind of baton, leading us on.

When I come to the final words of the refrain, I make a change. In deference to Catherine I "read": "Power to the Witch and to the *Bovine* in you!" This brings her to the height of delight, and she leaps around the workshop with Bovine grace, knocking everything out of place.

Wild Cat turns and stares at the cow. "All right," I say, "It's your turn, Now." So I sing the line that will give her her cue: "Power to the Witch and to the *Feline* in you!"

---

3. The Figureheads were designed, constructed, and attired by Anna Larson and Nicki Leone
4. NEMESIS HEX:

> On the Earth, in the Air,
> Through the Fire, by the Water
> We are vengeance, Hecate's daughters!
> For peace and love we ever yearned
> But some do wrong and never learn
> This Time it won't be us that burn
> The wrath of Nemesis is here!

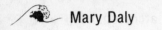

Then we dance in a circle and roll on the floor. I urge my companions to prance out the door. I return to my task of writing the story of "The Witches Return" on that evening of glory.

Logbook Entries on "The Witches Return" (continued)

As I was saying, the scene had been set for our Dramatic Indictment. A stern Bailiff (Krystyna Colburn) stalked to the lectern and shouted:

> Wild Witches will now expose and condemn the massacre of women's minds, bodies, and spirits. Bring in the accused!

Immediately there followed a loud beat of drums as the black-robed members of the Witches' Chorus carried the accused from the back of the theatre, down the aisle, and up the stairs of the stage, depositing the dummies in their assigned stand, and then seating themselves in the Witches' Chorus section, where they were joined by two Gossips.[5]

At the Bailiff's command – "All rise for the Chaircrones of the court!" – three Chaircrones, Emily Culpepper, Joyce Contrucci, and mySelf, wearing red flowing robes, tall black Wildly decorated Witches' hats, and holding Labryses aloft, swept onto centre stage to the sound of trumpet and drum. We then seated ourSelves at the judgment table and removed our hats. As High Chaircrone, seated in the center, I pounded the table with my Labrys, howling: "Disorder in the court!" three times.

Chaircrones Culpepper, Contrucci, and I each stood and Hexed the patriarchy. And then the Trial began.

In the course of the Trial each of the accused was brought before the judgment table. Chaircrones pronounced charges against them and each was allowed to "defend" himself briefly.[6]

The Trial was a high-powered dramatic exposé of patriarchal gynocide. The eight accused were forcefully denounced in seven electrifying speeches and Hexed by Grand Accusers.[7]

Throughout the Trial the audience participated Wildly. After each Grand Accuser finished her speech, one of the Chaircrones addressed the audience and Witches' Chorus:

---

5. Members of the Witches' Chorus were Leigh Anthony, Susan Messenheimer, Maria Moschoni and Georgia Stathopoulou. The Gossips were Niliah MacDonald and Suzanne Melendy.

6. The voice of the Accused was that of Julia Penelope, who read actual quotes from each of the criminals in appropriately satirical tones.

7. The Grand Accusers were Gail Dines (Pornographers), Melissa Fletcher (Rippers), Joyce Contrucci (Earth-rapers), Julia Penelope (Wit Dimmers), Bonnie Mann (Mind-fuckers), Emily Culpepper (Brain-drainers, Mary Daly (Soul-killers).

Members of the Jury. Witches of Boston. You have heard all the evidence against the accused. How do you find the accused? Guilty or Not Guilty?

The "Witches of Boston" yelled mightily each time: "Guilty!"

After each of the accused had been properly harangued, Hexed, and indicted – culminating with the Soul-killers – I addressed the audience:

How do you find ALL of the accused? Guilty or Not Guilty?

When the roaring of "Guilty!" had subsided, the Chaircrones put on our hats and retired to chambers to determine the sentence.

Interspersed throughout the first part of the Trial there had been powerful Hexes, Pronounced by Chaircrones and Grand Accusers, stirring voice and guitar music, blaring of horns, and explosive drumming.

When the Witches of Boston returned to their seats after intermission, there was an impressive Karate performance accompanying a reading from Monique Wittig's *Les Guérillères*.

At the Bailiff's call the Chaircrones then swooped back into court, Labryses again held high. Standing and addressing the Witches' Chorus, I Hexed:

North South East West
Spider's web shall bind them best.
East West North South
Hold their limbs and stop their mouths
Seal their eyes and choke their breath
Wrap them round with ropes of Death.

The entire Witches' Chorus rushed the accused, wrapping them with yarn to signify the muting of the mutilators. After this, as High Chaircrone, I sentenced these figureheads to de-heading.

"Off with their heads!" shouted the women, as the jailors, flourishing sharp-edged Labryses, descended upon the accused and popped their balloon heads. As one woman wrote: "The action, intense and furious, was like an enormous exhalation, breathing out pent-up Rage and frustration."[8]

There was an enormous relief of tension as the lights went out and the jailors dumped the de-headed figureheads behind their stand. Then we all left the stage. When the lights went on again Diana Beguine sang her inspiring song, "Celestial Time Tables". I spoke briefly about the Moments of Exorcism and Ecstasy that constitute the Spiral Galaxies of the Voyaging of Wild Women.

The entire cast returned on stage chanting: "POWER TO THE WITCH AND TO THE WOMAN IN ME." Then the whole audience joined in the chanting. As they left Sanders Theatre, with the sounds of "The Witching Hour" in their ears, women's eyes were shining.

As one woman said: "Patriarchy doesn't exist Here, Now."

This statement could have applied to the 1975 Forum on Women and

---

8. This description was written by Annie Milhaven in an unpublished article describing the event.

Higher Education. It could also have applied to the 1979 Rally, "We Have Done with Your Education". Both the 1975 and 1979 events were Sparkling triumphs over patriarchal oppression. They seemed to represent the utmost in transcendence at their respective Times. They were both Third Galactic phenomena.

In fact, however, this Stunning statement was made in 1989, because at this Time Something Other did happen. Our dramatic indictment was created with utterly Fiercely Focused Rage and Elemental, Creative Power. What conditions came together to allow us to bring this about?

On the foreground level the oppression of women and of nature was more atrocious and more obvious. We knew much more about the pornography industry and its vile effects, about serial killers, about the Earth-rapers. We knew more about connections, for example, between the mind-mutilating media and rape. Moreover academic and churchly malevolence did not escape being judged in this context of interconnectedness.

So in 1989, in the foreground Age of Dis-memberment, we Leaped into participation in Nemesis. We – the Witches – returned to judge and mete out the death punishment to the gynocidal killers of women's minds, bodies, and spirits. We Hexed them with Force and Fury. When we de-headed the dummies this was a Metaphor with Terrifying Power. The Witches of Boston had pronounced them GUILTY – without qualification.

Evelyn Wight had spoken to us of the very real, malignant killing of her sister. [9] The Daring Dramatic Production was regal, riotous and Rage-full. We broke Terrible Taboos.

And after *this* event more than one woman actually did say: "Patriarchy doesn't exist Here, Now." Because this was a Moment, or rather, a cluster of Moments, of Be-Dazzling, many women entered a Door to Four. So it is Be-Dazzling Now, in the Expanding Now.

---

9. In a telephone conversation, in February 1992, Evelyn Wight told me that the opportunity to speak that night had enabled her to see beyond her own blinders and to Realize that there is a whole world of women, Lesbians in particular, who have been deeply affected by the murder of Rebecca. She had felt isolated in her grief before that, but then had felt the tremendous compassion and energy of the women Present when she spoke. Just before Evelyn went on stage to give her talk, Lierre, one of the musicians who was part of the Event, went backstage and sang for her a song which she had written about the murder of Rebecca, who had been killed exactly a year and a day before "The Witches Return" at Sanders Theatre. That evening Evelyn had been able, for the first time, to cry about her sister's violent death.

Robyn Rowland

The Burying of Hughes*

*(for Sylvia Plath
Stall Hapton, Hebden Bridge)*

... five women stood
in the grey morning mist of a
Yorkshire fall ...

Such a simple act of identity it was ...

... call it political, call it artistic, call it
the act women do and redo
to name themselves or take back their
names, though some would call that
desecration, & the hammer did ring out too
loud at each tap & the women did hold
their breath as the postman passed, but
the letters were cheap leading & fell easily.

Then silence. For a moment they stood with leaves
clustering & the sun beginning to stir among the graves &
a heavy kind of sigh fell while
they gathered each her letter, & the H
was hard & bent where the chisel
almost broke its back, & the hand that held
it felt the sigh & the chill air warming
into day, & the eye saw the work done
where it says "In Memory Of
Sylvia Plath" – & the faint passing across
the stone of the imprint of "Hughes".

---

* Excerpted from *Up From Below: Poems of the 1980s* (1987). By June 1995, the name "Hughes" had
been replaced on the tombstone ...

A Po-mo Quiz

[*Scene Change*] There follows a Po-mo quiz, wherein the Editors offer, for your enjoyment, a selection of the entries from our Contributors. Responding to our request for multi-choice questions that might assist the reader in working through the complexities of post-modernism, we received many items. We regret that we can not share all of them. Some were funny but not true, others funny and true, many were libellous and still others employed language that was not in our spell check, let alone our vocabularies!

Q. How many Po-mos does it take to change a lightbulb?
(a) None, because the lightbulb, which both typifies the weary technological inventiveness of a dead modernism and also serves as the iconic representation of modern thought ("idea") is utterly meaningless in a post-modern world;
(b) None, they wouldn't bother because it's essentialist and ahistorical to think that you can't see in the dark;
(c) None, the Enlightenment is dead!

Q. Essentialism is wrong because
(a) it's wrong;
(b) the truth is, it's not true;
(c) it's a moral evil;
(d) post-modernists say so;
(e) there aren't any reasons;
(f) it's not wrong at all if you call it ontology.

Q. Why do Po-mos see Radical Feminists as bad and wrong?
(a) Because Radical Feminism is biological determinism;
(b) Because Radical Feminism is foundationalism;
(c) Because Radical Feminism is essentialism;
(d) Because Radical Feminism not only sees the problems but offers solutions.

Q. If the original meaning of torture is to separate the mind from the body, then is reading Po-mo material torture?
(a) Yes;
(b) Kia Ora (Maori);
(c) Oui;
(d) Ja;
(e) 'Ae (Hawai'ian);
(f) Yeah!

Q. "Gender" means
(a) anything;
(b) everything;
(c) nothing;
(d) not sex;
(e) women;
(f) men too;
(g) something superficial so you can change it at will;
(h) all of the above.

Q. Why do Po-mos love looking in mirrors and glassy surfaces?
(a) They are essentially narcissistic;
(b) The mirror does not reflect the soul;
(c) They are vain;
(d) They are prone to zits.

Q. If Po-mos extol the virtues of multivocality, how come they don't want to hear what Radical Feminists have to say?
(a) They are deaf, textually speaking;
(b) They are in denial;
(c) They are frightened;
(d) They wouldn't know truth if they saw it.

Q. If Foucault is right and power is everywhere why do we all have to pay electricity bills?

Q. What is so threatening about political activism for Po-mos?
(a) It might require moving their butts off the chair and into the street;
(b) It has mass appeal;
(c) It threatens their superiority and elitism;
(d) They'd rather be shopping.

Q Why do Po-mos love repetition and sacrifice so much?
(a) They secretly worship the bible;
(b) They offer up all women as sacrifice to their egos;
(c) They like word games;
(d) Repetition helps to reinforce nonsense.

Q. If the prick is a god and god doesn't exist, then does Po-mo philosophy exist?
(a) Ask Derrida;
(b) Ask Foucault;
(c) Ask De Sade. Yes – he's dead;
(d) No.

Q. When booking an airline ticket, which of a person's multiple subject positions travels first-class?

Q. Why do Po-mos write so many books?
(a) to self-abnegate;
(b) to prove that truth is unimportant;
(c) to practise their spelling.

Q. If the author is dead who gets the royalty cheque?
(a) The tax man;
(b) ducks;
(c) cheques are texts, stupid.

Q. Where do you find a Po-mo feminist?
(a) In the nearest menstrual hut;
(b) the fourth floor of the National History Museum;
(c) Grand Central;
(d) Grand Canyon.

Q. Are Po-mos universally anti-environment?
(a) Yes (ask the trees which have been pulped);
(b) The land is for inscription not for conservation;
(c) No because the environment does not exist.

Q. Why do Po-mos enjoy blatant consumptionism?
(a) When the going gets tough, the tough go shopping;
(b) The more Toyotas purchased, the better their BMWs stand out;
(c) It shows power over;
(d) It shows superiority.

Q. If there are only texts, what does it mean when the FBI reports a 120% increase in violent crimes against women between 1993 and 1994?

Q. Why does Derrida call women the "name for that untruth of truth"?
(a) He has a problem knowing what truth is;
(b) He hates his mother;
(c) He hates his sister;
(d) He hates himself;
(e) He needs therapy.

Q. If there is no such thing as truth, why can you be incarcerated for perjury?
(a) Because judges have not read Foucault;
(b) Because jail is just a text;
(c) Because you deserve it.

Q. What is "phallic drift"?

(a) A powerful subterranean force capable of moving continents;

(b) a wandering dick;

(c) a pen (which) is in motion;

(d) the powerful tendency for public discussion of gender issue to drift, inexorably, back to the male point of view.

And now for your essay topics

Write a fragment on one of the following topics in about 50,000,000 words. Do not attempt to make sense of anything whatsoever, and avoid all substantiating examples. Students are advised that there will be a penalty imposed on sections which (a) attempt to achieve clarity, or (b) are not fragmentary.

(1) *The Sexed Sky*, or the problematics of post-descendency de-realisation in the ethereal text.

(2) The theory of engendered sustenance, ie: all the women are fruit, all the men are vegetables, and tomatoes are still puzzled.

(3) Regimes of difference: the significance of cucumber, chicken, chocolate *or* chips in the lives of global women.

Lastly, how was *Radically Speaking* reviewed?

(a) With the true generosity of spirit that characterises po-mo pronouncements: "Let a thousand flowers bloom."

(b) Objectively: "I didn't have to read it to know what it was about."

(c) Subjectively: "There go those victim feminists again!"

(d) From multiple subject positions: "This hurts."

Bibliography

Aaron, Jane and Sylvia Walby. (Eds.) (1991). *Out of the Margins: Women's Studies in the Nineties.* London: Falmer Press.

Abbot, Pamela and Claire Wallace. (1990). *An Introduction to Sociology: Feminist Perspectives.* London: Routledge.

Abdalla, Raqiya Hajji Dualeh. (1982). *Sisters in Affliction.* London: Zed Press.

Accad, Evelyne. (1978). *Veil of Shame: The Role of Women in the Contemporary Fiction of North Africa and the Arab World.* Sherbrooke: Naaman.

Accad, Evelyne. (1988 and 1992). *L'Excisée.* Paris: L'Harmattan. (English translation *The Excised.* 1994. Colorado: Three Continents Press).

Accad, Evelyne. (1990). *Sexuality and War.* New York: New York University Press.

Accad, Evelyne. (1993). *Blessures des Mots: Journal de Tunisie.* Paris: Côté femmes.

Adler, Rachel. (1983). Jew Who Wasn't There. In Susannah Heschel (Ed.) *On Being a Jewish Feminist.* New York: Schocken Books.

Afkhami, Mahnaz and Erika Friedl. (Eds.) (1994). *In The Eye of the Storm: Women in Post-Revolutionary Iran.* Syracuse, New York: Syracuse University Press.

Agosín, Marjorie. (1989). *Women of Smoke: Latin American Women in Literature and Life.* Stratford, Ontario, Canada: Williams and Wallace Publishers.

Agosín, Marjorie. (1992). *Circles of Madness.* Fredonia, New York: White Pine Press.

Akhter, Farida. (1987). Statistics for Wheat: A Case Study of Relief Wheat for Attaining Sterilization Target in Bangladesh. In Patricia Spallone and Deborah L. Steinberg (Eds.) *Made to Order.* Oxford and New York: The Athene Series, Pergamon Press.

Akhter, Farida. (1992). *Depopulating Bangladesh.* Dhaka: Narigrantha Prabartana.

Akhter, Farida. (1995). *Resisting Norplant: Women's Struggle in Bangladesh Against Coercion and Violence.* Dhaka: Narigrantha Prabartana.

Albury, Rebecca. (1987, Autumn). Babies on Ice: Aspects of Australian Press Coverage of IVF. *Australian Feminist Studies,* 4 64.

Alcoff, Linda. (1988). Cultural Feminism vs Post-Structuralism. *Signs, 1* (3), 405-36.

Alcoff, Linda. (1990). Feminist Politics and Foucault: The Limits to a Collaboration. In Arleen B. Dallery and Charles E. Scott (Eds.) with P. Holley Roberts. *Crises in Continental Philosophy.* Albany: State University of New York Press.

Allan, Jeffner and Iris M. Young. (Eds.) *The Thinking Muse, Feminism and Modern French Philosophy.* Bloomington: Indiana University Press.

American Academy of Religion Committee on the Status of Women in the Profession. (1994). Harassment and Violence Against Women Scholars. *Religious Studies News, 9* (4), 15.

Amnesty International. (1995). *Human Rights are Women's Rights*, London: Amnesty International.

Andreasen, Tayo *et al.* (Eds.) (1991). *Moving On: New Perspectives on the Women's Movement.* Denmark: Aarhus University.

Andrews, Lori. (1986). My Body, My Property. *Hastings Center Report.* 28-37.

Andrews, Lori. (1988). Alternative Modes of Reproduction. In *Reproductive Laws for the 1990s: A Briefing Handbook.* Newark, New Jersey: Women's Rights Litigation Clinic, Rutgers Law School.

Ang-Lygate, Magdalene, Chris Corrin and Millsom Henry. (Eds.) (1996). *Desperately Seeking Sisterhood: Still Challenging and Building*, London: Taylor and Francis.

An-Na'im, A. A. (Ed.) (1992). *Human Rights in Cross-cultural Perspectives.* Philadelphia: University of Pennsylvania Press.

Anzaldúa, Gloria and Cherrie Moraga (Eds.) (1981). *This Bridge Called My Back: Writings by Radical Women of Color.* Massachusetts: Persephone Press.

Anzaldúa, Gloria. (1988). *La Frontera/Borderlands.* San Francisco: Spinsters Ink.

Anzaldúa, Gloria. (Ed.) (1990). *Making Face, Making Soul, Haciendo Caras.* San Francisco: Aunt Lute Foundation.

Appignanesi, Lisa. (Ed.) (1989). *Postmodernism, ICA Documents.* London: Free Association Books.

Ardill, Susan and Sue O'Sullivan. (1987). Upsetting an Applecart: Difference, Desire and Lesbian Sadomasochism. In *Feminist Review.* (Ed.) *Sexuality: A Reader.* London: Virago.

Arditti, Rita, Renate Duelli Klein and Shelley Minden. (Eds.) (1984). *Test-Tube Women: What Future for Motherhood?* London and Boston: Pandora Press.

Armanda, Asja. (1992). Interview for ZDF German Television Emission Mona Lisa.

Armanda, Asja and Natalie Nenadic. (1994, November). Activists Warn Not to be Fooled by Genocide/Rape Revisionists. *Northwest Ethnic News Seattle,* 2.

Armstrong, Louise. (1963). *A Child's Guide to Freud.* New York: Simon and Schuster

Armstrong, Louise. (1975). *How to Turn Lemons Into Money: A Child's Guide to Economics.* New York: Harcourt Brace Jovanovitch.

Armstrong, Louise. (1978a). *How to Turn Up Into Down Into Up: A Child's Guide to Inflation, Depression and Economic Recovery.* New York: Pocket Books.

Armstrong, Louise. (1978b). *Kiss Daddy Goodnight.* New York: Hawthorn. Re-released (1979 and 1987) New York: Pocket Books.

Armstrong, Louise. (1979a). *How To Turn War Into Peace: A Child's Guide to Conflict Resolution.* New York: Harcourt Brace Jovanovitch.

Armstrong, Louise. (1979b). *Solomon Says: A Speakout on Foster Care*, New York: Pocket Books.

Armstrong, Louise. (1983). *The Home Front: Notes from the Family War Zone.* New York: McGraw-Hill.

Armstrong, Louise. (1993). *And They Call It Help: The Psychiatric Policing of America's Children.* New York: Addison-Wesley.

Armstrong, Louise. (1994). *Rocking The Cradle of Sexual Politics: What Happened When Women Said Incest.* New York: Addison-Wesley.

Armstrong, Louise. (1995). Incest: A journey to Hullabullloo. *Women and Therapy, 17* (1/2).

Ås, Berit. (1975). On Female Culture: An Attempt to Formulate a Theory of Women's Solidarity and Action. *Acta Sociologica, 18* (2-3), 142-61.

Ås, Berit. (1985a/1989). The Feminist University. *Women's Studies International Quarterly, 8* (4). Oxford: Pergamon Press. Reprinted in Renate Klein and Deborah Steinberg (Eds.) *Radical Voices: A Decade of Feminist Resistance from Women's Studies International Forum,* Oxford: The Athene Series, Pergamon Press.

Ås, Berit. (1985b). Mobilizing Women for Action. In Aisla Thomson (Ed.) *The Decade for Women, CCLOW: Canadian Congress for Learning Opportunities for Women.* Special Report: The UN Decade for Women.

Ås, Berit. (1990). A Feminist University in Norway. In Suzanne Stiver Lie and Virginia E. O'Leary (Eds.) *Women in the Academic World.* London: Kogan Page.

Atkinson, Judy. (1989). Violence in Aboriginal Australia. Draft manuscript. (Revised and published as Atkinson 1990b and c).

Atkinson, Judy. (1990a). Violence against Aboriginal Women: Reconstitution of Customary Law – The Way Forward. *Aboriginal Law Bulletin, 2* (46), 6-9.

Atkinson, Judy. (1990b and c). Violence in Aboriginal Australia: Colonisation and Gender. *The Aboriginal and Islander Health Worker,* Part 1, *14* (2), 5-21; Part 2, *14* (3), 4-27.

Atkinson, Judy. (Ed.) (1990d). *Beyond Violence: Finding the Dream.* Video and booklet produced by the Aboriginal and Islander Subprogram, National Domestic Violence Education Program. Canberra: Office of Status of Women.

Atkinson, Ti-Grace. (1974). *Amazon Odyssey.* New York: Links Books.

Atwood, Margaret. (1986). *Handmaid's Tale.* London: Jonathan Cape.

Australian. (1995, 18 December). Garner Wins Eros. 3.

Backhouse, Constance. (1992). *Challenging Times: The Women's Movement in Canada and the United States.* Montreal: McGill–Queen's University Press.

Balasubrahmanyan, Vimal. (1984). Women As Targets in India's Family Planning Policy. In Rita Arditti, Renate Duelli Klein, and Shelley Minden (Eds.) *Test Tube Women,* London and Boston: Pandora Press.

Balendra, Jaya. (1990, August, 2). Aboriginalities: Black Violence at Home. *Independent Monthly.*

Banner, Lois. (1989). A Reply to "Culture et Pouvoir" from the Perspective of United States Women's History. *Journal of Women's History, 1* 101-7.

Baraka, Imamu Amiri (LeRoi Jones). (1964). Black Dada Nihilismus. In *The Dead Lecturer.* New York: Grove Press.

Barrett, Michèle. (1988). *Women's Oppression Today: The Marxist/Feminist Encounter.* London: Verso.

Barrington, Judith. (Ed.) (1991). *An Intimate Wilderness: Lesbian Writers on Sexuality.* Portland, Oregon: The Eighth Mountain Press.

Barry, Kathleen. (1979). *Female Sexual Slavery.* New York and London: New York University Press.

Barry, Kathleen. (1989). Tootsie Syndrome, or "We Have Met the Enemy and They are Us." *Women's Studies International Forum 12* (5), 487-93.

Barry, Kathleen. (1990, Winter). The New Historical Synthesis: Women's Biography. *Journal of Women's History, 1* (3), 74-105.

Barry, Kathleen. (1991). Deconstructing Deconstructionism (or, Whatever Happened to Feminist Studies?). *Ms. Magazine, 1* (4), 83-5.

Barry, Kathleen. (1995). *The Prostitution of Sexuality. The Global Exploitation of Women.* London: New York University Press.

Bart, Pauline B. (1970, November–December). Portnoy's Mother's Complaint. *Trans-Action, 7* (13).

Bart, Pauline B. (1971a). Depression in Middle-Aged Women. In Vivian Gornick and B. K. Moran (Eds.) *Woman in Sexist Society: Studies in Powerlessness.* New York: Basic Books.

Bart, Pauline B. (Ed.) (1971b). Sexism and Social Science: From the Gilded Cage to the Iron Cage – The Perils of Pauline. In *Journal of Marriage and the Family, 33* (4).

Bart, Pauline B. (1986). Will the Real Radical Feminist Stand Up? Urbana: National Women's Studies Association.

Bart, Pauline B. (1987). Seizing the Means of Reproduction: An Illegal Feminist Abortion Collective – How and Why it Worked. *Jane, 10* (4), 339-57.

Bart, Pauline B. (1989). Rape as a Paradigm of Sexism in Society – Victimisation and its Discontents. In Renate Klein and Deborah Lynn Steinberg (Eds.) *Radical Voices.* Oxford: The Athene Series, Pergamon Press.

Bart, Pauline B. (1994). Introduction. In Julia Penelope (Ed.) *Out of the Class Closet.* Freedom, California: The Crossing Press.

Bart, Pauline B. and Linda Frankel. (1972). *The Student Sociologist's Handbook.* Morristown, New Jersey: General Learning Press.

Bart, Pauline B. and B. K. Moran. (1993). *Violence Against Women: The Bloody Footprints.* London: Sage.

Bart, Pauline and Patricia O'Brien. (1985). *Stopping Rape: Successful Survival Strategies.* Oxford and New York: The Athene Series, Pergamon Press.

Bartley, Paula. (1994, July). Review of *The Real Facts of Life.* In *Women's Studies Network (UK) Newsletter, 18.*

Barwick, Diane, Isobel White and Betty Meehan. (Eds.) (1985). *Fighters and Singers.* Sydney: Allen and Unwin.

Barykin, Konstantin. (1990, November). Seks podorozhal: reportazh srynka svobodnoi pornopressy. (Sex Has Become More Expensive: A Report from the Open Market for Pornographic Press.) *Ogonek, 46* 18-19.

Baudrillard, Jean. (1988). *Selected Writings.* (Edited by Mark Poster.) Stanford, California: Stanford University Press.

Baxter, Mark. (1990). Tak li Bezobidny "Eti Kartinki". (How Inoffensive are these Pictures.) *Abroad Magazine, 42* (1579), 19.

Beall, J. S. Hassim, and A. Toades. (1989). A Bit On The Side?: Gender Struggles in the Politics Of Transformation In South Africa. *Feminist Review, 33.*

Beechy, Veronica. (1986). Introduction. In Veronica Beechey and Elizabeth Whitelegg (Eds.) *Women in Britain Today.* Milton Keynes: Open University Press.

Behrendt, Larissa. (1993). Aboriginal Women and the White Lies of the Feminist Movement: Implication for Aboriginal Women in Rights Discourse. *The Australian Feminist Law Journal, 1* 27-44.

Bell, Diane. (1985). Topsy Napurrula Nelson: Teacher, Philosopher, Friend. In Diane Barwick, Isobel White and Betty Meehan (Eds.) *Fighters and Singers.* Sydney: Allen and Unwin.

Bell, Diane. (1988). The Politics of Separation. In Marilyn Strathern (Ed.) *Dealing with Inequality*. New York: Cambridge University Press.

Bell, Diane. (1990). Letter to the Editor. *Anthropological Forum, 6* (2), 158-65.

Bell, Diane. (1991). Intra-racial Rape Revisited: On Forging a Feminist Future Beyond Factions and Frightening Politics. *Women's Studies International Forum, 14* (5), 385-412.

Bell, Diane. (1992). Considering Gender: Are Human Rights for Women Too? An Australian Case Study. In A. A. An-Na'im (Ed.) *Human Rights in Cross-cultural Perspectives*. Philadelphia: University of Pennsylvania Press.

Bell, Diane. (1993). *Daughters of the Dreaming*. Minneapolis: University of Minnesota Press.

Bell, Diane. (1994). Representing Aboriginal Women: Who Speaks For Whom? In Oliver Mendelsohn and Uprendra Baxi (Eds.) *The Rights of Subordinated Peoples*. Delhi: Oxford University Press.

Bell, Diane and Topsy Napurrula Nelson. (1989). Speaking about Rape is Everyone's Business. *Women's Studies International Forum, 12* (4), 403-16.

Bell, Shannon. (1994). *Reading, Writing and Rewriting the Prostitute Body*. Bloomington and Indianapolis: Indiana University Press.

Beloff, Halla. (1993). Review of *Stolen Glances: Lesbians Take Photographs. Feminism and Psychology, 3* (2), 289-91.

Benjamin, Sophia. (1992). God and Abuse: A Survivor's Story. In Ellen M. Umansky and Diane Ashton (Eds.) *Four Centuries of Jewish Women's Spirituality – A Sourcebook*. Boston: Beacon.

Bennett, Catherine. (1994, May 28). Interview with Catharine MacKinnon. *Weekend Guardian* 20-27.

Bennett, Paula. (1993, Winter). Critical Clitoridectomy: Female Sexual Imagery and Feminist Psychoanalytic Theory. *Signs, 18* (2), 235–59.

Berkeley, George. (1770/1977). A Treatise Concerning the Principles of Human Knowledge. In Cahn (Ed.) *Classics of Western Philosophy*. Indianapolis: Hackett Publishing Co.

Bernard, Jessie. (1981). Introduction. *The Female World*. New York: Free Press.

Bertens, Hans. (1995). *The Idea of Postmodernism*. London and New York: Routledge.

Bhate, Kamakshi and Mona Daswani, Lakshmi Menon, Padma Prakash, Manisha Gupte, Rima Kashyap, Mira Savara, Vibuti Patel. (Eds.) (1987). *In Search of Our Bodies: A Feminist Look at Women, Health and Reproduction in India*. Bombay: Shakti.

Bhavnani, Kum-Kum. (1993). Talking Racism and the Editing of Women's Studies. In Diane Richardson and Victoria Robinson (Eds.) *Introducing Women's Studies: Feminist Theory and Practice*. London: Macmillan.

Biale, Rachel. (1984). *Women and Jewish Law*. New York: Schocken Books.

Biale, Rachel. (1989). Abortion in Jewish Law. *Tikkun, 4* (4), 26-8.

Birch, Helen. (Ed.) (1993). *Moving Targets: Women, Murder and Representation*. London: Virago.

Blaise, Suzanne. (1988). *Le rapt des origines ou le meurtre de la mère, De la communication entre femmes*. [The theft of origins or the Murder of the Mother. On Communication Between Women] Paris: self-published.

Bleier, Ruth. (1984). *Science and Gender: A Critique of Biology and its Theories on Women*. New York: The Athene Series, Pergamon.

Bleier, Ruth. (Ed.) (1986). *Feminist Approaches to Science*. Oxford and New York: The Athene Series, Pergamon Press.

Bligh, Vivien. (1983). Study into the Needs of Aboriginal Women Who Have Been Raped or Sexually Assaulted. In Fay Gale (Ed.) *We are Bosses Ourselves*. Canberra: Australian Institute of Aboriginal Studies.

Bly, Robert. (1992). *Iron John. A Book about Men*. New York: Random.

Bock, Gisela. (1989). Women's History and Gender History: Aspects of an International Debate. *Gender and History, 1* 7-30.

Boffin, Tessa and Jean Fraser (Eds.) (1991). *Stolen Glances: Lesbians Take Photographs*. London: Pandora.

Böhnisch, Lothar und Reinhard Winter (1993). *Männliche Sozialisation – Bewältigungsprobleme männlicher Geschlechtsidentität im Lebenslauf*. Weinheim und München: Juventa Verlag.

Bolger, Audrey. (1990). *Aboriginal Women and Violence: A Report for the Criminal Research Council and the Northern Territory Commissioner of Police*. Darwin: ANU.

Boone, Kathleen C. (1989). *The Bible Tells Them So: The Discourse of Protestant Fundamentalism*. Albany: State University of New York Press.

Bordo, Susan. (1990). Feminism, Postmodernism, and Gender Skepticism. In Linda J. Nicholson (Ed.) *Feminism/Postmodernism*. New York and London: Routledge.

Bordo, Susan. (1993). Material Girl: The Effacements of Postmodern Culture. In Cathy Schwichtenberg (Ed.) *The Madonna Connection: Representational Politics, Subcultural Identities, and Cultural Theory*. Boulder, Colorado: Westview Press.

Boris, Eileen. (1994). Gender, Race, and Rights: Listening to Critical Race Theory. *Journal Of Women's History, 6* 111-24.

Børrensen, Kari E. (1981). *Subordination and Equivalence: The Nature and Role of Women in Augustine and Thomas Aquinas*. Washington: University Press of America.

Boston Lesbian Psychologies Collective. (Eds.) (1987). *Lesbian Psychologies*. Chicago: University of Illinois Press.

Boston Women's Health Collective. (1969/1973/1992). *Our Bodies, Ourselves*. New York: Simon and Schuster.

Bousquet, Jean Pierre. (1982). *Las locas de la Plaza de Mayo*. Buenos Aires: El Cid.

Bowen, Angela. (1983, November 8). Take Your Pageant and Shove it. *Village Voice*.

Bowen, Angela. (1996). Enabling a Visible Black Lesbian Presence in Academia: A Radically Reasonable Request. In Bonnie Zimmerman and Toni McNaron. (Eds.) *Lesbian Studies*. New York: Feminist Press.

Bracht, Ulla und Dieter Keiner. (1994). *Jahrbuch für Pädagogik. Geschlechterverhältnisse und die Pädagogik*. Frankfurt am Main: Lang Verlag.

Braidotti, Rosi, Ewa Charkiewicz, Sabine Häusler and Saskia Wieringa. (Eds.) (1994). *Women, the Environment, and Development: Towards a Theoretical Synthesis*. London: Zed Books.

Braidotti, Rosi. (1991). *Patterns of Dissonance: A Study of Women in Contemporary Philosophy*. Cambridge: Polity Press.

Brampton, Sally. (1994, October 14). Vive les girls. *The Guardian*, 2-3.

Bright, Susie. (1993, November). Intruder in the Lust. *Express Books, 1* 11-13.

Briscoe, Joanna. (1994, November). The New Unisex. *Elle*, 91-6.

Bristow, Joseph and Angelia R. Wilson. (Eds.) (1993). *Activating Theory: Lesbian, Gay, Bisexual Politics*. London: Lawrence and Wishart.

Bristow, Joseph. (1992, May 3). Cross-dress, Transgress. *The Observer*, 27.

Brock, Rita Nakashima. (1988). *Journeys By Heart: A Chritology of Erotic Power*. New York: Crossroad.

Brod, Harry. (Ed.) (1987). *The Making of Masculinities: The New Men's Studies*. London: Routledge.

Brodribb, Somer. (1989). Delivering Babies: Contracts and Contradictions. In Christine Overall (Ed.) *The Future of Human Reproduction*. Toronto: Women's Press.

Brodribb, Somer. (1992). *Nothing Mat(t)ers: A Feminist Critique of Post-modernism*. Melbourne: Spinifex; New York: New York University Press; Toronto: Lorimer.

Broom, Dorothy H. (1991). *Damned If We Do: Contradictions in Women's Health Care*. Sydney: Allen and Unwin.

Brown, Joanne Carlson and Carole R. Bohn. (Eds.) (1989). *Christianity, Patriarchy and Abuse*. New York: The Free Press.

Brown, Laura. (1992). While Waiting for the Revolution: The Case for a Lesbian Feminist Psychotherapy. *Feminism and Psychology, 2* (2), 239-53

Brown, Laura and Maria Root. (Eds.) (1990). *Diversity and Complexity in Feminist Therapy: Part 1 Special Issue of Women and Therapy, 9* (1–2), 56-65.

Brown, Rita Mae. (1975). Living with Other Women. In Charlotte Bunch and Nancy Myron (Eds.) *Lesbianism and the Women's Movement*, Baltimore, Massachusetts: Diana Press.

Brownmiller, Susan. (1975). *Against Our Will: Men, Women and Rape*. New York: Simon and Schuster; (1976) Harmondsworth: Penguin.

Bunch, Charlotte. (1975a/1981a). Not for Lesbians Only. In *Building Feminist Theory: Essays from Quest, A Feminist Quarterly*. New York and London: Longman. (First published in *Quest: A Feminist Quarterly. II* (2). 50-56.)

Bunch, Charlotte. (1975b/1981b). The Reform Tool Kit. In *Building Feminist Theory: Essays from Quest, A Feminist Quarterly*. New York and London: Longman. (First published in *Quest: A Feminist Quarterly. I* (1). 37-51.)

Bunch, Charlotte. (1976a/1987). Beyond Either/Or: Nonaligned Feminism. In *Passionate Politics: Feminist Theory in Action*. (1987). New York: St Martins Press. First published in *Quest: A Feminist Quarterly, III* (1), 2-17.

Bunch, Charlotte. (1976b/1980/1987). Learning from Lesbian Separatism, *Ms. Magazine*. Reprinted (1980) in Sheila Ruth (Ed.) *Issues in Feminism: A First Course in Women's Studies*. Boston: Houghton Mifflin; (1987) in *Passionate Politics: Feminist Theory in Action*. New York: St Martins Press.

Bunch, Charlotte. (1983). Not by Degrees: Feminist Theory and Education. In Charlotte Bunch and Sandra Pollack (Eds.) *Learning Our Way: Essays in Feminist Education*. New York: Crossing Press.

Bunch, Charlotte. (1987). *Passionate Politics: Feminist Theory in Action*. New York: St Martin's Press.

Bunch, Charlotte and Nancy Myron. (Eds.) (1974). *Class and Feminism*. Baltimore, Massachusetts: Diana Press.

Bunch, Charlotte, and Nancy Myron. (Eds.) (1975). *Lesbianism and the Women's Movement*, Baltimore, Massachusetts: Diana Press.

Bundesministerium für Frauenangelegenheiten/Bundeskanzleramt. (1995). *Bericht über die Situation der Frauen in Österreich*. Frauenbericht. Wien.

Burack, Cynthia. (1992). A House Divided: Feminism and Object Relations Theory. *Women's Studies International Forum, 15* (4), 499-506.

Burns, Jan. (1992). The Psychology of Lesbian Health Care. In Paula Nicolson and Jane Ussher (Eds.) *The Psychology of Women's Health and Health Care*. London: Macmillan.

Burris, Barbara in agreement with Kathy Barry, Terry Moore, Joann DeLor, Joann Parent, Cate Stadelman. (1973). The Fourth World Manifesto. In Anne Koedt, Ellen Levine and Anita Rapone. (Eds.) *Radical Feminism*. New York: Quadrangle/The New York Times Book Co.

Butler, Marylou. (1985). Guidelines for Feminist Therapy. In Lynn Bravo Rosewater and Lenore Walker (Eds.) *Handbook of Feminist Therapy*. New York: Springer.

Butler, Judith. (1990). *Gender Trouble. Feminism and the Subversion of Identity*. London and New York: Routledge.

Butler, Judith. (1991). Imitation and Gender Insubordination. In Diana Fuss (Ed.) *Inside/Out. Lesbian Theories, Gay Theories*. London and New York: Routledge.

Butler, Judith. (1992). Contingent Foundations. In Judith Butler and Joan W. Scott, (Eds.) *Feminists Theorize the Political*. London: Routledge.

Butler, Judith. (1993a). *Bodies that Matter: On the Discursive Limits of "Sex"*. New York and London: Routledge.

Butler, Judith. (1993b). Critically Queer. *GLQ. 1* 17-32.

Butler, Judith and Joan W. Scott. (Eds.) (1992) *Feminists Theorize the Political*. London: Routledge.

Cahill, Lisa Sowle. (1990). Notes on Moral Theology: 1989. Feminist Ethics Issue. *Theological Studies, 51* 49-64.

Cahill, Tom. (1984). Cruel and Unusual Punishment – Rape in Prison. *Victimology, 9* (1), 8.

Cahn, Steven M. (Ed.) (1977). *Classics of Western Philosophy*. Indianapolis: Hackett Publishing Co.

Caine, Barbara and Rosemary Pringle. (Eds.) *Transitions: New Australian Feminisms*. Sydney: Allen and Unwin.

Cameron, Debbie. (1993). Telling It Like It Wasn't. *Trouble and Strife, 27* 11-15.

Campbell, Beatrix. (1987). A Feminist Sexual Politics: Now You See It, Now You Don't. In *Feminist Review. Sexuality: A Reader*. London: Virago.

Canaan, Joyce E. and Christine Griffin. (1990). The New Men's Studies: Part of the Problem or Part of the Solution? In Jeff Hearn and David Morgan (Eds.) *Men, Masculinities and Social Theory*. London: Unwin Hyman.

Canning, Kathleen. (1993). German Particularities in Women's History/Gender History. *Journal of Women's History, 5* 102-14.

Canning, Kathleen. (1994). Feminist History after the Linguistic Turn: Historicizing Discourse and Experience. *Signs, 19* 368-90.

Cantor, Aviva. (1983). The Lilith Question. In Susannah Heschel (Ed.) *On Being a Jewish Feminist*. New York: Schocken Books.

Capra, Fritjof. (1982). *The Turning Point*. New York: Simon and Schuster.

Cardea, Caryatis. (1985). The Lesbian Revolution and the 50-Minute Hour: A Working-Class Look at Therapy and the Movement. *Lesbian Ethics, 1* (3), 46-68.

Carmody, Moira. (1990). Keeping Rape on the National Agenda. *National Women's Conference 1990: Proceedings*. Canberra: Write People.

Carr, Anne. (1990). *Transforming Grace*. San Francisco: Harper and Row.

Cartledge, Sue and Joanna Ryan. (Eds.) (1984). *Sex and Love, New Thoughts on Old Contradictions*. London: The Women's Press.

Center for Anti-War Activities. (1992, July 14). *Save Humanity Report.* Sarajevo.

Chamberlin, Judy. (1977). *On Our Own.* London: MIND Publications.

Chapkis, Wendy. (1986). *Beauty Secrets: Women and the Politics of Appearance.* London: The Women's Press.

Chateauvert, Melinda. (1994). A Response to "Gender, Race, and Rights". *Journal of Women's History,* 6 133-34.

Chaucer, Geoffrey. (1951). *The Canterbury Tales.* (Translated by Nevil Coghill.) London: Penguin Books.

Chaudhuri, Nupur and Margaret Strobel. (Eds.) (1992). *Western Women and Imperialism: Complicity and Resistance.* Bloomington: Indiana University Press.

Chedid, Andrée. (1985). *La Maison Sans Racines.* Paris: Flammarion. Translated (1989). *House Without Roots.* London: Serpent's Tail.

Chernin, Kim. (1987). *Reinventing Eve: Modern Woman in Search of Herself.* New York: Harper and Row.

Chesler, Phyllis. (1972). *Women and Madness.* New York: Doubleday.

Chesler, Phyllis. (1986). *Mothers on Trial.* Seattle, Washington: Seal Press.

Chesler, Phyllis. (1994). *Patriarchy: Notes of an Expert Witness.* Munroe, Maine: Common Courage Press.

Chester, Gail. (1979). I Call Myself a Radical Feminist. In *Feminist Practice: Notes from the Tenth Year.* London: In Theory Press.

Christ, Carol P. (1979). Why Women Need the Goddess: Phenomenological, Psychological and Political Reflections. In Carol P. Christ and Judith Plaskow (Eds.) *Womanspirit Rising.* New York: Harper and Row.

Christ, Carol P. and Judith Plaskow (Eds.) (1979). *Womanspirit Rising.* New York: Harper and Row.

Christian, Barbara. (1987, Spring). The Race for Theory. *Cultural Critique,* 6 335-45; (1988) *Feminist Studies 14* (1), 67-80; (1989) In Linda Kauffman (Ed.) *Gender and Theory: Dialogues on Feminist Criticism.* Oxford and New York: Basil Blackwell; (1990) In Gloria Anzaldúa (Ed.) *Making Face, Making Soul, Haciendo Caras.* San Francisco: Aunt Lute Foundation.

Christian, Susan. (1991). Woman (Modified), *Yale Journal of Law and Feminism,* 4 1, 171-76.

Chung, Hyun Kyung. (1990). *Struggle to be the Sun Again: Introducing Asian Women's Theology.* Maryknoll: Orbis.

Cleaver, Eldridge. (1968). *Soul on Ice.* New York: McGraw Hill.

Clément, Catherine. (1983). *The Lives and Legends of Jacques Lacan.* (Translated by Arthur Goldhammer). New York: Columbia

Clément, Catherine and Hélène Cixous. (1986). *The Newly Born Woman.* (Translated by Betsy Wing.) Minneapolis: University of Minnesota Press. (Originally published as *La Jeune Née,* Union Génèrale d'Éditions, 1975.)

Cline, Sally and Dale Spender. (1987). *Reflecting Men at Twice Their Natural Size.* London: Andre Deutsch.

Cloudsley, Anne. (1981). *Women in Omdurman: Victims of Circumcision.* London: Cloudsley.

Cobbe, Frances Power. (1878, April). Wife Torture in England. *Contemporary Review, 32* 55-87.

Cocks, Joan. (1984). Wordless Emotions: Some Critical Reflections on Radical Feminism. *Politics and Society, 13* (1), 27-57.

Collins, Glenn. (1989, May 30). Soviet Actress Talks About Sex and Symbolism. *New York Times*, Section C.

Collins, Margery and Christine Pierce. (1976). Holes and Slime: Sexism in Sartre's Psychoanalysis. In Carol C. Gould and Marx W. Wartovsky (Eds.) *Women and Philosophy: Towards a Theory of Liberation*. New York: Perigee Books, GP Putnam and Sons.

Collins, Patricia Hill. (1990). *Black Feminist Thought: Knowledge, Consciousness and the Politics of Empowerment*. London: Routledge.

Coney, Sandra. (1990). *Out of the Frying Pan: Inflammatory Writing 1972–90*. Auckland: Penguin.

Cooper, Davina. (1995). *Power in Struggle*. Milton Keynes: Open University Press.

Cooper, Dennis. (Ed.) (1992). *Discontents: New Queer Writers*. New York: Amethyst Press.

Corea, Gena. (1977/1985). *The Hidden Malpractice: How American Medicine Mistreats Women*. New York: Harper and Row.

Corea, Gena. (1985). *The Mother Machine: Reproductive Technologies from Artificial Insemination to Artificial Wombs*. New York: Harper and Row.

Corea, Gena and Cynthia De Wit. (1988). Current Developments: German Police Raids. *Reproductive and Genetic Engineering 1* (2).

Corea, Gena, Renate Duelli Klein, Jalna Hanmer, Helen B. Holmes, Betty Hoskins, Madhu Kishwar, Janice Raymond, Robyn Rowland and Roberta Steinbacher. (1985). *Man-Made Women: How New Reproductive Technologies Affect Women*. London: Hutchinson; (1987) Bloomington: Indiana University Press.

Cornelius, Stella. (1986, April 3). In Deborah Wood. Tribal Elder of Peace Seeks Security for All. *Australian*.

Court, John. (1979). Pornography and Rape in White South Africa. *De Jure, 12* (2), 19, 236-41.

Coveney, Lal *et al.* (1984). *The Sexuality Papers: Male Sexuality and the Social Control of Women*. London: Hutchinson.

Crawford, Mary. (1993). Identity, "Passing" and Subversion. In Sue Wilkinson and Celia Kitzinger (Eds.) *Heterosexuality: A Feminism and Psychology Reader*. London: Sage.

Creed, Barbara. (1993, August 7). Paper delivered at Sexualities Conference, University of Melbourne.

Cronan, Sheila. (1973). Marriage. In Anne Koedt *et al.* (Eds.) *Radical Feminism*. New York: Quadrangle Press.

Cruikshank, Margaret. (Ed.) (1982). *Lesbian Studies*. New York: Feminist Press.

cunningham, e christi. (1991). Unmaddening: A response to Angela Harris. *Yale Journal of Law and Feminism, 4* 156-69.

Dahlerup, Drude. (1986). *The New Women's Movement*. London: Sage.

Dalton, Clare. (1987 – 88). Where We Stand: Observations on the Situation of Feminist Legal Thought. *Berkeley Women's Law Journal, 3* 1-13.

Daly, Martin and Dugald Jellie. (1993, September 23). Diggers Raped Japanese Women: Academic. *Age,* 1.

Daly, Martin and David Porter. (1993, September 24). Allies had to Protect Brothels: Academic. *Age,* 7.

Daly, Mary. (1968/1975). *The Church and the Second Sex: With a New Feminist Postchristian Introduction by the Author*. New York: Harper Colophon.

Daly, Mary. (1973). *Beyond God the Father: Toward a Philosophy of Women's Liberation*. Boston: Beacon.

Daly, Mary. (1978/1979). *Gyn/Ecology: The Metaethics of Radical Feminism*. Boston: Beacon; (1979) London: The Women's Press.

Daly, Mary. (1984). *Pure Lust: Elemental Feminist Philosophy*. Boston: Beacon.

Daly, Mary. (1991). New Intergalactic Introduction. In Mary Daly *Gyn/Ecology: The Metaethics of Radical Feminism*. London: Women's Press.

Daly, Mary. (1993). *Outercourse: The Be-dazzling Voyage. Containing Recollections from my Logbook of a Radical Feminist Philosopher (Being an Account of my Time/Space Travels and Ideas – Then, Again, Now and How)*. San Francisco: HarperCollins; Melbourne: Spinifex Press; London: The Women's Press.

D'Aprano, Zelda. (1977/1995). *Zelda*. Melbourne: Spinifex Press.

Dardigna, Anne-Marie. (1981). *Les châteaux d'Éros ou les infortunes du sexe des femmes*. [The castles of Eros or the misfortunes of women's sex] Paris: Maspero.

David, Barbara. (1992). Personal/Political Polarisation. *Journal of Australian Lesbian Feminist Studies, 2* (1), 24-41.

Davis, Dena. (1992). Abortion in Jewish Thought: A Study in Casuistry. *Journal of the American Academy of Religion, 60* (2), 313-23.

Davis, Horace. (1978). *Toward a Marxist Theory of Nationalism*. New York and London: Monthly Review Press.

Davis, Kathy. (1995). *Reshaping the Female Body: The Dilemma of Cosmetic Surgery*. London and New York: Routledge.

Daylight, Phyllis and Mary Johnstone. (1986). *Women's Business: Report of the Aboriginal Women's Task Force*. Canberra: Australian Government Publishing Service.

de Beauvoir, Simone. (1968). *Force of Circumstance*. Harmondsworth: Penguin. (Translated from the original 1963 edition.)

de Beauvoir, Simone. (1971). *The Second Sex*. (Translated and edited by H. M. Parshley.) London: Penguin.

Declaration of People's Perspectives. (1993, December). *People's Perspectives on Population 4 and 5*. Dhaka: UBINIG.

de Lauretis, Teresa (Ed.) (1986). *Feminist Studies/Critical Studies*. Bloomington: Indiana University Press.

de Lauretis, Teresa. (1989, Summer). The Essence of the Triangle or, Taking the Risk of Essentialism Seriously: Feminist Theory in Italy, the US and Britain. *Differences, 1* (2), 3-37.

de Lauretis, Teresa. (1991). Queer Theory: Lesbian and Gay Sexualities. An Introduction. *Differences, 3* (2), iii-xvii.

Deleuze, Gilles and Félix Guattari. (1988). *A Thousand Plateaus, Volume II of Capitalism and Schizophrenia*. (Translated by Brian Massumi.) London: The Athlone Press. (Originally published as *Mille Plateaux*, Editions de Minuit, 1980.)

Delmotte, Isabelle. (1993). *Chronological Skeleton of the Sensations Composing the Regaining of Consciousness after an Epileptic Fit*. Sydney. (Computer Art Project).

Delphy, Christine. (1984). *Close to Home: A Materialist Analysis of Women's Oppression*. London: Hutchinson.

Delphy, Christine. (1987). Protofeminism and Antifeminism. In Toril Moi (Ed.) *French Feminist Thought: A Reader*. New York: Basil Blackwell.

Delphy, Christine. (1993). Rethinking Sex and Gender. *Women's Studies International Forum, 16* (1), 1-9.

Denny, Elaine. (1994). Liberation or Oppression? Radical Feminism and In Vitro Fertilisation. *Sociology of Health and Illness: A Journal of Medical Sociology, 16* (1), 62-80.

Derrida, Jacques, with Geoff Bennington. (1989). On Colleges and Philosophy (Interview). In Lisa Appignanesi (Ed.) *Postmodernism, ICA Documents.* London: Free Association Books.

Derrida, Jacques. (1974). *Of Grammatology.* (Translated by Gayatri Chakravorty Spivak.) Baltimore: Johns Hopkins University Press. (Translation of original 1967 edition.)

Derrida, Jacques. (1978a). Becoming Woman. *Semiotext(e), 3* 128-37.

Derrida, Jacques. (1988, Spring). Like the Sound of the Sea Deep Within a Shell: Paul de Man's War. *Critical Inquiry, 14* (3), 590-652.

Derrida, Jacques. (1989). *Of Spirit, Heidegger and the Question.* (Translated by Geoffreyn Bennington and Rachel Bowlby.) Chicago: University of Chicago Press.

di Giovanni, Janine. (1992, December). Erotica: Pleasure or Porn? *Cosmopolitan,* 147, 198-99.

di Stefano, Christine. (1990). Dilemmas of Difference: Feminist, Modernity, and Postmodernism. In Linda J. Nicholson (Ed.) *Feminism/Postmodernism.* New York and London: Routledge.

Diamond, Irene and Lee Quinby. (Eds.) (1988). *Feminism and Foucault.* Boston: Northeastern University Press.

Dinnerstein, Myra. (1989, February). Questions for the Nineties. *The Women's Review of Books.*

Directorate-General of Budget, Accounting and Statistics, Executive Yuan, Republic of China. (1993). *Statistical Yearbook of the Republic of China.* Taipei.

Dollimore, Jonathan. (1991). *Sexual Dissidence: Augustine to Wilde, Freud to Foucault.* Oxford: Clarendon Press.

Domingo, Chris. (1984, August 25). *Anzac Day – Thinking About the Future – A Forum for Women.* Papers from A Forum for Women. Melbourne: YWCA.

Dostoyevsky, Fyodor. (1955). *The Idiot.* (Translated by David Magarshack.) Harmondsworth: Penguin.

Douglas, Carol Anne. (1993, February). I'll Take the Low Road: A Look at Contemporary Feminist Theory. *Off Our Backs. XXIII* (2), 16-17.

Douglas, Carol Anne. (1990). *Love and Politics: Radical Feminist and Lesbian Theories.* San Francisco: ism press.

Duberman, Martin Bauml *et al.* (Eds.) (1989). *Hidden from History: Reclaiming the Gay and Lesbian Past.* New York: New American Library.

Dubois, Ellen and Linda Gordon. (1983). Seeking Ecstasy on the Battlefield: Danger and Pleasure in Nineteenth Century Feminist Thought. In *Feminist Review, 13.*

Dunlop, Kim. (1993, March 9). Porn Stripped Bare: Women Used as Sexual "Porns". *Varsity, 52* (2), 9.

Dunsford, Cathie. (Ed.) (1986). *New Women's Fiction.* Auckland: New Women's Press.

Dunsford, Cathie. (Ed.) (1991). *Subversive Acts.* Auckland: Penguin.

Dunsford, Cathie. (Ed.) (1993). *Me and Marilyn Monroe.* Wellington: Daphne Brasell.

Dunsford, Cathie. (1994). *Cowrie.* Melbourne: Spinifex Press; Auckland: Tandem Press.

Dunsford, Cathie and Susan Hawthorne. (Eds.) (1990). *The Exploding Frangipani.* Auckland: New Women's Press.

DuPlessis, Rachel Blau. (1979). Romantic Thralldom in H.D. *Contemporary Literature, XX* (2), 178-203.

DuPlessis, Rachel Blau. (1986). *H.D. The Career of That Struggle*. Brighton: Harvester Press.

DuPlessis, Rachel Blau, and Susan Stanford Friedman. (1981, Fall). "Woman is Perfect": H.D.'s Debate with Freud. *Feminist Studies*, 7 (3), 417-30.

Dworkin, Andrea. (1974). *Woman Hating*. New York: Plume.

Dworkin, Andrea. (1976/1982). *Our Blood: Prophecies and Discourses on Sexual Politics*. 1982; London: The Women's Press.

Dworkin, Andrea. (1979). *Pornography: Men Possessing Women*. New York: Perigee Books; (1981). London: The Women's Press.

Dworkin, Andrea. (1983). *Right-Wing Women*. New York: Perigee; London: The Women's Press.

Dworkin, Andrea. (1986). *Ice and Fire*. London: Fontana.

Dworkin, Andrea. (1987). *Intercourse*. New York: Free Press and Macmillan.

Dworkin, Andrea. (1988). *Letters from a War Zone*. London: Secker and Warburg.

Dworkin, Andrea. (1990 Summer). Dworkin on Dworkin. *Trouble and Strife, 19* 2–13.

Dworkin, Andrea. (1991a). *Mercy*. London: Arrow Books.

Dworkin, Andrea. (1991b, December 5). Interview. *Guardian*, 21.

Dworkin, Andrea. (1993, September 5). The Real Pornography of a Brutal War Against Women. *Los Angeles Times*, M2.

Dworkin, Andrea and Catharine A. MacKinnon. (1988). *Pornography and Civil Rights: A New Day for Women's Equality*. Minneapolis: Organizing Against Pornography.

Dworkin, Ronald. (1993, October 21). Women and Pornography. *New York Review of Books*, 36-42.

Dworkin, Ronald. (1994, March 3). An Exchange. *New York Review of Books*, 47-8.

Dyer, Richard. (1991). *Believing in Fairies: The Author and the Homosexual*. In Diana Fuss, (Ed.) *Inside/Out*. London and New York: Routledge.

Eadie, Jo. (1993.) Activating Bisexuality: Towards a Bi/sexual Politics. In Joseph Bristow and Angelia R. Wilson (Eds.) *Activating Theory: Lesbian, Gay, Bisexual Politics*. London: Lawrence and Wishart.

Eardley, Tony. (1985). Violence and Sexuality. In Andy Metcalfe and Martin Humphries (Eds.) *The Sexuality of Men*. London: Pluto Press.

Ebert, Teresa L. (1991). Postmodernism's Infinite Variety: Review of *Feminism/Postmodernism. Women's Review of Books, 8* (4), 24.

Echols, Alice. (1983). Cultural Feminism: Capitalism and the Anti-Pornography Movement. *Social Text, 7* 34-53.

Echols, Alice. (1984). The New Feminism of Yin and Yang. In Ann Snitow *et al.* (Eds.) *Desire: Politics of Sexuality*. London: Virago.

Echols, Alice. (1989). *Daring To Be Bad: Radical Feminism in America 1967-1975*. University of Minnesota Press.

Eckermann, Elizabeth. (1994). Beyond Giddens: Differentiating Bodies. *Annual Review of Health Social Sciences, 4* 92-113.

Eisenstein, Hester. (1984). *Contemporary Feminist Thought*. London: Unwin Paperbacks.

El Dareer, Asma. (1982). *Woman, Why Do You Weep?* London: Zed Press.

Eldridge, Clever. (1967). *Soul On Ice*. (Introduction by Maxwell Geismar). New York: McGraw Hill.

Eller, Cynthia. (1993). *Living in the Lap of the Goddess: The Feminist Spirituality Movement in America*. New York: Crossroad.

Elliott, Beth. (1992). Holly Near and Yet So Far. In Elizabeth Reba Weise (Ed.) *Closer to Home: Bisexuality and Feminism*. Seattle: Seal Press.

Encyclopedia of Islam. (1975-76). Lieden: Brill.

Enders-Dragässer, Uta and Claudia Fuchs. (1988a). *Interaktionen und Beziehungsstrukturen in der Schule*. Eine Untersuchung an hessischen Schulen im Auftrag des Hessischen Instituts für Bildungsplanung und Schulentwicklung. Unter Mitarbeit von Petra Schmidt, Brigitte Schäfer, Sabine Hark, Sigrid Bachler, Susanne Odrich und Erika Bohrmann. Wiesbaden.

Enders-Dragässer, Uta and Claudia Fuchs. (1988b). *Jungensozialisation in der Schule. Eine Expertise*. Gemeindedienste und Männerarbeit der Evangelischen Kirche von Hessen und Nassau. Darmstadt, 2. Auflage Mai 1989, 3. Auflage Mai 1990.

Enders-Dragässer, Uta and Claudia Fuchs. (1989). *Interaktionen der Geschlechter. Sexismusstrukturen in der Schule*. Eine Untersuchung an hessischen Schulen im Auftrag des Hessischen Instituts für Bildungsplanung und Schulentwicklung. Unter Mitarbeit von Petra Schmidt, Brigitte Schäfer, Sabine Hark, Sigrid Bachler, Susanne Odrich und Erika Bohrmann. Veröffentlichungen der Max-Traeger-Stiftung. Herausgegeben von Dieter Wunder. Band 10. Weinheim und München: Juventa Verlag.

Enders-Dragässer, Uta, Petra Schmidt, Claudia Fuchs und Sabine Hark. (1986). *Konzeptionsbericht zur "Interaktionsstudie"*. Im Auftrag des Hessischen Instituts für Bildungsplanung und Schulentwicklung. Frankfurt.

Enloe, Cynthia. (1983/1988). *Does Khaki Become You? The Militarisation of Women's Lives*. London: Pluto Press; (1988), London: Pandora/Harper Collins.

Enloe, Cynthia. (1989). *Bananas Beaches and Bases: Making Feminist Sense of International Politics*. London: Pandora.

Enloe, Cynthia. (1993). *The Morning After: Sexual Politics at the End of the Cold War*. Berkeley: University of California Press.

Eridani. (1992). Is Sexual Orientation a Secondary Sex Characteristic? In Elizabeth Reba Weise (Ed.) *Closer to Home: Bisexuality and Feminism*. Seattle: Seal Press.

Erlich, Michel. (1986). *La femme blessée: Essai sur les mutilations sexuelles féminines*. Paris: L'Harmattan.

Ernst, Sheila, and Marie Maguire. (Eds.) (1987). *Living with the Sphinx: Papers from the Women's Therapy Centre*. London: The Women's Press.

Evans, David. (1993). *Sexual Citizenship: The Material Construction of Sexualities*. London: Routledge.

Evans, Mari. (Ed.) (1984). *Black Women Writers (1950-1980)*. New York: Anchor Press.

Evans, Mary. (Ed.) (1994). *The Woman Question*. Second edition. London: Sage.

Ezekiel, Judith. (1992, June 12). Comments on Claire Moses's paper. Berkshire: Berkshire History of Women Conference.

Fabella, Virginia and Mercy Amba Oduyoye. (Eds.) (1990). *With Passion and Compassion: Third World Women Doing Theology*. Maryknoll: Orbis.

FACT (Feminist Anti-Censorship Taskforce *et al.*). (1985). Brief Amici Curiae, No 84–3147, in the US Court of Appeals, 7th Circuit (Southern District of Indiana) at 4.

Faderman, Lillian. (1984). *Surpassing the Love of Men*. London: Junction Books. (1985). New York: Century America. (1992). London: Penguin.

Faderman, Lillian. (1991). *Odd Girls and Twilight Lovers: A History of Lesbian Life In Twentieth-Century America*. New York: Colombia University Press. (1992) London: Penguin.

Faderman, Lillian. (1993). The Return of the Butch and Femme: A Phenomenon in Lesbian Sexuality of the 1980s and 1990s. In J. Fout and M. S. Tantillo (Eds.) *American Sexual Politics: Sex, Gender and Race since the Civil War.* Chicago: University of Chicago Press.

Faludi, Susan. (1991/1992). *Backlash: The Undeclared War Against American Women.* New York, Crown; 1992, London: Chatto.

Faludi, Susan. (1995). I'm not a Feminist, but I play one on TV. *Ms Magazine.* March–April. 30-39.

Farias, Victor. (1989). *Heidegger and Nazism.* Joseph Margolis and Tom Rockmore (Eds.) (Translated by Paul Burrell and Gabriel R. Ricci). Philadelphia: Temple University Press.

Feminist Anthology Collective. (1982). *No Turning Back: Writings from the Women's Liberation Movement, 1975-80.* London: The Women's Press.

Feminist Practice: Notes From the Tenth Year. (1979). London: In Theory Press.

Ferguson, Ann. (1989). *Blood at the Root: Motherhood, Sexuality and Male Dominance.* London: Pandora Press.

Ferguson, Ann. (1993). Does Reason Have a Gender? In R. Gottleib (Ed.) *Radical Philosophy: Tradition, Counter Tradition and Politics,* Philadelphia: Temple University Press.

Ferry, Luc and Alain Renaut. (1988/1990). *Heidegger and Modernity.* (Translated by Franklin Philip. Originally published as *Heidegger et les modernes,* Editions Grasset and Fasquelle, 1988). Chicago: University of Chicago Press.

Fesl, Eve. (1984). Eve Fesl. In Robyn Rowland (Ed.) *Women Who Do Women Who Don't Join the Women's Movement.* London: Routledge and Kegan Paul.

Finkielkraut, Alain. (1992). *Remembering in Vain: The Klaus Barbie Trial and Crimes Against Humanity.* New York: Columbia University Press.

Finnane, Kieran. (1995). Domestic Violence: Hints for Our Finest. *Alice Springs News,* 2 (8), 3.

Fiorenza, Elisabeth Schüssler. (1983). *In Memory of Her: A Feminist Reconstruction of Christian Origins.* New York: Crossroad.

Firestone, Shulamith. (1970/1972). *The Dialectic of Sex: The Case for Feminist Revolution.* London: Jonathan Cape, New York: William Morrow; New York: Bantam; 1972, London: Paladin.

Flax, Jane. (1990). *Thinking Fragments: Psychoanalysis, Feminism and Postmodernism in the Contemporary West.* Berkley: University of California Press.

Flax, Jane. (1992). The End of Innocence. In Butler and Scott (Eds.) *Feminists Theorize the Political.* London: Routledge.

Fletcher, Beryl. (1991). *The Word Burners.* Wellington: Daphne Brasell.

Foote-Smith, Elizabeth and Lydia Bayne. (1991). Joan of Arc. *Epilepsia, 32* (6).

Forrest, Drew. (1992, December 23-29). And Now for the Good News ... *Weekly Mail,* 6.

Fortune, Marie. (1983). *The Unmentionable Sin.* New York: The Pilgrim Press.

Foster, Hal. (Ed.) (1983). *The Anti-Aesthetic, Essays on Postmodern Culture.* Seattle: Bay Press.

Fout, J. and M.S. Tantillo. (Eds.) (1993). *American Sexual Politics: Sex, Gender and Race since the Civil War.* Chicago: University of Chicago Press.

Frankfort, Ellen. (1973). *Vaginal Politics.* New York: Bantam.

Fraser, Jean and Tessa Boffin. (1991). Tantalizing Glimpses of Stolen Glances: Lesbians Take Photographs. *Feminist Review, 38* 20-32.

Fraser, Nancy. (1989). *Unruly Practices: Power, Discourse and Gender in Contemporary Social Theory*. Minneapolis: University of Minnesota Press; (1990) New York and London: Routledge.

Fraser, Nancy, and Linda Nicholson. (1988). Social Criticism Without Philosophy: An Encounter Between Feminism and Post-modernism. In Andrew Ross (Ed.) *Universal Abandon? The Politics of Post-modernism*. Minneapolis: University of Minnesota Press.

Frazier, Nancy and Myra Sadker. (1973). *Sexism in School and Society*. New York: Harper and Row.

Freeman, Alan. (1988). Racism, Rights and the Quest for Equality of Opportunity: A Critical Legal Essay. *Harvard Civil Rights – Civil Liberties Review, 23* 295-392.

French, Maggie. (1992). Loves, Sexualities and Marriages: Strategies and Adjustments. In Ken Plummer (Ed.) *Modern Homosexualities: Fragments of Lesbian and Gay Experience*. London: Routledge.

French, Marilyn. (1992). *The War Against Women*. London: Hamish Hamilton.

Freud, Sigmund. (1913). Totem and Taboo. *Standard Edition, 3* 1-161.

Friedman, Scarlet and Elizabeth Sarah. (Eds.) (1982). *On the Problem of Men*. London: The Women's Press.

Friedman, Susan Stanford. (1981). *Psyche Reborn, The Emergence of H.D.* Bloomington: Indiana University Press.

Friedman, Susan Stanford. (1985, Fall). Palimpsest of Origins in H.D.'s Career. *Poesis, 6* (3–4), 56-73.

Friedman, Susan Stanford and Rachel Blau duPlessis. (Eds.) (1990). *Signets, Reading H.D.* Madison: University of Wisconsin Press.

Frömelt, Michael. (1994). Männer–Väter–Vaterschaft. Eine Auswahlbibliographie. In Ute Gonser und Ingrid Helbrecht-Jordan. (Eds.) *". . . Vater sein dagegen sehr!" Wege zur erweiterten Familienorientierung von Männern*. Materialien zur Väter – und Männerarbeit in der Familien – und Erwachsenenbildung. Bielefeld: Kleine Verlag. 143-84.

Frug, Mary Joe. (1992). *Postmodern Legal Feminism*. Routledge: New York.

Frye, Marilyn. (1983). *The Politics of Reality: Essays in Feminist Theory*. New York: Crossing Press.

Fukia, Bunseki. (1991, February). Lecture: *Untitled Paper*. New York City: Caribbean Cultural Center.

Fuss, Diana. (1990). *Essentially Speaking. Feminism, Nature and Difference*. London and New York: Routledge.

Fuss, Diana. (Ed.) (1991). *Inside/Out. Lesbian Theories, Gay Theories*. London and New York: Routledge.

Gaitskell, Debora and Elaine Unterhalter. (1989). Mothers of the Nation, Race and Motherhood in Afrikaner Nationalism and The African National Congress. In N. Uval-Davis and F. Anthias. (Eds.) *Women-Nation-State*. London: Macmillan.

Gale, Fay. (Ed.) (1993). *We are Bosses Ourselves*. Canberra: Australian Institute of Aboriginal Studies.

Gallop, Jane. (1982). *The Daughter's Seduction*. Ithaca: Cornell University Press.

Gallop, Jane. (1988). *Thinking Through the Body*. New York: Columbia University Press.

Gardner, James B. and George Rollie Adams. (Eds.) (1983). *Ordinary People and Everyday Life*. Nashville: American Association for State and Local History.

Garner, Helen. (1995). *The First Stone: Some Questions about Sex and Power*. Sydney: Macmillan.

Garner, Shirley Nelson *et al.* (Eds.) (1985). *The M(o)ther Tongue.* Ithaca: Cornell University Press.

Gatens, Moira. (1996). *Imaginary Bodies: Ethics, Power and Corporeality.* London and New York: Routledge.

Gavey, Nicola. (1993). Technologies and Effects of Heterosexual Coercion. In Wilkinson, Sue and Kitzinger, Celia (Eds.) *Heterosexuality. A Feminism and Psychology Reader* London: Sage.

George, Sue. (1993). *Women and Bisexuality.* London: Scarlet Press.

Gergen, Mary. (1993). Unbundling Our Binaries – Genders, Sexualities, Desires. In Sue Wilkinson and Celia Kitzinger (Eds.) *Heterosexuality: A Feminism and Psychology Reader.* London: Sage.

Gilbert, L. A. (1980). Feminist Therapy. In Annette M. Brodsky and Rachel Hare-Mustin (Eds.) *Women and Psychotherapy: An Assessment of Research and Practice.* New York: Guilford Press.

Gillespie, Marcia Ann. (1994 May/June). The Posse Rides Again. *Ms. Magazine,* 1.

Gilligan, Carol. (1982). *In a Different Voice: Psychological Theory and Women's Development.* Cambridge, Massachusetts: Harvard University Press.

Gimbutas, Marija. (1974). *The Gods and Goddesses of Old Europe.* London: Thames and Hudson. Updated and re-released (1982) as *The Goddesses and Gods of Old Europe.* London: Thames and Hudson.

Gimbutas, Marija. (1989). *The Language of the Goddess.* San Francisco: Harper and Row.

Giobbe, Evelina. (1994). The Marketplace of Ideas. *Action Agenda, 1* (3), 3–4

Glumpler, Edith. (1995). Zukunftsfelder der feministischen Schulforschung. Universität Dortmund. Berichte aus dem IADS, Heft 1.

Goldenberg, Naomi R. (1979). *Changing the Gods: Feminism and the End of Traditional Religions.* Boston: Beacon.

Gonser, Ute und Ingrid Helbrecht-Jordan. (1994). *". . . Vater sein dagegen sehr!" Wege zur erweiterten Familienorientierung von Männern.* Materialien zur Väter – und Männerarbeit in der Familien – und Erwachsenenbildung. Bielefeld: Kleine Verlag.

Gordon, Linda. (1986). What's New in Women's History. In Teresa de Lauretis (Ed.), *Feminist Studies/Critical Studies.* Bloomington: Indiana University Press.

Gornick, Vivian and B. K. Moran. (Eds.) (1971). *Sexist Society: Studies in Power and Powerlessness.* New York: Basic Books.

Gottleib, R. (Ed.) (1993). *Radical Philosophy: Tradition, Counter Tradition and Politics,* Philadelphia: Temple University Press.

Gould, Carol C. and Marx W. Wartovsky. (Eds.) (1976). *Women and Philosophy: Towards a Theory of Liberation.* New York: Perigee Books, Putnam.

Grant, Jacquelyn. (1989). *White Women's Christ and Black Women's Jesus.* Atlanta: Scholars Press.

Gray, Francine du Plessix. (1990). *Soviet Women.* New York: Doubleday.

Green, Margaret. (1987). Women in the Oppressor Role: White Racism. In Sheila Ernst and Marie Maguire (Eds.) *Living with the Sphinx: Papers from the Women's Therapy Centre.* London: The Women's Press.

Greenberg, Blu. (1976). Abortion: A Challenge to Halakhah. *Judaism, 25* (9), 201-8.

Grevisser, Mark. (1991, May 3-9). Porn in the RSA. *The Weekly Mail,* 8.

Griffin, Gabriele. (Ed.) (1993). *Outwrite: Popular/izing Lesbian Texts.* London: Pluto Press.

Griffin, Susan. (1981). *Pornography and Silence: Culture's Revenge Against Nature*. London: The Women's Press; New York: Harper and Row.

Griffin, Susan. (1982). *Made From This Earth: Selections from her Writing, 1967-1982*. London: The Women's Press.

Grooms by Mail Agency at Nadhodka. (1990, December 7). *Daily Penn*.

Grosz, Elizabeth. (1989). *Sexual Subversions: Three French Feminists*. Sydney: Allen and Unwin.

Grosz, Elizabeth. (1990a). Contemporary Theories of Power and Subjectivity. In Sneja Gunew (Ed.) *Feminist Knowledge: Critique and Construct*. London: Routledge.

Grosz, Elizabeth. (1990b). *Jacques Lacan: A Feminist Introduction*. New York: Routledge.

Grosz, Elizabeth (1994). *Volatile Bodies: Toward a Corporeal Feminism*. Bloomington and Indianapolis: Indiana University Press; Sydney: Allen and Unwin.

Grosz, Elizabeth. (1995). *Space, Time and Perversion*. London and New York: Routledge; Sydney: Allen and Unwin.

Grosz, Elizabeth and Elspeth Probyn. (Eds.) (1995). *Sexy Bodies: The Strange Carnalities of Feminism*. London and New York: Routledge.

Guattari, Félix and Gilles Deleuze. (1983). *Anti-Oedipus, Capitalism and Schizophrenia. Volume 1*. (Translated from the French by Robert Hurley, Mark Seem and Helen R. Lane. Preface by Michel Foucault.) London: The Athlone Press. (Originally published in 1972.)

Gubar, Susan and Joan Hoff. (Eds.). (1989). *For Adult Users Only: The Dilemma of Violent Pornography*. Bloomington: Indiana University Press.

Gudorf, Christine E. (1992). *Victimization: Examining Christian Complicity*. New York: Trinity International Press.

Gudorf, Christine E. (1994). *Body, Sex and Pleasure: Reconstructing Christian Sexual Ethics*. Cleveland: The Pilgrim Press.

Guerlais, Maryse. (1991). Vers une nouvelle idéologie du droit statutaire: "Le temps de la différence de Luce Irigaray". *Nouvelles Questions Féministes*. 16–18.

Gunew, Sneja. (Ed.) (1990a). *Feminist Knowledge: Critique and Construct*. London: Routledge.

Gunew, Sneja. (Ed.) (1990b). *A Reader in Feminist Knowledge* London: Routledge.

Gunew, Sneja and Anna Yeatman. (Eds.) (1993). *Feminism and the Politics of Difference*. Sydney: Allen and Unwin.

Gustavsson, Kersten. (1989, June 11). The Most Beautiful. *Moscov News*, *24* (3376), 13.

Gutman, Roy. (1993). *A Witness to Genocide*. New York: Macmillan.

H.D. (1956). *Tribute to Freud*. Boston: David R. Godine.

H.D. (1981, Fall). The Master. *Feminist Studies*, *7* (3), 47–416

Hagan, Kathy. (1988). *Internal Affairs: A Journalkeeping Workbook for Self Intimacy*. San Francisco: Harper Row.

Hall, Jacquelyn Dowd. (1986). Women's History Goes to Trial: *EEOC v. Sears Roebuck and Co. Signs*, *11* 751-79.

Hampton, Fred. (1968-71). A Nation of Law? In *Eyes on the Prize-Part II*. Video.

Hanmer, Jalna. (1990). Men, Power and the Exploitation of Women. In Jeff Hearn and David Morgan (Eds.) *Men, Masculinities and Social Theory*. London: Unwin Hyman.

Haraway, Donna. (1988, Fall). Situated Knowledges: The Science Question in Feminism and the Privilege of Partial Perspective. In *Feminist Studies*, *14* (3).

Haraway, Donna. (1991). A Cyborg Manifesto: Science, Technology and Socialist-Feminism in the Late Twentieth Century. In Donna Haraway. *Simians, Cyborgs, and Women: The Reinvention of Nature.* New York: Routledge.

Haraway, Donna. (1991). *Simians, Cyborgs, and Women: The Reinvention of Nature.* New York: Routledge.

Harding, Sandra. (1991). *Whose Science? Whose Knowledge? Thinking from Women's Lives.* Milton Keynes: Open University.

Harding, Sandra. (1986). *The Science Question in Feminism.* Ithaca: Cornell University Press.

Harding, Sandra and Merrill B. Hintikka. (Eds.) (1983). *Discovering Reality: Feminist Perspectives on Epistemology, Metaphysics, Methodology and Philosophy of Science.* Boston: D. Reidel Publishing Co.

Harding, Susan. (1990). Starting Thought From Women's Lives: Eight Resources For Maximising Objectivity. *Journal of Social Philosophy, 21* (2 and 3), 140-9.

Harris, Angela P. (1990). Race and Essentialism In Feminist Legal Theory. *Stanford Law Review, 42* (3), 581-616.

Harrison, Beverly Wildung. (1983). *Our Right to Choose: Toward a New Ethic of Abortion.* Boston: Beacon.

Harrison, Beverly Wildung. (1985). Misogyny and Homophobia: The Unexplored Connections. In Carol S. Robb (Ed.) *Making the Connections: Essays in Feminist Social Ethics.* Boston: Beacon.

Hartmann, Betsy. (1995). *Reproductive Rights and Wrongs: The Global Politics of Population Control.* Boston: South End Press.

Hartstock, Nancy C. M. (1990). Foucault on Power: A Theory for Women. In Linda J. Nicholson (Ed.) (1990). *Feminism/Postmodernism.* New York: Routledge.

Hawkins, Elaine. (1992). Dicing with Madonna. *Trouble and Strife, 14* 25-9.

Hawley, John Stratton. (1994). *Fundamentalism and Gender.* New York: Oxford University Press.

Hawthorne, Susan. (1976/1990). In Defence of Separatism. Unpublished Honours Thesis. Melbourne: La Trobe University. (Excerpt published in Sneja Gunew (Ed.) (1990). *A Reader in Feminist Knowledge.* London: Routledge.

Hawthorne, Susan. (1991). What Do Lesbians Want? *Journal of Australian Lesbian Feminist Studies, 1* (2).

Hawthorne, Susan. (1992). *The Falling Woman.* Melbourne: Spinifex Press.

Hawthorne, Susan. (1993a). The Language in My Tongue. In *Four New Poets.* Melbourne: Penguin.

Hawthorne, Susan. (1993b). Meditation on Falling. In Roberta Snow and Jill Taylor (Eds.) *Falling for Grace: An Anthology of Australian Lesbian Fiction.* Sydney: Blackwattle Press.

Hawthorne, Susan. (1993c). Wild Politics – A Manifesto. In *People's Perspectives.* No. 4 and 5, 1993, 26-27. Dhaka: Ubinig; (1995). *Broadsheet.* (Autumn/Ngahuru). 52-3.

Hawthorne, Susan. (1994). Variations. Unpublished.

Hawthorne, Susan and Renate Klein. (Eds.) (1991). *Angels of Power and Other Reproductive Creations.* Melbourne: Spinifex Press.

Hearn, Jeff. (Ed.) (1991). *Critical Studies on Men.* London: Routledge.

Hearn Jeff and David Morgan. (Eds.) (1990). *Men, Masculinities and Social Theory.* London: Unwin Hyman.

Hekman, Susan J. (1990). *Gender and Knowledge, Elements of a Postmodern Feminism*. Boston: Northeastern University Press.

Henderson, Lorna. (1993). Justify Our Love: Madonna and the Politics of Queer Sex. In Cathy Schwichtenberg (Ed.) *The Madonna Connection: Representational Politics, Subcultural Identities, and Cultural Theory*. Boulder, Colorado: Westview Press.

Heschel, Susannah. (Ed.) (1983). *On Being a Jewish Feminist*. New York: Schocken Books.

Hessisches Institut für Bildungsplanung und Schulentwicklung – Im Auftrag des Hessischen Kultusministers. (1986). *Konzept zum Vorhaben Verwirklichung der Gleichstellung von Schülerinnen und Lehrerinnen an hessischen Schulen*. Sonderreihe Heft 21, Wiesbaden.

Heywood, Carter. (1991). The Erotic As Sacred Power: A Lesbian Feminist Theological Perspective. In Judith Barrington (Ed.) *An Intimate Wilderness: Lesbian Writers on Sexuality*. Portland, Oregon: The Eighth Mountain Press.

Higonnet, Margaret Randolph *et al.* (Eds.) (1987). *Behind the Lines: Gender and the Two World Wars*. New Haven: Yale University Press.

Hill, Marcia. (1990). On Creating a Theory of Feminist Therapy. In Laura Brown and Maria Root. (Eds.) Diversity and Complexity in Feminist Therapy: Part 1 *Special Issue of Women and Therapy*, 9 (1–2), 56-65.

Hirsch, Marianne, and Evelyn Fox Keller. (Eds.) (1990). *Conflicts in Feminism*. New York and London: Routledge.

Hoagland, Sarah. (1988). *Lesbian Ethics: Toward New Value*. Palo Alto: Institute of Lesbian Studies.

Hoagland, Sarah Lucia and Julia Penelope. (1988). *For Lesbians Only: A Separatist Anthology*. London: Onlywomen Press.

Hobby, Elaine and Chris White. (Eds.) (1991). *What Lesbians Do in Books*. London: The Women's Press.

Hochschild, Arlie. (1989). *The Second Shift*. New York: Viking.

Hoff, Joan. (1989). Why is There No History of Pornography? In Susan Gubar and Joan Hoff (Eds.) *For Adult Users Only: The Dilemma of Violent Pornography*. Bloomington: Indiana University Press.

Hoff, Joan. (1991). *Law, Gender, and Injustice: A Legal History of US Women*. New York: New York University Press.

Hoff, Joan. (1992). Introduction: An Overview of Women's History in the United States. *Journal of Women's History Guide To Periodical Literature*. Bloomington: Indiana University Press.

Hoff, Joan. (1993, October 20). The Pernicious Effects of Poststructuralism. *The Chronicle of Higher Education*. B1-2.

Hoff, Joan. (1994). Gender as a Post-modern Category of Paralysis. *Women's Studies International Forum*, 17 (4), 443-47; (1994, June) *Women's History Review*, 3 (2), 149-68.

Hoff, Joan and Christie Farnham. (1990). Theories About the End of Everything. *Journal of Women's History*, 1 6-10.

Hoffman, John. (1975). *Marxism and the Theory of Praxis*. New York: International Publishers.

Holland, Sue. (1991). From Private Symptoms to Public Action. *Feminism and Psychology*, 1 (1), 58-62.

Holloway, Wendy. (1984). Heterosexual Sex: Power and Desire for the Other. In Sue Cartledge and Joanna Ryan (Eds.) *Sex and Love, New Thoughts on Old Contradictions*. London: The Women's Press.

Holloway, Wendy. (1993). Theorizing Heterosexuality: A Response. *Feminism and Psychology, 3* (3), 412-17.

hooks, bell. (1984). *Feminist Theory: From Margin to Centre.* Boston, Massachusetts: South End Press.

hooks, bell. (1990). *Yearning, Race, Gender and Cultural Politics.* Boston: South End Press.

hooks, bell. (1992). Madonna. Plantation Mistress or Soul Sister? In *Black Looks: Race and Representation.* Boston: South End Press.

hooks, bell. (1994). *Outlaw Culture: Resisting Representations.* New York: Routledge.

Hosken, Fran P. (1982/1994). *The Hosken Report: Genital and Sexual Mutilation of Females.* Lexington, Massachusetts: Win News.

Hubbard, Ruth. (1990). *The Politics of Women's Biology.* New Brunswick: Rutgers University Press.

Huggins, Jackie. (1987). Black Women and Women's Liberation. *Hecate, 13* (1), 77-82. (Reprinted, (1990) in Sneja Gunew (Ed.) *A Reader in Feminist Knowledge.* London: Routledge.

Huggins, Jackie. (1990a). International Indigenous Women's Conference. *Australian Feminist Studies, 11* 113-4.

Huggins, Jackie. (1990b, May). Are all Women White? *The Coming Out Show.* Australian Broadcasting Corporation, Women's Broadcasting Unit, September. (In conversation with bell hooks.)

Huggins, Jackie. (1990c). Questions of Collaboration: An Interview with Jackie Huggins and Isabel Tarrago. *Hecate, 16* (1–2), 140–47.

Huggins, Jackie. (1991a). Theories of Race and Gender. *Olive Pink Society Bulletin,* (91), 6-15.

Huggins, Jackie. (1991b). Pretty Deadly Tidda Business. *Hecate, 17* (1). (Reprinted 1993, in Sneja Gunew and Anna Yeatman (Eds.) *Feminism and the Politics of Difference.* Sydney: Allen and Unwin.

Huggins, Jackie. (1992a). Letters to Diane Bell, June 14 and 15.

Huggins, Jackie. (1992b). Towards a Biography of Rita Huggins. In Susan Margary, with Caroline Guevin and Paula Hamilton. (Eds.) *Writing Lives: Feminist Biography and Autobiography.* Adelaide: Australian Feminist Studies.

Huggins, Jackie, Jo Willmot, Isabel Tarrago, Kathy Willetts, Liz Bond, Lillian Holt, Eleanor Bourke, Maryann Bik-Salik, Pat Fowell, Joann Schmider, Valerie Craigie and Linda McBride-Levi. (1990). Letter to the Editor. *Women's Studies International Forum, 14* (5), 506-7.

Hulme, Keri. (1985). *the bone people.* Auckland and London: Spiral in conjunction with Hodder and Stoughton.

Humm, Maggie. (Ed.) (1992). *Feminisms: A Reader.* London: Harvester Wheatsheaf.

Humphries, Martin. (1985). Gay Machismo. In Andy Metcalf and Martin Humphries (Eds.) *The Sexuality of Men.* London: Pluto Press.

Hunt, Margaret. (1990). The De-Eroticization of Women's Liberation: Social Purity Movements and the Revolutionary Feminism of Sheila Jeffreys. *Feminist Review,* (34), 23-46.

Hunter, Allan. (1993). Same Door, Different Closet: A Heterosexual Sissy's Coming-out Party, in Sue Wilkinson and Celia Kitzinger (Eds.) *Heterosexuality. A Feminism and Psychology Reader.* London: Sage.

Hunter, Dianne. (1985). Hysteria, Psychoanalysis and Feminism: The Case of Anna O. In Shirley Nelson Garner *et al.* (Eds.) *The M(o)ther Tongue.* Ithaca: Cornell University Press.

Huyssen, Andreas. (1990). Mapping the Postmodern. In Linda J. Nicholson (Ed.) *Feminism/ Postmodernism*. New York and London: Routledge.

Hyman, Prue. (1994). *Women and Economics. A New Zealand Feminist Perspective.* Wellington: Bridget Williams Books.

Inquiry into Prostitution in Victoria. (1985). Report. Melbourne: Government Printer.

Irigaray, Luce. (1981, Autumn). And the One Doesn't Stir without the Other. *Signs, 7* (1), 60-67.) (Translated by Hélène Vivienne Wenzel.) Special issue on French Feminism.

Irigaray, Luce. (1985a/1974). *Speculum of the Other Woman.* (Translated by Gillian C. Gill.) Ithaca, NY: Cornell University Press (Originally published as *Speculum de l'autre femme.* [1974], Les Editions de Minuit).

Irigaray, Luce. (1985b/1977). *This Sex Which Is Not One.* (Translated by Gillian C. Gill.) Ithaca: Cornell University Press. (Originally published as *Ce sexe qui n'en est pas un* [1977] Les Editions de Minuit.)

Irigaray, Luce. (1993a). Divine Women. In *Sexes and Genealogies.* New York: Columbia University Press.

Irigaray, Luce. (1993b). *Je, tu, nous: Toward a Culture of Difference.* New York: Routledge.

Jacklin, Carol Nagy. (1993). How My Heterosexuality Affects My Feminist Politics. In Sue Wilkinson and Celia Kitzinger (Eds.) *Heterosexuality: A Feminism and Psychology Reader.* London: Sage.

Jackson, Margaret. (1990). *The Political Versus the Natural: Case Studies in the Struggle for Female Sexual Autonomy (1800-1940).* Unpublished Ph.D. dissertation, University of Birmingham, England.

Jackson, Margaret. (1994). *The Real Facts of Life.* London: Taylor and Frances.

Jackson, Robert H. (1946). Foreword. In Sheldon Glueck *The Nuremberg Trial and Aggressive War.* New York: Alfred A. Knopf.

Jackson, Stevi. (1983). The Desire for Freud: Psychoanalysis and Feminism. *Trouble and Strife, 1* 32-41.

Jackson, Stevi. (1992). The Amazing Deconstructing Woman. *Trouble and Strife,* (25), 25-31.

Jackson, Stevi. (1995). Gender and Heterosexuality: A Materialist Feminist Analysis. In Mary Maynard and June Purvis (Eds.) *(Hetero)Sexual Politics.* London: Taylor and Francis.

Jaggar, Alison. (1983). *Feminist Politics and Human Nature.* Totowa, New Jersey: Rowman and Allan.

Jaggar, Alison. (1989). Love and Knowledge: Emotion in Feminist Epistemology. In Alison Jaggar and Susan Bordo (Eds.) *Gender/Body/Knowledge.* New Brunswick: Rutgers University Press.

Jaggar, Alison and Susan R. Bordo. (Eds.) (1989). *Gender/Body/Knowledge.* New Brunswick: Rutgers University Press.

James, Joy. (1993a). Teaching Theory, Talking Community. In Joy James and Ruth Farmer. (Eds.) *Spirit, Space and Survival: African American Women in (White) Academe.* New York: Routledge.

James, Joy and Ruth Farmer. (Eds.) (1993b). *Spirit, Space and Survival: African American Women in (White) Academe.* New York: Routledge.

Janeway, Elizabeth. (1980). *Powers of the Weak.* New York: Alfred A. Knopf.

Jardine, Alice A. (1985). *Gynesis: Configurations of Woman and Modernity.* Ithaca: Cornell University Press.

Jay, Karla and Joanne Glasgow. (Eds.) (1990). *Lesbian Texts and Contexts. Radical Revisions.* New York: New York University Press.

Jayawardena, Kumari. (1986). *Feminism and Nationalism in the Third World.* London: Zed Books.

Jeffreys, Sheila. (1985). *The Spinster and Her Enemies: Feminism and Sexuality 1880-1930.* London: Pandora.

Jeffreys, Sheila. (1990). *Anticlimax: A Feminist Perspective on the Sexual Revolution.* London: The Women's Press.

Jeffreys, Sheila. (1993). *The Lesbian Heresy: A Feminist Perspective on the Lesbian Sexual Revolution.* Melbourne: Spinifex Press; (1994) London: The Women's Press.

Jeffreys, Sheila. (1994). The Queer Disappearance of Lesbians: Sexuality in the Academy. *Women's Studies International Forum, 17* (5), 459-72.

Jeffs, Sandy/Deborah Staines. (1993). *Poems from the Madhouse/Now Millennium.* Melbourne: Spinifex Press.

Jelin, Elizabeth. (1976). *Los nuevos movimientos sociales.* Buenos Aires: Centro Editor de América Latina.

Jewish Community Relations Council San Francisco. (1992, July 27). Cattle Cars. Editorial. *San Francisco Chronicle.*

Johnson, Angela. (1992, January). For Feminists, Talk is Cheap: But in Therapy It'll Cost You $38 an Hour (and That's on a Sliding Scale). *Off Our Backs,* 8-9.

Johnson, Elizabeth A. (1992). *She Who Is: The Mystery of God in Feminist Theological Discourse.* New York: Crossroad.

Johnson, Elliot. (1991). *Royal Commission into Aboriginal Deaths in Custody,* National Report. Canberra: Australian Government Publishing Service.

Johnson, Elliott. (1992). *Royal Commission into Aboriginal Deaths in Custody.* Canberra: Australian Government Publishing Service.

Johnson, Sonia. (1986). Telling the Truth. *Trivia, 9* 9-33.

Jones, Ann Rosalind. (1981, Summer). Writing the Body: Toward an Understanding of *L'écriture féminine. Feminist Studies, 7* (2), 247-63.

Jones, Kathleen B. and Anna G. Jónasdóttir. (1988). *The Political Interests of Gender: Developing Theory and Research with a Feminist Face.* London: Sage.

Joseph, Gloria I. and Jill Lewis. (1981). *Common Differences: Conflicts in Black and White Feminist Perspectives.* Boston: South End Press. (1986), New York: Doubleday.

Joy, Morny. (1989). Reflections of an Unrepentant Feminist with Pluralistic Tendencies. *Herizons, 16* (2), 346-52.

Joy, Morny. (1994). Sainthood or Heresy: Contemporary Options for Women. In Morny Joy and P. Magee (Eds.) *Claiming our Rites: Essays on Religion by Australian Women Scholars.* Adelaide: Australian Association for the Study of Religion.

Joy, Morny. (1996). No Longer Docile Daughters or Handmaids of the Lord: Women in Religion Contest their Divine and Human Condition(-ing). Forthcoming in *Women's Studies International Forum.*

Joy, Morny and P. Magee. (Eds.) (1994). *Claiming our Rites: Essays on Religion by Australian Women Scholars.* Adelaide: Australian Association for the Study of Religion.

Joyce, James. (1934). *Ulysses.* New York: Random House.

Jungwirth, Helga. (1995). Neuere Studien zur und Problematisierungen der geschlechts-spezifischen Sozialisation. In Bundesministerium für Frauenangelegenheiten/Bundes-kanzleramt: *Bericht über die Situation der Frauen in Österreich.* Wien, 148-166.

K. v. Karadzic, 93 Civ. 1163 (S.D.N.Y. 1993).

Kader, Soha Abdel. (1988). Women in the Arab World. In *Survey of Trends in Research on Women*. Paris: UNESCO.

Kanter, Hannah, Sarah Lefanu, Sheila Shah, and Carole Spedding (Eds.) (1984). *Sweeping Statements. Writings from the Women's Liberation Movement 1981-83*. London: The Women's Press.

Kandiyoti, Deniz. (1991). Islam and Patriarchy. A Comparative Perspective. In Nikkie R. Keddie and Beth Baron (Eds.) *Women in Middle Eastern History Shifting Boundaries in Sex and Gender*. New Haven: Yale University Press.

Kaplan, Gisela T. and Lesley J. Rogers. (1990). The Definition of Male and Female: Biological Reductionism and the Sanctions of Normality. In Sneja Gunew (Ed.) *Feminist Knowledge: Critique and Construct*. London: Routledge.

Kaplan, Marion A. (1979). *The Jewish Feminist Movement in Germany, The Campaigns of the Jüdischer Frauenbund, 1904-1938*. Westport, Conneticut: Greenwood Press.

Kaplan, Temma. (1982). Female Consciousness and Collective Action: The Barcelona Casa 1910–1918. *Signs, 7* (3), 545–56.

Kappeler, Susanne. (1995). *The Will to Violence. The Politics of Personal Behaviour*. Cambridge: Polity Press; Melbourne: Spinifex Press; New York: Teachers College Press.

Kareta Feminist Group and International Initiative of Women of Bosnia and Hercegovina "Biser". (1994). Appeal by Sarajevo Women's Groups May 30, Sarajevo.

Katzenstein, Mary Fainsod and Carol McClurg Mueller. (Eds.) (1987). *The Women's Movements of the United States and Western Europe*. Philadelphia: Temple University Press.

Kauffman, Linda. (Ed.) (1989). *Feminism and Institutions: Dialogues on Feminist Theory*. Oxford and New York: Basil Blackwell.

Keddie, Nikkie R. and Beth Baron. (Eds.) (1991). *Women in Middle Eastern History: Shifting Boundaries in Sex and Gender*. New Haven: Yale University Press.

Keen, Sam. (1992). *Fire in the Belly: On Being a Man*. London: Piatkus Books.

Keller, Evelyn Fox. (1985). *Reflections on Gender and Science*. New Haven: Yale University Press.

Kelly, Liz. (1987, Summer). The New Defeatism. A Review of *Is the Future Female?* In *Trouble and Strife* (11), 23-8.

Kimmel, Michael. (1988a, September 29). The Gender Blender. *Guardian*, 20.

Kimmel, Michael. (Ed.) (1988b). *Changing Men: New Directions in Research on Men and Masculinity*. London: Sage.

Kinsey, Alfred C. Wardell B. Pomeroy, and C.E. Martin. (1948). *Sexual Behavior in the Human Male*. Philadelphia: W.B. Saunders Co.

Kipnis, Laura. (1988). Feminism: The Political Conscience of Post-modernism? In Andrew Ross (Ed.) *Universal Abandon? The Politics of Postmodernism*. Minneapolis: University of Minnesota Press.

Kirkwood, Julieta. (1984). *Las feministas y los partidos*. Santiago de Chile: Flacso.

Kitzinger, Celia. (1987). *The Social Construction of Lesbianism*. London: Sage.

Kitzinger, Celia. (1993). Depoliticising the Personal: A Feminist Slogan in Feminist Therapy. *Women's International Forum, 16* 486–96.

Kitzinger, Celia. (1994). Problematising Pleasure: Radical Feminist Deconstructions of Sexuality and Power. In H. Lorraine Radtke and Henderikus J. Stam (Eds.) *Power/Gender: Social Relations in Theory and Practice*. London: Sage.

Kitzinger, Celia, and Rachel Perkins. (1993). *Changing Our Minds: Lesbian Feminism and Psychology.* London: Onlywomen Press; New York: New York University Press.

Kitzinger, Celia and Sue Wilkinson. (1993). Theorizing Heterosexuality. In Sue Wilkinson and Celia Kitzinger (Eds.) *Heterosexuality: A Feminism and Psychology Reader.* London: Sage.

Kitzinger, Celia and Sue Wilkinson. (1994). Virgins and Queers Rehabilitating Heterosexuality? *Gender and Society, 8* (3), 444-62.

Kitzinger, Jenny and Celia Kitzinger. (1993). "Doing It": Representations of Lesbian Sex. In Gabriele Griffin (Ed.) *Outwrite: Popular/izing Lesbian Texts.* London: Pluto Press.

Klein, Renate. (Ed.) (1989). *Infertility: Women Speak Out About Their Experiences of Reproductive Medicine.* Pandora: London. (Distributed by Spinifex Press.)

Klein, Renate. (1990). Passion and Politics in Women's Studies in the Nineties. *Women's Studies International Forum, 14* (3), 125-34.

Klein, Renate and Susan Hawthorne. (1995). Bad/Old Girls Don't Get the Blues: Radical Feminism as an Alternative to De/Composition. *Proceedings New Zealand Women's Studies Conference.* Wellington, 198-203.

Klein, Renate and Susan Hawthorne. (1996). Reclaiming Sisterhood: Radical Feminism as an Antidote to Theoretical Embodied Fragmentation of Women. In Magdalene Ang-Lygate, Chris Corrin and Millsom Henry (Eds.) *Desperately Seeking Sisterhood: Still Challenging and Building.* London: Taylor and Francis.

Klein, Renate, Janice G. Raymond and Lynette J. Dumble. (1991). *RU 486: Misconceptions, Myths and Morals.* Melbourne: Spinifex Press; Amherst: Institute on Women and Technology; Dhaka: Narigrantha Prabartana.

Klein, Renate and Robyn Rowland. (1992, September). Feminist Theory into Action: The Politics of Engagement. AWSA Conference. University of Sydney.

Klein, Renate Duelli and Deborah Lynn Steinberg. (Eds.) (1989). *Radical Voices: A Decade of Feminist Resistance from Women's Studies International Forum,* Oxford: The Athene Series, Pergamon Press.

Kleinberg, Seymour. (1987). The New Masculinity of Gay Men and Beyond. In Michael Kaufman (Ed.) *Beyond Patriarchy. Essays by Men on Pleasure, Power and Change.* Toronto and New York: Oxford University Press.

Kline, Marlee. (1989, Spring). Race, Racism, and Feminist Legal Theory. *Harvard Women's Law Journal, 12* 115-50.

Kloepfer, Deborah Kelly. (1984, Spring). Flesh Made Word: Maternal Inscription in H.D. *Sagetrieb 3* (1), 27-48.

Koedt, Anne, Ellen Levine and Anita Rapone. (Eds.) (1973). *Radical Feminism.* New York: Quadrangle/The New York Times Book Company.

Kostovic, Ivica and Milos Judas. (Eds.) (1992). Mass Killing and Genocide in Croatia 1991–92: A Book of Evidence. In *Naklada.* Zagreb: Hrvatska Sveucilisna Naklada.

Kramer, Marieke and Jytte Larsen. (1992). *Resources for Providing Information and Documentation in the Field of Equal Treatment for Men and Women in the European Community,* DGV, Commission of the European Communities, V/602/92.

Kristeva, Julia. (1974/1981). La femme, ce n'est jamais [A woman can never be defined], an interview by "psychoanalysis and politics" in *Tel Quel,* Autumn, 1974. Translated and quoted in Elaine Marks and Isabelle de Courtivron (Eds.) *New French Feminisms: An Anthology.* New York: Schocken Books.

Kristeva, Julia. (1989). Women's Time. In Belsey and Moore *The Feminist Reader: Essays in Gender and Politics of Literary Criticism.* New York: Basil Blackwell.

Kriz, Heidi. (1992, December 4-10). The Censors See Dirty Pictures: The New Feminists See Liberation. *Weekly Mail*, 15.

Kroker, Arthur and Marilouise Kroker. (1987). "Theses on the Disappearing Body" in the Hyper-Modern Condition. In Arthur and Marilouise Kroker (Eds.) *Body Invaders*. New York: St Martin's Press.

Kroker, Arthur and Marilouise Kroker. (Eds.) (1987). *Body Invaders*. New York: St Martin's Press.

Kruks, Sonia. (1992). Gender and Subjectivity: Simone de Beauvoir and Contemporary Feminism. *Signs*, *18* (1), 89-101.

Kruks, Sonia. (1993). Genre et subjectivité: Simone de Beauvoir et le féminisme contemporain, *Nouvelles Questions Féministes*, *14* 3-28.

Ku, Yenlin. (Forthcoming). *Neither First nor Third World: The Feminist Experience of Taiwan.*

Kuykendall, Eleanor. (1989). Questions for Julia Kristeva's Ethics of Linguistics. In Jeffner Allan and Iris Marion Young (Eds.) *The Thinking Muse, Feminism and Modern French Philosophy*. Bloomington: Indiana University Press.

Kuznetsova, Larisa. (1990). Conversations in Front of the Mirror. Open Tribune. *Working Woman*, 3.

Kwok, Pui-Lan, (1992). *Chinese Women and Christianity, 1860-1927*. Atlanta: Scholars Press.

Lacan, Jacques. (1953). Some Reflections on the Ego. *International Journal of Psycho-Analysis*, *34* (Part II), 11-17.

Larbalestier, Jan. (1990). The Politics of Representation: Australian Aboriginal Women and Feminism. *Anthropological Forum*, *6* (2), 143-57.

Lawson, Olive. (1990). *The First Voice of Australian Feminism: Excerpts from Louisa Lawson's The Dawn 1888–1895*. Brookvale: Simon and Schuster.

Lazreg, Marnia. (1988, Spring). Feminism and Difference: The Perils of Writing as a Woman on Women in Algeria. *Feminist Studies*, *14* (1), 81-107.

Le Doeuff, Michèle. (1989). *The Philosophical Imaginary*. (Translated by Colin Gordon.) Stanford University Press. (Originally published as *L'Imaginaire philosophique*, 1980.)

Lebacqz, Karen. (1990). Love Your Enemy: Sex, Power and Christian Ethics. In *The Annual of the Society of Christian Ethics*. Washington: Georgetown University Press.

Lederer, Laura. (1980). *Take Back The Night: Women on Pornography*. New York: William Morrow and Co.

Leeds Revolutionary Feminist Group. (1979). *Love Your Enemy? The Debate Between Heterosexual Feminism and Political Lesbianism*. (Republished (1981) London: Onlywomen Press.)

Leghorn, Lisa and Katherine Parker. (1981). *Woman's Worth: Sexual Economics and the World of Women*. London: Routledge and Kegan Paul.

Lehman, David. (1991). *Signs of the Times, Deconstruction and the Fall of Paul de Man*. New York: Poseidon Press.

Leidholdt, Dorchen and Janice G. Raymond. (1990). *The Sexual Liberals and the Attack on Feminism*. New York: Athene Series, Pergamon Press.

Lengyel, Olga. (1947). *Five Chimneys: The Story of Auschwitz*. Chicago: Ziff-Davis.

Leonoff, Elena. (1990, November 9). Save Some Revulsion for the Strip-Joint Men. Letter to the Editor. *Age*.

Lerner, Harriet. (1990). Problems for Profit. *Women's Review of Books*, *VII* (7), 15-16.

Lessing, Doris. (1962). *The Golden Notebook*. London: Granada.

Li, Yuan-chen. (1992). *Intimate Talks about Love (Ai-ching Tsu-yu)*. Taipei: Tzu-li.

Lie, Suzanne Stiver and Virginia E. O'Leary (Eds.) (1990). *Women in the Academic World*. London: Kogan Page.

Lifton, Robert Jay. (1986). *The Nazi Doctors: Medical Killing and the Psychology of Genocide*. New York: Basic Books.

Lightfoot-Klein, Hanny. (1989). *Prisoners of Ritual: An Odyssey into Female Genital Circumcision in Africa*. New York: Harrington Park Press.

Lindbergh, Anne Morrow. (1955/1992). *Gift from the Sea*, London: Chatto and Windus.

Linden, Robin Ruth, Darlene R. Pagano, Diana E. H. Russell, and Susan Leigh Star. (Eds.) (1982). *Against Sadomasochism: A Radical Feminist Analysis*. Palo Alto, California: Frog in the Well Press.

Lionnet, Françoise. (1989). *Autobiographical Voices: Race, Gender and Self-Portraiture*. Ithaca: Cornell University Press.

Lionnet, Françoise. (1991). Feminism, Universalism and the Practice of Excision. *Passages, 1.*

Lloyd, Genevieve. (1984). *The Man of Reason, "Male" and "Female" in Western Philosophy*. Minneapolis: University of Minnesota Press.

Loewenberg, Bert J. and Ruth Dugin. (Eds.) (1976). *Black Women in Nineteenth Century American Life: Their Words, Their Thoughts, Their Feelings*. University Park: Pennsylvania State University Press.

Loncar, Mladen. (1993). *Medical and Psycho-Social Help for Male Victims of Sexual Assault*. Zagreb: Medical Center for Human Rights.

London Lesbian Offensive Group. (1984). Anti-lesbianism in the Women's Liberation Movement. In Hannah Kanter, Sarah Lefanu, Sheila Shah, and Carole Spedding (Eds.) *Sweeping Statements. Writings from the Women's Liberation Movement 1981-83*. London: The Women's Press.

Lonergan, Bernard. (1957). *INSIGHT: An Understanding of Human Knowing*. New York: Harper and Row.

Lorde, Audre. (1981). The Master's Tools Will Never Dismantle the Master's House. In Cherrie Moraga and Gloria Anzaldúa (Eds.) *This Bridge Called My Back: Writings by Radical Women of Color*. New York: Kitchen Table Press.

Lorde, Audre. (1984). *Sister Outsider: Essays and Speeches*. Trumansburg, New York: The Crossing Press.

Lorde, Audre. (1990). Speech from *Honoring Audre Lorde: The Making of a Global Conference*. (Video-in-progress. Produced and edited by Jennifer Abod).

Los Angeles Feminist Women's Health Center. (1981). *How to Stay Out of the Gynecologist's Office*. Culver City: Peace Press.

Lovell, Terry. (Ed.) (1990). *British Feminist Thought*. Oxford: Basil Blackwell.

Lowe, Sarah. (1991). Lesbian Identity. *Rebellious* (Special Women's Issue of La Trobe University Student Newspaper *Rabelais*, Melbourne).

Luker, Kristin. (1984). *Abortion and the Politics of Motherhood*. Berkeley: University of California Press.

Lyndon, Neil. (1992). *No More Sex War: The Failures of Feminism*. London: Sinclair-Stevenson.

Lyotard, Jean-François. (1984). *The Post Modern Condition: A Report on Knowledge*. (Translated by Geoff Bennington and Brian Massumi.) University of Minnesota Press. (*Theory and History of Literature, 10.*) (Originally published in 1979.)

MacCowan, Lyndall. (1992). Re-collecting History, Renaming Lives: Femme Stigma and the Feminist Seventies and Eighties. In Joan Nestle (Ed.) *The Persistent Desire: A Femme-Butch Reader*. Boston, Massachusetts: Alyson Publications.

MacCurtain, Margaret and Mary O'Dowd. (1992). An Agenda for Women's History in Ireland: Part I: 1500–1800. *Irish Historical Studies, 27* 1-18.

MacKenzie, Jean. (1995, June 25). Playboy of the Eastern World Does Cover-Up. *Sunday Times*.

MacKinnon, Catharine A. (1982). Feminism, Marxism, Method and the State: An Agenda for Theory, *Signs, 7* (3), 515-44.

MacKinnon, Catharine A. (1987). *Feminism Unmodified: Discourses on Life and Law*. Cambridge, Massachusetts: Harvard University Press.

MacKinnon, Catharine A. (1989a). *Toward a Feminist Theory of the State*. Cambridge, Massachusetts: Harvard University Press.

MacKinnon, Catharine A. (1989b). Pornography: Not a Moral Issue. In Renate Duelli Klein and Deborah Lynn Steinberg (Eds.) *Radical Voices*. Oxford: The Athene Series, Pergamon Press.

MacKinnon, Catharine A. (1991a). Reflections on Sex Equality Under Law. *Yale Law Journal 100* (5), 1281-1328.

MacKinnon, Catharine A. (1991b) From Practice to Theory or What is a White Woman Anyway? *Yale Journal of Law and Feminism*, (4), 13-22.

MacKinnon, Catharine A. (1993a). Crimes of War, Crimes of Peace. In Stephen Shute and Susan Hurley (Eds.) *On Human Rights: The Oxford Amnesty Lectures 1993*. New York: Basic Books.

MacKinnon, Catharine A. (1993b). *Only Words*. Cambridge, Massachusetts: Harvard University Press.

MacKinnon, Catharine A. (1994a, Spring). Rape, Genocide, and Women's Human Rights. *Harvard Women's Law Journal, 17* 5-16.

MacKinnon, Catharine A. (1994b March 3). An Exchange. *New York Review of Books*, 47-8.

MacKinnon, Catharine and Andrea Dworkin. (1994a, December 10–1995, March 8). Women's Equality Day in the US. *Woman and Earth Almanac, 3* (1), 35.

MacKinnon, Catharine and Andrea Dworkin. (1994b, Fall). Statement on Canadian Customs and Legal Approaches to Pornography. *Action Agenda, 1* (3), 5, 8-9.

Madonna. (1992). *Sex*. (Photographed by Steven Meisel.) New York: Warner Books.

Mahony, Pat. (1992). Which Way Forward? Equality and Schools in the 90s. *Women's Studies International Forum, 15* (2), 293-303

Mainardi, Pat. (1970). The Politics of Housework. In Robin Morgan (Ed.) *Sisterhood is Powerful*. New York: Vintage Books.

Mairs, Nancy. (1990). *Remembering the Bone House: An Erotics of Place and Space*. New York: Harper and Row.

Mairs, Nancy. (1992). On Being a Cripple. In *Plaintext*. Tucson: University of Arizona Press.

Mamonova, Tatyana. (1984). *Woman and Russia*. Boston: Beacon

Mamonova, Tatyana. (1992). *Russian Women's Studies: Essays on Sexism in Soviet Culture*. New York: Teachers College Press.

Mamonova, Tatyana. (Ed.) (1995, March 8). *Woman and Earth Almanac: 15 Years Anniversary Issue, 3* (1), 70.

Mandzuik, Roseann M. (1993). Feminist Politics and Postmodern Seductions: Madonna and the Struggle for Political Articulation. In Cathy Schwichtenberg (Ed.) *The Madonna Connection: Representational Politics, Subcultural Identities, and Cultural Theory.* Boulder, Colorado: Westview Press.

Mann, Bonnie. (1986). The Radical Feminist Task of History: Gathering Intelligence in Nicaragua. *Trivia, 9* 46, 60.

Maracle, Lee. (1990, September). Oratory: Coming to Theory. North Vancouver, B.C: Gallerie Women Artists' Monographs. Issue 1.

Marchiano, Linda. (Linda Lovelace). (1980). *Ordeal: An Autobiography.* New Jersey: Citadel Press.

Marks, Elaine and Isabelle de Courtivron. (Eds.) (1981). *New French Feminisms.* New York: Schocken Books.

Martin, Biddy and Chandra Talpade Mohanty. (1986). Feminist Politics: What's Home Got to Do with It? In Teresa de Lauretis (Ed.) *Feminist Studies/Critical Studies.* Bloomington: Indiana University Press.

May, Margaret. (1978). Violence in the Family: An Historical Perspective. In J. P. Martin. *Violence and the Family.* Chichester: John Wiley and Sons.

Maynard, Mary and June Purvis. (Eds.) (1995). *(Hetero)sexual Politics.* London: Taylor and Francis.

McAllister, Pam. (1982). *Reweaving the Web of Life.* New York: New Society Publishers.

McBride, James. (1995). *War, Battering, and Other Sports: The Gulf Between American Men and Women.* Atlantic Highlands, New Jersey: Humanities Press International.

McDowell, Colin. (1994, February 6). Bad Boys and Screen Queens. *Observer Magazine,* 8-14.

McNaron, Toni. (1982). Out at the University. In Margaret Cruikshank (Ed.) *Lesbian Studies.* New York: Feminist Press.

Meese, Elizabeth A. (1990a). *Crossing the Double-Cross: The Practice of Feminist Criticism.* University of North Carolina Press.

Meese, Elizabeth. (1990b). Theorizing Lesbian: Writing – A Love Letter. In Karla Jay and Joanne Glasgow (Eds.) *Lesbian Texts and Contexts. Radical Revisions.* New York: New York University Press.

Meese, Elizabeth A. (1990c). *(Ex)Tensions: Re-Figuring Feminist Criticism.* Urbana: University of Illinois Press.

Mendelsohn, Oliver and Uprendra Baxi. (Eds.) (1994). *The Rights of Subordinated Peoples.* Delhi: Oxford University Press.

Mercer, Jan. (Ed.) (1975). *The Other Half.* Ringwood: Penguin.

Mercer, Kobena. (1992). Just Looking for Trouble: Robert Mapplethorpe and Fantasies of Race. In Lynne Segal and Mary McIntosh (Eds.) *Sex Exposed. Sexuality and the Pornography Debate.* London: Virago.

Merck, Mandy. (1993). *Perversions: Deviant Readings.* London: Virago.

Metcalfe, Andy and Martin Humphries. (Eds.) (1985). *The Sexuality of Men.* London: Pluto Press.

Metz-Göckel, Sigrid and Maria Anna Kreienbaum. (1991, December). Herkömmliche Geschlechterpolarisierungen und neue Differenzierungen. Ulf Preuss-Lausitz' Fragen: ein Pamphlet gegen die Frauenzentrierung der Frauenforschung. *Pädextra, 12* (19), 16-18.

Mies, Maria. (1982). (Ed.) *Fighting on Two Fronts: Women's Struggles and Research.* The Hague: Institute of Social Studies.

591

Mies, Maria. (1986). *Patriarchy and Accumulation on a World Scale: Women in the International Division of Labour.* London: Zed Books.

Mieth, Dietmar and Jacques Pohier. (Eds.) (1989). *Changing Values and Virtues. Concilium 191.* Edinburgh: T. and T. Clark.

Milan Women's Bookstore Collective. (1990). *Sexual Difference: A Theory of Social-Symbolic Practice.* (Translated from the Italian by Patricia Cicogna and Teresa de Lauretis). Bloomington: Indiana University Press.

Miller, Alice. (1987). *For Your Own Good: The Roots of Violence in Child Rearing.* London: Virago.

Miller, Elaine and Lynne Harne. (Eds.) (1995). *All the Rage: The Backlash and Lesbian Feminist Resistance.* London: The Women's Press.

Millett, Kate. (1970/1971). *Sexual Politics.* Garden City, New York: Doubleday; London: Abacus; (1971) New York: Avon Books.

Min Sheng Daily. (1987, May 30). To Our Teachers With Love.

Mitchell, Juliet and Ann Oakley (Eds.) (1986). *What is Feminism?* Oxford: Blackwell.

Mitchell, Susan. (Ed.) (1984). *Tall Poppies.* Ringwood: Penguin.

Modleski, Tania. (1991). *Feminism without Women: Culture and Criticism in a "Postfeminist" Age.* New York: Routledge.

Mohanty, Chandra Talpade. (1984). Under Western Eyes: Feminist Scholarship and Colonial Discourses. *Boundary 2: A Journal of Post-Modern Literature and Culture, 12-13* 333-59.

Mohanty, Chandra Talpade, Ann Russo and Lourdes Torres. (Eds.) (1991). *Third World Women and the Politics of Feminism.* Bloomington: Indiana University Press.

Moi, Toril. (1985). *Sexual/Textual Politics.* London: Methuen.

Moi, Toril. (Ed.) (1987). *French Feminist Thought: A Reader.* Cambridge, Massachusetts: Basil Blackwell.

Moi, Toril. (1988, Spring). Feminism, Postmodernism and Style: Recent Feminist Criticism in the United States. *Cultural Critique,* 3-22.

Molyneux, Maxine. (1985, Summer). Mobilization Without Emancipation? Women's Interests, the State, and Revolution in Nicaragua. *Feminist Studies, 11* 227-540.

Morales, Rosario. (1981). We're all in the same boat. In Gloria Anzaldúa and Cherrie Moraga (Eds.) *This Bridge Called My Back: Writings by Radical Women of Color.* Massachusetts: Persephone Press, 91-6.

Morgan, David H.J. (1992). *Discovering Men.* London: Routledge.

Morgan, Robin. (1970). Goodbye to All That. In Robin Morgan (1992). *The Word of a Woman: Selected Prose 1968-1992.* London: Virago.

Morgan, Robin. (Ed.) (1970). *Sisterhood Is Powerful: An Anthology of Writings from the Women's Liberation Movement.* New York: Random; New York: Vintage.

Morgan, Robin. *Monster.* (1972). New York: Random House.

Morgan, Robin. (ND). Monster. In *Monster.* Melbourne: Melbourne Radical Feminists (pirate edition).

Morgan, Robin. (1978). *Going Too Far: The Personal Chronicle of a Feminist.* New York: Vintage Books.

Morgan, Robin. (Ed.) (1984). *Sisterhood Is Global: The International Women's Movement Anthology.* New York: Doubleday. (1985). London: Penguin Books. (1993). *Mujeres del Mundo.* Madrid: Vindicacion Feminist/Hacer Editorial.

Morgan, Robin. (1990). *Upstairs in the Garden: Poems Selected and New 1968- 1988.* New York: W.W. Norton

Morgan, Robin. (1992). *The Word of a Woman: Selected Prose 1968-1992.* London: Virago.

Morris, Aldon. (1984). *The Origins of the Civil Rights Movement: Black Communities Organizing for Change.* New York: Free Press.

Morrison, Toni. (1992). *Race-ing Justice, En-gendering Power: Essays on Anita Hill, Clarence Thomas and the Construction of Social Reality.* New York: Pantheon.

Morrison, Toni. (1984). Rootedness: The Ancestor as Foundation. In Mari Evans (Ed.) *Black Women Writers (1950-1980).* New York: Anchor Press.

Moses, Claire. (1992a, 12 June). "French feminism" in US Academic Discourse. Paper presented at Berkshire History of Women Conference, Berkshire.

Moses, Claire. (1992b, Winter). Debating the Present, Writing the Past: Feminism in French History and Historiography. In *Radical History Review, 52* 79-94.

Naroyan, Uma. (1989). The Project of Feminist Epistemology: Perspectives from a Non-western Feminist. In Alison Jagger and Susan Bordo (Eds.) *Gender/Body/Knowledge.* New Brunswick: Rutgers University Press.

National Research Bureau Inc. (1992). *Working Press of the Nation: Magazine and Editorial Directory, II.* Burlington, Iowa.

Nelson, Topsy Napurrula. (1990a). My Story. In Shelley Schreiner and Diane Bell (Eds.) *This is My Story.* Geelong: Centre for Australian Studies, Deakin University.

Nelson, Topsy Napurrula. (1990b). Letter to the Editor. *Women's Studies International Forum, 14* (5), 507.

Nestle, Joan. (Ed.) (1992). *The Persistent Desire: A Femme-Butch Reader.* Boston: Alyson.

Newton, Helmut. (1976). *White Women.* New York: Stone Hill.

Newsweek. (1992, November 29). The Rites of Americans.

Nichols, Margaret. (1987). Lesbian Sexuality: Issues and Developing Theory. In Boston Lesbian Psychologies Collective (Eds.) *Lesbian Psychologies.* Chicago: University of Illinois Press.

Nicholson, Linda J. (Ed.) (1990). *Feminism/Postmodernism.* New York and London: Routledge.

Nicolson, Paula and Jane Ussher. (Eds.) (1992). *The Psychology of Women's Health and Health Care.* London: Macmillan.

Nietzsche, Friedrich. (1990). Interpretation. In Gayle L. Ormiston and Alan D. Schrift (Eds.) *Transforming the Hermeneutic Context.* New York: State University of New York Press.

Nye, Andrea. (1989). *Feminist Theories and the Philosophies of Man.* New York: Routledge. (First published by Croom Helm, 1988.)

Nyssen, Elke. (1991, December). ". . . und sie wurden gewahr, dass sie nackt waren (*Altes Testament, Genesis,* v. 2, 3)." Ist die feministische Schulforschung eine Schimäre? *Pädextra, 12* (19), 13-15.

O'Brien, Mary. (1981). *The Politics of Reproduction.* Boston: Routledge and Kegan Paul.

O'Brien, Mary. (1989). *Reproducing the World: Essays in Feminist Theory.* Boulder, Colorado: Westview Press.

O'Donnell, Guillermo. (1986). *Transition from Authoritarian Rule.* Baltimore: Johns Hopkins University Press.

O'Neill, Rosemary. (1994, June 18–19). Our Shame: How Aboriginal Women and Children are Bashed in their Own Community – Then Ignored. *Weekend Australian Review,* 1-2.

Ormiston, Gayle L. and Alan D. Schrift. (Eds.) (1990). *Transforming the Hermeneutic Context.* New York: State University of New York Press.

O'Shane, Pat. (1976, September). Is There Any Relevance in the Women's Movement for Aboriginal Women? *Refractory Girl,* 31-4.

O'Shane, Pat. (1984). Autonomy. In Susan Mitchell (Ed.) *Tall Poppies.* Ringwood: Penguin.

O'Shane, Pat. (1988). Report on Aboriginal Women and Domestic Violence. Unpublished manuscript.

Oakley, Ann. (1982). *Subject Women. A Powerful Analysis of Women's Experience in Society Today.* London: Fontana Paperbacks.

Ogunyemi, Chikwenye Okonjo. (Forthcoming). *Ectomies: A Treasury of Juju Fiction by Africa's Daughters.*

Omerdic, Muharem. (1992, June 1). Another Genocide Against Muslims: Let it Be Known and Never Repeated. *Preporod.*

Omerdic, Muharem. (1992, June 29). Muslims in Concentration Camps. Sarajevo: SDA Information Center.

Onlywomen Press. (Ed.) (1981). *Love Your Enemy? The Debate Between Heterosexual Feminism and Political Lesbianism.* London: Onlywomen Press.

Overall, Christine. (Ed.) (1989). *The Future of Human Reproduction.* Toronto: Women's Press.

Owens, Craig. (1983). The Discourse of Others: Feminists and Postmodernism. In Hal Foster (Ed.) *The Anti-Aesthetic, Essays on Postmodern Culture.* Seattle: Bay Press.

Padesky, Christine A. (1989). Attaining and Maintaining Positive Self-Identity: A Cognitive Therapy Approach. *Women and Therapy,* 8 145-56.

Paglia, Camille. (1992). *Sex, Art and American Culture.* New York: Vintage Books.

Paine, Thomas. (1791). *The Rights of Man.* Harmondsworth: Penguin.

Parnaby, Julia. (1993, Summer). Queer Straits. *Trouble and Strife,* (26), 13-16.

Pateman, Carole. (1988). *The Sexual Contract.* Cambridge: Polity Press.

Patrick, Anne E. (1989). Narrative and the Social Dynamics of Virtue. In Dietmar Mieth and Jacques Pohier (Eds.) *Changing Values and Virtues. Concilium 191.* Edinburgh: T. and T. Clark.

Patton, Cindy. (1993). Embodying Subaltern Memory: Kinesthesia and the Problematics of Gender and Race. In Cathy Schwichtenberg (Ed.) *The Madonna Connection: Representational Politics, Subcultural Identities, and Cultural Theory.* Boulder, Colorado: Westview Press.

Pavel, Thomas. (1990). *The Feud of Language: A History of Structuralist Thought.* (Translated by Linda Jordan and Thomas Pavel.) Oxford: Basil Blackwell. (Originally published as *Le Mirage linguistic: Essai sur la modernisation intellectuelle,* Minuit, 1988.)

Payne, Sharon. (1990). Aboriginal Women and the Criminal Justice System. *Aboriginal Law Bulletin, 2* (46), 9-11.

Pelka, Fred. (1995, March–April). Voices from a War Zone. *The Humanist,* 6-10.

Penelope, Julia. (1990). *Speaking Freely: Unlearning the Lies of the Fathers' Tongues.* New York: The Athene Series, Pergamon Press.

Penelope, Julia. (Ed.) (1994). *Out of the Class Closet: Lesbians Speak.* Freedom, California: The Crossing Press.

Perkins, Rachel. (1991). Therapy for Lesbians? The Case Against. *Feminism and Psychology, 1* (3), 325-28.

Perl, Gisella. (1948). *I was a Doctor in Auschwitz.* New York: Arno Press.

Petschesky, Rosalind. (1987). Fetal Images: The Power of Visual Culture in the Politics of Reproduction. *Feminist Studies, 13* (2), 280.

Pickering, Brian. (1992, September 8). Queer Street Fighters. *Guardian,* 23.

Picq, Françoise. (1993). *Libération des Femmes: Les années-mouvement.* Paris: Seuil.

Piercy, Marge. (1979). *Woman on the Edge of Time.* London: The Women's Press.

Piercy, Marge. (1982). *Circles on the Water: Selected Poems of Marge Piercy.* New York: Alfred A. Knopf.

Pietila, Hilkka and Jill Vickers. (1990). *Making Women Matter: The Role of the United Nations.* London: Zed Books.

Pityana, N. B. M Ramphele, M. Mpumlwana and L. Wilson. (Eds.) (1990). *Bounds of Possibility: The Legacy of Steve Biko and Black Consciousness.* Cape Town: David Phillip.

Plaskow, Judith and Carol P. Christ (Eds.) (1989). *Weaving the Visions: New Patterns in Feminist Spirituality.* New York: Harper and Row.

Plaskow, Judith. (1990). *Standing Again at Sinai: Judaism from a Feminist Perspective.* San Francisco: Harper.

Plaskow, Judith. (1992). The Coming of Lilith: Toward a Feminist Theology. In Carol P. Christ and Judith Plaskow (Eds.) *Womanspirit Rising – A Feminist Reader in Religion.* New York: Harper and Row.

Playboy in South Africa. (1993, January 8-14). *Weekly Mail,* 3.

Pleck, Elizabeth H. (1983). Women's History: Gender as a Category of Analysis. In James B. Gardner and George Rollie Adams (Eds.) *Ordinary People and Everyday Life.* Nashville: American Association for State and Local History.

Plummer, Kenneth. (Ed.) (1992). *Modern Homosexualities.* London: Routledge.

Prengel, Annedore. (1986). Konzeptionelle Planung der Untersuchungen des Feministischen Interdisziplinären Forschungsinstituts (FIF). In Hessisches Institut für Bildungsplanung und Schulentwicklung – Im Auftrag des Hessischen Kultusministers: *Konzept zum Vorhaben Verwirklichung der Gleichstellung von Schülerinnen und Lehrerinnen an hessischen Schulen.* Sonderreihe Heft 21, Wiesbaden, 21-53.

Prengel, Annedore. (1994). Universalität – Kollektivität – Individualität. Dimensionen demokratischer Differenz in der Bildung. In Ulla Bracht und Dieter Keiner. *Jahrbuch für Pädagogik 1994. Geschlechterverhältnisse und die Pädagogik.* Frankfurt am Main: Lang Verlag, 139-51.

Preuss-Lausitz, Ulf. (1991, December). Der Kaiserin neue Kleider? Fragen an die feministische Schulforschung beim Blick auf die Jungen. *Pädextra, 12* (19), 5-12.

Probyn, Elspeth. (1987). Bodies and Anti-Bodies: Feminism and the Postmodern. *Cultural Studies, 1* (3), 349-60.

Questions Feministes. (1980). Editorial: Variations on Some Common Themes. *1* (1), 1-19.

Radtke, H. Lorraine and Henderikus J. Stam. (Eds.) (1994). *Power/Gender: Social Relations in Theory and Practice.* London: Sage.

Radford, Jill and Diana E. H. Russell. (1992). *Femicide: The Politics of Woman-Killing.* New York: Twayne.

Radicalesbians. (1970). The Woman Identified Woman. (Leaflet). Reprinted in Sarah Lucia Hoagland and Julia Penelope (Eds.) (1988). *For Lesbians Only: A Separatist Anthology.* London: Onlywomen Press.

Ramazanoglu, Caroline. (1993). Theorizing Heterosexuality: A Response to Wendy Hollway. In Sue Wilkinson and Celia Kitzinger (Eds.) *Heterosexuality: A Feminism and Psychology Reader.* London: Sage.

Ramphele, Mamphele. (1990). The Dynamics of Gender Within Black Consciousness Organizations: A Personal View. In N. B. Pityana, M. Ramphele, M. Mpumlwana and L. Wilson. (Eds.) *Bounds of Possibility: The Legacy of Steve Biko and Black Consciousness.* Cape Town: David Phillip.

Raphaely, Jane. (1992, December). Our Cosmo World. Editorial. *Cosmopolitan,* 12.

Rapp, Rayna. (1988, April). A Womb of One's Own. A Review of *Made to Order* and *Reproductive Technologies. The Women's Review of Books,* 5 (7).

Raymond, Janice G. (1979/1982/1994a). *The Transsexual Empire: The Making of the She-male.* Boston: Beacon; (1982) London: The Women's Press; (1994a) New York and London: Teachers College Press.

Raymond, Janice G. (1986/1991). *A Passion for Friends: Toward a Philosophy of Female Affection.* Boston: Beacon; London: The Women's Press.

Raymond, Janice G. (1989a). At Issue: Reproductive Technologies, Radical Feminism and Socialist Liberalism. *Reproductive and Genetic Engineering,* 2 (2), 133-42.

Raymond, Janice G. (1989b). Putting the Politics Back into Lesbianism. *Women's Studies International Forum,* 12 (2), 149-56. Reprinted in *Journal of Australian Lesbian Feminist Studies,* 1 (2).

Raymond, Janice G. (1993/1994b). *Women as Wombs: Reproductive Technologies and the Battle over Women's Freedom.* San Francisco: HarperCollins; Melbourne: Spinifex Press.

Reagon, Bernice Johnson. (1991, June). "Nobody Knows the Trouble I See" or "By and By I'm Gonna Lay Down My Heavy Load." In *Journal of American History,* 78 (1), 111-19.

Redstockings. (Eds.) (1978). *Feminist Revolution.* New York: Random House.

Reich, June L. (1992). Genderfuck: The Law of the Dildo. *Discourse,* 15 (1), 112-27.

Reinharz, Shulamit. (1993). How my Heterosexuality Contributes to my Feminism and Vice-Versa. In Sue Wilkinson and Celia Kitzinger (Eds.) *Heterosexuality. A Feminism and Psychology Reader,* London: Sage.

Report of the Inquiry into Prostitution in Victoria. (1985). Melbourne, Australia: Government Printer.

Rhodes, Dusty and Sandra McNeill. (Eds.) (1985). *Women Against Violence Against Women.* London: Onlywomen Press.

Rich, Adrienne. (1976/1977). *Of Woman Born: Motherhood as Experience and Institution.* New York: W. W. Norton; (1977) London: Virago.

Rich, Adrienne. (1979). *On Lies, Secrets, and Silence: Selected Prose 1966–78.* New York: Norton.

Rich, Adrienne. (1979a). Disloyal to Civilization: Feminism, Racism, Gynophobia. In *On Lies, Secrets and Silence.* New York: W. W. Norton.

Rich, Adrienne. (1979b). Motherhood in Bondage. In *On Lies, Secrets and Silence.* New York: W. W. Norton. 195-7.

Rich, Adrienne. (1980). Compulsory Heterosexuality and Lesbian Existence, *Signs,* 5 (4), 631-60.

Richardson, Diane. (1992). Constructing Lesbian Sexualities. In Kenneth Plummer (Ed.) *Modern Homosexualities.* London: Routledge.

Richardson, Diane. (Ed.) (1995). *Theorizing Heterosexuality: Telling it Straight.* Milton Keynes: Open University Press.

Richardson, Diane and Victoria Robinson. (Eds.) (1993). *Introducing Women's Studies: Feminist Theory and Practice.* London: Macmillan.

Richardson, Diane and Victoria Robinson. (1994). Theorising Women's Studies, Gender Studies and Masculinity: The Politics of Naming. *European Journal of Women's Studies, 1* (1), 11-27.

Richter, Judith. (1996). *Vaccination Against Pregnancy: Miracle or Menace?* London: Zed Press; Melbourne: Spinifex.

Rittner, Carol and John K. Roth. (Eds.) (1993). *Different Voices: Women and the Holocaust.* New York: Paragon House.

Robb, Carol S. (Ed.) (1985). *Making the Connections: Essays in Feminist Social Ethics.* Boston: Beacon.

Robinson, Victoria. (1993). Heterosexuality: Beginnings and Connections. In Sue Wilkinson and Celia Kitzinger (Eds.) *Heterosexuality: A Feminism and Psychology Reader.* London: Sage.

Robinson, Victoria. (1993). Introducing Women's Studies. In Diane Richardson and Victoria Robinson (Eds.) *Introducing Women's Studies: Feminist Theory and Practice.* London: Macmillan.

Rodgerson, Gillian and Elizabeth Wilson. (Eds.) (1991). *Pornography and Feminism: The Case Against Censorship.* London: Lawrence and Wishart.

Roggenkamp, Viola. (1984). Abortion of a Special Kind: Male Sex Selection in India. In Rita Arditti, Renate Duelli Klein, and Shelley Minden (Eds.) *Test-Tube Women: What Future for Motherhood?* London and Boston: Pandora Press.

Roiphe, Kate. (1994). *The Morning After: Sex, Fear and Feminism.* London: Hamish Hamilton.

Romano, Carlin. (1993, November 15). Between the Motion and the Act. *Nation,* 563-70.

Romano, Carlin. (1994, December 27). Exchange. *Nation,* 786, 816.

Rorty, Richard. (1991). Feminism and Pragmatism. *Michigan Quarterly Review, 30* 231-34.

Rose, Hilary. (1987/1988). Victorian Values in the Test-Tube: the Politics of Reproductive Science and Technology. In Michelle Stanworth (Ed.) *Reproductive Technologies: Gender, Motherhood and Medicine.* Minneapolis: University of Minnesota Press.

Rose, Hilary. (1993, June). Thinking Global: Acting Local: Paper presented at the KEGME/ UNESCO Conference Gender Studies Towards The Year 2000. Athens.

Rose, Sonya O. (1993). Gender History/Women's History: Is Feminist Scholarship Losing its Critical Edge? *Journal of Women's History, 5* 89-101.

Rosenau, Pauline Marie. (1992). *Post-modernism and the Social Sciences: Insights, Inroads, and Intrusions.* Princeton: Princeton University Press.

Rosewater, Lynn Bravo and Lenore Walker. (Eds.) (1985). *Handbook of Feminist Therapy.* New York: Springer.

Ross, Andrew. (Ed.) (1988). *Universal Abandon? The Politics of Postmodernism.* Minneapolis: University of Minnesota Press.

Rosser, Sue. (1990). *Female Friendly Science. Applying Women's Studies Methods and Theories to Attract Students.* New York: Athene Series, Pergamon.

Rowbotham, Sheila. (1990). *The Past is Before Us: Feminism in Action Since the 1960s.* Harmondsworth: Penguin.

Rowland, Robyn. (1984). *Women Who Do and Women Who Don't Join the Women's Movement.* London: Routledge Kegan and Paul.

Rowland, Robyn. (1987a). Technology and Motherhood: Reproductive Choice Reconsidered, *Signs, 12* (3), 512-28.

Rowland, Robyn. (1987b). The Burying of Hughes. In *Up from Below: Poems of the 1980s*. Sydney: Women's Redress Press.

Rowland, Robyn. (1988). *Woman Herself: A Transdisciplinary Perspective on Women's Identity*. Melbourne: Oxford University Press.

Rowland, Robyn. (1990). Lesbianism and Feminism: A Woman-Centred Sexuality, A Woman-Centred Politics. In *Women and Social Change Study Guide*, Geelong: Deakin University.

Rowland, Robyn. (1991-92). Correspondence. *Anthropological Forum, 6* (3), 429-35.

Rowland, Robyn. (1992/1993). *Living Laboratories. Women In Reproductive Technologies*, Bloomington: Indiana University Press, London: Limetree, Cedar Press; Sydney: Pan Macmillan, distributed by Spinifex Press.

Rowland, Robyn. (1993). Radical Feminist Heterosexuality: The Personal and the Political. In Sue Wilkinson and Celia Kitzinger (Eds.) *Heterosexuality*. London: Sage.

Rowland, Robyn. (1995, August). Human Rights Discourse and Women: Challenging the Rhetoric with Reality. *Australian and New Zealand Journal of Sociology, 31* (2), 8-24.

Rowland, Robyn. (1996). A Politics of Relationship: Reproductive and Genetic Screening Technology. In Magdalene Ang-Lygate, Chris Corrin and Milsom Henry (Eds.) *Desperately Seeking Sisterhood: Still Challenging and Building*. London: Taylor and Francis.

Rowland, Robyn and Renate Klein. (1990). Radical Feminism: Critique and Construct. In Sneja Gunew. (Ed.) *Feminist Knowledge: Critique and Construct*. London: Routledge.

Rowland, Robyn and Alison Thomas. (Eds.) (1996). Mothering Sons: A Crucial Feminist Challenge, *Feminism and Psychology, 6* (1), 93-154.

Rubin, Gayle. (1984). Thinking Sex: Notes for a Radical Theory of the Politics of Sexuality. In Carole Vance (Ed.) *Pleasure and Danger: Exploring Female Sexuality*. London: Pandora.

Rubin, Gayle. (1991). Misguided Dangerous and Wrong. In Gillian Rodgerson and Elizabeth Wilson (Eds.) (1991). *Pornography and Feminism: The Case Against Censorship*. London: Lawrence and Wishart.

Rubin, Gayle. (1992). Of Catamites and Kings: Reflections on Butch, Gender and Boundaries. In Joan Nestle (Ed.) *The Persistent Desire: A Femme-Butch Reader*. Boston: Alyson.

Ruether, Rosemary Radford. (1974). Misogynism and Virginal Feminism in the Fathers of the Church. In Rosemary Radford Ruether (Ed.) *Religion and Sexism: Images of Women in the Jewish and Christian Traditions*. New York: Simon and Schuster.

Ruether, Rosemary Radford. (Ed.) (1974). *Religion and Sexism: Images of Women in the Jewish and Christian Traditions*. New York: Simon and Schuster.

Ruether, Rosemary Radford. (1983). *Sexism and God-Talk: Toward a Feminist Theology*. Boston: Beacon.

Russ, Joanna. (1989). Letter to the Editor. *Women's Review of Books, 6* (7), 4.

Russell, Diana E.H. (1991). Rape and Child Sexual Abuse in Soweto: An Interview with Community Leader Mary Mabaso. *South African Sociological Review, 3* (2), 64-83.

Russell, Diana E. H. (1993). *Making Violence Sexy. Feminist Views on Pornography*. New York: Athene Series, Teachers College Press.

Russell, Letty (Ed.) (1985). *Feminist Interpretation of the Bible*. Philadelphia: Westminister Press.

Ryan, Barbara. (1992). *Feminism and the Women's Movement: Dynamics of Change in Social Movement Ideology and Activitism.* New York: Routledge.

Saadawi, Nawal El. (1982). *The Hidden Face of Eve: Women in the Arab World.* Boston: Beacon.

Sandroff, Ronni. (1994). Beware of phallic drift. *On the Issues: The Progressive Women's Quarterly, 3* (2), 2.

Santa Barbara Rape Crisis Centre. (1994, Mayo/May). Mission Statement. *Outcry,* 1, 6.

Sappho. Fragment 31. Translated by Gillian Spraggs. In Divine Visitations: Sappho's Poetry of Love. In Elaine Hobby and Chris White (Eds.) (1991). *What Lesbians Do in Books.* London: The Women's Press.

Sarachild, Kathie. (1978). Consciousness-Raising: A Radical Weapon. In Redstockings (Eds.) *Feminist Revolution.* New York: Random House.

Sartre, John-Paul. (1948/1960). *Anti-Semite and Jew.* (Translated by George J. Becker.) New York: Grove Press

Saurel, Renée. (1985). *Bouches Cousues: Les mutilations sexuelles féminines et le milieu médical.* Paris: Tierce.

Save Humanity Report. (1992, July 14). Sarajevo: Center for Anti-War Activities.

Sayer, Susan. (1990). La Ngu Age. In Cathie Dunsford and Susan Hawthorne (Eds.) *The Exploding Frangipani.* Auckland: New Women's Press.

Sayers, Janet. (1982). *Biological Politics: Feminist and Anti-feminist Perspectives.* London and New York: Tavistock.

Scarf, Mimi. (1983). Marriages Made in Heaven? Battered Jewish Wives. In Susannah Heschel (Ed.) *On Being a Jewish Feminist.* New York: Schocken Books.

Schechter, Susan. (1982). *Women and Male Violence: The Visions and Struggles of the Battered Women's Movement.* Boston: South End Press.

Schor, Naomi. (1989). This Essentialism Which is Not One. *Differences, 1* (2), 38–58.

Schreiner, Shelley and Diane Bell. (Eds.) (1990). *This is My Story.* Geelong: Centre for Australian Studies, Deakin University.

Schüssler, Marina and Kathrin Bode. (1992). *Geprüfte Mädchen – Ganze Frauen. Zur Normierung der Mädchen in der Kindergynäkologie.* Zürich and Dortmund: eFeF Verlag.

Schwartz, Stephen. (1992, August 4). Arrest of Bosnia Jews Denounced: Anti-Semitic Propaganda Reported in Serbian Media. *San Francisco Chronicle.*

Schwichtenberg, Cathy. (Ed.) (1993a). *The Madonna Connection: Representational Politics, Subcultural Identities, and Cultural Theory.* Boulder, Colorado: Westview Press.

Schwichtenberg, Cathy. (1993b). Madonna's Postmodern Feminism: Bringing the Margins to the Center. In Cathy Schwichtenberg (Ed.) *The Madonna Connection: Representational Politics, Subcultural Identities, and Cultural Theory.* Boulder, Colorado: Westview Press.

Scott, Hilda. (1984). *Working Your Way to the Bottom: The Feminisation of Poverty.* London: Pandora Press.

Scott, Joan Wallach. (1986). Gender: A Useful Category of Historical Analysis. *American Historical Review, 91* 1053-75.

Scott, Joan Wallach. (1987). Rewriting History. In Margaret Randolph Higonnet *et al.* (Eds.) *Behind the Lines: Gender and the Two World Wars.* New Haven: Yale University Press.

Scott, Joan Wallach. (1987, October). Critical Tensions. *Women's Review of Books,* 5 17-18.

Scott, Joan Wallach. (1988a). *Gender and the Politics of History.* New York: Columbia University Press.

Scott, Joan Wallach. (1988b, Spring). Deconstructing Equality-versus-Difference: Or, The Uses of Poststructuralist Theory for Feminism. *Feminist Studies 14* (1), 33-50.

Scott, Joan Wallach. (1991). The Evidence of Experience. *Critical Inquiry, 17* 773-98.

Scott, Sarah and Tracy Payne. (1984). Underneath We're all Lovable: Therapy and Feminism. *Trouble and Strife, 3* 21-24.

Scully, Diana. (1980/1994). *Men Who Control Women's Health: The Miseducation of Obstetrician-Gynecologists.* Boston: Houghton Mifflin; (1994) New York: Athene Series, Teachers College Press.

Sculthorpe, Heather. (1990). Review of Domestic Violence Resource Materials. *Aboriginal Law Bulletin, 2* (46), 15-16.

Scutt, Jocelynne A. (1983/1990). *Even in the Best of Homes: Violence in the Family.* Ringwood: Penguin Books; (1990) Carlton: McCulloch Publishing.

Scutt, Jocelynne A. (Ed.) (1987). *Different Lives: Reflections on the Women's Movement and Visions of its Future.* Ringwood: Penguin.

Scutt, Jocelynne A. (1994). *The Sexual Gerrymander.* Melbourne: Spinifex Press.

SDA. (1992a). Bulletin no. 24, June 26. Sarajevo: SDA Information Center.

SDA. (1992b). Bulletin no. 25, June 29. Sarajevo: SDA Information Center.

Seager, Joni and Ann Olsen. (1986). *Women in the World: An International Atlas.* London and Sydney: Pan Books.

Seager, Joni. (1993). *Earth Follies: Coming to Feminist Terms with the Global Environment.* New York: Routledge.

Sedgwick, Eve Kosofsky. (1993). Queer Performativity: Henry James's *The Art of the Novel. GLQ,* (1) 1-16.

Segal, Lynne. (1987). *Is the Future Female? Troubled Thoughts on Contemporary Feminism.* London: Virago.

Segal, Lynne. (1994). *Straight Sex: Rethinking the Politics of Pleasure.* London: Virago.

Segal, Lynne and Mary McIntosh. (1992). *Sex Exposed: Sexuality and the Pornography Debate.* London: Virago.

Seidler, Victor. (1989). *Rediscovering Masculinity: Reason, Language and Sexuality.* London: Routledge.

Seidler, Victor. (1992, June 30). Sobs for the Boys. *Guardian,* 20.

Seidler, Victor. (Ed.) (1991). *Male Orders.* London: Routledge.

Sethna, Christabelle. (1992). Accepting "Total and Complete Responsibility": New Age Neo-Feminist Violence against Women. *Feminism and Psychology, 2* (1), 113-19.

Shange, Ntozake. (1981). *Three Pieces.* New York: St Martins Press.

Sharpe, Gene. (1980). *Social Power and Political Freedom.* Boston: Sargent Publishers.

Shiva, Vandana. (1988). *Staying Alive: Women, Ecology and Development.* London: Zed Books; New Delhi: Kali for Women.

Showalter, Elaine. (Ed.) (1986). *The New Feminist Criticism: Essays of Women, Literature & Theory.* London: Virago Press

Silveira, Jeannette (now "Fox"). (1985). Lesbian Feminist Therapy. *Lesbian Ethics, 1* (3), 22-27.

Simpson, John and Jana Bennet. (1985). *The Disappeared and the Mothers of the Plaza.* New York: St Martin's Press.

Skinningsrud, Tone. (1984, August). Girls in the Classroom: Why They Don't Talk. Paper presented at the Second International Interdisciplinary Congress on Women, Groningen. Published in German as: Mädchen im Klassenzimmer: warum sie nicht sprechen. In *Frauen und Schule, 3* 21-3.

Smith, Paul. (1988). *Discerning the Subject*. Minneapolis: University of Minneapolis Press.

Smith-Rosenberg, Carroll. (1985). *Disorderly Conduct: Visions of Gender in Victorian America*. New York: Oxford University Press.

Smith-Rosenberg, Carroll. (1989). Discourses of Sexuality and Subjectivity: The New Woman: 1870-1936. In Martin Duberman *et al.* (Eds.) *Hidden from History: Reclaiming the Gay and Lesbian Past*. New York: NAL.

Smyth, Ailbhe. (1992). A (Political) Postcard from a Peripheral Pre-Post-modernist State (of Mind) or How Alliteration can Knock you down Dead in Women's Studies. *Women's Studies International Forum, 15* 331-37.

Smyth, Ailbhe. (1993, October). Haystacks in My Mind or How to Stay SAFE (Sane, Angry and Feminist) in the 1990s. Paper presented at WISE Conference, Paris.

Smyth, Cherry. (1992). *Lesbians Talk: Queer Notions*. London: Scarlet Press.

Snitow, Ann. (1992). Retrenchment vs. Transformation: The Politics of the Anti-pornography Movement. In FACT Book Committee (Eds.) *Caught Looking: Feminism, Pornography and Censorship*. East Haven, Connecticut: Longriver Books.

Snitow, Ann, Christine Stansell and Sharon Thompson. (Eds.) (1983). *Powers of Desire: The Politics of Sexuality*. New York: Monthly Review Press.

Snow, Roberta and Jill Taylor. (1993). (Eds.) *Falling for Grace: An Anthology of Australian Lesbian Fiction*. Sydney: Blackwattle Press.

Snyder, Sarah. (1987, March 13). Baby M Trial Hears Closing Argument. *Boston Globe*.

Sofia, Zoë. (1995). Of Spanners and Cyborgs: "De-homogenising" Feminist Thinking on Technology. In Barbara Caine and Rosemary Pringle (Eds.) *Transitions: New Australian Feminisms*. Sydney: Allen and Unwin.

Spallone, Patricia and Deborah L. Steinberg. (Eds.) (1987). *Made to Order: The Myth of Reproductive and Genetic Progress*. Oxford and New York: The Athene Series, Pergamon Press.

Spelman, Elizabeth V. (1988). *Inessential Woman: Problems of Exclusion in Feminist Thought*.

Spence, Jo. (1990, July). Sharing the Wounds. Interviewed by J. Z. Grover in *Women's Review of Books VII*, 38-9.

Spender, Dale. (1980b/1988). *Man Made Language*. London: Routledge and Kegan Paul; 1988, London and New York: Routledge.

Spender, Dale. (Ed.) (1981). *Men's Studies Modified: The Impact of Feminism on the Academic Disciplines*. London: The Athene Series, Pergamon Press.

Spender, Dale. (1982). *Women of Ideas and What Men have Done to Them*. London: Ark Paperbacks; (1983) London: Routledge and Kegan Paul.

Spender, Dale. (Ed.) (1983). *Feminist Theorists: Three Centuries of Women's Intellectual Traditions*. London: The Women's Press.

Spender, Dale. (1983). Modern Feminist Theorists: Reinventing Rebellion. In Dale Spender (Ed.) *Feminist Theorists: Three Centuries of Women's Intellectual Traditions*. London: The Women's Press.

Spender, Dale. (1984). Mit Aggressivität zum Erfolg: über den doppelten Standard, der in den Klassenzimmern operiert. In Senta Trömel-Plötz. *Gewalt durch Sprache. Die Vergewaltigung von Frauen in Gesprächen*. Frankfurt: Suhrkamp.

Spender, Dale. (1985a). *Frauen kommen nicht vor. Sexismus im Bildungswesen.* Frankfurt: Fischer Verlag.

Spender, Dale. (Ed.) (1985b). *For the Record: The Making and Meaning of Feminist Knowledge.* London: The Women's Press.

Spender, Dale. (1995). *Nattering on the Net: Women, Power and Cyberspace.* Melbourne: Spinifex Press; Toronto: Garamond Press.

Spender, Dale and Elizabeth Sarah. (1980a). *Learning to Lose.* London: The Women's Press.

Spiegel, Gabrielle M. (1990). History Historicism and the Social Logic of the Text in the Middle Ages. *Speculum, 65* 59-86.

Spivak, Gayatri. (1988). Can the Subaltern Speak? In Larry Grossberg and Cary Nelson (Eds.) *Marxism and the Interpretation of Culture.* Urbana: University of Illinois Press.

Spoden, Christian. (1993). Jungenarbeit in Schulen als Prävention von Gewalt an Mächen. Gutachten für die Senatsverwaltung Arbeit und Frauen. Berlin: Senatsverwaltung Arbeit und Frauen.

Spraggs, Gillian. (1991). Divine Visitations: Sappho's Poetry of Love. In Elaine Hobby and Chris White (Eds.) *What Lesbians Do in Books.* London: The Women's Press.

Spretnak, Charlene. (1991). *States of Grace: The Recovery of Meaning in the Post-modern Age.* San Francisco: HarperSanFrancisco.

Sprinkle, Annie. (1992). My First Time with a F2M-Transsexual-Surgically-made Hermaphrodite. In Dennis Cooper (Ed.) *Discontents: New Queer Writers.* New York: Amethyst Press.

Stacey, Jackie. (1993). Untangling Feminist Theory. In Diane Richardson and Victoria Robinson (Eds.) *Introducing Women's Studies: Feminist Theory and Practice.* London: Macmillan.

Stacey, Judith. (1986). Are Feminists Afraid to Leave Home? The Challenge of Conservative Pro-Family Feminism. In Juliet Mitchell and Ann Oakley (Eds.) *What is Feminism?* Oxford: Blackwell.

Stacey, Judith and Barrie Thorne. (1985). The Missing Feminist Revolution in Sociology. *Social Problems, 32* (4), 301-16.

Stanko, Elizabeth A. (1985). *Intimate Intrusions – Women's Experience of Male Violence.* London: Routledge Kegan and Paul.

Stanley, Liz. (1982). Male Needs: The Problem and Problems of Working with Gay Men. In Scarlet Friedman and Elizabeth Sarah (Eds.) *On the Problem of Men.* London: The Women's Press.

Stanworth, Michelle. (1987/1988a). The Deconstruction of Motherhood. In Michelle Stanworth (Ed.) *Reproductive Technologies: Gender, Motherhood, and Medicine.* Oxford: Polity Press; Minneapolis: University of Minnesota Press.

Stanworth, Michelle. (1987/1988b). (Ed.) *Reproductive Technologies: Gender, Motherhood, and Medicine.* Oxford: Polity Press; Minneapolis: University of Minnesota Press.

Star, Susan Leigh. (1990). The Politics of Right and Left: Sex Differences in Brain Asymmetry. In Sneja Gunew. (Ed.) *A Reader in Feminist Knowledge.* London and New York: Routledge.

Steedman, Caroline. (1984). *Policing the Victorian Community: The Formation of English Provincial Police Forces 1856–1880.* London: Routledge and Kegan Paul.

Steedman, Caroline. (1986). *Landscape for a Good Woman: A Story of Two Lives.* London: Virago.

Steinem, Gloria. (1992). *Revolution from Within: A Book of Self-Esteem.* London: Bloomsbury.

Stens, Katharina. (1989). Give Me Children, Or Else I Die. In Klein (Ed.). *Infertility: Women Speak out About Their Experiences of Reproductive Medicine*. London: Pandora.

Sternhall, Carol. (1992). Review of Gloria Steinem's *Revolution from Within. Women's Review of Books, IX* (9), 5-6.

Strathern, Marilyn. (Ed.) (1988). *Dealing with Inequality: Analysis of Gender Relations in Melanesia and Beyond*. New York: Cambridge University Press.

Strauss, Murray. (1978). Stress and Assault in a National Sample of American Families. In *Colloquium on Stress and Crime*. Washington, DC: National Institute of Law Enforcement and Criminal Justice – MITRE Corporation.

Sykes, Bobbie. (1975). Black Women in Australia: A History. In Jan Mercer (Ed.) *The Other Half*. Ringwood: Penguin.

Taking Liberties Collective. (1989). *Learning the Hard Way: Women's Oppression in Men's Education*. London: Virago.

Tallen, Bette. (1990a). Twelve Step Programs: A Lesbian Feminist Critique. *NWSA Journal, 2* (3), 390-407.

Tallen, Bette. (1990b). Codependency: A Feminist Critique. *Sojourner, 15* 20-1.

Tamez, Elsa. (1989). *Through Her Eyes: Women's Theology from Latin America*. Maryknoll: Orbis.

Taub, Nadine and Sherrill Cohen. (Eds.) (1988). *Reproductive Laws for 1990s: A Briefing Handbook*. Newark: Rutgers University.

Tavris, Carol. (1992, February 20). Has Time Stood Still for Women? *Los Angeles Times*.

Te Awekotuku, Ngahuia. (1991). *Mana Wahine Maori: Selected Writings on Maori Women's Art, Culture and Politics*. Auckland: New Women's Press.

Terborg-Penn, Rosalyn, Sharon Harley and Andrea Benton Rushing. (Eds.) (1987). *Women in Africa and the African Diaspora*. Washington, DC: Howard University Press.

Thiam, Awa. (1978). *La parole aux négresses*. Paris: Denoël/Gonthier.

Thiam, Awa. (1986). *Black Sisters Speak Out: Feminism and Opression In Black Africa*. London: Pluto Press.

Thistlethwaite, Susan Brooks. (1985). Every Two Minutes: Battered Women and Feminist Interpretation. In Letty Russell (Ed.) *Feminist Interpretation of the Bible*. Philadelphia: Westminister Press.

Thomas, David. (1993). *Not Guilty: In Defence of the Modern Man*. London: Weidenfeld and Nicolson.

Thompson, Denise (1991). *Reading Between the Lines. A Lesbian Feminist Critique of Feminist Accounts of Sexuality*. Sydney: Gorgon's Head Press.

Thompson, Denise. (1993). Against the Dividing of Women: Lesbianism, Feminism and Heterosexuality. In Sue Wilkinson and Celia Kitzinger (Eds.) *Heterosexuality: A Feminism and Psychology Reader* London: Sage.

Thompson, Denise. (1994, August 1). Asking Questions about Racism. Paper presented at International Feminisms Conference, Australian Women's Research Centre. Melbourne: Deakin University.

Tokarczyk, Michelle M. and Elizabeth A. Fay. (1992). (Eds.) *Working Class Women in the Academy: Laborers in the Knowledge Factory*. Amherst, Massachusetts: University of Massachusetts Press.

Tomes, Nancy. (1978). A "Torrent of Abuse": Crimes of Violence Between Working Class Men and Women in London, 1840–1975. *Journal of Social History, 11* (3), 328-45.

Tong, Rosemary. (1989). *Feminist Thought: A Comprehensive Introduction.* Boulder, Colorado: Westview Press.

Travis, Ellen. (1994, Fall). The Backlash on Campus: Climate Report Opens Floodgates. *Herizon,* 29-9, 46-7.

Trnka, Susanna. (1992). A Pretty Good Bisexual Kiss There . . . In Elizabeth Reba Weise (Ed.) *Closer to Home: Bisexuality and Feminism.* Seattle: Seal Press.

Tsoulis, Athena. (1987, June). *Spare Rib,* 179.

Turkle, Sherry. (1996, January). Who Am We? *Wired,* 149-52, 194, 196-99.

Tushnet, Mark. (1984). An Essay on Rights. *Texas Law Review,* 63 1363-82.

Tuttle Lisa. (1986/1987). *Encyclopedia of Feminism.* London: Longman; (1987) London: Arrow Books.

Tyler, Carol-Anne. (1991). Boys Will Be Girls: The Politics of Gay Drag. In Diana Fuss (Ed.) *Inside/Out.* London and New York: Routledge.

Umansky, Ellen M. and Diane Ashton. (Eds.) (1992). *Four Centuries of Jewish Women's Spirituality – A Sourcebook.* Boston: Beacon.

UNESCO and Coalition against Trafficking in Women. (1991). *International Meeting on Sexual Exploitation, Violence and Prostitution.* The Penn State Report, Pennsylvania: State College.

Unger, Roberto Mangabeira. (1986). *The Critical Legal Studies Movement.* Cambridge, Massachusetts: Harvard University Press.

UNICEF. (1988). *State of the World's Children.* New York: United Nations University Press.

US Bureau of the Census, Current Population Report. (1991). Sex. In *Money Income of Households, Families, and Persons in the United States.*

Ussher, Jane. (1991). *Women's Madness: Misogyny or Mental Illness?* New York: Harvester Wheatsheaf.

Vance, Carole S. (Ed.) (1984). *Pleasure and Danger: Exploring Female Sexuality.* London: Pandora.

Vance, Carole S. (1992). More Danger, More Pleasure: A Decade After the Barnard Sexuality Conference. In Carole S. Vance. (Ed.) (1984). *Pleasure and Danger: Exploring Female Sexuality.* London: Pandora. (Reprinted with additions in 1992).

VanEvery, Jo. (1995). *Heterosexual Women Changing the Family: Refusing to be a Wife!* London: Taylor and Francis.

Varikas, Eleni. (1993). Féminisme, modernité, post-modernisme: pour un dialogue des deux côtés de l'océan. In *Féminismes au présent.* (Special Issue) *Futur Antérieur,* 63.

Victorian Attorney-General. (1986, July). Press Release. Melbourne. Australia.

Vicuña, Francisco Orrego. (Ed.) (1985). *Transición a la democracia en América Latina.* Asunción, Paraguay: Grupo Editoria Latinoamericano.

Vitaliev, Vitali. (1987). Chuma liubvi: Blesk i nishcheta Sovrvemennykh Kurtizanok. (Love's a Plague: The Splendour and destitution of Modern-Day Courtesans.) *Krokodil,* (9).

Vitaliev, Vitali. (1990, October 29). King's Cross Strikes an Unwitting Blow for Russian Correspondent. *Age,* 10.

von Eissele, Ingrid and Rudolf Müller. (1994, August 25). Die Russen-Mafia in Deutschland, Mädchenhandel, Prostitution, Killerkommandos. *Stern.*

Waithe, Mary Ellen. (Ed.) (1987). *A History of Women Philosophers.* Volume 1: Ancient Women Philosophers 600 BC.–500 AD. Boston: Martinus Nijhoff Publishers.

Walker, Alice. (1992). *Possessing the Secret of Joy.* New York: Harcourt Brace Jovanovich.

Walkerdine, Valerie. (1990). *Schoolgirl Fictions.* London: Verso.

Wallace, Michele. (1979). *Black Macho and the Myth of the Superwoman.* London: John Calder.

Ward, Elizabeth (Biff). (1984). *Father–Daughter Rape.* London: The Women's Press.

Waring, Marilyn. (1988). *Counting for Nothing. What Men Value and What Women are Worth.* Wellington, New Zealand: Allen and Unwin.

War Crimes Investigation Bureau. (1992). *Fourth Exodus of the Jews: War in Bosnia-Herzegovina.* Sarajevo: War Crimes Investigation Bureau.

Waters, Lindsay. (1994, December 27). Exchange. *The Nation,* 786.

Watson, Lilla. (1987). Sister, Black is the Colour of my Soul. In Jocelynne A. Scutt (Ed.) *Different Lives: Reflections on the Women's Movement and Visions of its Future.* Ringwood: Penguin.

Waugh, Evelyn. (1977). *Brideshead Revisited.* New York: Penguin.

Weedon, Chris (1987). *Feminist Practice and Poststructuralist Theory.* Oxford: Basil Blackwell.

Weise, Elizabeth Reba. (Ed.) (1993). *Closer to Home: Bisexuality and Feminism.* Seattle: Seal Press.

Weisstein, Naomi. (1970). "Kinder, Küche, Kirche" as Scientific Law: Psychology Constructs the Female. In Robin Morgan. (Ed.) *Sisterhood is Powerful.* New York: Random.

Wenz, Kathie. (1988). *Women's Peace of Mind: Possibilities in Using the Writing Process in Counselling.* Association for Women in Psychology, Arizona Chapter Regional Conference, Arizona State University.

Wigg, Louise. (1995). The Acquisition of Body Image in Children and Adolescents. Unpublished Minor Thesis, Women's Studies. Melbourne (Rusden): Deakin University.

Wilkinson, Sue. (1995). Bisexuality as Backlash. In Elaine Miller and Lynne Harne (Eds.) *All the Rage: The Backlash and Lesbian Feminist Resistance.* London: The Women's Press.

Wilkinson, Sue and Celia Kitzinger. (Eds.) (1993). *Heterosexuality: A Feminism and Psychology Reader.* London: Sage.

Williams, Dolores. (1993). *Sisters in the Wilderness: The Challenge of Womanist God-Talk.* Maryknoll: Orbis.

Williams, Elizabeth. (1987). Aboriginal First, Woman Second. In Jocelynne A. Scutt (Ed.) *Different Lives: Reflections on the Women's Movement and Visions of Its Future.* Ringwood: Penguin Books.

Williams, Linda. (1992). Pornographies On/scene, or Diff'rent Strokes for Diff'rent Folks. In Lynne Segal and Mary McIntosh (Eds.) *Sex Exposed: Sexuality and the Pornography Debate.* London: Virago.

Williams, Patricia J. (1991). *The Alchemy of Race and Rights.* Boston: Harvard University Press.

Williams, Patricia J. (1993). A Rare Case Study of Muddleheadedness and Men. In Toni Morrison (Ed.) *Race-ing, Justice, En-Gendering Power.* London: Chatto and Windus.

Williams, Robert A. Jn. (1989). Taking Rights Aggressively: The Perils and Promise of Critical Legal Theory for Peoples of Color. *Law and Inequality Journal, 5* 103-34.

Willis, Ellen. (1983). Feminism, Moralism, and Pornography. In Snitow *et al. Desire: the Politics of Sexuality.* London: Virago.

Wittig, Monique. (1976/1982/1992). The Category of Sex. In *The Straight Mind and Other Essays.* Boston: Beacon.

Wittig, Monique. (1979). The Straight Mind. *Feminist Issues, 1* (1), 103-11.

Wittig, Monique. (1981). One is Not Born a Woman. *Feminist Issues, 1* (2), 47-54.

Wittig, Monique. (1992). *The Straight Mind and Other Essays.* Boston: Beacon.

Wolf, Margery. (1972). *Women and the Family in Rural Taiwan.* Stanford: Stanford University.

Wolf, Naomi. (1990). *The Beauty Myth.* London: Chatto and Windus.

Wolf, Naomi. (1993). *Fire with Fire: New Female Power and How It Will Change the 21st Century.* London: Chatto and Windus.

Wollstonecraft, Mary. (1790/1891). *A Vindication of the Rights of Man.* London: Fawcett (with an Introduction to the Second Edition by Millicent Garret).

Wood, Deborah. (1986, April 3). Tribal Elder of Peace Seeks Security for All. *Australian.*

Woolf, Virginia. (1929). *A Room of One's Own.* London: The Hogarth Press.

Woolf, Virginia. (1947/1966). *Three Guineas.* London: The Hogarth Press; New York: Harbinger.

Woolf, Virginia. (1958). The Narrow Bridge of Art. In *Granite and Rainbow.* London: The Hogarth Press. (Originally published 1927. In *New York Herald Tribune,* August 14).

Yeatman, Anna. (1993). Voice and Representation in the Politics of Difference. In Sneja Gunew and Anna Yeatman (Eds.) *The Politics of Difference.* Sydney: Allen and Unwin.

Young, Iris Marion. (1990). The Ideal of Community and the Politics of Difference. In Linda Nicholson (Ed.) *Feminism/Postmodernism.* New York and London: Routledge.

Yuval-Davis, Nira. (1993). The (Dis)Comfort of Being "Hetero". In Sue Wilkinson and Celia Kitzinger (Eds.) *Heterosexuality: A Feminism and Psychology Reader.* London: Sage.

Zilbergeld, Bernie. (1983). *The Shrinking of America.* Boston: Little Brown.

Zimmerman, Bonnie. (1984). The Politics of Transliberation: Lesbian Personal Narratives, *Signs, 9* (4), 668-82.

Zimmerman, Bonnie and Toni McNaron. (Eds.) (1996). *Lesbian Studies.* New York: Feminist Press.

Zipper, Juliette and Selma Sevenhuijsen. (1987/1988). Surrogacy: Feminist Notions of Motherhood Reconsidered. In Michelle Stanworth (Ed.) *Reproductive Technologies: Gender, Motherhood and Medicine.* Oxford: Polity Press; Minneapolis: University of Minnesota Press.

Contributors

Evelyne Accad was born and raised in Beirut, Lebanon. She has been Professor at the University of Illinios Champaign-Urbana since 1974, in French, Comparative Literature, African Studies, Women's Studies, Middle East Studies, and the honors program. Her publications include: *Blessures des Mots* (1993); *Sexuality and War* (1990); and *Veil of Shame* (1978). She is also a songwriter and interpreter of both music and lyrics.

Mahnaz Afkhami is currently the Executive Director of the Sisterhood Is Global Institute, Executive Director of Foundation for Iranian Studies, and a member of the Advisory Committee for the Women's Project of Human Rights Watch. She is the author of *Women in Exile* (1994), co-editor of *In The Eye of the Storm* (1994) and editor of *Faith and Freedom: Women's Human Rights in the Muslim World* (1995). Afkhami founded the Iranian University Women's Association and was the secretary-general of the Women's Organization of Iran and Minister of State for Women's Affairs of Iran during the period 1976 to 1979.

Marjorie Agosin, poet and human rights activist, is Professor of Literature at Wellesley College and author of almost twenty books of poetry and literary criticism including: *Women of Smoke: Latin American Women in Literature and Life* (1989) and *Circles of Madness* (1992). She is from Chile which in her own words is a country of poets, clowns and dictators.

Since the mid-1970s, **Louise Armstrong's** work has focused on incest and issues of violence against women and children, and the role assigned psychiatry/psychology as society's clean-up crew on these issues. She has spoken widely at conferences as well as colleges and universities. Her most recent book is *Rocking the Cradle of Sexual Politics: What Happened When Women Said Incest* (1994).

Berit Ås: Born: too early. Belongs to the 23rd century. Place: A patriarchal and authoritarian country which fosters creativity by suppression. Education: From science-fiction books and teaching at universities between the North Pole and the Black Bible Belt. Activities: professional, 1st female party leader in Norway. Founder of The Feminist University.

A founder of the Coalition Against Trafficking in Women **Kathleen Barry** is a sociologist at Penn State University and the author of *Female Sexual Slavery* (1979); *Susan B. Anthony. A Biography of a Singular Feminist* (1988) and *The Prostitution of Sexuality* (1995).

Pauline B. Bart is a radical feminist grandmother who has told the truth and paid the consequences. Her work as a feminist sociologist has led her to study an illegal feminist abortion collective, depression in middle-aged women and effective strategies against rape. Pauline has written three books, two with students: *The Student Sociologist's Handbook* (1972); *Stopping Rape: Successful Survival Strategies* (1985) and more recently *Violence Against Women: The Bloody Footprints* (1993). She is currently studying the liquidity of female sexuality – Protean women.

Diane Bell is currently the Henry Luce Professor of Religion, Economic Development and Social Justice at the College of the Holy Cross, Worcester, Massachusetts, USA. On the basis of extensive fieldwork with Indigenous Peoples in Australia and comparative work in the USA, she has published widely. Her books include *Law: The Old and the New* (1980/4) (co-author), *Daughters of the Dreaming* (1983/1993); *Religion in Aboriginal Australia* (1984) (co-editor); *Generations: Grandmothers, others and Daughters* (1987); *Gendered Fields: Women, Men and Ethnography* (1993) (co-editor). She has a habit of speaking about and acting on outrageous ideas like "women are people".

Suzanne Bellamy is an Australian artist/writer somewhat weary of self-definition. She struggles with the dynamic conflicts of dual creativity, living matter, monumental and miniature sculpture, thinking and observation, the written and spoken word, where ideas come from, and the destiny of our planet.

Angela Bowen, a PhD candidate in Women's Studies at Clark University, Worcester, Massachusetts, in the USA, is writing her dissertation on Audre Lorde and contributing to a book on Audre Lorde in the Sage series, *Women of Ideas*, edited by Dale Spender and Liz Stanley. Bowen's ongoing research focuses on the lives of Black lesbians.

Somer Brodribb teaches feminist theory/politics and women's social and political thought at the University of Victoria, Canada.

Deirdre Carraher is a graduate of Holy Cross College specializing in Women in French History. As a radical feminist, she is dedicated to increasing awareness of issues that women face in their daily life, particularly sexual harassment.

Barbara T. Christian is Professor of African American Studies at the University of California, Berkeley. She is the author of *Black Women Novelists: The Development of a Tradition* (1980); *Black Feminist Criticism: Perspectives on Black Women Writers* (1985) and editor of *Alice Walker's Everyday Use* (1994).

Sandra Coney is one of New Zealand's most well-known feminists – one of the founders of the long-running feminist magazine *Broadsheet*, and the co-author of an article on an unethical experiment at the country's major women's hospital which led to major medico-legal reforms. She is the author or editor of nine books including *The Unfortunate Experiment* (1988), *Out of the Frying Pan* (1990), *The Menopause Industry* (1991) and *Standing in the Sunshine* (1993). She is also the Director of the women's health advocacy group, Women's Health Action.

Sharon Cox is a graduate of Holy Cross College in Worcester, Massachusetts. As an athlete and a feminist she is interested in women and sport. She is a Mathematics Major as well as a Women's Studies Concentrator.

Elizabeth C. Daake, is a radical feminist from Holy Cross College, Massachusetts who hopes to pursue graduate work in Women's Studies and has worked consistently and creatively to raise women's issues within her community.

Mary Daly, a Nag-Gnostic philosopher, is the author of six Radical Feminist books, including *The Church and the Second Sex* (1968); *Beyond God the Father* (1973); *Gyn/Ecology* (1978); *Pure Lust* (1984); *Webster's First New Intergalactic Wickedary of the English Language* (1987) (conjured in Cahoots with Jane Caputi); and *Outercourse* (1993). This Pirate/Voyager Craftily pursues her own intellectual Quest and disturbs the peace by lecturing irregularly to audiences around the United States and Europe and by teaching Feminist Ethics at Boston College.

Christine Delphy is an activist and full-time researcher. She is the editor of France's only Women's Studies journal, *Nouvelles Questions Féministes*. Her latest book is *Familiar Exploitation: A New Analysis of Marriage in Contemporary Western Societies* with Diana Leonard (1992). Although she does not have any cats at the moment, she thinks of herself as a (good) radical feminist.

Carol Anne Douglas has worked on the feminist newspaper, *Off Our Backs*, since 1973. She also teaches feminist theory at George Washington University and within the Washington DC community. She is the author of *Love and Politics: Radical Feminist and Lesbian Theories* (1990).

Cathie Dunsford is Director of Dunsford and Associates Publishing Consultants, a feminist based and run company which searches for, assesess, edits and seeks to sell feminist texts to the publishing industry. She taught literature at Auckland University from 1978 to 1983 and was a Fulbright Post-Doctoral Research Fellow at the University of California, Berkeley, from 1983 to 1986. She is the co-editor of four anthologies; the author of a novel, *Cowrie* (1994) and a collection of poetry, *Survivors/Überlebende* (1990).

Andrea Dworkin is a radical feminist activist and author of many books, amongst them *Pornography: Men Possessing Women* (1979); *Intercourse* (1987); and the novels *Ice and Fire* (1986) and *Mercy* (1991). She is also co-author with Catharine MacKinnon of the first law recognizing pornography as a violation of the civil rights of women.

Uta Enders-Dragässer is a feminist sociologist, educationalist and activist with a special interest in girls' and boys' gender socialisation in school. She has drafted recommendations on gender equality in education for the Council of Europe in 1993 and 1994 and is the co-founder of GSF (Gesellschaft für sozialwissenschaftliche Frauenforschung – Association for Feminist Research in the Social Sciences) in Frankfurt.

Beryl Fletcher is a full-time novelist and feminist activist. In 1992 she was awarded the Commonwealth Writer's Prize for the best first book published in South Asia and the South Pacific for her novel, *The Word Burners* (1991). In 1994 she was Writer in Residence for New Zealand at the International Writing Program at the University of Iowa. She is also the author of *The Iron Mouth* (1993) and *The Silicon Tongue* (1996).

Michele Gagne is an English Major and Women's Studies Concentrator at Holy Cross College in the US. She is interested in a career in broadcast journalism.

Marcia Ann Gillespie, editor of *Ms Magazine*, has written extensively on issues of gender and race, and is currently at work on a history of the women's movement to be used as a textbook for high school students.

Evelina Giobbe is the founder and current Director of Education and Public Policy at WHISPER (Women Hurt in Systems of Prostitution Engaged in Revolt). Her research into commercial sexual exploitation has been published in numerous academic, legal and popular texts. She is currently collecting oral histories of prostituted women for a forthcoming book.

Patricia Good is an English Major and Women's Studies Concentrator at Holy Cross College, Worcester, Massachusetts.

Jalna Hanmer is Professor of Women's Studies at the University of Bradford. She began to actively participate in the Women's Liberation Movement in Britain in the early 1970s. She writes on violence against women; reproduction, science and technology; and Women's Studies.

Susan Hawthorne is a writer, publisher, teacher, festival organiser and circus performer. Her books include a novel and a collection of poetry, both of which focus on her experience of epilepsy, *The Falling Woman* (1992) and *Language in My Tongue* (1993, published in the volume, *Four New Poets*). She is the (co)-editor of five anthologies and the author of *The Spinifex Quiz Book* (1993). She lectures in creative writing and publishing at Victoria University of Technology in Melbourne.

Joan Hoff is Professor of History at Indiana University, Bloomington, and co-editor of the *Journal of Women's History*. She is a specialist in twentieth-century US foreign policy and politics, and women's legal history. Her books on women include *Law, Gender and Injustice* (1991); *The Rights of Passage: The Past, Present and Future of the ERA* (1986); *Without Precedent: The Life and Career of Eleanor Roosevelt*, co-edited with Marjorie Lightman (1984) and *For Adult Users Only: The Dilemma of Violent Pornography*, co-edited with Susan Gubar (1989).

Joy James teaches Women's Studies at the University of Massachusetts, Amherst. She is co-editor of *Spirit, Space and Survival: African American Women in (White) Academe* (1993) and author of *Resisting State Violence in US Culture: Anti-Racism, Feminism(s) and Political Coalitions* (1996).

Sheila Jeffreys has been active in the Women's Liberation Movement since 1973 mainly in campaigns against male violence. She has written three books on the history and politics of sexuality; *The Spinster and Her Enemies: Feminism and Sexuality 1880–1930* (1985); *Anticlimax: A Feminist Perspective on the Sexual Revolution* (1990) and *The Lesbian Heresy* (1993). She was a founding member of the London Lesbian Archive and the London Lesbian History Group, and now lives in Australia where she is a Senior Lecturer in the Department of Political Science at the University of Melbourne. She is currently working on prostitution within a human rights context.

Morny Joy is Associate Professor in the Department of Religious Studies at the University of Calgary, Canada. She has published many articles on women and religion, feminist theory and contemporary continental philosophy. Morny is President of the Canadian Society for the Study of Religion and Director of the Institute for Gender Studies at the University of Calgary.

Celia Kitzinger is Director of Women's Studies at Loughborough University UK. Her books include *The Social Construction of Lesbianism* (1987); *Changing Our Minds* with Rachel Perkins (1993); *Heterosexuality* (1993); and *Feminism and Discourse* (1995), both co-edited with Sue Wilkinson and published by Sage Press.

Renate Klein has degrees in biology, sociology and Women's Studies from Zürich and London Universities and the University of California (Berkeley). She works as a Senior Lecturer and Deputy Director of the Australian Women's Research Centre at Deakin University and is the (co)-author/(co)-editor of four books of feminist theory and six books on reproductive medicine. For the past twelve years she has been part of an international feminist network (FINRRAGE) exposing the inhumane nature of population control policies.

Yenlin Ku is a first generation feminist living in Taiwan and a pioneer in teaching Women's Studies. She is co-founder of the Women's Research Program and the Awakening Foundation. She is also Board Director of Fembooks and the Feminist Studies Association. She is currently Professor of Women's Studies at National Chiao Tung University, Hsinchu, Taiwan.

Tania Lienert began her work on radical feminist theory in her Honours year in Women's Studies at Deakin University in 1993. She has also researched feminist ethics, queer politics and lesbian activism. She has taught Women's Studies at Deakin, been a journalist and a community arts worker and is now doing her PhD, where she will investigate women's friendships and lesbian ethics.

Catharine A. MacKinnon currently Professor of Law at the University of Michigan, is a lawyer, teacher, writer, activist and expert on sex equality. Since the mid 1970s MacKinnon, through litigation, legislation, and policy development, has been a pioneer for women's human and civil rights domestically and internationally. She is currently representing *pro bono* Croatian and Muslim women and children victims of Serbian genocidal sexual atrocities. She is the author of *Sexual Harassment of Working Women* (1979); *Feminism Unmodified* (1987); *Toward a Feminist Theory of the State* (1989); *Pornography and Civil Rights* with Andrea Dworkin (1988) and *Only Words* (1993) as well as numerous articles.

Pat Mahony is Professor of Education Studies at Roehampton Institute, London. She has written extensively in the fields of sexual violence in school and teacher education. Her books include *Schools for the Boys?* (1985) and *Learning Our Lines* with Carol Jones (1989).

Teboho E. Maitse is a South African presently completing a PhD at the University of Bradford, UK on violence against Black women in South Africa. She is a member of the African National Congress and the African National Congress Women's League. She has acted as the organisation's spokesperson in West Yorkshire over the past three years.

Tatyana Mamonova is a writer, poet and feminist leader exiled from Russia for publishing the Almanac *Woman and Russia* (1985) (now an international and yearly production called *Woman and Earth* printed in New York City in several languages). She is also an editor, lecturer, a Harvard University-Bunting Institute fellow (1984–1985), videographer and artist.

Sigrid Markmann was born in the northern part of Germany. She has studied and raised a daughter. She is currently Chair of the English Department, Universität Osnabrück, Germany. Her main fields of research are teaching Women's Studies, new literatures in English and Pacific Literary Studies. She is the editor of OBEMA (Osnabrück Bilingual Edition of Marginalised Authors).

Jessie McManmon, the oldest of five children, is interested in issues of childcare. She was captain of the women's soccer team at Holy Cross College and is a Women's Studies Concentrator and a proud feminist.

Katja Mikhailovich teaches in the School of Community and Health Studies at the University of Canberra, Australia. She is currently completing her PhD, her areas of research interest include violence against women, women and mental health and lesbian and gay studies.

Robin Morgan, a founder of the contemporary women's movement, has been a feminist theorist and activist in both the US and international feminist movements for over twenty five years. She has compiled and edited two now-classic anthologies. An award-winning poet, she has published twelve other books, encompassing fiction, poetry, and radical feminist theory. Her most recent works include *The Demon Lover: On the Sexuality of Terrorism* (1989) and *The Word of a Woman* (1993).

Natalie Nenadic is a coordinator of the US based Rape/Genocide Law Project. She is a graduate student at Yale University.

Nganampa Health Council: The committee members of the Nganampa Health Council work as Senior Health Workers and Women's Council Executive members. They are women who are comfortable to teach and learn as they go. They navigate both on traditional ground and the relatively new territory of cancer, infertility, STDs and HIV. They live and work in the remote north west of the Pitjantjatjara Freehold Lands in South Australia. Tjikilyi is the kind of senior woman and teacher Sandra describes. In 1994 she was awarded an Order of Australia for many years' work in women's and family issues.

Marjorie O'Connor is an English Major and a Women's Studies Concentrator from Holy Cross College. She grew up in Bronxville, New York, in a family with six kids. She hopes to continue the struggle for the advancement of women.

Janice G. Raymond is Professor of Women's Studies and Medical Ethics at the University of Massachusetts, Amherst. A longtime feminist activist, she is one of the founders of FINRRAGE and currently Co-Executive Director of the Coalition Against Trafficking in Women. She is the author of five books, her most recent being *Women as Wombs* (1993).

Diane Richardson is Senior Lecturer in the Department of Sociological Studies at the University of Sheffield, UK. Together with Victoria Robinson she co-edited *Introducing Women's Studies: Feminist Theory and Practice* (1993). Her other books include *Women and the AIDS Crisis* (1989); *Safer Sex* (1990); *Women, Motherhood and Childrearing* (1993) and *Theorizing Heterosexuality* (1996).

Powhiri Wharemarama Rika-Heke: Her mother is Nellie Young (nee Rika). Her father is Tiakitai Moana Kamiro AKA Cyril Campbell. She was raised by her maternal grandfather, Hemi Ngapine Rika-Heke on their family dairy farm in the Mangakahia, Aotearoa. That's me, she says.

Victoria Robinson teaches Women's Studies at the Division of Adult Continuing Education at the University of Sheffield, England. She has worked with women in the local community, establishing Women's Studies as a field of enquiry. In 1993, she co-edited with Diane Richardson, one of the first British textbooks on the subject, *Introducing Women's Studies: Feminist Theory and Practice* (1993). She has recently had a son, Eddie Joe.

Robyn Rowland is the Director of the Australian Women's Research Centre at Deakin University, Geelong. She has taught Women's Studies for twenty years and written on women's human rights, women's identity, sexuality and feminist ethics. For fifteen years she has been a leading radical feminist voice against reproductive technology. Her books include *Woman Herself* (1989), *Living Laboratories: Women and Reproductive Technology* (1992) and two volumes of poetry.

Diana E. H. Russell, is the author/editor/co-editor of twelve books including *Rape in Marriage* (1982); *The Secret Trauma: Incest in the Lives of Girls and Women* (1986); *Femicide: The Politics of Women Killing* with Jill Radford (1992); *Making Violence Sexy: Feminist Views on Pornography* (1993) and *Against Pornography: The Evidence of Harm* (1994).

The Santa Barbara Rape Crisis Center/Centro Contra la Violación is dedicated to helping people survive the trauma of sexual assault and to eliminating this brutal crime from our society.

Susan Sayer is a fiction writer and a DPhil candidate researching lesbian writings in the postcolonial context of Aotearoa/New Zealand. She was a member of "Scratching the Surface", a lesbian writing group, and has been part of a feminist theory group for over ten years. She is a welfare rights and anti-racist activist and most recently has been guest editor of a special issue of *Australian Women's Book Review* (1995).

Jocelynne A. Scutt is Australia's best known feminist lawyer. She is widely admired for her work raising issues around violence against women. She is author and editor of many books including *Even in the Best of Homes* (1983); *The Baby Machine* (1988); *Women and the Law* (1990); *The Sexual Gerrymander* (1994) and the *"Women's Lives"* Series, (Artemis).

Brigitte Sellach is a social worker, feminist sociologist and activist. Once a high-ranking Green politician, she made a recent comeback as a feminist researcher with a special interest in social politics, women's family work and women and migration. She is a co-founder of GSF (Gesellschaft für sozialwissenschaftliche Frauenforschung/the Association for Feminist Research in the Social Sciences).

Ailbhe Smyth Irish bourgeois(e) by birth; Academic reluctantly; Writer uncertainly; Activist passionately; Lesbian by desire; Radical feminist by conviction, choice and great serendipity.

Charlene Spretnak is author of *Lost Goddesses of Early Greece* (1981); *The Spiritual Dimension of Green Politics* (1986); and *States of Grace: The Recovery of Meaning in the Post-modern Age* (1991). She is also co-author of *Green Politics (1984)* and editor of an anthology, *The Politics of Women's Spirituality* (1981).

Inés Maria Talamantez is currently Assistant Professor in the Department of Religious Studies at the University of California, Santa Barbara, where she established the concentration in Native American religions. Her field research and interest in contemporary Native American issues have connected her to the boards of three Native American organisations as a consultant and an adviser. Since 1978 she has been on the editorial staff of *New Scholar* and presently serves as its Managing Editor.

Ngahuia Te Awekotuku was raised in an extended family of weavers, dancers and storytellers, in Ohinemutu village, Rotorua. She was founding member of Aotearoa's Women's Movement (second wave) and Gay Liberation, and she spoke for Aotearoa and the Pacific at the Stonewall Rally, 1994 in New York City. She has written two books, *Tahuri: Stories* (1989) and *Mana Wahine Maori: Selected Writings on Maori Women's Art Culture & Politics* (1991), as well as a resource book, *He Tikanga Whakaaro: Research Ethics in the Maori Community* (1991). Her work, both fiction and non-fiction, appears in many local and international journals and anthologies. She teaches Art History at Auckland University, and indulges in cats, leather and chocolate.

Denise Thompson is in her glorious fifties and lives and works in Sydney, Australia. She is a radical feminist theorist who has always worked outside an academic institution. This has its advantages in that she can say and write what she thinks, but it also has its disadvantages in that it means no status, little recognition and no money. Her published works include *Reading Between the Lines* (1991). She is currently working on a book addressing the question of the meaning of feminism.

Ellen Travis currently lives in Toronto, Canada, where she is a doctoral student in Social and Political Thought at York University.

UBINIG – the Policy Research for Development Alternative – is a policy research organization – founded in 1984 – in Bangladesh that works directly with the people, promoting research, supporting campaigns on social issues and organising workshops and international conferences on women's health, reproductive technologies and genetic engineering and population control. UBINIG's Executive Director, Farida Akhter also runs a feminist bookstore and the publishing company Narigrantha Prabartana.

Kristin Waters is an independent scholar and lecturer who has taught mainly in the Northeastern United States at a number of colleges and universities including Bard College, Clark University and the College of the Holy Cross. A philosopher by training though not by temperament, she writes on issues in feminist ethics and epistemology.

Sue Wilkinson is based in the Social Sciences Department at Loughborough University, UK. She is the founding and current editor of *Feminism and Psychology* and the *Gender and Psychology* book series. Her books include *Heterosexuality* (1993) and *Feminism and Discourse* (1995) both edited with Celia Kitzinger.

Christine Zmroczek is Senior Lecturer in Women's Studies at Roehampton Institute, London and Managing Editor of *Women's Studies International Forum*. She has published on Women's Studies, technology, oral history and with Pat Mahony she is editor of *Class Matters: Working Class Women and Social Class* (forthcoming), and a new book series, *Women and Social Class*. Her current research interests include household technologies as well as women and class issues. In 1994–1995 she was the Chair of the Women's Studies Network (UK) Association.

Index

ejaculatory politics, 207
elocution lessons, 74
empowerment, 99-101
  see also power
epilepsy, 483-4, 487-93
equality and inequality, 46-7, 79-80, 168,
    198-9, 202, 211-12, 219-22, 374, 402-3
  see also power
erotic power, 119
Erotica, 195
erotica, 150, 210-11
essentialism, 143-6, 156, 157-9, 160, 164,
    166, 167, 168, 330-1, 334-5, 336, 362,
    370-1, 372, 386
ethnic issues
  see Aboriginal; African American;
      Black; indigenous; Maori; race

F
FACT, 241
False Memory Syndrome, 90
family, 28, 31-2
  ideology, 15
  incest, 87-91
  violent institution, 103-4
  see also incest; marriage; motherhood;
      patriarchy
fashion
  queer notions, 379
  see also clothes
female impersonators, 272-3
femicide, 456-64
'feminazi', 142, 197, 270
femininity, 362, 364, 366
feminism
  see definitions
Feminist Archive, 546-50
Feminist University, 535-45
fiction, 215
FINRRAGE, 26, 232, 236
First Amendment, 204-5, 206, 220
food production, 18
  see also work
Fourth World, 58
Fourth World Manifesto, 157, 161
freedom of speech, 200-2, 203-5, 215, 219,
    220, 226, 250-1, 273, 435, 451, 452
  see also academic freedom; silence
French feminism, 383-92
friendships, 9, 28, 29, 79, 82, 251
Frug, Mary Joe, 295
Fuchs, Claudia, 254-61
fucking with gender, 151, 375, 377-8

G
Gay Black Group, 372
gay liberation, 364
gay masculinity, 364, 374
'gay sexualities', 373-4
gender, 33, 49-50, 178-80, 188, 192, 272-3, 559
  freedom of speech, 251-2

post-modernism, 329
post-modernism and lesbianandgay
    theory, 359-74
poststructuralism, 393-412
queer theory, 375-82
race, 251
schools, 254-61
gender, fucking with, 151, 375, 377-8
gender benders
  see fucking with gender
gender relations
  sexual practices, 153
gender studies, 184-7, 189
'gendered bodies', 350-2
'genderfuck'
  see fucking with gender
Generation X, 195, 196, 197
genital mutilation
  see sexual mutilation
genocide, 456-64
German educational research, 254-61
Germany, 510-13
global issues, 6, 18-22, 26
  Muslim perspective, 525-7
  population control programs, 519-24
  pornography, 448-55
God
  see religion
Gross Domestic Product, 7
growth movement, 96-7
Gyn-affection, 29

H
harassment
  see sexual harassment; violence
hatred, 199
  see also rage
health, 7-8, 22-3, 26, 239, 346
  Aboriginal project, 516-18
  post-modernism, 346-58, 347
  sexual mutilation, 465-8
  see also bodies; mental health;
      reproductive technology
hegemony, academic, 312
hegemony, claim of
  radical feminism, 150
hermaphrodites, 378
hetero-reality, 9, 15-17, 29, 79, 81, 350-2
heterofeminism, 27-8
heterosexual women
  see privilege
heterosexuality, 15-17, 27, 31-2, 77-86, 149-
    50, 210, 382
  as institution, 27-9, 371, 374
  post-modernism, 360-2
  see also incest; rape
hierarchy, 270
  see also patriarchy
history
  poststructuralism, 393-412
  women's liberation movement, 546-50